Editor's Study

Editor's Study

by

William Dean Howells

Edited, with an Introduction by

James W. Simpson

The Whitston Publishing Company
Troy, New York
1983

TABLE OF CONTENTS

INTRODUCTION

The American authors that rose to eminence in the 1840's and 1850's fulfilled the role of the artist and commented upon their social environment without benefit of the moral and physical alienation that later artists found necessary. Nathaniel Hawthorne spent practically his whole creative life ensconced in the proto-establishment towns of Salem and Concord, Massachusetts. Lowell, Emerson, Whittier, and the other Brahmins clustered around Boston's literary hub and reflected and established the social and moral judgment of the nation. Few questioned the propriety of the artist's retaining his social position.

Part of the reason that it was possible for these and other important and undoubted artists to operate from within, indeed at the very center of, the society of which they were the arbiters of conscience lies in the then still unshaken optimism of the nineteenth century mind. The brunt of the thrust to settle the frontier areas was still in the future, and the challenge to society's institutions that resulted from people seeking and believing in better opportunities elsewhere had not arisen. The robber barons, Rockefeller, Carnegie, and the others, who were to fleece the country's people as well as its institutions during the Gilded Age, had just been born, so the limits of the efficacy of gluttony and greed in amassing personal gain had not been tested. The great labor movements of the 1870's and 1880's that assaulted the collective national conscience with revelations of the conditions endured by the laboring classes, and resulted in the spilling of the blood of working men, strikebreakers, Pinkerton detectives, and innocent bystanders alike, were still in the future. But perhaps most important of all, the world of Hawthorne, Emerson, and their contemporaries then had not undergone the immense national trauma of the Civil War. The illusion that the forces of established society were in the end righteous and worthy of trust and capable of meeting any divisive challenge had not been destroyed by the spectacle of one half of the nation making war upon the other.

Literary artists in this milieu of optimism without serious challenge felt justified in turning their attention to the "higher pursuits of man," and in viewing as relatively inviolable the basic tenets of the American republic. Hawthorne felt secure enough in his own society to turn to the Puritan founders of another century for a source of conflict and challenge to moral rectitude. Melville's best works symbolically portrayed earth-wide quests for moral salvation and the resulting betterment of man, but left untouched the contemporary problems of the Missouri Compromise and Bleeding Kansas. These apparent oversights along with those of other writers of the period do not represent a shortcoming of artistic values or a condemnation of a limited view of mankind. The writers were integral parts of the society which they reflected, and without a moral movement to an external position of observation, they could establish no other viewpoint. At least for several decades, there was little impetus for such movement.

The naturalistic writers of the generation after that of Henry James, Mark Twain, and William Dean Howells from the first had social comment as their *raison d'être*. Frank Norris in *The Octopus* and *The Pit* struck out at the predatory practices of the business enterprises that had arisen after the Civil War, and at the society that caused otherwise moral people to behave as animals. Stephen Crane and Theodore Dreiser had similar themes in *Maggie: A Girl of the Streets* and *Sister Carrie*, respectively. Both were first novels, and in each case the author portrays society not as a competent, trustworthy set of institutions, but as a predator that cruelly brings down its prey with inexorable unopposability.

The events that brought about this drastic change in outlook in American literature are the same events that the young American Romanticists predated and that the same writers when older largely chose to overlook: the Western movement, the Gilded Age, the labor movement, and the Civil War. The Naturalist's outlook upon society is as explicable as his Romantic predecessor's. But the generation of Norris, Crane, and Dreiser did not directly follow that of Hawthorne, Emerson, and Melville. The intervening generation, born between 1835 and 1845, was

first impressed with and clearly a part of the Romanticists'
optimism, but in the prime of middle age its members lived
through the same illusion-destroying events that later caused the
Naturalists to depict social forces as essentially inimical. Circumstances forced James, Twain, and Howells to witness the
dissolution and dismemberment of the social ideals that had
prevailed during their formative years and into the beginning
of their professional lives—ideals that the writers they idolized
and sought to emulate expertly assured them to be universal.
For this intervening generation, more so than for the ones immediately before and after, the changing social climate induced
a personal moral trauma. Products of the Romantic optimism
of the years before the Civil War, they were forced in mid-stride
either to throw off the old idealism that they had every reason
to believe would be the guiding forces throughout their lives,
and take their places in the newer more pessimistic generation,
or to ignore and excuse the profound social changes around
them, cling to established values, and be left behind and forgotten by exponents of the new outlook.

In spite of being the co-author of the book that gave the
Gilded Age its name, Twain's crisis as he faced the dilemma of
the artists of his generation was much later and more profound
than James'. One primary reason is that while James is the
epitome of the conscious artistic craftsman, Twain remained for

Henry James was probably the first major writer of his
generation to realize the increasing shortcomings of American
society. His 1879 critical work on Hawthorne asserts that the
lack of American institutions such as a sovereign, aristocracy,
and national literature leaves the artist emasculated and without basis for moral presentation. He might well have added that
what few institutions Americans did have were and would continue to be challenged and destroyed by the growth of social
conscience and the demise of optimism. His solution was to become an expatriate. Living most of the time in England, his
physical alienation became a manifestation of the moral alienation that literary artists found necessary beginning in the late
nineteenth century. James' expatriation produced tangible results in the series of international novels, which portrayed American characters against a European background, thus delineating
the American character from a new viewpoint.

In spite of being the co-author of the book that gave the
Gilded Age its name, Twain's crisis as he faced the dilemma of
the artists of his generation was much later and more profound
than James'. One primary reason is that while James is the
epitome of the conscious artistic craftsman, Twain remained for

most of his creative life an artistic genius whose artistry was largely unconscious. Part of the reason that Twain was able to retain his nineteenth century outlook much longer than James is that while James' subject matter was entirely contemporary, dealing with an American confrontation of the society of Europe, Twain's still largely concerned the boyhood world of Tom Sawyer, and of Mark Twain himself, in the 1850's. At the same time that James dealt critically with the shortcomings of the society that had kept Hawthorne from reaching his full potential as an artist, Twain published *The Adventures of Tom Sawyer* and *A Tramp Abroad,* both still mid-nineteenth century in their outlook. The older values in Mark Twain's artistic consciousness fought a longer and more brutal struggle for dominance, and left him all the more disillusioned and pessimistic. His incipient pessimism was evident by the time he wrote "The Man That Corrupted Hadleyburg," and fully mature in "The Mysterious Stranger," posthumously published. By the time Twain reached his seventies, he sought to surround himself with the symbols of the innocence (for example, his "little fish") that his own artistic environment had failed to provide. Twain's achievement of cultural alienation was clearly a case of his finally realizing that his moral world had crumbled around him without his knowing it.

While James decided early in his life that as an artist he could only operate from a position of moral (and in his own case physical as well) alienation, Twain spent most of his creative life without realizing that alienation was necessary. Therefore on the one hand (James) there exists a literary canon which in its artistic values and outlook belongs wholly to the twentieth century, and on the other hand (Twain) a collection of literature almost as entirely belonging to the nineteenth century.

William Dean Howells, however, furnishes an example of a writer who began his literary career at the very center of the nineteenth century literary establishment, as editor of *Atlantic Monthly,* who underwent his cultural crisis in the 1880's, as opposed to James' crisis in the 1870's and Twain's in the late 1890's, and whose creative period extended far enough into the new period to furnish, at least theoretically, a basis for comparison of the two cultural periods. A very important approach to the tracing of the moral development of these three writers, or

of any writer, is the examination of their fiction. The fiction of
James and of Twain primarily furnishes examples of either the
late period, or the earlier one, but not both. Howells' fictional
output, then, because of the timing of his crisis of cultures, and
the length of his career, might be expected to furnish the best
example of an artist being forced to abandon the optimistic
values he began with and to adopt those of the coming generation. Indeed, a diligent search of Howells' fiction reveals strong
elements of both periods. But because his literary output is so
very large (thirty-five novels, ten travel books, eight volumes of
short stories, eight volumes of criticism, five volumes of autobiographical writings, and additional critical and autobiographical works published only in magazines), and because there are
so many examples of relapses from one artistic outlook to the
other and back again, results of such analysis can be qualified,
inconclusive, and even contradictory. For example, *A Modern
Instance,* published in 1882, is in many ways a very courageous
novel delving into a subject taboo in polite nineteenth century
society, namely divorce. But in the following year came *A
Woman's Reason,* demonstrating none of the tendency toward a
less optimistic outlook evident in the preceding novel. There are
many more examples of such anomalies: *The Rise of Silas Lapham* followed by *Indian Summer, The Minister's Charge* followed
by *April Hopes, A Traveler from Altruria* followed by *The Day
of Their Wedding.* Examples of the relationship we are looking
for in Howells' fiction can be complex and obscured by concurrent, though relatively minor, trends. But there is other evidence.

Howells made his monthly contribution to the "Editor's
Study" department of *Harper's Magazine* from January, 1886
through March, 1892, a period that corresponds closely to the
series of crises and developments that slowly changed the way
he viewed the world. Foremost among the crises, of course, was
the erosion of the optimistic values prevalent in the nineteenth
century and their replacement by realization of the shortcomings
of the human spirit and of the American republican values. To
appreciate and ultimately be able to evaluate the unique position of the "Editor's Study" columns in the works of Howells
and in American literature of the late nineteenth century, it is
first necessary to represent the column's production against
the background of the concurrent events and crises in Howells'

life.

When James Russell Lowell in August, 1859 accepted for
that most prestigious of Boston journals, *Atlantic Monthly,* a
single poem called "Andenken" submitted by an unknown Ohio
poet named William Dean Howells, he completed Howells' first
link with the literary establishment of the East, and at the same
time founded a father-son-like friendship that was of primary
importance to Howells' early career. Shortly before, *Atlantic*
had accepted the contribution of Howells' friend, John J. Piatt,
and before the end of the year the Columbus, Ohio publishing
firm of Follett, Foster, and Company had brought forth the joint
volume called *Poems of Two Friends.* Howells' position with
this firm became the conduit through which he managed to
escape the relative provinciality of the Ohio frontier. The firm
asked him to write a campaign biography of the Republican
candidate in the 1860 Presidential race, Abraham Lincoln. As a
result of the biography, Howells, working through Secretary of
the Treasury Salmon P. Chase, and Lincoln's two young secre-
taries, John Milton Hay and John George Nicolay, acquired the
appointment as consul to Venice. The Civil War was in its early
stages when he left for Venice in November, 1861, and all but
its lasting animosities were over when he returned to Boston in
August, 1865.

James T. Fields had succeeded Lowell as editor of *Atlantic,*
and fairly consistently throughout Howells' stay in Venice, Fields
had rejected the poems that Howells submitted to him for publication in *Atlantic.* In spite of his early publication in *Atlantic*
and the important encouragement from Lowell, Howells did not
feel in 1865 that he had any particular friends on the magazine's
staff, and instead sought employment in New York. The offer
that finally did come from Fields, conveyed through the young
employee of Ticknor, Fields and Company, James R. Osgood,
stipulated $2500 a year for services as assistant editor of the
magazine.[1]

With Howells' acceptance of Fields' offer, he had successfully made the difficult transition from an outland helper in his
father's various print shops and newspaper enterprises to the
country's center of literary opinion and prerogative. His position
there was hard won, and achievement of it was in spite of con-

stant self-doubt and self-consciousness in the chronically insecure Howells. Indeed, Howells did lack almost everything that
had heretofore been necessary to Boston literary life: breeding,
background, formal education, influence. But in fact he soon
became the quintessential figure of the literary establishment.

In his letter to Fields accepting the position of assistant editor, Howells enumerated what he understood to be his duties:

> These duties I understand to be: examination of mss. offered to
> the *Atlantic;* correspondence with contributors; reading proof
> for the magazine after its revisal by the printers; and writing the
> *Reviews and Literary Notices,* for which I am to receive fifty dol-
> lars a week, while I am to be paid extra for anything that I may
> contribute to the body of the magazine.[2]

Clearly his was to be a responsible and demanding position.
Kenneth Lynn, in his biography, further indicates that there was
a "gentlemen's agreement" between Howells and Fields that
when the latter relinquished the editorship, as he intended to do
a few years hence because of failing health, Howells would get
the position.[3] Considering the degree of responsibility that he
got from the first at *Atlantic,* and the further promise of the
editorship in the near future, his financial and professional
future was secure enough, although his artistic posture was still
in some question.

Fields' steady rejection of his poetry after 1862 had led to
the decision by the time he returned to the United States that
his ultimate artistic endeavors would not be poetic. The Venetian stay had produced only two travel books, *Venetian Life* and
Italian Journeys, which while erudite and delicately phrased were
still only travel books in the final analysis, not genuine artistic
creations. Given his situation and the heavy editorial responsibilities assigned by Fields, his creative endeavors would have to
be spare time affairs; he did not even have an established genre
within which to work. Furthermore he was cast firmly now into
the gentleman of letters mold. Extricating himself from that
mold was to be one of his life's most arduous experiences.

With the assumption of duties on the *Atlantic Monthly,*
Howells' first transition was complete. In one respect he had

sacrificed an initial advantage, that of being born outside the
literary establishment. He relinquished this advantage willingly
enough, and probably even viewed it as a liability. But it might
have given him a source of artistic alienation necessary to exercise moral judgments in literature.

Howells' influence upon the magazine and upon literary
events in general increased rapidly and steadily as a result of his
performance at *Atlantic*. He read every manuscript that writers
of the period submitted, and while the decision that he made
about its acceptability was technically only a preliminary one, in
practice it became more and more definitive, because of Fields'
slowly decreasing role in editorial capacities. It was Howells,
not Fields, who did all the corresponding with contributors, the
result being that even such literary powers as Emerson and
Lowell began to regard him as the editorial force behind *Atlantic*. The authors with whom he exercised such increasing influence, while still largely members of the Boston literary establishment, now frequently included newer and more provincial
figures such as Mark Twain, Bret Harte, and John William De
Forest, so Howells' scope of influence was larger than might
be expected of the assistant editor of a magazine whose circulation was still only 12,000.[4]

While his power and influence increased, his critical prerogative did not. His primary contribution to the finished magazine,
apart from a great deal of technical work such as verification of
facts, dates, and terms, proofreading, and supervision of the
printers, was the book review column entitled "Reviews and
Literary Notices." The column under Lowell and later Fields
had always been respected, but under Howells' hand it gained
enormously in prestige and influence. Because the *Atlantic's*
book reviews were so widely read and because the readers of the
reviews associated them closely with the magazine itself, Fields
and his predecessors had always been unwilling to permit viewpoint and tone to vary as the reviewer's job changed hands.
The *Atlantic*, therefore, had a "house voice" which amounted
to a loosely defined critical approach and taste, and a more precisely defined list of subjects and authors that could not be included in the reviews. Thus when Howells wrote a review of a
book for the column, he had first to choose that book on the
basis of a "standard of decency," and then to express opinions

on the book's quality representing not necessarily his own beliefs, but instead the adherence to the standards of the "house."

Lynn observes "that he was under an obvious obligation to continue writing favorable reviews for, as well as accepting the contributions of, the romantic authors who had first made the magazine famous."[5]   Clearly it would not require very many offended Romanticists boycotting the magazine because of unfavorable reviews to do serious damage to the publication's standing.

On the other side of the coin, *Atlantic* was a rather small enterprise of a book publishing company, Ticknor and Fields (later Fields, Osgood, and Company). The editors quite understandably had to be sensitive about matters contrary to the publishing company's best interests. One of the items on the parent company's forbidden list was the reviewing, favorably or otherwise, of books published by subscription companies. These subscription publishers used high pressure tactics to sell their books on a door-to-door approach, and many established publishers felt that they both provided unfair competition and gave the book publishing business in general a bad name. The American Publishing Company of Hartford was one of these companies, nominally run by Mark Twain's son-in-law, but in reality a business enterprise of Twain's. On the one hand, then, the pressures of the business world forced Howells to review favorably books he might not otherwise have been inclined to, and on the other hand, similar pressures from another quarter prevented him from reviewing books he might otherwise have chosen.

Even within these confining limits, however, Howells managed to inject life into the *Atlantic's* review column. On occasion he gave bitingly hostile reviews, especially when he saw the chance to elaborate upon his growing dislike of English literature and writers. And on other occasions he overlooked the ban on subscription books and gave favorable reviews of Twain's *Innocents Abroad* and Grant's *Memoirs of U. S. Grant*,[6] the latter perhaps as a result of Grant's being the Republican nominee for President in 1868 and Howells' being a lifelong Republican of the staunchest conviction.

Howells made the best of a confining situation. He raised the column of reviews to the highest level, making it well known for its wit and virility, and still managed to avoid offending delicate (often financial) sensibilities. But the column hardly added to his own stature as a free-thinker or a critical power to be reckoned with. He was not to get that opportunity until he began the "Editor's Study."

Through a complex series of reorganizations and dissolutions, the firm that had been Ticknor and Fields when Howells began as assistant editor in 1866 became Houghton, Osgood and Company in 1878. This partnership was no more stable than its forerunners, and in 1881 Henry O. Houghton withdrew from the partnership to form Houghton, Mifflin and Company, while Osgood formed James R. Osgood and Company. The *Atlantic Monthly* part of the business went with Houghton, and there was some contention whether the services of its now-valuable editor, William Dean Howells, belonged to Houghton or to Osgood. Uneasy as an object of contention, and perhaps ready for a chance to leave the magazine's burden of responsibilities, Howells resigned the *Atlantic* editorship in February, 1881.

Howells had throughout the corporate machinations felt more loyalty to Osgood than to any other person in the company. Even before Howells became assistant editor, he had been finally persuaded to accept the job not by Fields, toward whom there was perhaps still a vestige of ill will because of his rejection of Howells' poetry in the 1860's, but by Osgood. Osgood had now embarked upon the difficult task of creating a major publishing house in Boston, when the tide of literature was definitely rising in New York. Howells signed a book contract with Osgood after leaving *Atlantic*, partly out of personal loyalty, and partly from his belief that Osgood had the makings of a great publisher.

As circumstances developed he was only partly right. While editorially sound, Osgood lacked the business acumen necessary to compete with the New York publishing houses, and his firm went bankrupt in the middle of 1885. Though the time was financially trying for Osgood, it was artistically an important time for Howells. He had determined, upon returning to this country after the war, that his future did not lie in poetry, and his main production during the busy first years at *Atlantic* was in the form of travel books. But he realized in the 1870's that the next logical step after travel books was novels, and though his early novels still retained a travel book flavor, he soon developed the theme of the American girl in Europe that Henry James would adopt and develop more fully.

In his increasing artistic awareness he turned to more complex and socially vital subjects for his novels, and during the Osgood period he produced *Doctor Breen's Practice, A Modern Instance, A Woman's Reason,* and *The Rise of Silas Lapham.* True to Howells' on-and-off pattern two of the novels were highly successful and two were failures, but Howells had finally established himself as an artist. He had himself decided to put poetry aside, and it was primarily for his abilities as an editor and a printer that Fields had hired him at *Atlantic.* But the Osgood years gave him a chance to create a name for himself as a creative man, and not just an administrator of other creative men.

Although generally successful artistically, the years with Osgood were not without their hardships. On November 15, 1881 he wrote his father to cancel a planned visit because he was "down with some sort of fever."[7] A month later he wrote to Horace Scudder to thank him for correcting proof that he had been unable to do.[8] At the end of the letter he added, "I feel like a diluted shadow."

The proof that Scudder corrected for Howells was probably that of the monthly serialization of *A Modern Instance* which was then appearing in *Century.*[9] Kenneth Lynn in his biography attaches a great deal of importance to this illness, and goes so far as to call it "the breakdown precipitated by *A Modern Instance.*"[10] In a letter to Twain dated January 31, 1882, two and a half months after he complained of being ill to his father, Howells said that he "had written 1466 MS. pages before I fell sick,"[11] and this point in the manuscript corresponds to the point in *A Modern Instance* where Bartley Hubbard deserts his family. Putting the two facts together Lynn concludes that "it is clear that Bartley's flight set in motion an anxiety that completely overran the castle of Howells' defenses."[12] In other words, Lynn contends that Howells' malady was mental and emotional as well as physical.

There can be little doubt that Howells' 1881-82 illness was
a serious one. He wrote to John Hay that it kept him in bed for
"seven endless weeks."[13]   Just as certainly the illness affected
his fiction, notably the ending of *A Modern Instance.* The pressure to finish the book was all the greater because serialization
began before it was finished, and therefore Howells could not
afford the recuperation time he may have needed before taking
up work again. But to assert that the illness was "precipitated
by *A Modern Instance*" implies that the physical disease played
a lesser role. To further assert that the incident represents a
supposed renunciation by Howells as drastic and cataclysmic
as that of Bartley Hubbard is probably reading too much into
the coincidence of the two situations, one real and the other
fictional.

A similar overreading on the part of Lynn concerns the
year 1885, while another Howells novel, *The Rise of Silas Lapham,* was being serialized in *Century.* Lynn takes Howells' own
1896 statement to a reporter that "the bottom dropped" as indication of a sort of moral renunciation, a basic change in moral
viewpoint, on the part of Howells. At least from a psychological
standpoint the 1885 interruption was more significant than the
one in 1881. A closer look at the report of Howells' original
words will indicate the source of the misunderstanding.

> The Altrurian's doctrine. . .is an answer to grave questions that had
> arisen in the author's own mind. . . . They made their demand—
> these questions and problems—when Mr. Howells was writing *Silas
> Lapham.* His affairs prospering, his work marching as well as heart
> could wish, suddenly and without apparent cause, the status
> seemed wholly wrong. His own expression, in speaking with me
> about that time was, "The bottom dropped out!"[14]

Lynn's quotations of the passage begins with "They" in the
second line above, thus omitting reference to *A Traveler from
Altruria,* in the first line. The author of the words, Marrion Wilcox, was writing for *Harper's Weekly* a resumé of the books
Howells had published between 1860 and 1896. The words
quoted above came at the end of Wilcox's discussion of *A Traveler from Altruria,* published in 1894. Howells was not, as Lynn
implies, telling the story of his breakdown to Wilcox. Apart
from the passage quoted above, the entire article deals with

Howells' fiction, not his mental health.

Lynn is not the first of Howells' biographers to feel the need of an explanation of the changed behavior that Howells exhibited after 1885. Everett Carter attributes the change to Howells' reaction to the Haymarket Affair:

> The exact occasion for the transformation of Howells from conservative to radical. . .was at some time between the summer of 1886 and the summer of 1887. In this year he came to realize that an America which could present only smiling aspects to the realist was no longer.[15]

Howells did not write the "smiling aspects" passage to which Carter alludes until June, 1886 (for publication in the September, 1886 "Editor's Study"), so at least according to Carter's timetable Howells was not long in refuting it.

Both writers depict Howells' "great change" as a rather immediate, catastrophic occurrence, although Carter places it in time roughly a year later than Lynn. The explanation for Carter's different timing is obvious, and realization of the point indicates the shortcomings of both hypotheses: having undergone such a major sudden change, Howells could hardly so soon after have written the optimistic smiling aspects passage, and the many other passages like it.

The truth is that the 1881 illness, the 1885 collapse, and Howells' part in the Haymarket Affair reaction were all contributing factors to a much more protracted and complex change of outlook and values on the part of Howells. There were many other factors that contributed to the change that were equally important: Howells' reading of Tolstoy's fiction, his impression with Tolstoy's personal example of socialistic theory, his interest in other social theories, the death of his sister Victoria, the tragedy of his daughter Winifred, and the personal life that circumstances forced him to live throughout the 1880's.

Howells' change, or rather his assumption of moral alienation, was a long agonizing process, caused not so much by a revolutionary light of realization as by a years-long accumulation of physical and emotional trials. There was a long period of visible change, corresponding roughly with the years that Howells spent his first time with Harper's.

When Howells decided almost twenty years before that Boston was the literary pinnacle to which he aspired, he had made a wise decision. But in 1885 the older Brahmin culture was breaking up, the writers who had flourished twenty and even thirty years before were far past their prime, and more importantly the Boston publishing houses were finding it increasingly difficult to stay in business faced with the highly organized New York firms. Lynn's observation that "In the autumn of 1885, Howells abruptly began to deviate from accustomed patterns of behavior"[16] is certainly correct, but the "deviations" were more for personal and business reasons than for emotional.

Besides being a productive editor-author, Howells had always shown business acumen, a skill probably fostered in the early days when he helped his peripatetic father run their succession of printing and newspaper establishments. The urge to remain in Boston must have been strong, but in the end no rival was able to match the offer made by Harper and Brothers in New York. In return for the serialization rights to one novel and one farce a year, Howells received $10,000. In addition Harper's pressed him to add to his duties a monthly column for *Harper's Monthly,* the content of which he was to control. Howells agreed, with some reservations since he had ever since the *Atlantic* days begrudged the time he spent away from his current novel, in return for an additional $3000 annually, bringing his total salary to $13,000, this apart from the usual royalties he got from the hard cover publication of his books. He did relinquish the right, though, to have his name appear anywhere except over the Harper's imprint.

The amount of production and work that he committed himself to here was hardly less than it had been at *Atlantic.* He was still obligated to release the first chapters of a novel for serialization before he had completed the later ones, and so never had the opportunity to collect his thoughts and contemplate, being always committed to at least a chapter a month. The commitment was made doubly difficult because of increasing pressures and expenses from Winifred's lingering illness, but Howells for the whole of his life was nothing if not prolific, and he never fell behind schedule.

He made another beginning in the final months of 1885, the reading and the revolutionary appreciation of the works of Tolstoy. Howells wrote ten years later in *My Literary Passions,* "I do not know how to give a notion of his influence without the effect of exaggeration. As much as one merely human being can help another, I believe that he has helped me."[17]

Understanding Howells' passion for Tolstoy is probably the most helpful key to the comprehension of the pain, guilt, and self-doubt that Howells underwent during the last half of the 1880's. His first mention of Tolstoy in the "Editor's Study" was in the column for February, 1886 (written in late November, 1885). Thereafter Tolstoy's name and a great many of his works appeared in fully thirty of the seventy-five monthly columns, far more frequently than other favorites such as Henry James, Mark Twain, and Palacio Valdés. This surprising frequency was in spite of Howells' having read the works from translation of the Russian into French; Tolstoy's works were then largely unavailable in English.

Many of Tolstoy's works of fiction express against some remarkably grandiose backgrounds exactly the dilemma that his autobiographical works express in detail, a dilemma that was just beginning to dawn upon Howells when he first picked up a Tolstoy volume. With the increased awareness of the gross inadequacies of many of society's institutions comes a simultaneous revelation of the personal tragedy endured by the very people least able to cope with their hardship, the poor working class. To such an intensely perceptive and introspective man as Tolstoy, suffering as he did from almost unresolvable tensions between the two facets of his personality, the social distance between his station in life as a nobleman in Czarist Russia and that of the Russian peasantry living on his estates must have demanded correction. Tolstoy in his own infinitely inconoclastic way arrived logically at a solution to such intolerable differences in social station:

> He himself made an attempt consciously to impose upon humanity his own reasoned-out theory of life, the final aim of which was not only to scrap civilization, but to make history itself impossible.

> All differentiation should be abolished. There should be neither
> social nor functional difference between one individual and an-
> other. Tolstoy even went so far as to efface the line between
> manual and mental work in the society to come. Everybody
> should till the ground with his own hands in order to obtain the
> food he eats, for in this he saw the law of life.[18]

Tolstoy's social awareness, then, was so strong that he went
beyond the demands of even the wildest anarchist in his formula
for rectification.

If living in Czarist Russia can be considered an advantage
in cultivating an increased social awareness, it was not one that
Howells enjoyed. Conditions in the United States in the 1880's
were a far cry from those of Russia during the same period, and
at the same time Howells' own sense of social wrong was in-
finitesimal compared to Tolstoy's radical zeal. Still Howells
had been disturbed enough by his country's comparatively mild
social injustices to recognize in Tolstoy a leader whose example
he might follow.

Tolstoy on the one hand was the geatest of voluptuaries,
prone to excesses temporal and sexual, and brimming over with
a passion for being alive, but on the other hand he was also the
most demanding ascetic, requiring the strictest morality, celibacy, and complete atonement for real or imagined transgres-
sions. In his extensive diaries (the writing of which must have
provided a valuable therapeutic effect), Tolstoy the ascetic established rules and calendars of behavior for one day, two days,
as long at a time as he thought he might manage. At the end
of the period he reported back to himself concerning the success or failure of the last schedule, and then set himself another.

The tensions in Howells' own personality were far from
being as strong as this, but after he began to write about unhappy
marriage in *A Modern Instance* (1882), and the excesses and suffering possible in the world of business in *The Rise of Silas Lapham* (1885), his indignation was strong enough that he began to
search for solutions, a search that reflects itself in the "Editor's
Study" in a great many reviews of books of social commentary,
socialistic theory, and works of European naturalism showing

the other side of life.

Howells would have viewed Tolstoy more as an example than a furnisher of solutions. The example that must have most impressed Howells was Tolstoy's renunciation of his title, lands, and money and moving to the country to lead the life of a peasant. Howells discusses this extraordinary act in his review of *Que Faire?* and he clearly regarded the act as something he should himself be able to do, but alas was not. The guilt of simply having a position and social and financial security when others worked their lives away in intolerable conditions for not one tenth as much began to weigh more heavily upon him. As his newly found awareness of social injustice became more acute, the burden grew ever heavier.

Tolstoy tells in *Que Faire?* (*What Then Must We Do?*) of trying as a nobleman to raise materially the level of Moscow's poor, and in doing so and seeing some slight progress begins to think of himself as a better and more moral person for having done so. Thus the social distance between himself and the poor increased all the more. His only solution was the extreme one of renouncing all his worldly holdings and setting an example that others might follow. Howells took the example to heart, but never developed more than a regret of his own moral weakness in not taking a similar step.

In fact the ascetic side of Tolstoy's character had not over-balanced the Epicurean side to an extent sufficient to allow him either to renounce so much. He did live for the rest of his life upon the family's baronial estate in Yasnaya Polyana (the rest of his life, at least, until he fled his home in 1910, aged eighty-two, caught pneumonia in a railway station, and died), but the only actual renunciation he made was to sign his property over to his wife. His lifestyle after his renunciation was as unpeasantlike as his morals were un-Christian after his conversion. Nevertheless, Tolstoy was a very important force in the process of Howells' social maturity. Howells stated his dilemma in a letter to Henry James on October 10, 1888:

> I'm not in a very good humor with "America" myself. It seems to be the most grotesquely illogical thing under the sun. . . . After fifty years of optimistic content with "civilization" and its ability

to come out all right in the end, I now abhor it. . . . Meantime, I
wear a fur-lined overcoat, and live in all the luxury my money can
buy.[19]

Another stone added to the burden carried by Howells,
and also one that added to his sense of social injustice, was the
death in December, 1886 of his sister Victoria. Howells was
close to his sister, and stayed with her in the final stages of her
illness in the old home town of Jefferson, Ohio. Her death was
all the more pathetic because thirty of her forty-eight years were
spent caring for their helpless idiot brother, Henry Israel Howells.
One life unavoidably wasted because of mental retardation was
bad enough, but the wasting of another one needlessly because
society had no provision for caring for its helpless members
doubled the loss.

The 1880's found Howells developing an acute social conscience, but the changes were more gradual and even occasional
than revolutionary. Nor were they entirely the result either of
Howells' disturbance over the Haymarket Affair and the subsequent trials, or of a sudden change of insight brought about by
a nervous collapse, although such incidents did play a part. A
letter that Howells wrote to his father in the summer of 1884
indicates that his social conscience was bothering him even as he
was taking the house at Boston's 302 Beacon Street, only a few
doors away from Oliver Wendell Holmes. Howells' family was
in Kennebunkport, Maine while he was alone in the Boston
house readying it for occupancy.

> There is not only nobody else in the house, but nobody else I
> know sleeps in town. Altogether the effect is queer. There are
> miles of empty houses all around me. And how unequally things
> are divided in this world. While these beautiful, airy, wholesome
> houses are uninhabited, thousands upon thousands of poor crea-
> tures are stifling in wretched barracks in the city here, whole fami-
> lies in one room. I wonder that men are so patient with society as
> they are.[20]

Perhaps implicit in the last line is a complaint against himself
for being "so patient with society" for so many years.

As early as 1878 while still at *Atlantic* Howells had worked

on *A Woman's Reason,* the story of a wealthy Boston girl forced
by the death of her family and loss of fortune to live among the
Boston working class. He could not finish the novel then, but
did return to it in the early 1880's when he tried to acquaint
himself more fully with the kinds of people and situations that
the novel demanded.[21]   The book finally made an appearance in
1883, but as a revealing study of Boston's "other half" it was a
failure. Howells' own psychological distance from the problems
involved is parallel to the distance he maintained between the
upper class Helen Harkness and what few members of the working class she was exposed to. In any case it was only an unpleasant interlude, since her lover rescues her, having been lost then
found again at sea. Thus the book fails on two counts: one, the
book's viewpoint acts to prevent identity with working people;
and two, it loses the sense of hopelessness and inevitability that
are the real hardships of being poor.

But Howells' distance from the working class decreased.
The years at *Atlantic* and shortly after had been busy times,
filled with still unaccustomed success. By 1886 the success that
he had wanted so badly was no longer a new sensation, and the
flush of success was being replaced by the guilt of it.

Chicago's Haymarket Affair and Howells' part in it represented a remarkable departure for a man identified so closely
with the establishment point of view. Briefly, the background of
the riots and subsequent trials and executions is this: on May 3,
1886 workers were striking the McCormick Reaper Works in
Chicago in support of the eight-hour working day. There was a
fight between the strikers and the company-hired strikebreakers,
and when the police moved to break up the fight, one striker
was shot and killed. Strikers held a meeting the following day
near Chicago's Haymarket to plan their strategy, and a large
squad of policemen moved to break up the meeting. Someone,
it was never proven who, threw a bomb into the crowd of policemen, killing or fatally injuring seven and wounding many more.

The nation's press had for some years illogically associated
the term "unionism" with "socialism" and "anarchy." When
the news from Chicago reached them, many blew the incident
out of all proportion to reality, and incited unreasoning fear and
hatred and a call for reprisal. In response to this call, the Chicago

police arrested eight "anarchists" and charged them with the murder of one of the policemen.

The mood of popular opinion was such that the eight were convicted in spite of the prosecution's furnishing no evidence that any of them had had anything to do with the bombing. They were, in short, condemned for their political beliefs. The court sentenced seven to be hanged, and the eighth to a prison term. One of the seven condemned men committed suicide, four others were executed on November 11, 1887, and two had their sentences commuted to life imprisonment, which they served until pardoned by the Illinois governor in 1893. The eighth defendant, against whom the prosecutor had presented no evidence at all, received a fifteen-year prison sentence, which he served until he was pardoned with the others.

In a letter to Judge Roger A. Pryor, who was to represent the defendants in their Supreme Court appeal of a technicality, Howells stated, "I have never believed them guilty of murder, or of anything but their opinions."[22] But the Supreme Court failed to overturn the conviction, which prompted Howells to write the following letter to the *New York Tribune:*

> To the Editor of the *Tribune:*
> Sir: I have petitioned the Governor of Illinois to commute the death-penalty of the Anarchists to imprisonment and have also personally written him in their behalf; and now I ask your leave to express here the hope that those who are inclined to do either will not lose faith in themselves, because the Supreme Court has denied the condemned a writ of error. That court simply affirmed the legality of the forms under which the Chicago court proceeded; it did not affirm the propriety of trying for murder men fairly indictable for conspiracy alone; and it by no means approved the principle of punishing them because of their frantic opinions, for a crime which they were not shown to have committed. The justice or injustice of their sentence was not before the highest tribunal of our law, and unhappily could not be got there. The question must remain for history, which judges the judgment of courts, to deal with; and I, for one, cannot doubt what the decision of history will be.
> But the worst is still for a very few days reparable; the men sentenced to death are still alive, and their lives may be finally

saved through the clemency of the Governor, whose prerogative is
now the supreme law in their case. I conjure all those who believe
that it would be either injustice or impolicy to put them to death,
to join in urging him by petition, by letters, through the press, and
from the pulpit and the platform, to use his power, in the only
direction where power can never be misused, for the mitigation of
their punishment.[23]

William Dean Howells

Howells had originally intended the letter to the *Tribune* to
be a joint letter with John Greenleaf Whittier, the old crusader
against slavery, and George William Curtis, long-time author of
the companion in *Harper's* to the "Study," the "Editor's Easy
Chair." While both men admitted their concern that justice was
not being served, neither was willing to allow his name to appear
under the letter above, so in the end only Howells signed it.

The mood of popular opinion was such that an appearance
of support for the Anarchists was taken as open threat and hos-
tility. Newspapers, magazines, and people in general were
astounded by Howells' stand.[24] And their sense of outrage
doubled when Whittier announced to the press that Howells had
tried to persuade him to join the letter in question, but that he
had refused.

Howells had signed his contract with Harper's less than a
year before, and reaction now was so strong against his stand
that there was an open question in the minds of some about
whether it was appropriate for him to continue at the conservative publishing house. The firm never directly voiced any objections to the stand, but there may have been serious consideration of dismissal, at least in the mind of the editor of *Harper's
Monthly,* Henry Mills Alden.[25] But in the winter of 1887, with
the offenders either hanged or imprisoned, animosity abated
somewhat, although there must have remained a measure of
distrust of Howells.

The Haymarket Affair marked the first time that Howells'
social awareness that later turned to social guilt became active
participation. But even then the change to social activism was
neither absolute nor irrevocable. There continued to be periods
of the old optimism commingled with the newer trends. His

fiction after 1887 generally reflected a more somber tone than
before. The period coincides roughly with the publication of
The Minister's Charge, which turned new ground for Howells,
but following immediately was *April Hopes,* a slight comedy of
manners, and such travel pieces as "A Little Swiss Sojourn,"
all of which show the rising and falling nature of Howells' moods
and convictions.

Much of the explanation for such lesser works is the pressure he was under to produce. A novel a year would be task
enough for the normal writer, and Howells' production was more
difficult because the serialization that all his books of this period
went through before hardback publication required that the production be steady; there could be no sabbaticals to collect
thoughts. Apart from additional works of criticism and introductions to the books of the many friends who asked him,
he also produced a steady stream of farcical dramas (thirty-five
in his career) which, though Howells considered then subliterary,
continuously provided him with an appreciable income from
the royalties of productions by amateur and small professional
theatre companies.

Although after Howells made his deal with Harper's he told
Twain that he had "contracted to take all of Harper & Bro.'s
money,"[26] which amounted to a $13,000 annual salary plus
generous royalties, his income was never more than just equal to
his financial drain. He paid a great deal of the living expenses of
his none-too-careful father, supported his mentally deficient
brother and his sister Victoria, who cared for him, provided
many considerations such as servants because his wife, Elinor's,
health was always delicate, in the years between 1880 and 1889
engaged a series of very expensive specialists for treatment of
Winifred's illness, and after the failure of the Osgood firm lived
in luxury and resort hotel suites, rented mansions, and houses
on Long Island and in Maine.. When he abruptly resigned his position with Harper's and accepted the editorship of *Cosmopolitan* in 1891, it was largely because the magazine's owner, John
Brisben Walker, offered him a $15,000 basic salary compared to
Harper's $13,000.[27]

The point is not that Howells was ever financially deprived
or debt ridden; he was not. But there were many members of the

Howells family who depended entirely upon the writer for their existence. Any decision corresponding to the one he thought Tolstoy had made and urged upon others would have directly and drastically affected at least seven dependents, and of course it was a decision that no man of responsibility could make. Still, only a week after the execution of the Chicago Anarchists he wrote to his sister Annie, "Elinor and I both no longer care for the world's life, and would like to settle somewhere very humbly and simply, where we could be socially identified with the principles of progress and sympathy for the struggling mass." But the rest of the letter reveals his dilemma. Winifred was in an expensive sanatorium in Dansville, New York, and he and Elinor were staying in Buffalo in "this wonderful new hotel, the most exquisite place of the sort that I was ever in."[28] Responsibilities and personal habits combined to prevent Howells absolutely from taking any positive action to relieve the guilt of being physically a member of the aristocracy and emotionally with the masses.

The illness and eventual death of the Howellses' oldest child, Winifred, did as much as anything to dispel the notion that things would "come out all right in the end." Illness forced her to withdraw from school in 1880 when she was sixteen. Doctors diagnosed her problem as neurasthenia, for which the prescribed cure was complete bed rest and forced feeding. After spending two years in bed she was well enough to make her social debut in 1883, soon after the family moved to the house at Boston's 302 Beacon Street. Prospects for her complete recovery seemed good, but at about the time Howells signed the Harper's contract she grew suddenly worse, and the family was forced to move away from Boston in the hope that a different climate would help her. This move from Boston to Auburndale, Massachusetts was the first in a practically endless series of moves from one temporary place to another, some made for Winny's health, others largely from discontent.

The character of the illness was such that there was a series of relapses and recoveries, each recovery being less satisfactory than the one before. Doctors believed that the illness was largely nervous and mental rather than physical. At one point in spite of terrible pain doctors prescribed that she keep up a cheerful demeanor and engage in "stimulating" conversations with family and friends. The belief that the illness was mental, and therefore largely not understood, promoted in Howells the fear that he had somehow failed her by spending so much time away from her with his work. The double burden of his daughter's illness and his own guilt became even harder to bear because of the times when remission seemed imminent and there was cause for hope.

Her status grew very much worse late in 1887, so much so that she went to the sanatorium in Dansville, New York. Howells for a time accompanied his daughter in Dansville, and as circumstances developed it was from there that he fought his lonely and unpopular fight for the lives of the Chicago Anarchists. Finally in 1889, after untold pain and suffering, Winifred died. That her illness was then shown to have been purely organic did little to correct almost ten years of agony and guilt.

Elinor Howells had never been hardy (one letter from Venice says that her weight was down to eighty-two pounds), and the blow of Winifred's death was one from which she never fully recovered. For the last twenty years of her life she was a practical invalid.

The nature of Howells' work with Harper's did not absolutely require that he move from Boston to New York, but coincident with the signing of the contract was the worsening of Winny's health and the resulting need to move frequently. After they moved from the house on Beacon Street, the Howells family never again really lived in a home of their own for very long. They passed perhaps a season or several months at a time in upstate New York, at the seashore, in Maine, in summer houses on Long Island, or in rented apartments in New York City. They did at several times buy houses, but the health of either Winny or Elinor, or sometimes literary business or visits, conspired to keep the family on the move, but judging from the quantity and never faltering steadiness with which he met his obligations he must have developed the ability early in his career of working whenever he got the chance. In a newspaper interview of 1886, he described his workday thus: "I work from 9 in the morning until 1 or 2 in the afternoon; after that the work does not seem to be in me." And he added, "I read nearly all the afternoon. . . . Russian books in the French. . .Spanish books. . .Italian always. . .and every notable American and English book that comes out; they all go to the making of my 'Study' work." He added at the end, "Yes, my health is good."[29]   The time of the interview, August 4, 1886, corresponds roughly to the time of his supposed "breakdown." It seems clear that anyone able to perform such a demanding regimen of work is not one in nervous despair or unable to discharge his responsibilities.

Although the break with Boston was slow in coming, Howells did spend an increasing portion of his time in New York. This pleased J. W. Harper, the head of the publishing firm, who it is evident from his contract with Howells and his later one with Twain, was eager to receive as much return upon his investment as possible. It had been Harper in conjunction with Henry Mills Alden who had persuaded Howells against his better judgment to add a monthly column of criticism for *Harper's Monthly* to the already agreed upon production of fiction. Howells was reluctant to take on work resembling the job he had done at *Atlantic,* where both the quality and the quantity of his fiction suffered, but the extra $3000 must have been a strong factor, considering his continual need for money.

"Editor's Study," though, was not just another book review column of the sort that he had done for years at *Atlantic.* Beginning it was not a matter of settling back into an old routine, although Howells himself may not have been particularly aware of the differences at first. In the August 4 interview he said, "When I began to write the 'Study' I was a little out of practice in that kind of writing. When I first took hold of the *Atlantic Monthly* I wrote all the book notices. Then when I left the magazine I ceased writing any and did not do any sort of critical work for four or five years."[30]   He had made certain with Harper and Alden that he was to be allowed to write whatever he wanted in the column, without the publishing house restrictions against subscription publishers. In fact, he devoted part of his December, 1886 column to an explanation of the subscription book business; Harper said nothing. Nor was he under the obligation to cultivate the good will of the friends of and contributors to *Harper's Magazine,* and he could write about whatever he liked, whether or not it was currently topical.

Opponents of the column viewed it as a personal display of one man's literary prejudices, and certainly some of Howells' less congenial prejudices are strongly represented, for example, his recurring strikes against English fiction, and against the English themselves. Defenders of the column, some of them already friends and followers of Howells, saw the column as a breath of hope in a literarily airless atmosphere. But few were unable to find something with which to disagree, and the rebuttals of the many offended parties assured the continuing level of controversy that hovered over the "Study" throughout its tenure.

II.

Even though "Editor's Study" was the object of much of the criticism heaped upon Howells during the late eighties and early nineties, the opinions expressed there were not always the true cause of the scorn. In this country many critics roundly criticized one or the other of his books, before and just after the beginning of the column, and this scorn left its impression in the minds of other would-be judges. Perhaps the single most damaging element to Howells' image as the kindly old "Dean" of American letters was his part in the protest over the handling of the Haymarket Affair, which was a case in which even the average citizen felt a threat to his way of life, caused largely by the hysterical reaction of the press. The amalgam of these objections and latent fears formed the atmosphere into which "Editor's Study" boldly set its course.

Resentment had been building in England perhaps longer than it had in this country. Howells had maintained an ill-disguised dislike for things and people associated with the English ways of literary life, and these dislikes often made appearances even as early as the book reviews he did for *Atlantic* in the late sixties and throughout the seventies. But in those cases the impact of a provincial American magazine, culturally important though it was, was not as great as it might have been, especially considering *Atlantic's* rather small circulation. But one of Howells' jabs at the English escaped the notice of almost no English literary eye.

Richard Watson Gilder became editor of *Century* in 1881 and soon after commissioned a series of critical evaluations of the three leading writers of the day, Twain, James, and Howells, all of whom, as it happened, were then devoting a great deal of their production to *Century*. T. S. Perry wrote the article on Howells, and Howells himself contributed the pieces on Twain and James. The essays on Howells and Twain appeared first and were normally received, but Howells' essay on James caused an uproar in England. The bulk of the essay is a thoughtful and penetrating evaluation of James' fiction, and while one paragraph toward the end of the article is no less thoughtful—in fact it turned out to be prophetic—it was certainly more controversial.

> The art of fiction has, in fact, become a finer art in our day than it was with Dickens and Thackery. We could not suffer the confidential attitude of the latter now, nor the mannerism of the former, any more than we could endure the prolixity of Richardson or the coarseness of Fielding. These great men are of the past—they and their methods and interests; even Trollope and Reade are not of the present.[31]

So innocently and genuinely had Howells added this evaluation to the article, that when the deluge of reaction began he had to write for a copy of the magazine to see what the controversy was about.[32]

The indignation caused by the audacity of an American suggesting that the fiction of Henry James was comparable to, let alone greater than, that of Dickens and Thackery, and to compound the offense by including a list of the most revered English authors and assert that their relevancy had passed, was loud and long, and its effects enduring. The British newspapers fired the first shots of rebuttal until the heavier, more important reaction was established by the British literary quarterlies, notably *Blackwood's,* which said that Howells' remarks were intended as self-aggrandizement, saying in effect that his own fiction, not just James', was better than its English counterpart.[33]

The straightforwardness and innocence apparent in Howells' evaluation of James at the expense of the English, together with his inability to even guess which of his statements had caused the reaction, indicates that in 1882 Howells did not fully realize that his genuinely held literary views constituted a visible threat to the world of letters as it was then established. The year of 1882 was not a particularly trying time for Howells: Winifred's health seemed to be a problem no longer; he finished and published *A Modern Instance,* the first of his "major" novels; the illness of 1881 had passed and the crises of 1885 still lay in the future; and for the first time in many years he was free of editorial responsibility and could concentrate upon his novels. Thus, at least in an incipient sense, Howells' sense of alienation was an outgrowth of his own artistic tenets, and while they were specified and codified by the trying events to come, they were not solely a product of them.

Howells' accusation of English fiction becomes to some critics evidence that he was in a conscious struggle to establish the long-sought "American critical standards." While efforts in "Editor's Study" and elsewhere did contribute to the attitude that American literature was a separate discipline from English fiction, not necessarily judged by the same standards, it is a distortion to view this movement as Howells' primary goal. Howells was always a very sensitive and precise observer of people, and he took genuine fascination in recording their everyday actions and motives. Very early in his career he took offense at the depiction of superhuman and subhuman characters by Romantic writers like Scott. He was unable to appreciate the viewpoint that any ultimate truth could be conveyed through exaggerated actions and motives. His criticism continually accuses such writers of a lack of truth, and by this he did not mean the capitalized Truth in the sense of a moral lesson, but a basic adherence to the example provided by people everywhere. The attitude that Truth could only be gotten from actuality perhaps betrays a failure of the tolerant attitude in Howells. This failure was older and more basic than the desire to escape from under the critical thumb of the mother country; it was a personality trait, and probably the source of some of the most damning criticism to be levelled against Howells and his works.

The pages of *Century* were the source of adverse reaction to Howells in 1882. *A Modern Instance,* serialized by *Century* in 1881-82, was the first American novel dealing completely and specifically with the problem of divorce. While many of Howells' friends and literary acquaintances wrote to praise the novel, among them, James, Twain, and John Hay, there were many others who resented the subject's having been opened, as for example, Robert Louis Stevenson, who wrote on December 4, 1882 to say:

> My wife did me the honour to divorce her husband in order to marry me. It will be a sincere disappointment to find that you cannot be my guest. I shall bear up however; for I assure you I desire to know no one who considers himself holier than my wife.[34]

Many other reviewers less personally affronted than Stevenson pronounced the book depressing and dealing with subject matter that ought properly to be left untouched.

Howells had been developing the idea for the book for about five years before he actively began to write it. During its production he became ill, from overwork as he told his father, and by all indications the book had been a difficult one for him to produce. He may have been spared part of the adverse criticism, since the letters of praise from friends came directly to him, and the essays of condemnation were for the most part in newspapers and periodicals, and Howells was not in as close contact with these as he might have been, since he had taken the opportunity, no longer having a magazine to edit, and Winifred's apparently having recovered from her two year illness, to take an extended trip to Europe. But whether Howells was immediately aware of the criticism or not, attitudes of censure on the part of a large section of the reading public were becoming less and less vague, and together they formed the atmosphere prevalent considerably before the first installment of "Editor's Study" was written. The opinions expressed in the "Study" certainly did their part to win some friends and alienate some others, but judging their impact would be difficult without an idea of the critical context into which they appeared.

If Howells' novels caused more controversy than they had before, one reason for it was that far more people were reading them. The circulation of *Century* in the early 1880's was about 200,000, compared to 12,000 for *Atlantic Monthly*.[35] Also the attitude of *Century's* editor, Richard Watson Gilder, did nothing to alleviate the controversy. Proud of having the three foremost writers of the day in his publication, he rightly assumed that controversy sells magazines.

If *A Modern Instance* raised the most controversy in the first half of the decade, the holder of the title in the last half of the 1880's would surely be *The Minister's Charge*, which appeared in 1886. The central figure, Lemuel Barker, is a young farm lad who comes to Boston in search of a literary career. Filling the role of the satiric innocent, he encounters prostitutes and con-men in Boston, and lands in jail on a trumped-up charge. There the Reverend Mr. Sewell takes charge of both Lemuel and the rest of the novel. From a modern view the fault of the novel is that having gotten off to a good start in telling Lem's story, Howells then adopts the middle class attitudes and standards of Sewell, and therefore prevents the story from making a statement of how the "other half" lives. But by the then-current standards, the affront to the proper Bostonians that Howells had once cultivated as friends was unforgivable. They objected to being shown in their literature what they had carefully insulated themselves from in real life, and for an author, himself a Bostonian, to destroy the illusion, even if tentatively and with forebearance, was a breach of trust. And soon the breach was widened and the suspicions then only loosely held were confirmed.

The *Modern Instance* controversy, which touched both sides of the ocean, had not subsided before the shouts started from England objecting to Howells' assessment of James. Then came the gentler rumblings aroused by *The Rise of Silas Lapham,* which depicted ingrown malfeasance in the business world, besides an unusual amount of sexual imagery, followed by the more violent storm of the first iconoclastic installments of "Editor's Study," and the confirming transgression of *The Minister's Charge.* And then, sin of sins, Howells took the side of the convicted anarchists and murderers of the Haymarket Affair. The blows which transformed Howells' image from that of a diffident man of letters into that of a radical, berserk, social and literary rebel were as regular and effective as the blows from a blacksmith's hammer. To view the change from *Atlantic Monthly* to *Harper's Monthly* as that of an establishment reviewer of books in Boston becoming an establishment reviewer of books in New York is dangerously wrong. The Howells who left *Atlantic* was not the same as the Howells who took up residence in Harper's "Study," and he was to be different yet before he left the column.

Often the monthly pronouncements from "Editor's Study" took the form of a general dialogue in print between Howells on the one hand and his many detractors on the other. The newspaper drama and book critics sometimes saved their Sunday editions to reply to Howells' latest attacks. For example in the "Study" for August, 1891, Howells launched an attack on the medium of legitimate drama, saying in effect that is conventions assigned it to the realm of subliterature. Soon after publication, the *New York Times* drama critic ran underneath the headline "Mr. Howells At It Again" a story containing his rebuttal, along with the statement, "Indeed, Mr. Howells' false judgments of literature and art sometimes make us fear that his observations of contemporary life are not so true as we have been striving to believe."[36] Such public arguments usually ended with the statement by one side and a reaction by the other, but occasionally Howells, in his less immediate forum, opened the question again, having seen the printed reply to his first statement, albeit between the two statements several months had passed because of the time lag in printing.

The *Times* statements above reveals a fairly common trait in the printed reactions to the "Study," namely an attack upon Howells' work in other areas because of statements Howells made as a literary critic. The relationship also works in reverse. Under the guise of reviewing a work by Howells, reviewers often slipped in strikes at his other areas of endeavor. For example, an earlier edition of the *New York Times* reviewed his ballet, "A Sea Change," with the statement, "His effort in the composition of one [ballet] naturally takes the color of his severely chaste and frigid mind."[37] The ostensible review of the ballet ends with the statement:

> The novelist who contents himself with a plain statement of facts within the reach of everybody can scarcely be said to fulfill all the obligations a literary artist owes to the world and to himself.[38]

So eager is the *Times* reviewer who signed himself "E.A.D." to do damage to Howells wherever possible that he includes the observation, "Surely the pitiable tale of his doings [Bartley Hubbard's] is not. . .worth telling. . . ."[39]

The *Times* of May 25, 1890 contained a reply to a statement made by Howells in the installment of the "Study" for June, 1890: "Mr. William Dean Howells has the faculty of saying more in a few words and less in many than any other American author of this time."[40] That the reply practically coincided with the magazine's appearance on the newsstands suggests that the duel of words amounted to more than casual comments.

The "Study" for August, 1890 contained Howells' attack upon those critics who reviewed works anonymously while hiding behind the prestige of a respected journal. (He cannot have forgotten about his book reviews, all unsigned, that appeared in *Atlantic*.) This time *Nation* was ready with a fast defense:

> The fact is that Mr. Howells, in nearly all his criticisms during the last five years, has illustrated, by his lack of it, one great advantage of anonymous criticism. . . . He has expressed his personal opinions without let or hindrance; and the result has been a mass of judgments upon great and petty authors which is remarkable for eccentricity, dogmatism, and the spirit of faction.[41]

But the most vicious attack came not from a critic who was an enemy, but from a friend, who was an author. In the "Study" for February, 1889, Howells included Ambrose Bierce in a list of thirteen outstanding American humorists. Bierce was apparently not impressed, for on May 23, 1892 he wrote:

> The master of this detestable school of fiction [Realism] is Mr. Howells. Absolutely destitute of that supreme and sufficient literary endowment, imagination, he does not what he would but what he can. . . . For years this diligent insufferable has been conducting a department of criticism in *Harper's Magazine* with the sole purpose of expounding. . .the offspring of his own limitations.[42]

To summarize, then, the context into which the first installments of "Editor's Study" appeared was always latently, sometimes openly, hostile. From the public's point of view, Howells' good name and dependable image had received a succession of body blows that left an image of immorality, depravity, anarchism, social offense, and poor taste. Howells still had his friends and followers, but the people who had before been merely neutral were now both afraid and unfriendly. Howells felt compelled to write to his father in 1887 to reassure him lest he be disturbed by what he read of his son in the papers.[43] Newspaper and journal critics strove to be the first to take a stand against a particular view that he had expressed, and sometimes produced attacks at the *ad hominem* level. During this difficult period in his life, Howells had many friends and admirers, but he also had many more very vocal and very irate opponents.

III.

In October of 1885 when Howells signed his contract with J. W. Harper, he was reluctant to add to the considerable duties already specified the responsibility for a new department for *Harper's Monthly.* His concern, of course, was with the amount of energy diverted every month away from his production of fiction. The writing itself was not seriously time consuming. The monthly production of three to five printed pages was only the work of a day or two, but the necessity of keeping up with all the works of all the current authors *was* time consuming, and he had learned from the years at *Atlantic* how demanding a task it could be. Perhaps the consideration of time was foremost on his mind when he asked for, and received, assurance from Harper that the column was to be entirely under his control, and he would not be obligated to review any certain number of books, or indeed books at all. According to his own description of his work habits, his best hours for production of fiction were in the morning, so with further work on novels out of the question, his afternoons might as well be spent in preparing for his "Study" column.

He moved out of his Boston house at about the time his work on the "Study" began, and thereafter frequent moves became the rule, due largely to Winifred's health. So, while production of fiction went ahead almost every day that he was healthy, it was never done at the same place for any length of time. The fanciful description of a sumptuously furnished study, with windows overlooking the "confluence of the Hudson and Charles Rivers," heavy rugs underfoot, and richly carved mahogany table, bears no resemblance whatever to the place where the columns were actually composed.

In a letter to Twain dated May 23, 1886, Howells says, "Tomorrow I have to switch off and do a 'Study'."[44] The switching off to which he refers in this case was of the writing of *April Hopes.* Taking the 24th of a month as a typical beginning date for the writing of the "Study," and remembering that a "Study" written on a particular day was for publication in the issue date the third month hence, yields a general idea about when Howells actually made the statements appearing in the "Study." Thus, the fictive description of the study that appeared in the January, 1886 issue was actually written around October 24, 1885. The material that he had to "switch off" *April Hopes* to produce appeared in the August, 1886 issue, and so forth. Considering Howells' nomadic life, some of the columns must have been produced in trains and rooms of various resort hotels. He adds in the Twain letter referred to above, concerning the column, "What a fool I was to undertake that!"[45] He wrote the letter just in the midst of a long sequence of abuses in the press that were a result of both his novels and the column. Before the storm abated, he must have felt even sorrier for taking the responsibility.

Howells says in the first installment that novels rather than "solider" forms of literature would occupy his main attention, and novels do, in the final analysis, form the bulk of the raw material upon which he comments. Contending strongly for second place are short story collections, biographies, and works of history. Relatively few important substantive statements relate to poetry, perhaps at first glance peculiar in view of his being a "disgruntled" poet. He does devote one column to the "strange" poetry of Emily Dickinson, which had just appeared, but for the most part the poems that he quotes in the column and the collections he reviews are not matters likely to cause controversy.

If novels, then, form Howells' main body of data, the group

of novels within that body most remarkable for its size is the foreign novels. Works of Palacio Valdés, Tolstoy, Dostoyevsky, Turgenev, Zola, and Boyeson recur again and again as illustrations of Howells' ideas of propriety in literature. Many of the works of these authors and the other foreign writers represented were not available to the American reading public when the columns appeared. Some, notably those of Tolstoy, were not even available in English anywhere. Fortunately, Howells was an amazingly efficient self-taught linguist. His formal education amounted to less than two years while he lived in Ohio,[46] but nevertheless he could read and speak several languages including French, Spanish, and Italian with perfect fluency. He set up regular correspondence with writers such as Armando Palacio Valdés, whose works were almost entirely unknown, and certainly entirely unavailable in English.

One of the reasons for the continuing animosity with the English was Howells' assertion that the most important developments in European literature came not from England, but from the Continent. Victorian Englishmen regarded European authors such as Zola as hopelessly and criminally immoral, and the very thought that such literature could rightly sit on the same shelf as the works of, say, Thackery, was an intolerable affront. But Howells continued to champion the European cause and the change in literary standards that it represented, even when, as Carter reports,[47] Henry Mills Alden set aside his promise of non-interference with Howells' column, and objected to favorable statements Howells made concerning Zola's *La Terre*.

One place where Howells saw promise in American literature was with the local color writers, as they later came to be called. Regionalists such as Sarah Orne Jewett, Mary Noailles Murfree, Rose Terry Cooke, and John William De Forest were the objects of his continuing attention, because they, he felt, told the truth about people.

At first look Howells' liking for local color writers may seem anomalous. Surely the stock in trade of the regionalists is the tall tale about the larger-than-life hero, and as such must be a good approximation of the novels of Romance, such as those of Scott. But Howells applauded the tendency to deal with ordinary people rather than kings and princes and to have them speak

in at least an approximation of colloquial speech. Even Howells'
special friends and favorites, Mark Twain, James Russell Lowell,
and John Hay, were cast in this regional mold.

One way to become a subject of one of the essays in "Editor's Study" was to display in almost any forum promise toward
achieving Howells' ideal. Many little known and anonymous
writers received some of their earliest notices because of the
closeness of Howells to the publishing industry all over the
country. But another and perhaps more certain way to get into
the column was to be one of his special friends or acquaintances.
The people appearing in the column often appeared in other
capacities in Howells' life. A partial list of these "friends of the
'Study' " follows:

> Thomas Bailey Aldrich — Howells' friend since both were early
> contributors to New York's *Saturday Press.* He succeeded
> Howells as editor of *Atlantic Monthly* when Howells left in
> 1881.

> Hjalmar Hjorth Boyeson — a young, Norwegian-born novelist
> whom Howells befriended while he was *Atlantic* editor in 1871.
> They were thereafter close friends.

> George Washington Cable — actually a closer friend of Twain's, but
> there existed for a while a plan for a company of speakers for
> the lecture circuit, to include Twain, Howells, Cable, and several
> others. Eventually only Twain and Cable went on the tour.

> Samuel Langhorne Clemens — Howells' closest friend. Each had an
> important influence upon the work of the other. They planned
> many joint business and literary ventures, most of which never
> materialized.

> Hamlin Garland — became a devotee of Howells after reading one
> of his novels in 1881. While his early work was strongly de-
> pendent upon Howells' directives, later pieces showed progres-
> sively less influence.

> Richard Watson Gilder — became editor of *Century* in 1881, and
> published in serial form all the novels Howells wrote between
> leaving *Atlantic* and joining *Harper's.*

John Hay — Abraham Lincoln's secretary. It was through Hay that Howells secured his appointment as consul to Venice. Hay's *Pike County Ballads* and his poetry were favorites of Howells.

Oliver Wendell Holmes — Howells first met Holmes through the agency of Lowell on the first trip to Boston. Holmes was the epitome of the proper Bostonian, an image which Howells emulated for several years.

Henry James, Jr. — The James family became important to Howells while he was in Boston. Discussions of literary theory with Henry provided a useful training ground in the days when most of Howells' efforts went to the production of travel books. After James moved more or less permanently to England, the relationship took the form of long personal letters.

William James — elder brother of Henry, and a specialist in psychology.

Sergei Mikhailovich Kravchinski — used the pseudonym "Stepniak." He stayed with Howells in Boston while on an American lecture tour about the people and literature of his native Russia.

James Russell Lowell — Howells' lifelong mentor. Lowell was editor of *Atlantic* when the young Howells submitted his first poem, and later introduced him to the Boston literary powers. Howells felt uneasy at filling the job at *Atlantic* that Lowell had once held.

S. Weir Mitchell — a notable physician who treated Winifred Howells during much of her long illness. It was his famous "rest cure" that necessitated her staying in bed and eating eight meals a day.

Louise Chandler Moulton — in editing a collection of poems in 1891 asked for and received permission to include some of the poems written by Winifred.

John George Nicolay — other secretary to Abraham Lincoln while he was President. He collaborated with Hay on *Abraham Lincoln: A History.*

Albert Marshman Palmer — theatrical producer who in 1886 sponsored a series of "Author's Matinees," in Madison Square Theatre. The first play in the series was Howells' dramatization of *A Foregone Conclusion.*

Edmund Clarence Stedman — third in the trio of contributors (Howells, Aldrich, Stedman) to the *Saturday Press* in the 1850's who became lifelong friends.

Armando Palacio Valdés — Howells did not meet Palacio Valdés until 1911, but for twenty-five years before, they had a constant correspondence. Palacio Valdés' first letter to Howells was to thank him for his reviews in "Editor's Study."

These are some of the people to whose works Howells refers again and again. When Howells makes a point about the preferability of colloquial language, Lowell's name, or Hosea Biglow's, inevitably occurs. A point concerning truth of motive often involves Palacio Valdés. These writers form the backbone of the "Editor's Study."

The tone that Howells used in writing the columns was often aggressive and defiant. The installments have little of the fastidious politeness shown in some of the novels and farces. In the opening number he says:

If the reader disagrees. . .upon any point, he will be allowed to write for publication. . ., when, if the editor can not expose the reader's folly, he will be apt to suppress his letter.

The mood here, of course, is in the same half-jocular mood as the fanciful description of the study itself which precedes it. But in fact the jocularity disguises a grain of truth. The "Study" was never conciliatory, even when Howells was forced to retract factual errors.

Part of the cause of the independent and defiant tone is that several political issues find their forum in the "Study." Loudest and longest of the political fights in the column is over the enactment of an international copyright law. Countries of the world had reached such an agreement before the "Editor's Study" finished its run in 1892, but before the law, authors were apt to have their works pirated.

American publishers producing books by American authors made the usual agreement with the author about how he was to be paid for his work. The agreement normally was for a sum of money plus a royalty arrangement on the sale of books. But if an American publisher wanted to publish a book by, say, an English author, there existed no assurance that the foreign writer would be paid at all. Publishing houses did sometimes make some sort of minimal payment to the author, but the author was hardly in a position to bargain. If he objected the publisher simply published anyway and paid him nothing.

Of course, the same situation might work in reverse; that is, British publishers were free to publish American books without payment, but in fact the British market for American books was then comparatively small. Howells argued for the enactment of an international agreement whereby an author, whatever his nationality, received just recompense for the sale of his work. With Howells the question was largely one of conscience; he had worked for one major publishing house or another throughout most of his career, and his employers stood to lose money should the agreement be reached. But also on his mind was the improvement of American literature. Publishers who could no longer make money by bringing out cheap foreign editions would have to turn elsewhere for their raw material, to the young and regional writers of this country, as well as to the established authors.

A cause upon which Howells had much less visible success was socialism. This campaign on the part of Howells was largely an outgrowth of the importance that Tolstoy played in this part of his career, but in looking for less radical solutions to the problems of morality raised by Tolstoy, he found more practical socialists such as Laurence Gronland and William Morris. The fight for social reform was a much longer and more complicated fight than the international copyright question. Howells' generation and many after it would live to see only slight progress.

The important factor to remember about Howells' arguments for socialism is the unpopularity of and fear for the cause. Newspapers lumped socialists together with anarchists, ignoring the diametrically opposing philosophies, and almost anyone who threw a bomb or committed a crime of violence was an "anarchist." Howells had, almost without realizing it, become a genuine social and literary radical.

A corollary problem to any edition of "Editor's Study" is the book called *Criticism and Fiction*. The book has almost certainly done more damage to Howells' reputation than the most irresponsible of his critics. *Criticism and Fiction* contains pasted together statements that seemingly belie all the important and drastic changes in outlook that Howells underwent in the 1880's. Carter devotes a section of his Fourth Chapter to invalidating the book,[48] and the points he makes there are well taken. Haste and the unwillingness to establish the book's continuity were the most serious problems, but the idea of making a coherent statement from material that itself serves as an example of Howells' changes and growth is wrong.

The remaining problem with Carter's invalidation and those of Howells' other biographers is that in the end it cannot be ignored, because Howells himself was responsible for the book. The present edition indicates by brackets which portions of the original "Editor's Study" text found their way into *Criticism and Fiction* and the notes associated with the passages indicate where in the book they may be found. It cannot really be shown conclusively that *Criticism and Fiction* is not a fair representation of Howells' beliefs at the time in question, without demonstrating both the source and the destination of Howells' words.

NOTES

[1] Kenneth S. Lynn, *William Dean Howells: An American Life* (New York: Harcourt Brace Jovanovich, Inc., 1971), p. 135.

[2] Mildred Howells, ed., *Life in Letters of William Dean Howells* (Garden City, New York: Doubleday, Doran & Company, Inc., 1928), I, p. 105.

[3] Lynn, p. 135.

[4] Lynn, p. 266.

[5] Lynn, p. 186.

[6] [William Dean Howells], "Reviews and Literary Notices," *Atlantic Monthly*, 24 (December, 1869), pp. 765-766.

[7] Mildred Howells, ed., I, p. 303.

[8] Mildred Howells, ed., I, p. 305.

[9] *Scribner's Monthly* changed its name to *Century* beginning with the November, 1881 issue. To prevent confusion the publication shall hereinafter be referred to as *Century*, whether the reference in question was before or after the change.

[10] Lynn, p. 258.

[11] Mildred Howells, ed., I, p. 307.

[12] Lynn, p. 258.

[13] Mildred Howells, ed., I, p. 310.

[14] Marrion Wilcox, "Works of William Dean Howells - (1860-96)," *Harper's Weekly*, 40 (July 4, 1896), pp. 655-656.

[15]Everett Carter, *Howells and the Age of Realism* (Philadelphia: J. B. Lippincott Company, 1954), p. 183.

[16]Lynn, p. 282.

[17]William Dean Howells, *My Literary Passions* (New York: Harper and Brothers, 1895), p. 250.

[18]Janko Lavrin, *Tolstoy: An Approach* (New York: The Macmillan Company, 1946), p. 109.

[19]Mildred Howells, ed., I, p. 417.

[20]Mildred Howells, ed., I, pp. 363-364.

[21]Lynn, p. 275.

[22]Mildred Howells, ed., I, p. 393.

[23]Mildred Howells, ed., I, pp. 398-399.

[24]Lynn, p. 291.

[25]Carter, p. 184.

[26]Mildred Howells, ed., I, p. 372.

[27]Edward Wagenknecht, *William Dean Howells: The Friendly Eye* (New York: Oxford University Press, 1969), p. 58.

[28]Mildred Howells, ed., I, p. 404.

[29]*The New York Times*, August 4, 1886, p. 4.

[30]*The New York Times*, August 4, 1886, p. 4.

[31]William Dean Howells, "Henry James, Jr.," *Century* 24 (November, 1882), p. 28.

[32]Edwin H. Cady, *The Road to Realism* (Syracuse, New York: Syracuse University Press, 1956), pp. 218-219.

[33]T. M. Coan, "Studies in Literature," *Blackwood's Magazine* 133 (January, 1883), pp. 136-161.

[34]Mildred Howells, ed., I, pp. 332-333.

[35]Lynn, p. 266.

[36]"Mr. Howells At It Again," *The New York Times,* August 9, 1891, p. 13.

[37]*The New York Times,* July 15, 1888, p. 10.

[38]*The New York Times,* July 15, 1888, p. 10.

[39]*The New York Times,* July 15, 1888, p. 10.

[40]*The New York Times,* May 25, 1890, p. 13.

[41]Anonymous, *Nation* 51 (August 7, 1890), pp. 111-112.

[42][Ambrose Bierce], *The New York Times,* May 23, 1892, p. 5.

[43]Lynn, p. 286.

[44]Mildred Howells, ed., I, p. 384.

[45]Mildred Howells, ed., I, p. 384.

[46]Cady, p. 25.

[47]Carter, pp. 185-190.

[48]Carter, pp. 185-190.

January, 1886

Editor's Study.

I.

THERE are few words so sympathetically compliant with a varied need as the word used to conceal the real character of this new department of the *New Monthly*. In almost every dwelling of any pretensions to taste there is nowadays a study, charmingly imagined by the architect and prettily equipped by the domestic powers, where the master of the house lounges away his leisure, scanty or abundant, and nobody apparently studies. From a very early time, or at least from the opening of the present genteel period when the whole race began to put on airs of intellectual refinement, the "study" has been known; and even in the *Book of Snobs* we read of Major Ponto's study, where "the library consisted mostly of boots," gardening tools, fishing-rods, whips, spurs, and pots of blacking; and such branches of literary inquiry were discussed as the fate of the calf or the sentence of the pig. This, to be sure, was the study of a country gentleman, and the study of an editor of such a magazine as ours is necessarily somewhat different, though its appointments are equally expressive, we hope, of cultivated pursuits. It is, in any case, not at all the kind of place which the reader, with his mind full of the Grub Street traditions of literature, would fancy—a narrow den at the top of the house, where the occupant, piled about with books and proofs and manuscripts, darkles in a cloud blown from his own cigar. The real editor, before whom contributors tremble, may be something like this in his habitat and environment; but the unreal editor, the airy, elusive abstraction who edits the Study, is quite another character, and is fittingly circumstanced. Heavy rugs silence the foot upon his floor; nothing but the costliest masterpieces gleam from his walls; the best of the old literatures, in a subtly chorded harmony of bindings, make music to the eye from his shelves, and the freshest of the new load his richly carved mahogany table. His vast windows of flawless plate look out upon the confluent waters of the Hudson and the Charles, with expanses, in the middle distance, of the Mississippi, the Great Lakes, and the Golden Gate, and in the background the misty line of the Thames, with reaches of the remoter Seine, and glints of the Tiber's yellow tide. The peaks of the Apennines, dreamily blending with those of the Sierras, form the vanishing-point of the delicious perspective; and we need not say that the edifice in which this study luxuriously lurks commands the very best view of the Washington Monument and the two-pair-front of the national Capitol. As a last secret we will own that the edifice is an American architect's adaptation of a design

by the poet Ariosto, who for reasons of economy built himself a very small house in a back street of Ferrara, while he lavished his palaces on the readers of his poetry at no expense to himself; it was originally in the Spanish taste, but the architect has added some touches of the new Renaissance, and has done what he could to impart a colonial flavor to the whole.

In such keeping, the editor of the Study proposes to sit at fine ease, and talk over with the reader—who will always be welcome here —such matters of literary interest as may come up from time to time, whether suggested by the new books of the day or other accidents of the literary life. The reader will, of course, not be allowed to interrupt the editor while he is talking; in return the editor will try to keep his temper, and to be as inconclusive as possible. If the reader disagrees with him upon any point, he will be allowed to write to him for publication, when, if the editor can not expose the reader's folly, he will be apt to suppress his letter. It is meant, in other terms, to make the Study a sort of free parliament, but for the presiding officer only; or, a symposium of one.

The editor comes to his place after a silence of some years in this sort, and has a very pretty store of prejudices to indulge and grudges to satisfy, which he will do with as great decency as possible. Their victims will at once know them for prejudices and grudges, and so no great harm will be done; it is impartiality that is to be feared in these matters, and a man who likes or dislikes can never be impartial—though perhaps a woman might. The editor will not deny that in addition to his prejudices and grudges he has some opinions, honest as opinions go, but cherished possibly because he has had no opportunity to exchange them with others. With a reader reduced to silence, the affair of their expression will be very simple; the reader will accept them or not as he likes, and having no chance to reply, will not be argued into them. While the editor's guest, he is invited to look at the same books and consider the same facts with him, and—tacitly, of course—may disable his judgment as much as he will. If he is not content with this, there will always be a vast body of literature not under discussion, and he may turn for relief to that.

II.

If any one, for example, prefers the *History of England*, which Major Ponto had been reading all the morning when he asked Mr. Snob into his study, there is certainly no reason why he must join the editor in turning over the novels which happen for the most part to cumber his table. If himself a novelist, he will probably not care so much for them as for some solider sorts of literature; he will choose almost any history, or biography, or travels, or volume of *mémoires pour servir*, which will feed his imagination and afford him material, like so much life; if he is an unsuccessful novelist, he will in this way spare himself the sting of envy, which certain of the books before us might inflict. Yet, if he is not this, if he is a reader who reads novels, and not a reader who writes them, we think he will do himself a pleasure by looking at a few of them with us.

For our own part, these novels strike us in their range and tendency as admirable. We will[1] not say they are all good, or that any of them is wholly good; but we find in nearly every one of them a disposition to regard our life without the literary glasses so long thought desirable, and to see character, not as it is in other fiction, but as it abounds outside of all fiction. This disposition sometimes goes with poor enough performance, but in some of the books it goes with performance that is excellent; and at any rate it is for the present more valuable than evenness of performance. It is what relates American fiction to the only living movement in imaginative literature, and distinguishes by a superior freshness and authenticity this group of American novels from a similarly accidental group of English novels, giving them the same good right to be as the like number of recent Russian novels, French novels, Spanish novels, Italian novels, Norwegian novels. If we take[2] one of the best of these new fictions of ours, like Miss Murfree's *Prophet of the Great Smoky Mountain*, we shall hardly find it inferior in method or manner to the best of the new fictions anywhere; it is, in fact, a charming effect of literary skill working simply and naturally, and marred only here and there by the traditions of the bad school we were all brought up in. It is well to call things by their names, even if they are spades, and when Miss Murfree, having arrived at a thrilling, triumphant moment with her lovers, breaks bounds and tells us that the "wild winds whirled around the great Smoky Mountain, and the world was given over to the clouds and night, and the rain and the drops splashed with a dreary sound down from the eaves of the house," we know whom she learned that poor business of—who the great master was, that, having done a fine thing, abandoned himself to hysterical emotionality over it, or what people call "sympathy with his characters," and presently wandered off into a waste of hollow and sounding verbiage. We have some fear, also, that Dickens, with his Victor Hugoish martyr of a Sidney Carton, was not wholly absent when the last end of Miss Murfree's *Prophet* was imagined, though probably enough he was not present to the author's consciousness. It is not in such romantic wise that men really die for men; the real sacrifices, indeed, have been offered for races, not for persons; it is not after this manner that even a saint gives his life to save his enemy's. If Kelsey's substitution of himself for Micajah Green, whom the Cayces meant to kill, was insanely voluntary, it was not interesting, for no act of lunacy is so, except pathologically; if it was voluntary, it was romantic, which is worse than uninteresting; if it was accidental, it was insignificant. But it is really the least important matter of a

freshly delightful and artistic book, dealing so strenuously with a strange world that even in our strangeness to it we have the courage to call it faithful. The author has painted us those Tennessee mountaineers of hers before, but never a group so bold and cognizable as the tranquil-conscienced, not unamiably homicidal Cayces, with their brush-whiskey still; the implacably jealous Rick Tyler; the brutally avaricious blacksmith Fletcher; and the whole neighborhood of lank-bodied, religious, unmoral, primitive-passioned people; and that dreamy yet clear-headed, simply generous, and thoroughly sensible beauty, Dorinda. The girl is, in fact, the best figure of the story: when it touches her, it rises and brightens; a note limpid and serene strikes above the mingling of harsh sounds; a light, cool yet tender and lovely, throws its effluence across the rude picture. It does not matter, after one has valued her aright, that the Prophet himself remains misty rather than mystical, and seems to have been scarcely worth the pains taken with him. The art of the book is, for the most part, very good; there is little comment; the people speak for themselves. If we are perhaps called too often to look at the landscape, the landscape is certainly always worth looking at, and the book, wherever it escapes from tradition, both satisfies and piques. After one has finished it, one wants to know what Miss Murfree's next book will be like.

Through such work as hers and Mr. Cable's the South is making itself heard in literature after a fashion likely to keep attention as well as to provoke it. These writers, while they study so carefully the actual speech and manners of the people they write of, still permit themselves a certain romance of motive; but the other day there came to us—or was it the other week or month? the succession of these things is so rapid—another Southern book, very well written too, which concerned itself with some phases of our varied national life, and with characters moved by the natural impulses that we see at play in the people about us. The authoress of *Across the Chasm*[3] overdoes her Northern hero somewhat, and makes him a bit of a prig—a good deal of a prig; but the Southern personages she contrasts him with are obviously true and well done both as to their good and their bad qualities. She has also finely guessed and happily suggested the Northern people, whom she was not so much concerned to make impressive as her hero, and she has used them as a foil to her Southerners, who think themselves ladies and gentlemen because their families and neighborhoods think them so, and who have none of the social anxiety, the wish to be of vogue, which attends the citizens of our wider and richer and more knowing world. They are all brought on the scene at Washington—very good ground for fiction still, if one will honestly subsoil it—where the Southerners come up with a humorously recognized air of coming back to their own, and are shown poor, provincial, a little bewildered, and rather braggart, but touched with a patriotic tenderness which also shows them wholly free from the snobbishness that mars the good-breeding of the Northerners. Snobbishness is rather a hard word for it, perhaps; it is not really so bad as that. A distinguished and polished Bostonian like General Gaston is flattered at a certain piece of social attention which leaves

3

the imagination of an Alabama brigadier quite unmoved—possibly because the Alabamian has not the perspective for viewing it aright. The hand that can give us actualities like Charley Somers, the local adorer of the heroine in the Southern village where she has lived, and Major King, the shabby, arrogant rebel soldier who comes to call upon her in the evening, at Washington, and stays till eleven o'clock, is destined to better work hereafter, and should not trouble itself with such conventional figures as Louis Gaston, the hero-prig from Boston, and Alan Decourcey, the too fascinatingly wicked and fine-worldly unreality from Baltimore.

Not that we would be exacting with a very clever little book that had given us pleasure. Perhaps two or three thoroughly well represented people are all that one has a right to ask of a novel; though in that case they ought to be the principal people. We should not have asked more from Dr. Weir Mitchell, if he had no more to give us in his novel *In War Time*, than the perfectly divined character of Ezra Wendell, for example. It was a new thing to attempt to paint a cowardly nature like that; and it was no less the affair of a good art than of a humane spirit to do justice to the gentleness that goes with the timidity, the sensibility that accompanies the falseness, the good-will that qualifies the selfishness. It is a very deep and awful tragedy, that poor soul's, and if it does not bring conviction of sin to the reader, in an age too enlightened for that, it can hardly fail to stir him with the wish to be a little truer; and this, young ladies and gentlemen who intend writing novels for the consideration of our successors, is a finer thing for the novel to do than "to be entertaining," which is well enough too. One feels in the portrayal of Wendell a touch, steady and strong, which has equal force in the characterization of his sister Ann. These represent in two extremes the decay of Puritanism; in one the moral nature almost paralyzed, in the other, hysterically active—a conscience divided from reason, working automatically, with a sort of stupefied helplessness. It is not strange if two personages depicted with so much power as these southward-drifted New-Englanders should remain the chief effect of the book in the reader's mind; though it is true that the whole atmosphere of the story is, as some one has acutely said, Philadelphian as distinguished from the Bostonian or Southern or Western atmosphere. This decided localization is most valuable; more valuable still is the artistic quiet of the book, which takes at once a high level, and keeps it without the emotional foolishness of manner or the contorted pseudo-dramaticism of method which cause the compassionate to grieve over so much of our fiction, especially our lady-fiction.

The grip—we might almost say the clutch—of a hand not new in fiction, but here making itself felt with novel power, is laid upon the reader of *A Wheel of Fire*. It is the most intense, the most absorbing, by far, of the stories we have lately read; and we think no one can read it without recognizing in it a distinct and individual quality, which, whatever it is, ought to be hereafter known as Mr. Bates's. He has taken a lurid theme, the dark problem of hereditary insanity, and he studies it with relentless vigor in the story of a young girl who goes mad at last, on her wedding day, through fear of the family taint. He wisely refuses to ask us to be interested in her a moment after her madness comes upon her, but we know all her anguish and despair up to that moment. He has imagined a lovely figure, noble and full of pathos, but as natural and probable as the coquettish cousin who supplies what relief the tragedy has in her flirtations and quarrels with the doctor in charge of Damaris Wainwright's insane brother. These characters are both very well managed—the girl with her heartless teasing and mischievous experiments upon the doctor's temper, and he with his thorough science counterbalanced by a certain native brutality and social inferiority: the reader who is not charmed with them is made very skillfully to feel the charm they have for each other. The motive of the book is almost romantic, but the treatment is not at all romantic; it is scientific, naturalistic; it has its lapses of art, but the lurid theme is kept in the full light of day, and in this sort there is something apparently still to be done with the romantic motive, so apt otherwise to turn allegoric and mechanical on its victim's hands. The scene of the story is largely in Boston, and for the rest at an old country house not far away, and the social *entourage* is perceptibly Bostonian.

III.

In these books and in Mr. Picard's unequally managed novelette of *A Mission Flower* (he managed *A Matter of Taste*, his first book, better upon the whole); in a painfully faithful but not finally unhopeful little study of Yankee village life called *A New England Conscience*, by Miss Belle C. Greene; in Mr. Edgar Fawcett's *Social Silhouettes*, which, in spite of their high coloring and the overdramatization of the patrician quality of Mr. Manhattan, the supposed author, do strongly suggest certain probable phases of New York society—in all these books we find not only that disposition to look at life which we have noted, but a disposition to look at it keenly and closely in the right American manner, and to question the results with the last fineness for their meaning and their value. There is conscience and purpose in it all, and it is all far from the make-believe "Greek" theory of art for art's sake—as if the Greekest of the Greek art were not for religion's sake, as the Greeks understood it. Moreover, in this American fiction, American life is not only getting looked at, but getting fairly well represented, not in some typical embodiment long dreamed of as the business of a great American novel, but in details of motive and character slowly and honestly assembled by many hands from its vast spaces and varieties. We shall probably never have a great American novel as fancied by the fondness of critics, and for our own part we care no more to have it than to have "a literary centre," which from time to time the injudicious set about fixing in this place or that, but mainly establishing in New York, to the lasting shame and loss of Boston. It is not a question that need be seriously discussed, but we invite the friends of a literary centre to observe that literary centres and artistic centres and scientific centres and religious centres and political centres have hitherto been the creations of monarchies, not to say despotisms, and that they are quite alien to the spirit of the federal nationalities. These nationalities, in Italy and Germany, got on extremely well without such centres, and it is probable that if we once had a literary centre irremovably fixed in New York, we should next have a sceptred Boss sitting in the City Hall, with a poet employed to cover it with verses in his praise. But with a literary centre scattered all over the country, as our political centre now is, there is no danger of this; and instead of having one poor Westminster Abbey on One-thousandth Street, or that neighborhood, we shall be able, when a sufficient number of us die, to fill the whole land with well-stocked Westminster Abbeys. We imagine, in fact, that one reason why so many distinguished gentlemen, when asked the other day to pronounce for or against an American Westminster Abbey, failed to favor it, was not so much because they objected to one another being interred there, or elsewhere, as because they foresaw that if the desire for a literary centre fulfilled itself, the Abbey would have to be built in New York, where the celebrities would be convenient for sepulture in it, and where there are already several extinct celebrities keeping about the streets for want of fitting tombs to lie down in. It is a spirit of jealousy, we admit, and it operates fatally in the case of a National New York Grant Monument. The same spirit, however, kept Italy glorious through all her mediæval life, when not Rome or Naples or Florence or Milan was the intellectual centre, but every rock-built or sea-girt provincial city exulted to be the home of the letters and the arts. That civilization, which ours resembles more than any other in its intense localism, gave certain memorable names to the world, and without prophesying that our resemblance to it will be of as much effect, we are very willing to go without a literary centre for a while yet.

IV.

We have the more patience because we hope that our inherited English may be constantly freshened and revived from the native sources which literary decentralization will help to keep open, and we will own that as we turned over those novels coming from Philadelphia, from New Mexico, from Boston, from Tennessee, from rural New England, from New York, every local flavor of diction gave us courage and pleasure. M. Alphonse Daudet, in a conversation which Mr. Boyesen has set down in a recently recorded interview with him, said, in speaking of Tourguéneff: "What a luxury it must be to have a great big untrodden barbaric language to wade into! We poor fellows who work in the language of an old civilization, we may sit and chisel our little verbal felicities, only to find in the end that it is a borrowed jewel we are polishing. The crown jewels of our French tongue have passed through the hands of so many generations of monarchs that it seems like presumption on the part of any late-born pretender to attempt to wear them."

This grief is, of course, a little whimsical. M. Daudet was expecting Mr. Boyesen to say, as he immediately said, that M. Daudet was himself a living refutation, and so forth, and so forth; yet it has a certain measure of reason in it, and the same regret has been more seriously expressed by the Italian poet Aleardi:

"Muse of an aged people, in the eve
Of fading civilization, I was born.

. . . . . . Oh, fortunate,
My sisters, who in the heroic dawn
Of races sung! To them did destiny give
The virgin fire and chaste ingenuousness
Of their land's speech; and, reverenced, their hands
Ran over potent strings."

It will never do to allow that we are at such a desperate pass in English, but something of this divine despair we may feel too in thinking of "the spacious times of great Elizabeth," when the poets were trying the stops of the young language, and thrilling with the surprises of their own music. We may comfort ourselves, however, unless we prefer a luxury of grief, by remembering that no language is ever old on the lips of those who speak it, no matter how decrepit it drops from the pen. We have only to leave our studies, editorial and other, and go into the shops and fields to find the "spacious times" again; and from the beginning Realism, before she had got a name or put on her capital letter, had divined this near-at-hand truth along with the rest. Mr. Lowell, the greatest and finest realist who ever wrought in verse, showed us that Elizabeth was still Queen where he heard Yankee farmers talk; and without asking that our novelists of the widely scattered centres shall each seek to write in his local dialect, we are glad, as we say, of every tint any of them gets from the parlance he hears; it is much better than the tint he will get from the parlance he reads. One need not invite slang into the company of its betters, though perhaps slang has been dropping its *s* and becoming language ever since the world began, and is certainly sometimes delightful and forcible beyond the reach of the dictionary. We would not have any one go about for new words, but if one of them came aptly, not to reject its help. For our novelists to try to write Americanly, from any motive, would be a dismal error, but being born Americans, we would have them use "Americanisms" whenever these serve their turn; and when their characters speak, we should like to hear them speak true American, with all the varying Tennessecan, Philadelphian, Bostonian, and New York accents. If we bother ourselves to write what the critics imagine to be "English," we shall be priggish and artificial, and still more so if we make our Americans talk "English." There is also this serious disadvantage about "English," that if we wrote the best "English" in the world, probably the English themselves would not know it, or, if they did, certainly would not own it. It has always been supposed by grammarians and purists that a language can be kept as they find it; but languages, while they live, are perpetually changing. God apparently meant them for the common people—whom Lincoln believed God liked because He had made so many of them; and the common people will use them freely as they use other gifts of God. On their lips our continental English will differ more and more from the insular English, and we believe that this is not deplorable, but desirable. Our tongue will [4] always be intelligible enough to our cousins across seas to enable them to enjoy this department of the *New Monthly*, and we should not fear a diminished circulation of the Magazine among them if we became quite faithful in our written English to the spoken English of this continent.

V.

We wish we could find something as national as the novels give us in either the performance or the promise of the illustrated books with which the season loads the editor's table and the bookseller's counter; but except in the American excellence of engraving we shall hardly discover it. The books are so like the books of former holidays that we might imagine ourselves very much younger than we are in turning them over. In what wise do these sumptuous volumes of 1885 differ from the sumptuous volumes of 1875 or 1865? With a single exception, not certainly in novelty of conception or design, though generally the mechanical beauty of their execution has distinctly increased. We think, upon the whole, that Messrs. Houghton, Mifflin, and Co. have made the handsomest book of the sort in the illustration of Dr. Holmes's poem of *The Last Leaf* which has yet issued from our press; but, on the other hand, in their volume of Mr. Whittier's *Poems of Nature* they have made almost the ugliest. The interior of that volume, with the text covering the page from top to bottom in large print, is like a child's book; and the pleasure one might get from the faithful landscapes of Mr. Kingsley is quite spoiled by this setting. We should say it was the very ugliest book we had seen, if we had not suffered from the cover of *Favorite Poems* from Miss Ingelow, which Messrs. Roberts Brothers have illustrated: a *chef-d'œuvre* of tastelessness, where a deeply relieved metalized effigy of St. Botolph's Church in old Boston looks like a silver-plated geyser. The pictures within are some good and some bad, after the manner of pictures made to poems; but one remains resenting the cover while looking at them. Mr. Boughton's *Sketching Rambles in Holland*, from the press of Messrs. Harper and Brothers, with his own pictures and Mr. Abbey's in abundance, is in its sort perhaps the most attractive; they draw the meaning as well as the form of things; and in Mr. Howells's *Tuscan Cities* Mr. Pennell has done some of his best work, which is always gay, bright, honest, and expressive of the joy of doing. Of the text it will not do for us to speak, but we may praise that of Mr. Hamerton's *Paris in Old and Present Times*, which Messrs. Roberts Brothers give us with many interesting reproductions of old prints, engravings, and etchings. Messrs. Putnam's Sons publish a luxurious edition of D'Amicis's *Spain and the Spaniards*, exquisite in printing, paper, and binding, and unique in the little Japan-proof wood-engravings with which each chapter is prefaced; but not so good in its other illustrations. Messrs. Ticknor and Co., who publish *Tuscan Cities*, have issued *Childe Harold* in an illustrated volume, which is not of a new fashion; it is, in fact, of the old tradition of illustration, which many people will always like; and so are nearly all the other holiday books that we have seen, except Mr. Howard Pyle's quaint children's book, *Pepper and Salt*. He has gone to the useful Japanese for some hints in his amusing pictures, and in the text with which he has blended them he has employed his own invention and that of legend with equal charm. But we must return to *The Last Leaf*, which has been touched with graphic felicity in every reticulation by Mr. F. Hopkinson Smith and Mr. George Wharton Edwards, for the chief impression of originality we are to get from the holiday books. In this an elder and statelier Boston is charmingly reflected in certain visages and vistas, and the light of a colonial time is thrown fancifully over all.

So far as it is colonial it is ours; it is imagined in delightful sympathy with the poem, and delightfully realized; but another year we would gladly see something still more authentic in the association of art with literature —something distinctive in our holiday books, as our illustrated magazines are distinctive and pertinent to our date and life. The multitude and popularity of our holiday books are characteristically American; can they not begin to be American in something else? Of course it is first of all desirable that a thing of that sort should be beautiful, even before it is national; but with us it is so often neither!

---

[1] William Makepeace Thackery, <u>The Book of Snobs</u> (New York: D. Appleton, 1852). Originally published as "The Snobs of England," <u>Punch</u>, Nos. 242-294 (March 7, 1846 to February 27, 1847). The book version omits installments XVII - XXIII of the <u>Punch</u> version.

[2] William Dean Howells, <u>Criticism and Fiction</u> (New York: Harper and Brothers, 1891), pp. 123-124.

[3] [Julia Magruder], <u>Across the Chasm</u> (New York: C. Scribner's Sons, 1885).

[4] <u>Criticism and Fiction</u>, pp. 134-138.

February, 1886

Editor's Study.

I.

IF there should happen to be among the million readers (*à peu près*) of this Magazine two or three young men who are presently

> "Waiting to strive a happy strife,
> To war with falsehood to the knife,
> And not to lose the good of life,"

we think we can tell them of a new book which will interest and help them. It is the *Life and Correspondence of Louis Agassiz*, of which Mrs. Agassiz modestly calls herself editor rather than author. They will find it a romance, full of the high joy of achievement; of youth, brilliant, vivid, glad with utter self-forgetfulness, kept beyond gray hair and fading eyes, to the very moment of death; in other words, the story of a man born poor in money, but incalculably rich in the impulse to know and to use knowledge to the highest end, and so happily framed that he could always prefer his object to himself, could attain his results without apparently leaving upon them any stain of egotism. This simplicity, this purity of motive, won not only brains and pockets to his service wherever he went, but all hearts. People saw that the sole aim he had in view was the truth, and that he was not pursuing it for his own sake, but for any other sake sooner. The secret of his success, which is the only sure and sovereign formula for the finest success, has been open from the beginning of time; but it has rarely been able to commend itself so attractively to the young imagination as in Agassiz's life. It has had so often to insist upon itself in spite of neglect, of obloquy, of martyrdom; but here it is the talisman of unbroken prosperity. We do not mean that Agassiz had not his early struggles and renunciations; the son of a poor Swiss *pasteur*, sensitively conscious that his home was cramped to open his path through the schools, could not be without these; but wide recognition came to him very early. "To do all the good you can to your fellow-beings, to have a pure conscience, to gain an honorable livelihood, to procure for yourself by work a little ease, to make those around you happy—that is true happiness; all the rest but mere accessories and chimeras," his mother tenderly, warningly wrote him, when at twenty-one his thoughts began to turn from the profession for which he was fitting himself, to the science that afterward engrossed his life, and he answered: "I wish it may be said of Louis Agassiz that he was the first naturalist of his time, a good citizen, and a good son, beloved of all who knew him." A year later, the value of his first work

on fishes was acknowledged by Cuvier, and hard upon this came the cordial acclaim of Humboldt, who formed for the young naturalist an affection which strengthened through all his remaining years. The constantly recurring evidence of this in the letters of Humboldt now first printed is a lovely strain in the book, where at times one is tempted to complain that there is too little of Agassiz's personal life, till one remembers that his whole life was scientific, and rich and ample as his nature was, it must leave chiefly that record. We learn more about him by the letters to him than by the letters from him; these are the expression of his impassioned ambition as a naturalist almost from the first. We have only glimpses of his beloved home by the Swiss lake, but its sober peace and reasonable piety remain from these a light upon him through all the succeeding events.

After Agassiz came to America his life was no longer a romance; it was a fairy tale, whose incidents are known to all of us; for Agassiz, through his hold upon the sympathies and imaginations of men, became a public man here, as politicians and soldiers and divines are public men, but scientists never before. Private fortunes were opened to him as freely as if they had been the treasures of princes; money honestly amassed in commerce was offered as munificently as if it had been wrung from subject populations; legislatures gave as if they had been individuals, fascinated by the charm of high, unselfish intents. It is a great example, and much courage can be taken from it. Perhaps the time has really come in the history of our race when the man of grand aims, of purposes not even immediately beneficent, but wholly altruistic, may hopefully appeal to his fellow-men for their help in realizing them. Agassiz believed that he could do this, and his faith was justified, not only with millionaires and general courts, but with hard-working people of all sorts, like his enthusiastic students and assistants, like the carpenters at Penikese, who, when he called them together and told them that the Summer School there "was neither for money nor the making of money,.... it was for the best interests of education, and for that alone," took off their Sunday coats and labored from dawn till dark to finish his buildings for him on the Sabbath day.

II.

Agassiz found this new world of ours full not merely of vast physical activities, but of eager and thorough scientific work by men who, he tells his European friends, would be noted in science anywhere, and whom he found employed in public enterprises undertaken by popular governments. He had been used to the munificence of kings, as science may experience it; but this liberality of legislatures composed of farmers and country lawyers amazed him, at nearly the same moment when poor M. de Bacourt, Minister from France to these States, was asking his Maker what a person of his quality could have done that he should be forced to live among such people as the Americans, so sordid, so ignorant, so barbarous!

Madame la Comtesse de Mirabeau, who obliges us with the *Souvenirs of a Diplomate,* after they had remained unpublished in his private letters for nearly fifty years, prefaces them with a sketch of M. de Bacourt's life—a life passed in courts, near the persons of princes, and perfumed throughout, except for those odious years in America, with the odor of salons and the incense of a rehabilitated Church. M. de Bacourt was a gentleman of birth and fortune, a reactionary in politics and religion, who believed in himself and his king and his confessor, and adored the memory of the great and good Prince Talleyrand. Whether M. de Bacourt's Maker was ever able to justify to that gentleman his exile in this country there is now no means of knowing, but no reader of his amusing book can be ungrateful to the providence that brought him here to write these letters about the United States under Van Buren and Tyler. They show us not only how a man of his sort regarded us then, but how such a man must always regard us; for under our system the strong, rude native life will always be working to the top, especially in politics. Very probably it will come to the top now and then in society, and if this keeps on happening till we learn that no class of Americans is to be polished alone, but that we are all bound together, high and low, for barbarism or civilization, it will be perhaps no bad thing.

However this may be, few of our witnesses have been or will be able to dislike us so comprehensively as M. de Bacourt. The weather behaved almost as badly as an American statesman at the very moment of his arrival in the country; it turned in a single day of June from very cold to intensely hot. This was in New York, where everything, even in 1840, "is a weak imitation of the English, ... an England and Englishmen of second and third rate," and where, after twenty-four hours, he has "seen none of the much-talked-of American beauties" in the street. On the railway to Philadelphia "cinders penetrate the cars, and at the end of the journey one has the appearance of a coal-heaver.... Then don't forget that all Americans chew tobacco, and spit continually around them, and it is difficult to keep out of this filth." From the very first, Washington is his "penitentiary," with its wide, dusty, broiling streets, its mean houses, and its life neither of city nor village. He begins to meet there the giants of those days, whose extinction we deplore in our moments of depression, and although Mr. Clay's "proclivities are very French, ... his exterior is that of an English farmer," while in the House and Senate our lamented publicists not only keep their hats on after the fashion "imported from England," but they "sit with their legs in the air, and others, stretched out, sleep as if in

their beds; .... they all spit everywhere," and it is the sound of this spitting which most shocks M. de Bacourt. He finds no one but the President who is "exempt from this vice"; but "Mr. Van Buren, though the son of an innkeeper, and himself even trained to the family calling, has acquired to an astonishing degree the ways of the world." Mr. de Muhlenberg, formerly United States Minister to Austria, makes M. de Bacourt's blood run cold by saying: "You want to know what I think of Prince Metternich? Well, he is a hog." At a fashionable evening party in Washington, "the women, ridiculously dressed, stood around the room hanging on their husbands' arms. Perhaps it was very moral, but I assure you it was very grotesque. There are no young people in the French provinces who have not better manners." "The celebrated Mr. Webster is pompous to the last degree, and ill at ease" in company. "All the distinguished men in this country would be only second or even third class in England. They give themselves the airs of importance one sees in the brewers of London, with their vanity, vulgarity, and absurdity." At six o'clock in the morning—good heavens!—M. de Bacourt meets "Miss Meade, one of the beauties of Washington, alone in the street, going or coming from I do not know where. Free manners!" While he is calling upon a member of Mr. Tyler's cabinet, "three of his colleagues came in—Mr. Badger smoking a cigar, which he did not extinguish; Mr. Bell lay down on a sofa, with his feet over the arms, and thus presenting the soles of his boots to us; as to Mr. Crittenden, finding it too warm, he took off his coat, and pulled a great roll of tobacco from his pocket, put it in his mouth, and commenced chewing. They were very merry and facetious, and as I did not wish to hurt the feelings of men who were so influential in commercial questions, I joined in with them." One fancies the strain it must have been to M. de Bacourt, who is treated throughout by such people exactly as they treat one another, with no apparent sense of his quality, and who must bear it all, if he will keep them from levying duties on French wines and silks; and all in vain, for they levy the duties at last, and perhaps have chuckled in their shirt sleeves at the notion of his cajoling them. At a dinner in the White House our god-like Daniel embraces M. de Bacourt, and hiccoughs over him the professions of a very tender friendship, apparently unfelt before the third bottle of Madeira. He was forced to meet such persons as "a Mr. and Mrs. Bayard, who have the impudence to call themselves descendants of Chevalier Bayard," not knowing that he had never married. At Rockaway Beach he sees the gentlemen take off their coats and vests and join the ladies at a game of ten-pins. On a journey to Niagara he can not get a cutlet, or even an egg. At Boston, where he might otherwise have had a moment of happiness, he finds that "the inhabitants of this elegant and charming city hate the French, and what is worse, they despise them." In a prison at Philadelphia the stamp of crime is much more pronounced on the convicts' faces than in Europe. The American steamboats continually agitate M. de Bacourt by blowing up, and there is a mania for suicide among the few refined people in the country, which he can account for only by supposing them bored to madness by the social conditions.

It is impossible to rehearse all his griefs with us, and, so far as it goes, it is impossible to deny the truth of the portrait he draws. We may say it is not flattered, but in our hearts we can not deny that he saw all these terrible and ugly and ridiculous features in us. He saw nothing else, because he was M. de Bacourt, and was bred to believe that "politeness in social relations.... is the fundamental basis and the most indispensable element" of life. Rained down in the midst of a new people, each bent by so much of the divine purpose as was in him to help accomplish with tireless work of head and hand the destiny of the greatest free nation which had ever been, he saw—poor little diplomatic reactionary—nothing but the abundance of our bad manners, which, even after fifty years, might still strike him. He prophesied that a people with manners like ours must go to the dogs; he beheld us well on our way to the dogs; and so did some other prophets who visited us at the same time, and conspicuously the prophet Dickens, whom M. de Bacourt found made more of by the Americans than Fanny Elssler, Lafayette, and Prince de Joinville all put together. The caricaturist was right in his picture of us, as the diplomatist was; but their study is a faithfuler portrait of themselves even than of us.

Perhaps, indeed — the temptation to construct the theory rushes overpoweringly upon us—the foreign critic's measure of America is always the measure of himself. So far as he perceives that this is the opportunity of the whole human race, not merely to enjoy and ornament itself for the satisfaction of its higher vanity, but chiefly to work and to help itself unhampered by tradition—so far as he shows himself a man who has lived in realities, and not in bubbles, however iridescent, literary, social, or diplomatic—so far he will be consoled for our uncouthness. Occasionally even poor M. de Bacourt has a perception of magnitudes transcending "politeness in social relations," and it affords him a momentary comfort in the midst of suffering otherwise incessant. In one of these intervals he can say: "The Anglo-American race is, in my opinion, charged with a special providential mission—that of peopling and civilizing this immense continent; they are proceeding in the accomplishment of this work undisturbed by any obstacle, and this explains the anomalies so easy to observe and criticise. But it is not fair to judge from details; one must see the whole, and this whole is grand, majestic, and imposing.... The only fault of the Americans is that they will not rest satisfied with their success, but will always, in comparing themselves with European nations, claim superiority over them in everything. This is their great weakness, and encourages writers who come here to find fault."

We have now become so modest—partly from the chastisements of foreign critics, but chiefly, we must believe, through our native virtue—that it is incredible we should have ever had the fault which M. de Bacourt here imputes to us, and we hardly know how to yield, such is our present diffidence, even to the French, in a fine sense of national deficiencies and a generous habit of self-disparagement.

III.

It is some such reluctance, perhaps, which renders us sensitive to the compliment lately paid our poor American language by two English novelists. These writers have wished to reproduce the accents and expressions which we commended last month to the attention of our native authors, and they have imagined several American characters entirely for the purpose of having somebody speak American. Our foreign compatriots are not much like the fellow-citizens we know at home, but it can be honestly said of them that they are as like us as their talk is like our untutored speech. We believe it was Mr. Robert Buchanan who, feeling that the language of Shakespeare and Milton would no longer serve as a means of international *rapprochement*, was the first Briton to write in the New England dialect; at any rate he produced a poem in it which he was not able to tell from one of Mr. Lowell's; and now Mr. Black, in his *White Heather*, has a character who speaks perceptible American; only, he is a man, and he speaks young-lady American as often as masculine American. To us the two sorts are distinct enough, but Mr. Black, who has no doubt heard most of the former in praise of his agreeable books, is not so much to blame for getting them mixed. He makes Mr. Hodson say a London fog is "just too dismal for anything," but we feel that it was his daughter who supplied Mr. Black with that phrase; and when the young lady says, "You bet your pile on that," we suspect that Mr. Black really had the expression from her younger brother.

As for Mr. Grant Allen, who has made a country boy from northern New York the hero of his novel *Babylon*, we should not know exactly where or how he got his Americanisms. There are some tokens of a visit or sojourn here in his decorative use of our birds and flowers; but our phrases seem rather to have been studied from such widely representative authorities as Mark Twain, Dr. Eggleston, Bret Harte, Sam Slick, and Charles Dickens. A farmer in "Geauga County," New York, asks "Whar's Hiram?" as if he were in the heart of the bluegrass region; and this deacon of the church adds that he has an itching "to give that thar boy a durned good cowhidin'," as if he were a Pike accustomed to "exhort the impenitent mule." Hiram is in the blackberry patch, but Mr. Allen calls it the blackberry *lot*, because, as he understands, "lot" is the American for "field, meadow, croft, copse, paddock, and all the other beautiful and expressive Old-World names for our own time-honored English inclosures," though we believe Americans, when foreigners are not by, speak among themselves of meadows, fields, pastures, wood pastures, girdlings, loppings, clearings, intervales, and other features and subdivisions of the landscape as they have occasion to specify them. Mr. Allen, however, has heard of bottom-lands, and he tells us that in Rome his hero's thoughts turned fondly to the "old blackberry bottom"; and he has "cranberry-trees" growing in his cranberry marsh. His deacon addresses a group of trappers as "Gents, all"; and his talk is delicious with such native flavors as "Wal, this do beat all, really"; "He's progressin' towards citizenship now, and I've invested quite a lot of capital in his raisin';" "Wal, I should appreciate that consid'able;" "I des-say that thar boy;" and "It allus licks my poor finite understanding altogither why the Lord should have run this continent so long with nothin' better'n Injuns. . . . Why a lad, that's been brought up a Chrischun and a Hopkinsite, should want to go grubbin' up their knives and things in this cent'ry is a caution to me, that's what it is—a reg'lar caution." It all sounds amazingly American, and probably Mr. Allen could not be persuaded that it is not so. His people are Americans of the sort that the accurate English eye has seen and the delicate English hand has drawn ever since we were first portrayed in *Martin Chuzzlewit*.

IV.

Apparently Mr. Allen has not thought it a serious thing to write a novel, nor human nature worth that honest inquiry which has given him an honorable name in science. This is a mistake which we hope he will come to regret, and which will certainly cause his friends to grieve. It is not quite enough in itself, however, to make one despair of English novelists, and we have read within the year two English books by an unknown hand which may yet mark a new era in English fiction. We hardly know, indeed, whether to call them fiction, they carry so deep a sense of truthfulness to the reader, they are so far in temper from any sort of mere artistry, so simply and nobly serious. The books are the *Autobiography of Mark Rutherford* and *Mark Rutherford's Deliverance*, the one being the rather unsatisfying sequel to the other. Yet it is unsatisfying only as the incompleteness, the brokenness of life, which it perfectly counterfeits, is unsatisfying. There never were books in which apparently the writer has cared so little to make literary account of himself, cared so little to shine, to impress, wished so much to speak his heart plainly out to the heart of his reader. There is absolutely no study of attitude, no appeal to the dramatic or the picturesque, no merely decorative use of words. When you have read the books you feel that you have witnessed the career of a man as you might have witnessed it in the world, and not in a book. We could not give too strong an impression of this incomparable sincerity.

The history is that of an Englishman of the lower or lowest middle class, who is bred to the ministry, but who is constrained by lapses of belief first to abandon his evangelical pulpit, and then to give up a Unitarian parish, and who at the close of his autobiography is the clerk of an atheistical bookseller in London. *Mark Rutherford's Deliverance*, which appeared last summer, four years after the publication of the *Autobiography*, takes up his story at the point where he becomes the Parliamentary correspondent of two provincial newspapers, and follows him through the failure of this employment, his marriage with the woman to whom he had been betrothed in his youth, and his final toil at hateful work under a hard master, to his sudden death. There is no "incident" in the story; there is neither more "plot" nor less than there is in the experience of God's creatures generally, so generally ignored by "imaginative" writers in their "powerful" inventions. It can not, therefore, find favor with readers who like to be "amused," and to "have their minds taken off themselves." We warn them that the story

of Mark Rutherford will fix their "minds" all the more intensely upon themselves, and will stir them deeply, without in the least "amusing" them. Or rather it will do this with readers who can think and feel; and the other sort had better go to the theatre and see a modern play.

Nothing of Mark Rutherford's error or weakness is concealed in these extraordinary books, and in him we have more distinctly got rid of that barbaric survival, the "hero," than in any other figure of fiction—if he is really fictitious. If you pity him, and even love him for his truth and purity and right endeavor, it is because you are sufficiently mature, sufficiently civilized, to see the beauty of these things in their union with tremulous nerves, irresolute performance, vague aspiration, depression, frequent helplessness, faltering faith. He is only one of ten or twelve other persons drawn with the same wise faithfulness, and presented to us with the belief that we shall have enough inconsistencies in ourselves to account for all the inconsistencies in them. When the author has to tell us that a certain man of clear, strong, disciplined mind is a journeyman printer, he seems not to feel bound to explain the fact that he can be both one and the other, and he has no excuses to make for asking us to be interested in the psychological experience of a waiter, a salesman, a porter, who are never at all romanced, but are considered simply in their quality of human beings, affected in due degree by their callings. But such a man as Marden, living and dying in gentle, serene, patient, agnosticism; such a man as McKay, groaning over the misery of London, and inventing out of his own poverty and helplessness a way to help it some little, however little; such women as Mary Marden, Theresa, and Ellen, taking quietly, strongly, unspectacularly, their share of the common burden of common life, have more of consolation and encouragement in them than all the "ideal" figures that ever "helpless fancy feigned" out of proportion to the things that are. The story where they move naturally, from real impulses and with genuine interests, is not gloomy, with all its unrelenting seriousness, and it would be very unjust to leave the reader with the notion that it is inimical to religion. It is very religious. We do not see how Christianity could be more subtly and profoundly comprehended, and throughout his doctrinal stumblings and gropings Mark Rutherford finds his happiness only in that highest good which Christ taught in the highest degree— good to others. This is the key-note of his story, touched throughout, but never with maudlin pathos or rhetorical flourish.

People who like genteel company in novels will not find him in it; there is not a "gentleman" or a "lady" in either of the books, and the plain, poverty-bound lives which they have to do with are considered as inapologetically in their struggles with real sorrows and troubles as if they were all so many gentlemen and ladies of leisure longing to get married or unmarried. If there is no false shame in depicting these common people and conditions, neither is there any boastfulness, or anything of the foolish superstition that there is merit in narrow circumstances of themselves. Perhaps the self-respectful attitude in regard to this material is kept so well because it is the inner life of these men and women that is portrayed — that experience so sweet, so bitter, so precious, of almost any human soul, which we should always be better and wiser for knowing, but which we so often turn from in the stupid arrogance of our cultures and respectabilities.

At times the author seems to have no art in presenting his facts, he does it so barely and bluntly, but he never fails to make you understand just what he means, and he never offends against that beautiful "modesty of nature" which, when one has once really valued it, one can not see offended in literature without a sense of outrage.

V.

A great master may sin against it as well as a bungling apprentice; and if the reader will turn from these books to Balzac's *Le Père Goriot*, of which a new translation has lately appeared, we think he will feel the truth of this painfully enough. In the atmosphere, sane if sad, of the English story, there is in high degree the quality of repose with which the Greeks knew how to console tragedy in every art; but the malarial restlessness of the French romance is as destitute of this as the theatre. After that exquisitely careful and truthful setting of his story in the shabby boarding-house, the author fills the scene with figures jerked about by the exaggerated passions and motives of the stage. We can not have a cynic reasonably wicked, disagreeable, egoistic; we must have a lurid villain of melodrama, a disguised convict, with a vast criminal organization at his command, and

"So dyèd double red"

in deed and purpose that he lights up the faces of the horrified spectators with his glare. A father fond of unworthy children, and leading a life of self-denial for their sake, as may probably and pathetically be, is not enough; there must be an imbecile, trembling dotard, willing to promote even the *liaisons* of his daughters to give them happiness and to teach the sublimity of the paternal instinct. The hero can not sufficiently be a selfish young fellow, with alternating impulses of greed and generosity; he must superfluously intend a career of iniquitous splendor, and be swerved from it by nothing but the most cataclysmal interpositions. It can be said that without such personages the plot could not be transacted; but so much the worse for the plot. Such a plot had no business to be; and while actions so unnatural are imagined, no mastery can save fiction from contempt with those who really think about it. To Balzac it can be forgiven, not only because in his better mood he gave us such biographies as *César Birotteau* and *Eugénie Grandet*, but because he wrote at a time when fiction was just beginning to verify the externals of life, to portray faithfully the outside of men and things. It was still held that in order to interest the reader the characters must be moved by the old romantic ideals; we were to be taught that "heroes" and "heroines" existed all around us, and that these abnormal beings needed only to be discovered in their several humble disguises, and then we should see every-day people actuated by the fine frenzy of the creatures of the poets. How false that

notion was few but the critics, who are apt to be rather belated, need now be told. Some of these poor fellows, however, still contend that it ought to be done, and that human feelings and motives, as God made them and as men know them, are not good enough for novel-readers.

VI.

This is more explicable than would appear at first glance. The critics—and in speaking of them one always modestly leaves one's self out of the count for some reason—when they are not elders ossified in tradition, are apt to be young people, and young people are necessarily conservative in their tastes and theories. They have the tastes and theories of their instructors, who perhaps caught the truth of their day, but whose routine life has been alien to any other truth. There is probably no chair of literature in this country from which the principles now shaping the literary expression of every civilized people are not denounced and confounded with certain objectionable French novels, or which teaches young men anything of the universal impulse which has given us the books, not only of Zola, but of Tourguéneff and Tolstoï in Russia, of Björnsen in Norway, of Valera in Spain, of Verga in Italy, of the unknown Englishman who wrote *Mark Rutherford*. Till these younger critics have learned to think as well as to write for themselves they will persist in heaving a sigh, more and more perfunctory, for the truth as it was in Sir Walter, and as it was in Dickens and in Hawthorne. Presently all will have been changed; they will have seen the new truth in larger and larger degree, and when it shall have become the old truth, they will perhaps see it all.

In the meanwhile they are not such bad fellows with us, and though one might perhaps count our critical authorities upon rather less than the thumbs of one hand, we believe there is no country in the world where an author finds completer recognition at least. Our critics must still make each his manners, more or less comical, to the awful form of precedent; but when this is once done, they do collectively find out what is good in a piece of literature. In a thousand newspapers, scattered over the whole country, they utter so vast an amount of fresh and independent impression that every part of the author's work is touched, nothing of his intention or performance is lost. It will often be deplored as mistaken and of wrong direction or slighter value, but it will have been felt to the last, lightest insinuation.

This is another advantage of a literary centre distributed almost as widely as the Presidential patronage. There is no critical leadership among us. Chicago frankly differs from Boston about a book, and St. Louis can not do less than differ from Chicago; San Francisco has no superstition about the opinions of New York; Buffalo and New Orleans have each its point of view. Comment is almost co-extensive with reading in our country; and from the newspapers the author may learn fairly well what this vast, sympathetic, eager people are saying and thinking of his book. This will always, however, be far less than he would have imagined.

[1] Sam Slick is a character from the sketches of Thomas Chandler Haliburton, and later those of Samuel Adams Hammett.

[2]*Criticism and Fiction*, pp. 25-28.

March, 1886

Editor's Study.

I.

WE may safely leave out of the question those half-dozen conditional reputations which Dr. Holmes's new romance would have made for as many unknown men, at least till the number of persons in Massachusetts who could have written the plays of Shakespeare has been ascertained. No other hand could have given us that charming introduction to *A Mortal Antipathy;* no other art would have been equal to that whimsical study of the novelist's limitations in the use of actual figures and traits; no other mind could have inquired so curiously, and not too seriously, into the facts of mortal antipathies, with just that careful balancing of the documents between the tolerant fancy and the reticent science; and who else could have bestowed those touches of humor, of poetry, of sense, which please on every page? The perpetual play of his wit flushes the horizons of thought all round us like a genial heat-lightning, which nowhere falls in a killing bolt, but passes harmless, leaving the air full of exhilarating ozone.

It will probably not frighten even the young creatures who are now dusting off their poems on Autumn, and seeing how they will make over for Spring; we suspect they will read with a painless smile the invective of one of the Autocrat's old Professors when he declares that he "recognizes a tendency to rhyming as a common form of mental weakness, and the publication of a thin volume of verse as *prima facie* evidence of ambitious mediocrity, if not inferiority.... The presumption," he maintains, "is always against the rhymester, as compared with the less pretentious person about him or her, busy with some useful calling.... The sight of a poor creature grubbing for rhymes to fill his sonnet.... makes my head ache and my stomach rebel."

These are hard sayings, but the most conscience-stricken offenders know the Autocrat better than to take him at his Professor's word. In fact, it is not a prospective want of poetry which we are disposed to deplore in our time, but the lack of the good old-fashioned criticism which we once had. We can remember the day when every quarterly, monthly, weekly, had its gridiron well heated, and its tender young poet or poetess always grilling over the coals for the amusement of the spectators. But what journal now keeps a hot gridiron, or broils bards of any sex or age? Ours, we are ashamed to say, has been lost so long that it was not to be found the other day when we wished to wreak a personal revenge on Mr. Robert Buchanan, though we looked the Study high and low for it. In this state of things, we leave all anxiety for the poetic

future to Mr. Stedman; we forebode not a famine, but a gross surfeit of poets, and great ones at that, all of the most unmistakable "genius," unless the sort of criticism which we lament can be restored. But who will begin? Who will strike the first blow to save us from the horde of nascent immortals now threatening to possess the earth? We see how playfully the Autocrat's hand descends; but perhaps that is because he remembers the pleasant sins of his own youth. What we need for this work is some dull, honest, ferocious brute, whose thick head no pretty fancy ever entered into; who observes only that where the lilies and daisies are, the grass isn't so good; and who can't see a bit of gay color anywhere without longing to get the points of his horns well under the wearer. Unless we can have him, and soon, there is no hope for us.

II.

But if the danger we fear isn't really at hand, if, on the contrary, we are at the end of our great poets for the present, we do not know that we shall altogether despair. There are black moments when, honestly between ourselves and the reader, the spectacle of any mature lady or gentleman proposing to put his or her thoughts and feelings into rhymes affects us much as the sight of some respected person might if we met him jigging or caracoling down the street, instead of modestly walking. This rhyming is not a thing to call the keepers of the mad-house for, to prescribe chains and stripes and a straw bed on the floor till the patient begins to talk prose again; but isn't it all the same a thing to blush and grieve for at this stage of the proceedings? So we ask ourselves in those black moments which pass and leave us to the beneficent magic which bathes all life in the light that never was on sea or land, the charm which none but dolts deny. What we ask is, hasn't there perhaps been enough of it? If there should be no more great poetry, haven't we all the great poets of the past inalienably still? We can think of a single small volume of early verse which ought to supply any reasonable demand for poetry many years, and almost any middle-aged literary man can think of another.

III.

But if we are altogether wrong in asking this question—and we won't readily allow that we are—we are afraid that with the present critical apparatus it is quite impossible to forecast the poetical probabilities. Neither Mr. Stedman, in the last very interesting chapter of his *Poets of America*, nor Mr. William John Courthope, in his less considerable essays on the *Liberal Movement in English Literature*, is able to prophesy with any comforting measure of assurance that we shall soon have some more great poets; they both hope that we shall, though Mr. Courthope doesn't try to conceal from us that the great Romantic movement just ended, which began as a protest against convention, has grown "through the force of circumstances into a revolt against society." This, to be sure, is not the crime it was once thought—say about the time when the good Man of the 2d December was trying to "save society"; but if the great new poets when they come are to be the apostles of Socialism, we shall all the more lament the absence of the gridiron in criticism; and we take this to be the attitude of a good citizen. Mr. Stedman, to be sure, does not shake us with any apprehension for the social fabric in reasoning upon the absence and prospects of new poetry; he rather thinks it will be a good thing when we get it; and he advises any one who suspects himself of having it in him "not to believe in limitations; a few by ignoring them will reach the heights." This seems to be the greatest encouragement he can offer; and the prophet who knows will not come till we have a complete literary bureau, something like our weather bureau, we suppose, with stations all over the country. There may be at this very moment a poetic storm central in Dakota, a lyric wave moving eastward from the region of the great plains, with lower dramatic pressure in the Middle States, and occasional or local rhymes for New England, and dialect pieces for the Gulf States; but till we have some system of observation perfected, we shall not know it till the great new poetry is hard upon us; and in the mean time all prognostications must be made in the conditional mood of the *Old-Farmer's Almanac*.

IV.

We should be very sorry if we had seemed to treat Mr. Stedman's book slightly or lightly, for that is certainly not the spirit of his own criticism, which, indeed, we could not praise too highly. Commonly the critic approaches his subject with a violent liking or dislike; but, so far as we have noted, Mr. Stedman never does this. He is singularly judicial; to the best of his knowledge he is just. He has no quarrels, and he picks none. He tries to ascertain the place and the qualities of each poet whom he considers, and when this is done, his work is done. He may be wrong or he may be right about Bryant or Longfellow or Emerson, but no one who likes either of these poets better than the other two can say that his favorite has suffered to their glory. Mr. Courthope spends some time and temper in knocking Mr. Swinburne about the head for saying that Shelley is a better poet than Byron, or that figs are better than pomegranates; but our saner American leaves you to indulge your own taste in fruits, merely ascertaining whether this peach or that melon is good of its kind.

He does not wear "a foolish face of praise," his soul is his own in all presences, contemporary or past; and he has made a remarkably honest book. His subject has been well studied historically; and he has given us a sufficiently luminous prospect of the whole field he has worked, as well as a vivid idea of particular corners of it. You can not read his book without acquainting yourself with the significant phases of American poetry, or at least renewing your acquaintance with them. He has not effected this as a scholar or inquirer simply; he has brought to the study the poet's quick sympathy, his generous ardor, his fine unerring pleasure in beauty. He is not harsh or arrogant; he remembers to be a gentleman even in his censure; he is unfailingly decent.

We don't see how we could say very much more for Mr. Stedman as a critic, unless we said that his book gave us an impression of freshness which we failed to get from Mr. Courthope's; perhaps because Byron and Shelley, Scott and Wordsworth, Keats and Coleridge, have been so much more written about than Bryant and Emerson, Holmes and Whittier, Poe and Whitman, Lowell and Longfellow. But Mr. Courthope, beyond a peculiarly happy gift for quotation, seems to have brought little of his own to his task except an uncertain temper, a belated Toryism, very honest and very droll, and a "nice derangement of epitaphs." He calls the dry formalists of the last century Realists, and relegates Wordsworth to the company of the Romanticists; and he has a little theory that the Romantic movement was revolutionary, and neither Scott nor any other Romantic reactionary of the endless list on the Continent is suffered to be a stumbling-block in his way.

V.

But what won't a man sacrifice to a theory, especially a wrong one? We see the lengths to which even so fair a spirit as Mr. Stedman will go in humoring his notion that the present suspense of poetry is largely conscious, if not partially intentional. The poets, we understand from him, who might be the Longfellows and Emersons of the next generation, perceive—the sly rogues!—that the popular tendency is toward prose, and so leave off singing; and Mr. Howells has deliberately taken up the trade of noveling because it pays better than versing. If we were authorized to speak for Mr. Howells, we think we should appeal from the court on this point, where the judge perhaps nodded over his notes. As between the novelist and the public, the matter isn't very important; as between him and other poets now intending to follow his mercenary example, it is more so; and it is of infinite moment as between him and his own literary conscience—if the lady newspaper correspondents who think his female characters so much inferior to themselves will allow that he has a conscience of any kind.

We should warn, more or less solemnly, any sweet bird singing in the bare ruined choirs that now shake against the cold prosaic time not to imagine that he can become a novelist, even of Mr. Howells's quality, by leaving off being a poet; and we should very much doubt if that faltering and imperfect writer ever proposed to himself any such thing as Mr. Stedman fancies. He may be quite the thrifty time-server he is represented; but we suspect that he did not take to noveling because he thought it was a good way of making a living, and jumped with the humor of the time, or because he was "wise in his generation," as Mr. Stedman scripturally phrases the treason. It was a different affair altogether, we imagine, though quite as simple. We should say, judging from a casual acquaintance with his early attempts in fiction, that it was from always trying his hand in that sort, and finding pleasure and, at last, apparent success in it, that he kept on, and that he left off versing because it no longer interested him so much. We are not sure, but we fear that any poet who should be tempted by Mr Stedman's philosophization of Mr. Howells's career to turn novelist, from the motive attributed to him, would bring up in the poor-house, or at least in the chair of criticism. Nothing but a love of it beyond all other arts and industries, or any branch of the show business, will bring him success in it; without that, he may be certain that he will not do good work, and he will not deserve to do it. If practicable, he ought to believe that to write the great possible novel is to surpass all make and manner of versing whatsoever, hitherto accomplished or imagined. He need not be afraid that he will really write it.

VI.

If we are actually upon that suspense of poetry which Mr. Stedman and Mr. Courthope both forebode, we ought to get a little altruistic consolation from such a delightful book as Mr. Edmund Gosse has written about a similar suspense in the period *From Shakespeare to Pope*. Will it not be something for us to supply, by a century or two of inanity and insipidity, the materials for such a gracious and charming spirit to work with? In this way we should "join the choir invisible" of those whose pangs of non-existence hereafter will be assuaged by not-feeling that they survive in their usefulness to the race. This sounds like nonsense, but it is the English of the condition that George Eliot aspired to; and not to have been poets ought now to be a fine satisfaction to those poor seventeenth-century nonentities, if they could only know how exquisitely Mr. Gosse has employed their absence of poetic quality. We had almost said that this lack in his subject is necessary to show Mr. Gosse at his best, but we remembered in time his other *Seventeenth Century Studies* and his beautiful *Life of Gray*. Yet we still think he has made the art of rendering such barren fields enchanting his own; and this is chiefly because he brings to it that fine spirit of humor which is wanting in Mr. Stedman and Mr. Courthope. In the light of this, Cowley is translucent, Waller is amusing, Denham is charming, and Davenant is not dull. The whole artificial and vapid group is endeared to us. We perceive that they are not great poets, but there is no doubt about their being well-meaning men, and in their day and generation useful and even indispensable. Mr. Gosse, more than either of his brother—or step-brother—critics, uses the humane modern method in dealing with those severally tiresome people; and in considering them as part of the history of poetry, of literature, of the human mind and race, as perfectly inevitable as Shakespeare or Dante or Goethe, he is able to treat them tenderly and sweetly, after the natural prompting of the heart he puts in all his work.

VII.

In all these books, but not so much in Mr. Gosse's as in Mr. Stedman's or Mr. Court-

hope's, for obvious reasons, there is talk from time to time of something these authors call "genius." It seems from their account to be the attribute of a sort of very puissant and admirable prodigy which God has created out of the common for the astonishment and confusion of the rest of us poor human beings; but do they really believe it? Can they severally lay their hands upon their waistcoats and swear that they think there is any such thing? Would they like, when upon oath, to declare that what they call a "genius" is at all different from other men of like gifts, except in degree? Do they mean anything more or less than the Mastery which comes to any man according to his powers and diligence in any direction, conscious or unconscious, nature has given him? If not, why not have an end of the superstition which has caused our race to go on so long writing and reading of the difference between talent and genius? It is within the memory of middle-aged men that the Maelstrom existed in the belief of the geographers, but we now get on perfectly well without it; and why should we still suffer under the notion of "genius," which keeps so many poor little authorlings trembling in question whether they have it, or have only "talent"?

VIII.

We have just read a book by one of the greatest captains who ever lived—a plain, taciturn, simple, unaffected soul — who tells the story of his wonderful life as unconsciously as if it were all an every-day affair, not different from other lives, except as a great exigency of the human race gave it importance. So far as he knew, he had no natural aptitude for arms, and certainly no love for the calling. But he went to West Point because, as he quaintly tells us, his father "*rather thought he would go*"; and he fought through one war with credit, but without glory. The other war, which was to claim his powers and his science, found him engaged in the most prosaic of peaceful occupations; he obeyed its call because he loved his country, and not because he loved war. All the world knows the rest, and all the world knows that greater military mastery has not been shown than his campaigns illustrated. He does not say this in his book, or hint it in any way; he gives you the facts, and leaves them with you. But these *Personal Memoirs of U. S. Grant*, written as simply and straightforwardly as his battles were fought, couched in the most unpretentious phrase, with never a touch of grandiosity or attitudinizing, familiar, homely, even common in style, is a great piece of literature, because great literature is nothing more nor less than the clear expression of minds that have something great in them, whether religion, or beauty, or deep experience. Probably Grant would have said that he had no more vocation to literature than he had to war. He owns, with something like contrition, that he used to read a great many novels; but we think he would have denied the soft impeachment of literary power. Nevertheless, he shows it, as he showed military power, unexpectedly, almost miraculously. All the conditions here, then, are favorable to supposing a case of "genius." Yet who would trifle with that great heir of fame, that plain, grand, manly soul, by speaking of "genius" and him together? Who calls Washington a genius? or Franklin, or Bismarck, or Cavour, or Columbus, or Luther, or Darwin, or Lincoln? Were these men second-rate in their way? Or is "genius" that indefinable, preternatural quality, sacred to the musicians, the painters, the sculptors, the actors, the poets, and above all, the poets? Or is it that the poets, having most of the say in this world, abuse it to shameless self-flattery, and would persuade the inarticulate classes that they are on peculiar terms of confidence with the deity? No doubt ⌐[1]

> "The poet in a golden clime was born,
> With golden stars above,"

and they are in some sort creditable to our species. If we should have no more poets we might be less glorious as a race, but we should certainly be more modest — or they would. At least a doctrine wholly opposed to the spirit of free institutions and the principles of civil service reform would go out of the world with them; but since we shall probably have them to the end of the story, let us try to rid ourselves of it as we may. There is no Maelstrom sucking down ships and vomiting up bottles with MSS. in them; there is only a bad current off the coast of Norway. There is no "genius"; there is only the mastery that comes to natural aptitude from the hardest study of any art or science; "genius" exists chiefly in the fancy of those who hope that some one else will think they have it. The men who do great things as quietly as they do small things do not commend themselves to the imagination as geniuses; there must be something spectacular in them, or they must have some striking foible or vice or disability united with their strength before they can be so canonized. Then for some reason we are expected to recognize them as different in essence from other men, as a sort of psychical aristocracy, born gentle, while the rest of us were born simple.

IX.

But as we come to know great men better, we come to see that, after all, they are of one blood with the well-known human race, and no miracles of creation. They seem each thoroughly of his time and place, and this or that tendency of civilization appears merely to have found its most striking expression in them. Napoleon was the creature of the French Revolution, as Grant was the creature of our civil war; and not, as Grant was not. The great shaping exigency found each admirably prepared material to mould a master out of; but the Revolution and the Union would have prevailed in civilization, though their instruments might not have been named Napoleon or Grant. How many generals were nearly as great as they! How many dramatists of Shakespeare's time were Shakespearean!

It does not detract from greatness to say this of it; and Mr. John C. Ropes, who has just given us an admirable book on *The First Napoleon*, has pursued the right modern method with his subject, to the signal advantage of Napoleon's fame. He studies him as the representative and inevitable outcome of certain tremendous conditions, and he sympathizes with him because he believes he was more nearly right than his enemies. We do not see how any one can read his extremely temperate and conscientious chapters on the principal facts of Napoleon's career without agreeing with him. Certainly Mr. Ropes's attitude is not obviously the attitude of an advocate. He criticises as freely as he praises, and he has a sincerity in either that wins him your liking throughout.

It is needless to say that he has taken an un-English view of Napoleon; for the English view of any contemporary foreign civilization and character, as no one should know better than ourselves, is pretty sure to be the wrong view. When you have read his book, you no longer feel—or you no longer feel so sure—that Napoleon was seeking his sole glory and advantage. It looks very much as if his enemies were the enemies of human progress, for the most part. But if any reader differs with us, his quarrel is with Mr. Ropes, to whom we very willingly leave him.

---

[1] *Criticism and Fiction*, pp. 88–91.

April, 1886

Editor's Study.

I.

THE evolution of a believer in a God sensible to human need and in the life hereafter, from a metaphysician so purely scientific as Mr. John Fiske, is certainly one of the most interesting phases of Darwinism. Of course it proves nothing very conclusive, but for the moment one does not realize this; and if one's heart is not altogether at rest in orphanage and nonentity, as we suppose very few hearts are, it comforts, it encourages. So many scientists have denied so many things that it is hard to understand that Science herself denies nothing, to begin with, but seeks only and always to know the truth. The emotions and desires concerning our origin and destiny which seem innate are as fit subjects for her inquiry as the material world; it was to the satisfaction of these that Mr. Fiske lately addressed himself in his little book on *The Destiny of Man as viewed in the Light of his Origin*, and now again he addresses himself to the same end in *The Idea of God as affected by Modern Knowledge*. We need not say what spirit he has brought to his work, or what literary grace: his humane and high intent, his admirable art, are present in all he does; and we do not think they have ever been more sympathetic than in this essay, where he arrives at the conviction that "the everlasting source of phenomena is none other than the infinite Power that makes for righteousness," or that "however the words may stumble in which we try to say it, God is in the deepest sense a moral Being." This will not seem much to those who are accustomed to accept God from authority, and who have always believed what they were bid (which is no bad thing, perhaps, and seems to save time); but it is a good deal as the result of reasoning that begins and ends outside of all authority except that of fact scientifically ascertained; and it is still more as an induction from the Darwinian theory, which teaches Mr. Fiske that in natural selection psychical variations were preferred to physical variations, that infancy was prolonged in the interest of the family and morality, and that man, thus differentiated from the other creatures, has been perfected by the gradual predominance of the soul over the body; that the long period of his development is closing; that strife and the habits bred of war must cease as naturally as they began, and that "a stage of civilization will be reached in which human sympathy shall be all in all, and the spirit of Christ shall reign supreme through the whole length and breadth of the earth."

Throughout his essay it is interesting to find Mr. Fiske unable to language his thoughts of infinity at supreme moments except in the words of the old Book of those Semitic tribes so remote from Darwin; and it is remarkable that modern light and knowledge have no hope or type more sublime than Christ and His millennium. At the moment when we were reading the argument which could culminate in nothing higher than faith in these, there came to us another book which we think others may find it well to read together with Mr. Fiske's. It is not a new book in Europe, but we believe the American translation gives it for the first time to English readers, and it may not be superfluous to say that the great Russian novelist, incomparably the greatest writer living in that sort, who has set forth in it his doctrine of the right life, is fully a believer in Christianity; too fully, perhaps, for those who believe it ought to be believed, but not that it ought to be practiced. He supposes that Jesus Christ, being divinely sent to make God known to man, was serious when He preached meekness, submission, poverty, forgiveness, charity, and self-denial; and that He actually meant what He said when He bade us resist not evil, eschew courts of law, forbear judgment, refuse to make oath, take one wife and cleave to her till death, have no respect to persons, but love one another. The author says all this is not only possible, but easy, and he does not relegate the practice of the Christian life to some future period, but himself attempts it here and now. This must of course strike Christians who kill, and litigate, and divorce, and truckle to rank, and hate, and heap up riches, as very odd; but none of the sort who take Christ in the ironical way can help being startled by the attitude of this literalist, and suffering perhaps some pangs of disagreeable self-question. We can not help being moved by certain appeals which the author of *My Religion* makes to our experience and our reason in behalf of the life taught by Him who said His yoke was easy and His burden was light; he certainly seems to show that the yoke of the world is not easy and its burden is not light. He tells us that in this century thirty millions of men have perished in war; and he asks us how many have given up their lives for Christ's sake. These things give one pause, but probably an average American humorist could dispose of his arguments in a half-column funny article. A graver critic might point out that the Society of Friends, except in the single matter of heaping up riches, which they have been rather fond of, long lived the life he commends; and that it is no new thing, either, in the practice of the Moravians, who were possibly somewhat nearer his ideal. One might readily believe one's self to be reading the confession of an early Quaker or a despised Herrnhuter in these passages from the pen of one of the subtlest, the deepest, the wisest, students of human nature in our time : "Everything that once seemed to me important, such as honors, glory, civilization, wealth, the complications and refinements of existence, luxury, rich food, fine clothing, etiquette, have become for me wrong and despicable. Everything that once seemed to me wrong and despicable, such as rusticity, obscurity, poverty, simplicity of surroundings, of food, of clothing, of manners, all have now become right and important to me. . . . I can not, as I once did, recognize in myself or others titles or ranks or qualities aside from the quality of manhood. I can not seek for fame or glory ; I can no longer cultivate a system of instruction which separates me from men. . . . I can no longer pursue amusements which are oil to the fire of amorous sensuality, the reading of romances and the most of poetry, listening to music, attendance at balls and theatres. . . . I can not favor the celibacy of persons fitted for the marriage relation. . . . I am obliged to consider as sacred and absolute the sole and unique union by which man is once for all indissolubly bound to the first woman with whom he has been united."

But it is not Thomas Ellwood, or Zeisberger, the Apostle to the Delawares, who says these things ; it is Count Leo Tolstoï, a Russian nobleman of our day, born rich, an accomplished scholar, a brave soldier, a brilliant man of society, the greatest creative talent in fiction which his country, fertile in such talents, has produced, except, perhaps, Tourguéneff. To him the dream of the Christ-life on earth, the heavenly vision which again and again has visited generous souls, comes once more ; and in his hope of realizing it he has turned from the world and its honors and embraced poverty and toil. He works with his own hands among his peasants in the fields, and he celebrates his happiness in this life as a final fruition, for, strangely and sadly enough, this latest of the apostles does not believe in the personal or individual life after death. At the time when Mr. Fiske finds the hope of this in Evolution, Count Tolstoï discovers no promise of it in Scripture, but regards it as a survival from savage times, when death and sleep were confounded in the minds of men.

II.

This curious trait of agnosticism in such a devout Christian seems like a survival itself, a projection into the hopefulness and ardor of the early Christianity which Tolstoï's doctrine and practice recall, of the vast, passive Asiatic melancholy which seems to tinge all Russian character. One is familiar with it in Tourguéneff's people, and it is a pensive light, if not a positive color, on the wonderful pages of Tolstoï's novels, where a good heart and a right mind, sensible from the first word, console and support the reader against it. After one has lived a certain number of years, and read a certain number of novels, it is not the prosperous or adverse fortune of the characters that affects one, but the good or bad faith of the novelist in dealing with them. Will he play us false or will he be true in the operation of this or that principle involved? We can not hold him to less account than this:

he must be true to what life has taught us is the truth, and after that he may let any fate betide his people ; the novel ends well that ends faithfully.

It is this conscience, present in all that Tolstoï has written, which has now changed from a dramatic to a hortatory expression. The same good heart and right mind are under all and in all. Their warmth and their light are not greater in *My Religion* than in *Anna Karenine*, that saddest story of guilty love, in which nothing can save the sinful woman from herself—not her husband's forgiveness, her friends' compassion, her lover's constancy, or the long intervals of quiet in which she seems safe and happy in her sin. It is she who destroys herself, persistently, step by step, in spite of all help and forbearance ; and yet we are never allowed to forget how good and generous she was when we first met her, how good and generous she is, fitfully and more and more rarely, to the end. Her lover works out a sort of redemption through his patience and devotion ; he grows wiser, gentler, worthier, through it ; but even his good destroys her. As you read on you say, not, "This is like life," but, "This is life." It has not only the complexion, the very hue, of life, but its movement, its advances, its strange pauses, its seeming reversions to former conditions, and its perpetual change ; its apparent isolations, its essential solidarity. A multitude of figures pass before us recognizably real, never caricatured or grotesqued, or in any wise unduly accented, but simple and actual in their evil or their good. There is lovely family life, the tenderness of father and daughter, the rapture of young wife and husband, the innocence of girlhood, the beauty of fidelity ; there is the unrest and folly of fashion, the misery of wealth, and the wretchedness of wasted and mistaken life, the hollowness of ambition, the cheerful emptiness of some hearts, the dull emptiness of others. It is a world, and you live in it while you read, and long afterward ; but at no step have you been betrayed, not because your guide has warned or exhorted you, but because he has been true, and has shown you all things as they are.

III.

At the close of some vivid *Scenes of the Siege of Sebastopol*, lately translated in the *Revue des Deux Mondes*, Tolstoï, who had seen what he describes, and had been part of it, exclaims : "It is not Kalougine, with his brilliant courage, his *bravura* of gentleman, his vanity, the principal motive of all his actions ; it is not Praskoukine, null and inoffensive, albeit he fell on the field of battle for the faith, the throne, and the country ; nor Mikhaïlof, so timid ; nor Pesth, that child without conviction and without moral principle—who can pass for traitors or heroes. No, the hero of my tale, that which I love with all the strength of my soul, that which I have sought to reproduce in all its beauty, that which has been and ever will be beautiful, is the True."

It is the might of this literary truth, which is also spiritual truth, that has made the Russians so great in fiction, so potent to move the heart and the conscience. In another paper of the *Revue*, on "Les Écrivains Russes Contemporains," which we commend to any one interested to know the sources of the present universal literary movement, the writer says of Nicolas Gogol: " A realist in the best sense of the term, he has furnished a fit instrument for the thought and the art of our time; he has clearly foreseen its future use; he has discerned the issue in Russia, at least, of that exact study of phenomena and of men which he began. If any one doubts it, let him take this sentence, one of the last that fell from his pen, in *The Confession of an Author:* 'I have pursued life in its reality, not in the dreams of the imagination, and I have thus arrived at Him who is the source of life.'" The sentence is valuable to the reader of Tolstoï's last book, and is full of suggestion for all. In another place Gogol, who began to write realistically fifty years ago, said of himself and his public: "Thankless is the fate of the writer who ventures to show what passes at each moment under his eyes.... The contemporary judge will treat his creations as low and useless; he will be assigned a despised rank among the writers who defame humanity; he will be denied all soul, heart, talent.... The reader is revolted by the meanness of my heroes.... He could have forgiven me if I had shown him picturesque rascals; he can not forgive me for showing him base ones."

The Russian criticism of 1836 was in fact as immature as much American criticism of 1886. It did not wish to see men and things in fiction as they really are: it wished to see them as the romancers had always made believe they were; it still cried for its Puss in Boots and its Jack the Giant-Killer, and would have them in some form or other.

IV.

The Russians who have followed Gogol and learned from him, as now the whole world must learn from them, have not heeded those childish demands, and they form a group from which one can hardly turn to other literatures without feeling that he enters an atmosphere of feigning, of insincere performance and ignobler ideals. The French, with their convention of indecency, the English, with their convention of propriety, alike dwindle—all except that colossal George Eliot woman—before these humane, simple masters, who have no convention, but wish merely to be true.

It is a long step to descend from them to American fiction; one holds one's breath and looks anxiously to see if there is really any footing down there; but again we can console ourselves with the fact that what our writers are doing is mostly in the right direction. The author of *Margaret Kent* has gone rather far in it, though she (the pseudonym of Henry Hayes [4] does not hide the fluctuation of feminine draperies) seems to have been frightened back at times. This story, very clever in spite of its defects, is the story of a beautiful and unwise young grass-widow who lives in New York by her pen, while her husband lives in Rio Janeiro no one knows how. They are Southern people, who were married too young, and the wife has everything to regret in her marriage except the little girl whom it has left her—a child truthfully and winningly portrayed, and one of the successes of the book. Margaret Kent has more men to her friends than women; there is no harm in her,

but a great deal of wandering, selfish good intention. One of the men, not knowing her husband's survival, wishes to marry her, and she palters for a moment with the notion of a divorce. The husband suddenly comes back, recalled by a childish appeal from the little daughter, who has been always longing and grieving for the father she has not seen—her part in this is very touching—and begins to waste his wife's earnings as he had already wasted her fortune. A mortal peril which he falls into recalls her from her scorn of him; she tries to love him, and succeeds in being good to him. When he gets well he goes South, and dies opportunely of yellow fever. The lover gets back from Europe (whither the lovers of ladies unprepared to marry have gone a great deal in novels), and after the rescue of the little Gladys by his science from diphtheria, Margaret and he are married.

The temper of the book is romantic, but many of its phases are naturalistically studied; the women figures are very well done; the men figures are such men as women draw, except always the handsome, boyish scamp-husband: he is a triumph. The lover is a doctor, of the masterful species prevalent in novels ever since Charles Reade invented it. He is not new, and neither, quite, is Mrs. Kent's dragon, the old artist whom she lives with, and who supplies with her brush the gaps that Mrs. Kent's pen leaves in their common gains; but we are compensated for her conventionality by the freshness of the portrait of Mrs. Townsend, the society newspaper correspondent; and again we say the book, as a whole, is very clever; and if it is not safe to let ladies believe that unloved husbands will die about the time that self-banished lovers wish to come home from Europe, still there is a moral sense in the story very uncommon in women's novels. We have some suspicion that if the burden of tradition had not been upon the author—if she had not been enslaved to the theatre-goer's ideal that a story should "end up" well—so skillful an artist, so fine a student of woman nature, if not human nature, as she shows herself to be, might have given us a conclusion more in keeping with what she must know of life.

V.

We admit that it would have been difficult with a novel-reading public like ours, well-meaning, sympathetic, appreciative, but superabounding in a fibreless soft-heartedness that can not bear to have pretty women disappointed in fiction; yet from a writer like the author of *Margaret Kent* we have a right to expect entire fidelity. Till we have that from our clever writers we shall have clever writers and nothing more, and we must turn elsewhere for examples of what fiction may be at its best.

One would not perhaps look first to find them in Spain, but we have just been reading a Spanish novel which is very nearly one. Of course it is a realistic novel; it is even by an author who has written essays upon realism, and who feels obliged, poor fellow, in choosing a theme which deals with the inside rather than the outside of life, to protest that the truth exists within us as well as without, and is not confined to the market-houses, the dram-shops, the street corners, or the vulgar facts of existence. Don Armando Palacio Valdés believes that his *Marta y Maria* is a [5] realistic novel, although it is not founded upon current and common events, and that the beautiful and the noble also lie within the realm of reality. We should ourselves go a little farther, and say that they are to be found nowhere else; but we have not at present to do with our opinions, or even the prologue to Señor Valdés's novel, though we should be glad to reproduce that in full, it is so good. We must speak, however, of the admirable little illustrations of his book, so full of character and spirit and movement. They are badly printed, and the cover of the book, stamped in black and silver, is as ugly as a "burial casket," but our censure must almost wholly end with the mechanical execution of the book. The literature is delightful: full of charming humor, tender pathos, the liveliest sympathy with nature, the keenest knowledge of human nature, and a style whose charm makes itself felt through the shadows of a strange speech. It is the story of two sisters, daughters of the chief family in a Spanish sea-port city: Maria, who passes from the romance of literature to the romance of religion, and abandons home, father, and lover to become the spouse of heaven, and Marta, who remains to console all these for her loss. We do not remember a character more finely studied than that of Maria, who is followed, not satirically or ironically, through all the involutions of a conscious, artificial personality, but with masterly divination, and is shown as essentially cold-hearted and selfish in her religious abnegation, and as sensuous in her spiritual ecstasies as she was in her abandon to the romances on which she first fed her egoistic fancy. But Marta—Marta is delicious! We see her first as an awkward girl of thirteen at her mother's *tertulia*, helplessly laughing at some couples who give a few supererogatory hops in the dance after the music suddenly stops; and the note of friendly simplicity, of joyous, frank, sweet naturalness, struck in the beginning, is felt in her character throughout. Nothing could be lovelier than the portrayal of this girl's affection for her father and mother, and of the tenderness that insensibly grows up between her and her sister's lover, left step by step in the lurch by the intending bride of heaven. One of the uses of realism is to make us know people; to make us understand that the Spaniards, for example, are not the remote cloak-and-sword gentry of opera which romance has painted them, abounding in guitars, poniards, billets, *autos-da-fe*, and confessionals, but are as "like folks" as we are. It seems that there is much of that freedom among young people with them which makes youth a heavenly holiday in these favored States. Maria's lover has "the run of the house," in this Spanish town, quite as he would have in Chicago or Portland, and he follows Marta about in the frequent intervals of Maria's neglect; he makes her give him lunch in the kitchen when he is hungry, this very human young Marquis de Penalta; he helps her to make a pie, the young lady having a passion for all domestic employments, and to put away the clean clothes. Her father, Don Mariano Elorza, has a passion for the smell of freshly ironed linen, much as any well-domesticated American citizen might have, and loves to go and put his nose in the closets where it hangs. His wife has been a tedious, complaining invalid all her married

life, but he is heart-broken when she dies; and it is at this moment that Maria—who has compromised him in the Carlist movement because that is the party of the Church, and has tried in the same cause to make her lover turn traitor to the government which he has sworn as citizen and soldier to defend—comes ecstatic from the death-scene to ask his permission to complete her vocation in the convent. He gives it with a sort of disdain for her pitiless and senseless egotism. The story closes with the happy love of Marta and Ricardo, clasped to the old man's breast and mingling their tears with his; and the author cries, "O eternal God, who dwellest in the hearts of the good, can it be that these tears are less grateful to Thee than the mystical colloquies of the Convent of St. Bernard?"

A sketch of the story gives no idea of its situations, or, what is more difficult and important, the atmosphere of reality in which it moves. The whole social life of the quiet town is skillfully suggested, and an abundance of figures pass before us, all graphically drawn, none touched with weakness or exaggeration. It is a book with a sole blemish—a few pages in which the author thinks it necessary to paint the growth of little Marta's passion in too vivid colors. There is no great harm; but it is a lapse of taste and of art that libels a lovely character, and seems a sacrifice to the ugly French fetich which has possessed itself of the good name of Realism to befoul it.

VI.

We must not close the door of the Study this month without speaking of some other books that have been giving us pleasure. Chief of these is Mr. T. W. Higginson's admirable *Larger History of the United States*, which has gone far to make us believe with him that our national story is "more important, more varied, more picturesque, and more absorbingly interesting than any historic subject offered by the world beside." He has at least made a thoroughly delightful book about it, and has approached it with a fresh sense, and treated it with a charming ease and familiarity which it seems impertinent to say is never trivial, and which knows how to rise at the right moments into all the necessary dignity and force. We can promise the reader that in Mr. Higginson's handling he will not find the "commonplace" story of these States less fascinating than, for example, the romantic *Story of the Fourth Crusade*, though Mr. Edwin Pears has told that again extremely well. He raises the regret, the pang, without which one can not read of that conquest of Constantinople by the French and Venetians. That calamity wrecked an ancient civilization, retarded learning, darkened Christianity, and opened to the Turk the garden lands which his presence has blighted for four centuries; and the new historian of the event shakes us anew with the doubt whether the course of events is always, even finally, the accomplishment of good, and whether the effect of this or that great crime or error is not lastingly bad.

To those who think that the career of Bonaparte was such a crime or error, *A Short History of Napoleon the First*, by Professor John Robert Seeley, will bring greater conviction, perhaps, than to Mr. John C. Ropes, say, whose Napoleon we commended last month. Professor Seeley rapidly narrates the facts of Napoleon's life, and then in a second part makes a study of his character and place in history. Briefly, he finds that if there had not been Napoleon, there would have been somebody else to do his work, and that almost any soldier of great ability could have done it better. He leaves very little of Napoleon, who looms up again as soon as Professor Seeley has done with him.

We have two excellent books which we still wish to speak of, if the reader has a moment left: *Japanese Homes and their Surroundings*, by Edward S. Morse, and *Chosön, the Land of the Morning Calm*, a sketch of Korea, by Percival Lowell. Mr. Morse's book is a store of facts concerning Japanese houses, great and simple, in city and country, which seems to comprise all that is knowable on the subject; and the driest details are so admirably treated that we can not forgive him for leaving these houses uninhabited; he should have filled them with the life of the people he knows so well, and no other could have described so interestingly. He still owes this to the public. In the mean time his volume is a treasure of architectural facts, and could not be too highly valued. Mr. Lowell, with some posturing which we could wish absent, has made a book of unique freshness and interest. Korea was about the only untravelled land; now he has been there and surprised its whole secret, which he tells again: its strange, melancholy, womanless civilization, its null commerce, its arrested art, its passive religion, the entire circle of its negations. The book is wonderfully full of novel material, well philosophized, and has a value which now can not belong to any future book of travel till we begin to explore the moon.

[1]*Criticism and Fiction*, pp. 85-86.

[2]Léon Tolstoi, "Scenes du Siege de Sébastopol," *Revue des Deux Mondes*, Ser. 9, No. 72 (December 1, 1885), 481-513.

[3]Eugene-Melchior de Vogüé, "Les Ecrivains Russes Contemporains--Nicolas Gogol," *Revue des Deux Mondes*, Ser. 9, No. 72 (November 15, 1885), 241-279.

[4]Henry Hayes is a pseudonym of Ellen Warner Kirk.

[5]The title of the English translation is *Marquis of Peñalta*.

May, 1886

Editor's Study.

I.

MR. ROBERT LOUIS STEVENSON in his new romance, *The Strange Case of Dr. Jekyll and Mr. Hyde,* follows the lines explored by Mr. Edward Bellamy in his romance of *Miss Ludington's Sister.* But the Patent-office abounds in simultaneously invented machinery, and, at any rate, Mr. Stephenson may claim an improvement upon the apparatus of Mr. Bellamy. The American writer supposed several selves in each human being, which died successively and became capable of meeting one another in a different state of existence. Mr. Stevenson immensely simplifies the supposition by reducing these selves to the number of two—a moral self and an unmoral self. The moral self in the *Strange Case* was Dr. Jekyll, who, by the use of a certain drug, liberated Mr. Hyde, his unmoral self or evil principle, in whom he went about wreaking all his bad passions, without the inconvenience of subsequent remorse; all he had to do was to take the infusion of that potent salt, and become the good Dr. Jekyll again. The trouble in the end was that Mr. Hyde, from being at first smaller and feebler than Dr. Jekyll, outgrew him, and formed the habit of coming forth without the use of the salt. Dr. Jekyll was obliged to kill them both.

The romancer cannot often be taken very seriously, we suppose; he seems commonly to be working out a puzzle, and at last to have produced an intellectual toy; but Mr. Stevenson, who is inevitably a charming and sympathetic writer, and whom we first knew as the author of certain poems full of deep feeling and sincerity, does something more than this in his romance; he not only fascinates, he impresses upon the reader the fact that if we indulge the evil in us it outgrows the good. The lesson is not quite new, and in enforcing it he comes dangerously near the verge of allegory; for it is one of the hard conditions of romance that its personages starting with a *parti pris* can rarely be characters with a living growth, but are apt to be types, limited to the expression of one principle, simple, elemental, lacking the God-given complexity of motive which we find in all the human beings we know.

Hawthorne, the great master of the romance, had the insight and the power to create it anew as a kind in fiction; though we are not sure that *The Scarlet Letter* and the *Blithedale Romance* are not, strictly speaking, novels rather than romances. They do not play with some old superstition long outgrown, and they do not invent a new superstition to play with, but deal with things vital in every one's pulse. We are not saying that what may be called the fantastic romance—the romance that descends from *Frankenstein* rather than *The Scarlet Letter* — ought not to be. On the contrary, we should grieve to lose it, as we should grieve to lose the pantomime or the comic opera, or many other graceful things that amuse the passing hour, and help us to live agreeably in a world where men actually sin, suffer, and die. But it belongs to the decorative arts, and though it has a high place among them, it cannot be ranked with the works of the imagination—the works that represent and body forth human experience. Its ingenuity can always afford a refined pleasure, and it can often, at some risk to itself, convey a valuable truth.

II.

We can be glad of it even in a writer of our time, but it would be hard to forgive a contemporary for a bit of theatricality like that which the new translation of Balzac offers us in *The Duchesse de Langeais.* It is worse, if anything could be worse, than *Père Goriot*—more artificial in motive, more malarial, more oblique in morals. In fact, the inversion of the principles of right and wrong, the appeal made to the reader's sympathy for the man who cannot ruin the married coquette he loves, is as bad a thing as we know in literature. But it has its value as part of the history of Balzac's evolution, which was curiously fitful and retarded. It is a survival of romanticism, and its Sworn Thirteen Noblemen, who abduct the Duchess at a ball and bring her back before supper, and who are pledged to defend and abet each other in all good and ill, are the sort of mechanism not now employed outside of the dime fictions.

It must by no means be supposed, in fine, that because Balzac was a realist, he was always a realist. As a matter of fact, he was sometimes a romanticist as flamboyant as Victor Hugo himself, without Victor Hugo's generous sympathy and noble faith; and we advise the reader that a more depraving book could hardly fall into the hands of the young than *The Duchesse de Langeais*—more false to life, more false to art. It is a pity that it is bound up in the Boston edition with *The Illustrious Gaudissart,* a charming piece of humor and nature.

III.

It is droll to find Balzac, who suffered such bitter scorn and hate for his realism while he was alive, now become a fetich in his turn, to be shaken in the faces of those who will not blindly worship him. But it is no new thing in the history of literature: whatever is established is sacred with those who do not think.

At the beginning of the century, when romance was making the same fight against effete classicism which realism is making to-day against effete romance, the Italian poet Monti declared that "the romantic was the cold grave of the Beautiful," just as the realistic is now supposed to be. The romance of that day and the realism of this are in certain degree the same. Romance then sought, as realism seeks now, to widen the bounds of sympathy, to level every barrier against æsthetic freedom, to escape from the paralysis of tradition. It exhausted itself in this impulse; and it remained for realism to assert that fidelity to experience and probability of motive are essential conditions of a great imaginative literature. It is not a new theory, but it has never before universally characterized literary endeavor. When realism becomes false to itself, when it heaps up facts merely, and maps life instead of picturing it, realism will perish too. Every true realist instinctively knows this, and it is perhaps the reason why he is careful of every fact, and feels himself bound to express or to indicate its meaning at the risk of over-moralizing. In life he finds nothing insignificant; all tells for destiny and character; nothing that God has made is contemptible. He cannot look upon human life and declare this thing or that thing unworthy of notice, any more than the scientist can declare a fact of the material world beneath the dignity of his inquiry. He feels in every nerve the equality of things and the unity of men; his soul is exalted, not by vain shows and shadows and ideals, but by realities, in which alone the truth lives. In criticism it is his business to break the images of false gods and misshapen heroes, to take away the poor silly toys that many grown people would still like to play with. He cannot keep terms with Jack the Giant-Killer or Puss in Boots, under any name or in any place, even when they reappear as the convict Vautrec, or the Marquis de Montrivaut, or the Sworn Thirteen Noblemen. He must say to himself that Balzac, when he imagined these monsters, was not Balzac, he was Dumas; he was not realistic, he was romantic.[2]

IV.

Such a critic will not respect Balzac's good work the less for contemning his bad work. He will easily account for the bad work historically, and when he has recognized it, will trouble himself no farther with it. In his view no living man is a type, but a character; now noble, now ignoble; now grand, now little; complex, full of vicissitude. He will not expect Balzac to be always Balzac, or Tennyson to be always Tennyson; and in his scheme of criticism the laureate's last work, with its pathetic echoes of his past work, will interest him hardly less than that.

It is by no means necessary to compare the "Tiresias" with the "Ulysses," or the "Balin and Balan" with the "Morte d'Arthur"; one need not be brutal in confessing their inferiority. They are perhaps what the Tennysonian art must come to; but one must not forget how lovely that art was at its best. Its sweetness is in the nerves of every refined man and woman of his generation, and is perhaps all the more inalienably theirs if a younger generation does not feel its witchery so keenly. The race has its moods, and it cannot prolong them or recur to them; but it was in a high and hopeful mood when Tennyson pleased it to its heart's core, and no doubt something is lacking in it as well as in him if he no longer pleases so much. We would rather compare him with anything that we have the reasonable hope of in the future, and bear the consequent discouragement as we may, than decry what has been so good, and is so good. If the latest verse of this illustrious poet came to us as the earliest verse of a poet quite unknown, we should welcome it, not as the promise, but as the performance, of fine things. When shall we have from another a lyric of such noble note as "Freedom" in this book? Or an elegiac of such tender feeling as the "Prefatory Poem to my Brother's Sonnets"? Or a didactic of such high wisdom as "The Ancient Sage"? By-and-by, in the general account with Tennyson which time shall square, these things will be valued aright, and they will have their place, not as his best, but among his best. For the present it can be justly said of the book generally that there is more of Tennyson's manner than of Tennyson in it. His manner, which was always so much, has become more and more with him; and in this he is different from Longfellow, with whom manner became less and less, so that his latest poems were the simplest and most direct expressions of his poetic quality, absolutely purified, in the case of some of his sonnets, from posturing. But Tennyson's manner was always much of his charm, and here it charms the old reader still, and is as full of memory, as historical, as a perfume. Whether it has the same fascination for a younger reader, it must remain for the younger reader to say.

V.

We, at least, would not willingly leave out some of his most manneristic poems, if we were to have any share in that process of elimination which must finally await modern literature of every kind. The volume of this has now grown so enormous, and there is so very much of what is so very good, that the race must in self-defence eventually reject all but the best. We hope even in our own day to see an edition of those unwieldy immortals, the British Classics, in which they shall be reduced and exalted by the rejection of what is dull and what is indecent in them. Then one may read all of them that is worth reading, and feel that he knows English literature, and is none the worse for it. We have been encouraged to the expression of this hope, long secretly cherished, by some words of excellent wisdom which Professor Max Müller has lately written in answer to an inquiry for his opinion of Sir John Lubbock's list of the Best Hundred Books. "If I were to tell you,"[3] he says, "what I really think of the best books, I am afraid you would call me the greatest literary heretic or an utter ignoramus. I know few books, if any, which I should call good from beginning to end. Take the greatest poet of antiquity, and if I am to speak the truth, the whole truth, and nothing but the truth, I must say there are long passages even in Homer which seem to me extremely tedious. Take the greatest, or at all events one of the greatest, poets of our century, and again I must confess that not a few of Goethe's writings seem to me not worth a second reading. There are gems in the most famous, there are gems in the least known, of poets, but there is not a single poet, so far as I know, who has not written too much, and who could claim a place for all his works in what may be called a library of world literature."

Every now and then in a world of affectations and pretences the truth comes out, and we all rather wonder that it has not come out before. It comes out in these days somewhat oftener than in former times, because it is now, on the whole, less dangerous to speak it; but Professor Müller must not expect an unalloyed gratitude from our generation even. He must expect, on the contrary, to be asked whether he thinks himself greater than Homer and Goethe, and if he has the full advantage of " criticism," he will learn that a person of his opinions cannot be a person of his science. He will be challenged to write anything half as good as the worst of Homer and Goethe, and he will be taught that burglary and blasphemy are light offences compared with his, in the eyes of those who know Homer and Goethe by hearsay. Nevertheless, what he says of poetry, of all literature, will remain true, and the time will come when an ultimate Sir John Lubbock will set down for us a list of the best hundred pieces instead of the best hundred books. An ultimate Prince of Wales will then not be obliged to exclude the whole of Thackeray on account of the lectures on *The Four Georges*, and we shall be allowed, even by the ultimate New York Anglomaniacs, to read passages of the *Book of Snobs*. ⁴

VI.

Apropos of the future of poetry, there are some passages from a little book published in Florence on *Berlioz et le Mouvement de l'Art Contemporain*, by Georges Noufflard, which we commend to the notice of those now engaged in prophesying on the subject. In that absence of a Meteorologico-literary Bureau which we have already deplored, the ideas of M. Noufflard, who has a number of very good ideas of his own, may be useful; and suggesting as they do a further poetical development, through reversion to a primitive phase, they may console, they may even encourage.

"I believe," he says, "that the future of absolute music and poetry will have the same fate as sculpture, and this for reasons analogous to those I have alleged against the last— the means of action at their disposal are insufficient. In effect, if sculpture can only represent life by depriving it of its colors and placing it in the void, music can only paint feeling in an abstract fashion. . . . Poetry, that is, the art of working in verse, has no other expression of its own but that which may result from the sonorousness and rhythm which it obtains by the choice and the grouping of words. Now these, whatever may have been their origin, are to-day certainly nothing more than conventional signs, capable of analyzing, but not of directly representing, our sensations. If poetry had no other basis than its expression, it is evident that it would not exist; its object is to arrange words in regular and symmetrical groups. Born with the dance and with music, it is, like these, when it stands alone, an art essentially decorative. It may be said that in verse there is a music marked and perceptible, and yet so controlled that the meaning is not lost in the sound. But it seems to me that all the effects of this sort may be achieved with greater force either by veritable music or by prose—prose, for exam-

ple, like that of the De Goncourt brothers. . . . The decadence of poetry and music are two related facts arising from the decadence of ornamental art itself. Considered separately, music and poetry have both reached the limit of their development; but associated intimately enough to form a single art, they may in the future vigorously make head against prose. All the objections that can be advanced against music and poetry, when separated, disappear when they are united. The significance of music is not less sufficient when words determine it, and the direct expression of sense is not degraded when, instead of relying wholly upon the resources of the spoken tongue, it rests upon all the means of action proper to music. Are my theories too bold? It seems to me that we need only look around us to see that they are confirmed by the facts. Sculpture is nowhere alive to-day except in Italy and France; and what has it produced that is truly original without betraying tendencies that its means of action will not allow it to realize fully? On the other hand, painting is everywhere flourishing. . . . The comedy in prose and the novel have already taken the place of the tragedy and the epic poem; no one any longer composes absolute melodies even in Italy, and the need of music to rest upon words shows itself even in the symphony. . . . The modern spirit tends farther and farther from the arts that can express a theme only by halves, to concentrate itself upon those that can show it in its entirety. Prose, painting, and poetry, blended with music, will, I am convinced, be the three principal organs of the thought of the twentieth century. Prose has the advantage over its rivals which its universality gives; it knows no limits but those of the human spirit. On the other hand, it cannot represent directly. An artificial product of the intelligence, its danger is that of being more and more engrossed by science. Witness, for example, the scientific preoccupations which Zola has introduced into the novel. It is true that if science ever comes to be complete, if it ever goes to the bottom, to the soul of things, if the broken fragments it now gives us are ever assembled, it will be poetry, as it was in the time of Dante. To painting belongs fully the exterior world; it not only shows us the man living and individual, but it places him in the *milieu* where he belongs, and where his personality continues and affirms itself. And the new art resulting from the intimate union of music and poetry will, thanks to its double organ and to the special faculties of music, be able to represent completely all the phenomena of the inner life."

VII.

One of the serious disadvantages of infallibility is that one has no sooner laid down any general principle than some signal and quite irreconcilable exception is pretty sure to arise. Mr. Froude's *Oceana*, for example, comes hard upon the doctrine of this Study, pronounced only a month or two ago, that the English view of any foreign civilization is sure to be the wrong view. If we had not warned the reader at the start that we were always to be understood as speaking humanly, we should now have some difficulty in owning that this great Englishman's view of our greatness through the Union, and of our individual consequence through our federal greatness, is so gratifying that it must be correct. As it is, it is simply a pleasure to recognize the fact. His cursory chapter on the United States comes at the close of the story of his wanderings from England to the Cape of Good Hope, from the Cape to Australia, from Australia to New Zealand, and from New Zealand to California; but it is in some sort the key-note of the whole book, which affirms and reaffirms that the hope of England and her colonies is in a federation as like our own as possible. The book is agreeable reading enough as a book of travels, but its chief value is political. The most interesting chapters are those recounting and condemning the facts of English policy in South Africa. Australasian affairs are more rose-colored to Mr. Froude's eye; he finds society and politics even exuberantly loyal; but he too is speaking humanly, and he recognizes exceptions in which the colonists declare that they are merely waiting their own convenience to be independent, and take the United States rather than England for their exemplar of greatness.

But if Mr. Froude is too hopeful in his politics, there is no error in his attitude toward the civilization of the new countries he visits. He perceives, as we think no Englishman has before, the real solidarity of the Anglo-Saxon civilization, and the simultaneity of its characteristics. He cannot see that men or their interests are less modern or advanced in Melbourne than in London, and he crosses our own continent without finding us anywhere merely grotesque or sordid, or even unintelligible. *Oceana* may be held to mark the beginning of a new era in English travel when its author can say of another people: "The dimensions and value of any single man depend on the body of which he is a member. As an individual his horizon is bounded by his personal interests; he remains, however high his gifts, but a mean creature. . . . A man, on the other hand, who is more than himself, who is part of an institution, who has devoted himself to a cause—or is a citizen of an imperial power—expands to the scope and fulness of the larger organism; and the grander the organization, the larger and more important the unit that knows that he belongs to it. His thoughts are wider, his interests less selfish, his ambitions ampler and nobler. . . . Behind each American citizen America is standing, and he knows it, and is the man that he is because he knows it. The Anglo-Americans divided might have fared no better than the Spanish colonies. The Anglo-Americans united command the respectful fear of mankind, and, as Pericles said of the Athenians, each unit of them acts as if the fortunes of his country depended only on himself. A great nation makes great men, a small nation makes little men."

[1] *Criticism and Fiction*, pp. 115-116.

[2] *Criticism and Fiction*, pp. 14-17.

[3] Sir John Lubbock, "On the Pleasure of Reading," *Contemporary Review*, 49 (February, 1886), 240-251.

[4] See note 1, p. 5.

June, 1886

Editor's Study.

I.

THE lectures of the Concord School of Philosophy on the *Life and Genius of Goethe* form a book which is notable for its limitations as well as its excellences, but is always curious and interesting. It is what Professor White thinks of Goethe's Youth, Mr. Albee of his Self-Culture, Professor Davidson of his Titanism, Dr. Bartol of Goethe and Schiller, Dr. Hedge of Goethe's Märchen, Mr. Sanborn of his Relation to English Literature, Mr. Partridge of his qualities as a Playwright, Mrs. Cheney of his Ewig-Weibliche, Mr. Emery of his Elective Affinities, Mrs. Sherman of his treatment of Child Life, Mr. Snider of the Faust Poem, Mrs. Julia Ward Howe of his Women, Professor Harris of his Faust. Each of these lectures has its value, and if their fortuitous combination does not enhance their worth, we cannot say that it necessarily detracts from it. They seem to us, so far as they severally go, to embody a good deal of original if not novel impression, and to have each a certain adequacy; it is the whole book that is a little insufficient. Dr. Hedge's elucidation of the allegory which he explains is as unquestionably interesting as the Märchen itself is tiresome, even now when its cloudy prophecies concerning the rehabilitation of Germany seem fulfilled. Mr. Sanborn's inquiry as to Goethe's influence on English literature is interesting, though it fails of indicating the one certain effect which, directly or indirectly, Goethe's method in fiction is having in these latest times. He taught us, in novels otherwise now antiquated, and always full of German clumsiness, that it was false to good art—which is never anything but the reflection of life—to pursue and round the career of the persons introduced, whom he often allowed to appear and disappear in our knowledge as people in the actual world do. This is a lesson which the writers able to profit by it can never be too grateful for; and it is equally a benefaction to readers; but there is very little else in the conduct of the Goethean novels which is in advance of their time; this remains almost their sole contribution to the science of fiction. They are very primitive in certain characteristics, and unite with their calm, deep insight, an amusing helplessness in dramatization. "Wilhelm retired to his room, and indulged in the following reflections," is a mode of analysis which would not be practiced nowadays; and all that fancifulness of nomenclature in *Wilhelm Meister* is very drolly romantic and feeble. The adventures with robbers seem as if dreamed out of books of chivalry, and the tendency to allegorization affects one like an endeavor on the author's part to escape from the unrealities which he must have felt harassingly, German as he was. Mixed up with the shadows and illusions are honest, wholesome, every-day people, who have the air of wandering homelessly about among them, without definite direction; and the mists are full of a luminosity which, in spite of them, we know for common-sense and poetry. What is useful in any review of Goethe's methods is the recognition of the fact, which it must bring, that the greatest master cannot produce a masterpiece in a new kind. The novel was too recently invented in Goethe's day not to be, even in his hands, full of the faults of apprentice work.

Among these Concord essays, we believe we have liked Mrs. Howe's almost the best, because we have found it one of the clearest and frankest. She thinks that Goethe differs from most men who have written about women in not satirizing them; but she does not blink the fact that whatever Goethe's ideal women were, his treatment of real women was not ideal. To our own mind it is no defence of him to say that many other known and unknown men were as bad or worse, or to imply that much must be forgiven to his "genius." Nothing must be forgiven to a man's "genius." The greater his power, the greater his responsibility before the human conscience, which is God in us. But men come and go, and what they do in their limited physical lives is of comparatively little moment; it is what they say that really survives to bless or to ban; and we wish that some of our good Concord philosophers—pure souls and right minds as they all are—had thought it well to recognize the evil that Wordsworth felt in Goethe, and that must long survive him. There is a kind of thing—a kind of metaphysical lie against righteousness and common-sense—which is called the Unmoral, and is supposed to be different from the Immoral; and it is this which is supposed to cover many of the faults of Goethe. His *Wilhelm Meister*, for example, is so far removed within the region of the "ideal" that its unprincipled, its evil-principled, tenor in regard to women is pronounced "unmorality," and is therefore inferably harmless. But no study of Goethe is complete without some consideration of the ethics of his great novel, and in this particular the Concord study of his life and genius is signally defective. There is no lecture on *Wilhelm Meister*, no recognition of the qualities which caused Wordsworth to hurl the book across the room with an indignant perception of its sensuality. Yet such a recognition might have come most fitly from the group who preferred rather to burn incense at his shrine. For the sins of his life Goethe was sufficiently punished in his life by his final marriage with Christiane; for the sins of his literature many others must suffer; and we think it would have been well for the worshippers of his "genius" to lift a voice of warning against them in behalf of the votaries whom they will draw to his cult. Of course people who assemble to celebrate "genius" could not be expected to interrupt the rites with too severe a scrutiny of the obliquities of the god.

II.

We do not despair, however, of the day when the poor honest herd of humankind shall give universal utterance to the universal instinct, and shall hold selfish power in politics, in art, in religion, for the devil that it is; when neither its crazy pride nor its amusing vanity shall be flattered by the puissance of the "geniuses" who have forgotten their duty to the common weakness, and have abused it to their own glory. In that day we shall shudder at many monsters of passion, of self-indulgence, of heartlessness, whom we still more or less openly adore for their "genius," and shall account no man worshipful whom we do not feel and know to be good. The spectacle of strenuous achievement will then not dazzle or mislead; it will not sanctify or palliate iniquity; it will only render it the more hideous and pitiable. A life at once good and great will no longer strike us as something so anomalous that we shall be tempted to question either its goodness or its greatness, and in that desirable time we shall know fully how to appreciate the unblotted sublimity of a career like Longfellow's. Even now the careful reader of the *Life* which the poet's brother has lately given us will feel that grandeur if he will put all the false and misshapen ideals of "genius" out of his mind. At first the story moves slowly and even coldly, but the charm of that unerring loveliness of spirit, that never-clouded right-mindedness, that unfaltering loftiness of purpose, grows upon you unawares, and it holds you closer and closer to the end. There is never anything spectacular or agonized or contorted in that life, though it knew sorrow doubly tragic by contrast with the long flow of its prosperity, and was fretted in its undercurrents, as all lives are, by the troubles which "genius" has so often exploited as its peculiar griefs.

Not much more in outline appears in Mr. Samuel Longfellow's two volumes than we knew of Longfellow already; but the detail which he loved—" Oh, give *details* of thy life, dear friend, and not generalities, which in no wise satisfy!"—is here in delightful fulness. It abounds in the letters which he wrote home on his youthful wanderings in Spain, in the journals and letters of his subsequent journeys and sojourns in Italy, in France, and in Germany, and those of the long period of his residence in Cambridge, with its manifold friendships, its beloved duties, its poetic delights, its heavy sorrow, its days of uncomplaining pain. There was nothing to be hidden, and nothing is kept from us that could throw light upon his life, whose beauty was so great, whose incidents were so simple and few. The story of his first love and marriage is given with unstudied pathos, and with the perfect taste which marks the biographer's handling of his material throughout; and then there is not much more to tell except the story of his coming to Cambridge, and of his union with the Mary Ashburton of his beautiful romance. The chief events of his life there were the poems which the world knows; and in the abundant record there is nothing to change the impression which his work gives of him, certainly none of those anomalies and contradictions of temper and performance which have made modern biography such lurid reading. He is a man to whom you have nothing to forgive, not even a feeble quality in his irreproachable goodness; for there is nothing more striking in Longfellow's life than the manly strength which governed it. He was full of fancy, and he had an optimistic gayety of heart, but neither his imagination nor his faith misled him in large things or small, personal or public, literary or moral, æsthetic or political. His philosophy of life was very simple, but entirely adequate: to do good and to be good, and then "learn to enjoy the present—that little space of time between the great past and the still greater future." There is no rancor expressed against any human creature, except " the nasty little professor in a dirty schlafrock" at Heidelberg, who, in bidding the poet farewell, "took his pipe out of his mouth and kissed" him on the lips. "I had a great mind to take him by the ears," he adds, and it must be owned the offence was great. But no one else is visited with like severity; not even Poe, whose bitterness never imparted itself to Longfellow. Now and again there is a touch of his delicate humor; and the letters and journals grow more interesting as time advances and the fermentation of youth subsides, leaving the poet clear as to his purpose and destiny. He was not always so sure of either, for in 1829 he wrote, "My poetic career is finished," and for six years after he made no more verses.

While the details of his life will not change the feeling toward him, they will deepen it; for the reader will find here abundant and fresh reason to confirm himself in reverence for one of the noblest and simplest souls. Longfellow was never known, for instance, as a champion of the antislavery cause; but early in his literary career he threw down his gage in the *Poems on Slavery;* and throughout its existence he was the fast friend of those that hated it and fought it. In 1837, at the time of the Lovejoy meeting, he wrote home to his father, " The Little Peddlington community of Boston is in a great toss .... about Dr. Channing and the abolitionists; Boston is only a great village; the tyranny of public opinion there surpasses all belief"; and throughout the long struggle he stood by the righteous, and defended them, with serene dignity and courage, when scorn covered them. In the teeth of Boston respectability, which had loved him, he never faltered in his fealty. What that respectability was—its culture, its barbarism, its refinement, its meanness, its servility, its arrogance—is now pretty historical; what respectability was elsewhere in 1842 may be inferred from the fact that the editor of *Graham's Magazine* excused to Longfellow a notice of his book, which had to be made very guarded, because "the word *slav-*

ery was never allowed to appear in a Philadelphia periodical, and the publisher objected to have even the name of the book appear in his pages." As time passed, and the infamy of Northern complicity with slavery was brought home to the North by the now incredible Fugitive Slave Law, Longfellow wrote in his journal, under date of February 15, 1851: "I learn that a fugitive slave, or a man accused of being one, escaped to-day from the court-room during the recess, aided by other blacks. Very glad of it. This government must not pass laws that outrage the sense of right in the community." This slave was Shadrach. Of the rendition of Simms he wrote, April 4th, of the same year: "There is much excitement in Boston about the capture of an alleged fugitive slave. O city without soul! When and where will this end? Shame that the great republic, the 'refuge of the oppressed,' should stoop so low as to become the hunter of slaves! .... Troops under arms in Boston; the court-house guarded; the Chief-Justice of the Supreme Court forced to stoop under chains to enter the temple of justice! .... Alas for the people who cannot feel an insult! While the 'great Webster' comes North to see that the work is done!'

To a friend who had blamed him for his *Poems on Slavery*, he replied, declining argument, but stating his moral and political creed concerning it, which was that of Sumner and the other statesmen who first organized a practical opposition to it. But these were Longfellow's own opinions, and he based his action upon a principle that underlay his whole life. "I have great faith in doing what is righteous, and fear no evil consequences." It underlay his literature as well as his life, and it was a conscience that resulted not only in the highest conduct, but the finest art. With nothing narrow, and with finally nothing moralistic, he achieved in the poetry he has left us a blended ideal of goodness and of beauty which is incomparably perfect. It has for some time been the silly fashion in criticism to depreciate it; but those who have sneered at it have unwittingly paid it the highest tribute, for they have called it the poetry of the average human life; and this, without their knowing it, is the universal poetry.

A great part of his biography consists of passages from Longfellow's diaries, which are more interesting, because more intimate, than his letters. The records are often mere comments on the books he is reading; and these comments, without affecting profundity or finality, are often of the last wisdom. Criticism has only in these times learned to value Bulwer aright; but in 1849 Longfellow said of *The Caxtons:* "It has well-drawn characters in it, but the style produces upon me the effect of a flashy waistcoat festooned with gold chains." His judgments were seldom so harsh as these, but they were always clear and decided. He was never swayed by personal feeling, nor by that larger cockneyism which calls itself patriotism, though he was an American, zealous and strenuous to the last degree, where the good and honor of his country were concerned. He abhorred "the unrighteous Mexican war," and found it "melancholy to see how little true Christian feeling there is on the subject in the country." But even in small things he liked a thorough Americanism. When Sumner returned from his social triumphs in England in 1840, Longfellow recorded: "I fear that his head is a little turned, and no wonder; but he is a strong man, and will see in the end that there is something better than breakfasting at ten and dining at six."

Longfellow had not only great faith in men, but patience as vast and kindly as Lincoln's. Neither the foibles nor the sins of his fellow-mortals shut his heart against them, or inclined him to distinguish himself from them. He expressed in his life and in his literature that perfect toleration which was the only virtue left for the Americans to invent. Doubtless he said to himself that he too had his foibles like the rest; in fact, a tradition of his gaudiness in neck-ties and waistcoats survived his youth in Cambridge, and his biographer does not blink it. But there was nothing in that blameless life to blink, nothing to palliate, nothing to deprecate. It was filled full with a most ardent and generous love of letters, but a love of men mingled and interfused itself with this, so that it could never become reckless or cruel. He

"Whose smoothest verse was harsher-toned than he,"

left no heart to burn at the mention of his name. Yet, as we have suggested, no estimate of his character could be more mistaken than a conception of his goodness as a weak mildness, "a mush of concession." This gentlest of men was one of the manliest. It was his strength that was kind; and it not only softened him to the folly of others, but armed him with pity against their envy and malice and ingratitude, all which he felt in full measure throughout his life. It enabled him also to bear with dignity the uninstructed arrogance in criticism which found the pure and serene beauty of his work unsatisfying, and hankered for something contorted and passion-stricken.

It will be long, probably, before the Concord School of Philosophy will study Longfellow's life and genius; and perhaps it will begin by denying him the latter; but in the former it will have to leave no chapter untouched. In the mean time we can commend it to the unphilosophical without reservation, and especially we can ask the young to teach themselves from his career, not the greatness, of which he alone had the secret, but the goodness, which is open and possible to all, and which no one can read his life without feeling in supreme degree.

III.

Now that we have the new Boston translation of *César Birotteau*, we are reminded again how Balzac stood at the beginning of the great things that have followed since in fiction. There is an interesting likeness between his work in this and Nicolas Gogol's in *Dead Souls*, which serves to illustrate the simultaneity of the literary movement in men of such widely separated civilizations and conditions. Both represent their characters with the touch of exaggeration which typifies; but in bringing his story to a close, Balzac employs a beneficence unknown to the Russian, and almost as universal and as apt as that which smiles upon the fortunes of the good in the *Vicar of Wakefield*. It is not enough to have rehabilitated Birotteau pecuniarily and socially; he must make him die triumphantly, spectacularly, of an opportune hemorrhage, in the midst of the festivities which celebrate his restoration to his old home. Before this, human nature has been laid under contribution right and left for acts of generosity toward the righteous bankrupt; even the king sends him six thousand francs. It is very pretty; it is touching, and brings the lump into the reader's throat; but it is too much, and one perceives that Balzac lived too soon to profit by Balzac. The later men, especially the Russians, have known how to forbear the excesses of analysis, to withhold the weakly recurring descriptive and caressing epithets, to let the characters suffice for themselves. All this does not mean that *César Birotteau* is not a beautiful and pathetic story, as stainless as a French story can well be, full of shrewdly considered knowledge of men, and of a good art struggling to free itself from self-consciousness. But it does mean that Balzac at his best was under the burden of traditions which he has helped fiction to throw off. He felt obliged to construct a mechanical plot, to surcharge his characters, to moralize openly and baldly; he permitted himself to "sympathize"

with certain of his people, and to point out others for the abhorrence of his readers. This is not so bad in him as it would be in a novelist of our day. It is simply primitive and inevitable, and he is not to be judged by it. ⌐5

In fact, there is also something of nationality in the 'too visibly *operated* incidents of César Birotteau's rehabilitation, if we are to believe an eminent critic of the same nation. In his essay on *Les Grands Maîtres de la Littérature Russe*, M. Ernest Dupuy, speaking of the mechanical methods of French novelists, says: "Our good romancers are such skilful carpenters; they construct works so regular, so ingeniously arranged for effect, where the interest is managed with so much address, where the action moves with a step so sure toward a logical close suspected or desired from the first word! We find ourselves at the outset ill at ease in these Russian romances, full of art, but stripped of the little artifices; whose development resembles the course of life; where the personages hesitate, sometimes remain quiet; where the action proceeds without haste, and the author does not trouble himself to round off and finish up. It is enough for them to note facts and express character."

[1]The Concord School of Philosophy was an annual colloquium of idealists and transcendentalists begun by Amos Bronson Alcott on July 15, 1879, and continuing into the twentieth century. Its publications are reprinted in Concord Harvest, Kenneth Walter Cameron, ed. (Hartford, Conn.: Transcendental Books, 1970).

[2]Criticism and Fiction, pp. 22-24.

[3]Criticism and Fiction, p. 86.

[4]Criticism and Fiction, pp. 86-87 (abridged).

[5]Criticism and Fiction, pp. 18-20.

July, 1886

Editor's Study.

I.

MR. SIDNEY LUSKA'S *Mrs. Peixada* is a novel so good in some things that it is a pleasure to recognize its fresh ground, its unworn *personnel*, its generous passion, its vivid incident, and the strong young *go* of the whole affair; for Mr. Luska—who is not Mr. Luska, we believe, but some one much nearer us poor Gentiles in name if not in sympathy—is clearly a young man, and has the chance of better and better work before him. He has the reasonable hope of it too; and we take all the more heart for him because in this second venture of his he has left the region of music and romance, where he dwelt in his first story, and has stepped quite out into the light of our common day, which, as we have several times assured the guests of this Study, is preferable to any manner of moonshine or alabaster lamps, or even the latest improvement in electrics. We are glad, however, that Mr. Luska has kept to his chosen people, and that he gives us Jews again in his novel. The heroine is a Jewess, and nearly all the characters in the book are New York Jews, finely distinguished one from another, and very neatly accented. In fact, Mr. Luska's mastery is in the treatment of his various Israelites, in their presentation individually, and in their collective localization here in New York. They are neither flattered nor caricatured; they are simply portrayed with truth by a hand that is already firm, and that gives promise of greater and greater skill. After them comes the plot, intricate and thrilling enough to enrapture the inexperienced, and not such as to give the old novel reader a moment's anxiety for the outcome. By-and-by Mr. Luska will probably evolve his plot from his personages, rather than involve them in it; and then he will touch hearts instead of merely shaking nerves. His present situations could all have grown out of the same number of Gentiles quite as well; but the plot is valuable because it exacts from him the study of many local conditions and characters, and he makes this study very faithfully and graphically. His art lapses most in the narrative dramatized in the reported evidence of the murder trial, and in the autobiography of Mrs. Peixada; in these the literary man keeps coming to the front; and at other times he has a consciousness that is not altogether pleasant. His best work is in the subordinate figures; these are the *characters;* the principal people are only types of this or that passion: they do not remain in the mind like the others; they have the conventional singleness of motive noticeable in the people of a modern stage play.

II.

In fact, *Mrs. Peixada* would make into a very good play, and if as a drama it could keep the novel's variety of uncaricatured personages, and its glow of genuine, decent passion, untouched by sentimentalism, it would be a drama which would send the poor, patient metropolitan play-goer home with a real emotion under his waistcoat. He would feel that he had seen a bit of life, if the stage could show him those Beekman Place interiors, with the eating and smoking that goes on in them, and those Beekman Place figures of naturalized German Jews. If he could have also the scenes in the lonely suburban house when the tortured woman kills her hideous husband and his accomplice in self-defence, and then the scenes in court when she pleads guilty, he would have tragic "action" enough, and what such action does not always give—pathos and genuine tragedy.

Perhaps Mr. Luska's next essay may be dramatic in form as well as in spirit. Then we should have at least one phase of that American play which we are all beginning to long for, or to think we long for. In fact, with a great and unquestionable love of the theatre, we doubt if there is much love of the drama among us, and we are sure there is less knowledge. So the managers have continued to give us the theatre and not the drama; very good acting, but little or nothing worth acting. Probably if Mr. Luska wrote a very good play, fresh, native, true, he could not get it played, for there has been so little that is fresh, native, and true on the stage for so long that the managers might not know what to make of the piece; and it is to the manager, not the public, that the playwright appeals. In every other art the artist's censor is the world. He makes a statue or paints a picture, and somewhere, somehow, it meets the eye of general criticism; he writes a book, and if no publisher will have it, there are means of cheap publication by which it can still reach the light without ruining the author. But no one, unless he is rich enough to write history, can hire a theatre and produce his play. Its fate lies in the judgment, the taste, the theory, of the manager. He is eager, on his part, only too eager, to please the public, and not knowing what new thing will offend, he keeps offering it the old thing over and over in some form or other. The literary motives, outgrown and cast off in every other department of literary art, have formed so long the prosperity of the theatre, the art of the stage, that it is no wonder the manager cannot believe his public would like anything better. He knows per-

29

fectly well that it is abject trash he gives; for whatever the manager is he is very commonly not a fool. He is often a man of taste and of sufficient reading; he knows quite well what is good literature. He merely believes that it is not adapted to the stage; it might have been adapted to the stage once, he admits, but now, not. He will tell you that the public wishes merely to be amused, and does not care for the literary quality of a play. "What pleases the public, it thinks is good, and it thinks all the rest is 'rot.'" The manager is right; but the author who wishes to give his piece literary quality, to be faithful to life and to art, as he would be in writing a novel, is right too in asking the manager to let the public decide whether it likes this quality or not.

But here is another difficulty. The manager cannot afford to experiment with literary quality; for it costs so much to "stage" a play in these days of a material theatre but no drama, that he can only risk giving the old rubbish in some novel disguise. If a play could be put upon the stage cheaply, he might let a really new play make its appeal to the public; he might try half a dozen new plays during the season. But with the present expensiveness of setting, a failure is ruinous, and nothing really new can be risked. So much money has to be put into the frame of the picture that only the well-known chromo-effects in sentiment, character, and situation can be afforded in the picture. It is as if all new books were published in *éditions de luxe*, and consequently all new books were compilations and rehashes of old books. That is what he believes plays must be, compilations and rehashes of old plays, in order to stand any chance of success with the public.

III.

The outlook is not hopeless, however. We will not speak of Mr. Gilbert's exquisite ironies; he is an Englishman, and we are talking now about the American drama, or non-drama; for, in spite of theatres lavishly complete in staging, and with all the sanitary arrangements exemplary—the air changed every fifteen minutes, and artificially refrigerated in the summer—we have still no drama. Yet we have the prospect of something of the kind, and naturally we have it in accordance with the existing conditions. We have an abundance of most amusing sketches and extravaganzas, embodying more or less of our grotesque life; and amongst these, saving the respect of all the gentilities, are Mr. Hoyt's *Rag Baby*, and other absurdities. But, most hopeful of all the promises, we have the plays of Mr. Edward Harrigan. Our one original contribution and addition to histrionic art was negro minstrelsy, which, primitive, simple, elemental, was out of our own soil, and had the characteristics that distinguish autochthonic conceptions. But that is a thing almost of the past, and we have now to do with a novel contribution to the drama, and not to the art of the drama. It is peculiarly interesting, because it is morally, though not materially, the contribution most possible under our peculiar circumstances, for it is the work of a man in whom the instincts of the author combat the theatre's traditions, and the actor's experience censures the author's literary vanity. Mr. Harrigan writes, stages, and plays his pieces; he is his own playwright, manager, and comedian.

He has his own theatre, and can risk his own plays in it, simply and cheaply, in contempt of the carpenter and upholsterer. Not that he does treat these useful personages with contempt, but he subordinates them. In his theatre the highly decorated husk and gilded shell are not everything, nor the kernel attenuated to the last degree of innutritiousness. But the setting is at the same time singularly perfect and entirely sufficient. Mr. Harrigan accurately realizes in his scenes what he realizes in his persons; that is, the actual life of this city. He cannot give it all; he can only give phases of it; and he has preferred to give its Irish-American phases in their rich and amusing variety, and some of its African and Teutonic phases. It is what we call low life, though whether it is essentially lower than fashionable life is another question. But what it is, it is; and it remains for others, if they can, to present other sides of our manifold life with equal perfection; Mr. Harrigan leaves a vast part of the vast field open. In his own province we think he cannot be surpassed. The art that sets before us all sorts and conditions of New York Irishmen, from the laborers in the street to the most powerful of the ward politicians and the genteelest of the ladies of that interesting race, is the art of Goldoni—the joyous yet conscientious art of the true dramatist in all times who loves the life he observes. The old Venetian filled his scene with the gondoliers, the serving-folk, the fish-women, the trades-people, the quacks, the idlers, the gamesters, of his city; and Mr. Harrigan shows us the street-cleaners and contractors, the grocery-men, the shysters, the politicians, the washer-women, the servant-girls, the truckmen, the policemen, the risen Irishman and Irish woman, of contemporary New York. Goldoni carried through scores of comedies the same characters, the masks of the older drama which he drove from the stage, and Mr. Harrigan instinctively repeats the same personages in his Mulligan series. Within his range the New-Yorker is not less admirable than the Venetian. In fact, nothing could be better than the neatness, the fineness, with which the shades of character are given in Mr. Mulligan's Irish people; and this literary conscientiousness is supplemented by acting which is worthy of it. Mr. Harrigan is himself a player of the utmost naturalness, delicate, restrained, infallibly sympathetic; and we have seen no one on his stage who did not seem to have been trained to his part through entire sympathy and intelligence. In certain moments of *Dan's Tribulations* the illusion is so perfect that you lose the sense of being in the theatre; you are out of that world of conventions and traditions, and in the presence of the facts.

All the Irish aspects of life are treated affectionately by this artist, as we might expect from one of his name; but the colored aspects do not fare so well under his touch. Not all the Irish are good Irish, but all the colored people are bad colored people. They are of the gloomy, razor-bearing variety; full of short-sighted lies and prompt dishonesties, amusing always, but truculent and tricky; and the sunny sweetness which we all know in negro character is not there. We do not wholly object to the one-sided picture; it has its historical value; and so has the contemptuous prejudice of both Irish and ne-

-groes for the Italians, which comes out in the *Leather Patch;* that marks an epoch and char-acterizes a condition.

The *Leather Patch* is not nearly so good as the Mulligan series, though it has very good things in it. The author seems to have labor-ed for incident and effect in a plot, whereas all that the heart asked of him was to keep his de-licious Irish folks on the scene and keep them talking. As it is, some passages of the piece are extremely good; and it is as a whole in the good direction. The material is rude, very rude; we repeat that; it is the office or it is the will of this artist to work in that material; but it is the artist and not the material which makes the work of art. The error of the dramatist has been that he has at times not known how to hold his hand; he has given us the whole truth where part of it would have been enough; he might have spared us some shocking suggestions of the undertaking business. At other times he quite forgets his realism: the whole episode of the colored wake, with its plantation spirituals, is real and excellent; but when the old-clothes men and women of Chatham Street join in a chorus, one perceives that the theatre has come to the top, and the poet has lapsed.

In spite of such lapses, however, we recog-nize in Mr. Harrigan's work the spring of a true American comedy, the beginning of things which may be great things. We have more than intimated its limitations; let us say that whatever its offences, it is never, so far as we have seen it, indecent. The comedies of Edward Harrigan are, in fact, much decenter than the comedies of William Shakespeare.

They are like Shakespeare's plays, like Mo-lière's plays, in being the work of a dramatist who is at the same time a manager and an actor. Possibly this is the only way we can have a drama of our own; it is not a bad way; and it is at least a very natural way. At any rate, loving reality as we do, we cannot do less than cordially welcome reality as we find it in Mr. Harrigan's comedies. Consciously or un-consciously, he is part of the great tendency toward the faithful representation of life which is now animating fiction.

Yet because it is so very good, one must not forget anything else that is good; and it is a pleasure to recognize the success of an-other playwright, who, without having the threefold qualification of those we have named, has at least worked with as intimate a relation to the theatre as Goldoni, or as the dramatists of the days when literature still found expression in the drama. Mr. Bronson Howard's *One of our Girls* touches the chord which has already vibrated in the pages of our international novelists, and contrasts the opposite civilizations of France and America in their ideal of love and marriage. It is a subject that will always interest, and Mr. Howard has handled it with distinct force. His play is extremely well knit; it is thor-oughly right-minded, and it has literary qual-ity. No one can be the worse for seeing it, and many might be very much better. It is of the good order of English plays which gave Robinson his just fame, and it is better litera-ture, with a spirit and a nature of its own. We need not say that it proves the superior-ity of "the American plan" in the important matters it treats; and if its satire is rather more mordant, its irony more obvious, than

the author would have found it necessary to make them in a book, we must not forget the intelligence of the ordinary play-goer. The excess will enlighten this, and it is not so great as to offend the quicker perception of others, who can enjoy the very nice work of the piece in other respects. The charac-terization in some of the people, while al-ways a little too satirical, is charming; and in the performance, as we saw it at the Ly-ceum Theatre, the author's intention was in-terpreted by most of the players with the most sympathetic accuracy; there was an ad-mirable evenness in the work, becoming truly exquisite under the touch of Mr. Sothern in his part of the slow, brave, loyal, very single-minded English captain of hussars. In fact, here as elsewhere, in our theatres, one must be struck with the enormous improvement in the average acting within a dozen years past. It is quite up to the level of Mr. Harri-gan's or Mr. Howard's work for it; and it is far higher than that of most work given it to do; it is equal even to the perfect *entourage*.

IV.

But we feel that we ought to ask the read-er's patience with our digression about New York theatres. The real drama is in our novels mostly. It is they chiefly which ap-proach our actual life, and interpret it so far as it has yet been represented to the vast majority of our intelligent public; it is in them alone that a number, only a little less than that majority, will ever see it repre-sented. The theatre is the amusement of the city, of people whose lives are crowded with pleasures and distractions; but the novel is the consolation, the refuge, of the fine spirits that pine in the dulness of small towns, or the monotony of the country, where other intel-lectual resources are few, and the excitements none. It is therefore of little consequence to the great mass of those who truly love litera-ture whether the theatre is good or bad; they will never see it; they will never suffer from it, or profit by it. We in the great cities long for a renewal of the glories that surrounded it in the days when it was a living interest; but that is an affair of sentiment merely, and it would not greatly matter if the theatre re-mained always what it has long been—a mere diversion, neither affecting our life, nor affect-ed by it. Perhaps the theatrical drama will never revive. We have noted some signs of re-newed respiration, but we should not think it quite cataclysmal if, after a few gasps, it ceased to breathe again. We should certainly regret to see any art perish, but it is for the arts, like the interests, to assert their own vitality and maintain it; and if the drama, with all our lavish love of the theatre, cannot hold its own there, and prosper and advance, as the novel has prospered and advanced, in spite of the unfriendly literary conditions, it simply proves that the drama is an outworn literary form. It cannot be willed back to life by criticism, censured back, or coaxed back. It must take its chances; it must make them.

We do not know that we should wish Mr. Luska, for his own sake, to give his next essay dramatic form; he will meet a wider audience in the novel, and more intelligent; there can be no doubt of that. The novelist's audience is now so great and so good that it is quite worth his while to do his best for it; and we

have the hope that Mr. Luska's clever work
will be more than clever. We wish him a little more repose, a little more perfect dramatization, a little stronger belief that the ordinary complexion of human affairs is the thing
that is now newest in fiction, and will remain
so. It is not easy to catch.

For Mr. Wolcott Balestier, another young
writer whom we have been reading, we could
desire something of Mr. Luska's vigorous
touch and security of direction from the start.
A true poetical atmosphere is not wanting in
his pure and sympathetically suggested story
of *A Victorious Defeat;* and he has new ground
among his Moravians of the early years of our
century. But for a long time the figures have
a teasing vagueness, and perhaps they never
quite lose it. He lingers upon them with a
hand that is tender and decorative, but not so
sure as we hope it will be; and he has a very
good, self-respectful, impersonal way of treating them. His work is suffused with a sense
of what is fine and delicate in literature and
in life; he has a just feeling for the value of
the common materials that life is made of,
and for the simple means. He has a strong
situation in the attitude of the Moravian minister whom the Moravian usage of marriage
by lot has given the girl he loves, and who
finds it in his heart to give her up because
she does not love him. That is natural and
probable. It is possible, but neither natural
nor probable, that he should wish afterward to
marry her to the man she does love; and Mr.
Balestier, with his good feeling for the minor
realities, should never propose to himself anything less than nature and probability in great
things. To have the minister die soon after is
a concession to the weakness of novel readers;
he should have lived on, as men generally do,
even after signal sacrifices.

V.

We deal attentively with the work of those
young writers, because if criticism is to affect
literature at all, it must be through the writers
who have newly left the starting-point, and
are reasonably uncertain of the race, not with
those who have won it again and again in
their own way. Mr. Luska and Mr. Balestier
may possibly think there is something in what
we say; but older writers probably would not.
In fact, criticism can, after all, do very little
toward forming or reforming any writer; if it
could, we are painfully aware that we should
ourselves be very different from what we are.
More and more it must content itself with ascertaining currents and tendencies, and not
proposing to direct or stop them; more and
more it must realize that it is not a censorship. It will not find its work lighter for this
shrinkage in its apparent importance. It is
so much easier to say that you like this or
dislike that, than to tell why one thing is, or
where another thing comes from, that many
flourishing critics will have to go out of business altogether if the scientific method comes
in, for then the critic will have to know something beside his own mind, which is often
but a narrow field. He will have to know
something of the *laws* of that mind, and of its
generic history. Nothing less is required of [2]
him in the example lately set him by Mr.
Hutcheson Macaulay Posnett, whose work on
Comparative Literature is calculated, we fear,
to make many complacent authorities' heads

ache and hearts fail them. Before speaking
of his book it is only fair to recognize what a
thoroughly equipped critic of our own has
done on the same lines, and to remind the
reader of Mr. T. S. Perry's work in his essays
on *English Literature in the Eighteenth Century,* and in his smaller volume of studies of
German literature *From Opitz to Lessing.*
There could not be a more interesting illustration of the principles held by both of these
writers than the fact that Mr. Posnett should
have been advancing contemporaneously, under the same general influences, toward the
very positions taken by Mr. Perry three years
ago. His field is vastly wider, for he attempts
to explain and account for the whole course
of literature, but we cannot see that his method
is different, or that his application of scientific
theories to literature is different. One in America and the other in England has been the first
to respond to ideas now everywhere appealing
to the human reason. "A genius," said Mr.
Perry, three years ago, " in the future as in the
past, is bound by the necessity of building on
the foundations that society is laying every
day. Every apparently insignificant action
of ours contributes its mite to the sum of circumstances which inspire the writer, whose
vision may be dim or inaccurate, but who can
see only what exists or may exist, and is limited
by experience, whether this be treated literally or be modified by imagination." "By neg-
lecting the influences of social life on literature," says Mr. Posnett, "Greek criticism fostered the deadly theories that literature is
essentially an imitation of masterpieces, that
its ideals are not progressive, but permanent,
that they have no dependence on particular
conditions of human character, on the nature
of that social instrument language, on circum-
scribed spheres of time and space." In other
words, both of these writers, whose books will
form epochs for any one who comes fresh to
their principles, hold alike that literature is
from life, and that it is under the law as every
part of life is, and is not a series of preposterous miracles.

Mr. Posnett, for his part, is not hopeful of
a ready assent to his method. But he is not
dismayed for that reason: "To our friends,
the men of Literature, we would say that nothing has contributed more largely to lower
the value of their studies in the eyes of thinking men than the old-fashioned worship of
imagination, not merely as containing an element of mystery, but as altogether superior
to conditions of space and time; that, under
the auspices of this irrational worship, the
study of Literature tends to become a blind
idolatry of the Unknown, with a priesthood
of textual pedants who would sacrifice to ver-
balism the very deity they affect to worship;
but that the comparative study of Literature
not only opens an immense field of fruitful labor, but tends to foster creative imagination."

The treatise which is the fruit of this well-
grounded belief is divided into five books.
The first is introductory, and deals with the
nature of literature, its relativity, the principle
of its growth, and the comparative method.
Applying this method, Mr. Posnett studies in
the four succeeding books Clan Literature,
the literature of the City Commonwealth,
World Literature, and National Literature,
with chapters subdividing each of these topics. We cannot give a just idea of the learning, the sympathy, the logic, brought to the

inquiry, and we will not try. But we are sure that the book will make a fame for itself which will not suffer any lover of literature to neglect it, and we leave our readers to make its acquaintance at first hand. We can promise them that they will be much the wiser for doing so; we could even imagine an average romantic critic coming away from it with some hopeful misgivings, some vague preference of principles to impressions in considering literature. It will, of course, shake somewhat his prepossessions as to the nature and essence of literature; but he will be none the worse for that.

"The theory that literature," says Mr. Posnett, "is the detached life-work of individuals who are to be worshipped like images fallen down from heaven, not known as workers in the language and ideas of their age and place, and the kindred theory that imagination transcends the associations of space and time, have done much to conceal the relation of science to literature, and to injure the works of both. But the 'great-man theory' is really suicidal; for, while breaking up history and literature into biographies, and thus preventing the recognition of any lines of orderly development, it would logically reduce not only what is known as 'exceptional genius,' but all men and women, so far as they possess personality at all, to the unknown, the causeless—in fact, would issue in a sheer denial of human knowledge, limited or unlimited."

This is in substance what Mr. Perry has also repeatedly maintained; and these two authors stand together in a conscious perception of principles which others have been feeling more or less blindly, and which are really animating and shaping the whole future of criticism.

With their clear perception of the origin of literature comes a just and high sense of its office, which Mr. Posnett expresses in words that have the thrill and glow of a religious conviction. "It will be clear to any reader of this book that its author is far from regarding literature as the mere toy of stylists, far from advocating the 'moral indifference' of art. In his eyes literature is a very serious thing, which can become morally indifferent only in ages of moral indifference. 'Let the world go its way, and the kings and the peo-

ples strive, and the priests and philosophers wrangle; at least to make a perfect verse is to be out of time, master of all change, and free of every creed.' * Such was Gautier's view; but it is stamped false by the whole history of literary development. Whether men like it or not, their literary efforts at ideal beauty in prose or verse must involve ideals of human conduct. Action, speech, and thought are too subtly interwoven to allow their artistic severance aught but fancied truth; if it were otherwise, literature might indeed have been the product of a Cloud-cuckoo-town in which historical science and morality would be equally out of place. But, it may be said, your science cuts at the roots of moral conduct by treating the individual as made by conditions over which he has no control. Far from it. Our science traces a growth of social and individual freedom so far as the conditions of human life have hitherto allowed them to grow together. Nothing is really gained for morality or religion by assuming that the life with which they deal is unlimited, unconditioned; nay, such limitless pretensions have hitherto proved very fatal to morality by fostering suicidal extremes of social and individual thinking. How are these suicidal extremes to be best kept in check? By insisting on the social and physiological limits within which man moves and has moved; by answering the admirers of universal shadows, in which morality itself becomes shadowy, in the words of the Hebrew prophet: 'Who hath heard such a thing? What hath seen such things? Shall a land bring forth in a day? or a people be born in a moment?'"

At the close of his preface Mr. Posnett tells us that he leaves Trinity College, Dublin, while his work is going through the press, for New Zealand, where we believe he is to have a literary professorship in a colonial university. It is one of the superb conditions of modern civilization, however, that so important a man can be equally valuable in London or New York or Auckland, and can speak as easily to the whole world from one place as the other. He must not look for ready acceptance from the Maori, anywhere; but he may be assured that the less barbarous races in different quarters of the globe will be very glad to hear from him again. In the mean time they cannot do better than study his present book.

* Dowden, *Studies in Literature*, 1789-1877, p. 401.

---

[1] Howells probably meant to refer to Thomas William Robertson, not Robinson.

[2] Criticism and Fiction, p. 38.

August, 1886

Editor's Study.

I.

ONE of the minor regrets which the observer of contemporary literature must feel in view of the fact that he will probably not be alive a hundred years hence is that he cannot know what is to become of all the estimable books which the press is now pouring out. If he is himself an author, he knows that his own books must at least perish in the second glacial epoch; and he cannot help the foreboding that much besides which is excellent and much which is beautiful will be lost before that time in the mere excess of beauty and excellence. The greatest excellence and the greatest beauty are still perhaps as rare as in the past, but we think that the literary average is in some ways higher than ever it was. More honest and faithful and skilful work is done, and more of it. The penetrating spirit of democracy has found its expression in the very quality of literature; the old oligarchic republic of letters is passing; already we have glimpses of the Commune. If the reader has noted the optimistic tone of these essays he will conceive that we are not wholly dismayed at the prospect, and that we find a consolation in recognizing what seems good now, when the difficult business of forecasting its future perplexes and saddens. Our chief concern is that we cannot recognize all the good there is in all the books that come to us; but if the public will keep our secret, we will confess that we believe this will have very little to do with their destiny. The fittest, in literature as in everything else, will survive, as it has always done; and for all our confident air in saying this is well and that is ill, we understand perfectly that we are not dealing final doom. We are saying what our experience of literature and of life has persuaded us is the truth; but these books are also the expression of literature and of life, and we will confess again, if again the public will keep our secret, that sometimes the crudest expression in that sort seems better than the finest comment upon it. We have sometimes suspected that more thinking, more feeling certainly, goes to the creation of a poor novel than to the production of a brilliant criticism; and if any novel of our time fails to live a hundred years, will any censure of it live? Who can endure to read old reviews? One can hardly read them if they are in praise of one's own books. It is not, then, with a wholly impersonal pang, dearly beloved brother immortals, that we sit here in our Study sorrowfully regarding your multitude, and misgiving which of you shall survive. You cannot all, that is certain; and more and more pensively we perceive that it is not absolutely for us to say which; but to use what patience we may if the poets, the historians, the novelists, the essayists, are not able to keep their number within bounds. It is vain, at any rate, to preach Malthusianism to them, and we willingly relinquish to the reader the problem of their future, if, as seems very likely, they should multiply rather than decrease. It is already quite impossible to do more than touch contemporary literature at a few points, to speak of what seems characteristic, or what seems promising; but the author neglected or overlooked need not despair for that reason, if he will reflect that criticism can neither make nor unmake authors; that there have not been greater books since criticism became an art than there were before; that in fact the greatest books seem to have come much earlier.

II.

That which criticism seems most certainly to have done is to have put a literary consciousness into books unfelt in the early masterpieces, but unfelt now only in the books of men whose lives have been passed in activities, who have been used to employing language as they would have employed any implement, to effect an object, who have regarded a thing to be said as in no wise different from a thing to be done. In this sort we have seen no modern book so unconscious as *General Grant's Personal Memoirs*, which is now complete in its second volume. We have already spoken of the first volume, and of the simplicity which distinguished it. The same unimpassioned, singular directness characterizes the story to its end. The author's one end and aim is to get the facts out in words. He does not cast about for phrases, but takes the word, whatever it is, that will best give his meaning, as if it were a man or a force of men for the accomplishment of a feat of arms. There is not a moment wasted in preening and prettifying, after the fashion of literary men; there is no thought of style, and so the style is good as it is in the Book of Chronicles, as it is in the *Pilgrim's Progress*, or in a novel of De Foe's, with a peculiar, almost plebeian, plainness at times. There is no more attempt at dramatic effect than there is at ceremonious pose; things happen in that tale of a mighty war as they happened in the mighty war itself, without setting, without artificial reliefs, one after another, as if they were all of one quality and degree. Judgments are delivered with the same unimposing quiet; no awe surrounds the tribunal except that which comes from the weight and justice of the opinions; it is al-

34

ways an unaffected, unpretentious man who is talking; and throughout he prefers to wear the uniform of a private, with nothing of the general about him but the shoulder-straps, which he sometimes forgets.

We have heard a great deal about what the American was to be in literature when he once got there. What if this were he—this good form without formality, this inner dignity, this straightforward arrival, this mid-day clearness? We find much of these qualities in the two large volumes of Lieutenant Greely's *Three Years of Arctic Service;* so much that we are not sure but West Point might be a good training school for our literati, as it has certainly been for our soldiers. The annual appointment of a literary cadet from each Congressional district would probably give us a permanent body of writers whom we could draw upon for all departments, with a reasonable assurance that they had been rigidly trained to express themselves with distinctness and sincerity; and this our present happy-go-lucky fashion of getting our literary men hardly does. The idea is one which must not be pressed too far, or suffered to interfere with a more serious expression of the respect we feel for Lieutenant Greely's telling of his wonderful story; but still we think there must be something due to the high and wholesome discipline of two men, alike in little else in their past, when they come to the same effect in their reader's mind. The effect is all the more noticeable because the method of the books is so different. Lieutenant Greely's story is not a continuous, full narrative, told without stopping, as it were, from memory. Some day, we hope, he will give us this, or something like it in unity and compactness; but for the present we have a mass of details, patched and pieced together from various diaries, with loose threads of statement, and weighted with facts of scientific interest only, from which, however, the heroic experience of that three years' service disentangles itself in the retrospect, and remains an impression as clear as that given by Grant's unbroken memories of the war. We do not know why this should be unless it is from the same habit, inbred in both writers, of looking to one end only—the presentation of the facts without regard to the effects. In this way their work has the advantage over literary writing that scientific writing must always have: they are both possessed of their subject rather than possessed of their manner.

It is not strange that Lieutenant Greely's narrative should have the fascination it has; a potent charm always invests the experience of a life or a group of lives isolated from all others, and striving to be self-sufficient in circumstances that forbid hope or help from without. When the exploring party are settled for the first winter at Fort Conger, one feels a sort of pleasure in their snug security, with their forays into the realms of cold and night, a sense of cosiness expanding into sympathetic rapture when the brief arctic summer drops suddenly upon them, and fills the air with birds, and floods the waste with blooming grasses and wild flowers. We think Lieutenant Greely, more than any former explorer, realizes to the reader this brief flush of glowing and throbbing vitality in regions which the fancy had delivered over to perpetual death and "ever-during dark"; but he uses no rhetoric upon it, and it becomes of itself a tragic light and color in the background when the retreat begins, when the pleasant safety and plenty of Fort Conger are abandoned for the struggle southward through the freezing wilderness to the famine and despair of Cape Sabine. It is in this part of the story that the observer interested to know how simply great things happen, how hunger, cold, and death are really met by the human weakness and the human will confronted with them, will find the greatest instruction. It is not all one uninterrupted course toward the catastrophe, spectacular, with an exterior of impressive dramatic unity; it is relieved by little respites, by little reversions of prosperity; even at the worst, hope remains, and character and discipline persist. The gay young fellow who lies dying in the arms of his comrade, far from the wretched camp, in the midst of an arctic storm, keeps up his American habit of joking to his last breath; certain men are helpful to the rest as naturally and unconsciously as women in a sick-room; there is weakness and selfishness of the sort we find everywhere; the "villain" is as absent as the "hero," but there is a starving thief who is found stealing the portions of his companions, and will not stop; he is sentenced, and two dying men put him to death, in a perfectly business-like way. All goes on orderly, and with a ghastly conformity to the life-long usages and habits. The hunters kill a little game, and the doom is stayed a while. They catch shrimps and live on them till their bait fails; then they live on boiled lichens, and the cripple who has lost both his hands and feet by freezing is quite cheerful when one of the others ties the spoon to the stump of his wrist, so that he can help himself to the stew of lichens and seal-skin. At last the seven men left out of twenty-five lie pinned to the ground in their sleeping-bags, under their fallen tent, waiting for death, when rescue comes instead. We need not recite the points of the story so well known; and for a full sense of what that tremendous passage of human experience was we must send the reader to the book itself.

What chiefly strikes one in it is that everything seems like everything else; that neither this thing nor that has projection or relief. Given the conditions, the events seem to proceed naturally and in a proper sequence. It seems in keeping with all the rest that the welcome home of the leader of the expedition should have been imbittered by calumny, and that the soldiers who suffered with him should still be the objects of private charity, disabled for life, their allowances for arctic service unpaid, and their pensions not awarded.

III.

Upon the whole, the effect is something like the effect studied in the best modern novels; only the reality takes all the color out of realism, and we should be doing injustice to the most vivid invention if we placed it beside such experience. The reader will therefore kindly suppose a considerable interval of time and space between the consideration of Lieutenant Greely's history of *Three Years of Arctic Service* and Miss Woolson's story of *East Angels,* though, after all, if he likes to bathe his fancy immediately in the warm air and tepid sea of the Florida coast, there are reasons why he may do so without prejudice to the first great romance of that region. He will find himself in a peculiar atmosphere, very faithfully and perfectly rendered, and amidst interesting groups of the sex necessarily excluded from arctic adventure; and that will be certainly a pleasure if not wholly an advantage. Of the ladies of East Angels several are freshly and singularly charming, whom the reader will like if he is a man, and there is at least one very heroic, whom she may adore if she is a woman. Margaret Harold, martyr-wife of that chief of scapegraces Lansing Harold, is a figure that ought to console such of her sex as have heart-hungered for grand and perfect women in fiction perhaps ever since George Eliot drew Romola. She not only dedicates her life to the invalided age of the unloved husband who has insulted her by the precept as well as the example of gross indifference, she not only very rightly drives from her the man she loves, but she proposes to the young widow who jilted him that she shall try to get him back and marry him, and promises that their children shall be a consolation to her. If this is not enough for the worshippers of grand and perfect women, we cannot imagine what they want more.

For ourselves we will confess that it is too much, and that we are better satisfied with the man who guesses this plan for his consolation, and finds it revolting, though he is too much in love with Margaret Harold to feel its absurdity. It was perhaps the supposed necessity of keeping the chief person exemplary and sublime which caused the error. Neither Margaret nor Winthrop her lover appeals to our sympathy, perhaps because we cannot believe in them; they form for us the one false note of the book. The other people, men and women, are all better, and they are for the most part, in mood and motive, like people one meets. The least important figure among them is sketched with a feeling for character which leaves it distinct and memorable. Many of the studies in this sort have an uncommon value, like Mrs. Thorne, the poor little lady who supposed she had lived English and Southern, but who perceives in dying that she has always been immutably New England and Northern. There is a delicate pathos in the treatment of her character which moves the heart, and is the right complement of the delicate humor which differentiates the comic points of the two young Spaniards, Ernesto de Torres and Manuel Ruiz, without caricaturing either of them, and depicts the intellectual commonplace of the Rev. Mr. Moore while divining his rare and exalted goodness. A purely artistic temperament like Lucian Spenser is caught as unerringly as if by some instantaneous process, and a big, dull girl, like Rosalie Bogardus, even more difficult to catch, is given again to the reader with none of her compensating traits and qualities forgotten. We speak of these minor persons in the book because it is in the excellence of all the minor persons that the charming mastery of the author is shown. She cannot do an injustice, and this keeps her faithful and patient with Garda Thorne, and will not suffer her to make that light, chameleon nature merely typical of a race or a latitude, but exacts in it the representation of a distinct, individual life, which has nothing of flirtation's badness, and, slight as it is, wishes to be generous, and is sincere. Garda is a masterpiece, and the triumph of the book. For our own selfish pleasure we prefer a novel where there is less going and coming, and there are fewer people, and the webs of so many different lives are not intertangled. Yet we are obliged to own that the small isolated group is less life-like, and that if Miss Woolson can paint a multitude of figures so well, that is a sufficient reason for her introducing them. The story is full of delightful moments, of interesting moments, and there are great moments in it. But, above all, there is, except in the heroine, the respect for probability, the fidelity to conditions, human and social, which can alone justify the reading or writing of novels; there is the artistic conscience, and the other conscience without which art is merely pernicious.

Both kinds of conscience are felt also in *Constance of Acadia*, a romance which an unknown hand gives us. Whether it is an unpractised hand we are not so sure, nor whether it is the hand of a man or of a woman; but this does not matter if it is apt and true. The story is that of Constance, the Huguenot wife of Charles la Tour, Governor of Acadia under Louis XIII. He is Huguenot too, but primarily ambitious trader and wily politician; and by her help holds his own against his father, coming from the English to take his fort from him, and against Charnacé, who comes from the Jesuits with designs upon both his fort and his wife; for Charnacé, who has not completed his ecclesiastical vows, loved Constance in La Rochelle long before, and has not ceased to love her. Acadia, apparently, is not only inexhaustible in romance, but it has a history that blends so happily with its romance that in this writer's hands it is all one web, and the less-learned reader will do well not to attempt to say which is which. What strikes one no less than the poetic beauty of the book is this mastery of the historical situation. The thoroughness with which the author has assimilated the facts of that remote time and scene is of the same effect in his art as close observation of contemporary life would be, and there is a comfortable reality in the people very uncommon in historical fiction. The La Tours, father and son, are admirably of their time, and Charnacé, wavering between passion and devotion, and now man and now Jesuit, is a peculiarly seventeenth-century personage. Some passages, fundamentally historical, lift the curtain upon the Boston and the Boston traits of that day, and there is a very pleasant humor mixed with the more heroic strain of the book. This strain is single only in the character of Constance, which is yet so well managed that it does not lose in probability or lovableness. The figures are not always distinctly outlined; and withdrawn so far into the past, the action has a dimness except in certain details upon which the light is strongly thrown. Yet within the vague you are somehow assured of a veritable human life, and we welcome in the book a fresh and brilliant achievement in a sort that has long seemed obsolescent, if not obsolete. It is a pleasure to come upon good work in any direction, and if the direction of the historical romance is one which fiction seems not likely to explore again very extensively, still we must admire the success of an occasional daring foray like this. We do not know that we should altogether regret it if this were the precursor of adventure by other and lesser talents. Perhaps the whole region of historical romance might be reopened with advantage to readers and writers who cannot bear to be brought face to face with human nature, but require a mist of distance or a far perspective, in which all the disagreeable details shall be lost. There is no good reason why these harmless people should not be amused, or their little preferences indulged. [2] In the mean time we can praise *Constance of Acadia* as a beautiful and touching story.

IV.

Mr. H. H. Boyesen's *Story of Norway* reads like another historical romance, so picturesque and poetic is the wild past of the land of fiords and mountains. We do not know that it would have been possible to treat it in the modern spirit which presents historical events as illustrations of conditions, and gives greater prominence to peoples than to heroes; but it is certain that the author has not chosen to do this. He has, however, supplied such abundant material that the reader can philosophize the facts for himself, and arrive at the solution of all the problems involved. They are not very intricate, for the story is that of a rude race living in almost incomparable degree in an imagination stormily sublime and grotesque, and striving to realize their tremendous dreams in their deeds. They had an ideal of valor, of endurance, of power, which Mr. Boyesen lets declare itself in that texture of record and legend forming his story. This is the poet's way, and Mr. Boyesen is first of all a poet, and delights in the feats he recounts as if he had invented them. His book is the prose epic of his race—a race so passionately enamored of individual liberty that it could not fail in time to submit itself to law for the sake of freedom to all, and in this way emerge from war and barbarism into peace and civilization. Mr. Boyesen does not fail to claim as a final expression of this once turbulent and always mighty passion of the Norsemen the glory of constitutional freedom in England and America; and we do not know that the claim can be altogether denied: our German kindred have never known freedom or unity at home, and, as he points out, they exist nationally now only as a great military despotism.

A very interesting inquiry into the operation of the political instinct in the Anglo-Saxon race, wherever that instinct comes from, is to be found in Professor Josiah Royce's *History of California*, in Mr. Scudder's "American Commonwealth Series." His method is so exactly opposite that of Mr. Boyesen that we could almost wish it were less so. It seems to us that the early life of California could have been advantageously painted to the exclusion of great part of that painfully traced coil of intrigue and violence by which, to be sure, Spanish California came to be American, but which the reader follows with difficulty and impatience, feeling that it could all be much more briefly and distinctly told. No doubt it helps to give effect to the spectacle of the rise of a civilized state from conditions of as rascally barbarism as an educated race could well lapse into; but the absence of background is felt throughout till we come to the story of the great Vigilance Committee, which marked a final phase in the evolution of order. Professor Royce frankly calls his volume a study of American character, and doubtless did not feel at all bound to present a dramatic synthesis. This final passage, however, as compared with the rest of the book, illustrates the difference between history and a historical study, and the vastly greater advantage of the former to the reader. It is a beautifully compact, vigorous, and effective piece of writing, and embodies the action and its significance in thoroughly vivid form. There is, indeed, hardly a page of the book which is not illuminated by shrewd and just thinking; and there is always frank courage of statement and characterization. It is the story of a community clothing itself anew in civilization and decency, after a debauch of disorder. The reader never fails of the author's intention, and if he feels that he is made too much a partner in the enterprise, as a French critic acutely said of the poetry of Mr. Walt Whitman, that is at least a tribute to his intelligence. In a fair half of the volume, from where the study of "The Struggle for Order" begins, to the end, his complicity is not invoked, and the volume closes with a passage or two which are as characteristic of the author as they are true:

"The race that has since grown up in California, as the outcome of these early struggles, is characterized by very marked qualities of strength and weakness, some of which, perchance, even a native Californian like the author, who neither can nor would outgrow his healthy local traits, may still be able to note and confess. A general sense of social irresponsibility is, even to-day, the average Californian's easiest failing. Like his father, he is probably a born wanderer, who will feel as restless in his farm life, or in his own town, as his father felt in his. He will have little or no sense of social or of material barriers, he will perchance hunt for himself a new home somewhere else in the world, or in the old home will long for some speculative business that promises easy wealth, or, again, on the other hand, he will undertake some great material labor that attracts him by its imposing difficulty. His training at home gives him a curious union of provincial prejudice with a varied if not very exact knowledge of the sorts of things that there are in the world. For his surroundings from infancy have been in one sense of a cosmopolitan character, while much of his training has been rigidly or even narrowly American. He is apt to lack a little, moreover, complete devotion to the life within the household, because, as people so often have pointed out, the fireside, an essential institution of our English race, is of such small significance in the climate of California. In short, the Californian has too often come to love mere fulness of life, and to lack reverence for the relations of life.

"And yet, as we have seen, the whole lesson of his early history, rightly read, is a lesson in reverence for the relations of life. It was by despising, or at least by forgetting them, that the early community entered into the valley of the shadow of death; and there was salvation for the community in those days only by virtue of its final and hard-learned submission to what it had despised and forgotten. This lesson, I confess, has come home to me personally, as I have studied this early history, with a quite unexpected force. I had always thought of the old days as times of fine and rough labors, amusements, and crimes, but not as a very rational historical process. I have learned, as I have toiled for a while over the sources, to see in these days a process of divinely moral significance. And, as a Californian, I am glad to be able to suggest what I have found, plain and simple as it is, to any fellow-Californian who may perchance note in himself the faults of which I make confession. Here in the early history are these faults, writ large, with their penalties, and the only possible salvation from them.

" After all, however, our lesson is an old and simple one. It is the State, the Social Order, that is divine. We are all but dust, save as this social order gives us life. When we think it our instrument, our plaything, and make our private fortunes the one object, then this social order rapidly becomes vile to us; we call it sordid, degraded, corrupt, unspiritual, and ask how we may escape from it forever. But if we turn again and serve the social order, and not merely ourselves, we soon find that what we are serving is simply our own highest spiritual destiny in bodily form. It is never truly sordid or corrupt or unspiritual; it is only we that are so when we neglect our duty."

Here, it seems to us, are not only right feeling and plain speaking, but thinking of a sort which is likely to invite the reader to do some thinking of his own. There is a ring of earnestness unafraid and unashamed in it all, which is the key-note of the best modern writing in all kinds, and which, more than anything else, characterizes the real literary endeavor of an epoch serious, sympathetic, and conscientious beyond those that have gone before it.

[1] Criticism and Fiction, pp. 42-44 (abridged).

[2] Criticism and Fiction, pp. 116-117.

September, 1886

Editor's Study.

I.

THE readers of Tourguéneff and of Tolstoï must now add Dostoïevsky to their list if they wish to understand the reasons for the supremacy of the Russians in modern fiction; and we think they must put him beside these two, and not below either, in moral and artistic qualities. They are all so very much more than realists that this name, never satisfactory in regard to any school of writers, seems altogether insufficient for them. They are realists in ascertaining an entire probability of motive and situation in their work; but with them this is only the beginning; they go so far beyond it in purpose and effect that one must cast about for some other word if one would try to define them. Perhaps humanist would be the best phrase in which to clothe the idea of their literary office, if it could be limited to mean their simply, almost humbly, fraternal attitude toward the persons and conditions with which they deal, and again extended to include a profound sense of that individual responsibility from which the common responsibility can free no one. The phrase does not express that artistry which one feels in them, and it can only group them loosely in a single characteristic; but it certainly hints at what one feels most of all in the latest known of these great masters. At the same time, if it suggests anything of sentimentality, it is wholly and mischievously false. For instance, in *Le Crime et le Châtiment*, which we have just been reading, and which, besides *Les Humiliés et Offensés*, is the only book of Dostoïevsky's yet given in French, the author studies the effect of murder in the assassin, who is brought to confession and repentance by a hapless creature whom poverty has forced to a life of shame. Yet there is nothing of the maudlin glamour of heroism thrown about this pair; Raskolnikoff is the only man who has not been merely brutal to Sonia, and she divines his misery through her gratitude; this done, her one thought, her only hope, is not to help him hide his crime, but to help him own it to the law and to expiate it. She sees that there is no escape for him but this, and her inspiration is not superior to her; it is not from her mind, but from her soul, primitively good and incorrupt, amidst the hideous facts of her life, which, by-the-way, are in nowise brought forward or exploited in the story. Raskolnikoff is not her lover; he becomes so only when his expiation has begun; and the reader is scarcely allowed to see beyond the first breaking down of his egotistic self-justification in the Siberian prison. He has done the murder for which he suffers upon a theory, if not a principle:

the theory that the greatest heroes and even benefactors of the race have not hesitated at crime when it would advance their extraordinary purposes or promote their development. He is a student, forced to quit the university by his poverty, and he reasons that it is better he should complete his career, destined, as he feels, to be useful and splendid, than that a certain old woman who keeps a pawnbroker's shop should continue to live and to prey upon the necessities of others. He asks himself which of the extraordinary men who have set the world forward would have stopped at putting her out of his way if he had found it to his advantage, and he kills her and robs her; he kills her half-witted sister too, the harmless thing that comes in upon him and his first victim through the door he has forgotten to lock. His punishment begins with this deed, which he had never counted upon, for the wickedness of the old usuress was largely his defence for taking her off; but it cannot properly be said that Raskolnikoff feels regret or even remorse for his crime until he has confessed it. Till then his terrible secret, which all the accidents and endeavors of the world seem conspiring to tear from him, forms his torment, and almost this alone. His repentance and his redemption begin with his penalty. The truth is a very old one, but what makes this book so wonderful is the power with which it is set forth. The story is not merely an accumulation of incident upon incident, a collection of significant anecdotes, as it might be in the hands of an inferior artist, but a mounting drama, to the catastrophe of which all the facts and characters tend, not mechanically or intentionally, but in the natural and providential way; it is only in the latter half of the story that you suspect a temptation in the author to intensify and to operate. At moments the stress of the story is almost intolerable; the misery of Raskolnikoff is such that you suffer all Sonia's despair when he comes back from the police office without having confessed, and you scarcely breathe till he makes the second attempt and succeeds. The arrival of his mother and sister in the midst of his wretchedness, to be the loving and trusting witnesses of suffering of which they cannot understand the cause, is merely one of the episodes of the book which penetrate the soul by their reality, by their unsparing yet compassionate truth. But the impressive scenes abound so that it is hard to name one without having seemed to leave a finer one unmentioned. Perhaps there is nothing of higher and nobler strain than that series of passages in which the Judge of Instruction, softened and humanized by the familiarity with crime which hardens so many, tries to bring Raskolnikoff to confess for his own sake the murder which the Judge is sure he committed. Other passages are of a pathos intense beyond anything else that we can remember in fiction, and chief among them, perhaps, are those in which Sonia's step-mother goes mad after her drunken husband's death, and leads her little children, fantastically tricked out in tattered finery, through the street to sing and dance. She is herself dying of consumption; terrible fits of coughing interrupt her ravings, and the weird escapade is the precursor of her death; she ceases to live the same night. Between her and her step-daughter, whom her wild appeal drove to ruin that the others might not starve, there exists an affection which no sense of wrong done and wrong suffered can weaken; their love for each other is a consolation when they have no friend or helper but the impenitent assassin who wreaks upon them the desire to do good, to help some one, which is one of the most subtly divined traits of a soul at war with itself.

It is a lurid chapter of human life certainly, but the light of truth is in it; and in the ghastliest picture which it presents there is the hope, the relief, that human sympathy gives, and everywhere there is recognition of the fact that behind the supreme law is the supreme love, and only there. It is therefore by no means a desperate book, nor a wholly depressing book. It not only clearly indicates the consequences of sin, but it attempts to define their bounds, the limits at which they seem to cease. Raskolnikoff suffers, but we reach the point at which he begins not to suffer. He makes others suffer, but we see where the suffering which his guilt inflicts must naturally end. It leaves him at the outset of a new life, the life of a man who has submitted to punishment, and has thereby won the privilege to repent. It is the reverse of a pessimistic book.

II.

The reader of such a story will hardly be satisfied without knowing something of the author, and in an article of the *Revue des Deux Mondes* for January 15, 1885, M. Eugène-Melchoir de Vogüé will tell him the hardly less tragical story of Dostoïevsky's own life. It seems that he was born at Moscow, in a charity hospital, in 1821, and to the day of his death he struggled with poverty, injustice, and disease. His first book, *Poor People,* which won him reputation and the hope of better things, was followed within a few years by his arrest for Socialism. He was not really concerned in Socialism, except through his friendship for some of the Socialists, but he was imprisoned with them, and after eight months of solitude in the casemate of a fortress—solitude unrelieved by the sight of a friendly human face, or a book, or a pen—he was led out to receive his sentence. All the prisoners had been condemned to death; the muskets were loaded in their presence, and levelled at their breasts; then the muzzles were struck up, and the Czar's commutation of their sentence was read. They were sent to Siberia, where Dostoïevsky spent six years at hard labor. There he made his studies among the prisoners for his book *The Humil-*

iated and the Wronged, which the French have now translated with *The Crime and the Punishment.* At the end of this time he returned to St. Petersburg, famous, beloved, adored, to continue his struggle with poverty and disease. The struggle was long, for he died only five years ago, when his body was followed to the grave by such a mighty concourse of all manner of people as never assembled at the funeral of any author before: " Priests chanting prayers; the students of the universities; the children of the schools; the young girl medical students; the Nihilists, distinguishable by their eccentricities of costume and bearing—the men with their shawls, and the women with their spectacles and close-clipped hair; all the literary and scientific societies; deputations from all parts of the empire—old Muscovite merchants, peasants, servants, beggars; in the church waited the official dignitaries, the Minister of Public Instruction, and the young princes of the imperial family. A forest of banners, of crosses, and of crowns waved over this army in its march; and while these different fragments of Russia passed, you could distinguish the gentle and sinister faces, tears, prayers, sneers, and silences, tranquil or ferocious.... What passed was the spectacle of this man's own work, formidable and disquieting, with its weakness and its grandeur; in the first rank, without doubt, and the most numerous, his favorite clients, the *Poor People, The Humiliated and the Wronged,* even *The Bedeviled*"—these are all titles of his books —" wretched beings happy to have their day, and to bear their defender on the path of glory, but with them and enveloping them all that uncertainty and confusion of the national life such as he has painted it, all the vague hopes that he had roused in all. As the czars of old were said to gather together the Russian earth, this royal spirit had assembled the Russian soul."

III.

M. Vogüé writes with perhaps too breathless a fervor, but his article is valuable for the light it casts upon the origins of Dostoïevsky's work, and its inspirations and motives. It was the natural expression of such a life and such conditions. But it is useful to observe that while *The Crime and the Punishment* may be read with the deepest sympathy and interest, and may enforce with unique power the lessons which it teaches, it is to be praised only in its place, and its message is to be received with allowances by readers exterior to the social and political circumstances in which it was conceived. It used to be one of the disadvantages of the practice of romance in America, which Hawthorne more or less whimsically lamented, that there were so few shadows and inequalities in our broad level of prosperity; and it is one of the reflections suggested by Dostoïevsky's book that whoever struck a note so profoundly tragic in American fiction would do a false and mistaken thing—as false and as mistaken in its way as dealing in American fiction with certain nudities which the Latin peoples seem to find edifying. Whatever their deserts, very few American novelists have been led out to be shot, or finally exiled to the rigors of a winter at Duluth; one might make Herr Most the hero of a labor-question romance with perfect impunity; and in a land where journeymen carpenters and plumbers strike for four dollars a day the sum of hunger and cold is certainly very small, and the wrong from class to class is almost inappreciable. We invite our novelists, therefore, to concern themselves with the more smiling aspects of life, which are the more American, and to seek the universal in the individual rather than the social interests. It is worth while, even at the risk of being called commonplace, to be true to our well-to-do actualities; the very passions themselves seem to be softened and modified by conditions which cannot be said to wrong any one, to cramp endeavor, or to cross lawful desire. Sin and suffering and shame there must always be in the world, we suppose, but we believe that in this new world of ours it is mainly from one to another one, and oftener still from one to one's self. We have death too in America, and a great deal of disagreeable and painful disease, which the multiplicity of our patent medicines does not seem to cure; but this is tragedy that comes in the very nature of things, and is not peculiarly American, as the large, cheerful average of health and success and happy life is. It will not do to boast, but it is well to be true to the facts, and to see that, apart from these purely mortal troubles, the race here enjoys conditions in which most of the ills that have darkened its annals may be averted by honest work and unselfish behavior. |2

It is only now and then, when some dark shadow of our shameful past appears, that we can believe there ever was a tragic element in our prosperity. Even then, when we read such an artlessly impressive sketch as Mrs. Sarah Bradford writes of Harriet Tubman—once famous as the Moses of her people—the self-freed bondwoman who led three hundred of her brethren out of slavery, and with a price set upon her head, risked her life and liberty nineteen times in this cause; even then it affects us like a tale

"Of old, unhappy, far-off things,
And battles long ago,"

and nothing within the date of actual history. We cannot realize that most of the men and women now living were once commanded by the law of the land to turn and hunt such fugitives back into slavery, and to deliver such an outlaw as Harriet over to her owner; that those who abetted such outlaws were sometimes mulcted to the last dollar of their substance in fines. We can hardly imagine such things now for the purposes of fiction; all troubles that now hurt and threaten us are as crumpled rose leaves in our couch. But we may nevertheless read Dostoïevsky, and especially our novelists may read him, to advantage, for in spite of his terrible picture of a soul's agony he is hopeful and wholesome, and teaches in every page patience, merciful judgment, humble helpfulness, and that brotherly responsibility, that duty of man to man, from which not even the Americans are emancipated.

IV.

There are some very interesting passages concerning this obligation in Vernon Lee's last book, *Baldwin*, where she speaks through several dialogic personages about novels, and claims for them an influence in deepening and refining human feeling which we suppose no one can successfully deny. "They have, by

playing upon our emotions, immensely increased the sensitiveness, the richness of this living key-board, even as a singing-master, by playing on his pupil's throat, increases the number of the musical intervals which he can intone. . . . Believing as I do in the power of directing human feeling into certain channels rather than certain others, believing especially in the power of reiteration of emotion in constituting our emotional selves, in digging by a constant drop, drop, such moral channels as have been already traced, I must necessarily also believe that the modern human being has been largely fashioned in all his more delicate peculiarities by those who have written about him, and most of all, therefore, by the novelist. I believe that were the majority of us educated and sensitive men and women able to analyze what we call our almost inborn, nay, automatic, views of life, character, and feeling, able to scientifically assign its origin to each and trace its modifications—I believe that were this possible, we should find that a good third of what we take to be instinctive knowledge, or knowledge vaguely acquired from personal experience, is really obtained from the novels which we or our friends have read."

There are a great many just and true things in this talk about novels, as there are in the other papers which discuss such topics as the responsibilities of unbelief and the consolations of belief, vivisection, the value of the ideal, and doubts and pessimism; and we think there is sense, if not final wisdom, in this conclusion: "To make the shrewd and tolerant a little less shrewd and tolerant, to make the generous and austere a little more skeptical and easy-going, this seems to me pretty well the chief problem of life, and also the chief use of the novel."

V.

It is an interesting proof of the intimate hold which fiction has taken upon life that when we wish to praise a true story we say that it reads like a novel. By this we do not at all mean always that it is very exciting or very romantic, but often merely that it is ideally charming. This is the quality of Miss Louise Livingston Hunt's memoir of her great-aunt, Mrs. Edward Livingston, the daughter of an old and noble French house, colonialized in San Domingo, and surrounded there by all that we fancy of tropical ease and state. The patriarchal family dwelt in a white marble palace, surrounded by a village of eight hundred slaves, to whom harshness was unknown, and among whom they led such lives of dreamful splendor as are dreamily suggested in the enchanted pages of *Prue and I*. Her daughter was a widow of sixteen—she was a bride three years earlier—when the insurrection of the blacks broke out; and she escaped to New Orleans in time to see the transfer of Louisiana to the United States. Life in the old Franco-Spanish town was then hardly less idyllic (with the plague-spot of slavery on it, of course) than it had been in San Domingo, and the memoir offers quaint glimpses of the simple, sensuous, pleasure-loving society, in which the ladies walked to balls in their "white satin slippers behind slaves carrying lanterns; . . . . when it rained, or the weather was bad, the ball did not take place," and "this was announced by a crier through the streets to the sound of a drum." The young widow from San Domingo married the most brilliant of the young Americans who came in with the new rule, and she saw the success of the young Republic's arms in the defeat of the British in 1815.

Thereafter, as the wife of a rising statesman, great part of her life was passed in Washington, where she was a leader while her husband was Secretary of State under Jackson. Life in Washington was then as simple, if not as idyllic, as in New Orleans, and Mrs. Livingston's friends were charming and cultivated people, who founded the tradition of social freedom and equality which makes Washington still the most delightful city in the world. There is no doubt but Jackson, who broke up the old official life, and has the shame of introducing the spoils system, should have the credit of liberating society from the trammels of etiquette that even Jefferson had left. The reader of this memoir will find some letters of the old warrior in it which will show him in a new light, for one thinks of his saying things roughly and forcibly rather than with the delicacy and dignity which these letters attest. Mrs. Livingston afterward shone at the French court, when her husband was sent thither as minister, and she died, an old woman, in 1860, at her country place on the Hudson. An attractive feature of the memoir is in the letters given of those which she and her husband daily exchanged in their frequent separations: hers especially have a literary grace which, if a little studied, a little academic, is very, very lovely. In her whole character were united that elegance and strength which were the best effect of the best eighteenth-century education in women, and one cannot read of it without a sense of its refining and ennobling influence, or without a sigh for an amiable type which is necessarily extinct.

VI.

It was an aristocratic type, adapting itself sincerely and patriotically to our conditions, but not springing from them, nor from such aristocratic conditions as are known to our rude Anglo-Saxon race elsewhere. What types these produce the reader may learn from General Adam Badeau's very entertaining, if perhaps a little too gossipy, study of *Aristocracy in England*. It is, of course, imprudent to prophesy anything in particular of human nature, but it does not seem as though this ugly relic of feudalism, if it should ever be cast down, could be regretted by the fondest of its idolaters. One fancies the thing itself feeling a sort of relief if its reign were once well over, and it were reduced to its merely human elements once more.

In General Badeau's book, which does not differ from other impartial observers' accounts of the English social system, we see how very much less respectable than ordinary human beings men are apt to become by assuming to be something more. Not that he paints the English aristocracy very black or intentionally bad; it is probably bad, where it is bad, in spite of a great deal of personal good intention. But he shows satisfactorily that the so-called aristocratic virtues do not exist, and there really never were any virtues which society would not have had without the aristocracy. The aristocrats have been supposed to be preëminently courageous; but Thackeray noticed long ago that the plough-boy seemed to die quite as bravely as the lord who led him into battle. They have been honored for their veracity and generosity; but wealth need not deny itself to give, and generosity is self-denial; as for lies, why should a man tell them whose standing and prosperity could hardly be imperiled by speaking the truth? We are brave and true when we are so to our possible ruin, and what aristocracy was ever more so than the lowest democracy? An undoubted frankness the English aristocrats seem, from General Badeau and other students of them, to have; they do not trouble themselves to hide their bad qualities. They would probably not be worse than the average of society if public opinion forbade them; but the corrosion of English life by snobbishness is the great mischief resulting from their existence, and it is certain that public opinion spoils them. When it comes to a question of rank, the natural self-respect of the English people seems eaten away, from the highest to the lowest; and the meanest lackey is not of a meaner soul before a lord than the lord is before royalty. This spiritual abasement is open and undeniable; it is defended and perpetuated by the whole ecclesiastical and political civilization of England; and probably General Badeau touches the very heart of the matter, the vital difference between English and American things, when he says that though with us some people may look down upon their fellows, their fellows (who feel that they are only the other fellows) do not look up. As long as this is the fact we are safe; and till a thoroughly stupid millionaire can inspire social reverence, or anything but a more or less jocular curiosity, in most Americans, we can still hold up our heads. Till then we need only hang them in shame for the truly great Englishmen, the princes of letters and of arts, who tell us that it refines people to revere rank, to exalt a class of titled persons necessarily their intellectual and moral inferiors, and worship them as their betters, because reverence is a good thing. Reverence for good is a good thing, but even then it had better be good in the abstract, lest at the very best it savor of that respect to persons abhorred of the apostle. This is the important lesson which General Badeau's book teaches; and it might be a very much less admirable book than it is and still be commendable for teaching it. As it is, it groups a great number of facts together, and reasons justly and good-humoredly enough from them. If the facts were less notorious, if they did not qualify the whole of English life and literature, if they were told of some unknown people otherwise great and noble, they would simply seem preposterous. Such a story as Dostoïevsky's leaves one braced and strong by a sense of the self-help in human nature; but General Badeau's study is curiously depressing. It is not even a comfort to feel that one has not a part in that particular squalor.

[1] Eugene-Melchior de Vogue, "Les Ecrivains Russes Con-
temporains--F. M. Dostoievsky," Revue des Deux Mondes, Ser. 9,
No. 67 (January 15, 1885), 312-356.

[2] Criticism and Fiction, pp. 127-129. Howells changed
the wording of this famous passage significantly in preparing
the text for book publication. See Edwin H. Cady, "A Note on
Howells and 'the smiling aspects of life,'" American Literature,
17 (May, 1945), 175-178.

October, 1886

Editor's Study.

I.

THERE comes to us from Venice, in these summer months which will be autumn months before our words reach the reader, a book which the author hopes may become, so to speak, "the Bible of all lovers," and which we think may be at least praised to the race at large as a work of monumental industry and prodigious scholarship, not to speak of its artistic qualities. It is, in its way, one of those feats in which the Italians come to the front, apparently when they will, and claim in this sort or that their world-old primacy; or if the reader will not allow that, then it is one of those achievements of patient learning and of thorough intelligence in which they are now rivalling the Germans. It is called *Il Libro dell' Amore*, and it consists of versions into Italian of twenty-eight hundred poems in celebration of the well-known passion of love in every phase, from more than ninety languages, and seven hundred and fifty poets, not to speak of unknown and popular origins. The versions, save some eight or ten, were made by the compiler, Professor Marco Antonio Canini, and if we may judge by the translations from the English (to omit the other forty or fifty languages familiar to us), they are all not only "very choice Italian," but extremely spirited and faithful. In the case of poems from the Latin, ancient Greek, Neo-Hellenic, Greek vernacular, French, Spanish, old and modern Provençal, Romansch, Roumanian, Catalan, Portuguese, Gallegan, Creole, German, and English, he has translated from the original text, and in the others he has used such versions as he could find in other European tongues.

We cannot wonder, as he says in his most delightful introduction, that if he could have confronted the idea of the work such as it now is, before putting hand to it, he would have turned from it in despair. But Professor Canini is an old scholar inured to heroic toil in the compilation of his *Dizionario Etimologico di Vocaboli Italiani*, and in his *Solution de Cent Problèmes Étymologiques;* he is the author of a volume of amorous verse, fitly entitled *Amore e Dolore*, and he was therefore equipped for the work that grew upon him, by his science and his imaginable acquaintance with the subject—to which few of us, indeed, are altogether strange. Let us add, however irrelevantly here, that he is of that noble tradition of Italian authors who have suffered for their country, and let us remember, as we turn over the pages of his work, that he was banished after the fall of the Venetian republic of '48, and that his *Vingt Ans d'Exil* is an autobiographical contribution to the knowledge of

"come sa di sale
Lo pane altrui, e quanto è dura calle
Lo scendere e il salir per l' altrui scale."

In his introduction, which is not only a formal exposition of his literary ideas and the scope of his work, but at times a charming and touching personal confidence, he tells us: "My labor was more difficult, because performed in Italy, than it would have been in Paris or London or Berlin or Vienna, on account of the difficulty of finding the necessary books, and above all because performed at Venice, rather than in some large city of Italy, for the same reason. My outlay to procure even a part of these books has been very great." He proclaims, with a pride which the sympathetic reader will find as amiable as it is just, that he is "the first to publish a collection so ample of lyrical love-poems, whether popular or written by educated poets, in the principal languages of the world, distributed under a certain number of heads, and translated, where foreign, by the collector himself. There will pass," he goes on to say, "under the reader's eye the love-poetry of all times, from the remotest antiquity to our own days, ...and as to distant epochs, so to various and far-off climes do the verses of this collection belong....Poets of all social conditions, the highest and the lowest, are united here. I have given the verses of famous princes, like Solomon King of Jerusalem, Soliman II. the Magnificent, Sultan of the Turks, and the Grand Mogul Shah Alam II., as well as those of obscure peasants and workmen, in Italy and elsewhere, even to the miserable blacks. And, to confess the truth, the songs of the Pauv' Zizi, the Louisiana slave, move me more than those of the two mighty Mussulman emperors."

It will be perceived that Professor Canini writes like a poet; but he works like a savant, and his subject is scientifically treated. This subject, he says, is the love of a man for a woman, or a woman for a man, and excludes the sensualized mysticism of many devotional poems, as well as all other forms of human love. To keep the book still more within bounds, he rejects romances and ballads as being primarily narrative and only secondarily lyrical, and he admits only a few passages from the Iliad and the great Sanscrit poems. The entire work is in two volumes, and as "all the world loves a lover," the reader will wish to know that the first is divided into eight chapters, namely, What is Love? Beauty and Woman; Need of Loving; First Love; Spring and Love; The Two Loves, Sensuous and Platonic; Expressions of Love in Sonnets; Expressions of Love in Various Metres; while the second volume treats in twelve parts of Love-Songs after the Oriental; The Kiss; Hope Fulfilled; Marriage; Disdain and Infidelity; Reconciliation and Love Renewed; Death of the Beloved; The Widow and the Widower; New Love; Love in Old Age; Memories.

Professor Canini confesses difficulties in the work of selection and rejection, arising chiefly from the delicacy of the theme and the indelicacy of the poets, into which we need not follow him; it is enough that he decided to restrict the expressions of sensuous love, and that, therefore, as he quaintly acknowledges, this division of his work is somewhat wanting. The *naïveté* with which he gives his reasons upon this and other points in his introduction is always charming. "Let no one marvel," he says, "that I have translated so few sonnets. Nothing is more difficult than to translate a German or an English sonnet into an Italian sonnet, because of the different nature of the tongues. For example, the English say with one syllable, *spring,* what we must say in four, *primavera.* To render the conceit of fourteen German or English verses into fourteen Italian verses you must lay them on a very bed of Procrustes." And, again, he says of his chapter on Love in Old Age: "Let no one be surprised that I have given this a special heading. I will not repeat the sophisms of the Gérontes of Molière, or those of Bajazet II., Sultan of the Turks—and poet, as were other sultans—to prove that a woman should prefer the love of an old man to any other. Not so; suffice it to affirm that an elderly man can inspire love in a young girl. Even an elderly woman can enamour a young man, but this case is rarer. It is enough to cite the instance of the son of Madame de Sévigné, who killed himself for Ninon de l'Enclos when she was already of mature age. Love in old age is not rare, especially in the poets, who are gifted with a livelier fancy than most other men."

These flavors of a Montaignesque simplicity and frankness are to be tasted in many passages of Professor Canini's essay; and it is full of curious and striking observations. He notes that the popular poetry is always more sincere than that of the more lettered Muse, and he invites us to notice that in the premeditated art the poetesses are always fewer than the poets, while the contrary happens in popular poetry. Then he adds, with a generosity that ought to endear him to the sex which has not always received from criticism that overrunning measure of justice which it likes when the justice is in its favor: "Woman, according to my thinking, expresses love more naturally, more tenderly, and more vividly than man. I believe that some of the most ancient erotic poems which remain to us—Chinese, Egyptian, Hebrew—are the work of women"; and we, for our part, make bold to say that if any fair reader has conceived a rancor in her heart against Professor Canini for more than insinuating that an old woman is less capable of inspiring love than an old man, she ought straightway to unpack it in the handsomest words she can think of.

The remarks and judgments of Professor Canini on the qualities and relative excellence of the different poets and the different races in the business of making love-songs are all worth attention; and he believes rightly that his work will serve a useful end in the study of comparative literature, that latest of the sciences, which we are beginning to hear something of on many sides nowadays. "In this phase of the lyrism of each people there is a special character, but it all has a common ground: an Italian in love might often, to express his feelings, make use of forms invented by a Turk, and *vice versa.* Therefore the study of contrasted literatures, in what concerns the utterance of love, is a new proof of the unity of the human race, and ought to contribute to the fraternization of men."

He gives a third of his entire space to the Italian poets in pursuance of a design to present a history of love-poetry from the earliest traces of it among his compatriots to its latest achievements; but he frankly says that the German love-songs have been the best of our century, in the literary sort. "Nothing surpasses the *Lied.* Among us, Leopardi alone is not inferior to the Germans;" yet at the present moment he declares without hesitation that "the Hungarian and the Portuguese are the first literatures in the poetry of love. There is, in the Hungarian songs, passion, power, originality; they portray the national character, so vivacious, sometimes so violent.... I consider as the greatest living poet, not only in Portugal, but in all Europe, Giovanni de Deus." The cognate Brazilians are impassioned and full of fire; the Spaniards are not now at their best; the Spanish Americans are careless, but abound in fantasy and passion; the popular love-poetry of the modern Turks is good, but the lettered sort, on the other hand, is a "mixture of Turkish, Arabic, and Persian —a curious mosaic which records the successive dominations of the Turanian, Semitic, and Aryan races"; some of the poems of the Circassians and Georgians are among the most beautiful of all, in Professor Canini's opinion; "in the Sanscrit and Pracrit love-poetry there is not only the ardor of the senses, but lively sentiment and affection. ... In the Hindu songs fancy prevails; in those of the old Aryan or Dravidic populations, tenderness." He finds few love-songs of merit in the Russian, except some that lament the death of the beloved, which curiously attests the universal sadness of Russian literature. The Malaysian lyrics "show a deep tenderness and a refined art;" the Chinese are passed without comment; the Japanese are slighted as rather poor stuff; those of the Patagonians and Araucanians are full of fancy and sentiment; but Professor Canini blames us Americans of both continents for having profited so little by "the poetic treasures of the nations who preceded" us here.

He recognizes the new life of Scandinavian poetry in Björnson, Tegnér, and Oehlenschläger, but regards the literary love-poetry of France, except the new Provençal, as mostly an intellectual toy. What he says of the Anglo-American is worth reproducing at length, as a means of judging his judgments of other literatures. "The Scotch love-songs," he says, "would be much more numerous in my book if I had not been obliged, as noted above, to exclude ballads. Of the English love-literature I have given various pieces from the sixteenth century onward. Readers acquainted with Shakespeare only as a dramatic poet may see that he was also an excellent love-poet in his sonnets and songs. Sufficiently numerous are the pieces which I have given from Burns and from Moore, whom I believe the best of the English love-poets. It grieves me to see how the fame of Moore has for some time declined in England. I have translated almost entire an exquisite lyric of Shelley's, written as it was for an Italian lady, Emiliana Viviani, of Pisa. I have not failed to give some of the best love-poems of Byron, and to offer examples of the more modern poets, as Tennyson, considered the first English poet living; Browning, profound and bizarre; Barrett-Browning, his predeceased wife, whose Sonnets from the Portuguese (really original English poems) are *chefs-d'œuvre ;* G. Dante **2** Rossetti; and Swinburne. The last two have been praised to the skies by many critics, including Italians. To tell the truth, Rossetti seems to me too labored and sometimes too sibylline; I have attempted, not too successfully, I fear—others, including the able critic Nencioni, have judged the task impossible—to translate some of his sonnets. Perhaps the poems of Rossetti's first youth were less artificial and simpler. When he had risen in renown his friends urged him to publish them, but he said that the only copy in existence was enclosed in the casket which the woman he loved had begged in dying to have buried with her. The grave was opened, and it was found that the hair of the poor dead thing had grown so long and had twined itself around the box so closely that this could not be opened without cutting off the tresses. I will say also that Swinburne as a lyric poet does not please me overwell; as a dramatist this is not the place to speak of him. Certainly he has a rich fancy, and a style harmonious and correct; but I think that in his poems the images are heaped up too much, and the conceits rather too sixteenth-century-ish, just as they are in Victor Hugo, of whom Swinburne is a great admirer. For my part, I stick to the half-forgotten Moore—yes, and to Burns: I like the simple verse that gushes from the heart. I offer the reader some poems from the American poets who have written in English, which are lovely indeed. But Walt Whitman is not a love-poet; the love-songs of Longfellow are few ; and Russell Lowell, who is the first of their love-poets, has greater fame as a humorist."

II.

From the most if not the whole of this it will have been seen that Professor Canini knows what he is talking about, and if his knowledge of other literatures is as wide and as critical, he is authorized to speak with the decision he uses. We cheerfully let him speak for us, since we have not, as we must own, read above two thousand, if so many as that, out of the twenty-eight hundred love-poems in his collection. At the age of fifty, or thereabouts, there comes a distinct abatement, as some poets have themselves noted, in the appetite for love-poetry, however voracious it may once have been. We should say that two or three hundred love-songs are then quite enough at a sitting, and we should admire the digestion that could compass more, without wishing to rival it at the risk of a surfeit.

"As long as the sun shines upon our planet," says Professor Canini, at the close of that essay which we should so much rath-er read than the songs that follow it, " as long as plants and animals feel a new life in the spring-time, as long as the birds sing among the April leaves, the human heart will be wrought, now to rapture and now to anguish, by the need of loving. And as long as the world endures, man will strive to express, to utter in rhythmic phrase, the sentiment, mixed of earth and heaven, which gives him his keenest joys and his cruelest pangs, Love." Yet while confidently prophesying to this effect, our poet-savant does not conceal from himself that " the decadence of this as well as other kinds of poetry is a fact general in Europe ;.... in no place is it so evident as in Italy. ... Will it always remain there, as it actually is, more or less, in all the other countries of Europe, hectic and infirm ? I do not think so: there have been other like periods of decadence, on which have followed epochs of fresh and glorious efflorescence."

This seems, indeed, to be the mood, trustful and amiable, of all the critics now vaticinating on the subject of poetry; and it is notably the mood of Mr. G. P. Lathrop, whose introduction to Miss Jeannette L. Gilder's collection of *Representative Poems of Living Poets* we have been reading with so much pleasure and respect. The volume is peculiarly interesting because the selections were all made, at Miss Gilder's invitation, by the poets themselves, and are accompanied by fac-similes of their autographs, the sole exception being that of Lord Tennyson, who would not choose, but who sent word by his son that the list chosen for him, and submitted to him, " would answer the purpose." We think, saving his lordship's respect, it answers the purpose very ill; and perhaps the most striking thing in this collection is how very unfit most of the poets seem to have been to make the choice asked of them. We are not saying that any universally satisfactory selection could have been made ; we are merely saying that in many cases there could hardly have been a less satisfactory one. It is, of course, quite impossible that any man should know what is the most characteristic thing in his own work, and yet this is just what other people would like him and expect him to know. Nevertheless, in its way, this collection is one of unique value, and if no poet has given us only his best, each has given us some of his best, and none certainly has offered us his worst. We have that to be glad of; and if we could know upon what theory of himself or his powers each of the poets had acted, we should have still greater cause for gratitude. But this theory, naturally, the editor is not able to reveal.

Among those poets who have made acceptable, or more or less acceptable, selections may be mentioned Mr. Aldrich, who includes his weird little poem of " Identity," and sonnet on " Sleep"—one of the great sonnets of the language. Mrs. Akers Allen gives, with others, her beautiful poem " Among the Laurels," which subtly expresses one of the sweetest and truest moods known to rhyme. Mr. Bunner rests content with one piece, " The Way to Arcady," which, indeed, for a bewitching grace and movement is enough for half a dozen poets. Mr. Cranch puts in his " Bobolinks," which is also a happy representation of his quality. Mr. Dobson gives us " A Dead Letter" and " The Ballad of Prose and Rhyme," with four other poems of happy choice. From Dr. Holmes the choice of "The Chambered Nautilus," "The Last Leaf," "Old Ironsides," and "The Voiceless" is altogether good; and Mr. Lowell is quite as satisfactory with his extract from the "Commemoration Ode," "A Parable," "The Present Crisis," "What is so rare as a Day in June?" and "The Courtin'." Mr. Lathrop places first of his four poems "The Singing Wire," an admirable piece, meriting remembrance for its imaginative modernness. Mrs. Piatt's choice is very characteristic of her, and Mr. Stoddard's, containing his noble ode on "Abraham Lincoln," and that exquisitely tender little sigh, "The Flight of Youth," is entirely acceptable. "Atalanta," "A Prelude," and "Wild Honey" suggest fairly well the range from elegant to sylvan of one of our most charming and original poets, Mr. Maurice Thompson. Mr. Trowbridge with "The Vagabonds," and Mr. Whittier with "My Playmate," place themselves perfectly before us in at least one phase of their best. The others go from tolerably good to bad and worse, with quite marvellous maladroitness in some instances.

The next most surprising thing after the inability of the poets is their very great number. We had not the least notion there were so many living English and American poets, of all ages and sexes, especially since our violent explosion against their tribe in the March or February number of this Study. It shows what a really poor article of dynamite we use in these outbursts. Judging from the vehemence of our feelings on that occasion, we should say that a few tattered scraps of laurel, and some splintered and blackened lyres, picked up in the adjoining counties, ought to be all that was left of the twanging and twittering crew; but even in this volume alone we count no less than seventy-eight poets and poetesses, most of them in the full vigor of youth, and all apparently in perfect repair. In view of a fact so bewildering, so discouraging, our sole consolation comes from the patriotic pride which will be flattered in every true American by the immense numerical superiority of our poets and poetesses. We have no less than sixty — a round sixty — to the paltry eighteen of the English.

III.

But this idle talk is keeping us from the essay of Mr. Lathrop, which, like most of his critical work, is mostly well felt and well thought. If it does not always impart to the reader the seriousness of the writer, that is the fault of the subject, about which it requires a deliberate and careful resolution to be serious. When it comes to asking whether we are going to have any more poetry, and if not, why, one must remember to be grave, or one is apt to smile. When it comes to specifics for its production, one must stuff one's handkerchief in one's mouth. The critics are all alike droll at that pass; and it is difficult to keep one's countenance even with a lady who, like Madame Bentzon, has written so much and so amicably of American literature, when she prescribes what we ought to do if we wish to create poetry. At the close of her late review of Mr. Stedman's *American Poets* in the *Revue des Deux Mondes* she warns us not to be too American if we wish to be at all, and to beware of making Americanism a fanatic cult, as Walt Whitman does. Guard against the dangerous facility of assimilation, says she; and then guard against an abuse of dialect. Let your poetry, says she, become what it must in entire freedom. By observing these three simple rules we shall see what we shall see.

Mr. Lathrop is not so didactic with us. He seems to think, with Mr. Stedman, that a great deal can be done in poetry by thinking you can do a great deal, or that "the genesis of the greatest poetry involves, first of all, an unbounded, although silent and devout, confidence, in the mind of the artist, that he can rise to the loftiest heights of thought and feeling on wings of the most musical expression. He must believe implicitly that he will one day reach those upper spheres if left to his own manner of flight." Certainly the experiment is worth trying, though we suspect that the difficulty would always be in first getting your silent and devout confidence; plenty of the other sort we see all round us. However, we quite agree with Mr. Lathrop that "if we are constantly telling" the intending poet "that the state of the atmosphere is such as absolutely to prevent any one's rising above a certain plane, or that careful research has disclosed a fatal weakness in the wing-power of the present generation, or that the measurements of his throat demonstrate that he can never give more than a small volume of sound—if we are always doing this, we shall be doing what we can to destroy that native faculty of self-reliance and joyous inspiration that makes him a poet." We not only agree with Mr. Lathrop in this position, but we think that most of his positions are sound and good, and merit entirely serious assent. He invites us to observe that in all ages the poetic future has always been a dark one, just like the political future and the moral future, which are at this very moment simply Egyptian in their blackness. He speaks interestingly and usefully of the critical future, which he finds in even a worse way than the poetic, and he would have us begin its reform "by abolishing superstitions" such as "that we must make unreasoning reference of all new work to the standard of supposed flawless examples produced in the past," and here he stands on the solid ground taken by Mr. Posnett and Mr. Perry. "The rational development of poetry cannot be a climbing backward along the slope that leads to some peak far behind us," he says; and he says this after saying some things of the impeccable masters which will strike many devout and venomous persons as little short of flat burglary, if not beyond it. "To speak frankly, I am not of those who in commending some beautiful example of modern song—eminent, it may be, for a single well-defined quality—feel constrained always to make the reservation that it is the best of its kind 'after Shakespeare.' .... Much of the popular indifference to poetry in our day comes indirectly, I think, from this servile attitude toward writers of the past.... There is scarcely a poet who does not pour us out a measure of dross with his gold. Even in Shakespeare—the very part of him which is generally admitted to be his true body—may be found an occasional mixture of triviality, doggerel or bombast, *which would not be tolerated in a modern poet of high standing.*"

IV.

It is we who have italicized those last terrible words.

Does Mr. Lathrop perhaps remember how a few years ago the British Isles were shaken to their foundations, and their literary dependency here quaked

"From one to the other sea,"

and all the dead conventionalities rose to a sitting posture in their graves with horror, because some one casually said that the "mannerism of Dickens and the confidential attitude of Thackeray would not now be tolerated," fiction having become "a finer art than it was in their day"? Has Mr. Lathrop forgotten that awful moment? Are we to have that day of wrath all over again? Mr. Lathrop

is a poet, and at times a very charming one: does he realize that he has placed himself in a position to be asked whether he thinks he writes greater poetry than Shakespeare? Is he aware that to many worthy persons he will actually seem to have said so?

Its former occupant might well take pleasure in stepping out of the pillory of which Mr. Lathrop seems emulous, and in turning to heave the first half-brick at him. He is young, and has his best work before him, and brickbats will do him good, if he keeps on speaking the truth and saying things which, if said on any other subject, would seem the stalest truisms. The world moves—this terrestrial ball — that was settled by science, which knows; the æsthetic world does *not* move— that was settled by taste, which does not need to know.

---

[1] "come sa di sale/ Lo pane altrui, e quanto e dura calle/ Lo scendere e il salir per l'altrui scale." - how tastes of salt/ Another's bread, and how arduous/ The descending and climbing of another's stairs.

[2] "G. Dante Rossetti" should refer to Dante Gabriel Rossetti.

[3] Thérèse Bentzon, "Les Poètes Americains," <u>Revue des Deux Mondes</u>, Series 9, No. 75 (May 1, 1885), 80-115.

November, 1886

Editor's Study.

I.

IN *The Mayor of Casterbridge* Mr. Hardy seems to have started with an intention of merely adventurous fiction, and to have found himself in possession of something so much more important that we could fancy him almost regretting the appeal first made to the reader's wonder. Henchard's sale of his wife is not without possibility, or even precedent; Mr. Hardy sufficiently establishes that; and yet when the grave, every-day problems resulting from that wild act began to grow under his hand, so fine an artist might well have wished them derived from some fact more commonly within the range of experience. After you have said this, however, you can have very little else to say against the story; and we are not strenuous that this is much against it. We suppose it is a condition of a novelist's acceptance by the criticism of a country now so notably behind the rest of Europe in fiction as England that he must seize the attention in an old-fashioned way; and we willingly concede to Mr. Hardy the use of the wife-sale for this purpose, though we are not sure that the non-professional readers of his book, even in England, would have exacted so much of him. The tangled web woven from Henchard's error is of the true modern design and honesty of material; and one forgets that he sold his wife in following all the consequences to his innocent and beneficent after-life, and to the good and guiltless lives of others. The wrong he has done cannot be repaired, because it cannot, to his mistaken thinking, be owned; and in the tragedy of its expiation your pity is more for him than for all the others. That wrong pursues him, it hunts him to death, with what natural reliefs and pauses the reader knows. Mr. Hardy has never achieved anything more skilful or valuable in its way than the recognition and development of these in his last story; we are not sure that he has not placed himself abreast of Tolstoï and the greatest of the Continental realists in their management.

Then the book is full of his proper and peculiar charm, which is for us always very great. It is a quality which, if he had no other great quality, would give him a claim upon his generation hardly less than that of any other contemporary novelist. It seems to exist apart from any beauty of style or felicity of phrase, and is like the grace of his women, which remains in your thought when you have ceased to think of their different pretty faces and variously alluring figures. It would be as hard to say what it is as to say what that grace is,

and we can only suggest that it is a very frank and simple way of dealing with every kind of life, and of approaching men and women as directly as if they had never been written about before. In fact, thanks no doubt to his early training in another profession (Mr. Hardy was an architect), his first sense of people is apparently not a literary sense, but something very much more natural. He studies their exterior graphically, and deals with their souls as we do with those of our neighbors, only perhaps a little more mercifully. This absence of literosity, if we may coin a word as offensive as the thing, accounts for an occasional bluntness of phrase, which we have sometimes felt in Mr. Hardy's work, and for here and there an uncouthness of diction—or call it awkwardness; but we gain infinitely more than we lose by it. His natural method gives us in this story country folks as veritable as those in *Far from the Madding Crowd*, or *Under the Greenwood Tree*, never ironically or sentimentally handled, but left to make their own impression, among scenes and in surroundings portrayed as sympathetically and unconventionally as themselves. In fact, his landscapes are no more composed than his figures, and share evenly with them the charm of his treatment; no one except Tourguénief gives a fact or trait of nature with a more living freshness.

We should say that *The Mayor of Casterbridge* was not inferior to any other story of Mr. Hardy's in its grasp of character; and his humanity is so very pervasive that each of the leading personages has almost to the same degree that charm of his which we have not been very successful in defining. Henchard is brutal only in our first moments of him; his life, after these, is a willingness, if not an effort, to repair his wrong to his wife; and the heart aches with him through all his necessary ruin to the pitiable end of the old, broken, friendless man. Then that young Scot, Farfrae, gay, thrifty, and good, who supplants his benefactor in business, in love, and in public honors, without intending harm to Henchard, is one of the freshest and most clean-cut figures in recent fiction; if you have known any bright young Scotchman, this one will make you think of him. Henchard's wife is one of those women, single-minded, unknowing, upright, which Mr. Hardy has the secret of divining and presenting to us in all their probability; there is not much of her, but every word of that little seems true. There is not very much of Lucetta either, but she too is every word true; she is perhaps only too captivating in that combination of shrewdness and blind imprudence, of fickleness and tender-heartedness, of fascinating grace and helplessness. She is of the order of women whom Mr. Hardy is rather fond of drawing, like Bathsheba in *Far from the Madding Crowd*, like Fancy in *Under the Greenwood Tree*, like Elfride in *A Pair of Blue Eyes*, and some delicious young person in nearly every one of his books; the sort who guiltlessly compromise themselves by some love impulse, and then more or less amusingly, more or less distressingly, pay for it, but remain in the reader's mind an appealing, a distracting presence. Nothing is better in the book than Lucetta's dropping Henchard, and her conquest of the young Scotchman, whom she wins away from Henchard's putative daughter, Elizabeth Jane, such being the fond and foolish heart of man in the thriftiest and best of us. But Elizabeth Jane, with her unswerving right-mindedness and her never-failing self-discipline, is a very beautiful and noble figure; and Mr. Hardy has made her supremely interesting merely by letting us see into her pure soul. Hers is the final triumph, unmixed with remorse, because nothing but goodness like hers could come unscathed out of all that sorrow and trouble. The author who can discover such a type, on whom the reader's liking may wholesomely rest, has done his public a real favor. It is a very great thing to show goodness and justice and mercy like hers in their actual relation to other lives, and lovable; and it is all the more useful to know Elizabeth Jane because her limitations are more than suggested, and she is not made St. Elizabeth Jane.

II.

In turning from a book like this, in which the allegiance to the lessons of life is so deeply felt, to a story like *Pepita Ximenez*, one is aware of the need of applying more purely literary criterions to Señor Don Juan Valera's brilliant work, if one would judge it fairly. Yet we doubt very much whether any one will be able to regard it simply as a work of art, though the author frankly declares himself "an advocate of art for art's sake." We heartily agree with him that it is "in very bad taste, always impertinent and often pedantic, to attempt to prove theses by writing stories," and yet we fancy that no reader whom Señor Valera would care to please can read his *Pepita Ximenez* without finding himself in possession of a great deal of serious thinking on a very serious subject, which is none the less serious because it is couched in terms of such delicate irony. If it is true that "the object of a novel should be to charm through a faithful representation of human actions and human passions, and to create by this fidelity to nature a beautiful work," and if "the creation of the beautiful" is solely "the object of art," it never was and never can be solely its effect as long as men are men and women are women. If ever the race is resolved into abstract qualities, perhaps this may happen; but till then the finest effect of the "beautiful" will be ethical, and not æsthetic merely. Morality penetrates all things, it is the soul of all things. Beauty may clothe it on, whether it is false morality and an evil soul, or whether it is true and a good soul. In the one case the beauty will corrupt, and in the other it

will edify, and in either case it will infallibly and inevitably have an ethical effect, now light, now grave, according as the thing is light or grave. We cannot escape from this; we are shut up to it by the very conditions of our being. What is it that delights us in this very *Pepita Ximenez*, this exquisite masterpiece of Señor Valera's? Not merely that a certain Luis de Vargas, dedicated to the priesthood, finds a certain Pepita Ximenez lovelier than the priesthood, and abandons all his sacerdotal hopes and ambitions, all his poetic dreams of renunciation and devotion, to marry her. That is very pretty and very true, and it pleases; but what chiefly appeals to the heart is the assertion, however delicately and adroitly implied, that their right to each other through their love was far above his vocation. In spite of himself, without trying, and therefore without impertinence and without pedantry, Señor Valera has proved a thesis in his story. They of the Church will acquiesce with the reservation of Don Luis's uncle the Dean that his marriage was better than his vocation, because his vocation was a sentimental and fancied one; we of the Church-in-error will accept the result without any reservation whatever; and we think we shall have the greater enjoyment of the delicate irony, the fine humor, the amusing and unfailing subtlety, with which the argument is enforced. In recognizing these, however, in praising the story for the graphic skill with which Southern characters and passions are portrayed in the gay light of an Andalusian sky, for the charm with which a fresh and unhackneyed life is presented, and the unaffected fidelity with which novel conditions are sketched, we must not fail to add that the book is one for those who have come to the knowledge of good and evil, and to confess our regret that it[1] is so. It would be very unfair to it, however, not to say that though it is of the elder tradition of fiction in this, it is not conscienceless, or forgetful of what so many good old British classics, for instance, which we are so much advised to go back to, trampled under their satyr-hoofs; even "art for art's sake" cannot be that in these days, and the "beautiful work" created by "fidelity to nature" must pay its devoir to what is above nature.

In the preface to the American edition, which is also a new translation of the novel, Señor Valera addresses himself to our public with a friendly directness which cannot fail of sympathetic response, and with a humor of attitude and wit of phrase which will pleasantly recall the prefatory moods of Cervantes. After the fashion of that master, he gives us the genesis of his romance, and he lets us see that if it is not his favorite, it is at least very near to his heart. Yet we feel that this novel, so full of joyous charm, so brilliant in color, so vivid in characterization, is far from representing its author fully, and we hope his publishers will not be slow to follow it up with his *Doña Luz*, which is in some sort a pendant of *Pepita Ximenez*, with a heroine who is the counterpart of that impassioned little personality. The fascination of Doña Luz and her history is that of a most tender and tragic beauty; it is again the story of a priest's love, but Doña Luz and her lover meet long after his vocation has been decided, and there is nothing for him but to die with his secret. We know hardly any figure in fiction more lovely and affecting than Doña Luz, a beautiful girl growing old in a small country place, and marrying in her second youth a wretch infamously unworthy of her love, and suffering patiently and helplessly on. All her traits are studied with a minute and respectful compassion which leaves the reader a fast friend of the author, and, as it were, her intimate acquaintance. It is a character which makes that of Pepita seem slight and narrow, by comparison with a certain noble depth of feeling in it, and all the tones of the picture are graver. Like the story of Pepita, it presents a small group of persons, but each of these is strongly realized, and is made the exponent of local conditions in which the reader seems to live. It is all very fine and masterly work, scarcely to be matched in the contemporary fiction of our language, if that is not putting the case too faintly.

Señor Valera, who, as the reader may know, has been the Minister of Spain in this country for several years past, and has now left us for a diplomatic post in Europe, is one of those many-sided publicists of southern Europe beside whom our own politicians do not seem so gigantic as we like to think them when the other party is not running them for office. He has passed his life, we believe, in the public service, yet he has not only found time to write the two novels we have mentioned, but four or five others, as well as a treatise on the Poetry and Art of the Arabs in Spain and Sicily, a volume of Critical Studies, a volume of Literary Judgments and Dissertations, another of Poems, another of Dramas. We cannot attempt to ascertain his standing as an author in Spain; that is a thing for the Spaniards to do; but no reader of his books, even at second hand and in translation, can fail to perceive in them a very great talent. Whatever his theories of literary art may be, about the creation of the beautiful and all that, he works primarily, as all the great talents work now, in the interest of what is true, and with a poetic fidelity to facts and conditions. In this way the fiction of our time, such of it as is worth reading, is constituting itself, as never before, the interpreter of history; so that hereafter public events can be accurately read in its light, and whoever would know what this or that people were, at the time they made such and such laws and wars and treaties, may learn their intimate life from the report of their novels.

III.

We are glad to see announced a translation of *Marta y Maria*, the excellent story of Don Armando Palacio Valdés, which we praised some months ago; and we wish we could praise in equal terms two other stories of Señor Valdés which have since come to our hands. One of these is certainly charming as a picture of Spanish life, and would be utterly so but for the leprous taint of illicit intrigue which seems to infect all Latin work. It is called *Riverita*, after the hero, whose career is portrayed from his childhood to his marriage with delightful sympathy and humor, and with a fidelity to circumstance which does not allow itself to be doubted. The Spanish boy, it seems, is very like the American boy, and there are familiar episodes of this book in which he takes a lively part. The scene of the story is in Madrid, and there are immense-

ly amusing sketches in it of Madrid journalism and journalists, of amateur bull-fighting, and of domestic and social life. It is all very modern, but enough of the inalienable Spanish flavor—the tang of the wine-skin—remains to make the reader feel that he is with old friends.

The other book is *José*, a study of people in a little fishing village on the Spanish coast, and the story of two humble lovers there. All the figures are struck out with refreshing vigor, to which one forgives an occasional unsparing truth of line and color. But the author helps himself out with a romantic and superfluous bit of self-sacrifice, and spoils the pleasure of the judicious in his work by the final behavior of an otherwise admirably studied hidalgo, the decayed gentleman of the place. Still, the story is worth reading if one has the Spanish for it.

If one has the Italian for it, the study of people in a little fishing village on the Italian coast, by Verga, is better worth reading. It is called *I Malavoglia*, and is not so new a book as *José*. It is simply the history of a poor family struggling to pay off an unjust debt, and patiently suffering and even perishing in the long struggle. Some passages are of harrowing pathos, and others of a noble sublimity. The father lost at sea; two of the brothers conscripted, and one killed in battle and the other growing desperately up to vice and crime; the devoted mother dying of cholera; the eldest daughter giving up her lover to become the stay of the tottering home; the youngest driven to shame; and the old grandfather submissively, heroically toiling on till the hospital receives him, and he dies away from the *tetto natio*, which the youngest of the Malavoglia retrieves at last, are the incidents of this simple and beautiful story of those common people whom vulgar people call commonplace. It has an incomparable grasp of Italian actualities, as they present themselves on such a small stage—social, political, domestic, and religious—and there is, so far as we remember, "no offence in it." The book is eminently worthy of translation.

A curious contribution to international fiction is the little volume of *Misfits and Remnants*, in which Messrs. L. D. Ventura and S. Shovitch, an Italian and a Russian naturalized among us, have embodied eight or ten interesting sketches of life in New York. These studies are chiefly of poor and friendless foreigners, and have a prevailing charm, in spite of their slightness, and of something like amateurishness at times. The prettiest and best of them is Peppino, a little Italian bootblack, in whom the graceful fidelity of a race whose very vices are engaging is affectionately recognized. There is heart-breaking truth in the history of Bobbo and Rita, the small slaves of a brutal padrone, into whose hands the child-exiles have fallen in the strange, great city; and the Herr Baron is a picturesque nobleman who has lost his fortune at play, and has come over to recover it as waiter and then owner in a New York restaurant. It would be invidious to distinguish between the authors of this pleasant and amiable book, but we may say that Mr. Shovitch seems to ply the laboring oar in sentiment, and that Mr. Ventura has the lighter touch for national character, with which he deals honestly as well as tenderly.

Whilst we are about speaking of novels and novelists of the living sort, let us commend to the reader M. Ernest Dupuy's volume of essays on *Les Grands Maîtres de la Littérature Russe,* of which an American version has appeared, and *La Roman Russe,* sketches and criticism by M. Eugène-Melchior de Vogüé, which has not yet been translated. M. Dupuy speaks of Gogol, Tourguénief, and Tolstoï; M. de Vogüé takes rather a wider range and includes Dostoïevsky. Together, the books form a most valuable commentary upon authors and works of unrivalled mastery, and Mr. Dole, who translates the essays of M. Dupuy, adds to the interest of the volume by collecting into an appendix many facts relating to the writers discussed. These are chiefly from Russian sources, but in the case of Tourguénief he turns to French witnesses of that author's long Parisian exile, and in one place he quotes from M. Viardot words which have a bearing upon matters often discussed in this Study. "Plots, Tourguénief thought, spoiled novels, which were *peintures de mœurs,* and he was glad to see that the taste for them was dying out.... The plot was necessary for a drama, but in the way of a novelist, who should above everything else keep the truth in view. .... Tourguénief was of opinion that a splendidly picturesque country was a bad soil for literary or artistic production. Strong emotions or sensations tended to dethrone the faculty of exact observation, upon which we are dependent for æsthetic enjoyments in flat districts.... 'My first acquaintance with the skylark was precisely in looking about for compensation for the ugliness of a flat near Berlin. I shall never forget the broadening out of the æsthetic faculty on this occasion.... I then remarked the beauty of the sky and of many other things which I should not otherwise have noticed.'"

Here is consolation—if they merit consolation—for the feeble-hearted who complain that there is no inspiration in our level social and moral landscape.

IV.

The prospect is not wanting, indeed, in elements of tremendous drama, which in the apparently fortuitous combinations of life sometimes assume the proportions and majesty of the noblest tragedy for those who have the eyes to see. Life, after all, is the greatest of masters, and now and then one of its facts has shape so perfect that it makes all imitation of life seem clumsy prentice-work, and all comment upon the imitation idle chatter. Such a fact comes to us in the biography of Judge Richard Reid, of Kentucky, by his wife, Elizabeth Jameson Reid, who gives the cruel story with a richness and minuteness of detail intensified in its effect by the artlessness of the work. It is a book that burns and thrills in every leaf with an inextinguishable sense of wrong, with a most impassioned tenderness and devout reverence for the martyr whose suffering it commemorates. This we cannot give again, either directly or at second-hand, for it is so pervasive and so wrought into the very texture of the narrative that it must remain there for the reader; and we wish, for the sake of civilization, of religion, that the book might have as wide a currency as our praise of it.

Very probably our readers have forgotten the name of Richard Reid, but they cannot have forgotten his tragedy, and we need only remind them that he was the Kentucky justice who two years ago was attacked and beaten by a brother lawyer in the little country town where they lived together in civic amity and church fellowship. This lawyer, whom, when she does not name him, Mrs. Reid always speaks of as "the murderer," believed himself injured in fortune and repute by a decision of the court; and although Judge Reid was not sitting in the case, he attributed the decision to him. He decoyed him into his office, and while the judge sat looking over the papers that the lawyer had submitted to him, the latter began to beat him on the head with a heavy cane. The stunned and stupefied man staggered to his feet and blindly struggled into the street, the lawyer following with a cowhide, that he might add the shame of a public chastisement to the injury he had already inflicted. There would then have naturally remained but one thing for the victim of an assault like that, in a community like that, to do. It was wonderful that he had not been killed; having survived, he must kill his assailant.

Judge Reid seems to have been a man of the local civilization, gentle, indeed, of blameless life, and refined by a love of letters and a Christian conscience as regards most affairs of life, but not different probably from many of his neighbors, and probably not better. He himself owned that the natural and established thing for him to do was to take his gun and shoot his enemy on sight. He had always abhorred violence, but it does not appear that he had strongly felt the enormity of a system of violence like slavery, and when the rebellion broke out he was prevented from taking part in the war to perpetuate slavery only by physical disability. He was, as we have said, a man of his time and place; and yet he found it impossible to kill his deadly enemy, as was so natural and customary. He perceived that as a judge he must not break the law, he saw that as a Christian he must not shed blood. He obeyed his revelation; he submitted. He did not submit or take up his cross willingly, and he took it up far from triumphally; but he took it up, and he bore it before the people.

The election for judge was coming on, and he was a candidate. He determined to make his canvass practically upon the principle which forbade him to repay wrong for wrong, or to take vengeance upon his enemy in a community where, whatever was the reasoned approval of his course, there must have been an instinctive contempt for it at the bottom of men's souls, and, worse yet, of women's souls. The heads were all right, and hundreds of letters manifest the abhorrence in which the outrage was held in every part of Kentucky; but the victim believed that there was a slight for his righteousness in these hearts inured to private war, to feuds fought out in village streets and country lanes, to shame washed out in blood. This belief preyed upon his bruised and tortured brain, but still he held out. He had not only to forbear from vengeance, but he had to stay the hands of others, willing and eager to avenge him. The hour came when, in sight of his political triumph, he could bear the stress no longer, and the atrociously injured man took his own life. This is what publicly appeared, though there is a possibility that he did not lift his stainless hand against himself, but perished by some unknown assassin. To such a possibility the author of this most moving book clings with all the faith of a love that suffered unto death with the victim. In either case, Richard Reid fell the prey of implacable hate, and an offering in the cause of civilization and religion. His enemy was tardily expelled from the church where they had communed together; being tried in the court for his crime, he received a sentence of three years' imprisonment, from which he appealed to a higher court, and is still unpunished. This, again, though an unspeakable wrong, is a matter of comparative indifference. The great matter is that magnanimity like that of Richard Reid should be recognized as less than none in human history, and honored as a supreme public benefaction. In this age many things are denied and many are doubted, but more and more one truth shines inextinguishable: that whatever the public interest in a wrong may be, there can be no end to it but forgiveness between him who suffers and him who injures. That is not only religion, but that is also reason; and the martyrdom of Richard Reid dedicates it anew to the human mind and conscience. As for the people of the section in which he lived and died, and which has been so often stained with the blood of private vengeance, they could not do better than leave all commemoration of civic and military greatness among them, and join in raising some imperishable monument to his righteousness.

V.

An interesting study of their character and conditions is unconsciously made in the autobiography of Cassius M. Clay, of Kentucky, the first volume of which has appeared. It is this volume which will chiefly interest the reader; the writings and speeches of which the second is to be made up may be unenviously left to posterity. They had their use in their day, but what Cassius M. Clay was is much more important at present than what he said. His autobiography has the merits of the best in that kind, and is frank and bold even in its reticence, of which there is very little. Mr. Clay has not found it necessary to withhold himself on many points, and he is as explicit concerning his *domestici affanni* and his quarrel with his wife as he is about the difficulties which he has at different times conducted to a more successful issue with the bowie-knife and shot-gun and revolver. He is now mainly a historical figure, and in spite of his foibles he is a striking figure in our history. It was a great and a noble thing for him, a slave-holder, and bred to all the social traditions of his section, to renounce slavery, its principles and prejudices, forty years ago, and join himself with the despised abolitionists of the North in the crusade against it. He was not content with freeing his slaves and bearing a silent witness against their wrongs. He remained in Kentucky, where he was born and reared, to fight slavery and slave-holders in the opinions and persons of his old friends, his kinsmen, and his neighbors; and he fought them not only with the tongue and pen, but literally with fire and sword. He renounced slavery,

but he did not renounce the slave-holder's code of honor; he was prompt with knife and pistol; he was ready for rencontre and duel; he carved up his adversaries in the flesh as well as the spirit; he did not fly from any danger; and further to establish his thrice-approved courage to their sense, this soldier of freedom became a soldier of slavery, and did valiant service in the war with Mexico, begun and carried on that new lands might be brought under its blight and ban. In the later war for freedom he bore a comparatively slight part, and he can hardly be said to have shone above his fellow-statesmen in the diplomatic service of his country. The last fact that brought him prominently before the country was his shooting a negro whom he believed guilty of poisoning one of his family. His later political life, however sincere, has been eccentric and uncertain, and he is not a figure of contemporary importance.

In some aspects he is not a contemporary at all, but purely mediæval, like the society from which he sprang; as mediæval as Uguccione or Castruccio, as feudal as a Donati or an Uberti. But in his way he is always heroic; he has his magnificently generous side, which suffers nothing in his robust and positive representation. This or that chance might have been better for his fame than what actually happened, but nothing that has since happened can obscure the lustre of the fact that when he saw the right he dared all for it, and was willing either to live or to die for it. He came out from the South politically, but geographically he has never ceased to be a Southerner, and socially he is one of the most distinct Southern types.

His book is thoroughly interesting, and has a unique value as a contribution to the history of American civilization. It is not possible always to agree with Mr. Clay about himself, but he is a man, and it is no harm that he should know it. One need not care that he is not aware of his limitations, that he speaks with equal confidence on all points, and that his bold ideas of art and literature are somewhat grotesque. When others, who knew art and literature so very much better, were cowering before that hideous idol of slavery, he rose and dealt it a deadly blow in its sanctuary, among worshippers whose hands were instantly lifted against his life. About a book or a statue we can let him be mistaken, since he was right about humanity.

He was not altogether right, and his heroism was on a lower level than that of Richard Reid. We must not forget that. We cannot pay him that reverence which must be forever the due of such a martyr, and yet we can fitly recognize in him the moral sense, which, if sometimes too strongly qualified by virile force, was yet an extraordinary moral sense.

We commend both of these books to the reader in spite of literary disabilities and æsthetic lapses which it would be easy to point out. We can readily forgive Mrs. Reid her adoration of her husband, since she does not exaggerate his suffering and the value of his example, and we do not object to Mr. Clay's appreciation of himself which sometimes seems inordinate, for he has lived some great things. At the end of the ends, and with all their faults, the books are of the kind which uncommon lives can alone add to literature.

[1]<u>Criticism and Fiction</u>, pp. 82-85.

December, 1886

Editor's Study.

I.

THE reader who likes to think that the most and the best to be done in the world is to help one's self without hurting others will find support in the *Voyages of a Merchant Navigator,* by H. W. S. Cleveland. It is the story of Richard J. Cleveland's life, and it is not only the affectionate tribute of a son to his father's memory, but is in its way a monument to democracy.

At fourteen this typical New-Englander left the common schools of Salem with such learning and love of it as the common schools seemed to impart oftener in that day than in ours, and entered a counting-room of the old town. At eighteen he went to sea, and at twenty-four he was the master of a vessel. His career began in the troubled times following the American Revolution, and it led him with varying fortune through the picturesque and dramatic perils of the next thirty years in nearly every sea that washes the globe. During the English wars with the French republic, the English wars with Napoleon, the English wars with ourselves, the Spanish wars with their revolted South American provinces, the French wars with everybody, he trafficked in every port open to honest gain. Sometimes he sailed under one flag, and sometimes under another; now he was an American citizen, and now a Danish subject; he now carried despatches for the French Directory, and now he protected himself with an English register. He turned every phase of the shifting politics and hostilities of the time to account; he was ready for any opportunity or any emergency; he was alert, prompt, prudent; but he kept through all a conscience unsullied by baseness or dishonesty. He kept something more—a faith in human nature unshaken by wrong, and a generosity which the epithet of knightly would cheapen. On one side he was a shrewd Yankee adventurer; on the other, he was as fine and high a spirit as ever dared danger in any cause.

In that day commerce was still a romance, with thrilling chances, unknown prizes, unknown losses. The world was not penetrated by instant intelligence in every part; a voyage was not merely a passage to this port or that, with the market ascertained at either end: it was an adventure which demanded forecast and sagacity; it meant splendid success or ruinous disaster to the owner of the cargo, who was oftenest master of the ship. There were still pirates at sea and savages ashore, and trade was harassed by risks in war and restrictions in peace. Cleveland encountered these in twice making and twice losing a fortune which was thought handsome in those simpler days. But he never lost heart;

he never forgot himself in despair; he never forgot others in any mood. He writes his father, when making his first voyage, that he would rather work for the Derbys, in whose counting-room he had been so well used, than for any other house at twice the pay; he is always writing to his father to make use of the money he sends him as if it were his own; he writes his wife to do what she will with the thousands he has dared so much to gain—spend them or throw them away: to give her pleasure is all that he cares for. The letters, in which the book abounds, are not remarkable for the expression of his gentle and manly spirit only, but for the good sense, the advanced religious thought, the just and intelligent observation, in them. He was the author of *A Narrative of Voyages and Commercial Enterprises,* which was praised in its time for these qualities, and which ought not to be forgotten in ours.

II.

But what makes this old ship's captain so interesting and instructive a figure is not his intellectual character, hardly his moral character, but that nobility of heart which lifted him above every chance, and kept him master of himself in every circumstance of prosperity and disaster. It is not certain that every one can have it by trying, but it is worth trying for, and the book might be very well put into the hands of all people not too old for making the attempt—say people anywhere between eighteen and eighty. But it ought to be given them with an admonition against looking for anything spectacular in the manifestation of this magnanimity. Our sailor-merchant seems never to have thought that he was doing anything out of the common when he proved himself equal to occasions that were very much so; he is so simple and modest about himself that certain epithets which admiring criticism keeps in stock look rather tawdry when one dusts them off with the intention of applying them to him. After all, you cannot say anything better of bread than that it is good; and to be a just man and kind is more than to be a gentleman. Honesty was before honor, and never yet had the alloy of egotism which debases the latter. What consoles, what exalts, in the story of a life like Cleveland's is that its qualities are within the reach of all classes if any; and we have a right to be proud of him as a democratic type, as distinctively democratic as another navigator, whose life came into our hands at the same time, was aristocratic.

We think Mr. Edmund Gosse, whose touch is always charming, has seldom done a more agreeable piece of work than the sketch of the career of Sir Walter Raleigh which he contributes to Mr. Andrew Lang's series of English Worthies. It is thoroughly sympathetic, without being for a moment sentimental; it is delightfully sane and just; and when one thinks of the pseudo-picturesqueness with which such figures as Raleigh used to be treated only a little while ago, one experiences a profound gratitude for Mr. Gosse's clear sense of the difference between the inkstand and the palette—or say paint-pot, for the colors were laid on as if to be seen "from the front" in the studies now fortunately obsolete. There is no effort to make out a case for Raleigh (whose name, by-the-way, we pronounce Rawley as he did, while modern Englishmen call it Rally), and you are suffered to see that he was never so great as in the hour of his death, if indeed he was not a thought too epigrammatic on the scaffold; though one ought not to be critical of people's behavior there, and Raleigh had certainly a dauntless courage. Where he had not courage was in the presence of the truculent and ridiculous old maid Elizabeth, on whom he fawned with a pretence of passion sufficiently revolting. This is, of course, saying that Raleigh was a courtier and a man of his own epoch. His love of splendor, which was at the bottom of his highest achievements, which made him a dreamer and a poet, made him also a rather greedy and shameless office-seeker, and a rather selfish adventurer. He was a man of his epoch in being bloodily cruel against the hapless Irish, in spite of his better nature, and in being implacable against Spain, which was well enough. Mr. Gosse makes us feel, with his delicate skill, all the dramatic pathos of Raleigh's suffering for a supposed conspiracy in the interest of the power which he had hated his whole life, and of his dying at the demand of Spain for a really reprehensible offence to her. Even in that day of license it was too gross to attack the colony of a prince with whom one's king was at peace, especially when one had given one's word not to do anything of the kind. Still, after all you can admit against Raleigh, his tragical fate strongly moves you; after two hundred and fifty years your spirit pines with his in his long imprisonment, and the pang of his death is vivid yet.

III.

Another pleasant book, which we have been reading with these two, is the *Memoirs and Letters of Dolly Madison*, edited by her grandniece, in which we have found something of the flavor of Mrs. Hunt's *Memoir of Mrs. Edward Livingston*. But though the eighteenth century gives its charm to the letters of the most brilliant lady who ever reigned in the White House, there is a more native flavor in them than that which one tastes in the letters of the fascinating Creole. Dolly Madison was born a Quaker; she came of a titled Scotch family; but her father was so averse to the world and its spirit that he freed his slaves and left his Virginia manor to come and live in Philadelphia, where he spent his remaining days in straitened circumstances. There his daughter grew up, and there she first married, with one of their own sect, who died after a year or two, and left her a rich and beautiful young widow, to take in due time the fancy of "the great little Madison," as Burr called

the future President. When Jefferson was inaugurated he chose Madison his Secretary of State, and after that the greater part of Mrs. Madison's life was passed in Washington. Neither of Jefferson's daughters could come to the White House with their widowed father, and he called upon Mrs. Madison to help him out in hospitable exigencies, sending her little notes like this, in which the simplicity, if rather premeditated, is also charming:

May 27, 1801.

"Thomas Jefferson begs that either Mrs. Madison or Miss Payne will be so good as to dine with him to-day, to take care of female friends expected."

There would be more state about a Presidential invitation in our own day, when democracy has so much more firmly established itself, but Jefferson was then laying its foundations, and he did not know how much room the superstructure might need. For instance, in the "Canons of Etiquette to be observed by the Executive," he ordained some customs which we do not find it necessary to follow: "At dinners, in public or private, and on all other occasions of social intercourse, a perfect equality exists between the persons composing the company, whether foreign or domestic, titled or untitled, in or out of office. To give force to the principle of equality, or *pêle-mêle*, and prevent the growth of precedence out of courtesy, the members of the Executive, at their own houses, will adhere to the ancient usage of their ancestors—gentlemen *en masse* giving place to the ladies *en masse*." It seems a trifle grotesque, when put down in cold black and white, and yet much might be alleged to prove that there was more common-sense, more self-respect, and more picturesqueness even in the *pêle-mêle* plan than in the precedency which we now ape in going out to dinner. Thomas Jefferson and Dolly Madison made the White House a cheerfuler place than it had been under the solemn ceremonial of the Washington and Adams administrations, and when Madison became President the easy and friendly conditions were kept up. His wife "returned all calls made by her own sex, and the 'dove parties,' composed of the wives of cabinet officers and foreign ministers, when their lords were engaged in formal dinners, were exceedingly lively and popular. Her private parties, and the lotteries in which every guest received a 'cadeau,' are still remembered with great pleasure by a few. Though in no sense a learned woman, nor one who cared at any time for study, or even reading, Dolly Madison was eminently a talented woman, full of a most delicate tact, and so warm-hearted and amiable that even her early Quaker friends were induced to condone what they feared was 'an undue fondness for the things of this world.' She dressed handsomely and 'in the mode,' clinging for a time to the pretty little Quaker cap, but discarding that even, when she went into the White House, as unsuitable to her surroundings.... She delighted in company, and her table fairly 'groaned,' as the saying is, with the abundance of its dishes. The serious, thoughtful Madison, physically weak, and harassed and worried by the many cares crowding upon him at this time, often said that a visit to his wife in her sitting-room, where he was sure of a bright story and a good laugh, was as refreshing as a long walk.... To cheer and amuse her husband she kept a pleasant party of friends constantly with her, making them feel that her home was theirs in the warmth of her hospitality. She superintended all her domestic arrangements before breakfast, and while her guests were still sleeping."

We are now richer and prouder and more artificial than we were in those days; people lie abed longer in the morning, and wives no longer seek so much to "cheer and amuse" their husbands. These things are of the past; yet some small merit we should like to claim for our generation somewhere; and suppose we have the hardihood to say that a British admiral would not now burn a defenceless town, as Admiral Cockburn wantonly burned Washington in Madison's time? The story of his barbarity is told again in these memoirs with fresh effect, and does not commend itself to American liking any better than at first; it is all the more pathetic for the keener sense we have of the poor beginnings of a national capital which Washington then was. It seems as if a more reflective admiral than Cockburn might have decided that the little town stuck about in the deep mud at random ought to be sufficiently humiliating to our national pride as it was, and so let it be; but Admiral Cockburn set it on fire, and burned Mrs. Dolly Madison out of house and home. It was near the end of her husband's second term, and the White House was put in repair only in time for his successor. He then retired to his estates in Virginia, whence, after his death, his widow returned to Washington, and ended her long life there in 1846. It was, as the world goes, a beautiful and prosperous life, and the character which it developed was lovely and good. Yet it was so full of care and sorrow and vexation, through being merely a human life, that near its close one of the cheerfulest of women could say to a young girl who came to her for sympathy in some little grievance: "My dear, do not trouble about it; there is nothing in this world really worth caring for. Yes, believe me, I, who have lived so long, repeat to you that there is nothing in this world here below worth caring for."

IV.

Sweet Mrs. Dolly Madison only reiterated the experience of mankind. It is certainly best not to take very seriously the things of life that are not necessarily serious, and we can commend as exemplary the mood in which Mr. T. S. Perry approaches the treatment of a matter that in and out of print has long engaged the more or less amused attention of mankind. He deals, in a very attractive little book, with the *Evolution of the Snob*, bringing to his inquiry the wide knowledge and the scientific methods that distinguish his work in criticism from the *ad captandum* expression of likes and dislikes generally received as criticism among us. His theory is not that snobbishness always existed unrecognized in our race, as Thackeray holds, but that it existed undeveloped, and that the period of its first efflorescence was when the French Revolution had destroyed the prestige of the aristocrats, and had made it possible for the commonalty to aspire successfully to their society. As his business is mainly with the snob in our immediate Anglo-Saxon family, he gathers his proofs mainly from English literature, and their array is very curious and interesting. The sycophant and the parasite, whom he delicately differentiates from the

snob, were well known in all the ancient and mediæval societies, but the snob is strictly modern, though he is to be recognized in a sort of arrested development in the early days of the Roman Empire, with the same relation to our actual snob as the stamping of pottery among the Romans bears to the art of printing. Mr. Perry traces the gradual growth of the snob as it has been observed by the satirists and philosophers, and after quoting from Goldsmith a description of the sort of toad-eater common in his day, he continues with some passages worth reproducing in illustration of his particular theory on the subject and his general critical attitude:

"But this coarse barter of food, drink, and shelter for flattery and subserviency is yet remote from the subtler development of personal indignity that was at this period making ready to burst upon the nineteenth century. Even the famous conversation of Miss Skeggs and Lady Blarney in the *Vicar of Wakefield*, chap. xi., at which Mr. Burchell continually said 'Fudge!' indicates merely the widespread curiosity about 'anecdotes of lords, ladies, and Knights of the Garter,' which the Vicar gratified by recording these fantastic speeches. Snobbishness was not yet fully formed: it was in the same incomplete condition as democracy, traces of which abound in all the writings from which these quotations have been made; and it is important to understand how thoroughly the importance of 'the great' was an object of veneration. Some of these quotations may appear to magnify the importance of the small: yet it is never to be forgotten that there is no moment on which one can put his finger and say, 'Here is something absolutely new, something never thought of before, that appeared without preparation.' No conscientious historian will begin the history of the American Revolution in 1775, or of the French in 1789: to understand either, it is necessary to go back indefinitely, and to trace the many currents leading to those grand events from a very remote past. There is no one day in which a man becomes old, no one measurement which declares a growing boy tall. All the developments of literature in this century carry us back by curious ramifications to obscure, half-forgotten attempts of writers in the last. We say Wordsworth introduced the love of nature; but the most indifferent examination shows us the feeling growing up for many years, to find full expression in him and his contemporaries. Hence it is, because growth is gradual, that everything which is called a novelty is always attacked as trite and untrue by energetic conservatives. The future as well as the past is implicit in everything that happens; and if we were to quote from every book written in the last two hundred years, it would be as impossible to say 'Here is the first outburst of snobbishness,' as it would be to find the first statement of democracy."

All this, we submit, is very suggestive, if not convincing, and carries weight with it. Of course we shall none of us willingly abandon our belief in the antiquity of the snob; but in the mean time we commend our author's ideas to the reader. His book is not a satire, but a serious though not at all solemn investigation of a very striking phase of modern civilization. It ends with an expression of belief in the final disappearance of snobbishness through the realization of democratic ideals in society. The worthlessness of the distinctions for which people now abase themselves will be seen more and more, and the honor of being kicked by a duke will be felt less and less, as the levelling-up process is accomplished, though it is uncertain how long some may continue to preach that it is well to have a class in whose presence one may feel mean. The late Mr. Trollope, who was perhaps the greatest and the truest artist in English fiction of his time, went far to prepare us for this attitude of snobbishness in his Life of Thackeray, where he deprecates the elder [2] novelist's irreverence for aristocracy and even royalty. In his development the snob has become aggressive; from the snob quiescent we have passed to the snob agonistic, the snob militant. Is this possibly his ultimate or penultimate phase? What a strange world it would be without him! One would hardly know it; we might look for the reappearance of the snob as the hero of romantic fiction, and we might see him, say, risking his life to get to a duchess's ball, or slowly dying of a broken heart at not being received in fashionable society at Newport. This apotheosis would prove how really dead he was.

V.

The editor of a future work like Gateley's *World's Progress* might then include some such [3] study as Mr. Perry's in his valuable record of human advance, together with the chapters on Geology, Society, Agriculture, Manufacturing, Mining, Trade, Commerce, Statistics, Biography, Literature, Architecture, and Costume; but now he only gives an essay from him on Literature. The book is of that uncomfortable bulk which demands for the family Bible and the unabridged dictionary the monumental occupation of the " centre table" in houses to which the subscription book usually penetrates, and this is to be regretted in a volume which has so little else in common with the ordinary subscription book of North America. That is to say, each chapter in this very well imagined work is a real contribution to general knowledge on the subject it treats of, and is not only interesting, but in its popular way authoritative. For example, no one among us has given greater or more intelligent attention to the matter than Mr. Frank D. Millet, who writes of "Progressive Changes in Costumes and Customs"; Mr. Clarence Cook has established himself as a prophet concerning "House Architecture and Decoration"; Mr. Carroll D. Wright has an equal vocation to speak of "Inventions and Discoveries in Manufacturing"; Professor Packard has due authority to tell people of the " Prehistoric Progress of the Earth"; Dr. George P. Fisher is peculiarly well equipped for the task of handling topics like " The Formation, Growth, and Character of Nations," and " Moral, Social, and Intellectual Progress"; Mr. E. V. Smalley has an excellent and interesting paper on the " Trade of Ancient and Mediæval Nations"; while Professors Sanborn, Heinrich, and Ely treat of Mining, Agriculture, and Manufacturing; Mr. Charles E. Beale, the editor, of Comparative Statistics and Biography. It seems to be throughout a work not only of serious intention, but very honest and interesting performance. "The Progress of Literature" is the department assigned to Mr. Perry, and we confess that it is this which has chiefly attracted us. Like the other contributions to the massive volume, it is itself the substance of a book, and with its abundant illustrations from the authors of all times and peoples it is of unique value as a survey of world literature. At least we should not know where to match it in English, and it is admirable for its

vast scope and effective grasp. Mr. Perry is distinctly an apostle of the comparative method in criticism, and if, as he continually insists, there is no first time or first one in anything, but all is a development from beginnings indefinitely remote, still it is apparent that he is one of the first to give this method recognition and consciousness. In an essay ranging from the Chinese to the Americans, through the whole course of the Sanscrit, Greek, Roman, Mediæval and Renaissance, Romantic and Modern literatures, with all their European subdivisions, he has had to use a condensation dangerously near to desiccation; yet his theory of literary progress is so clear, and its application is so novel and refreshing in the midst of the general empiricism, that the perilous limit is not touched. Toward the close of the essay, what seems an editorial exigency has separated Mr. Perry's succinct comments on the different authors by wide tracts of quotation from them, with an effect that is rather distracting, though it does not necessarily impair their value. This, like that of the whole essay, consists largely in the intelligent and perfectly probable point of view. The critic regards literature with a historical interest mainly, as the reflection, sometimes conscious and sometimes unconscious, of the several periods and peoples among whom it arose—as their involuntary expression of their conditions and aspirations and affections, and not as merely the product of certain men who set themselves about making poems, plays, and novels. Even when most artificial, it is the genuine expression of an artificial mood ; and with its infinite variety of shades and tones, it has the final unity of human nature, in which all the strangest and remotest things are akin. Mr. Perry is strongest, perhaps, and most original in his sense of the simultaneity of the great literary movements or aspects, as the Classicistic, the Romantic, the Realistic; and he delights to find proofs of the almost instant communication of these impulses from one country to another, and the contemporaneous advance from widely different quarters toward the same end. He concerns himself little or not at all with the admiration of "exquisite passages," and as little or less with that censure of special defects which forms the stock in trade of the peevish race hitherto mostly accepted as critics; to him these are incidents without general import, and a cruel jibe or supercilious sneer is impossible to his sane and generous intelligence. It is indeed a new voice, a new temper, and almost unique, in literary criticism, with which one cannot acquaint himself without enlarging his horizons, and seeing literature in a novel light.

VI.

Gateley's World's Progress signalizes an advance in the quality of subscription books, of which there have been already some other tokens, and we could wish it well, if for no other reason than that its success will make it easier for other honest books to reach the mass of the people through an avenue by which so much that is worthless has found its way to them. The sale of a successful subscription book is something unrivalled by that of any book in the trade; as compared with the one, the other mode of publication is, as Mark Twain has said, merely printing for private circulation. The present subscription system is the American development of one of the oldest methods of publication, if not the first; and perhaps, if we continue without an international copyright law, it may be the refuge and the hope of literature among us. When the cheap reprints have made it more and more difficult to publish copyright works, for which the publisher pays the author, at a living profit, they may both be glad to invoke the aid of the despised book agent, who carries literature from door to door, and urges it upon the popular favor with an eloquence which is very effective. In the cities and large towns he is voted a bore and a nuisance; private houses of any gentility are all shut against him; brutal placards on shop and office doors and elevator shafts class him with the forbidden peddler and beggar; if he penetrate by chance or artifice to the prohibited interiors, sharp words and short shrift await him; insult is his meat and contumely is his drink; he is a hissing and a by-word, a proverb of the undesirable. But in the smaller towns and in the country, where people have all the time there is, and the ladies something more, no "pampered menial" shuts the door in his kindly face, but the mistress of the house throws it wide open to him, and he is a welcome visitor. She is glad to see him, and so are the daughters and the half-grown boys; and they willingly suspend their work while he sits down in the village parlor or the farm kitchen and unfolds his samples of print, illustration, and binding, and expatiates upon the incomparable merits of the work. He is armed at all points against criticisms and objections; he has got by heart a whole budget of secret instructions, in which not only are these supposed and confuted, but human nature is subtly studied, and he is taught to play upon its amiable weaknesses and vanities. He is skilled to turn a pretty compliment to the lady and her daughters; to be struck by the beauty and intelligence of her child when it comes into the room; to be surprised at the age of her father or mother, whom he would have thought much younger. He is instructed when and how to turn easily aside from urging them to subscribe, and to talk of the great world of news and the little world of gossip, and then adroitly get back to the book. The weather and the crops are for discussion with the master of the house, whose interest is solely to be consulted in persuading him to give his influential name to the enterprise. In these houses the book agent is not only tolerated, but welcomed; not only asked to sit down on a specially dusted chair, but bidden draw it up to the table when overtaken by dinner in the midst of his eloquence. He takes leave an honored friend, and they are glad to see him the next year.

Perhaps he would not have to practise all his arts if his book were better; perhaps he would have to use more. The subscription publishers are not certain; they are in the mood of the managers, who are beginning to wonder whether the public really prefers trash: once they had no doubt of it. We must wish them a hopeful solution of their doubt, and give a cordial greeting to any experiment in the right direction. They wield an enormous machinery, of which the finest and best literature we can offer the people may yet be eager to avail itself. The phenomenal success of such a book as Grant's *Memoirs* is full of suggestion. The reader who now goes to a bookseller and asks the clerk what is new and what he had better buy may live to find it safe to take the advice of a book agent; and the author who pines on a sale of fifteen or twenty-five hundred may thrive upon the added cipher, and may yet roll in riches. In that event, we have a plan for a new Study, with a refectory attached, in which we shall ask all our readers, and even our adverse critics, to sit down to our Christmas dinner; and no Barmecide feast, we promise them, of Ideals and Romance, but a Realistic banquet.

[1] Andrew Lang, ed., English Worthies (9vols.; London: Longmans & Co., 1885-87). Individual titles: Charles Darwin, by Grant Allen; Marlborough, by George Saintsbury; Admiral Blake, by David Hannay; Ben Jonson, by John Addington Symonds; Raleigh, by Edmund Gosse; Richard Steele, by Henry Austin Dobson; Shaftsbury, by H. D. Traill; George Canning, by Frank H. Hill; Claverhouse, by Mowbray Morris.

[2] Anthony Trollope, Thackery, in English Men of Letters Series, John Morley, ed. (London: Macmillan & Co., 1878-1919).

[3] Charles E. Beale, ed., Gately's World's Progress (Boston: M. R. Gately; New York: Gately and Williams; [etc.], [etc.], [c1886]).

January, 1887

Editor's Study.

I.

IT would be interesting to know the far beginnings of holiday literature, and we commend the quest to the scientific spirit which now specializes research in every branch of history. In the mean time, without being too confident of our facts, we venture to suggest that it came in with the romantic movement about the beginning of this century, when mountains ceased to be horrid, and became picturesque; when ruins of all sorts, but particularly abbeys and castles, became habitable to the most delicate constitutions; when the despised Gothick of Addison dropped its *k*, and arose the chivalrous and religious Gothic of Scott; when ghosts were redeemed from the contempt into which they had fallen, and resumed their place in polite society; in fact, the politer the society, the welcomer the ghosts, and whatever else was out of the common. In that day the Annual flourished, and this artificial flower was probably the first literary blossom on the Christmas Tree which has since borne so much tinsel foliage and painted fruit. But the Annual was extremely Oriental; it was much preoccupied with Haidees and Gulnares and Zuleikas, with Hindas and Nourmahals, owing to the distinction which Byron and Moore had given such ladies; and when it began to concern itself with the actualities of British beauty, the daughters of Albion, though inscribed with the names of real countesses and duchesses, betrayed their descent from the well-known Eastern odalisques. It was possibly through an American that holiday literature became distinctively English in material, and Washington Irving, with his New World love of the past, may have given the impulse to the literary worship of Christmas which has since so widely established itself. A festival revived in popular interest by a New-Yorker to whom Dutch associations with New-year's had endeared the great German ideal of Christmas, and whom the robust gayeties of the season in old-fashioned country houses had charmed, would be one of those roundabout results which destiny likes, and "would at least be Early English." If we cannot claim with all the patriotic confidence we should like to feel that it was Irving who set Christmas in that light in which Dickens saw its æsthetic capabilities, it is perhaps because all origins are obscure. For anything that we positively know to the contrary, the Druidic rites from which English Christmas borrowed the inviting mistletoe, if not the decorative holly, may have been accompanied by the recitations of holiday triads. But it is certain that several plays of Shakespeare were produced, if not written, for the celebration of the holidays, and that then the black tide of Puritanism which swept over men's souls blotted out all such observance of Christmas with the festival itself. It came in again, by a natural reaction, with the returning Stuarts, and throughout the period of the Restoration it enjoyed a perfunctory favor. There is mention of it often enough in the eighteenth century essayists, in the *Spectators*, and *Idlers*, and *Tatlers;* but the *World* about the middle of the last century laments the neglect into which it had fallen. Irving seems to have been the first to observe its surviving rites lovingly, and Dickens divined its immense advantage as a literary occasion. He made it in some sort entirely his for a time, and there can be no question but it was he who again endeared it to the whole English-speaking world, and gave it a wider and deeper hold than it had ever had before upon the fancies and affections of our race.

II.

The might of that great talent no one can gainsay, though in the light of the truer work which has since been done his literary principles seem almost as grotesque as his theories of political economy. In no one direction was his erring force more felt than in the creation of holiday literature as we have known it for the last half-century. Creation, of course, is the wrong word; it says too much; but in default of a better word, it may stand. He did not make something out of nothing; the material was there before him; the mood and even the need of his time contributed immensely to his success, as the volition of the subject helps on the mesmerist; but it is within bounds to say that he was the chief agency in the development of holiday literature as we have known it, as he was the chief agency in universalizing the great Christian holiday as we now have it. Other agencies wrought with him and after him; but it was he who rescued Christmas from Philistine distrust, and humanized it and consecrated it to the hearts and homes of all.

Very rough magic, as it now seems, he used in working his miracle, but there is no doubt about his working it. One opens his Christmas stories in this later day -- *The Carol, The Chimes, The Haunted Man, The Cricket on the Hearth,* and all the rest — and with "a heart high-sorrowful and cloyed," asks himself for the preternatural virtue that they once had. The pathos appears false and strained; the humor largely horse-play; the character theatrical; the joviality pumped;

the psychology commonplace; the sociology alone funny. It is a world of real clothes, earth, air, water, and the rest; the people often speak the language of life, but their motives are as disproportioned and improbable, and their passions and purposes as overcharged, as those of the worst of Balzac's people. Yet all these monstrosities, as they now appear, seem to have once had symmetry and verity; they moved the most cultivated intelligences of the time; they touched true hearts; they made everybody laugh and cry.

This was perhaps because the imagination, from having been fed mostly upon gross unrealities, always responds readily to fantastic appeals. There has been an amusing sort of awe of it, as if it were the channel of inspired thought, and were somehow sacred. The most preposterous inventions of its activity have been regarded in their time as the greatest feats of the human mind, and in its receptive form it has been nursed into an imbecility to which the truth is repugnant, and the fact that the beautiful resides nowhere else is inconceivable. It has been flattered out of all sufferance in its toyings with the mere elements of character, and its attempts to present these in combinations foreign to experience are still praised by the poorer sort of critics as masterpieces of creative work.

In the day of Dickens's early Christmas stories it was thought admirable for the author to take types of humanity which everybody knew, and to add to them from his imagination till they were as strange as beasts and birds talking. Now we begin to feel that human nature is quite enough, and that the best an author can do is to show it as it is. But in those stories of his Dickens said to his readers, Let us make believe so-and-so; and the result was a joint juggle, a child's-play, in which the wholesome allegiance to life was lost. Artistically, therefore, the scheme was false, and artistically, therefore, it must perish. It did not perish, however, before it had propagated itself in a whole school of unrealities so ghastly that one can hardly recall without a shudder those sentimentalities at second-hand to which holiday literature was abandoned long after the original conjurer had wearied of his performance.

Under his own eye and of conscious purpose a circle of imitators grew up in the fabrication of Christmas stories. They obviously formed themselves upon his sobered ideals; they collaborated with him, and it was often hard to know whether it was Dickens or Mr. Sala or Mr. Collins who was writing. The Christmas book had by that time lost its direct application to Christmas. It dealt with shipwrecks a good deal, and with perilous adventures of all kinds, and with unmerited suffering, and with ghosts and mysteries, because human nature, secured from storm and danger in a well-lighted room before a cheerful fire, likes to have these things imaged for it, and its long-puerilized fancy will bear an endless repetition of them. The wizards who wrought their spells with them contented themselves with the lasting efficacy of these simple means; and the apprentice-wizards and journeyman-wizards who have succeeded them practise the same arts at the old stand. The English Christmas book of last year was of the same motive and purport as the English Christmas book of twenty years ago, but the ethical

intention which gave dignity to Dickens's Christmas stories of still earlier date has almost wholly disappeared. It was a quality which could not be worked so long as the phantoms and hair-breadth escapes. People always knew that character is not changed by a dream in a series of tableaux; that a ghost cannot do much toward reforming an inordinately selfish person; that a life cannot be turned white, like a head of hair, in a single night, by the most allegorical apparition; that want and sin and shame cannot be cured by kettles singing on the hob; and gradually they ceased to make believe that there was virtue in these devices and appliances. Yet the ethical intention was not fruitless, crude as it now appears. It *was* well once a year, if not oftener, to remind men by parable of the old, simple truths; to teach them that forgiveness, and charity, and the endeavor for life better and purer than each has lived, are the principles upon which alone the world holds together and gets forward. It was well for the comfortable and the refined to be put in mind of the savagery and suffering all round them, and to be taught, as Dickens was always teaching, that certain feelings which grace human nature, as tenderness for the sick and helpless, self-sacrifice and generosity, self-respect and manliness and womanliness, are the common heritage of the race, the direct gift of Heaven, shared equally by the rich and poor. It did not necessarily detract from the value of the lesson that, with the imperfect art of the time, he made his paupers and porters not only human, but superhuman, and too altogether virtuous; and it remained true that home life may be lovely under the lowliest roof, although he liked to paint it without a shadow on its beauty there. It is still a fact that the sick are very often saintly, although he put no peevishness into their patience with their ills. His ethical intention told for manhood and fraternity and tolerance, and when this intention disappeared from the better holiday literature, that literature was sensibly the poorer for the loss.

It never did disappear wholly from the writings of Dickens, whom it once vitally possessed, and if its action became more and more mechanical, still it always had its effect with the generation which hung charmed upon his lips, till the lips fell dumb and still forever. It imbued subordinate effort, and inspired his myriad imitators throughout the English-scribbling world, especially upon its remoter borders, so that all holiday fiction, which was once set to the tunes of *The Carol* and *The Chimes*, still grinds no other through the innumerable pipes of the humbler newspapers and magazines, though these airs are no longer heard in the politer literary centres.

This cannot go on forever, of course, but the Christmas whose use and beauty Dickens divined will remain, though Christmas literature is going the way of so much that was once admired, like the fine language, the beauties of style, and the ornate manners of the past, down through the ranks of the æsthetical poor, whom we have always with us, to the final rag-bag of oblivion.

III.

It is still manufactured among us in the form of short stories; but the Christmas book, which now seems to be always a number of paste gems threaded upon a strand of tinsel, must be imported from England if we want it. With the constant and romantic public of the British Islands it appears that spectres and imminent dangers still have favor enough to inspire their fabrication, while if we may judge from an absence of native phantasms and perils, the industry has no more encouragement among us than shipbuilding, though no prohibitive tariff has enhanced the cost of the raw materials, or interfered to paralyze the efforts of the American imagination. Whether or not we get enough | [1] of the domestic article in the monthlies and weeklies, which feel the journalistic impulse to be seasonable in this as in other respects, at any rate it is certain that we do not get it in more permanent form. With us it is *not* customary " for the purveyors of amusing literature—the popular authors of the day—to put forth certain opuscules, denominated 'Christmas Books,' with the ostensible intention of swelling the tide of exhilaration, or other expansive emotions, incident upon the exodus of the old or the inauguration of the new year," as the noble-languaged critic of *The Kickleburys* [2] *on the Rhine* said in *The Times* when that holiday trifle appeared. No more in the burlesque mood of Thackeray than in the more Ercles vein of the other master do our popular authors put forth opuscules of the sort described. It is difficult for us even to fancy one of our authors doing it. It is not supposable of Dr. Holmes or of Mr. Lowell; nothing could be farther from the natural make and temper of Mr. James; Mr. Aldrich would smile to think of himself doing it; we cannot conceive of Mark Twain's writing a holiday opuscule for the subscription trade; and which of the ladies whose literature delights us could we expect such a thing from ?

Have we, then, come to our literary growth too late for pleasure in these amusements of our nonage, or is the English mind, which still toys with them, unriper than ours ? The latter would be such an agreeable thing to believe that we must not rashly refuse it credence out of modesty, even though we suspect that it is the former which is true.

IV.

Without inquiring too nicely into the reasons of the fact, we can all recognize the fact. The American holiday book is quite another affair, and is graphic rather than literary. It naturally took the form of illustration, because for a long time our conditions were not very fruitful in literature of any sort, and it was easier and cheaper for the publisher to get designs for some popular poem or story than to get the poem or story written. The Annuals had their day with us too; the Annuals and the Gift-books and the Keepsakes, with their mezzotinted simpers and dimples, their steel-plate maidenhoods and motherhoods and childhoods; and then we began to attempt the wood-cut illustration in which the *Century* and *Harper's New Monthly* have finally made us the masters. Our earlier attempts in that kind are not such as we can flatter ourselves upon, however fond of praise we may be. From year to year, almost, the difference is so great that it is a little painful to look at the past achievements which once gave us so much pleasure. The excellence of the performance has constantly advanced the ideal, and now any eye which has followed the progress of the art is impatient of less than the best. We cannot tell how general this trained feeling is, but the fact that the best is so well liked is significant of a wide appreciation of differences. No doubt many copies of the finest holiday publications, which are beautiful works of art, are bought because a handsome book is justly believed to be the most fitting holiday gift; but there can be no doubt, either, that a great deal of personal preference goes with the purchase, and, it is to be supposed, some personal taste and knowledge, though it would not be safe to say how much.

The holiday books of this year are not very different in scope from those of last year. There are books relating to the history of art, like Mrs. Erskine Clement's *Stories of Art and Artists;* books of travel, like Mr. Benjamin's *Persia and the Persians;* illustrations of classical pieces of literature, like *The Lay of the Last Minstrel* and *She Stoops to Conquer ;* and [3] certain other volumes with greater originality of plan. One of these is Mr. F. Hopkinson Smith's *Well Worn Roads*, which, perhaps from our readier sense of what is good in literature, we are inclined to value more for its literary than its artistic qualities. Whoever else might have thought of making those pleasant sketches in Spain, Venice, Holland, and Belgium, it was to Mr. Smith that it occurred to accompany them with study of the life about him while he was making them. He has told simply what happened to him then and there, and he has told it with spirit, with light humor, and with a genial sympathy which are very charming indeed. The result is as pleasant as the intention is novel, and in these little contributions to our knowledge of the scenes and people among which he went sketching he has become part of the great movement in literature whose prime traits are fidelity and sincerity.

This is what Mr. Charles Dudley Warner has done too in *Their Pilgrimage.* With all the good æsthetic theories in the world, to which he has heretofore given some cogent expression, in the presence of life at our seaside and mountain and inland lake resorts he finds himself " photographic." He not only shows the surface of things with instantaneous vividness, and with all the modern advantages of the dry-plate process, but he looks below the surface with an eye that does not always seek amusement or alone the entertainment of the reader. In his first essay in the field of fiction he turns out an actualist, whose first wish seems to be truth to his facts and the meaning of them. This was perhaps inevitable from the scheme of his work, but it was partly inevitable from his having something to say in a country and in a time when what is worth saying in fiction cannot very well be said in any other way. The effect is in harmony with Mr. Reinhart's illustrations. The artist has been faithful like the author, and the book which has resulted is one of rare excellence in a kind of which the examples are few and the difficulties many. To keep a pleasant story current through the study of conditions which form the groundwork of the design, and not to let it stagnate in levels of comment or the descriptions of the landscape and the spectators—to know when to drop the narrative and when to take it up—was the little miracle demanded of Mr. Warner in this prospect of our summer leisure, which seems so simple and so easy, and which must have been a labor full of the anxiety no one sees. The romantic fervors of *Corinne* and the poetic pensiveness of *Hyperion*—the great prototypes of what we may call travel-fiction — would alike have been false colors in this picture of our cheerful prosperity. A light touch, a friendly humor, and a keen eye for the beauty as well as the vulgarity of our watering-place commonplace, in all its curious variety of traits, and its inexhaustible picturesqueness of environment, were the gifts needed for such a book as Mr. Warner and Mr. Reinhart have given us.

In its peculiar union of literary and graphic charm we fancy that hardly any book of the year will dispute its supremacy, but in a different effect these qualities appear again in the *Tile Club Book*, which Mr. Edward Strahan and Mr. F. Hopkinson Smith have written, and all the members of that famous society have drawn. The tone and the flavor of studio talk have got thoroughly into the letter-press, and the phototype and other processes have rendered the sketches again with the perfection which is not the less perfection because it is no longer a surprise. The full-page illustrations are reproductions of well-known pictures by different members of the Club, while the text is profusely illuminated with " bits" from those spirited and fertile pencils, and occasionally the effective face of one of the contributors. On the fly-leaves the effigies and blazons of the Club appear in a lavish texture of decorative work; and the cover of the book is a triumph of sober richness and beauty. The volume is of the same general style as Mr. Hopkinson Smith's *Well Worn Roads*, and his illustration of *The Last Leaf*, which we praised last year; everything about it is artistic, and everything about it is American in ideal and in execution. It marks the extreme advancement of taste in its sort among us, and when we have seen it surpassed we shall believe that something finer has been done.

A book altogether different in design is Goldsmith's famous comedy as illustrated by Mr. E. A. Abbey. Like his Herrick, it seems a series of studies begun without certain intention of completion, and continued out of love of doing them till all were done as if by separate and original impulses. Whether this is the true history of them or not we will not be positive, but there is an effect of fresh, un-

jaded interest in the work which lends a color of probability to our conjecture. Like other conjectures of criticism in regard to artistic work, it does not greatly matter. What is unquestionable is the arch humor, the delicate sense of character, and the relish for broad fun which Mr. Abbey has brought to the interpretation of a masterpiece of literature, most distinctly of its own time in its eighteenth-century spirit, and of all times in its human nature. Written to displace the sentimental comedy which had inundated the English theatre with the tears of Sensibility, Goldsmith's play had no chance of success but in the boldest truth to the conditions of English life, with its gross eating and drinking, its rude arrogancies and familiarities, its naked passions, its practical jokes, its artificial civilities, and that essential core of kindness which the poet must divine chiefly from his sense of it in himself. Mr. Abbey's work is simply the graphic appreciation of all this, to which he has applied such skill and such sympathy that he has fairly made himself a partner of the dramatic enterprise. His pictures play the comedy for us, and whoever sits down to the pleasant spectacle will hardly see the characters again in any guise but that his pencil has given them. His pencil has had the immense advantage of the eighteenth-century costumes, and the scene is full of that silken pomp, that stately grace, that quaintness and grotesqueness. At the first page it is as if the curtain lifted upon all those familiar people, and at the last we rise with a sigh as at its fall upon their final grouping behind the foot-lights. It is a very perfect illusion of an illusion.

Mr. Ipsen's decorative illustration of Mrs. Browning's *Sonnets from the Portuguese* is another work which has the same charm of unity in execution, and of evident affection for the literary material in the enterprise. Each page of the book is the framework of a sonnet, and expresses with infinite variety of " leaf-fringed legend" the dominant feeling or idea of the poem: it is the prolongation, in the designer's art, of the music which breaks from the beautiful lines, and loses itself in bud and berry and blossom, and in gracious glimpses of sentient beauty. The artist has not wished to interpret or to represent; he has richly contented himself with setting the poet's pictures, and in the performance of a labor as strictly ornamentative as that of an old missal, he has achieved an effect full of distinction and charm.

---

[1] Criticism and Fiction, pp. 171-182.

[2] The Kickleburys on the Rhine, by William Makepeace Thackery.

[3] The Lay of the Last Minstrel, by Sir Walter Scott, and She Stoops to Conquer, by Oliver Goldsmith.

February, 1887

Editor's Study.

I.

THE reader of Miss C. F. Woolson's short stories, lately reprinted in two volumes, must have felt the mastery which she shows in them; and perhaps, pausing from the pathos of "Solomon" or "Wilhelmina," or from the fascination of "The South Devil," he may have let his thoughts run to the vast amount of work which other Americans have done in that kind. This work, indeed, is so great in quantity and so excellent in quality that we are tempted to claim a national primacy in short-story writing; and we do not easily content ourselves with the belief that we have merely done better in writing short stories than in writing long ones. The rest of mankind might dispute our claim, and our novelists, but for the modesty native in novelists, might refuse our conclusion as injurious. We will not insist upon either; perhaps neither is true; and if this is the case, we should like to hold Miss Woolson's charming volumes responsible for both. One of her books groups under the title of *Castle Nowhere* nine stories of the great lake country, from the southern shores of Erie to the further coasts of Superior; the other, called *Rodman the Keeper*, is a series of studies and brief romances of the South, from Florida northward to the Carolina mountains. The collections are different and alike in their fidelity to the physical and social conditions of these diverse regions; these are sometimes involved in romantic mists, and sometimes they are unsparingly distinct, but the sensitive and sympathetic spirit of the author, her humanity, her passion for nature, her love of beauty, and her delight in color, characterize all. Several of the stories in time past have given us very great pleasure, especially the "Solomon" and the "Wilhelmina," which we have mentioned, and which are pictures of life in the community of the Separatists at Zoar, in Ohio, and "The Lady of Little Fishing," a romance placed beyond the reach of the gazetteer on an island of Lake Superior; and we have been reading them over again with a satisfaction not diminished by the greater intelligence which the ten or fifteen years passed since their first publication may be supposed to have brought even to a critic. In fact, their assemblage under one cover somehow throws a new light on all the stories, and one sees, or seems to see—it is best not to be positive—that their final value, or the merit that they have in supreme degree, is to have caught and recorded in very clear and impressive terms the finest poetry which stirs in the heart of wild, new countries. This poetry is a religious aspiration or possession, often grotesque and delusive, but always touched with sublimity and sanctified by impulses of unselfish sincerity. The reader will feel it most in the study of "St. Clair Flats" and in the pathetic romance of "The Lady of Little Fishing"; but a sense of it imbues and qualifies nearly the whole book, which assumes a historical importance from it, as "Rodman the Keeper" and the companion pieces achieve vastly more than their æsthetic interest by eternizing that moment of heart-break and irreconciliation in the South when its women began to realize all their woe and loss through the defeat of their section in the war. Something more and something better than the literary instinct helped our author to the perception of things which give both of these books their uncommon claim to remembrance; she has made them necessary to any one who would understand the whole meaning of Americanism, or would know some of its most recondite phases by virtue of qualities which are felt in all her work, and at which we have hinted. These qualities, which are above artistry, to our thinking, need not make one indifferent to that; one would lose a great deal that is beautiful and valuable if they did. Miss Woolson deals with nature and with human nature in a fresh way, or at least a way of her own, which is at once simple in its kindliness and conscious of the limitations of all human judgment, where it ceases to be a question of suffering, sin, love, and hate, and becomes a question of sufferer, sinner, lover, and hater, with their relation to the frame of things, and to that material aspect of the universe, which now seems so deaf and blind to humanity, and now so full of poignant sympathy. The landscape is apt to grow sentient under her touch, which in the portrayal of that beautiful and deadly Florida swamp in "The South Devil" is really life-giving: the wicked, brilliant thing becomes animate. In this a writer who has since evolved for herself one of the most interesting phases of realism is romantic, but her epoch is distinctly marked by her forbearance in another respect: she does not extort an allegory from the malign morass, as Hawthorne must have done in obedience to the expectation of his time, nor suggest a psychical significance in it, as the romance of a little later period would have done. It is a merely animal life which "The South Devil" lives.

II.

Another group of short stories, called *Poverty Grass*, by Mrs. Lillie Chace Wyman, a writer not otherwise known, but destined to be less and less unknown if she keeps on writing, seems in its absolute and unswerving realism like the effect of a vow not to take from the truth one jot or tittle, or add to it any shadow of fancy in character or condition. The "Child of the State," though not the first in order in the book, is first in importance for its revelation of the author's power to deal faithfully yet not repulsively, pathetically yet not sentimentally, with one of the most awful problems of civilization. No one who read it, when first published in *The Atlantic Monthly* some years ago, can have forgotten it: the thing has a kind of monumental strength and quiet, and stands arraigning creed and law for their helplessness or hurtfulness with unsparing insistence. The other stories in the volume are mostly like it: simple, grim, true to misery, toil, pain, vulgarity, savagery, and the tenderness and beauty coexisting with these in the barest, bleakest, commonest lives. It is surely not a book for those who would like fiction to make out that life is a pretty play or an amusing game, and would have all sorrows end well, that their sensibilities may be tickled and pampered. But men and women who wish to meet other men and women in literature, and to hear them speak out the heart of human passion in the language of life, need not be afraid of these powerful sketches. They cannot help being better men and women for reading them, if only in awakened pity and good-will.

A gentler pathos, a pensiveness lit with the humor which is absent from Mrs. Wyman's work, breathes from Miss Jewett's latest book. *A White Heron, and Other Stories*, is not the volume which we would praise as showing the author at her best, and yet some of the pieces could hardly be better. One may say that certain of them are slight and tame to the point of fragility and the temper of the cosset, but others are exquisitely good. "The Dulham Ladies," whose final and most thrilling adventure is buying two frizzes of a deceiving French hair-dresser; "Martha and Mary," to whom the god appears in a reconciled cousin with the gift of a sewing-machine, are masterpieces of a kind that one would simply like to go on reading forever in that quiet, restful, humorously appreciative style of Miss Jewett. They are as satisfying at once and as appetizing as "March Rosemary," where the material of a much longer tale is wildly flung away in the story of the poor old maid who marries the worthless young sailor, and who makes a long journey to expose him to the second wife after he abandons her, and then seeing their happy home through the window, with its promise of usefulness for the man, returns to her desolation without taking her revenge.

III.

It is this occasional lavishness in the writers of short stories which gives one question whether a branch of the art of fiction tempting to such profusion ought to be encouraged. The motives which are both great and simple are not so many that the profession can afford to waste them in the narrow limits of a tale or sketch, and we conjure the writer of short stories to make sure that he has not one of these in hand before he casts his plot irrevocably in that miniature mould. We think a little question will usually enable him to decide whether he has hold of a short-story motive or a long-story motive. We believe the two are readily distinguishable, though not so easily definable. The short story should perhaps involve merely an episode, a phase; what is more, and especially what contains the germ of much conditioning or characterization, belongs to the novel.

Commonly, however, the matter will decide itself through the age of the writer. The novelette, like the poem or the romance, may come from youth and the first acquaintance with life, but the novel is of years and experience. There are, of course, exceptions, in which what is or seems a novel is the work of a youthful hand; and if any one were to think that women, by reason of their more restricted lives and necessarily narrower outlook into the world, were more successful with the novelette than the novel, he had better not say it, because it might displease a whole sex, and it might not be true. Better reserve such a thought, we should say, for further meditation in secret. What is certain is that almost all novelists who begin early begin by writing short stories or novelettes, and that some of the most brilliant achievements in that sort have been the work of women. The sort seems immemorial, but not to go further back than Boccaccio and the other Italian novelists, we find it the form which prose fiction took. These novelists, and their imitators in France and Spain, gave prose an ease and grace and naturalness which it did not show till very much later in English, when the essayists of the *Spectator* began to tell their little stories with a finer characterization of the personages than had yet been employed; for the Latin novelists, with all their delightful literary skill, dealt mainly with types well known and generally accepted. It became and remained in most countries the receptacle of the marvellous and the typical, though Zschokke in Germany deepened the lines of the short story, and found more room in it for character than had perhaps found place there before him. The Germans of the romantic school infused in it a mysticism which still often qualifies the English and American short story.

The great English novelists of the period just before ours served their apprenticeship in the short story, but the work of Dickens and Thackeray in that way is apprentice-work, and does not bear the relation to their novels which the stories of George Eliot bear to hers. The first of these masters continually recurred to the minor form with varying success; but Thackeray did not go back to it from the room and greater freedom of the novel. Mr. Black, we believe, does not write short stories at all; Mr. Hardy writes them, and always charmingly; Mr. Anstie writes them, and always amusingly. In France, Zola has not reverted even to the comparatively long short stories of his first period; Daudet almost as rarely does them; and in Italy, Verga, in some respects a greater master than either, has made powerful studies and sketches, rather than told tales, in his short stories. Tourguénieff's are studies and sketches too, rather than tales, and striking as they are, they are distinctly inferior to his novels. In Auerbach's village tales one has the sense of being among pigmy folk; the traits and conditions are all well ascertained, but the scale is small, and the persons seem not related to human nature at large. That colossus of the north, Björnstjerne Björnson, knows in supreme degree how to fill the little limits of the short story with powerful figures and the great motives of universal experience; some of his briefest tales, three or four pages long, have an immeasurable depth and distance in them.

IV.

But we are not sure, after all, as we hinted in the beginning, that the Americans have not brought the short story nearer perfection in the all-round sense than almost any other people, and for reasons very simple and near at hand. It might be argued from the national hurry and impatience that it was a literary form peculiarly adapted to the American temperament, but we suspect that its extraordinary development among us is owing much more to more tangible facts. The success of American magazines, which is nothing less than prodigious, is only commensurate with their excellence. There can be no question that it is one effect of the highest editorial skill, when each of the two great illustrated American periodicals attains a currency as large as that of the *Family Herald* in England, or the *Petit Journal* in France. This sort of success is not only from the courage to decide what ought to please, but from the knowledge of what does please; and it is probable that, aside from the pictures, it is the short stories which please the readers of our best magazines. The serial novels they must have, of course; but rather more of course they must have short stories, and by operation of the law of supply and demand, the short stories, abundant in quantity and excellent in quality, are forth-coming because they are wanted. By another operation of the same law, which political economists have more recently taken account of, the demand follows the supply, and short stories are sought for because there is a proven ability to furnish them, and people read them willingly because they are usually very good. The art of writing them is now so disciplined and diffused with us that there is no lack either for the magazines or for the newspaper "syndicates" which deal in them almost to the exclusion of the serials. In other countries the *feuilleton* of the journals is a novel continued from day to day, but with us the papers, whether daily or weekly, now more rarely print novels, whether they get them at first hand from the writers, as a great many do, or through the syndicates, which purvey a vast variety of literary wares, chiefly for the Sunday editions of the city journals. In the country papers the short story takes the place of the chapters of a serial which used to be given.

This demand, so great that it is not easily calculable, accounts for the quantity of our short stories, but it is to the taste with which our magazines are made that we mainly owe their quality; and in establishing and elevating this taste we must recognize as very eminent the influence, now as always sane and good, of the *Atlantic Monthly.* The *Galaxy* did much to the same end in its time; *Lippincott's Magazine* much also; and we expect nothing but good in this way from our neighbor, the new *Scribner's.*

It would not be easy to name all the novelists among us who have first made themselves known in this sort, and the enterprise would not be altogether safe, for we should be sure to forget some of them. It is not easy, either, to think of their admirable performance and not wish to recognize it. In some cases they have surpassed it in their novels; in others their short stories remain their best work. To take them alphabetically, in the right democratic fashion, we suppose it must be an open question whether Mr. Aldrich has "broken his record" in any of the novels he has written since *Marjorie Daw,* and the other short stories only less admirable than that because in its way that is unique. Another novelist of what may be called the *Atlantic* school, Mr. W. H. Bishop, has proved himself of the longer breath requisite for the novel, but his *Detmold,* his *House of a Merchant Prince,* and his *Golden Justice* can not make us forget how good *One of the Twenty Pieces* was, how delicious *The Battle of Bunkerloo.* Mrs. Rose Terry Cooke's stories have, we believe, the competition of no novel from her hand; *Freedom Wheeler's Controversy with Providence* is a masterpiece, and we think that the best of her stories are destined to a recognition which will not finally be affected by the inequality of her work. The novels of Charles Egbert Craddock (if we are to spell Miss Murfree's name with a C, as she prefers) have not yet outrivalled her first short stories in boldness and strength of outline, nor in value of detail uncheapened by its excess. Caroline Chesebro' was the author of short stories of original quality and most honest workmanship. *The Great Doctor,* by Alice Cary, is one of the best stories of life in the middle West ever written. Mrs. Rebecca Harding Davis has written stories which, if of an effect too nearly immediate, are very intense. J. W. De Forest, a novelist whose work has in some respects not only not been surpassed, but not approached, among us—a realist before realism was named, and an admirably equipped artist—is the author of a score or so of short stories, among which the veteran magazine reader will recall *My Neighbor the Prophet, The Taillefer Bell Ringers, The Drummer Ghost, The Lauson Tragedy,* and others of a force now mystical and now grimly satirical, but always true to human nature. Mr. P. Deming in his Adirondack studies and stories impresses, again, with his absolute faithfulness, with a most conscientious simplicity, and touching tenderness; he unites to much of Auerbach's charm and minor truth much of the virtue of Björnson's universality. He is not known at all as a novelist; but in a literature less rich in short stories than ours he would have achieved a repute indefinitely greater than the modest recognition which he now enjoys. Mr. Bret Harte's novels are of course inferior to his short stories, written in the spirit of expiring romance, and profoundly moving the reader with the types of that school transplanted into novel circumstance and seen through a new atmosphere. Mr. E. E. Hale's short stories, again, are better than his larger work, and have a charm which is altogether their own, and a singular vitality; their power of establishing in the reader's consciousness any given impossibility as a fact is an extraordinary triumph of the delightful fancy with which they are written. Mr. Edward H.

House has written stories of Japanese life full of novelty and humorous sympathy. Mr. James's short stories, especially *A Passionate Pilgrim* and *The Romance of Certain Old Clothes*, are of the highest quality in the highest sort; we should hardly know how to match them for effects at once imaginative and realistic, and for a sympathy all the deeper for the self-control in which they are written; one also feels in them the unjaded youthful joy of doing a new kind of thing vigorously. Of Miss Jewett's exquisite sketches we need hardly speak; they are as clearly a find as anything else in our literature, and entirely her own. Ralph Keeler's *Confessions of a Patent Medicine Man* was of a sort which, if he had lived, he might have won lasting repute from. Mr. Lathrop, who has done so much so respectably in so many ways, is at his best, we think, in a short story of his called *Left Out* — the simple study of a man whom the whole world has passed by; and his apparently slight sketch *In a Market Wagon* has a tenderness and delicate naturalness which leave the impression of far more spacious work. *The Case of John Dedlock* and *The Autobiography of a Quack*, among the short stories of Dr. Weir Mitchell, are of equal masterliness in their several ways. Mrs. Prescott Spofford, in the earlier and perhaps easier days, made a national reputation with her *In a Cellar* and *The Amber Gods*, and yet we are not sure that the achievement was less difficult than it would be now, when we recollect that Fitz-James O'Brien wrote *The Diamond Lens* at the same period. This was a sort of last refinement upon the manner and material of Poe, whose stories evolved a fantastic effect from a highly elaborated mechanism, still more subtly contrived and adjusted by the later artist. Another famous story of O'Brien's was that of the grewsome goblin which could be felt but not seen; and in proper scientific evolution from this appeared, not many years ago, one of the most striking achievements of fantasy which we can recall, namely, Mr. C. De Kay's *Manmatha*, a study of the survival of the most transparent. We mention him here out of his order in the almanac and the alphabet lest we might otherwise fail to pay a just tribute to his ingenious work. Of Miss E. S. Phelps's short stories we like most *In the Gray Goth*, an incident of life among the lumbermen of the Maine woods, very simple, powerful, and affecting, and of an unstrained human quality which the gifted author too seldom consents to give us. Of Mr. F. R. Stockton's stories what is there to say but that they are an unmixed blessing and delight? He is surely one of the most inventive of talents, discovering not only a new kind in humor and fancy, but accumulating an inexhaustible wealth of details in each fresh achievement, the least of which would be riches from another hand. *The Man who Stole the Meeting-House* is the best of all of Mr. J. T. Trowbridge's short stories, among which we remember few poor ones. Both of these charming writers seem at their most charming in their stories, and less successful in their novels, as was also the case with Bayard Taylor. It is not a question with regard to Uncle Remus, for Mr. Harris

writes no novels, and as yet Mr. Thomas N. Page, who is one of the writers advancing the name of the new South in literature, has not attempted anything but short stories. *Our Phil* and *Marty's Various Marcies*, by Mrs. Olive A. Wadsworth, are delicious pieces of colored character; and Mrs. S. B. Wister's *Carnival of Rome* and *Carnival of Venice* are uncommon realizations of uncommon people: the apparently insipid, passionately romantic English woman who chiefly figures in the latter is a personage whom one remembers like few heroines of novels.

V.

No doubt we have failed to mention writers whose names will occur to the reader, but we have mentioned enough to show that our claim for American excellence in short stories is not founded solely in our patriotism. An interesting fact in regard to the different varieties of the short story among us is that the sketches and studies by the women seem faithfuler and more realistic than those of the men, in proportion to their number. Their tendency is more distinctly in that direction, and there is a solidity, an honest report of observation, in the work of such women as Mrs. Cooke, Miss Murfree, Miss Jewett, and Miss Woolson which often leaves little to be desired. We should, upon the whole, be disposed to rank American short stories only below those of such Russian writers as we have read. These perhaps seem fresher because [3] they are stranger, but we think that Tolstoï has deepened and widened the possibilities of achievement within narrow limits beyond any other writer. We have heretofore spoken of his Scenes of the Siege of Sebastopol, of their powerful characterization and their absolute verity. Lately the French have translated *Deux Générations*, the study of an abominable father, and a son differently abominable through the change from earlier to later customs and ideals; and *La Mort d'Ivan Illitch*, which cannot fail to leave the profoundest impression with every reader. This last is an account of the mortal sickness of Ivan Illitch, in which the man almost sensibly suffers and dies before you. Its unsparing force searches the heart, and humbles it with such a sense of mortality as rarely penetrates to it through the world and its manifold vanities and the habit of life. It is full of touches of the truest pathos, and the master and teacher who speaks to us in it shrinks from no fact of the situation that can verify it to the imagination and the conscience. You go down into the valley of the shadow with Ivan, and you know him and all his household as if you had dwelt with them. We can hardly say how this intimacy is established; perhaps through the sincerity of the writer, who does not once strike an erring note, and who wastes no stroke in ornament or literary prettiness. The effects in this simple study are as deep and broad, as far-reaching, as in a tragedy of Shakespeare, which it about equals in length. It is a prodigious lesson in life and in letters, and the best of our short-story writers might conceive from it possibilities for his art undreamt of before.

[1]"Anstie" probably refers to Thomas Anstey Guthrie, on the staff of Punch from 1887 to 1930, where he used the pseudonym "F. Anstey."

[2]Criticism and Fiction, pp. 131-133.

[3]Criticism and Fiction, p. 134.

Editor's Study.

I.

THE ten or twelve books of verse on our table have an outward prettiness so great that it keeps the eye lingering on the creamy vellum and the delicately tinted cloth of their covers when it ought to be impatient for their printed pages. In fact, one of them, called *The Old Garden*, is so very daintily quaint in its caprice of gayly sprigged muslin or chintz that one must ask himself whether the Muse had really better be so charmingly dressed if she wishes people to listen to what she has to sing. That is something for the Muse to think of: a simple dove-colored gown, or a sober dress of black, even, would not that be more fortunate for a Muse who was very much in earnest? But perhaps this Muse would rather not be taken too seriously, and in that case criticism far sterner than that of the Study might consent to be ungrudgingly pleased by the gayety of her apparel. After all, the Muse is not a Quakeress or a Nun, and in this lyric mood of hers she might claim that her coquettish garment was strictly in keeping. Daintiness and quaintness, a little conscious, a very, very little *poseueses*, characterize all the graceful and fanciful rhymes of the book, and play in as many airy conceits with the ideas of such archaic blooms as pansies, myrtle, morning-glories, sweet-peas, rosemary, mignonette, growing in an old city garden. If this were saying that the poems expressed merely a literary interest in the themes, it would be doing them wrong; there are odors and flavors in them fetched from far—as far as the fields and parterres of seventeenth-century poetry—but there is a direct and personal knowledge too, and real love of the things dealt with, and real pleasure in them. Upon the whole, the opening poem, which the book takes its name from, is the best in it, and here is a passage from this poem which is full of sensitive feeling and delicate accuracy of touch:

"Still from the far-off pastures comes the bee,
   And swings all day inside the hollyhock,
Or steals her honey from the winged sweet-pea,
   Or the striped glory of the four-o'clock;
The pale sweet-william, winged with pink and
     white,
   Grows yet within the damp shade of the wall;
And there the primrose stands that, as the night
   Begins to gather and the dews to fall,
Flings wide to circling moths her twisted buds,
   That shine like yellow moons with pale, cold
     glow,
And all the air her heavy fragrance floods,
   And gives largess to any winds that blow.
Here in warm darkness of a night in June,
   While rhythmic pulses of the factory's flame

Lighted with sudden glare of red the gloom,
   And deepened long black shadows, children
     came
To watch the primrose blow. Silent they stood,
   Hand clasped in hand, in breathless hush
     around,
And saw her shyly doff her soft green hood
   And blossom—with a silken burst of sound."

This could hardly be better in its way, though we doubt that silken burst a little. There are four other sections of the book, called severally "Nature," "Love Songs," "Poems of Life," and "Verses of Children"; and from the first of these we take a picture which is simply perfect as far as it goes, and apparently goes as far as the painter meant:

"AUGUST WIND.

"The sharp wind cut a pathway through the cloud,
   And left a track of faintly shining blue;
The nun-like poplars swayed and bowed,
   And low the swallows flew.

"The sudden dust whirled up the stony road,
   And blurred the brightness of the golden-rod;
And ripening milkweed bent and sowed
   Winged seeds at every nod;

"Backward the maple tossed her feathery crown,
   Then flung her branches on the streaming air;
The brittle oak leaves, dry and brown,
   Rustled with break and tear.

"Each way-side weed was twisted like a thread;
   Then, suddenly, far up the pasture hill,
Quick as it came, the gust had fled,
   And all the fields were still."

II.

Among the other poems we found nothing that pleased us so much, and we found many things that pleased us less; we found some things that even fatigued us, particularly among the love poems. But everywhere we found, or seemed to find, among the faint and fainter echoes of an older time no reverberation of that music which has so long attuned all the tongues attempting to sing in English speech. For Mrs. Margaret Deland it is almost as if Tennyson had not lived; and his direct influence is so little felt in any of these volumes of verse that it might be said the only poet who now imitates Alfred Tennyson is Lord Tennyson. Twenty years ago, fifteen, ten, five years ago, this would have been very different. Then all young poets and many elderly poets shone more or less with his reflected light. Here and there one reflected Browning, one Emerson, one Longfellow, one Mrs. Browning; but it was Tennyson who glared or glimmered from most pages which honestly supposed themselves to be giving out a ray of their own. Now he seems at last to have paled from them; and a long literary period is closed in his evanescence. But, in fact, it is noticeable of these new poets that they do not take their color from any other master, and that whatever, much or little, is in them is their own. This is true not only of Mr. Cranch, of Miss Nora Perry, of Mrs. Celia Thaxter, and of Mrs. Akers Allen, who each contribute a volume to the collection, but of the names which are not yet fames. If the reader is disposed to take courage from this fact, we will not oppose him. It might very well mean that we have here a beginning as well as an end, and that these notes we hear are not only dying falls, but joyous preludings; there is a twilight of the morning as well as of the evening.

They are of rather uncertain direction, these essays in song, and of their common character it can be safely said only that it seems intensely subjective. Where the poets turn from their self-contemplation a moment, it is to see a picture and describe it, as in the poem last quoted, and in this from Miss Rachel Reynear's *Chansons du Matin:*

"NOVEMBER.

" I walked beside the quiet dike.
  The sunset's golden arms did strike
  And smite the waters smooth and bright
  Into a streak of flaming light
  That cleft November's landscape gray,
  A radiant line of parting day.

" Above the sunset's ruddy light
  One mournful star throbbed large and white.
  To eastward, 'gainst the leaden sky,
  The purple furnace flame flared high,
  And far o'er level marshes gray
  The cattle homeward wound their way.

" Against the sunset's golden breast
  A child with fagots hurried west,
  Against the orange sky outlined,
  Sharply each little limb defined.
  All things went home to warmth and light,
  And left the land to cold and night."

Here is probably an effect in literature of that great impulse toward graphic expression which has swayed all sensitive spirits during the last decade. The piece is one of the best of the *Chansons du Matin*, which are not so much songs as inspected emotions of one kind and another, with promise of better things hereafter, but with nothing else quite so entirely good for the present.

III.

Two other books of verse out of those before us are like this one in presenting their authors' thoughts about feeling rather than their feelings. Mr. Arlo Bates calls his poems *Berries of the Brier*, but is surpassed in titular humility by the nameless author of *The Heart of the Weed.* As a matter of fact there is nothing chance or wilding about either, and we should not have the courage to take them at their word, and treat them as sylvan growths. In both cases the poems have the effect which comes from cultivated and entire consciousness in an age when simplicity is impossible, and the air of it suggests affectation. Whatever else the reader questions in them, he will not question that the authors know what they are saying, and that they say it in verse because that seems the aptest instrument, and involves less waste of words than another.

A supreme instance of Mr. Bates's compression and distinctness offers itself in the little poem called

"RECOGNITION.

" Lover and mistress, sleeping side by side,
    Death smote at once; and in the outer air,
  Amazedly confronted, each to each,
    Their spirits stood, of all disguises bare.

" With sudden loathing stung, one spirit fled,
    Crying, 'Love turns to hate, if this be thou!'
  'Ah, stay!' the other wailed, in swift pursuit;
    'Thee I have never truly loved till now!'"

It seems to us that Mr. Bates has not attained anything so dramatic, so impersonal, so objective, at any other point. It is in these respects different from most of the other pieces in his book, and there are no others quite as finely wrought. If we wish to have poetry at all, we must be careful not to define it too illiberally, for then we shall end by denying ourselves a great deal that is beautiful. It was once said that poetry must be "simple, sensuous, passionate," but this was probably never entirely or solely true. Poetry may certainly now be complex, conscious, and intellectual. In fact, if it might not, we should not have had any poetry since Herrick, for ever since Herrick poetry has taken thought about itself, about its essence, its material, its form; and we do not believe that now it would be possible for any "genius," however "inspired" and "imaginative," to sit down and be simple, sensuous, and passionate. In fact, we doubt if poetry were ever so, not alone since Herrick, but since the poets learned to read and write. Chaucer probably knew what he was about, and probably "sweetest Shakespeare, fancy's child," as Milton patronizingly calls him (we should like to have heard what Shakespeare called Milton when he read it in Elysium), was quite well aware of himself in his work, though he keeps himself out of sight in it; Milton was unquestionably cultivated and conscious; Wordsworth was simple on principle; Keats was voluntarily sensuous; Mr. Swinburne is passionate of set purpose. All that we can fairly ask of a poet is that he shall express the æsthetic mood of his time, even if that mood is to travesty the mood of some other time. Just now, if he would be in sympathy with the contemporary refinement, he must be very perfect, under every apparent negligence, in form; he must be a little recondite in manner, but distinct and elect in diction; he must give his readers something to think about, and something to feel about. These virtues belong to the author of *The Heart of the Weed*, whose book is not sufficiently praised by saying that technically it is without comparison among the volumes of new verse. It is hard to give its range by example; but it is not unfairly characterized in the following sonnets, which express both its intellectualized spiritual fervor and its intense subjectivity. The reader will not fail to notice the literary perfection of the pieces:

"CAN THOSE ALONE BE SAVED?

" Can those alone be saved who *wish* aright?
  What if, with all our struggling, we are strong
  Only to keep our words and deeds from wrong,
  But over hopes and wishes have no might?

What if in dreams, like birds set free, at night,
Our thoughts sweep far afield, a joyous throng,
Toward that forbidden clime for which they long,
And harsh the waking in the wintry light?

"Hast Thou no mercy, Lord, for such as these,
Poor shivering souls who shrink, yet bear their
  lot;
Who stand upon temptation's edge and freeze,
With ne'er a cloak to hide their nakedness?
Share Thy cloak with them, Lord, and stoop to
  bless
Those who have loved Thee though they knew
  it not!"

"RETURN.

"Here on the steps I sit as long ago.
Some little change there seems; the vine its leaves
O'erhead flings broader, thicker darkness weaves,
And heavier branches sweep the path below;
While from its fragrant shade I watch the slow,
Long shadows of the elm creep o'er the grass,
And hear the tinkling cow-bells as they pass,
Like one who dreams but neither joys nor grieves.
"And still the same, but yet the same no more,
As when a girl I looked on through the years.
Some hopes I see fulfilled, and, ah! some fears,
Since last I sat in this familiar door.
I would not be a girl again, and yet
With sudden tears my folded hands are wet!"

There is a thrill of contagious pathos in the
last two lines; and in the book the reader
will find other things to move him as well as
stay him. What we have been trying to say
about it is that the heart of the weed has in
this instance got itself out on paper through
the head of a flower that has had the advantages of careful cultivation, and is none the
worse, but all the better, for it. No one can
pass it with indifference, after even a careless
glance. It arrests and interests by qualities
which are neither common nor trite.

IV.

It would be interesting to know how these
little books would affect an ingenuous and
intelligent youth; but probably he could not
tell if he read them. What one feels more
and more, as he grows older, is that the
new poetry does not seem to be made for
him; and he suspects a charm and virtue in
it that do not reach his soul through his
toughened sensibilities. Very likely they are
not in it, but he finds it to the advantage of
his spiritual health to imagine them there; and
he hopes to acquire merit by supposing that
some one else may feel them. It is certainly
not always easy to read this new poetry; but
honestly, between one and one's self, was poetry ever very easy reading? It is doubtless
easiest when read aloud to a person of the
other sex; then it is charming, if the person
of the other sex is charming; and it has its
attractions even when read aloud to a group
of attractive persons of the other sex. Or two
young men may read it together when they are
both in love, and in like manner two young girls.
But in one's closet (as one's room is called in
poetry, not the real closet where one's clothes
hang), in the solitude of one's chamber, would
not one far rather have a good novel, if he
wished to be either pleased or edified? This
is a very bold question, and it requires all our
hardihood to put it; but sooner or later some
one must ask it, for poetry is gradually changing its whole relation to life, which it no
longer depicts or expresses in the old way. It
no longer even represents literature, as it once
did. In the beginnings of modern literature

the mere poetic form was enough; metre and
rhyme meant scholarship, and men were
amazed, as children now are, at people who
could make them. Afterward thought and
feeling were demanded as well as metre and
rhyme; then elegance, then beauty, and beauty
more and more. There was a time when history was told in verse, and in the epics there
was a good deal of fact as well as fiction. In
our day *Aurora Leigh* and *Lucille* were at-[1,2]
tempts to give the poetic form to novels, and
the epic may be said to have expired in them;
their success ended the long tradition. The
pastoral was dead long ago, dead the satire,
dead the metrical drama. The tale in verse
ceased with Tennyson's Idyls, and his own and
other people's imitations of them. What we
have left is the essay, descriptive or subjective;
the sonnet, uttering in elaborate form a single
thought or emotion; the lyrical anecdote, the
lyrical conundrum, the lyrical picture, and the
lyrical cry or outburst. To this last the metrical shape still seems essential; it sings and
it pleases; but that it is really essential we do
not think any reader of Tourguénief's Poems
in Prose will maintain. Nevertheless it has
yet an undeniable value, though it can no
longer impart this value to thoughts in themselves poor and slight; and it is proof of the
intellectual and emotional merit of much in
this group of books that the charm seems inherent in the thought rather than the form.

V.

What charms us in Mr. Cranch's volume is
the gentle feeling which, with its pensive cast,
is still generous if not enthusiastic. Mr.
Cranch has been too long known to the public to need any special celebration of his qualities now: his sincere sympathy with nature,
his elevated conception of humanity, the aerial
touch of his humor, his constant faith, his vein
of clear and quiet thoughtfulness. All these
appear in the present book, ripened to much
of the exquisiteness which Longfellow's latest
verse attained, and moving the reader by like
simplicity of means and attitude, the same soft
dignity of mind, the same tranquil courage of
soul. In both cases it is the wisdom which
years alone can bring, looking at life serenely
and kindly, and claiming for its vision nothing transcendent or supernal. Without
quoting more largely than we may, we cannot
illustrate this fully; but if the reader will
turn to many of the sonnets in the book, and
to such poems as "After Life," "The Survival
of the Fittest," and "A Word to the Philosophers," he will understand what we intend.
In the mean time here is a little summer piece,
a picture painted with the feeling characteristic of an artist who is equally skilled with
pencil and with pen.

"AUGUST.

"Far off among the fields and meadow rills
The August noon bends o'er a world of green.
In the blue sky the white clouds pause and lean
To paint broad shadows on the wooded hills
And upland farms. A brooding silence fills
The languid hours. No living forms are seen
Save birds and insects. Here and there, between
The broad boughs and the grass, the locust trills
Unseen his long-drawn, slumberous monotone.
The sparrow and the lonely phœbe-bird,
Now near, now far, across the fields are heard;
And close beside me here that Spanish drone,
The dancing grasshopper, whom no care frets,
In the hot sunshine snaps his castanets."

Another mood of the poet's, equally characteristic in its smiling pensiveness, is reflected in these verses:

"TWO VIEWS OF IT.

"Before the daybreak, in the murky night,
My chanticleer, half dreaming, sees the light
Stream from my window on his perch below,
And taking it for dawn, he needs must crow.

"Wakeful and sad, I shut my eyes, and smile
To think my lonely vigil should beguile
The silly fowl. Alas! I find no ray,
Within my lamp or heart, of dawning day."

VI.

Almost the best thing in Mrs. Allen's volume is the last thing, which she calls

"ONE OF THREE.

"'I am not quite alone,' she said;
'I have fair daughters three:
And one is dead, and one is wed,
And one remains with me.

"'Awhile I watch, with tenderest care,
Her growth from child to maid,
And plait her fair and shining hair—
A long and golden braid—

"'(Ah! sweet the bloom upon the grape
Before it leaves the vine)—
And deck and drape her dainty shape
With garments soft and fine,

"'And keep her sacred and apart
Until some stranger's plea,
With flattering art, shall win her heart
Away from home and me,

"'Leaving her childhood's home and me
Forgotten and bereft;
Then there will be, of all my three,
Only the dead one left.

"'Why count the dead as lost? Ah me!
I keep my dead alone;
For only she, of all the three,
Will always be my own.

"'She will not slight, at morn or eve,
The old love for the new:
The living leave our hearts to grieve—
The dead are always true.'"

This suggests something of the author's quality, and it indicates the never-failing artistic grace of her work. That may always be taken for granted in what she does, and in what Mrs. Thaxter does, and what Miss Perry does. These writers have each given proof of the genuine feeling and the limpid thoughtfulness which, without being otherwise alike, they all have in common. Each has long been a distinct voice in our literature—so long that there is a chance it may not be valued aright, or valued so much as if it had not been heard before. Miss Perry interprets the moods and young ideals, the flushes and fine thrills, of girlhood as no one else has

done; to Mrs. Thaxter we owe a friendship with wild and strange aspects of nature, first touched in her verse with intimate love and knowledge; Mrs. Allen imparts the charm of a spirit, kindly human and finite, which shrinks within the safe bounds of reality, and dreamily conjectures of the secrets and wonders beyond; and each does much more than this. Their work no longer surprises, as it must if it came to us with an unknown name; but it is still admirable, and it continues the tradition of a waning period with a sweetness which will not let us forget how much it has been to the world.

VII.

Lord Tennyson might be hastily supposed to be trying to make us think it had been, or ought to have been, very little, in his echo of "Locksley Hall Sixty Years After." But it seems to us that his attitude in the poem has been misconceived, and that he has been thought to express a personal pessimism, when the poem was largely dramatic. As a poem it is very good in parts, better than its young readers, who have not lived long enough to regret their passions and prejudices, can know. It breathes the wisdom and the humility of age, as well as its foreboding and despair; if it judges the world harshly and hopelessly, it confesses and forgives with touching meekness the error and the loss of first love. For these virtues the imagined speaker may be allowed to fling about him somewhat crazily; to find all going wrong, as old men do, and to rail at the age as if God had made a mistake in letting it come to pass. We have heard a young philosopher, one of the new school abhorred by such old men for their desire to look facts in the face and try to see what they mean, declare that years need not always bring this despair; that the day may come when men instead of setting up some little ideal of æsthetics, or morals, or society, which must inevitably topple over in time, will regard each new development of seeming good or seeming ill as part of a design not inadvisedly conceived, and inevitably working from everlasting to everlasting; and that they will then not be shocked, but interested and eager for the next turn of affairs. If the hero of "Locksley Hall" were living in the possible future of this hopeful evolutionist, he would probably not scream at "author, atheist, essayist, novelist, realist," for being true to their knowledge of human nature, and would regard "the maiden fancies wallowing in the troughs of Zolaism" as perhaps no more dangerously employed than in conjecturing the precise character and experiences of such ladies as Vivien and Guinevere, Ettarre and Isolde.

---

[1] *Aurora Leigh*, by Elizabeth Barrett Browning.

[2] *Lucille* should read *Lucile*, by Edward Bulwer-Lytton.

April, 1887

Editor's Study.

I.

IT must have been a passage from Vernon Lee's *Baldwin*, claiming for the novel an indefinitely vast and subtle influence on modern character, which provoked the following suggestive letter from one of our readers:

"——, —— Co., Md., *Sept.* 18, 1886.

"Dear Sir,—With regard to article IV. in the Editor's Study in the September *Harper*, allow me to say that I have very grave doubts as to the whole list of magnificent things that you seem to think novels have done for the race, and can witness in myself many evil things which they have done for me. Whatever in my mental make-up is wild and visionary, whatever is untrue, whatever is injurious, I can trace to the perusal of some work of fiction. Worse than that, they beget such high-strung and supersensitive ideas of life that plain industry and plodding perseverance are despised, and matter-of-fact poverty, or every-day, commonplace distress, meets with no sympathy, if indeed noticed at all, by one who has wept over the impossibly accumulated sufferings of some gaudy hero or heroine.[1]

"Hoping you will pardon the liberty I have taken in addressing you, I remain,

"Most respectfully yours, —— ——."

We are not sure that we have the controversy with the writer which he seems to suppose, and we should perhaps freely[2] grant the mischievous effects which he says novel-reading has wrought upon him, if we were not afraid that he had possibly reviewed his own experience with something of the inaccuracy we find in his report of our opinions. By his confession he is himself proof that Vernon Lee is right in saying, "The modern human being has been largely fashioned by those who have written about him, and most of all by the novelist," and there is nothing in what he urges to conflict with her claim that "the chief use of the novel" is "to make the shrewd and tolerant a little less shrewd and tolerant, and to make the generous and austere a little more skeptical and easy-going." If he will look more closely at these postulates, we think he will see that in the one she deals with the effect of the novel in the past, and in the other with its duty in the future. We still think that there "is sense if not final wisdom" in what she says, and we are quite willing to acknowledge something of each in our correspondent.

But novels are now so fully accepted by every one pretending to cultivated taste—and they really form the whole intellectual life of such immense numbers of people, without question of their influence, good or bad, upon the mind—that it is refreshing to have them frankly denounced, and to be invited to revise one's ideas and feelings in regard to them. A little honesty, or a great deal of honesty, in this quest will do the novel, as we hope yet to have it, and as we have already begun to have it, no harm; and for our own part we will confess that we believe fiction in the past to have been largely injurious, as we believe the stage play to be still almost wholly injurious, through its falsehood, its folly, its wantonness, and its aimlessness. It may be safely assumed that most of the novel-reading which people fancy is an intellectual pastime is the emptiest dissipation, hardly more related to thought or the wholesome exercise of the mental faculties than opium-eating; in either case the brain is drugged, and left weaker and crazier for the debauch. If this may be called the negative result of the fiction habit, the positive injury that most novels work is by no means so easily to be measured in the case of young men whose character they help so much to form or deform, and the women of all ages whom they keep so much in ignorance of the world they misrepresent. Grown men have little harm from them, but in the other cases, which are the vast majority, they hurt because they are not true—not because they are malevolent, but because they are idle lies about human nature and the social fabric, which it behooves us to know and to understand, that we may deal justly with ourselves and with one another. One need not go so far as our correspondent, and trace to the fiction habit "whatever is wild and visionary, whatever is untrue, whatever is injurious," in one's life; bad as the fiction habit is, it is probably not responsible for the whole sum of evil in its victims, and we believe that if the reader will use care in choosing from this fungus-growth with which the fields of literature teem every day, he may nourish himself as with the true mushroom, at no risk from the poisonous species.

The tests are very plain and simple, and they are perfectly infallible. If a novel flatters the passions, and exalts them above the principles, it is poisonous; it may not kill, but it will certainly injure; and this test will alone exclude an entire class of fiction, of which eminent examples will occur to all. Then the whole spawn of so-called un-moral romances, which imagine a world where the sins of sense are unvisited by the penalties following, swift or slow, but inexorably sure, in the real world, are deadly poison: these do kill. The novels that merely tickle our prejudices and lull our judgment, or that coddle our sensibilities, or pamper our gross appetite for the marvellous, are not so fatal, but they are innutritious, and clog the soul with unwholesome vapors of all kinds. No doubt they too help to weaken the mental fibre, and make their readers indifferent to "plodding perseverance and plain industry," and to "matter-of-fact poverty and commonplace distress."

Without taking them too seriously, it still must be owned that the "gaudy hero and heroine" are to blame for a great deal of harm in the world. That heroine long taught by example, if not precept, that Love, or the passion or fancy she mistook for it, was the chief interest of a life which is really concerned with a great many other things; that it was lasting in the way she knew it; that it was worthy of every sacrifice, and was altogether a finer thing than prudence, obedience, reason; that love alone was glorious and beautiful, and these were mean and ugly in comparison with it. More lately she has begun to idolize and illustrate Duty, and she is hardly less mischievous in this new rôle, opposing duty, as she did love, to prudence, obedience, and reason. The stock hero, whom, if we met him, we could not fail to see was a most deplorable person, has undoubtedly imposed himself upon the victims of the fiction habit as admirable. With him, too, love was and is the great affair, whether in its old romantic phase of chivalrous achievement or manifold suffering for love's sake, or its more recent development of the "virile," the bullying, and the brutal, or its still more recent agonies of self-sacrifice, as idle and useless as the moral experiences of the insane asylums. With his vain posturings and his ridiculous splendor he is really a painted barbarian, the prey of his passions and his delusions, full of obsolete ideals, and the motives and ethics of a savage, which the guilty author of his being does his best—or his worst —in spite of his own light and knowledge, to foist upon the reader as something generous and noble. We are not merely bringing this charge against that sort of fiction which is beneath literature and outside of it, "the shoreless lakes of ditch-water," whose miasms fill the air below the empyrean where the great ones sit; but we are accusing the work of some of the most famous, who have, in this instance or in that, sinned against the truth, which can alone exalt and purify men. We do not say that they have constantly done so, or even commonly done so; but that they have done so at all marks them as of the past, to be read with the due historical allowance for their epoch and their conditions. For we believe that, while inferior writers will and must continue to imitate them in their foibles and their errors, no one hereafter will be able to achieve greatness who is false to humanity, either in its facts or its duties. The light of civilization has already broken even upon the novel, and no conscientious man can now set about painting an image of life without perpetual question of the verity of his work, and without feeling bound to distinguish so clearly that no reader of his may be misled, between what is right and what is wrong, what is noble and what is base, what is health and what is perdition, in the actions and the characters he portrays.

The fiction that aims merely to entertain— the fiction that is to serious fiction as the opéra bouffe, the ballet, and the pantomime are to the true drama—need not feel the burden of this obligation so deeply; but even such fiction will not be gay or trivial to any reader's hurt, and criticism will hold it to account if it passes from painting to teaching folly.

More and more not only the criticism which prints its opinions, but the infinitely vaster and powerfuler criticism which thinks and feels them merely, will make this demand. For our own part we confess that we do not care to judge any work of the imagination without first of all applying this test to it. We must ask ourselves before we ask anything else, Is it true?—true to the motives, the impulses, the principles that shape the life of actual men and women? This truth, which necessarily includes the highest morality and the highest artistry—this truth given, the book *cannot* be wicked and cannot be weak; and without it all graces of style and feats of invention and cunning of construction are so many superfluities of naughtiness. It is well for the truth to have all these, and shine in them, but for falsehood they are merely meretricious, the bedizenment of the wanton; they atone for nothing, they count for nothing. But in fact they come naturally of truth, and grace it without solicitation; they are added unto it. In the whole range of fiction we know of no *true* picture of life—that is, of human nature— which is not also a masterpiece of literature, full of divine and natural beauty. It may have no touch or tint of this special civilization or of that; it had *better* have this local color well ascertained; but the truth is deeper and finer than aspects, and if the book is true to what men and women know of one another's souls it will be true enough, and it will be great and beautiful. It is the conception of literature as something apart from life, superfinely aloof, which makes it really unimportant to the great mass of mankind, without a message or a meaning for them; and it is the notion that a novel may be false in its portrayal of causes and effects that makes literary art contemptible even to those whom it amuses, that forbids them to regard the novelist as a serious or right-minded person. If they do not in some moment of indignation cry out against all novels, as our correspondent does, they remain besotted in the fume of the delusions purveyed to them, with no higher feeling for the author than such maudlin affection as the *habitué* of an opium-joint perhaps knows for the attendant who fills his pipe with the drug.

II.

Or, as in the case of another correspondent of the Study, who writes that in his youth he "read a great many novels, but always regarded it as an amusement, like horse-racing and card-playing," for which he had no time when he entered upon the serious business of life, it renders them merely contemptuous. His view of the matter may be commended to the brotherhood and sisterhood of novelists as full of wholesome if bitter suggestion; and we urge them not to dismiss it with high literary scorn as that of some Bœotian dull to the beauty of art. Refuse it as we may, it is still the feeling of the vast majority of people for whom life is earnest, and who find only a distorted and misleading likeness of it in our books. We may fold ourselves in our scholars' gowns, and close the doors of our studies, and affect to despise this rude voice; but we cannot shut it out. It comes to us from wherever men are at work, from wherever they are truly living, and accuses us of unfaithfulness, of triviality, of mere stage-play; and none of us can escape conviction except he prove himself worthy of his time—a time in which the great masters have brought literature back to life, and filled its ebbing veins with the red tides of reality. We cannot all equal them; we need not copy them; but we can all go to the sources of their inspiration and their power; and to draw from these no one need go far—no one need really to go out of himself.

Fifty years ago, Carlyle, in whom the truth was always alive, but in whom it was then unperverted by suffering, by celebrity and despair, wrote in his study of Diderot: "Were it not reasonable to prophesy that this exceeding great multitude of novel-writers and such like must, in a new generation, gradually do one of two things: either retire into the nurseries, and work for children, minors, and semi-fatuous persons of both sexes, or else, what were far better, sweep their novel-fabric into the dust-cart, and betake themselves with such faculty as they have to understand and record what is true, of which surely there is, and will forever be, a whole infinitude unknown to us of infinite importance to us? Poetry, it will more and more come to be understood, is nothing but higher knowledge; and the only genuine Romance (for grown persons), Reality."

If after half a century fiction still mainly works for "children, minors, and semi-fatuous persons of both sexes," it is nevertheless one of the hopefulest signs of the world's progress that it has begun to work for "grown persons," and if not exactly in the way that Carlyle might have solely intended in urging its writers to compile memoirs instead of building the "novel-fabric," still it has in the highest and widest sense already made Reality its Romance. We cannot judge it, we do not even care for it, except as it has done this; and we cannot conceive of a literary self-respect in these days compatible with the old trade of make-believe, with the production of the kind of fiction which is too much honored by classification with card-playing and horse-racing.

III.

That fiction has made a good beginning in the right direction, as we have always said in the Study's darkest moods, we see fresh evidence in the group of novels which have accumulated during the last two or three months on our table. They are not the only novels, of course, which have been published within this period, but they fairly represent the American activity in that industry, and we think, upon the whole, the showing that they make for us is one that we need not be ashamed of in any general competition. When Mr. Henry James contributes a work to this *concours*, only Zola, or Daudet, or Tolstoï, or Thomas Hardy, can dispute the first prize with him; and when she who signs Charles Egbert Craddock gives us a book, it is sure to have certain traits of mastery beyond that of any other woman now writing. Her power of realizing the rough, native types with which she deals is known to all readers, as well as that subtlety by which she discerns the core of sweetness and goodness that is in them. They have so much in common, however, that every one may not recognize the skill with which she differentiates the types into characters, with the same mixture of motives which we find in the world. Her new book, *In the Clouds*, shows an advance in this over her former work, and we are not without hope that she will yet wholly escape from romantic ideals. It is much that in this book the hero dies *accidentally* in trying to save the man he hates; in an earlier book he would have died intentionally. To be sure, the heroine, the beautiful, bewildered, faithful, loving, fearless Alethea, with that quaint and fleeting charm which we have learned to know in her and her sister heroines, goes quietly mad, in the pathetic and attractive guise which insanity so often assumes in fiction. But we do not greatly object to this: young girls involved in such tragical coils do sometimes really go mad, though more commonly they marry after a time, and bring up families of children. A truer character than either of these is the country lawyer Harshaw, who is ascertained with extraordinary accuracy, and who lives in mind and person before us. He is the great figure of the book, though the pessimistic young legislator Kinsard, and Judge Gwinnan, who tried and sentenced Alethea's lover, and vaguely loved her himself, are both successful in a direction beyond the range that the author's stories usually take; they are both a little overcharged, and Kinsard's exits and entrances are managed with too much of the old romantic machinery. But the various groups in the mountaineers' cabins and moonshiners' caves, in the country court-room and the "settlemint" groceries, as well as in the mirrored vestibules of the Nashville hotels and the marble halls of legislation, are forcibly and faithfully done; and there is the love, intense and true, if too self-indulgent, of the scenes through which most of the figures move; the landscape is so marvellously painted that we can forgive its being a little painty. Some day, and not long hence, we believe that this gifted author will address herself yet more modernly to her work, and give us her mountain folk as she saw them before her fancy began to work upon them.

The value which fidelity to local circumstance can give is felt in a book which comes to us from Indianapolis, where it seems to have been written, as well as printed and published, with no apparent consciousness of different shades of civilization elsewhere. This is a great point gained for the author at the outset, for she is not tempted to patronize, to satirize, or to defend her characters, and the effect of verisimilitude from her simple directness is very great. Her problem, or theme, is largely, if not mainly, heredity, and she studies it in the family of a well-to-do farmer in central Indiana, emigrants from Virginia, as many of the settlers of that country were, and of sufficiently good blood, as those things go with us. The eldest son has been an army surgeon; in the South he married the daughter of a refugee planter, who proved to be a natural daughter by a slave mother; but before the story opens she dies, with her second child, whose reversion to the negro type reveals the truth of her origin to its father. She dies forgiven, with the secret in the keeping of her husband's family, leaving him a daughter whom it is his perpetual care to keep from knowing it.

The second son marries, for her money, a pretty slattern whom he does not love, and goes from bad to worse in his marriage and his business, till he runs away with his wife's seamstress, and gets a divorce further West, and marries her; his brother pays his debts, and all his family share his shame. So far so good, from an artistic point of view; but then follow lamentable passages of stage sentiment and stage incident. Yet even in these there is a truth to character and conditions that goes far to console the reader. It seems sometimes almost a helpless truth, and always quite an artless truth. The book is not "literature" in the conventional sense at all, perhaps; it is crude, and in a certain way common, if you will; but its people live in a living community; you do not mistake them one for another; and there is a sense of the physical conditions about them. The plain rich farm-house amidst its trees and harvests; the bustling little country town; the winter in Indianapolis when the husband of one of the daughters goes to the Legislature there—all this is so much better than "literature" that any one who reads *The Chamber over the Gate* will wish to see whatever Margaret Holmes may write hereafter. Her question of heredity solves itself with regard to the slave mother's child too melodramatically, too helplessly; but with regard to Hugh Gatsimer—the bad Gatsimer—it is interesting to find that his egotism is from that quiet self-will and self-love of his mother, who appears in a striking light as his champion and apologist in all his iniquities.

Another book, and again by a woman, deals again with the same question, in the intensely touching little story called *Towards the Gulf.* Again, too, there is a marriage with the descendant of a slave. The wife was born in England, and is as ignorant as her husband of her own origin; but the scene is in New Orleans and the Louisiana country, amid landscapes and figures with which Mr. Cable's magic has familiarized us. We will leave to the book its secret of how the truth became known to both husband and wife—an ineffaceable stain in his thought, and death to her. Their child lives, and the father lives to see in him the development of the traits of negroes and slaves—the tender affection, the light-hearted amiability, of the race, the furtive slyness of the servile caste. The little creature experiences his father's aversion, and begins to know the persecution of the world, which taunts him through his playmates, "*To bien habi, mais to negr' quand même,*" and then a merciful accident snatches him from both. The story is told with abundance of local color, and it is immensely pathetic.

There is no want of cleverness in any of the books on our list, but much of the cleverness is as deplorable as the costly decoration of a house of reeds would be; for the stories are not founded in human nature. One cannot, without great regret, see so brilliant a writer as the author of *Sons and Daughters* going so far about to get away from knowledge in the motives which actuate her people; they marry as people do on the stage, and love

and unlove as fantastically as the characters of Mr. Gilbert's burlesques; only, this author treats them seriously. The intrigue of Miss H. W. Preston's *Year in Eden* represents nothing representative in our life; the interest does not pass from the characters to the reader; their actions and their experiences do not implicate him; the obvious literary skill of the book is wasted. The author of *Constance of Acadia*, which we liked so much, toys quite as effectlessly with an incident of the Old Colony history in *Agatha and the Shadow,* withdrawing it from human sympathy in the mists of revery.

It is a waste of undoubted literary power; and Miss Charlotte Dunning is in danger of flinging still more away in her very well written story of *A Step Aside.* In this the wholesome atmosphere of reality in which the story moves, with its perfectly imaginable people, is vitiated by the attempt to have us believe that the hero could be a good fellow and yet steal in order to make a home for his affianced. There is commendable study of local conditions and local figures; it is actually New York where it all takes place, and the people are New-Yorkers of the various degrees of adoption—nobody, as is well known, being a born New-Yorker. The pretty little heroine is a very probable little heroine, and her lover is a flesh-and-blood lover, and they behave very naturally together till their ordeal comes, when they instantly turn into *dramatis personæ.* Mr. H. C. Bunner, with equal love for his city, studies another aspect of her multiform life in his *Midge.* He makes us pleasantly acquainted with the French quarter, and most of his persons are of one Latin race or another. But Midge, tiny morsel as she is, is too much; and in the characters generally the author abandons himself in regrettable degree to queerness and quaintness and picturesqueness. It is a clever pen, and it is a pity that the author should prefer to let it dwell upon the old *habitués* of fiction, in whatever new disguise, instead of the unhackneyed people, whom he gives, as it were, only a curb-stone ticket, like that delightful old priest of his, and the Secretary of the French Benevolent Society, and the Goubauds, and all the subordinate French and Italians of the story. Parts of the general study are extremely good, as, for example, the observation of the fact that the people of the French quarter should think evil of Dr. Peters's innocent relation to Midge, and yet not think evil of them for it. With all their imperfections both Mr. Bunner's book and Miss Dunning's are of the character of literary events: they achieve and they promise; they help, with Sidney Luska's work, to mark the beginning of something worth while, something new in New York.

IV.

The romantic machinery with which Mr. W. H. Bishop operates his story of *The Golden Justice* is as little obtrusive as machinery can be; and one can, by a slight inattention, quite ignore it. The interest of the tale, the life-like variety of motive and uncertainty of action in the persons, and, above all, the graphic effectiveness with which the whole aspect of a local civilization is painted, give most uncommon value to the book. As a study of a prosperous Western city, this picture of Keewaydin is unique in our literature; it is so sufficient that, lost in the movement of the social and commercial and political life in the streets and houses of Keewaydin, one forgets about the machinery, except for a vague discomfort, till, by-and-by, he comes back to its pivotal fact with an "Oh yes! that MS. in the Golden Justice!" The MS. was put there by the great citizen David Lane, when the statue was placed on top of the court-house; it is his confession of a sudden act of passion by which he unwittingly and involuntarily becomes the means of destroying a man's life; and the question is when it shall be found out, and yet not keep the son of his victim from marrying the homicide's daughter. That longing for atonement and expiation which Lane's confession represents, and that fearful hope of accidental detection which prompts its concealment, are very natural impulses of the complex heart of man; and Mr. Bishop has made us feel their poignancy with the sensibility and power of a true artist. Though he has chosen to follow tradition, to honor picturesqueness, and appeal to romance in working out the truth, he shall have sorrow and not anger from us; he is still a truthful observer and most conscientious reporter, and aside from the mere mechanism of his story, is thoroughly modern. The variety of figures moving through it; the sharply shown, delicately accented variety of social phases at Keewaydin; the business forces glimpsed at in their activity; the local politics so humorously studied in their manipulation by the men inside them; the delicious impudence of the local journalism; the corruption of the American leaders, and the easy, innocent corruptibility of the Bohemian and Polish voters; the scenes and characters drawn from these aliens, so characteristic of the West; even the love-making of the hero and heroine where it is not touched by the petrifying romance, and all the other love-making and flirting—are traits of mastery which cannot leave any critic doubtful of Mr. Bishop's power.

We find no fault with Mr. Henry James's *Princess Casamassima*: it is a great novel; it is his greatest, and it is incomparably the greatest novel of the year in our language. It has to do with socialism and the question of richer and poorer, which grows ever more burning in our day, and the scene is contemporary London. Its people are the types which the vast range of London life affords, and they are drawn not only from the highest and the lowest, but from the intermediate classes, who are so much more difficult to take alive. The Princess Casamassima is our old acquaintance Miss Light, of *Roderick Hudson* fame, come with her beauty and splendor to forget her hated husband in semi-sincere sympathy with the London socialists, and semi-personal love-making with two of the handsomest. The hero is the little, morbid, manly, æsthetic

bookbinder Hyacinth Robinson, son of an English lord and a French girl, who kills her betrayer. For the climax, Robinson, remembering his mother, kills himself—inevitably, not exemplarily—rather than shoot the political enemy whom the socialists have devoted to death at his hand. A striking figure is the plain, good, simple, romantic Lady Aurora, who goes about among the poor, and loves the tough-hearted chemist's assistant, Paul Muniment, and devotes herself to his sister, the unconsciously selfish little cripple. Another is Pynsent, the old dress-maker, who has brought Robinson up, and who lives and dies in awe of him as an offshoot of the aristocracy; another is Captain Sholto, the big, handsome, aimless swell, *dilettante* socialist, and hopeless lover of the Princess; another the Prince, with his passion for his wife and his coarse primitive jealousy of her; others yet are the real socialists—English, French, and German; and the ferment of the ideals and interests of all these is the story. From first to last we find no weakness in the book; the drama works simply and naturally; the causes and effects are logically related; the theme is made literature without ceasing to be life. There is an easy breadth of view and a generous scope which recall the best Russian work; and there is a sympathy for the suffering and aspiration in the book which should be apparent even to the critical groundlings, though Mr. James forbears, as ever, to pat his people on the back, to weep upon their necks, or to caress them with endearing and compassionate epithets and pet names. A mighty good figure, which we had almost failed to speak of, is the great handsome shop-girl Millicent Henning, in whose vulgar good sense and vulgar good heart the troubled soul of Hyacinth Robinson finds what little repose it knows.

Mr. James's knowledge of London is one of the things that strike the reader most vividly, but the management of his knowledge is vastly more important. If any one would see plainly the difference between the novelist's work and the partisan's work, let him compare *The Princess Casamassima* and Mr. W. H. Mallock's last tract, which he calls *The Old Order Changes*, and which also deals with socialism. No one can read it and deny Mr. Mallock's extraordinary cleverness, or its futility. His people are apparently real people till he gets them into his book, and then they turn into stalking-horses for his opinions, those who would naturally disagree with him coming helplessly forward to be overthrown by those wonderful Roman Catholics of his—so very, very fine; so very, very wise; so very, very rich; so very, very good; so very, very proud and well-born. We have some glimpses of an American girl, who seems at first a reality; but she ends by turning into an impossibility to oblige the author.

---

[1] Criticism and Fiction, pp. 92-93.

[2] Criticism and Fiction, p. 93.

[3] Criticism and Fiction, pp. 93-104.

May, 1887

Editor's Study.

I.

THE most important of the *Early Letters of Thomas Carlyle*, edited by Professor Charles Eliot Norton, are those that passed between him and the remarkable woman who became his wife. All the letters are in the interest of a kindlier view of Carlyle's character than that we get through Mr. Froude's life of him. They will not radically change the impression which this left, perhaps; but we think that the reader who has lived long enough to have learned for himself that the kindlier view of any man is apt to be the truer view will feel from them that this is peculiarly the case with Carlyle. In this conclusion he will not lack the help of very trenchant criticisms upon Mr. Froude's errors by Mr. Norton; in notes throughout the volumes, in a preface to the first, and in an appendix at the close of the second, the editor follows these so searchingly that one feels the need of gathering his dispersed compassion up for a kindlier view of Mr. Froude. He had a difficult task, and he does not seem really to have performed it with much discretion or accuracy; and yet, supplemented by the censures and the editorial labors of Mr. Norton, his book will always have a great value: a value hardly second to that of Boswell's life of Johnson. By his sins of commission—by the things which Mr. Norton believes he ought to have withheld, the intimate things, the sacred things—the world, which likes to rush in where angels fear to tread, has profited so far as such a world may; at least it has got a glut of one great man in all those relations and aspects from which more scrupulous biography withholds him. By Mr. Froude's sins of omission it need not suffer if it will read Mr. Norton's comments and contributions; and without reading these it clearly ought not to read Mr. Froude's book at all. They are so interesting a part of the whole truth that we could wish Mr. Froude the courage to embody them in his future editions; that would be a fine atonement, the only possible atonement; otherwise they must always accuse him of inattention, of indifference, of indelicacy, of callousness, even of rancor. Even then they might accuse him, but literature would then show that he had done what he could to right the wrongs they dwell on.

In the letters which they introduce, and which cover the period of Carlyle's life from the time he left home, early in the century, to that of his marriage, eighteen years later, we see him much the same Carlyle we knew already, but in a softer light. Between the harsh rugosities of his face we read a tenderness, a quivering sensibility, a strongly loving faithfulness, an impassioned affection; in the fierce, suffering eyes hovers a near relenting and humor. His young-men friends are dear to him; he writes them long, full letters brimming with himself and his regard for them; but it is upon father and mother, sisters and brothers, that he pours out his whole heart. He did love most fervently and constantly, root, trunk, and branch, flower and fruit and thorn, that tough peasant stock from which he sprang; and one cannot read without pathos and deep respect the letters to and from that poor, simple, honest, strong-headed, right-hearted home of his which is everywhere glimpsed in them. It is not an ideal or an idyllic picture at any time; there is plenty of British fussiness about details of health and personal concerns: the new socks and the mended old socks figure, along with a mother's interest for the son's soul; the carrier's remissness, and the hope that the mother will like the gift of the new hat, blend inextricably with the son's sweet and manly love, and his anxiety for her welfare; the cultivation of letters and the land, criticism and crops, intermingle in the missives to the men-folk on the farm at home. In short, and very thoroughly, all the Carlyles, including the greatest, were what vulgar people call "commonplace people," and their plain, wholesome, unromantic life is vividly, however fragmentarily, pictured in these letters. The high thinking that went along with the hard living, practised equally at Edinburgh and Ecclefechan, finds an expression in them as yet untainted by German idioms and wilful idiosyncrasies of speech; the style is clear, straight, and strong; and the perceptions of truth are not yet curdled into theories. There is abundant promise of the future Carlyle in them: the independence and the arrogance, the honesty and the bitterness, the true tender sympathy and the strong prejudice, the respect for right, the contempt for most men, the adoration of great power for good, and the inability to abhor great power of any kind—all the strange mixture of qualities which issued in tolerably disrespectful worship of the various military, political, theological, and literary mortals whom he vainly spent his great gifts in painting as heroes.

II.

The letters to Miss Welsh, replying to certain things in hers, dispose pretty effectually of the superstition that she married Carlyle while heart-broken for Irving. A girl who frankly owns to her lover that she once loved another man, but shows herself so far recovered from her first passion that she can make fun of her idol, is not a figure on which even sentimentality can waste many sighs;

and whatever was their influence upon each other in after-life, there can be no doubt for the reader of these letters that at the time they were written Carlyle's effect upon Jane Welsh's mind was altogether wholesome. They are rich in the proofs of his admiration for her brilliancy and versatility, but they are also full of warning and counsel for her against the exaggerations of her sensibility, her excesses of emotion, her intellectual exaltations, her perfervid ideals. She must have been a fascinating girl, but one sees that she had an immense capacity for unhappiness, with or without cause. She and Carlyle read the same books, and wrote to each other about them; he directed her reading somewhat, but he uses her with flattering deference as a mind equally clear and apt with himself. They tried treating some subjects poetically together, and he has some very wise words to her about poetry, and the potentialities of all in that sort, and the actualities of the few. Later she gets befogged and saddened with the calamities of authors, as Disraeli assembled them, and then Carlyle breaks out in a blaze of common-sense, which is perhaps the most luminous expression upon a matter that silly people have maundered so much about.

"I wish I had not sent you this great blubbering numbskull Disraeli.... Do you not see that his observations can apply only to men in whom genius was more the want of common qualities than the possession of uncommon ones, whose life was embittered not so much because they had imagination and sensibility as because they had not prudence and true moral principles? If one chose to investigate the history of the first twenty tattered blackguards found lying on the benches of the watch-house,... it would not be difficult to write a much more moving book on the calamities of shoemakers or street porters.... than this of Disraeli's on authors. It is the few ill-starred wretches, and the multitude of ill-behaved, that are miserable in all ranks, and among writers just as elsewhere. Literature, I do believe, has keener pains connected with it than almost any other pursuit; but then it has far livelier and nobler pleasures."

In another place he tells her the secret charm of art, so far as artists can ever tell it, and warns her not to hope for satisfaction in the applauses of others, not to think that " any man ever became *famous* entirely or even chiefly from the *love of fame. It is the interior fire, the solitary delight which our own hearts experience in these things, and the misery we feel in vacancy,* that must urge us, or we shall never reach the goal."

All the time this literary friendship was warming into love: a little more tardily in her than in him. The last of his letters to her is that which he writes the day before her wedding; and there can be no doubt of the truth which Mr. Norton finally expresses, with rare force and distinction, from knowledge and from insight that have not often the courage to be honest in dealing with such matters; for love seems to be set apart from the other principles in humanity, to be fabled about as superhuman. " There was much that was sorrowful in their inexperience, much that was sad in their relations to each other. Their mutual love did not make them happy, did not supply them with the self-control required for happiness. Their faults often prevailed against their love, and yet ' with a thousand faults they were both,' as Carlyle said to Miss Welsh, 'true-hearted people.'... One reads their lives wholly wrong unless he read in them that the love that had united them.... abided in the heart of each, and that in what they were to each other it remained the unalterable element."

III.

To turn from these letters of Carlyle to the *Democracy and Other Addresses* of Mr. Lowell is to find one's self again in the immediate presence of a great mind, which, in so far as repose is more beautiful than writhing, good-humor lovelier than ill-humor, hope fruitfuler than despair, daylight clearer than torch-light, and patience wiser than impatience, we find a more comfortable and edifying mind. The two might figure as opposing types of the Old World and the New, in that way in which we used to imagine them; but no one would be more reluctant in this office than Mr. Lowell, or more anxious to get down off his pedestal. The humor that everywhere lurks in these exquisite addresses, and suffuses them with the humanest kindness at whatever moment they are near lapsing into solemnity and severity, would not suffer him to stand for anything but himself; which, indeed, is quite enough for any one, as we each know in our smaller way.

The speeches have all been printed before; we have had in the newspapers the address on Democracy, which seemed the best "excuse for being" ever made for us; the tender and just words on Garfield; the generous words on Stanley; the apology for Fielding, which, owning his foulness, almost made us forget it; the eulogy and the confession of Coleridge; the passages, true and fine, about Wordsworth; the delightful talk about books and libraries; the admirable talk about Don Quixote; the frank, charming, and weighty address at the Harvard Anniversary. We tag each with an adjective which has ticketed many another fine achievement before now; but the reader will conceive that we do not think we have sufficiently qualified any. They are so full both of substance and of savor, of thought and suggestion, that it would be far beyond the scope of this Study, unless it were suddenly as big as all out-doors, to commend them fitly; but if we may not hope to speak at large of their matter, we may at least allow ourselves our poor say about their manner. This seems to us the last perfection in that kind, and the last perfection in any kind is simply getting back to nature. At the end you feel, " That is the way Mr. Lowell thinks to himself, and what wonderfully good company he must find himself!" The style is the "full-throated ease" of the best English prose, which is "far above singing"; every word is exactly yet freely used; the fancy glances everywhere; the pure wit sparkles and laughs like a brook at unexpected turns; the poetry which knows how to walk as well as to fly, the pathos which touches so lightly, so deeply, and above all and under all and through all, the unfailing good sense, are some of the charms that may be numbered, while the best, as the best always must, goes nameless and unnamed.

If the reader should happen to turn from the passages in Mr. Lowell's Harvard Anniversary Address where he speaks of the Puritan clergy of New England, to Mr. Brooks Adams's *Emancipation of Massachusetts,* he will be struck not only by the richer humor (that is putting it very mildly), but by the finer historical sense. Mr. Adams judges them, we think, too habitually by the incandescent electric light of the nineteenth century, instead of the glimmer of the seventeenth-century taper. It is to be said of them that they were no worse than most people of their time, and it was their peculiar misfortune that the haggard spirit of persecution in them should be immediately confronted with the heavenly-eyed angel of toleration here on this edge of the New World, where she first visited the earth. Yet, after making all the allowances for them, we must own that they did persecute very cruelly the Antinomians, the Quakers, and the victims of their witchcraft superstition. It has, to be sure, been shown that they would not have imprisoned the Quakers, or lashed their women at the cart's tail from town to town, or hanged either sex, if the Quakers had kept away from their jurisdiction; but the same reasoning would show that the Inquisition did not molest heretics who put themselves beyond its reach. In fact, the theocracy of New England seems to have been a pretty ugly mixture of the dregs of Mosaism and feudalism, all the bitterer because they were the dregs. The Puritan rulers, cleric and laic, were undoubtedly sincere, conscientious, and courageous; all this has been recognized in full measure, pressed down and running over, by their posterity; and it is well at last to have one of their descendants uncover their faults, show their limitations, and rebuke their errors, their wilful cruelties, their crimes against humanity. If he rather overdoes it, that is his defect of temperament; and it remains true, all the same, that their yoke was uneasy and their burden was sore on the necks of their generation. How both were shaken off by the old theological conservatives joining hands with the political liberals in the Revolution against the state which they hated along with the Church it established, and then falling by the free spirit they had evoked, is the story which Mr. Adams tells absorbingly, clearly, strenuously—not to say athletically.

IV.

There is a grim fantasy of Dostoïevsky's in [2] which he depicts the sudden appearance at the cathedral door in Seville of a man by whose look all the multitude are arrested with a thrill of instant recognition. It does not need the miracles which he performs on those pressing around him to convince them that he is Christ come again. They know it, and the Grand Inquisitor, passing by and seeing the unseemly disorder at the cathedral door, knows it too. But he does not hesitate; he has the stranger arrested, and the people sent home abashed and trembling. In the evening he visits his prisoner, and frankly says that he knows him. But he tells him that he has had his chance, that he was once offered all that the Church now possesses, and that he will not be suffered to disturb its hold upon the people; he will be burnt in the Plaza the next morning at ten.

The Quakers came preaching peace and equality and freedom to men who believed in war and rank and subordination; and they met the sort of welcome from the theocracy of old New England that we now see might have been expected in the seventeenth cen-

tury. They would not be hanged in Boston to-day; the Saviour of mankind would not be burned to-day even in Spain: so far has His spirit penetrated at last; but if the old history could be repeated in just the old way in any centre of modern civilization, it certainly would cause anxieties, it would cause misgivings.

The effort to realize any heavenly ideal of goodness is still very offensive to the world, because it is an unpleasant reflection upon the walk and conversation of some of the best people in it. The theocrats of New England treated greater goodness than their own, or different goodness, with ferocity, not because they were the Church, but because they were the World — a little, hard, merciless world of the seventeenth century set down here in the wilderness, with no larger world near to modify it. They had come out of the larger world, supposing themselves an Ark of the Lord; perhaps they were so at first; but as soon as the power was theirs they became a citadel of purely mundane strength and purpose. As part of their time, they were not so much to blame; but they are to be forever disowned as exemplars to this or any future time in things for which they have been warmly defended. In so far as they persecuted and maltreated their fellow-men they were neither brave nor self-devoted nor reverend; and Mr. Adams, who teaches that they were poorer in the Christian virtues than the poor common people of their state, less merciful, less tolerant, will have done mankind a great service if he has brought this phase of their character into lasting and indefeasible disrepute.

V.

Sore trials they had, no doubt, in the language and carriage of some of the hapless creatures whom they tortured and put to death; though, perhaps, not so heavy as they imagined, or has since been imagined for them: the world has never found difference of opinion agreeable in those who have helped it forward. We were reading, after we had finished Mr. Adams's robust arraignment of the New England theocracy, some of those limpid translations of Plato which an accomplished woman of Boston has given anonymously to the public; and in the account of Socrates's trial, and his account of himself in his Apology, we saw again what an intolerable nuisance wisdom and goodness must be to most respectable people. Here was a man who, by his own showing and the showing of all the witnesses of his life, dwelt in lasting poverty in order that he might have time to be wise and truly great; and not only this, but he spent the greater part of his vast leisure in going about and convincing some of the leading citizens, who had always supposed themselves wise and truly great, that they were really nothing of the kind. The religious state of the ancient Athens bore with Socrates a very long time; but we know what end he came to at last, and we feel sure that the religious state of the nascent modern Athens would have made much shorter work with him. He seems, like the Quakers, to have thought himself guilty of no wrong, and in his conscious innocence he refused to put himself beyond the jurisdiction of the worshipful magistrates and ministers; he escaped whipping at the cart's tail through Ipswich, Salem, and other towns, but he was put to death at last.

Was it on Boston Common? Not exactly, we believe; but there is an effect of something so recent, such an essential parity in all stories of human cruelty and folly, that we might well be excused a slight confusion of details. The little books themselves are somewhat to blame. That *Day in Athens with Socrates*, [3] those *Talks with Socrates about Life*, and that [4] first volume containing the Apology and the Phaedo, all strike a note so familiar, deal with questions so living, that they seem of present concern and of modern fact. Eminent scholars, men of much Latin and more Greek, attest the skill and truth with which the versions are made; we can confidently speak of their English grace and clearness. They seem a "model of style," because they are without manner and perfectly simple. Part of this virtue is Greek, no doubt, but it imbues the prefaces and introductions, and all the comments which illustrate every dark point in the text, and throws a welcome light of history on many facts which one politely supposes himself to have forgotten, but which perhaps he never knew.

VI.

Recurring once again to Tolstoï, as we own ourselves fond of doing, from the great reverence and honor in which we hold him, we wonder if there is yet an English translation of his pure and beautiful story of *Katia*, now in its seventh French edition. If not, we hope it will not be long till it is made known to American readers; that study of the romantic passion turning to family affection in two well-meaning but long-erring lives is something that might be very usefully known here, where the ideal of marriage is so exaggerated and unreasonable; and every page is a pleasure to those who can feel the beauty of truth.

This beauty in Tolstoï is unfailing; and we think our readers will be interested in competent witness to another aspect of it. We quote from the letter of a writer who is one of our chief novelists, and who was one of our bravest soldiers: [5]

"You do right to praise Tolstoï. Something that you wrote a while ago sent me to his *Peace and War*.... Let me tell you that nobody but he has written the whole truth about war and battle. *I* tried, and I told all I dared, and perhaps all I could. But there was one thing I did not dare tell, lest the world should infer that I was naturally a coward, and so could not know the feelings of a brave man. I actually did not dare state the extreme horror of battle, and the anguish with which the bravest soldiers struggle through it. His story of *Borodino*—the soldiers sitting hungry and white under that storm of death; the desperate struggles to keep the mind away from the horrors of the situation; the poor brave Prince pacing the meadow, counting his steps, etc.—it is the actual truth about the glories of war. I say it on the faith of a man who has seen it all a great many times by the hour together.... Oddly enough, the truth is not true to the uninformed. I recommended Tolstoï's *Borodino* to an educated, bright man of my acquaintance. He returned it with the remark that it seemed 'confused.' Well, that is just the truth, the supereminent, vital fact of the description. Nothing is more confounding, fragmentary, incomprehensible than a battle as one sees it. And you see so little, too, unless you are a staff officer and ride about, or perhaps a general. No two spectators ever fully agree in their story of a battle. Tolstoï must have been engaged many times. There are a thousand little touches which nobody could have guessed: the general who gives Pierre an angry glare; the staff officer who yells, 'What are you here for?' and rides off; the view of the charging enemy whom Pierre supposes to be Russians, and wonders why they are coming back—are touches which go to make up the picture of the haste, flurry, confusion, which a battle is. I am glad to have found Tolstoï."

VII.

Of subordinate fiction, of the sort which neither informs nor nourishes, a correspondent writes us, in sad conviction of the fact that the great mass of those who can read and write seem to ask for nothing better: "Do you think our novel-reading public cares much for any masterpiece? It appears to me that the ordinary or uncultivated mind revolts from anything much higher than itself. Here is another lofty stair to climb; here is a new dialect of thought, and even of language, to struggle with; here is somebody insulting us by speaking a foreign tongue." There is suggestion in this, and truth enough for serious pause; and yet we think that it hardly does justice to the power of the ordinary mind to appreciate the best. Much of the best fails of due recognition, but enough of the best gets it to make us hopeful that when literature comes close to life, even ordinary minds will feel and know its charm. We think that there is proof of this in the vast popularity of our humorists, in the fame of the greatest, whose pseudonym is at this moment as well known, in America at least, as the name of Shakespeare. We need not blink any of his shortcomings in recognizing that his books are masterpieces of humor; they are so, and yet our public does care for them in prodigious degree, and it cares for them because incomparably more and better than any other American books they express a familiar and almost universal quality of the American mind, they faithfully portray a phase of American life, which they reflect in its vast kindliness and good-will, its shrewdness and its generosity, its informality, which is not formlessness; under every fantastic disguise they are honest and true. That is all we ask of fiction—sense and truth; we cannot prophesy that every novel which has them will have the success of *The Innocents Abroad*, or of *Roughing It*, but we believe recognition wide and full will await it. Let fiction cease to lie about life; let it portray men and women as they are, actuated by the motives and the passions in the measure we all know; let it leave off painting dolls and working them by springs and wires; let it show the different interests in their true proportions; let it forbear to preach pride and revenge, folly and insanity, egotism and prejudice, but frankly own these for what they are, in whatever figures and occasions they appear; let it not put on fine literary airs; let it speak the dialect, the language, that most Americans know—the language of unaffected people everywhere—and we believe that even [6] its masterpieces will find a response in all readers.

[1]James Anthony Froude, <u>Life</u> <u>of</u> <u>Thomas</u> <u>Carlyle</u> (New York: N.P., 1882).

[2]Ivan relates the legend of the Grand Inquisitor to Alyosha in Book V, Chapter V of <u>The</u> <u>Brothers</u> <u>Karamasov</u>. The legend itself predates Dostoyevsky's publication of the novel in 1880.

[3]Plato, <u>A</u> <u>Day</u> <u>in</u> <u>Athens</u> <u>with</u> <u>Socrates</u>, Ellen F. Mason, trans. (New York: C. Scribner's Sons, 1883).

[4]Plato, <u>Talks</u> <u>with</u> <u>Socrates</u> <u>about</u> <u>Life</u>, Ellen F. Mason, trans. (New York: C. Scribner's Sons, 1886).

[5]Howells' correspondent was John William DeForest.

[6]<u>Criticism</u> <u>and</u> <u>Fiction</u>, p. 104.

June, 1887

Editor's Study.

I.

SOME months ago the Study made occasion to say certain things in praise of American criticism, which, so far as we could observe, displeased most of the American critics. This effect might well have discouraged a less ardent optimist, but, with a courage which we will own we admire, we have clung to our convictions, and should be willing to repeat our unwelcome compliments. They were qualified compliments, if we remember rightly; we should not even now like to commit ourselves to indiscriminate flattery of our fellow-critics; and if we were again to enter upon such dangerous ground, we should prefer to recognize a general amelioration of our dreadful trade on this continent rather than specify improvements. If we were to be quite honest (which is really *not* the best policy in some things), we should say to these brothers of ours that they were still rather apt to behave brutally in behalf of good taste and the best art; and that they were perilously beset by temptations to be personal, to be vulgar, to be arrogant, which they did not always overcome. Perhaps we might go so far as to say that their tone was sometimes ruffianly; though perhaps this would be going too far; perhaps one ought to add that it might not be consciously so. In this home of the amenities, this polite haunt of literary discernment, artistic sensibility, and moral purpose, the critic sometimes appears in the panoply of the savages whom we have supplanted; and it is hard to believe that his use of the tomahawk and the scalping-knife is a form of conservative surgery. It is still his conception of his office that he should assail with bitterness and obloquy those who differ with him in matters of taste or opinion; that he must be rude with those he does not like, and that he ought to do them violence as a proof of his superiority. It is too largely his superstition that because he likes a thing it is good, and because he dislikes a thing it is bad; the reverse is quite possibly the case, but he is yet indefinitely far from knowing that in affairs of taste his personal preference enters very little. Commonly he has no principles, but only an assortment of prepossessions for and against; and we grieve to say that this otherwise very perfect character is sometimes uncandid to the verge of dishonesty. He seems not to mind misstating the position of any one he supposes himself to disagree with, and then attacking him for what he never said, or even implied; the critic thinks this is droll, and appears not to suspect that it is immoral. He is not tolerant; he thinks it a virtue to be intolerant; it is hard for him to understand that the same thing may be admirable at one time

and deplorable at another; and that it is really his business to classify and analyze the fruits of the human mind as the naturalist classifies the objects of his study, rather than to praise or blame them; that there is a measure of the same absurdity in his trampling on a poem, a novel, or an essay that does not please him as in the botanist's grinding a plant underfoot because he does not find it pretty. He does not conceive that it is his business rather to identify the species and then explain how and where the specimen is imperfect and irregular. If he could once acquire this simple ideal of his duty he would be much more agreeable company than he now is, and a more useful member of society; though we trust we are not yet saying that he is not extremely delightful as he is, and wholly indispensable. He is certainly more ignorant than malevolent; and considering the hard conditions under which he works, his necessity of writing hurriedly from an imperfect examination of far more books, on a greater variety of subjects, than he can even hope to read, the average American critic—the ordinary critic of commerce, so to speak—is very well indeed. Collectively he is more than this; for, as we said once before, we believe that the joint effect of our criticism is the pretty thorough appreciation of any book submitted to it.

II.

The misfortune rather than the fault of our several or individual critic is that he is the heir of the false theory and bad manners of the English school. The theory of that school has apparently been that almost any person of glib and lively expression is competent to write of almost any branch of polite literature; its manners are what we know. The American, whom it has largely formed, is by nature very glib and lively, and commonly his criticism, viewed as imaginative work, is more agreeable than that of the Englishman; but it is, like the art of both countries, apt to be amateurish. In some degree our authors have freed themselves from English models; they have gained some notion of the more serious work of the Continent; but it is still the ambition of the American critic to write like the English critic, to show his wit if not his learning, to strive to eclipse the author under review rather than illustrate him. He has not yet caught on to the fact that it is really no part of his business to exploit himself, but that it is altogether his duty to place a book in such a light that the reader shall know its class, its function, its character. The vast good-nature of our people preserves us from the worst effects of this criticism without principles. Our critic, at his lowest, is rarely malignant; and when he is rude or untruthful, it is mostly without truculence; we suspect that he is often offensive without knowing that he is so. If he loves a shining mark because a fair shot with mud shows best on that kind of target, it is for the most part from a boyish mischievousness quite innocent of malice. Now and then he acts simply under instruction from higher authority, and denounces because it is the tradition of his publication to do so. In other cases the critic is obliged to support his journal's repute for severity, or for wit, or for morality, though he may himself be entirely amiable, dull, and wicked; this necessity more or less warps his verdicts.

The worst is that he is personal, perhaps because it is so easy and so natural to be personal, and so instantly attractive. In this respect our criticism has not improved from the accession of large numbers of ladies to its ranks, though we still hope so much from women in our politics when they shall come to vote. They have come to write, and with the effect to increase the amount of little-digging, which rather superabounded in our literary criticism before. They "know what they like" — that pernicious maxim of those who do not know what they ought to like—and they pass readily from censuring an author's performance to censuring him. They bring a lively stock of misapprehensions and prejudices to their work; they would rather have heard about than known about a book; and they take kindly to the public wish to be amused rather than edified. But neither have they so much harm in them; they too are more ignorant than malevolent.

III.

Our criticism is disabled by the unwillingness of the critic to learn from an author, and his readiness to mistrust him. A writer passes his whole life in fitting himself for a certain kind of performance; the critic does not ask why, or whether the performance is good or bad, but if he does not like the kind, he instructs the writer to go off and do some other sort of thing—usually the sort that has been done already, and done sufficiently. If he could once understand that a man who has written the book he dislikes, probably knows infinitely more about its kind and his own fitness for doing it than any one else, the critic might learn something, and might help the reader to learn; but by putting himself in a false position, a position of superiority, he is of no use. He ought, in the first place, to cast prayerfully about for humility, and especially to beseech the powers to preserve him from the sterility of arrogance and the deadness of contempt, for out of these nothing can proceed. He is not to suppose that an author has committed an offence against him by writing the kind of book he does not like; he will be far more profitably employed on behalf of the reader in finding out whether they had better not both like it. Let him conceive of an author as not in any wise on trial before him, but as a reflection of this or that aspect of life, and he will not be tempted to browbeat him or bully him.

So far as we know, this is not now the carriage of criticism toward authorship in any country but England and her literary colonies. Self-restraint, decency, even politeness, seem to characterize the behavior of critics elsewhere. They may not like an author's work, but they do not for that reason use him with ignominy or insult. Some extreme friends of civilization have insisted that a critic should not write of a book what he would not say to the author personally about it; but this is not possible; it is at least premature, if not a little unreasonable. All that we now suggest is that the critic need not be impolite, even to the youngest and weakest author. A little courtesy, or a good deal, a constant perception of the fact that a book is not a misdemeanor, a decent self-respect that must forbid the civilized man the savage pleasure of wounding, are what we ask for our criticism, as something which will add sensibly to its present lustre; or, if nothing can do that, will at least approach it to the Continental attitude, and remove it from the English. [1]

IV.

We do not really suppose that the inhabitants of the British Islands are all satisfied with their literary criticism; we suspect that many of them must have their misgivings when the *Saturday Review*, for example, calls names and makes faces because some one has, for instance, deplored the survival of the English aristocracy in our time. They must some of them feel that it is not a wholly terrible spectacle; that however right the *Review* may be, its behavior is a little ridiculous. But those islanders are very curious, and in some things quite remote; they may still think the tomtom a powerful argument, and the gourd-rattle the best means of carrying conviction to the minds of men. They may even admire the solemn port of the *Academy* when it knits [2] its classic front and tells an American novelist that "he is, to say the least, presumptuous" in questioning the impeccability of English fiction. What he would be, if the *Academy* were to say the most, one shrinks from guessing; but apparently the British aristocracy, which reads the British novel so little, and the British novel, which derides the British aristocracy so much, are twin monuments whose perfection no foreigner may doubt, under pain of British criticism's high displeasure.

It is no doubt partially in revolt from this severity that we call in question British criticism itself, and beg American criticism, which is still in the sap, to incline to other ways, to study different methods and different measures. At this stage of the proceedings, with the light of civilization flowing in upon us from the whole European continent, it would be a pity to continue in that old personal, arrogant, egotistical tradition; it would be something more than a pity, it would be a sin; and we tenderly entreat our brethren, from the highest to the lowest, to take thought of the matter, to reason with themselves, and to be warned by the examples which they have hitherto sought to imitate.

V.

Consider, dear friends, what you are really in the world for. It is not, apparently, for a great deal, because your only excuse for being is that somebody else has been. The critic exists because the author first existed. If books failed to appear, the critic must disappear, like the poor aphis or the lowly caterpillar in the absence of vegetation. These insects may both suppose that they have something to do with the creation of vegetation; and the critic may suppose that he has something to do with the creation of literature; but a very little reasoning ought to convince alike aphis, caterpillar, and critic that they are mistaken. The critic—to drop the others—must perceive, if he will question himself more carefully, that his office is mainly to ascertain facts and traits of literature, not to invent or denounce them; to discover principles, not to establish them; to report, not to create.

The history of all literature shows that even with the youngest and weakest author criticism is quite powerless against his will to do his own work in his own way; and if this is the case in the green wood, how much more in the dry! It has been thought by the sentimentalists that criticism, if it cannot cure, can at least kill, and Keats was long alleged in proof of its efficacy in this sort. But criticism neither cured nor killed Keats, as we all now very well know. It wounded, it cruelly hurt him, no doubt; and it is always in the power of the critic to give pain to the author—the meanest critic to the greatest author—for no one can help feeling a rudeness. But every literary movement has been violently opposed at the start, and yet never stayed in the least, or arrested, by criticism; every author has been condemned for his virtues, but in no wise changed by it. In the beginning he reads the critics; but presently perceiving that he alone makes or mars himself, and that they have no instruction for him, he mostly leaves off reading them, though he is always glad of their kindness or grieved by their harshness when he chances upon it. This, we believe, is the general experience, modified, of course, by exceptions.

VI.

Then, are we critics of no use in the world? We should not like to think that, though we are not quite ready to define our use. If we were to confess that we had none, we must not say, Let us not be like these English critics; but, Let us not be at all.

More than one sober thinker is inclining at present to suspect that æsthetically or specifically we *are* of no use, and that we are only useful historically; that we may register laws, but not enact them. We are not quite prepared to admit that æsthetic criticism is useless, though in view of its futility in any given instance it is hard to deny that it is so. It certainly seems as useless against a book that strikes the popular fancy, and prospers on in spite of condemnation by the best critics, as it is against a book which does not generally please, and which no critical favor can make acceptable. This is so common a phenomenon that we wonder it has never hitherto suggested to criticism that its point of view was altogether mistaken, and that it was really necessary to judge books not as dead things, but as living things—things which have an influence and a power irrespective of beauty and wisdom, and merely as expressions of actuality in thought and feeling. Perhaps criticism has a cumulative and final effect; perhaps it does some good we do not know of. It apparently does not affect the author directly, but it may reach him through the reader. It may in some cases enlarge or diminish his audience for a while, until he has thoroughly measured and tested his own powers. We doubt if it can do more than that; but if it can do that, we will admit that it may be the toad of adversity, ugly and venomous, from whose unpleasant brow he is to snatch the precious jewel of lasting fame.

We employ this figure in all humility, and we conjure our fraternity to ask themselves, without rancor or offence, whether we are right or not. In this quest let us get together all the modesty and candor and impartiality we can; for if we should happen to discover a good reason for continuing to exist, these qualities will be of more use to us than any others in examining the work of people who really produce something. __|3

[1] Criticism and Fiction, pp. 29-36 (abridged).

[2] William Sharp, "New Novels," The Academy, 30 (December 25, 1886), 423-424. This contains a review of Howells' own novel, The Minister's Charge, and the American who questioned the impeccability of English fiction was presumably Howells himself. There was a steady dialogue being published between Howells' attacks upon English fiction and critical standards, and the replies of various English journals, such as The Academy and Saturday Review.

[3] Criticism and Fiction, pp. 37-41.

Editor's Study.

I.

WE have been reading, with a pleasure which we should not quite know how to justify to the fastidious company usually assembled in this Study, Mr. Lee Meriwether's *Tramp Trip*, and Captain S. Samuels's account of his life *From the Forecastle to the Cabin*. Mr. Meriwether seems really to have walked over the greater part of Europe, and with some discomforts and humiliations to himself (which he never blinks), to have come much nearer its life, at a cost of fifty cents a day, than others do who travel through it in first-class railway carriages and stop at the best hotels. His book is apparently a mixture of observation and invention; apparently, if the thing that happens is not all that he or the reader could wish, he makes something more happen, and so there is a rounded incident in the end. It is not so good as if it were all true, or seemed true, but we are bound to say that most of the incidents do not have this effect of being "composed"; and there are some extremely interesting statistics with regard to the cost of living and the rate of wages among European artisans, which give a serious value to the book. Otherwise it is full of a youthful zest, and of a Western humor and audacity; and most modernly American as it is, it has a flavor one tastes in travels of former times, when the world was much newer than it is at present. Perhaps this is its charm; and perhaps this is the charm of Captain Samuels's memoirs, which are written with a more constant appeal to one's credence. Captain Samuels ran away to sea when he was a boy of eleven, and he rose, before he was of age, to be master of a ship; his manner is necessarily a mixture of the didactic and the romantic; he presents himself as at once an example and a warning; his adventures involve often some grave moral precept. But he is always interesting, and his experiences, too, have the flavor of an older time; they are as good reading in their way as those of Captain John Smith.

II.

In fact, next to autobiography, there is no better kind of reading than books of adventure, which are indeed passages of autobiography. They depict character, and deepen our knowledge of human nature in certain directions as no other books can do, if the narrator is himself the adventurer. It is of course character in exceptional action, and human nature under peculiar stress; and the knowledge gained is narrow in the ratio of its depth. Adventure, therefore, has not the usefulness, or to the more thoughtful mind the delightfulness, of autobiography, which presents life in its ordinary course, moved from within rather than from without, and swayed by normal interests and desires; yet it involves the dramatic moment, and is full of precious testimony to the existence of high qualities in all kinds of men: courage to do and to bear, self-sacrifice for wise and good ends, indomitable hope, persistent faith, gentleness, inexhaustible endeavor. It teaches, also, the essential parity of experience, and the sort of every-day simplicity with which the supreme exigencies present themselves. It shows that these come without heroic blazon of any sort, and without the theatrical effect of being different from other events. In the midst of them people are seen sorely tried, indeed, but still behaving like the people one knows, and not like people on the stage or in novels of adventure. But for the fact that they are adrift in an open boat, or attacked by savages in Central Africa, or lost on the plains, or afloat on an ice-floe, or aboard a foundering or burning ship, or besieged in a block-house by Indians, or wandering in the heart of Australia, or cast away on an uninhabited island, they would not affect us differently from any of the men or women whom we meet on the pavement or at dinner. There seems to be little exaltation, little excitement about them; they behave selfishly or generously according to their several dispositions, and the women are as brave and cheerful as the men.

It is one of the chief uses of real adventures to counteract the influence of fictitious adventures, and to disperse the many illusions bred of them; the facts of life seldom do any harm; it is the distempered imitations that are mischievous, with their exaggerated emotions, their false proportion, their absurd motives, their grotesque ethics. A few months ago we commended the memoirs of Captain Cleveland, the New England navigator, and now we commend the life of Captain Samuels, which on another level is also serious and important in its suggestion. We should commend with the same heartiness Mr. Meriwether's *Tramp Trip* if we could believe it all; but making allowance for the obvious "imagination" in it, we find it worth reading. It is valuable both as a picture of Europe from an uncommon point of view, and as a light upon the sort of American civilization which produced its author, with his helter-skelter encounter of facts, his shrewd examination of them, and his noteworthy deductions from them. Wherever he wandered, with his pack on his back, his light purse in his pocket, and his lighter heart in his breast, he inquired into the condition of the laboring-man, and found out what he could earn and what he must spend. He learned that in England, the only free-trade country, the working-man was better paid and better housed, clothed, and fed than anywhere else in Europe.

III.

The result was to make Mr. Meriwether a free-trader; and though he is not apparently a profound philosopher, though he is young enough to change his mind yet many times before he dies, still the result is interesting; and what is so sincerely offered must be respectfully received as one attempt to solve that "riddle of the painful earth" which now seems to be puzzling every one who thinks and feels. Very likely it is not the true answer; but if it is a part of that truth we have reason to be glad of it; and the remedy which it suggests, being public and political, is much easier of application than that proposed for the amelioration of human life by Count Tolstoï in his latest work. *Que Faire*, he calls it; and he believes that the first thing we are to do for the other sinners and sufferers is to stop sinning and suffering ourselves. He tells us, with that terrible, unsparing honesty of his, how he tried to do good among the poor in Moscow, and how he failed to do any good, because he proposed a physical instead of a moral relief, a false instead of a real charity, while he grew more and more into conceit of himself as a fine fellow. He wished to live in idleness and ease, as he had always lived, and to rid himself of the tormenting consciousness of the misery all around him by feeding and clothing and sheltering it. But when he came to look closer into the life of the poor, even the poorest, he found that two-thirds of them were hard at work and happy; the other third suffered because they had lost the wholesome habit of work, and were corrupted by the desire to live, like the rich, in luxury and indolence; because, like the rich, they despised and hated labor. No rich man, therefore, could help them, because his life and aims were of a piece with theirs, while a great social gulf, forbidding all brotherly contact, was fixed between them. Therefore this singular Russian nobleman concludes that it is not for him to try to make the idle poor better than the idle rich by setting them at work, but that as one of the idle rich he must first make himself better than the idle poor by going to work with his own hands, by abolishing his own nobility, and by consorting with other men as if he were born the equal of all. It is the inexorable stress of this conclusion which has forced him to leave the city, to forego his splendor in society and the sweets of his literary renown, to simplify his life, to go into the country, and to become literally a peasant and the companion of peasants. He, the greatest living writer, and incomparably the greatest writer of fiction who has ever lived, tells us that he finds this yoke easy and this burden light, that he is no longer weary or heavy laden with the sorrows of others or his share of their sins, but that he has been given rest by humble toil. It is a hard saying; but what if it should happen to be the truth? In that case, how many of us who have great possessions must go away exceeding sorrowful! Come, star-eyed Political Economy! come, Sociology, heavenly nymph! and soothe the ears tortured by this echo of Nazareth. Save us, sweet Evolution! Help, O Nebular Hypothesis! Art, Civilization, Literature, Culture! is there no escape from our brothers but in becoming more and more truly their brothers?

Count Tolstoï makes a very mortifying study of himself as an intending benefactor of the poor, and holds all the kindly well-to-do up to self-scorn in the picture. He found the poor caring for the poor out of their penury with a tenderness which the rich cannot know; he found a wretched prostitute foregoing her infamous trade, her means of life, that she might nurse a sick neighbor; he found an old woman denying herself that she might give food and shelter to a blind mendicant; he found a wretched tailor who had adopted an orphan into his large family of children. When he gave twenty kopecks to a beggar whom he met, the poor man with him gave three. But Count Tolstoï had an income of 600,000 rubles, and this poor man 150 rubles. He says that he ought to have given 3000 rubles to the beggar in order to have given his proportion. His wealth became not only ridiculous, but horrible, to him, for he realized that his income was wrung from the necessity of the wretched peasants. He saw cities as the sterile centres of the idleness and luxury of the rich, of the idleness and misery of the poor. He arraigned the present civil order as wrong, false, and unnatural; he sold all he had and gave it to the poor, and turned and followed Him. From his work-bench he sends this voice back into the world, to search the hearts of those who will hear, and to invite them to go and do likewise.

IV.

We will own that we do not like the prospect. If a very poor relation of the Study came into it, we should not know how to meet him gracefully, much as we should dislike to shut the door in his face; and we freely admit that *Que Faire* is another of those Russian books which have given some people the impression that Russia cannot be an agreeable country to live in. Like the rest of Russian literature, it seems intended to direct the mind to uncomfortable subjects, to awaken harassing thoughts in it. A comic opera is a great deal gayer; it will not compare even with an American novel or the criticism upon it for amusingness. After reading it you cannot be quite the same person you were before; you will be better by taking its truth to heart, or worse by hardening your heart against it.

There is a chapter in this book on the nature and meaning of money, which we dare say the political economist might laugh at, and which is nevertheless most interesting from the novelty, if nothing else, of its notions. Tolstoï holds that one man's money is not like another man's money; that the poor man's money is the proof of his toil, and the rich man's money is the certificate of his power to compel the labor of some one else; in other words, it is impersonal slave-holding. His whole essay is directed against riches and luxury, because these are produced by oppression and destitution, and must perpetuate suffering. Work, equality, brotherhood, are his ideals; and whatever may be said in ridicule or argument, it cannot be denied that the life he is living is in literal fulfilment of the teachings of Jesus Christ. This is what makes it impossible for one to regard it without grave question of the life that the rest of us are living; and we commend *Que Faire* to the attention of all our readers.

If one of them should happen to turn from it to the *Memoir of Charles Reade*, "dramatist, novelist, journalist," we think it will be with a vivid sense of the noisiness and futility of life as it goes on in the "great centres of civilization." It is an entertaining book, made up mostly of Reade's own letters, and the Rev. Compton Reade's comments and strictures in Reade's own manner; that is to say, it is not very significant of much besides the temperaments of the author and his editor, which seem to be of the same piece. A foreigner reading the book would not conceive very clearly of the literary period which Charles Reade belonged to, and would scarcely be able to place him in history. He would understand, perhaps, that there was a gentleman writing novels in English from 1850 to 1875, who was one of the most arrogant, kindly, egotistical, generous, impartial, and unjust members of that English race which foreigners find so droll. The novels he would not understand from this Memoir, and would have to be told that while they abounded in flashes of reality and traits of naturalness, they were, as a whole, untrue to life; that they tasted unpleasantly of the material which they were wrought out of—the undigested facts of multitudinous scrap-books; that they were mechanical in operation, and that their portrayal of character was capricious, slight, and theatrical; that for once they delighted, and perhaps would always amuse, but that they could not edify; that they were direct, immediate, and personal; and that on the ethical side they were either commonplace or grotesque. He might safely be told that they enlarged somewhat the bounds of toleration, and appealed to sympathy for much unmerited suffering; but that they were not to be quite trusted in behalf of any cause they befriended, or against any they attacked; that their philosophy was shallow, and even their prejudice not very profound.

Charles Reade was a fighter all his life long, and this book gives abundant proof of his warlike temper. Such a man never wanted occasion for quarrel in a world where most things ranged themselves for or against Charles Reade. Perhaps the most amusing instance of his suspicious and irascible temper was his belief that George Eliot wrote *Romola* largely for the purpose of superseding *The Cloister and the Hearth*, and capturing the "belt" of historical romance (if we may so express it, under strong temptation), which he had won by that novel. He seems really to have thought that there was a necessary rivalry between books so different in scope, intent, and effect, because they both dealt with mediæval life, and that it was an invasion of his province for another to write of the fifteenth century in the south of Europe. He allowed himself the poor revenge of calling Mrs. Lewes Georgy-Porgy, and the Rev. Mr. Compton Reade permits himself to talk of her as in great part the creature of skilful advertising, the spoiled child of the "anti-Christian" critics, and he falls into the grossness of speaking of her "animalism."

This is something for the Rev. Mr. Compton Reade to regret hereafter. For the rest, "the hypocritic days" will take care of George Eliot's name and fame. *Romola* is a sufficiently dull and tedious book in some respects, as

a historical romance must be; but it will always come as a revelation to the reader not wholly taken with the outside of things. It will matter less and less every day whether it is as vivid a picture of the Middle Ages as *The Cloister and the Hearth;* the great thing is that it is true to human nature in all times, and that in Tito Malemma it witnesses to every man the dangers of selfishness and falsehood in the softest and sweetest, and leaves him thrilling with fear and longing for escape from himself. It is calm and lucid where the other is boisterous and turbid; it is eternally true where that is temporarily true; it is deep where that is shallow; it moves naturally and livingly where that is operated and pushed from incident to incident; and its climax is in the reader's conscience, and not in his fancy or his love of excitement. In a very wide world there is plenty of room for both kinds of books, but not for question as to which is the greater kind.

We have been struck in thinking over Mr. Thomas Hardy's *Woodlanders*, which we read with the enjoyment that all his books give us, by the measure in which the principles of both of these writers are united in his work. They are no doubt his own principles too, and have an alternate attraction for him. In much of what is best in him we think he is better than either George Eliot or Charles Reade; his portrayal of simple life and his love of nature are more intimate and perfect than hers, and his operation of the plot is never so open and mechanical as Reade's. But about one-half of this story of the *Woodlanders*, in its sympathetic and conscientious study of village folk, will remind the reader of George Eliot; and the other half, in its manipulation of events, will recall Charles Reade. The inquirer into literary heredity will find here a very pretty study, and a proof that every writer is the creature of his time and its influences, while he will be rewarded with pleasures which no one but Thomas Hardy is able to impart. One of these will be the acquaintance with souls like Winterborne and Grace Melbury, so primitively good that a civic evil like divorce for the direct purpose of remarriage never occurs to them as wrong. Grace's father, with his ambition for her, so simple and sincere that it casts out selfishness, is excellent, and so are all the villagers; and up to the moment that the god comes out of the machine and smites Winterborne with fatal self-sacrifice, and the paramour of Grace's husband with death, that the married pair may be reunited, the progress of events is natural, and their proportion is life-like. There are also many excursions into the remoter regions of the human heart, like that which shows Grace really not jealous of her false husband, which have courage and absolute novelty. The husband is extremely well found, and his character is discovered to the reader with a subtle effect of unconsciousness on the author's part which is very remarkable.

The *Woodlanders*, in fact, is so consolingly good that it leaves us somewhat indifferent to the recent assumptions of the bold Mr. Rider Haggard in regard to the true function of fiction, though we had the greatest mind in the world to immolate him on the Study table this month. But he shall be spared to go on and write as many more *Shes* as he likes, and if people find pleasure in having their blood curdled for the sake of having it uncurdled again at the end of the book, we shall not interfere with their amusement. But we will say that the practice of sensation has not apparently left Mr. Haggard much time to inform himself in regard to the kind of fiction which he condemns, and which he finds exemplified only in its French and American phases; though he is very hard upon these, and it follows that he would be equally severe with the Russian, Spanish, Italian, and Norwegian realists if he had ever heard of them. The kind of novels he likes, and likes to write, are intended to take his reader's mind, or what that reader would probably call his mind, off himself; they make one forget life and all its cares and duties; they are not in the least like the novels which make you think of these, and shame you into at least wishing to be a helpfuler and wholesomer creature than you are. No sordid details of verity here, if you please; no wretched being humbly and weakly struggling to do right and to be true, suffering for his follies and his sins, tasting joy only through the mortification of self, and in the help of others; nothing of all this, but a great, whirling splendor of peril and achievement, a wild scene of heroic adventure, and of emotional ground and lofty tumbling, with a stage "picture" at the fall of the curtain, and all the good characters in a row, their left hands pressed upon their hearts, and kissing their right hands to the audience, in the good old way that has always charmed and always will charm, Heaven bless it!

No, we will not put our paper-knife—an exquisite Japanese conception—into Mr. Rider Haggard this month, or perhaps any other month. In a world which loves the spectacular drama and the practically bloodless sports of the modern amphitheatre he has his place, and we must not destroy him because he fancies it the first place. Others have made the like mistake before him, and he will not be the last to make it. In fact, it is a condition of his doing well the kind of work he does that he should think it important, that he should believe in himself; and we would not take away this faith of his, even if we could. As we say, he has his place. The world often likes to forget itself, and he brings on his heroes, his goblins, his feats, his hairbreadth escapes, his imminent deadly breaches, and the poor, foolish, childish old world renews the excitements of its nonage. Perhaps this is a work of beneficence; it is at least a work of mercy, however mistaken; and perhaps our brave conjurer in his cabalistic robe is a philanthropist in disguise.

V.

We do not know, but we should not like to affirm the contrary without reservation; for it would not be quite safe in these days when Creative Talent, or Genius, is apt to come back upon criticism with destructive violence. There is really no reason why Creative Talent, or Genius, should not do this; and from time to time we like to see it done. We have no statistics at hand by which to verify the results, and we cannot say what is commonly the effect upon criticism. It may not be so destructive as it seems, and commonly the effect with the public is at first amusement, and then extreme fatigue. The public is also of opinion that it involves loss of dignity to

Creative Talent, or Genius, but here again we are without the requisite statistics. Creative Talent, or Genius, may come off with all the dignity it went in with, and it may accomplish a very good work in demolishing criticism.

Our readers know what a modest opinion we have of criticism in general; how lowly we think its office; how slight its use; and we believe it would really be very interesting to know what was the precise effect of Mr. Edgar Fawcett's return upon the Boston critics of his play last April. Even at this late date the statistics are lacking, but their absence does not affect the principle upon which he acted.

We do not see really why it is not a just principle, or why it involves loss of dignity. In any other relation of life the man who thinks himself wronged tries to right himself, violently, if he is a mistaken man, and lawfully if he is a wise man or a rich one, which is practically the same thing. But the author, dramatist, painter, sculptor, whose book, play, picture, statue, has been unfairly dealt with, as he believes, must make no effort to right himself with the public; he must bear his wrong in silence; he is even expected to grin and bear it, as if it were funny. Everybody understands that it is not funny to him, not in the least funny, but everybody says that he cannot make an effort to get the public to take his point of view without loss of dignity. This is very odd, but it is the fact, and we suppose that it comes from the feeling that the author, dramatist, painter, sculptor, has already said the best he can for his side in his book, play, picture, statue. This is partly true, and yet if he wishes to add something more to prove the critic wrong, we do not see how his attempt to do so should involve loss of dignity. The public, which is so jealous for his dignity, does not otherwise use him as if he were a very great and invaluable creature; if he fails, it lets him starve like any one else. We should say that he lost dignity or not as he behaved, in his effort to right himself, with petulance or with principle. If he betrayed a wounded vanity, if he impugned the motives and accused the lives of his critics, we should certainly feel that he was losing dignity; but if he temperately examined their theories, and tried to show where they were mistaken, we think he would not only gain dignity, but would perform a very useful work.

If, for example, Mr. Fawcett, upon whose behavior we have no wish to pronounce, had brought against his critics a calm and clear statement of his ideas and motives in writing the play they condemned, we believe he would have won the favor of the public, and secured fresh attention to his work, and perhaps a reversal of judgment. There is at present hardly anything about which people are so little instructed as the drama, and about which they would so gladly know something. Mr. Fawcett has written two plays, one of which has been successful; and he cannot have written these plays without giving indefinitely more thought to the drama than all the dramatic critics in the country, simply because he has done what they have only talked about doing. He might be quite mistaken in his theories or principles, but about his practical knowledge there could be no mistake; and we think that the public, possessed of this by dispassionate and impersonal statement, would judge justly, generously, between him and his critics. Bad as the public is, it likes to have a man stand up for himself; and we should be glad to see it disabused of the superstition that an artist of any sort may not with perfect dignity defend himself against what he believes unfair or ignorant censure. This superstition is a survival of the doctrine that an author ought not to take money for his work, and is equally gross and foolish. We are glad then that Mr. Fawcett has had the courage to speak out in his own behalf. If he has not had the fortune to speak wisely, still he has had the courage to speak.

Another dramatist, Mr. Lathrop, in reply to a New York critic who condemned his play, has had both the fortune and the courage. His letter, in fact, was admirable in temper, and so perfect in logic that it makes one a little sorry for the critic, whom it convicted of an amount of unreason if not of error which it must have been uncomfortable to have so openly recognized.

VI.

As matters now stand, however, perhaps oblivion is still the author's best defence against dramatic criticism, the oblivion which comes to the critic as well as to the dramatist, although our dramatic criticism is probably the most remarkable apparatus of our civilization. We have no drama, and only the faintest promise of a drama, but we have a dramatic criticism which surpasses that of other countries as much as our fire department. A perfectly equipped critical engine stands in every newspaper office, with the steam always up, which can be manned in nine seconds, and rushed to the first theatre where there is the slightest danger of drama within five minutes; and the combined efforts of these tremendous machines can pour a concentrated deluge of cold water upon a play which will put out anything of the kind at once. But, as in a case of real fire, nobody remembers two days afterward whether the fire was put out or not, that is, nobody but the immediate sufferers, the author and the manager.

Not long ago a very dear and valued friend of the Study had a little play acted at a theatre in a great centre of dramatic criticism. Unless his fondness was abused, as it might very easily have been, for he thought well of his little play, the audience seemed to like it, and there was at least a pleasing illusion of success in the affair. But the next day the critics said that it was a dead failure. They owned that people appeared moved and interested by it, but that they were wrong to yield, and that whatever the little play was, it was not a play; that a play was this, that, and the other thing, and the little play was nothing of the kind. Our friend was surprised, but not convinced; he could not deny, however, that the critics were all agreed against his little play. Whatever differences of opinion those good men might have had in regard to religion, politics, or the civil service reform, they were of one mind in regard to his little play, and their mind was that it was not only not a play, but that whatever it was it was bad.

Our friend swallowed the bitter dose and made his wry faces in private, though he had been obliged to take it, as he fancied, in public, with a million people looking on. Not long afterward an acquaintance met him and congratulated him. "Play was a splendid success—wasn't it?"

"Were you there?" asked our friend.

"No; but I saw that all the critics praised it."

[1] Mrs. George Henry Lewes is the married name of Mary Ann Evans (pseudonym - George Eliot).

[2] Criticism and Fiction, pp. 105-106.

[3] Criticism and Fiction, pp. 106-107.

[4] Edgar Fawcett, "Should Critics Be Gentlemen?" Lippincott's Monthly Magazine, 39 (January, 1887), 163-177.

[5] Criticism and Fiction, pp. 53-55.

August, 1887

Editor's Study.

I.

A CORRESPONDENT suggests inquiry into a subject on which many others must have an opinion, or the materials for an opinion. "I believe," he writes, "that our best readers, the most appreciative, the most sympathetic, are not among the critics of the press, nor among the rich (who might be idle, but usually are not, and have too many occupations to read), nor among our leading lawyers, but among our parsons and teachers (teachers in a large sense) and clerks, and the officers of our army and navy. It is a fact that literature, imaginative literature, is supported by men and women of limited incomes."

If this is all true, it would be interesting to know how many and what kind of books are read in the enforced leisure of ward-rooms and garrisons, and whether the army and navy take to the literature that kills time merely, or to the robuster sort which is the supposed extremity of desolate islands. In the mean while some phases of the wide-spread passion for literature in civil life which our correspondent touches are such as no one can ignore. We think it is particularly true that, in America at least, rich people read very little, and they have still less to do with making literary reputations. Their social pleasures, or duties, or cares—whichever they are—leave them no time, as our correspondent says, for reading, and in this, as in everything else, most rich people are people of fashion. They read what gets talked about in their own set, what has vogue with persons known to them as persons of taste; the popularity, the fame of a book does not commend it to them unless it has this sanction; and their praise in turn does not penetrate beyond their own necessarily narrow circle. The rich buy pictures and statues and bric-à-brac; and some of them collect libraries, or *éditions de luxe*, or rare copies of books. But literature has nothing to hope or fear from them; they can do nothing toward making or marring the fortune of a new book.

We are inclined to think, however, that lawyers are fonder of imaginative literature than our correspondent seems to believe. We have been surprised to find how often jurists, even eminent jurists, are great novel-readers; they read novels for relaxation, and perhaps because they find a complete relief from the realities of life in the gross improbability of most of them. But the critics of the press are, as our correspondent justly affirms, not among the most sympathetic readers. In a certain way they may be said not to be readers at all. They are book-tasters; and as the tea-taster becomes indifferent to the cup that cheers in proportion to the growing skill of his palate

in distinguishing flavors, the book-taster is finally no lover of literature, though he may have begun with a real passion for it. Yet he has a vast influence in hastening or retarding the success of a book, at least temporarily, especially he of the daily press, as any librarian will testify. Probably he cannot ultimately decide its fate; in some cases he quite fails to affect it; and still his influence is vast. Most people do not know what to read; they are glad to be told, and he tells them promptly. His opinion is not to be undervalued because it would be so easy to overrate it; and he is undeniably a power.

He is so great a power that it might be well not to supersede him, perhaps, but to supplement him. This could be done by giving voice in print to the real lovers of literature, to those parsons, teachers, clerks, throughout the country, and above all to those intelligent and sympathetic women forming the unquestionable majority of the people of limited incomes who buy and read most of the new books.

In every community large enough to support a country printer there are three or four persons—oftenest women—whose acquaintance with such books is an intimacy almost unknown where the interests and amusements are more varied. In these places they read intensely, almost passionately, and they think and talk much of what they read. This is so not only in well book-clubbed New England, but throughout the whole North and older West; and it is a pity that their thinking and talking about books should not be invited into print. Much of it would be crude—very crude; but it would not differ in that from much of the other criticism now printed. Some of it would be good; we believe that most of it would be sincere; and we should hope (with no doubt an even chance of disappointment) that it would try books less and less by literary standards, which are necessarily unjust and inadequate, if the books are alive as well as new, and would test them by personal knowledge and experience.

There can be no doubt of the vastness of our reading public. In spite of all lamentations to the contrary, it is now not only positively greater, but relatively greater, than ever before. Not only are more newspapers and magazines read, but more books, and more good books. The general expression of his readers' minds about him would form a body of critical comment which, however imperfect, would still incorporate the public to the author, and confront him with those to whom he is such a living interest. The sum of it, the whole effect, we do not believe would

91

be mistaken; it would be the same verdict which now silently utters itself in failure or success. There is not a sufficient outlet for this opinion in the city press, but if the country newspapers made themselves its vehicle, if they accepted and encouraged it, there is no question but they could become a literary influence, and add indefinitely to their own interest and value. Publishers now lavish their new books upon the city press with the chance of comment upon one out of three or four; they rarely or never send to the country press, for the reason that the chance of their books receiving intelligent notice would be still less. But if the country editor who had no time or taste for the work had the habit of turning over any new publications he received to those persons known in every community for their love of reading, the field of criticism could be made commensurate with the map of the United States.

II.

The immediate result would not be ideal, and the ultimate result might not be ideal; but the present system of criticism is not ideal either. What is to be chiefly desired is the expression of real feeling about books, and it seems as if this might come from the people whom books most interest; it would not matter how broken or formless the expression was, or how brief. It is to be desired also that the tests of literature should not only be more and more practical, but more and more ethical. The notion of art for art's sake has probably never had any deep hold upon the popular fancy, and none at all upon the popular conviction; and if ministers are lovers of literature, there seems no reason why they may not also be its censors, on the moral side. They already concern themselves with the reading of their people in some degree; they encourage the circulation of sectarian newspapers and books among them; but the great body of literature is non-sectarian; and with this, as we understand, they do not concern themselves; they practically ignore the enormous influence which fiction, for example, has upon the young. Yet if a pastor knew a large portion of his flock to be feeding upon a certain popular book, why should he not taste it too, and tell them whether he thought it wholesome or unwholesome if a novel or a poem, and right or wrong if a work of polemics or metaphysics? Rev. Minot J. Savage, of Boston, has lately done something of this sort in regard to the ethical writings of Count Leo Tolstoï, and he has been the first to discuss before his people, so far as we know, those wonderful books *My Confession* and *My Religion*, which are such a potent appeal to the conscience of all Christendom. Mr. Savage considers them from the stand-point of radical Unitarianism; and when Tolstoï repeats the precepts of Christ, and insists that each man and the whole world should be ruled by them till the life of the race realizes the Saviour's ideal of meekness, of forgiveness, of charity, of humble toil and contented poverty, Mr. Savage answers him: Yes; these are unquestionably the precepts of Christ; but Christ believed that even in His own time the world was near its end; and His precepts were never meant for the founding of a civilization, but for the government of the little body of His immediate followers. Christ, he says, was a supremely good soul, but He was an inferior intellect; and Tolstoï, in attempting to rehabilitate Him as a practical reformer, is a still lower intellect. The world would be dull and ugly if they could have their way, and for himself he would prefer another planet, with our present diversity of aims and interests, even our present diversity of miseries and crimes. We wish merely to state Mr. Savage's position, of which Mr. Lowell might long ago have prophesied when he wrote,

> " John P.
> Robinson, he
> Says they didn't know everything down in Judee."

Mr. Savage believes that the world just as it is, with struggle, toil, sin, suffering, and death in it, is not only the world that God made, but the world that God meant; and that struggle, toil, sin, suffering, and death are to continue forever the school of the race, whose heaven is to be a perfect union of perfectly developed individualities. His position is entirely respectable for its honesty and courage, and no one can assail it on these grounds. But we suggest that the world could hardly be duller and uglier for those who now do the most of the hardest work in it even if it conformed to Christ's ideal.

III.

Tolstoï declares that he found its splendor and prosperity dull and ugly, and so devoid of real joy, so unsatisfying to his soul when his soul one day asked itself *What for*, and *What then*, that life became intolerable to him, and he meditated suicide. But, as we have already reminded our readers, in treating of Russian literature, the conditions of life here in this republic are so different from those of life there in that despotism as to be almost those of a better world in comparison. We have human nature and its temptations, and its passions and follies, as well as the Russians, but our civilization knows no such extremes as theirs; it has not their misdeeds, and need not have their remorse and despair. One should keep these facts in mind when reading Tolstoï's books, which fascinate by their right-mindedness and searching truth, and should use a reasoned conscience in regard to the ways and means of ameliorating life. We are still far from justice in our social conditions, but we are infinitely nearer it than Russia, and we have but to recognize that equality and fraternity in everything are the sole hope of the race in order to approach justice more and more.

One of the few points in which we resemble the Russians is in a multiplicity of religious sects; and we commend to the reader wishing to know something of the spiritual state of the community to which Tolstoï's primitive Christianity addresses itself Mr. Albert F. Heard's volume on *The Russian Church and Russian Dissent*. The chapters on the Erratic Sects are especially interesting, and a people who have produced Mormonism, Shakerism, and Materialization will recognize a kindred aspiration and chaos in the vagaries of those far-off fanatics. What seems strangest is that in the presence of an inflexible political despotism, which is also the framework of the Orthodox church, there should be so much religious liberty in Russia. Possibly the Russian rulers have found that human nature cannot be repressed at every point, and that its safest vent is in the direction of the other world. In any case, one cannot help feeling that not only the religion which Christ taught, but His political economy, which Mr. Savage thinks so ignorant and mistaken, might be tried in Russia with some hope of better things than now exist there. An argument which Tolstoï makes in favor of trying them somewhere is that they have never been tried anywhere. But, as we pointed out in speaking of *My Religion*, this seems an error. They have been tried by the Quakers and the Moravians, in whom they produced a high type of rather colorless and unpicturesque goodness. If these sects are now evanescent, the world is undoubtedly better for their past existence, and Mr. Savage, who likes diversity, would no doubt gladly keep them in his real-ideal world, at least in quality of contrasts. Tolstoï's word is evidently not the last word on this vital matter.

Even he does not accept the gospel *in toto*, as it is interpreted to us, for he doubts the immortality of the soul, while his bold critic strenuously affirms it. Perhaps here lies the great difference: we can endure much that is wrong and hideous here if we believe that it is merely temporary and disciplinary, and that it will be all right and beautiful hereafter.

IV.

An interesting confirmation of the theory that the direction of thought and its expression in literature is contemporaneous in places so widely separated as to be beyond one another's influence offers itself in Mr. Frank Wilkeson's *Recollections of a Private*. Mr. Wilkeson was an enlisted soldier of the Army of the Potomac, and although he won promotion long before the close of Grant's great campaign, he preferred to fight through it in the ranks. His story of the war, therefore, is the enlisted man's story, and it agrees with Tolstoï's *War and Peace* and *Scenes of the Siege of Sevastopol* in recognizing a battle, when once begun, as the work of the men fighting it, and not as the effect of generalship. The private soldiers, acting from individual intelligence and collective impulse, win the battle or lose it; the generals seldom realize their "plans" or carry them out after the first encounter. This was especially the case with our troops, in whom the grade of intelligence was so high, and who, Mr. Wilkeson seems to think, were seldom ably generaled. He makes it a reproach to the generals of our side that so few of them, in comparison with the Confederate generals, were killed; but this criticism is hardly just; the generals might retort that Mr. Wilkeson was not killed either. But the metal of the men on both sides, he says, was the same, except that on ours it was shamefully debased by the large alloy of bounty-jumpers, coffee-boilers, and bummers. Some passages of his book are not pleasant reading for those who believe that all the union soldiers were as good as their cause, or all the rebels as bad as theirs; but it will not offend patriots who mix common-sense with their love of country. He teaches that it was the common Americans—the American people—who fought the war through on both sides, and that the honor belongs to them. His book is well written—

very simply, very vividly, very graphically, and very, very frankly. In these times, when generalship is remembering and recording so much of the war, it is interesting, at least, to find the private soldier neither forgetful nor unable to speak. In the traits above mentioned this is one of the best books about the war which we have read; it would not perhaps be well to say it was the very best, though we do not know exactly why. The strain which runs through it is that which we hear from the beginning to the end of Tolstoï's *War and Peace*. "He knew that it was neither the plans of the commander, nor the placing of the troops, nor the number of guns, nor the amount of the slain, which decided the victory, but that imponderable force called the Spirit of the Army."

V.

In other words, that democracy which is the inspiration of our political frame asserts itself in Mr. Wilkeson's pages as the force which informed and guided the military life of the nation throughout the war. It is not for a civilian to decide whether Mr. Wilkeson is right or wrong in his doubt of generalship; there must be a great deal to say on the other side, and we merely note the temper of his book in its coincidence with that of the Russian soldier's, and as a sign of the times. The half-gods are going; will the gods arrive? Or is it the men who are to take their places, the plain, simple, common people, whom Lincoln thought their Creator must have loved because he made so many of them? At any rate hero-worship, in which this generation was dry-nursed, if not suckled, is a creed pretty well outworn. If it was a purely pagan superstition, we have not much to dread from it any more; we may approach it with sentiment, with a tenderness in which a measure of respect may safely mingle. It was not altogether a bad thing; it served its time. The great apostle of it, who became himself a sort of hero in his devotion to it, has been shown to be so wholly human by the records which have survived him that the heart must be hard indeed which does not now long to take Thomas Carlyle back to it, which does not welcome every word and fact casting a kindlier gleam upon his memory. It is droll, perhaps, for greatness to come to this effect; but no doubt greatness would often be found to end so if we knew it well. Because we have been so unsparingly acquainted with the greatness that was Carlyle, we have passed from the stupid and cruel stage in which we meaner men exulted to find him full of like frailties and errors with ourselves, and have come to that better mind about him in which we see that his defects were those common to the race, and that he had in high degree the uncommon will to live and to speak truly. He was not the prophet that many thought him; he was a Scotch peasant in blood and breeding who achieved the highest literary distinction without ceasing to be a Scotch peasant. For our own part we think this was as well for him as to start a Scotch peasant and end a Scotch lord; but that is a matter of taste upon which we do not insist. The inalienable peasant in him was ancestral, and what he did and wished to do was personal. The two were divinely mixed up in him; they formed his character, and together made Thomas Carlyle what he was; and we find that we cannot eliminate the peasant and bow down to the poet; but, again, for our own part, we have no desire to do this. We were glad of Professor Norton's labor in the publication of his *Letters*, not so much because they controverted Mr. Froude's defective biography as because they supplemented it; and we are glad now of the same conscientious editor's *Correspondence between Goethe and Carlyle*, because Carlyle's share in it makes us know him still better without making us know him differently. What Mr. Froude revealed (or exposed, if the reader finds that word more descriptive) remains Carlyle, but it no longer remains the whole of Carlyle. In this correspondence we find him taking an attitude manfully modest and self-respectfully reverent toward a man whom he regarded as truly great, and keeping it throughout an exchange of letters which must have had its disillusions and discouragements. The great Goethe as he shows himself here might oftener be called the good Goethe in the worst sense of that epithet, so wanderingly, putteringly benevolent are some of his letters. But only once, so far as we noted, does Carlyle suffer himself a cry of impatience and sardonic humor. This is when he has got Goethe's reply to a request for some expression to be used in his behalf as candidate for the Professorship of Moral Philosophy in the University of St. Andrews. "The old Sage," Carlyle writes to his brother John, then in Germany, "fills a whole sheet with his *Aeusserungen;* of which not quite one leaf belongs to me, the rest being, as it were, *Erklärungsbetrachtungen.....* To a certainty you must come round by Weimar and see this World's-wonder, and tell us on your sincerity what manner of man he is, for daily he grows more inexplicable to me. One letter is written like an oracle, the next shall be too redolent of twaddle..... Is he greater than man, or in his old days growing less than many men?"

Carlyle had of course answered himself this question in asking it: Goethe's letters are those of an old man. There is abundant kindness and good-will in them, and a sort of reflected glow from the writer's past; but there is little edification, and the reader must largely bring his own interest to them. They are much occupied with cataloguing the contents of boxes and parcels which he sends the "wedded pair" in Scotland, and with mild and friendly comment on the Englanders who keep turning up in Weimar; they are not, of course, without literary importance, and they are full of paternal affection for the Carlyles. They have their charm, and the situation on which the correspondence casts its light at Craigenputtock, whither Carlyle had gone that he need not be forced "to tell lies," need not be obliged to write for bread, has its dignity as well as its pathos. The humility with which Carlyle receives Goethe's letters, and the eagerness with which both he and his wife meet the great German's recognition of them in their poor proud life, as yet unconsoled by fame, are very touching. For how much neglect the maundering sage's goodness must have revenged them, of how much hope deferred must it have seemed the fruition, insipid and vacuous as it is to the reader! How hard those two keen wits must have striven to keep up the zeal of their gratitude to the end! The situation is one that no one would have thought of inventing, yet how interesting, how moving, how humorously suggestive, how natural and probable, it is when life has once framed it for us! Professor Norton, who arranges our point of view, has used unfailing skill and taste in his task. Every word of his own, and every word that he quotes from others, is luminous.

¹ See p. 103b for response.

𝕮𝖉𝖎𝖙𝖔𝖗'𝖘 𝕾𝖙𝖚𝖉𝖞.

I.

A WRITER in a Western periodical has[1] put into convenient shape some common errors concerning popularity as a test of merit in a book. He seems to think, for instance, that the love of the marvellous and impossible in fiction, which is shown not only by "the unthinking multitude clamoring about the book counters" for fiction of that sort, but by the "literary elect" also, is proof of some principle in human nature which ought to be respected as well as tolerated. He seems to believe that the ebullition of this passion forms a sufficient answer to those who say that art of all kinds should represent life, and that the art which misrepresents life is feeble art and false art. But it appears to us that a little carefuler reasoning from a little closer inspection of the facts would not have brought him to these conclusions. In the first place, we doubt very much whether the "literary elect" have been fascinated in great numbers by the fiction in question; but if we supposed them to have really fallen under that spell, we should still be able to account for their fondness and that of the "unthinking multitude" upon the same grounds, without honoring either very much. It is the habit of hasty casuists to regard civilization as inclusive of all the members of a civilized community; but this is a palpable error. Many persons in every civilized community live in a state of more or less evident savagery with respect to their habits, their morals, and their propensities; and they are held in check only by the law. Many more yet are savage in their tastes, as they show by the decoration of their houses and persons, and by their choice of books and pictures; and these are left to the restraints of public opinion. In fact, no man can be said to be thoroughly civilized or always civilized; the most refined, the most enlightened person has his moods, his moments of barbarism, in which the best, or even the second best, shall not please him. At these times the lettered and the unlettered are alike primitive, and their gratifications are of the same simple sort; the highly cultivated person may then like melodrama, impossible fiction, and the trapeze as sincerely and thoroughly as a boy of thirteen or a barbarian of any age.

We do not blame him for these moods; we find something instructive and interesting in them; but if they lastingly established themselves in him, we could not help deploring the state of that person. No one can really think that the "literary elect," who are said to have joined the "unthinking multitude" in clamoring about the book counters for the romances of no-man's land, take the same kind of pleasure in them as they do in a novel of Tolstoï, Tourguénief, George Eliot, Thackeray, Balzac, Manzoni, Hawthorne, Henry James, Thomas Hardy, Palacio Valdés, or even Walter Scott. They have joined the "unthinking multitude" perhaps because they are tired of thinking, and expect to find relaxation in feeling—feeling crudely, grossly, merely. For once in a way there is no great harm in this; perhaps no harm at all. It is perfectly natural: let them have their innocent debauch. But let us distinguish, for our own sake and guidance, between the different kinds of things that please the same kind of people; between the things that please them habitually and those that please them occasionally; between the pleasures that edify them and those that amuse them. Otherwise we shall be in danger of becoming permanently part of the "unthinking multitude," and of remaining puerile, primitive, savage. We shall be so in moods and at moments; but let us not fancy that those are high moods or fortunate moments. If they are harmless, that is the most that can be said for them. They are lapses from which we can perhaps go forward more vigorously; but even this is not certain.

Our own philosophy of the matter, however, would not bring us to prohibition of such literary amusements as the writer quoted seems to find significant of a growing indifference to truth and sanity in fiction. Once more, we say, these amusements have their place, as the circus has, and the burlesque, and negro minstrelsy, and the ballet, and prestidigitation. No one of these is to be despised in its place; but we had better understand that it is not the highest place, and that it is hardly an intellectual delight. The lapse of all the "literary elect" in the world could not dignify unreality; and their present mood, if it exists, is of no more weight against that beauty in literature which comes from truth alone, and never can come from anything else, than the permanent state of the "unthinking multitude."

II.

Yet even as regards the "unthinking multitude," we believe we are not able to take the attitude of the writer we have quoted. We are afraid that we respect them more than he would like to have us, though we cannot always respect their taste, any more than that of the "literary elect." We respect them for their good sense in most practical matters; for their laborious, honest lives; for their kindness, their good-will; for that aspiration toward something better than themselves which seems to stir, however dumbly, in every human breast not abandoned to literary pride or other forms of self-righteousness. We find every man interesting, whether he thinks or unthinks, whether he is savage or civilized; for this reason we cannot thank the novelist who teaches us not to know, but to unknow, our kind; and we cannot believe that Miss Murfree [2] will feel herself praised by a critic who says she has made her Tennessee mountaineers acceptable to us because she "has fashioned them as they are not." We believe that she has made them acceptable for exactly the opposite reason, and has taught us to see the inner loveliness and tenderness, however slight and evanescent, of those poor, hard, dull, narrow lives, with an exquisite sympathy which we are afraid must remain unknown to the lovers of the sweet-pretty. The perfect portrayal of what passes even in a soul whose body smokes a cob-pipe or dips snuff, and dwells in a log hut on a mountain-side, would be worth more than all the fancies ever feigned; and we value Miss Murfree's work for the degree in which it approaches this perfection. It is when she seems to have drawn upon romance and tradition rather than life for her colors that we have wished her to "give us her mountain folk as she saw them before her fancy began to work upon them." This may be "babbling folly," and "sheer, unmixed nonsense"; our critic is so sure of himself as to be able to call it so; but we venture to reaffirm it. It appears to us that the opposite position is one of the last refuges of the aristocratic spirit which is disappearing from politics and society, and is now seeking to shelter itself in æsthetics. The pride of caste is becoming the pride of taste; but as before, it is averse to the mass of men; it consents to know them only in some conventionalized and artificial guise. It seeks to withdraw itself, to stand aloof; to be distinguished, and not to be identified. Democracy in literature is the reverse of all this. It wishes to know and to tell the truth, confident that consolation and delight are there; it does not care to paint the marvellous and impossible for the vulgar many, or to sentimentalize and falsify the actual for the vulgar few. Men are more like than unlike one another: let us make them know one another better, that they may be all humbled and strengthened with a sense of their fraternity. Neither arts, nor letters, nor sciences, except as they somehow, clearly or obscurely, tend to make the race better and kinder, are to be regarded as serious interests; they are all lower than the rudest crafts that feed and house and clothe, for except they do this office they are idle; and they cannot do this except from and through the truth. [3]

III.

A more temperate critic than the one we [4] have been quoting deplores in a New York journal the danger which attends the new fiction of the South from its prompt and easy success. He calls himself a Southerner, and he thinks it would be well if there were a school of Southern criticism for the censure of Southern literature; but at the same time he is disposed to defend this literature against a charge which we agree with him cannot lie against it alone. It has been called narrow, and he asks: "Is not the broadest of the new American fiction narrow, when compared, as it should be compared, with the authors of Russian fiction, French fiction, English fiction? Is there a living novelist of the North whose largest boundaries do not shrink to pitiful dimensions when put by the side of Tolstoï's, or Balzac's, or Thackeray's?"

We do not know certainly whether a Southerner thinks narrowness a defect of Northern fiction or not, but upon the supposition that he does so, we remind him that both Thackeray and Balzac are dead, and that our recent novelists might as well, for all purposes of argument, be compared with Cervantes and Le Sage. Moreover, Balzac is rather a narrow writer in each of his books, and if we are to grant him breadth we must take him in the whole group which he required to work out his *comédie humaine.* Each one of Mr. Henry James's books is as broad as any one of Balzac's; and we believe his *Princess Casamassima* is of a scope and variety quite unknown to them. Thackeray, to be sure, wandered through vast spaces, but his greatest work was concerned with the very narrow world of English society; his pictures of life outside of society were in the vein of caricature. As for Tolstoï, he is the incomparable; and no novelist of any time or any tongue can fairly be compared with him, as no dramatist can fairly be compared with Shakespeare. Nevertheless, if something of this sort is absolutely required, we will instance Mr. J. W. De Forest, in his very inadequately named *Miss Ravenel's Conversion,* as presenting an image of American life during the late rebellion, both North and South, at home and in the field, which does not "shrink to pitiful dimensions" even when "put by the side of Tolstoï's" *War and Peace;* it is an admirable novel, and spacious enough for the vast drama glimpsed in it. Mr. Cable's *Grandissimes* is large enough to reflect a civilization; and Mr. Bishop, in *The Golden Justice* and *The House of a Merchant Prince,* shows a feeling for amplitude in the whole design, as well as for close and careful work in the details.

The present English fiction is as narrow [ ] as our own; and if a Southerner had looked a little farther abroad he would have found that most modern fiction was narrow in a certain sense. In Italy he would have found the best men writing novels as brief and restricted in range as ours; in Spain the novels are intense and deep, and not spacious; the French school, with the exception of Zola, is narrow; the Norwegians are narrow; the Russians, except Tolstoï, are narrow, and the next greatest after him, Tourguénief, is the narrowest great novelist, as to mere dimensions, that ever lived, dealing nearly always with small groups, isolated and analyzed in the most American fashion. In fine, the charge of narrowness accuses the whole tendency of modern fiction as much as the American school. But we do not by any means allow that this superficial narrowness is a defect, while denying that it is a universal characteristic of our fiction; it is rather, for the present, a virtue. Indeed, we should call the present American work, North and South, thorough, rather than narrow. In one sense it is as broad as life, for each man is a microcosm, and the writer who is able to acquaint us intimately with half a dozen people, or the conditions of a neighborhood or a class, has done something which cannot in any bad sense be called narrow; his breadth is vertical instead of lateral, that is all; and this depth is more desirable than horizontal expansion in a civilization like ours, where the differences are not of classes, but of types, and not of types either so much as of characters. A new method was necessary in dealing with the new conditions, and the new method is world-wide, because the whole world is more or less Americanized. Tolstoï is exceptionally voluminous among modern writers, even Russian writers; and it might be said that the *forte* of Tolstoï himself is not in his breadth sidewise, but in his breadth upward and downward. *The Death of Ivan Illitch* leaves as vast an impression on the reader's soul as any episode of *War and Peace*, which indeed can only be recalled in episodes, and not as a whole. In fine, we think that our writers may be safely counselled to continue their work in the modern way, because it is the best way yet known. If they make it true, it will be large, no matter what its superficies are; and it would be the greatest mistake to try to make it big. A big book is necessarily a group of episodes more or less loosely connected by a thread of narrative, and there seems no reason why this thread must always be supplied. Each episode may be quite distinct, or it may be one of a connected group; the final effect will be from the truth of each episode, not from the size of the group. | 5

IV.

Take, for instance, a number of studies like *A Humble Romance, and Other Stories*, by Miss Mary E. Wilkins, and you have the air of simple village life as liberally imparted as if all the separate little dramas were set in a single frame and related to one another. The old maids and widows aging and ailing and dying in their minute wooden houses; the forlorn elderly lovers; the simple girls and youths making and marring love; the husbands and wives growing apart and coming together; the quarrels and reconciliations; the eccentricities and the heroisms; the tender passions and true friendships; the funerals and weddings; the hates and spites; the injuries; the sacrifices; the crazy consciences; the sound common-sense—are all suggested and expressed in a measure which, we insist, does not lack breadth, though each sketch is like the sentences of Emerson, "an infinitely repellent particle," and will have nothing to do with any other, so far as community of action is concerned. Community of character abounds: the people are of one New England blood, and speak one racy tongue. It might all have been done otherwise; the lives and fortunes of these villagers might have been interwoven in one texture of narrative; but the work would not necessarily have gained breadth in gaining bulk. Breadth is in the treatment of material, not in the amount of it. The great picture is from the great painter, not from the extensive canvas. Miss Wilkins's work could hardly have given a wider sense of life in a Yankee village and the outlying farms if it had greater structural unity. It has unity of spirit, of point of view, of sympathy; and being what the author intended, we ask no other unity of it; many "broader" views lack this unity which is so valuable. Besides, it has humor of a quaint, flavorous sort, it has genuine pathos, and a just and

true respect for the virtues of the life with which it deals. We are tempted to give some passages illustrative of a very remarkable freshness in its description; they are abundant, but perhaps we had better content ourselves by referring the reader to the opening of the touching sketch, "A Far-away Melody." What is notable in all the descriptions is the absence of literosity; they are as unrhetorical as so many pictures of Tourguénief's, or Björnson's, or Verga's, and are interesting proofs of the fact that the present way of working is instinctive; one writer does not learn it from another; it is in the time, in the air, and no critic can change it. When you come to the motives of these little tales, the simplicity and originality are not always kept; sometimes they ring false, sentimental, romantic; but even then they are true in the working out of character, though this does not redeem them from the original error. For the most part, however, they are good through and through, and whoever loves the face of common humanity will find pleasure in them. They are peculiarly American, and they are peculiarly "narrow" in a certain way, and yet they are like the best modern work everywhere in their directness and simplicity. They are somewhat in the direction of Miss Jewett's more delicate work, but the fun is opener and less demure, the literature is less refined, the poetry is a little cruder; but there is the same affectionate feeling for the material, a great apparent intimacy with the facts, and a like skill in rendering the Yankee parlance. We have our misgivings, however, about "thar" and "whar" on New England tongues, though we are not ready to deny that Miss Wilkins heard them in the locality she evidently knows so well.

V.

We own our misgiving with misgiving; for so clever a writer has probably thought upon this point already. We do not suppose infallibility in clever writers; but we do suppose a greater intelligence concerning their own work than any critic can bring to it; their ignorance even may be more valuable than his information; it may keep them at least from attempting to do their own work in some one else's way, and that is a great matter. In fact, if our present literary condition were bad, North or South, we should have no such hope of its improvement from criticism as the Southerner whom we have been quoting. In his belief that severity of censure would avail much, he advises Southern writers to turn from the mistaken kindness of Northern editors, and if they cannot get wholesome castigation from their Southern contemporaries, to go back to Poe, "and take from his critical writings a certain standard of originality, contempt of mediocrity, and passion for beauty." But we doubt if it is possible to take any such standard, contempt, and passion from Poe, who, with great talent, had a perversity, arrogance, and wilfulness that render him wellnigh worthless as a censor of others' work, and a mechanical ideal that disabled him from doing any very noble work of his own. He was of his time, and his tales and poems remain a part of literary history; but if they were written to-day, most of them could not be taken seriously. Do not go to Poe, we should say to our Southern writers if we felt it our office to instruct them, but go to Life. Do not trouble yourselves about standards or contempts or passions; but try to be faithful and natural; and remember that there is no greatness, no beauty, which does not come from truth to your own knowledge of things. In the mean time, that "standard |6 of mere acceptableness at the hands of the great Northern magazines" which a Southerner laments as ruinous to Southern writers is, to our thinking, the best critical standard they could have; and although these magazines certainly do "publish, almost monthly, poems or short stories which never live as literature," this does not disable them as criterions. At least three-fifths of the litera- ture called classic, in all languages, no more lives than the poems and stories that perish monthly in our magazines. It is all printed and reprinted, generation after generation, cen- tury after century; but it is not alive; it is as dead as the people who wrote it and read it, and to whom it meant something, perhaps; with whom it was a fashion, a caprice, a passing taste. A superstitious piety preserves it, and pretends that it has æsthetic qualities which can de- light or edify; but nobody really enjoys it, except as a reflection of the past moods and humors of the race, or a revelation of the au- thor's character; otherwise it is trash, and often very filthy trash, which the present trash at least is not. The "standard of mere ac- |7 ceptableness at the hands of the great North- ern magazines" is a very high standard. They are not perfect; but there is an even texture in the quality of their literature which so wide a variety of literature has never presented be- fore. They are made with conscience and in- telligence, and with an instinctive preference for what is most modern as, upon the whole, the best. Any Southern writer who contributes to them may be sure that their editors will be the first to know when he is repeating him- self, when he is standing still, and when he is going backward, and may confidently await their warning signal.

The whole field of human experience was never so nearly covered by imaginative litera- ture in any age as in this; and American life especially is getting represented with unex- ampled fulness. It is true that no one writer, no one book, represents it, for that is not pos- sible; our social and political decentralization forbids this, and may forever forbid it. But a great number of very good writers are in- stinctively striving to make each part of the country and each phase of our civilization known to all the other parts; and their work is not narrow in any feeble or vicious sense. The world was once very little, and it is now very large. Formerly, all science could be grasped by a single mind; but now the man who hopes to become great or useful in sci- ence must devote himself to a single depart- ment. It is so in everything—all arts, all trades; and the novelist is not superior to the universal rule against universality. He con- tributes his share to a thorough knowledge of groups of the human race under conditions which are full of inspiring novelty and inter- est. He works more fearlessly, frankly, and faithfully than the novelist ever worked be- fore; his work, or much of it, may be destined never to be reprinted from the monthly maga- zines; but if he turns to his book-shelf and re- gards the array of the British or other classics, he knows that they too are for the most part

dead; he knows that the planet itself is des- tined to freeze up and drop into the sun at last, with all its surviving literature upon it. The question is merely one of time. He consoles himself, therefore, if he is wise, and works on; and we may all take some comfort from the thought that most things cannot be helped. Especially a movement in literature like that which the world is now witnessing cannot be helped; and we could no more turn back and be of the literary fash- ions of any age before this than we could turn back and be of its social, economical, or po- litical conditions. |8

VI.

These, like those, are greatly improved in the present everywhere, and how much they have been improved with us, at a focal point, the reader may learn from the entertaining *Reminiscences* of Major Ben: Perley Poore. That veteran journalist, who recently end- ed a long life of hard work performed with fidelity and constancy, was for sixty years the correspondent of various newspapers at the national capital, and saw Washington grow up from an uncouth village into the most charming city in the world. His recol- lections of more than half a century date from the inauguration of John Quincy Adams to that of Grover Cleveland; they are apparently im- partial, and certainly temperate and guarded. But their chief value is the panorama of events at Washington which they unfold from the year 1825 to the year 1885, and the encourage- ment they bring to the lover of his country and of his species. In nearly everything that dignifies and beautifies life the thronging fig- ures and incidents of this long canvas testi- fy to the immense improvement that has taken place in the nation as represented at the capi- tal. One cannot read the volumes and not be convinced that the tone of manners and morals is, on the whole, better at Washington now than it was sixty years ago, both in pri- vate and in public, and that through all appar- ent arrests and reactions the national con- scientiousness has made itself more and more felt at the national capital.

Major Poore was a good story-teller, and he tells stories without end, but his work is not a mere texture of long or short yarns. It is also a sketch of our history for the time being, which is to be praised for the ease and clear- ness with which now the personal and now the general side is shown, or the history is resumed and the anecdote is dropped. The work has no profundity, but a good deal of shrewdness; it is for the most part both out- spoken and amiable. Here and there the au- thor seems to be airing a personal prejudice, but not often; he either dislikes very few people, or else he keeps his dislikes to him- self. His work is done with tact and with good feeling, if not good taste, always.

A book of less consecutive interest and of less *bonhomie* than Major Poore's *Reminis- cences* is the late Henry B. Stanton's *Random Recollections*, which has the same sort of value as the materials of history. Mr. Stanton, who began political life an abolitionist and ended it a Tilden Democrat, seems to have touched at some point all the men and measures of his long day, and to have had a personal know- ledge of many things which posterity must not ignore in judging the past. Some celebrities, some fames, may suffer; we shall have rather fewer political heroes; but there will always be enough and to spare of these, and the race will, upon the whole, be the gainer through their decimation. Mr. Stanton was a keen observer, but he was not dispassionate, and there is not the effect of impartiality in his book which pleases in Major Poore's. Still he is of such an open make himself that no great harm is done; one sees what comes from his convictions, and what comes from his preferences. He bore courageously his part, which was perhaps all the harder to bear because it was not a leading part, in a political world which now seems as extinct as if it had perished very much more than ten years ago.

The country seems to have come of age in many ways during the war. Of what it was in art before that epoch the reader may get some glimpses in the pleasant collection of the *Letters of Horatio Greenough to his Brother Henry Greenough*, whose widow, Mrs. Frances Boott Greenough, accompanies the letters with biographical sketches and some illustrative contemporary correspondence, enabling us to know our first great American sculptor in many relations, at home and abroad. He was a man whose career was apparently marked out for him from the beginning, and neither the straitness of private circumstance nor the absence of incentive, in what was once perhaps the most provincial country in the world, could stay him in it. He went abroad at the age of twenty, and his after-life was passed in Italy, in steadfast devotion to his art, with brief visits to America, until he finally returned to die here in his forty-eighth year. It was mainly a serene and tranquil life; it had its sorrows, and it was vexed near its close by what the artist felt to be the shabbiness of our government in its dealings with him; but

it was never embittered, and he was in the joyous ardor of an enterprise at New York which consoled him for official reluctance at Washington when it suddenly ended. His letters bear witness to a spirit wholly unspoiled by success; and they signally record his fidelity to democratic traditions in a wily Old World which flatters so many successful Americans out of faith in them. There is a manly gentleness throughout, a tone of self-respect, a temperamental kindliness, with quick observation and good sense, and a lovely simplicity of expression, which make one think of Longfellow, with the difference that necessarily lies between the poet and the sculptor in everything relating to art. In the letters and in the graceful sketches which Mrs. Greenough contributes there are glimpses of the great political events which occurred at Florence during the artist's residence there; he saw the success and failure of the revolution of 1848; and the remote life of Boston, when Boston was only a large town, is attractively suggested. In these days, when the new science of heredity is perhaps disposed to vaunt itself a little, a fact which Mrs. Greenough notices in the family history has its interest. The sculptor and his five brothers, all of artistic bent, and all finally more or less devoted to art, sprang from a stock in which, so far as is known, the artistic impulse had never been felt before. Probably science would tell us that the impulse was always there, though unconscious and unrecognized, and that the removal of the Greenoughs from the country to the more favorable environment of the town freed and developed the latent gift. Boston was then a more purely intellectual centre than now; it had enthusiasms, especially æsthetic enthusiasms, and the local atmosphere must have been invigorating if not congenial for the young artist.

[1] Joseph Le Conte, "The General Principles of Art and their Application to the 'Novel,'" Overland Monthly, 5 (2nd series) (April, 1885), 337-347.

[2] Criticism and Fiction, pp. 107-112.

[3] Criticism and Fiction, pp. 187-188.

[4] Anonymous ("A Southerner"), "Literature in the South," The Critic, 10 (June 25, 1887), 322-324.

[5] Criticism and Fiction, pp. 141-143.

[6] Criticism and Fiction, p. 145.

[7] Criticism and Fiction, p. 146.

[8] Criticism and Fiction, pp. 143-145.

October, 1887

Editor's Study.

I.

IN his *Life of John Keats*, the latest issue of the "English Men of Letters" series, Mr. Sidney Colvin tells once more the most pathetic story in the annals of our literature, with a clearness, sympathy, and good sense which give it a fresh interest. We do not say that he makes Keats more known to us; the facts had been pretty thoroughly ascertained before; but he makes him better known, if there is such a difference; he makes us understand him. He does not write of him, as people must a generation ago, with heartbreak for his unfulfilled love and early death, with hot indignation for the malevolence of the criticism which was as savage as if it had really killed him, with idolatry for the beauty that divinely thrills and flushes in his verse. That personal mood is past, and Mr. Colvin lets us see him as a very natural phase of the great Romantic movement, quite inevitably arousing the hate of an equally natural phase of Classicism, in a conservative civilization shortly before frightened out of its decency by the spectre of revolution. It seems a far way about from Leigh Hunt's radical lampoon on the Prince of Wales to the high Tory attacks of *Blackwood* and the *London Quarterly* upon Keats, but the sequence through the friendship of the two poets is perfect, and one followed the other in the ordinary course of events. We have to imagine social conditions of a brutality which it is now hard to imagine before we can fully conceive of avenging a political difference by an assault on a poet's æsthetics, and by insult to his origin, and even to the profession he had abandoned, but any account of English society in George the Fourth's regency and reign will help us in the effort. When we have succeeded in making it, we shall perhaps understand how those attacks, which now seem so shallow and stupid, did really destroy, not Keats, but the public of Keats, and rendered him despicable to the average contemporary reader. No one at the time was more fully aware of this than he; and he accepted the fact with patience, while he felt in every nerve the atrocious injustice. He perceived that for the time it was literary death to him; but he met his fate manfully. He had the measure of himself, and he knew his own weaknesses better than the thick wits who outraged him for his virtues. He never denied that they wounded and discouraged him; he had not the folly of that hardihood, any more than the folly of that sensitiveness which once misrepresented him to most readers; but he was acquainted with the British public and its respect for authority, and he recognized that *Blackwood* and the *Quarterly* were authorities. It would not be safe to say that if Keats had been of a dif-

ferent political thinking these authorities would have praised him, but there can be no doubt that his liberalism embittered their spite. At any rate, he saw that he could have no present hope of success against them, and he submitted. He was dispirited; but his breaking health had quite other causes; he was the son of a consumptive mother; one of his brothers had died of consumption under his care, and the malady fastened itself upon him in the usual way; even the dramatic incident of his coughing up arterial blood and calling for a light and reading his doom in it, was one of a series of facts antedating it by several months.

Life was slipping from him, but fame was coming, to abide with his name while the language endures. It appears that all the adverse criticism, mixed with the cruelest obloquy, did not stay him nor swerve him for a moment. That was impossible; his whole intellectual being had resolved itself into his share of the work of liberating from forms and conventions the poetry which he enlarged with entrancing perspectives of unexpected phrase, and enriched with words so exquisitely chosen that they surprise like creations. He had his defects, his vices, of which he was conscious in part and partly not, and all of which his latest biographer notes with what we may call a sympathetic impartiality; but it was not for the reviewers and magazinists who could see nothing good in him to destroy him, though for the time they defeated him. He was part of the great tendency of his epoch, and his career illustrates the futility with which criticism opposes itself to any such tendency in any epoch or under any conditions. The end must always be the same; and we have a pleasure in helping to disabuse the reader, if any still linger in that superstition, of the old fabulous belief that Keats's critics compassed even Keats's death. They grievously hurt a generous spirit singularly susceptible to insult, but they had no other power upon him, and they did not change him one jot or tittle.

II.

The England of Keats's time, say from 1815 to 1825, the England of political reaction, is a region little explored by the curiosity of our time in those phases of passive or active protest which must have been very common among unstoried lives, and we therefore commend as a study of these a book which is otherwise very worthy of attention. It is called *The Revolution in Tanner's Lane*, and it is from the same hand that gave us the *Mark Rutherford* books already spoken of here. It is like these in its uncommon and unequal power, and in its unliterary naturalness, its deep feeling, and its novel material. The scenes lie again among the intellectualized artisans, of whom there are more than what calls itself culture suspects, and there are some important studies of English Philistinism, as well as of one type of high-caste radicalism, and types equally fresh and interesting of French refugee radicalism. We awkwardly indicate by these terms several characters vigorously painted and interestingly contrasted in a canvas where other figures are merely blocked out, and where there is an interrupted unity of design, as a whole. The book is, in fact, two fragments which scarcely supplement each other's incompleteness; and it is only fair to say that there is a courage in some of the thinking about the things of this life and the other in which some righteous souls might dread offence. But these ought to be the first to concede a sincerity that is so rare as to be almost precious in itself, and an honesty which is never irreverent. In a time when so little English fiction is strenuous or direct, it is almost a duty to praise a book dealing as originally with life as the Russians themselves, upon ground practically as new.

"How few materials," says Emerson, "are yet used by our arts! The mass of creatures and of qualities are still hid and expectant," and to break new ground is still one of the uncommonest and most heroic of the virtues. The artists are not alone to blame for the timidity that keeps them in the old furrows of the worn-out fields; most of those whom they live to please, or live by pleasing, prefer to have them remain there; it wants rare virtue to appreciate what is new, as well as to invent it; and the "easy things to understand" are the conventional things. This is why the ordinary English novel, with its hackneyed plot, scenes, and figures, is more comfortable to the ordinary American than an American novel, which deals, at its worst, with comparatively new interests and motives. To adjust one's self to the enjoyment of these costs an intellectual effort, and an intellectual effort is what no ordinary person likes to make. It is only the extraordinary person who can say, with Emerson: "I ask not for the great, the remote, the romantic; .... I embrace the common; I sit at the feet of the familiar and the low.... Man is surprised to find that things near are not less beautiful and wondrous than things remote.... The perception of the worth of the vulgar is fruitful in discoveries.... The foolish man wonders at the unusual, but the wise man at the usual.... To-day always looks mean to the thoughtless; but to-day is a king in disguise.... Banks and tariffs, the newspaper and caucus, Methodism and Unitarianism, are flat and dull to dull people, but rest on the same foundations of wonder as the town of Troy and the temple of Delphos."

Perhaps we ought not to deny their town of Troy and their temple of Delphos to the dull people; but if we ought, and if we did, they would still insist upon having them. An English novel, full of titles and rank, is apparently essential to the happiness of such people; their weak and childish imagination is at home in its familiar environment; they know what they are reading; the fact that it is hash many times warmed over reassures them; whereas a story of our own life, honestly studied and faithfully represented, troubles them with varied misgiving. They are not sure that it is literature; they do not feel that it is good society; its characters, so like their own, strike them as commonplace; they say they do not wish to know such people. [1]

III.

"English history," says Mr. J. W. De Forest, in a recent letter to the press, "is ancient, impressive, and far-famed, compared with our own; it is more agreeable to identify one's self with the ivy-grown castle than with the lowly and transitory log cabin. In the second place, an Englishman may be a noble, which is not possible with an American. When the New York dude puts on British costume and stutters in British accents, he is not trying to pass himself off for a London shopkeeper, but for a swell out of the English peerage or squirearchy. Now why are we so prodigiously impressed by the ivy-grown castle and by the class which belongs to it? It is because our minds are drenched from childhood with English fiction. In our reading we are still colonial; we have never had our war of independence. A host of English novelists fill the minds of our youth with English pictures of life, English ideas and preferences and prejudices. From the age of fifteen the American dude has been revelling by imagination in the aristocratic society of the mother-land, and learning to wish that he could attain to it. It is not to be expected that he should remain fervidly patriotic or democratic in his fancies and manners."

All this is perfectly true, and it is also true that the literary subjection in which we are to England has its lovely and charming phase as well as its odious aspect. We sit at the feet not only of the second-rate English novelists, but of the sympathetic and winning English essayists, the true and great English poets, and the ideal England is so endeared to us in earliest childhood by the very nursery rhymes, that when we come to the real England nothing is strange there but the Englishmen. We have known those gentle hills and streams, those green fields and hedges, those low, soft skies, those rooks and larks and nightingales, all our lives; and even if we are snobs, as most of us are, a genuine poetic strain in us is touched by the sight of noblemen's castles and gentlemen's places, and their parks and pleasances. Everything in England is appreciable to the literary sense, while the sense of the literary worth of things in America is still faint and weak with most people, with the vast majority who "ask for the great, the remote, the romantic," who cannot "embrace the common," cannot "sit at the feet of the familiar and the low," in the good company of Emerson. The effect is no doubt such as Mr. De Forest suggests, with these. We are all, or nearly all, struggling to be distinguished from the mass, and to be set apart in select circles and upper classes like the fine people we have read about. We are really a mixture of the plebeian ingredients of the whole world; but that is not bad; our vulgarity consists in trying to ignore "the worth of the vulgar," in believing that the superfine is better. [2]

IV.

Mr. De Forest makes the situation a text from which he preaches a brief sermon to the tough-conscienced fathers of the republic, urging them to pass an international copyright law, to the end that the English novel, which corrupts the fancy of the American dude, may become as costly as home fiction, and so be deprived of one ruinous advantage of stolen goods.

But there is another ground upon which we must always deplore the present pillage of English authors, and which Mr. De Forest would no doubt have touched if it had not seemed better, for the time, to limit himself to the point he was making. He, like every other honest man who thinks about the matter, must feel keenly the disgrace, now fairly shifted from the American publishers to the American public, of the wrong involved in the absence of an international copyright law. We prefer to put our demand for it upon this ground at once, because we believe we shall never have such a law till we appeal to the common conscience instead of the common interest. With the common conscience it now distinctly rests, for, however literary piracy grew up, in the days before the wrong had been duly considered, it must now be owned that American publishers, with but one or two exceptions, are in favor of its suppression. They stand with American authors in this, and it is now the American nation that wilfully perpetuates an abuse which in a small way is morally worse than slavery in a large way. Slavery compelled a man's labor, but it gave him in return food, shelter, and clothing, such as they were; literary piracy seizes the fruits of a man's labor, and gives him absolutely nothing in return. There can be no question of the nature of the wrong, and no justification of it. From time to time we hear that the English also pirate American books; but no one has the effrontery to urge this in defence of our piracy of English books; and every one knows that if the English continued to pirate our books for a hundred years the balance of guilt would still be upon our side. Moreover, every one knows that if we enacted justice to the English author, there would be an instant response on the part of England to our tardy reparation; in fact, prior publication in Great Britain already secures for the American author the protection which our law denies to the alien upon any condition.

We confess we have not much sympathy with the arguments of those who prove that foreign books would be just as cheap with a copyright law, and that we should somehow find our profit in doing justice to English authors. No doubt we should, if honesty is the best policy; but our people have no right to cheap literature by defrauding the author; they could have cheap silks and cheap wines by a like simple process. We are not to give over wrong-doing because it does not pay, but because it is wrong; and we are not to abandon literary piracy because it has disorganized the publishing business, but because it is a flagrant injustice, which no law, and no want of law, can change in its essence.

Those who appeal to the motives of self-interest in urging international copyright are like the philanthropists, of no great effect in their day and generation, who used to say that they did not care for the slaves, but were opposed to slavery because it was so ruinous to the masters. The masters smiled patiently under their burdens, and kept on holding slaves; and probably the literary pirates, un-

less they are rescued by a compassionate statute, will continue to bear their crushing load without murmuring. But the voluntary pirates are no longer numerous; they are very few; and this fact makes their offence more distinctly a national sin, because the nation could so easily suppress them. Some of us may seek to escape complicity in the sin by refusing to buy the cheap pirated editions of foreign books, as certain zealots used to refrain from the sugar and cotton produced by slave labor. But this privation had no perceptible effect upon the system of slavery, and for one just person who denies himself a ten-cent copy of an English novel because it pays the author nothing, a hundred of the wicked will buy it because it is a ten-cent copy.

It is the slow conscience of these hundreds and hundred thousands that we must reach before we can hope for an international copyright law; and we ought not to be discouraged because we are indefinitely remote from the desired end. After all, the American nation is not so wilfully as it is ignorantly guilty in this matter. The great mass of the people, even of those who buy books, have not the least notion what a pirated book is, or what the sacred principle which it outrages; they do not know what copyright is, international or otherwise. But they can be told; and we venture to suggest to our good friends of the International Copyright League that they prepare a very brief and very plain statement of the facts, such as the wayfaring man, though a fool, might not err in, to be printed in all the newspapers, and to be read in the churches throughout the country. We trust that few editors or ministers would refuse their aid to so good a cause, or would object to submit for signatures in their offices and vestries a petition to Congress for the passage of an international copyright law. The editor could readily illustrate the case by reference to some sketch or story reprinted in his paper from an English magazine without compensation to the author; and the minister could instance pirated reprints in the Sunday-school library in proof of the shameful wrong involved by the absence of such a law.

V.

We urge a little haste in the action of the League, because there has been proposed —ironically, perhaps—a "Bill for creating and maintaining National Free Circulating Libraries," which must have a great charm for the fancy of the cheap politician. This bill proposes to levy a tax, graduated to the bulk of the book, upon all foreign works imported or reprinted; but the money thus collected is not to be paid over to the foreign authors—that would be opposed to the whole tenor of our dealings with these outlaws—it is to be devoted to establishing, under the direction of the Secretary of the Treasury, free circulating libraries throughout the Union. By this simple and ready means a temple to our national discredit can be erected in every principal town in the country, and all our citizens can directly participate in the advantages of our common wrong-doing.

The chief difficulty in the way of believing the proposed bill a satire is its perfect consonance with the principles which have always governed us as a nation in our dealings with foreign authors. Long ago the respectable publishers among us began, in the absence of law, to pay these authors for their works; and even now, in the utterly disorganized state of that branch of the trade, when no comity protects one reprinter against another, the honorable publisher pays something—a little, but something. The nation, however, has never swerved from the position taken by the fathers, and has steadily authorized its citizens to take the literary property of the alien whenever they could lay hands upon it. It still authorizes them to do so, and we believe that if this bill to found national free circulating libraries by the official plunder of foreign authors were seriously introduced in Congress, it would meet with far greater favor from the average politician than any measure for the protection of those authors, and would have a better chance of passing both houses than a bill to establish international copyright.

It could be readily proved that the cause of education would be served by these free libraries, and there is no question but the great mass of those who used them would remain ignorant if not innocent of offence. It is even imaginable that Congress itself could pass such a bill without a sense of wrong, and we have no intention to arraign Congressmen as especially responsible for the want of international copyright. They are no worse than their constituents; we are all alike guilty, and ought all to be made to feel a modicum of the shame which comes home to the detected sinner. The wrong that our sin of omission involves should be made clear to every intelligence, every conscience; and we think that the friends of international copyright cannot begin to urge the moral aspect of the case upon the public too soon, for we do not believe that their cause will ever be won till this is done. We would have them put it at its worst; we would have them tell the people that this is the cause of the class which seems the strongest and is the weakest, that the class is small, and cannot hope to affect legislation in any ordinary way, that no politician sees any advantage in befriending it, that unless the American people take its cause to heart there is no chance for it with the American government. But let them add that it is one of the most righteous causes that ever appealed to the justice of a nation; that the wrong is as old as the nation; and that if English authors were paid up with interest for the piracies of the past, the award would be as just as that made us by England for the depredations of the *Alabama*.

Let the International Copyright League invoke the aid not only of the press and the pulpit, but of every social organization, and the whole educational mechanism of the country. Let it provide petitions for signature, and scatter them broadcast, in the schools, the libraries, the clubs, the churches, the post-offices; and then take care that these petitions are duly collected, and presented to Congress when the next bill for international copyright is introduced. Let it be known that every vested interest of piracy can be protected, and justice still be done; let it be understood that the friends of this most righteous cause will be humbly glad to accept any measure, however halting and imperfect, which tends toward righting the wrong of generations—and we do not believe that Congress will fail to respond to the popular demand.

VI.

"Since you are curious to know what is read in wardrooms," writes a naval officer, in reply to the inquiry suggested in the Study of our August number, "I will undertake to give you a general statement. Old newspapers, particularly local papers, and cheap novels, form the bulk of our literature. There are a few omnivorous readers among us, and now and then a critical one. I have a friend who enjoys the whole of Herbert Spencer, and in my last ship there were three who appreciated Stevenson, Meredith, and Jane Austen. Perhaps something of this latter result was due to missionary effort."

This is interesting, and not, on the whole, disappointing. We do not know in which sense our correspondent uses the word cheap, but if it is to indicate inexpensiveness simply, it is not necessarily to the disadvantage of the wardroom taste; almost any good reprint can now be bought for ten or twenty cents, whether it pays a copyright to the author, or a tax to the nation for the foundation of free circulating libraries. The old local newspapers are in the nature of old letters from home, and we suspect that the three who appreciated Stevenson, Meredith, and Jane Austen, together with the one who enjoyed Spencer, form a high average, not easily to be matched among readers elsewhere.

It is idle for literary people to deceive themselves, and we had better face the fact that many of those even who read appreciatively do not read intelligently. They feel that a thing is good, but they do not know how or why; very commonly they do not know the author's name or the title of the book, and they have never thought it important to know them. We literary folk make a great noise, and suppose ourselves to be generally understood in our relation to civilization, but there are vast numbers of our readers who do not even understand our relation to literature, or how literature becomes or exists. This is very unpalatable truth, but it is truth nevertheless, and until we have assimilated it we shall not be able to conceive of the almost immeasurable ignorance which lies between the popular conscience and a sense of the wrong done by the want of international copyright.

VII.

Probably the great difficulty of doing justice to the position of another, when there is the best will in the world to be just, would account for a vast deal of misrepresentation, and may be the obscure origin of a prevalent journalistic principle against making corrections of statement. The able editor instinctively feels that he will only be making bad worse by attempting to make it better, and he denies himself the satisfaction of the effort. But we have not this spirit of unselfish resignation, and we desire to recall to the reader the passage in the Study for August, intended to define the views of Rev. M. J. Savage concerning a point which he rightly feels to be important. Our summary of his sermon on Tolstoï was that he held Christ to be "a supremely good soul, but an inferior intellect," and Tolstoï "a still lower intellect in attempting to rehabilitate Him as a practical reformer." But in a passage of his discourse to which Mr. Savage calls our attention, he says that "it is no impeachment of his intellectual ability" to represent Christ as unpractical and mistaken in regard to the future, as "legislating for a passing phase of society instead of for the growing order of a developing civilization," which he did not foresee. Mr. Savage criticises Christ's "social and economical ideas precisely as he would those of Plato's Republic"; and he conceives that "this does not even raise the question of Christ's intellectual rank, any more than questioning some position of Kant or Bacon would be passing on their intellect. An inferior intellect to-day sees much that the greatest could not see one or two thousand years ago." So far as this is a question of words, we prefer that Mr. Savage's words should remain with the reader, and not ours.

---

[1] *Criticism and Fiction*, pp. 78-80.

[2] *Criticism and Fiction*, pp. 80-81.

[3] See pp. 92a-93a.

November, 1887

Editor's Study.

I.

AN ingenious writer in the *Christian Register*, of Boston, makes a passage in the Study for July the occasion for suggesting a new method in reviewing, or what he calls, very happily, Autographic Criticism. It seems to him that if authors were given their own books to review, there could at least be no complaint of "unjust and ignorant censure" from them, and that we might reasonably hope for the extinction of the professional critic by his venomous comment on his own performances. This would be delightful; and how practicable the plan is the writer illustrates by the review of a charming book of sketches by himself, *The Shaybacks in Camp*, namely. We cannot see that he overpraises his work; he treats it with apparent impartiality, and with an intelligence which could not reasonably be expected of a critic who had not read it. In fact, if he cannot hope to found a school of Autographic Criticism, Mr. Barrows may at least felicitate himself upon the success of his single experiment.

As usual, with a perfectly new thing, he is not the first to attempt it. We suppose that the prefaces of Dryden and Wordsworth may be taken as examples of indirect self-criticism, and Poe's analysis of his theories in writing *The Raven* is in the same sort. Charles Lamb's cheerful sibillation of his own farce is probably a doubtful fact; but in other literatures the attitude of self-criticism is far from uncommon. Two remarkable instances out of the Italian occur to us, and both in the case of dramatists. Goldoni, in his autobiography, analyzes and discusses nearly all his comedies; and Alfieri accompanies each of his tragedies with a full comment, in which its merits and demerits are very candidly and very self-respectfully debated. How far this kind of criticism could be carried with advantage to literature is another question, but, so far, every piece of it is interesting, and not only interesting, but vastly instructive. The autographic critic at least speaks with authority, and he tacitly puts himself upon honor not grossly to flatter; detraction, of course, is not to be feared from him; and we may be sure he will not try to exploit himself, to shine, to triumph at his own expense. He will not seek to show that he knows more than the author; he will not cram to read him down, or to overthrow him on his own ground, especially if it is ground where the general reader cannot meet him. As Mr. Barrows points out, he will be able in his review to clarify and enforce such parts of his work as he is conscious his creative art has left dim and halting. To a certain extent, indeed, this has been done by authors without actually taking up a position outside of their creative work. In George Eliot, for example, the perpetually recurring explanation of the characters' motives and feelings amounts to a critical comment on the course of the action and the nature of the problems involved, which we should have preferred to have in an appendix; and the essays with which Thackeray intersperses his narrative continually invite the reader's attention from what it is to what the author thinks of it. Autographic criticism in this shape is, of course, defective art, and yet who would not be glad to read an essay of Thackeray's upon his own work? Who would not be glad of a key from George Eliot to all the characters of her novels? Her poems, we own, we are not eager to unlock.

II.

If these things occur to the reader in regard to imaginative history, how much more must one desire the real historian to be the commentator of his own work! Who could speak of Mr. J. Addington Symonds's last volumes on the *Renaissance in Italy* half so well as Mr. Symonds himself? We have been reading these volumes (which he calls The Catholic Reaction, and in which he deals with the reconquest of the Latin mind by the Roman Church at the moment when the light of renascent art and learning shone brightest upon it) with the feeling that he alone could justly estimate his success and failure. Perhaps the first impression of the outside critic, deceived by the clearness with which the problem is treated, will be that, after all, it is a slight problem; but this impression will be lasting in proportion to his own ignorance, and his inability to seize the whole meaning of the situation. The books are, like all other histories, a study of what might have been, as well as what has been; and the pathos which no generous reader can fail to feel in them comes from the sense of this. To ask one's self what the world might have been now if the Inquisition and the Jesuits had never been in it, the one to crush out thought, and the others to pervert and falsify it, is to deal with the matter on the broad general ground where it presents itself to Mr. Symonds; and any one may do this, but no one else can bring to it the knowledge, the intelligence, the enlightened impartiality which we feel in him. We do not mean that he is ever lenient to either of those agencies; that would be a grotesque misconception of impartiality, and a lamentable misstatement of his position; but he is not blind to the evils that the Renaissance involved, and he is just to the motives and the professions even of those whose practice he abhors. He sees and he makes his reader see that they were not always malevolent or even selfish, and that the worldly ambition which triumphed in the Church by means of the Inquisition and the Jesuits turned to its account, with the well-known wisdom of the children of darkness, some of the best impulses of the children of light. There were good men in the Church who devoutly believed that if the world was to be saved from Protestantism it must be by the reform of the Church from within, and these righteous spirits played into the hands of the bigots and cynics who were aiming at temporal dominion and papal supremacy. Together, with the help of the irresistible forces of Spanish ignorance, cruelty, and violence, and the distrust, dissension, and treachery bred in Italian nature by mediæval feuds and wars, they succeeded in checking the intellectual expansion everywhere, in crippling and stupefying the conscience of the Latin race throughout Europe, and inducing upon the ruin, the misery, and despair a civilization of hypocrisy and pretence in letters, arts, and politics.

In this history we are asked to contemplate one of those triumphs of the wrong which from time to time shake the foundations of hope in the spectator, and make him doubt of the final prevalence of the right. But three hundred years after the Catholic reaction and the establishment of Spanish dominion, the free kingdom of Italy was imagined and accomplished; the good that had wrought for evil once had inscrutably survived, and the evil in turn had accomplished, in the inexhaustible patience and tolerance of the "somma sapienza e il primo amore," the ends of justice, liberty, and law. It is this final effect which Mr. Symonds wishes us to keep in mind while we read the dismal tale of repression, perversion, and cruelty which he tells.

His first volume is devoted to study of the Spanish ascendency in Italy, as confirmed by the reconciliation of Clement VII. and Charles V., the extension of the temporal power, the establishment of the Inquisition, the rise of the Jesuits, and the effect of all these political and religious changes upon social and domestic morals. The two chapters in which he paints the manners of the sixteenth century in Italy are less solid and masterly pieces of literature perhaps than those upon the Inquisition and the Jesuits, but they are even more astonishing, and their motive is prolonged into the sections of the following volume in which the characters and careers of Tasso, Bruno, Sarpi, and many poets, philosophers, and artists are portrayed. We cannot say that the second volume is more personal than the first, for Mr. Symonds is of those historians who have learnt that the history of mankind is the story of this man and that man and the other, but characters occupy larger space and events less. We do not mean, however, that Mr. Symonds regards any man as a hero; his heart is most of all with the steadfast courage and unfailing common-sense of that brave Paolo Sarpi who defended Venice against papal pretension, but even him he does not try to show above life-size; while such a saint of sentiment as Tasso, or such a martyr of abstract thinking as Bruno, he shows in all the deformity of his lunacy, in all the obliquity of his twofold, loose, wandering, and defeated life. The one was a great poet and

the other a great philosopher, to whom modern thought is vastly indebted, but besides this the one was a slavish courtier, a peevish hypochondriac, a complaining egotist, and a bore, and the other tried to carry water on both shoulders, to serve the Renaissance by denying Christianity, and to serve the Reaction by affirming Catholicism—to be both pagan and priest. To draw great men as they really were is of the utmost importance and value to all other men, and this is what we have mainly to thank Mr. Symonds for doing, for not adding to the empty idealization of men. Now at last we want the truth, for out of its absence nothing but folly ever came, and every figure of the past imposed upon the present as wholly grand, beautiful, or exemplary is an agency of mischief and deceit.

In the period with which he deals Mr. Symonds has had to deal, as material, with facts of incomparable horror and filthiness, and in making them clear he has had to use Scriptural plainness of speech at times. But any one who studies the same age in the Italian authorities will marvel at the slightness to which he has reduced the offence in his pages. He has not been weighed down by his material, or, rather, he has been supported in a slough where one might so easily bemire one's self, by a sense of his responsibility as a moralist and a scientist, if the terms are not now convertible. He is not discouraged by the corruption in which evil once so ruinously prevailed that it is hard to think of any future which it might not as successfully menace; but he perpetually points out that it is men's own lusts and passions and ambitions that betray them and others into slavery, and he shows that even this may be turned to good at last. The most interesting, the most important, lesson of his book is that, by repressing thought in the field of metaphysics, bigotry turned it aside to range at large in the ways of science. From the Renaissance in death a Renaissance sprang that can never die; and Italy became the mother of a civilization higher, deeper, truer, than the old—a civilization that no longer rests upon idealisms, but at every advance sets foot upon a fact, and cannot retrace its heaven-led steps. In fact, now at last that union of the kindred instincts of Renaissance and Reformation which Mr. Symonds dwells upon with so great and so just comfort seems to have been accomplished, and the freed soul and the freed mind of man are working together for the elevation of the race through conscience illumined by science.

III.

We are not willing to leave this excellent work without taking from it a passage bearing upon matters often discussed in the Study. In one of his most admirable chapters Mr. Symonds treats of the Bolognese school of painting, which once had so great cry, and was vaunted by a past criticism as the supreme exemplar of the grand style in art, but which is now fallen, as he believes, into lasting contempt for its emptiness and soullessness. The fact of its decadence leads him to inquire into the nature of criticism; he endeavors to determine whether there can be a final and enduring criterion or not, and his conclusion is as entirely applicable to literature as to the other arts:

"Our hope with regard to the unity of taste in the future then is, that all sentimental or academical seekings after the ideal having been abandoned, momentary theories founded upon idiosyncratic or temporary partialities exploded, and nothing accepted but what is solid and positive, the scientific spirit shall make men progressively more and more conscious of those *bleibende Verhältnisse*, more and more capable of living in the whole; also that, in proportion as we gain a firmer hold upon our own place in the world, we shall come to comprehend with more instinctive certitude what is simple, natural, and honest, welcoming with gladness all artistic products that exhibit these qualities. The perception of the enlightened man will then be the taste of a healthy person who has made himself acquainted with the laws of evolution in art and in society, and is able to test the excellence of work in any stage from immaturity to decadence by discerning what there is of truth, sincerity, and natural vigor in it."

IV.

While we are still upon Italian ground we wish to speak of Miss May Alden Ward's very clear, unaffected, and interesting sketch of *Dante, and his Life and Works*. It is not easy to trace the career of the poet in the vague and halting records, and it is harder still to free it from the attribution of ages of sentimentality and idealization, and present a probable likeness of the man in what he actually did and suffered. The effort is something comparable to those processes by which the stain and whitewash of centuries is removed, and the beauty and truth of some noble fresco underneath is brought to the light again. We do not mean to say that Miss Ward has given us another Dante of the Bargello, but she has wrought in the right spirit, and she shows a figure simple, conceivably like, and worthy to be Dante, with which she has apparently not suffered her fancy to play. To the life she has added a synopsis not only of the *Divine Comedy* and the *New Life*, but also of the poet's less famous works, *Il Convito*, and *De Monarchia*. The latter of these two embodies Dante's sufficiently mystical and impossible conception of a rehabilitated and purified Roman Empire, under which the primacy of the Italians should give the whole world peace; the former is his praise of love and learning, and would have been, probably, if completed, his theory of social life. Miss Ward notes what he says of nobility, which Frederic of Suabia had defined as "the possession of ancient wealth and fine manners," and some one else as ancient wealth alone, but which Dante declares to be the love and practice of virtue, holding that neither wealth nor birth can give it. "The family does not make the individual noble, but the individual ennobles the family.... A vile man descended of worthy ancestors ought to be hunted out by all." The Florentine citizen, who had seen the best government Florence ever enjoyed administered by the leader of the commonest of the people, speaks here more significantly to our time than the exile whom his wrongs had moved to put his faith in princes. It is very good Americanism for the thirteenth century, and it is very interesting as a proof of how far from feudal the ideal of Italy always was. In fact, Dante was then somewhat in advance of the *Saturday Review* of our time, which maintains that aristocracy is a thing too sacred to be criticised; but there is no saying what another five hundred years may not do for the *Saturday Review*.

V.

In these days of aspiration for a literary centre—which, if we could once get it, we should be pretty sure to have literature about—we find it interesting to note the geographical distribution of authorship upon each new occasion, and we find that Miss Ward, who gives such evidence of the love of scholarship, is from neither New York nor Boston, but from Ohio; and the author of one of the very best pieces of American fiction which has lately come to our hand, or which we have yet read, is from the South. Miss Frances Courteney Baylor has given hostages to criticism before this, but we had not read her other work, and we brought to her story a mind which, if unwilling through the aversion to unfamiliar fiction which grows upon one with the years, was at least unprejudiced. The story is of very simple life—very vulgar life, if you please—in a neighborhood of Virginia farmers, who have hardly risen above the condition of pioneers; but it has those evidences of fidelity in it without which a story of the very highest, the very superfinest, life is perhaps not worth reading, except by the very highest, the very superfinest, people. The character which must pass for that of hero, we suppose, is John Shore, a sensitive, soft-hearted, fiddling good-for-nothing, who is so broken by the loss of his young wife that he wanders away to Texas, leaving their babe to the mercies of chance hands, and returns, in a fit of untutored State patriotism, to lead the neighborhood to war, at the time of Virginia's secession. After the war he gives his farm to his son, grown up to be a dull, simple, kindly young man, fallen the matrimonial prey of a shrewish elderly widow, and wanders away again; but an incurable homesickness brings him back on the eve of a terrible railroad accident, in which a picnic party from his old neighborhood is slaughtered, and Shore loses his leg. He goes to live on the affection of his son and the unwilling charity of his son's wife, who puts him into a "shed-room" adjoining the cabin, with a little wretched orphan nephew of hers. He becomes great friends with this boy, and is consoled in all his wrongs and sorrows by the child's love and the music of his violin; and he is in the way to become a sentimental burden to the reader when he redeems himself by taking to drink; he has "sprees," as they are called, and then awful paroxysms of remorse and shame and reform, and then sprees again. At last, in one of these lapses, he loses his daughter-in-law's savings, which his son had given him to put in the bank; she meets his abject confession with a storm of fury, from which the hapless creature flies to drown himself. The situation is not unlike that of Polikouchka, in Tolstoï's heart-breaking story of the good-for-nothing serf; and it is treated with much of his mastery, though its reach and meaning are not so far. But John Shore is only one figure of the many powerfully studied in this very striking story. His dull, simple, kindly son, with his timid persistence against his wife's atrocious hate of the father, is not less successful than that pitiless termagant herself; and there are people of happier fate, and scenes of harmless if rude gayety, brought before us with the same unerring touch. Ignorant and pretty coarse the people all are, but with now and then a native beauty of soul, as in the poor foundling girl R. Mintah, who marries in grateful and reverent love the rich and powerful Jonah Newman in spite of his proud family; and in that old comrade of John Shore's, who is one of the killed in the railroad accident. This disaster, with the picnic preceding it, and R. Mintah's triumphant wedding, and the tragic scenes of John Shore's last day, are what remain clearest in our recollection out of many incidents which never seem feebly or falsely touched. The uncommon value of the book is in the conscientious art which portrays a whole community and a whole order of things without sentimentalizing them or seeking to idealize them, and which yet leaves us in sympathy with them through that divinely unifying "touch of nature." "They have this in them," says Charles Lamb, speaking of Hogarth's sketches, "that they bring us acquainted with the every-day human face; they give us skill to detect those gradations of sense and virtue (which escape the careless or fastidious observer) in the countenances of the world about us; and prevent that disgust at common life, that *tædium quotidianarum formarum*, which an unrestricted passion for ideal forms and beauties is in danger of producing." A sense of the poetry that is in all life dignifies and enriches the simple strain in which the story is written; and we must speak especially of the opening chapter, by which we are led into this vividly realized region "Behind the Blue Ridge," as in itself a lovely and winning idyl. It is in the spirit and form of some of Björnson's introductions to his Norwegian tales, and it personalizes with a poetry as delicate and genuine as his the history of the 'path that the wild things made through the mountain pass in its changes to the Indian trail, the way of the pioneer, the track of the emigrant, the country road, the macadamized highway of commerce, and the avenue of battle over which infantry, cavalry, and artillery found their destroying way back and forth in the great war. It is the allegory of our history, and it has a charm which we are aware our words do not impart.

VI.

It seems a vast distance from this picture of rude nature to the silhouettes and vignettes of a pleasant volume of "Society Verse" which we have been reading; and yet it is not necessarily so very far, if the society verse is as faithful to society as that is to nature. We do not suppose it is, quite. The attitude of the society versifier is inevitably a little artificial; he poses for a semi-humorous, self-satirical desolation, in a droll world of desperate pipes or cynical cigarettes, where trivial misunderstandings or worldly ambitions have divided youths and maidens, where the bouquets (preferably boutonnières nowadays) are mostly faded, the treasured gloves are faintly perfumed, the ribbons are crumpled, the immeritorious husbands are bald and fat, the young girls are agonizingly like their mothers of twenty years before. It is an amusing little make-believe Thackeray world, where elderly people are feigned to be still occupied with the disappointments of their teens, and where the heartlessness and heart-break are equally vast and not at all incompatible. Its flirtations are very dire indeed, and its marriages almost invariably of interest; its morals are somewhat disordered, but not to the point of anything really deplorable, and its experiences have a sad uniformity naturally productive of sameness in its records. The pattern of these was set long ago by the English masters, and in this collection of society verse by divers American hands the surprise ought to be that it has so much variety. Ballades and rondels and rondeaux and triolets we necessarily have, after the French studies of Mr. Dobson and Mr. Lang, but Mr. Ernest De Lancey Pierson, who edits the volume, has liberally interpreted the idea of society verse to include a number of pieces, lightly humorous, which are perhaps not strictly of that kind. He says, with possibly too great ingenuousness, that he has only "attempted .... to present the best productions of the younger school of poets and poetasters"; but we can reassure such "boding tremblers" as have had their misgivings concerning their classification in the editor's mind that we at least have found, with the exception of Blank, and Blank, and Blank, no poetasters in the book. It is, in fact, an uncommonly satisfactory collection of its sort. Wherever we come upon verse of Mr. Bunner's we are sure of a fresh and delicate pleasure, and he has three pieces here, among which "Just a Love Letter" is very charming indeed; Mr. Robert Grant's several rondeaux of Boston, Philadelphia, Baltimore, and New York are light, amiable, and graceful bits of satire; Mr. Dam's "Theosophic Marriage," if a little rougher in workmanship, is very amusing,

"She wore a wide and psychic smile"

being alone of inestimable value. Mr. Aldrich's "Intaglio Head of Minerva" is an old favorite, and as keenly, cleanly cut as if chiselled in the gem. Mr. Harrison Robertson's two triolets are delicious, and of quite aerial suggestiveness is "What She Thought":

"To kiss a fan !
    What a poky poet !
The stupid man,
    To kiss a fan,
When he knows—that—he—can—
    Or ought to know it—
To kiss a fan !
    What a poky poet !"

"On a Fly-Leaf of a Book of Old Plays," by Mr. Walter Learned, is a pretty picture, done with touch. "Her First Train," by Mr. A. E. Watrous, is also prettily picturesque, and also touchful; and "Her Bonnet," by Miss Mary E. Wilkins (she of the *Humble Romance, and Other Stories*, we suppose), is very arch and neat and demurely humorous:

"When meeting-bells began to toll,
    And pious folk began to pass,
She deftly tied her bonnet on,
    The little, sober, meeting lass,
All in her neat, white-curtained room, before her
        looking-glass. . . .

"So square she tied the satin strings,
    And set the bows beneath her chin !
Then smiled to see how sweet she looked;
    Then thought her vanity a sin,
And she must put such thoughts away before
        the sermon should begin. . . .

"Yet sitting there with peaceful face,
    The reflex of her simple soul,
She looked to be a very saint—
    And maybe was one, on the whole—
Only that her pretty bonnet kept away the
        aureole."

In fact, if it were not for fear of being thought a flatterer of the sex, we should say that not only for the finer humor, but for the broader fun, the ladies have the best of it in this collection of society verse. There is certainly nothing more amusing in it than Miss Helen Gray Coan's " Ballad of Cassandra Brown," or " The Stork's Jeremiad," by Miss Bessie Chandler. In the former we have an awful picture of the effects of Elocution, which we have all felt more or less in some young lady who has studied it ; and in the latter the heart-rending appeal of the protomartyr of decoration :

"'They've worked me standing, running, sleeping,
        flying ;
    Sometimes I'm gazing at a crewel sun ;
    They've worked me every way, I think, but dying ;
        And oh ! I wish they'd do that and be done !

"'I could forgive them all this bitter wronging
        If they would grant one favor, which I beg,
    Would gratify but once my soul's deep longing,
        Just to put down my cramped and unused leg.'

" A silence fell ; I gazed ; he had subsided ;
        I listened vainly ; all was dumb and still
    Upon the tidy where the stork resided,
        With upheld leg and red and open bill."

Mr. Pierson's volume is not, as he owns, fully representative, and he might make a larger one, which (as is too rarely the case with books of this or any kind) would be better ; but, upon the whole, this is by no means bad, and we are disposed, even in our quality of critic, to be grateful for it. We hope this is not beneath the dignity of a critic, which we should always like to be mindful of.

---

[1] The "ingenious writer" in *Christian Register* is Samuel June Barrows.

[2] *Criticism and Fiction*, pp. 1-2.

December, 1887

Editor's Study.

I.

THE question of a final criterion for the appreciation of art, or of a "unity of taste," which Mr. J. Addington Symonds treated with so much reason, in the passage quoted from his last volumes in the Study for November, is one that perpetually recurs to those interested in any sort of æsthetic work. The reader will remember that Mr. Symonds held, in brief, that simplicity and naturalness and honesty were the lasting tests; moods and tastes and fashions change; people fancy now this and now that; but what is unpretentious and what is true is enduringly beautiful and good, and nothing else is so. This is not saying that fantastic and monstrous and artificial things do not please; everybody knows that they do please immensely for a time, and then, after the lapse of a much longer time, they have the charm of the *rococo*. Nothing is more curious than the fascination that fashion has. Fashion in women's dress, almost every fashion, is somehow delightful, else it would never have been the fashion; but if any one will look through a collection of old fashion plates, he must own that most fashions have been ugly. A few, which could be readily instanced, have been very pretty, and even beautiful, but it is doubtful if these have pleased the greatest number of people. The ugly delights as well as the beautiful, and not merely because the ugly in fashion is associated with the young loveliness of the women who wear the ugly fashions, and wins a charm from them, not because the vast majority of mankind are tasteless, but for some cause that is not perhaps ascertainable. It is quite as likely to return in the fashions of our clothes, and houses and furniture, and poetry and fiction and painting, as the beautiful, and it may be from an instinctive or a reasoned sense of this that some of the extreme naturalists now refuse to make the old discrimination against it, or to regard the ugly as any less worthy of celebration in art than the beautiful; some of them, in fact, seem to regard it as rather more worthy, if anything. Possibly there is no absolutely ugly, no absolutely beautiful; or possibly the ugly contains always an element of the beautiful better adapted to the general appreciation than the more perfectly beautiful. This is a hazardous and somewhat discouraging conjecture, but we offer it for no more than it is worth; and we do not pin our faith to the saying of one whom we heard denying, the other day, that a thing of beauty was a joy forever. He contended that Keats's line should have read, "Some things of beauty are sometimes joys forever," and that any assertion beyond this was hazardous.

II.

We should, indeed, prefer another line of Keats's, if we were to profess any formulated creed, and should feel much safer with his "Beauty is Truth, Truth Beauty," than even with our friend's reformation of the more quoted verse. It brings us back to the solid ground taken by Mr. Symonds, which is not essentially different from that taken in a book read last summer, at the season when the newspaper noticers of the magazines suppose their conductors to be sharing the luxurious disoccupation of the daily journalists. It was at that season when these children of inspiration invariably announce that the July *Century* or *Atlantic* or *Harper* betrays the enervating influences of the weather in the lax and flimsy character of its contents (the number having actually been made up in the eager air of early May, when the sleepless energies of the editor were irritated to their highest activity by the conviction that the winter was going to last forever); and at the same time there came to us a carefully marked paragraph assuring us, in the usual confident and unsparing terms, that we were mistaken in supposing that literature should be true to life—"it should be true to art." Out of the envious spirit which will be readily attributed to us we suppress the name of the newspaper; but there is no reason why we should withhold that of the book, which every reader of taste will suppose an intimacy with, as we should ourselves have done six months ago. It was the great Mr. Burke's *Essay on the Sublime and the Beautiful*—a singularly modern book, considering how long ago it was wrote (as the great Mr. Steele would have written the participle a little longer ago), and full of a certain well-mannered and agreeable instruction. In some things it is of that droll little eighteenth-century world, when philosophy had got the neat little universe into the hollow of its hand, and knew just what it was, and what it was for; but it is quite without arrogance; it is not even so confident as the newspaper which we are keeping back the name of. It will be seen that Mr. Burke differs radically with this other authority, which, however, he unwittingly owns to be of the sort called critical, and might almost be supposed to have had prophetically in mind. "As for those called critics," he says, "they have generally sought the rule of the arts in the wrong place; they have sought among poems, pictures, engravings, statues, and buildings; *but art can never give the rules that make an art.* This is, I believe, the reason why artists in general, and poets principally, have been confined in so narrow a circle; they have been rather imitators of one another than of nature. Critics follow them, and therefore can do little as guides. I can judge but poorly of anything while I measure it by no other standard than itself. *The true standard of the arts is in every man's power; and an easy observation of the most common, sometimes of the meanest things, in nature, will give the truest lights,* where the greatest sagacity and industry that slights such observation must leave us in the dark, or, what is worse, amuse and mislead us by false lights."

III.

If this should happen to be true—and it certainly commends itself to our acceptance—it might portend an immediate danger to the vested interests of criticism, only that it was written a hundred years ago; and we shall probably have the "sagacity and industry that slights the observation of nature" long enough yet to allow most critics the time to learn some more useful trade than criticism as they pursue it. Nevertheless, we are in hopes that the communistic era in taste foreshadowed by Burke is approaching, and that it will occur within the lives of men now overawed by the foolish old superstition that literature and art are anything but the expression of life, and are to be judged by any other test than that of their fidelity to it. The time is coming, we trust, when each new author, each new artist, will be considered, not in his proportion to any other author or artist, but in his relation to the human nature, known to us all, which it is his privilege, his high duty, to interpret. "The true standard of the artist is in every man's power" already, as Burke says; Michelangelo's "light of the piazza," the glance of the common eye, is and always was the best light on a statue; Goethe's "boys and blackbirds" have in all ages been the real connoisseurs of berries; but hitherto the mass of common men have been afraid to apply their own simplicity, naturalness, and honesty to the appreciation of the beautiful. They have always cast about for the instruction of some one who professed to know better, and who browbeat wholesome common-sense into the self-distrust that ends in sophistication. They have fallen generally to the worst of this bad species, and have been "amused and misled" (how pretty that quaint old use of *amuse* is!) "by the false lights" of critical vanity and self-righteousness. They have been taught to compare what they see and what they read, not with the things that they have observed and known, but with the things that some other artist or writer has done. Especially if they have themselves the artistic impulse in any direction they are taught to form themselves, not upon life, but upon the masters who became masters only by forming themselves upon life. The seeds of death are planted in them, and they can produce only the still-born, the academic. They are not told to take their work into the public square and see if it seems true to the chance passer, but to test it by the work of the very men who refused and decried any other test of their own work. The young writer who attempts to report the phrase and carriage of every-day life, who tries to tell just how he has heard men talk and seen them look, is made to feel guilty of something low and unworthy by the stupid people who would like to have him show how Shakespeare's men talked and looked, or Scott's, or Thackeray's, or Balzac's, or Hawthorne's, or Dickens's; he is instructed to idealize his personages, that is, to take the life-likeness out of them, and put the literary-likeness into them. He is approached in the spirit of the wretched pedantry into which learning, much or little, always decays when it withdraws itself and stands apart from experience in an attitude of imagined superiority, and which would say with the same confidence to the scientist: "I see that you are looking at a grasshopper there which you have found in the grass, and I suppose you intend to describe it. Now don't waste your time and sin against culture in *that* way. I've got a grasshopper here, which has been evolved at considerable pains and expense out of the grasshopper in general; in fact, it's a type. It's made up of wire and cardboard, very prettily painted in a conventional tint, and it's perfectly indestructible.

It isn't very much like a real grasshopper, but it's a great deal nicer, and it's served to represent the notion of a grasshopper ever since man emerged from barbarism. You may say that it's artificial. Well, it *is* artificial; but then it's ideal too; and what you want to do is to cultivate the ideal. You'll find the books full of my kind of grasshopper, and scarcely a trace of yours in any of them. The thing that you are proposing to do is commonplace; but if you say that it isn't commonplace, for the very reason that it hasn't been done before, you'll have to admit that it's photographic."

IV.

As we said, we hope the time is coming when not only the artist, but the common, average man, who always " has the standard of the arts in his power," will have also the courage to apply it, and will reject the ideal grasshopper wherever he finds it, in science, in literature, in art, because it is not "simple, natural, and honest," because it is not like a real grasshopper. But we will own that we think the time is yet far off, and that the people who have been brought up on the ideal grasshopper, the heroic grasshopper, the impassioned grasshopper, the self-devoted, adventureful, good old romantic card-board grasshopper, must die out before the simple, honest, and natural grasshopper can have a fair field. We are in no haste to compass the end of these good people, whom we find in the mean time very amusing. It is delightful to meet one of them, either in print or out of it—some sweet elderly lady or excellent gentleman whose youth was pastured on the literature of thirty or forty years ago—and to witness the confidence with which they preach their favorite authors as all the law and the prophets. They have commonly read little or nothing since, or, if they have, they have judged it by a standard taken from these authors, and never dreamt of judging it by nature; they are destitute of the documents in the case of the later writers; they suppose that Balzac was the beginning of realism, and that Zola is its wicked end; they are quite ignorant, but they are ready to talk you down, if you differ from them, with an assumption of knowledge sufficient for any occasion. The horror, the resentment, with which they receive any question of their very peccable literary saints is to be matched only by the frenzy of the *Saturday Review* in defending the British aristocracy; you descend at once very far in the moral and social scale, and anything short of offensive personality is too good for you; it is expressed to you that you are one to be avoided, and put down even a little lower than you have naturally fallen.

These worthy persons are not to blame; it is part of their intellectual mission to represent the petrifaction of taste, and to preserve an image of a smaller and cruder and emptier world than we now live in, a world which was feeling its way toward the simple, the natural, the honest, but was a good deal "amused and misled" by lights now no longer mistakable for heavenly luminaries. They belong to a time, just passing away, when certain authors were considered authorities in certain kinds, when they must be accepted entire and not questioned in any particular. Now we are beginning to see and to say that no author is an authority except in those moments when he held his ear close to Nature's lips and caught her very accent. These moments are not continuous with any authors in the past, and they are rare with all. Therefore we are not afraid to say now that the greatest classics are sometimes not at all great, and that we can profit by them only when we hold them, like our meanest contemporaries, to a strict accounting, and verify their work by the standard of the arts which we all have in our power, the simple, the natural, and the honest. ⌐3

----

[1] See p. 107a.

[2] Criticism and Fiction, p. 1 (paraphrase).

[3] Criticism and Fiction, pp. 3-14 (abridged).

January, 1888

Editor's Study.

I.

IN the last number of the Study we tried, with the help of Edmund Burke and Mr. J. Addington Symonds, to persuade the reader that there was such a thing as a final criterion of art, to which, through every change of taste and fancy, we might confidently trust ourselves. Burke held that this standard was in every man's power, and that it was "an easy observation of the most common, sometimes of the meanest, things in nature." Mr. Symonds more broadly formulated the lasting test as a question of the presence or the absence of simplicity, naturalness, and honesty in any æsthetic performance.

With this test, not at all magic or difficult, which any one who is himself simple, natural, and honest can apply, we believe that one is able to judge intelligently of the worth of literature representing life wholly different from our own, and to feel the joy that truthful work always gives. By means of it we can measure the excellence of work like that of Armando Palacio Valdés, whose last book, *Maximina*, we have been reading, and appreciate the graphic fidelity of his pictures of life so remote as that of modern Madrid. We find it in essentials, which are always the universals, very like our own life, and this sweet and humorous and heart-breaking story of the young Spanish wife, Maximina, might with a few touches be naturalized among us so that it could pass for one of native origin.

Maximina's husband is that young Madrid journalist, Miguel Rivera, whose not altogether praiseworthy career was traced in the novel *Riverita*, mentioned in these pages last year, but who is mainly a good fellow, and who here falls in love with the child of very common people in an obscure little seaport where he is passing the summer. We cannot give, of course, the charm which takes him with her; that is indicated by a hundred little hints and touches; but it is chiefly her trusting goodness, her lovely diffidence, and her impassioned unselfishness which fascinate the shrewd and amiable young fellow with Maximina. They are married, and come up to live in Madrid, where he is a writer on a radical newspaper, with a small interest in its pecuniary adversity. Till they can get settled in a house of their own they stay for a short time with Rivera's high-tempered and high-handed step-mother, and then they go to housekeeping in a prettily appointed apartment, which we are invited sympathetically to assist them in furnishing, and to witness his extravagance and her anxiously deprecatory economy. The great day comes when they move in, and at night they find that they have forgotten the candles, and they sit down on the hearth together and talk long of their lives past and to come in the light of the fire.

Their life goes on from prettiness to prettiness, from sweetness to sweetness, like the new married life of fond young couples the world over. Miguel is working hard all the time at his newspaper office, and has to go away every day. "At times, to tease his wife, he would pretend to start without taking leave of her; but at the sound of the latch she dropped whatever she had in hand, in the dining-room, in the kitchen, or in her chamber, and flew to the door after him. When she did not hear the latch Miguel did all he could to make her hear. Maximina remained all the afternoon with the servants. At nightfall, when Miguel rang the bell, the young thing's heart gave a leap, and she ran herself to open the door. Sometimes she let the maid open it; but this was in order to hide behind the door, or in the next room. He knew by the maid's smiling face that his wife was somewhere near, and he would say, with a comic gesture, 'You are hiding Maximina here!' And he went straight to where she was, and caught her by the arm. 'I don't know how you always find me so soon,' she would say, with feigned disgust. At other times when he came she would open the little window over the street door and ask, 'What do you wish, sir?' 'Does Don Miguel Rivera live here?' Miguel himself would ask. 'Yes, sir; but he is not at home.' 'And Señora Rivera?' 'Señora Rivera is at home, but she is not receiving.' 'Please tell her that there is a gentleman down here who would like to give her a hug and a kiss.'"

Among many other incidents of their early house-keeping is a party which they give, and which is described with delicious humor and naturalness. The ostensible object of the affair is to let a disappointed poet read a play of his which the envious managers have rejected; but Miguel really wants to show off his beautiful young wife, who is in great terror of the occasion, but bears herself triumphantly. During the evening he flirts with the daughter of the countess living on the floor above, and Maximina is jealous; they have their first quarrel and their last, and he never again gives her cause to doubt his inalienable love. In due time the baby comes, and the glorious advent is celebrated with the most delicate sympathy, the most arch and smiling satire. Two rival forces invade the house and attempt mastery of the situation, the countess from overhead and Miguel's stepmother; the encounter between these ladies is a thrilling battle-piece; but calm returns with the indignant withdrawal of the countess, and all is well again. At two days old the baby smiles, and his young aunt Serafina rushes in with him, followed by all the servants, to announce the miracle.

"'He smiled, as surely as there is a God in heaven,' testified one of the servants. 'Go along; you're all crazy,' said Doña Martina. 'Why, he's only two days old.' 'It can't be,' said Maximina, but showing herself disposed to believe it. 'But he did, señora, he did,' they all broke out. 'This is the way it was,' said one of them, almost choking with excitement. 'Here was Señorita Serafina with the baby, so—see? And I came up and took it by the shoulder, so—see? And I lifted it up, and began to move it and say, "Chk, chk, chk! little rose-bud, little pink, do you want to be called Miguelito, like your papa?" And the baby didn't do anything. "Do you want to be called Enriquito, like your uncle?" It didn't do anything then, either. "Do you want to be called Serafin, like your aunt?" And then it opened its little eyes a little, and made a little mouth with its lips—but truly!' Maximina smiled as if she had been listening to a revelation from heaven. She and her aunt Martina were instantly convinced; but Miguel held out. 'In this matter of babies' smiles, especially when the babies have only been fifty-seven hours in the world, I have an inveterate skepticism. I am like St. Thomas—see and believe.' 'But he *did* smile, Miguel—he did indeed; I assure you he did,' said Serafina. 'You don't offer me sufficient guarantees of impartiality.' 'Very well, then, I'll make him do it again; then you'll see.' Serafina took the baby and

lifted it above her head with great decision, at the same time asking it if it wanted to be called Serafin, to which the baby did not judge it opportune to make any reply, perhaps from an excess of diplomacy, for possibly the name seemed to it ridiculous. Maximina was hanging on its lips. 'You try, Placida,' she said, trying to hide her affliction. Placida detached herself from the group like an actor at Price's circus when he comes out to execute a feat. She lifted the baby with surprising mastery, moved it from north to south, then from east to west, and then put the consecrated questions: 'Chk, chk, chk! little pet, little rose-bud, pink, do you want to be called Miguelito, like your papa? Do you want to be called Enriquito, like your uncle? Do you want to be called Serafin, like your aunt?' A lugubrious silence followed these words. All eyes were fastened upon the youthful interlocutor, who, far from showing a predilection for any of the names indicated, clearly manifested, though in an inarticulate fashion, that he found no reason for being bothered so with a mere question of names. 'You see?' said Miguel. 'It's because he isn't in the humor to smile now,' protested Maximina. '*You* don't smile either when you're told to. Besides, he must be hungry by this time. Give him to me—give him to me! Oh, my soul's little darling! my heart!'"

The tender irony with which this little scene is depicted, the perfect lightness, the unfailing accuracy with which the different persons are touched, the simple, natural, and honest art, are traits of the mastery which the book is full of. All the different people on the newspaper, and the people whom Miguel meets everywhere, especially a group of politicians, are sketched with the same unfailing skill, and Rivera is himself studied with an intimate sympathy that lets us into the soul of a man whose heart is generous and good, and whose will is better than his life has been, though his life has been better than that of his world in most things.

Miguel has been persuaded by the other owners of the *Independencia* to endorse their notes to the money-lender who supplies the funds for their failing enterprise; he does this against Maximina's instinct; he has to pay their notes, and he throws more good money after bad. At last he is ruined, and then all the loveliness, all the sublimity, of Maximina's character come out in the gladness with which she shares his poverty. In the midst of their privations their love and their happiness are without a blot; but now the worst of all comes. Maximina is taken with a nervous fever, and becomes dangerously sick; a certain palliative gives them both deceitful hopes of her recovery. After long watching Miguel falls into a heavy sleep; he is awakened by the call, "Señorito! señorito! the señorita is worse!" "The voice with which they rouse the doomed man to lead him to the scaffold never sounded more terrible than this cry sounded to Miguel. He leaped to his feet. He ran to her room. Maximina's eyes were closed. At his entrance she opened them and tried to smile; she closed them again, never to open them more. It was four o'clock in the morning. Juana ran to call the doctor. The widow of the colonel declared that it was only a faint; she and Miguel applied mustard draughts. The priest was sent for. A few minutes after, he came together with the doctor. What for? Miguel paced the corridor unceasingly, white as a ghost. Suddenly he stopped, and tried to re-enter his wife's room. The widow, the priest, and the doctor put their hands on his breast. 'No, no; don't come in, Rivera!' 'I know all. Let me pass!' They saw from his look and bearing that it was useless to oppose him. He flung himself upon the body of his wife, from which the warmth and life had not yet wholly faded, and for some minutes wildly continued to kiss it. 'Enough! enough! You are killing yourself!' At last they succeeded in pulling him away. ' Better than thou,' he cried aloud, giving her a last kiss, 'there never has been nor ever will be on the earth!' 'Happy those, my son, who can hear such words in death,' said the old priest. They led him away. He went to his study, and leaned against the window. Day had not yet fully dawned. Consternation had checked his tears. Immovable, with starting eyes, and with his forehead pressed against the pane, he stood long, listening to the revealing voice that speaks only in this supreme hour. At last he could have been heard to murmur hoarsely, 'Who knows? who knows?'"

It is impossible to give the different passages that lead to this, but the whole chapter that treats of Maximina's sickness is as inexpressibly touching as it is simple and real. Rivera lives on as he must for his child, but he becomes very poor. When the last extremity is reached one of the friends who ruined him has entered the cabinet, and he invites Rivera to be his secretary. "The flesh, weak, rebelled for an instant at this proposition. But in the end he subdued himself and accepted. Through hours of tears and meditation his inner life had freed itself from the dominion of pride. After terrible shocks his soul had broken the chains that had bound it to terrestrial passions. He had learned, never to forget it again, the sublime truth that rises eternally above human wisdom, and will ever be the sum of all truths, *the denial of self.*

His only thought from that time forward was to advance further and further on the path of freedom, till the hour of supreme emancipation should sound for him. The sole and most ardent desire of his life was to be able to love death. In the mean time he used the sacred and divine force of the imagination in creating a free world of his own where he lived with his wife in the sweet communion of other times, sharing his joys and sorrows with her. At every act of life he did not fail to ask himself, 'Would Maximina have approved it?' Daily he confessed himself to her, and told her the most intimate secrets of his soul. And whenever he had the unhappiness to fall into sin, a profound dismay overwhelmed him, thinking that he had that day separated himself a little from his wife. In this manner, participating like a divine creature in the august privilege of God, he was able to lend her new life, or rather keep her from having ever died. But like a human creature also, his spirit was shaken more than once by the storm of doubt. He suffered the cruel assaults of temptation, and faltered like the Son of God in the garden of Gethsemane—hours of agony that left him deeply crushed, and sapped if they did not wholly undermine his strength."

We will not look on at these, which the author describes with searching power, but will close our versions from the book with a passage treating of a time when Maximina was still alive on earth, but when their adversity had come upon them, and they were looking out of the window of their poor little house one night at the stars. "The wife became thoughtful, and said, after a pause, 'How can those worlds hold themselves up in space, and go on forever without clashing?' 'They are upheld and live by love—yes, by love,' he repeated, seeing the wonder in the eyes of his wife. 'Love is the law that rules the universe; the sublime law that unites your heart to mine is the same law that unites all the beings of the universe, and keeps them at the same time distinct. We are one in God, in the Creator of all things; but we enjoy at the same time the beautiful privilege of individuality. Yet this great privilege is at the same time our great imperfection, Maximina. By it we are separated from God. To live eternally united to Him, to rest on His breast like a child in its mother's arms, this is the constant aspiration of humanity. The man who feels this need the most livingly and imperiously is the best and the most just. What does abnegation mean, or self-sacrifice? Is it anything but the expression of this secret voice that dwells in the soul, and tells us that to love one's self is to love the finite, the imperfect, the ephemeral, and to love others is to unite ourselves by anticipation with the Eternal? Woe to the man who does not come at the call of that voice! Woe to him who shuts his ears to the breathings of his soul, and runs astray in chase of fleeting illusions! That man will always be the miserable slave of time and necessity.' They talked a long time; at last they suddenly stopped. They both remained silently contemplating the immensity of the heavens.... At the end of a moment Maximina asked, in a low voice, 'Miguel, don't you want to say a Pater-Noster?' 'Yes,' he answered, tenderly pressing her hand. The young wife repeated the Pater-Noster with true fervor; her husband responded with equal fervor. Never in his life, before or after, did Miguel find himself so near to God as in that moment. The night grew late. The clock in the study struck twelve. They shut the window, and lit their lamps to go to rest."

There are two subordinate stories interwoven with that of Maximina and Miguel in this beautiful book: the heart-breaking story of Miguel's sister, who is pursued and entrapped and ruined by her cousin; and the story of his own cousin Enrico's marriage with a girl of the people, a *chula* whom he falls in love with at her father's shop, where she sells milk. This is the comic strain in the lovely idyl, but this too is dignified and ennobled by Maximina's gentle and womanly attitude toward the bride. There is another comic character besides Enrico, and that is the poor young fellow who is in love with Julia Rivera, and who shoots himself when he hears of her ruin, and then does not want to die, and must die, turning tragedy at last, as comedy sometimes does in this finally rather serious world. These stories are both well enough done to make the fortune of an inferior writer, but it is in his treatment of the chief interest of his book that Valdés shows himself a master. We cannot say that *Maximina* is as great a book as his *Marta y Maria* (which the reader of the translation knows as the *Marquis of Peñalta*), but it is of the same admirable texture; the same unfailing right-mindedness characterizes it, the same clear and intelligent conscience. Some notion of the devout liberality of its religious feeling may be inferred from the passages we have given, but the reader must go to the book itself for a full impression of this. He must also go to it for a knowledge of all Maximina's unsentimentalized loveliness, and for a sense of the change operated by this and by the lessons of his life in Miguel's light, humorous, sarcastic spirit, teaching it patience and unselfishness and noble seriousness.

We hope that the book may be translated. There is not a word in it that offends against purity or good morals; there is a Latin frankness here and there concerning certain social facts which our own race has (we believe properly, on the whole) agreed to blink in fiction, but this could be easily silenced by a judicious pencil, and then the story would remain for all a flawless praise of marriage and wifehood, and one of the most exquisitely touching and consoling books ever written, "simple, natural, and honest," as only the fiction of our time knows how to be.

II.

It is needless for us to say, either to the many whom our opinions on this point incense or to the few who accept them, that we do not think the fiction of our own time even always equal to this test, or perhaps more than seldom so. But as we have before expressed, to the still-reverberating discontent of two continents, fiction is now a finer art than it has ever been hitherto, and more nearly meets the requirements of the infallible standard. We have hopes of real usefulness in it, because it is at last building on the only sure foundation; but we are by no means certain that it will be the ultimate literary form, or will remain as important as we believe it is destined to become. On the contrary, it is quite imaginable that when the great mass of readers, now sunk in the foolish joys of mere fable, shall be lifted to an interest in the meaning of things through the faithful portrayal of life in fiction, then fiction the most faithful may be superseded by a still more faithful form of contemporaneous history. We willingly, however, leave the precise character of this form to the more robust imagination of readers whose minds have been nurtured upon romantic novels, and who really have an imagination worth speaking of, and confine ourselves, as usual, to the hither side of the regions of conjecture.

III.

Among the recent fictions, besides that already noticed, the only one which seems perfectly to meet the requirements of the infallible standard is, of course, the last of Tolstoï's, *The Invaders*, which we have now in very good English. It is a group of studies and sketches, light, penetrating, and unsparingly true, pervaded by the sympathy and rectitude which characterize all the incomparable master's work. There is, properly speaking, only one story in the book—the austerely faithful, tenderly touching story of Polikushka, the weak, baddish serf, who loses the money of his mistress, and will not survive the ruin of having seemed to steal it. The story is for the rest fragmentary to the curiosity, but rounded to beautiful completeness for the heart and conscience. There is nothing more masterly than the closing episode of buying a substitute for the conscripted peasant, and we recommend this passage to the attention of the thoughtful reader, as well as that sketch of the cashiered officer in another study. This and the rest belong to contemporaneous history, however, rather than to fiction; they are evidently rescripts of fact, of experience, and they have the wild, simple charm of *The Cossacks;* they are mostly, like that, pictures of campaigning life in the Caucasus, but they seem maturer work —work in which the author has more clearly found out his meaning.

IV.

An American book to be praised for simplicity, naturalness, and honesty is Miss Esther Bernon Carpenter's *South County Neighbors,* or studies of a past generation in a Rhode Island country neighborhood. They are pervaded with the humor which is characteristic of the great Spaniard rather than the great Russian, and with the humanity which seems never absent from sincere work—which is indeed as much a part of realism as the truth itself; for it appears that we cannot learn to know others well without learning to pity and account for the defects in them which we must not excuse in ourselves. These *South County Neighbors* are valuable contributions to the history of a phase of things now almost, if not quite, vanished in New England, and they are delightful reading. They are worthy to be classed with Miss Wilkins's admirable New England studies, though they are contemplative rather than dramatic presentations of character; and Miss Jeannette H. Walworth's *Southern Silhouettes* is a series of sketches almost worthy to be classed with both. These are reflexes of a faded civilization too; but one feels that the negatives have been touched, and that is always to be regretted. So skilful a hand as Miss Walworth's should be taught when to hold itself.

V.

But what shall we say of Miss Octave Thanet and her *Knitters in the Sun?*

She has in some respects a greater power —or perhaps greater force is more accurate—than either of those just mentioned; and she writes with heart as well as brain. Putting out of the question the "goddess type" of dimly accounted for countess in the sketch, *The Communist's Wife* is something that may be read with equal pathos and instruction in these days of labor troubles, when Society is tempted to forget, in the duty of "saving itself," that the poor are also Society. *Schopenhauer on Lake Pepin,* the affecting story of the minister who loses his faith, is also of enduring significance. It is when we come to *Whitsun Harp, Regulator,* that we rebel against the author's spell. It is, briefly, the story of a man who believes that the Lord has called him to the work of reforming his Arkansas neighborhood by whipping wrong-doers with his own hand. One man on whom he inflicts a mistaken thrashing vows to kill him, but is kept from it by the prayers of a dying wretch who killed a man many years before, and now believes he shall find peace if he can save some one's life. As soon as the sick man dies, Lem Chinault goes to find Whitsun and kill him, and the effect of the situation is heightened for the reader by the knowledge that the men had been rivals in love. Before Chinault finds Harp, another's vengeance has overtaken the regulator; Chinault comes upon him just shot; his wife, who had followed to restrain him, comes up at the same moment, and in the lime-light which romantic fiction burns at such crises they are reconciled in the husband's gratitude that he has been saved from the crime of murder.

It brings the tear to the eye and the lump into the throat; but it is all wrong. When men are bent upon sin, not so does "the power, not ourselves, that works for righteousness" save them by melodramatic accident. It saves them in their own free wills, or, if they resist, it saves them not at all; and it is bad art and mistaken morality that teach otherwise. The Good Fairy conception of the Divine government of the world should be left to the cruder theologies: it is wholly unworthy of fiction. [4]

---

[1] Armando Palacio Valdes, The Marquis of Peñalta, Nathan Haskell Dole, trans. (New York: T. Y. Crowell & Co., [c1886]).

[2] Criticism and Fiction, pp. 186-187.

[3] Leo Tolstoy, The Invaders, and Other Stories, Nathan Haskell Dole, trans. (New York: T. Y. Crowell & Co., [c1887]).

[4] See p. 127b for retraction.

February, 1888

Editor's Study.

I.

WE have seldom read a biography in which life and character appeared with more completeness than in Mr. James Elliot Cabot's *Memoir of Ralph Waldo Emerson*. The work must have been all the more difficult because the life was so uneventful, and the character so essentially undramatic. Of course Mr. Cabot has allowed both to express themselves in Emerson's abundant letters and journals, but he has not abandoned his office to these, and what he has to say of Emerson from time to time, in comment and summary, is no less valuable for a right understanding of Emerson than what Emerson says of himself. Often it is more valuable, for Emerson still needs an apostle to the Gentiles. The literary merit of the book, which to our present thinking is always the least merit of a good book, is of a sort as uninsistent as Emerson could have wished that of a record of his life to be, and that is perhaps saying all that one need say of the clear style, the unaffected manner, and the candid attitude.

There is the advantage in the last that it leaves you assured of the estimates you form in Emerson's favor throughout; you feel that nothing has been done to force your liking or your duty to that illuminated conscience which Emerson was from first to last. He was the final and pre-eminent Puritan, with all that made Puritanism mean and harsh, cruel and hateful, eliminated from his righteous and gentle spirit; and this is what Mr. Cabot's memoir enables you to perceive in almost the same measure as if you had known the man. It was inevitable that such a man, with the defects as well as the virtues of his qualities, should seem placed out of time. He was, indeed, so much ahead of his time in his perceptions that we have not yet lived long enough to know how modern they were.

His sympathies perhaps lagged a little. He was not a man who *felt* his way; he had to *see* it; though when once he saw it, lions might be in it, but he went forward. His indifference to consequences came partly from his impersonality; he was so much an idealization of the ordinary human being that his fears were attenuated, like his sympathies. This again was Puritanism, which had so wholly died out of his creed that almost at the outset of his clerical career he found it impossible to go on making formal prayers in the pulpit, or administering the communion. Then he promptly turned his back upon this career, though with many a longing, lingering look over his shoulder for some ideal Church in which these functions would not be insisted on.

His evolution as an antislavery reformer is an even more interesting illustration of these facts of his character. When he was a very young man he came in contact with slavery in Florida, where he had gone one winter for his health; but he does not seem to have felt the horror, the crime of it, so much as he discerned its gross unreason, its inconsistency, its absurdity; and he was repelled from the abolitionists at first by his dislike of violence, even in convictions, and of the very appearance of disorder. But when once he had taken the measure of the affair with that telescopic eye of his, and had intellectually compassed its whole meaning to the very furthest and finest implication, his whole nature solidified against slavery. The man in whom conscience and intellect were angelically one perceived that the law and order which defied justice and humanity were merely organized anarchy, and that as a good citizen he could have no part in them. When the Fugitive Slave Bill became a law, "There is an infamy in the air," he said, at the indignation meeting in Concord. "I wake in the morning with a painful sensation, which I carry about all day, and which, when traced home, is the ignominy which has fallen on Massachusetts." It is a "filthy law," "a law which no man can obey, or abet the obeying, without loss of self-respect, or forfeiture of the name of gentleman." Later, at a Kansas relief meeting in Cambridge, he advised "the sending of arms to the settlers in Kansas for resistance to the pro-slavery raids from Missouri." After Harper's Ferry he said that if John

Brown should suffer, he would "make the gallows glorious like the cross," but he omitted this and other passages from the republished lecture, "distance of time," says his biographer, "having brought the case into juster perspective." With the light of our own time, and the modern improvements of the "perfection of reason" as applied by the courts, he might see cause to modify other expressions; but he spoke in days when good men thought that their sense of justice was pre-eminently binding upon their consciences, and brought all laws and decisions that conflicted with this sense into lasting discredit with those whom their teachings schooled.

II.

Emerson, though not one of the earliest, became easily one of the first of those men, and no doubt many a gray-bearded youth can remember with us the liberating thrill of his words, beautiful as sculptured marble, vivid as flame. Was it the poetry or the humanity which touched us most? Both, equally, we think; for again these were angelically one in the man, who could not have been a poet for beauty's sake alone, although he feigned that beauty was sufficient in and to itself. In humanity, as in his theories of what literature should be to us, Emerson is still the foremost of all our seers, and will be so a hundred years hence. He seems in these sorts to be almost a disembodied force, but this is an illusion of his extreme impersonality. It ought not to be necessary to explain that his intellectual coldness, which, whenever he would,

"Burned frore, and frost performed the effect of fire,"

did not chill his affectional make-up. Tender and faithful son, and loving servant of his widowed mother's narrow circumstance, he was always a devoted husband, and the fondest as well as wisest of fathers; but he found it difficult to make his shy heart go out beyond the bounds of kinship and old friendship. The gentlest of men could sometimes be as infinitely repellent a particle as one of his own sentences, and he whimsically confesses to his diary that while he gets on well enough with Man, he finds it hard to meet men half-way or upon common ground. Now we are beginning to know that there is no such thing as Man, that there are only men, but Emerson can, with all his shrinking from men, best teach us how to treat them, with a view to their highest good. Mr. Matthew Arnold gave him supreme praise when he said that those who wished to live in the spirit must go to Emerson, though many worthy persons were aggrieved that he should have said Emerson was not so great a poet as this, not so great an essayist as that, not so great a philosopher as the other. To live in the spirit is the lesson of his life as well as of his literature; his whole memory strengthens and purifies. You learn from it that one who lives in the spirit cannot be unfaithful to the smallest rights or interests of others; cannot ignore any private obligation or public duty without shame and pain.

Every new thing, every new thought, challenged him: abolition, Brook Farm, Walt Whitman: he was just to each, and, with Emerson, as with all high souls, to be just was to be generous. He was for a long time supposed to be the exemplar of Transcendentalism. People who did not know what he meant said that he meant Transcendentalism, and as nobody ever quite knew what Transcendentalism meant, they again said that it meant Emerson. But mental dimness was as foreign to him as moral dimness; all that he says is impatient, is tense with meaning.

"While self-inspection sucked its little thumb,
  With ' Who am I?' and ' Wherefore did I come?'"

Emerson was deeply employed in meditating the wisdom through which the mass of our stupidity and selfishness may finally be civilized into indifference to those questions, through a sense of duty to others. In a period still reeking with gross romantic individualism, when so many were straining to retch out the last rinsings of their sick egotism upon their fellows, he stood hale and serene and sane, elect and beautiful in every aspect of his mind. It is his impersonality, the quality that made him cold and unseizable to so many—it is this which makes him now and always our neighbor and our friend, the most imaginable person of his day. The value of Mr. Cabot's memoir is that it lets that sculpturesque figure grow fully upon you; and yet, even after reading this memoir, we should like to recur, for something more of color and warmth, to Henry James, Sen.'s incomparably vivid and suggestive essay on Emerson.* Written from the heartiest liking and the most tingling resentment of his elusiveness, the keenest perception, and the strictest limitations, and expressed from a lexicon peculiar to the author, this essay is of really unique value in the literature of biography.

III.

Perhaps Mr. Cabot imparts the same sense of Emerson, but the degree is wanting; and he has not touched at all one of the most interesting facts, from a literary point of view, in Emerson's history. His perception of the great and fruitful elements in Walt Whitman's work, when the "Leaves of Grass" first appeared, was long suffered to weigh with the public as unqualified praise; but Mr. Whitman has himself finally done justice to Emerson's

* *Literary Remains of Henry James.* Edited by WILLIAM JAMES.

exceptions. They concerned what may be called the manners, if not the morals, of Mr. Whitman's poetry; and we think they are still valid; but there is no doubt that Emerson felt a keen sympathy with the æsthetic revolt so courageously embodied in its form. His own verse, in a certain beautiful lawlessness, expresses now and again his impatience of smoothness and regularity, his joy in a fractured surface, a broken edge, his exultation in a pace or two outside the traces. Mostly, however, the freedom of his thoughts sufficed him; he submitted their utterance to the conventional measures; yet he could foresee the advantages of bringing poetry nearer to the language and the carriage of life, as Mr. Whitman's work seemed promising to do; and it was characteristic of him that he should not stint his congratulations to the author.

We have been thinking of them in connection with a passage of a recent criticism in the *World* newspaper reviewing one of the late translations of Tolstoï. The writer has discovered that "the Russian absolutely ignores all rules, all efforts at an artistic roundness and finish. He finds life without artistic roundness, and he draws it as he sees it. There is no composition, no grouping, merely stern verity." This cannot greatly surprise any reader of the Study; perhaps that reader will not even find wholly novel the assertion that beside this verity the realism "of the extremest French and American apostles shrinks into bald convention." But this is true, as a rule, and we are glad to have the *World's* critic say it and feel it, while we commend Mr. Whitman's work, both in verse and prose, as a signal exception to this rule.

As a whole we do not commend it, and for the very reason that we do commend Tolstoï as a whole. The American's frankness is, on its moral side, the revolt of the physical against the ascetic; the Russian's is the cry of the soul for help against the world and the flesh. The American is intolerant of all bonds and bounds, and he bursts them with a sort of Titanic rapture; the Russian's devotion to the truth is so single that he is apparently unconscious of the existence of limitations; but both of these masters, at opposite poles morally, are the same in æsthetic effect.

IV.

The question as to whether American writers or French writers can ever approach the directness of the Russian writers is one which involves the much larger question of literary consciousness. Walt Whitman's rebellion was itself a confession of this consciousness; and we ought to recognize that Tolstoï alone, even among Russian writers, seems wholly without it. Some philosophers have

attempted to explain his unconsciousness upon the theory that he has the good fortune to write in a language and land without a literary past, and is therefore wholly untrammelled by tradition; but these must have counted without the fact that Gogol, the father of Russian naturalism, who wrote fifty years ago, was as full of literary consciousness as Thackeray or Dickens. They ignore another fact, namely, that perhaps the book which most nearly approaches the simplicity of Tolstoï is *I Malavoglia*, by the Italian Verga, who has a literary past running back almost indefinitely. Near to this we think we should place *Maximina*, by Valdés, the Spaniard, who derives also from a remote literary antiquity. The only alloy in its unconsciousness is the humor which pervades it, and which perhaps disables the unconsciousness of the best American work, consciousness being the very essence of humor. Amongst Englishmen the author of the *Revolution in Tanner's Lane* and the *Mark Rutherford* books must be counted for his simplicity and directness. Amongst the French masters Daudet is always literose; and half the time Zola gives you the sense of book-making; the Goncourts are sincere, but still a little conscious; the repulsive masterpieces of Maupassant are as free from posing at least as Tolstoï's work.

If we come to the Americans, it is without the courage to make a very confident claim for any but the latest beginners, a Southerner here and there, and such a Northerner as Miss Wilkins, who, however, cannot always be trusted. We have something worse than a literary past: we have a second-hand literary past, the literary past of a rich relation. We are, in fact, still literary colonists, who are just beginning to observe the aspects of our own life in and for themselves, but who preserve our English ancestors' point of view, and work in their tradition.

Yet the future is ours if we want it, and we have only to turn our backs upon the past in order to possess it. Simplicity is difficult; some of the sophisticated declare it impossible at this stage of the proceedings; but it is always possible to be unaffected, just as it is to be morally honest, to put our object before ourselves, to think more of the truth we see than of our poor little way of telling it, and to prize the fact of things beyond the effect of things. What if, after all, Tolstoï's power came from his conscience, which made it as impossible for him to caricature or dandify any feature of life as to lie or cheat? What if he were so full of the truth, and so desirous to express it for God's sake and man's sake, that he would feel the slightest unfaithfulness to it a sin? This is not wholly incredible of such a man, though it is a hard saying for those who write merely from the low artistic motive long vaunted as the highest.

V.

Emerson felt the absence of the best motive, even in the greatest of the masters, when he said of Shakespeare that, after all, he was only master of the revels. The judgment is so severe, even with the praise which precedes it, that one winces under it; and if one is still young, with the world gay before him, and life full of joyous promise, one is apt to ask, defiantly, Well, what is better than being such a master of the revels as Shakespeare was? Let each judge for himself. To the heart again of serious youth, uncontaminate and exigent of ideal good, it must always be a grief that the great masters seem so often to have been willing to amuse the leisure and vacancy of meaner men, and leave their mission to the soul but partially fulfilled. This, perhaps, was what Emerson had in mind; and if he had it in mind of Shakespeare, who gave us, with his histories and comedies and problems, such a searching homily as *Macbeth*, one feels that he scarcely recognized the limitations of the dramatist's art. Few consciences, at times, seem so enlightened as that of this personally unknown person, so withdrawn into his work, and so lost to the intensest curiosity of after-time; at other times he seems merely Elizabethan in his coarseness, his courtliness, his imperfect sympathy. In these he was no greater [1] than his great contemporary, to whom Emerson's censure would far more strictly apply; and if Emerson had said of Cervantes that, after all, he was only the master of the revels, no one could have questioned his accuracy.

The new translation of *Don Quixote*, by [2] Mr. John Ormsby, brings Cervantes back into the literary world again as what the politicians call a "live issue," and his excellent introduction to the novel, his very interesting sketch of Cervantes's life, and his admirable essay on the master's masterpiece, supply fresh material for a bibliographical, biographical, and critical estimate of the whole case. The version recalls in flavor that of Jervas, which has so [3] long been the accepted English version; but this is proof that Jervas had imparted the true "tang of the wine-skin" to his work, rather than that Mr. Ormsby has caught his tone: the tone must be the tone of Cervantes, and the latest translator does full justice to the faithful predecessor whom he is destined to supplant. We may trust him when he tells us that all other English versions are worthless, for none other have survived; and without having compared his own with the Spanish, we may safely believe that he has conscientiously reported it. Those who

like can still read Cervantes in the original, though after reading Mr. Ormsby's essay they can hardly do so with the comfortable belief that its involved, careless, and rambling style is a *testa di lingua:* for that they had perhaps better go to any good modern Spanish novel. He has probably made a much better translation for us than more than two or three of us could make for ourselves; and after reading the novel nearly all through again in Mr. Ormsby's English, we feel no very lively regret for Cervantes's Spanish. We are really much obliged to Mr. Ormsby, not only for reflecting Cervantes so perfectly, but also for his sober and just criticism of the work. It is a relief to be freed from the hard necessity of supposing that the story of *The Curious Impertinent* (Ill-advised Curiosity, Mr. Ormsby calls it) is not very dull and characterless; that the other episodes, with the exception of the captive's story, are not very tiresome; and that the after-thought of that mechanism of Cid Hamet Ben-Engeli, with his Arabic manuscript, is not a direful bore. They are all each of these, in Mr. Ormsby's opinion, and we declare ourselves of it with a long breath of freedom. But for the sacrilege of mutilating a masterpiece, he intimates that the story of Don Quixote would be much better without them; and who that has taken the trouble of reading them, after having obeyed his first inspiration to skip them, can dispute this position? Mr. Ormsby is right not only in this, but in his feeling that they cannot be cut out by an editor. They are important as a part of literary history, if not literature; they mark a fashion, a stage of development, and belong properly enough with the crudity of much of the horse-play which deforms the exquisite beauty of the author's conception of Don Quixote and Sancho Panza. It must remain a question whether Cervantes would have put in the horse-play if left quite to his own taste, or if he had not felt obliged to consider the taste of his readers. Probably he was a man of his time, and liked horse-play himself, though, being the master he was, he probably liked better things better; and he half-humorously, half-seriously admits, in the discussion of the first part of the history by some of its characters in the second part, the justice of the censure it had brought him even among his contemporaries.

VI.

The sense of humor is something that the process of civilization has refined almost as much as the passion of love itself, which all connoisseurs now allow to be a very different thing from the passion of love known to even the free peoples of antiquity. The commonest newspaper funny man would now hardly offer to his readers the brutal pummellings, rib-breakings, jaw-smashings, vomitings, blanket-tossings, and worse, which the author of the supreme masterpiece of humor seems to have thought it amusing to portray. Doubtless he knew that as a bit of humor Sancho's coming out with the story of the punctilious clown, when Don Quixote was refusing the place of honor at the Duke and Duchess's table, was worth more than all these grotesque and barbarous inventions; but doubtless he liked them too. The memoirs and the novels testify how very lately such things were relished, and some college boys still think it droll to haze their fellows. Yet there has been a great advance, and the average humor of our time addresses itself habitually to the kindlier sense to which Don Quixote appeals only as a conception, and which his history touches only now and then.

VII.

As long as our modern humor does this it cannot become a serious question whether we are not too humorous, as a people, and whether, in our love of laughing, we have not lost some reverence for sacred and beautiful things. Apparently the sense of the grotesque is paramount in the Americans, just as that of beauty is in the Italians, and that of humanity is in the Russians, and that of science is in the Germans; and it is in the continual refinement of this sense that our safety from it lies. An old friend of the Study's, who loved the humorous with his full share of the national fondness for it, used to be troubled with serious doubts of its origin and its destiny. It seemed to him that the source of all derision was malignant, perhaps infernal; and he answered the fact that much humor was very kindly, with the argument that this kindness necessarily involved a degree of contempt, and that contempt was the one truly diabolical mood. He had grave misgivings as to the existence of humor in a heavenly state; an "affable archangel," yes; but he doubted about a funny one, though he owned, with the whimsicality which was his part in the sin, that he was afraid it might be dull in paradise without humor. His condition of mind was somewhat morbid, possibly; but it was no more difficult for him to mitigate the practical workings of his hypotheses than for a good Catholic to hope salvation for a heretical friend through the omnipotent mercy which can transcend its own laws. Humor and schism are alike bad, we may conclude, but not all humorists or schismatics must be lost. It is a very pretty inquiry, and we commend it to those now beginning to deal scientifically as well as ethically with the qualities and forces of the mind. In the

mean time we cannot see what harm there can be in a joke at some other's cost, or in that impersonal humor which plays luminously over many dark surfaces in life, and lights them up with a ray that neither kills nor scorches.

But humor, like every other gift, can continue valuable only as it becomes humanized and civilized. Like religion, it is always in danger of a relapse into barbarity; but its consciousness ought to save it; and the study of its own past can be very useful to it. The survival of old traits and the persistence of old forms in quite modern work is one of the interesting proofs of the irregular, hesitating, sometimes retrogressive character of all progress, and the reader who takes up the beautiful new Tappan-Zee edition of Irving's miscellaneous works must be struck by his fidelity to literary tradition if he comes to them from re-reading *Don Quixote*. It is not alone in his application of the Cervantean machinery to his comic history of New York, or the invention of a Knickerbocker Cid Hamet Ben-Engeli for the supposed authorship, that the American resembles the Spanish humorist; that is a device common to many; but there is a kindred love of horse-play in both. In Irving it is much tamer horse-play, the play of a horse much gentler and more politely bred, but still there is the same tendency to the broad, not to say the coarse, the same glance at drolleries which used to become the talk when the ladies left the table and the gentlemen began to enjoy themselves. It is just to Irving to recognize that this seems far more perfunctory in him than it does in Cervantes, in whom also it seems a concession largely to the coarseness of the general taste. But in higher qualities, as well as in these lower ones, we find the two men of the same lineage; and any sprightly *littérateur*, casting about for a subject, could not find a neater one than their community of humorous feeling. There has always been a strange affinity between the Anglo-Saxon mind and the Spanish mind; the two races brought the romantic drama to its highest perfection, and both rejected the classicistic, and the same comic strain seems to run through both people, so widely differenced by origin, by language, by religion, and by polity. As we suggested in the last Study, the humor of Valdés is of the same nature as that of some refined American humorist—say Mr. Warner, or Mr. Aldrich, or Mr. Cable—and we think the reader of Shakespeare and Cervantes will often be struck by the kindred qualities of their humor. It is then perhaps not through the imitation of Cervantes, so much as through the æsthetical affinity of the Iberian and Anglo-Saxon races, that Irving reflects some of his traits.

VIII.

A far nimbler spirit than either comes with them to the Study table, and makes itself Autocrat there, as elsewhere. In Dr. Holmes we have certainly the finest and sweetest expression of that sense which can touch such opposite extremes; and it has continually subtilized and humanized itself in his work, till at last it does not seem a laugh at anything, but only a gracious smile of sympathy with everything. All unkindness is gone; and one feels in it an increasing trust of different manners and conditions of men, and an absence of all former reservations concerning men whose manners were not the best, and whose conditions were not the most fortunate. The pure kindliness in Dr. Holmes's frank record of what happened to him in his recent visit abroad is the loveliest trait of *Our Hundred Days in Europe*, though we should find it hard to say whether this was more admirable than the almost miraculous tact with which it is expressed; both seem of a piece; one scarcely knows which is which. It would have been so easy to fill such a record with lasting offence to both hemispheres; but in perfect consistency with a delightful candor, both hemispheres are always rubbed the right way.

In each of Dr. Holmes's books there is an autobiographic quality which is most valuable, and of *Our Hundred Days in Europe* one can only say that it is a little more autobiographical than the rest. If he was to tell at all the story of the beautiful and spontaneous appreciation shown him in England, there was but one manner of doing it, and Dr. Holmes has rightly presented his hosts from the stand-point of a welcome guest whose heart has been deeply touched by his welcome, and who is incapable of abusing it. As the book is about what he heard and saw, the attitude is necessarily personal, but never was personal experience so graciously imparted to the reader before; it seems as if this egotism had somehow got itself transmuted to altruism through that fine sympathy, and that each of us had spent Dr. Holmes's Hundred Days in Europe.

The new *Don Quixote* came to us as such an exceptionally handsome piece of book manufacture that we were ill prepared to have it surpassed by the dainty beauty of the new edition of Irving, which is, up to the date of this writing, the happiest and tastefulest American achievement in that sort. It leaves behind even the style in which Dr. Holmes's publishers have hitherto led the fashion in clothing their authors; and we hope it will inspire them to give us at least the literature of the Autocrat in an exterior elegance and lightness expressive of its quality. The only unpleasant thing about *Our Hundred Days in Europe* is the commonness and inadequacy of its outside.

[1] *Criticism and Fiction*, pp. 113-114.

[2] Miguel de Cervantes Saavedra, *The Ingenious Gentleman Don Quixote of La Mancha*, John Ormsby, trans. (New York: Macmillan, 1885).

[3] Miguel de Cervantes Saavedra, *Adventures of Don Quixote de la Mancha*, Charles Jarvis, trans. (Chicago: Bedford, Clarke, 1887). Howells' "Jervas" should be Charles Jarvis.

[4] Washington Irving, *Works*, Tappan Zee Edition (New York: Putnam, 1887).

March, 1888

Editor's Study.

I.

MR. H. C. LEA'S *History of the Inquisition of the Middle Ages* is one of those books whose significance does not cease even with the suggestion of the remotest relations of its subject to the life of the period. One would read it to less than its whole purport if he failed to grasp the fact that underlying the cruelty of the Catholic Church in dealing with heresy were the primitive passions which stirred the heart of the Cave Dweller, and which still animate civilization in its social, commercial, and political rivalries and competitions. History, when it is wisely written, is both record and prophecy in its deeper implications. The aspects and forms change, but the motives remain the same, refined, indeed, and unconsciously masked, yet essentially what they were ever since one man found himself physically or mentally stronger than another, and sought to confirm his advantages by his brother's lasting subjection. He has never lacked the best reasons for this. The proofs that his self-seeking is for his brother's good are always so abundant that he is rarely driven to an open and cynical profession of an egoistic intention. In fact, when it comes to this with him, he is near to being a better man, for he then becomes intolerable to himself. But as long as he can make believe with any hopeful measure of success that he is somehow serving God, or humanity, or society, by the exploitation of his fears for his supremacy, by his lust of dominion, his state is not hopeful. We need not go far afield for exemplifications; if we cannot find them in our own hearts, we may see them in the lives of our neighbors all round us. The difference between the persecuting spirit of the past and the persecuting spirit of the present is largely a difference of ideals, of ends. A united Church was the most desirable thing on earth to the Romish clergy, and for the sake of it they seem to have been willing in former times to commit any crime, from stifling thought to burning the thinker. Whatever threatened that unity and its vested interests, temporal and spiritual, must be hunted down and exterminated. This ideal no longer inspires persecution; but persecution is not therefore extinct.

It is the fate of the Roman Catholic Church to bear forever before the world the chief burden of a sin which is no more Catholic than it is Protestant. The means of persecution were first at hand with that Church, and its hand was strongest; that is all. Every one knows that Lutheran, Calvinist, Anglican, and Puritan persecuted too, each in his turn. But these all came later; they were not only weaker in organization and numbers, but they were stayed sooner by the light of religious toleration, so tardily dawning as a principle on men's minds; yet their spirit was the same. We must keep this truth constantly before us if we would get all the good there is to be got from the story of the Inquisition as Mr. Lea tells it. We must not solace ourselves with the delusion that it is an accomplished and ended tragedy, or that it is a Catholic and Spanish or Italian crime; it flourished up from the profoundest depths of our common human nature, from the roots of greed and hate and fear that take hold on hell in every Protestant and Anglo-Saxon heart to-day as firmly as in the dark ages and the Latin races. Wherever one man hates another for his opinions, there the spirit of the Inquisition is as rife as ever.

Yet he may be a very good man in many things. The mortifying lesson of that interesting chapter of Mr. Lea's on the origin and rise of the Mendicant Orders in the Romish Church is its testimony to the fact that the men who became the most terrible instruments of persecution were men devoted to works of the most self-sacrificing mercy toward all but heretics; no form of suffering was too loathsome or dangerous for their care; they bore hunger and cold and denied themselves all their lives long for the poor; they established and realized an ideal of charity whose perfection has perhaps never been approached by men of more tolerant faith; yet they were the fiercest, most unrelenting foes of other men in whom one of the first signs of heresy was a life of purity, sobriety, and good works.

The reader might easily fail to do justice to the candor with which Mr. Lea deals with all the anomalies of his subject. His study of the corruptions in the Church which provoked heresy is perfectly temperate, and by its light we see how natural it was that the faithful should attack the heretics rather than the corruptions, the effects rather than the causes. This is still the way of intolerance in the world: its highest wisdom is to suppress the symptoms and to destroy the obnoxious theory in the person of the theorist.

But a notable thing is that in the very earliest ages, the Church, that afterward rioted in torture, shrank from punishing heresy with death, or with any penalty involving physical suffering. There seems to have been a time before intolerance wreaked itself, if not a time before intolerance began; and Mr. Lea is able to put his finger apparently on the instance in which the Christian Church first authorized the killing of men for their opinions. It was regarded with horror by all not immediately concerned in it, and it was reprobated by the highest authorities. But afterward, when heresy became formidable, the Church lost its sensibility, and abandoned itself to the atrocities of an inverted conscience. Mr. Lea makes a clear and impartial analysis of the different forms of heresy, and he gives an admirable chapter to the Albigensian crusades, not losing sight of the evils that were on the right side, nor the good that was on the wrong side; though he shows that the fault of the Albigenses was mainly with their rulers and allies, and the sincerity of the crusaders was as murderous as the defect of that virtue could well have been. Through this virtue was evolved the comfortable principle that the Divine wisdom would repair any mistakes of massacre made by the faithful, and that if the crusaders would kill all in sacking a heretical city, God would take care of the souls of such true Catholics as happened to perish in the promiscuous slaughter. It would not be easy to estimate the strength which the recognition of such a principle must have imparted to the nascent Inquisition, which Mr. Lea seems to regard as having its origin in the persecution of the Albigenses; together with the other great idea of relaxing heretics to the secular arm for punishment, it might well constitute an impregnable defence for the inverted consciences of the sincere and merciful men whose goodness is inextricably mixed up with the pitiless cruelties of the Holy Office.

Mr. Lea traces the rise of the Inquisition through that of the mendicant orders and their works of charity, and dispassionately studies its organization, its processes in taking evidence and admitting — or rather refusing — defence, its methods of executing sentence on quick and dead, and its confiscations. He lets us see, without denunciation or apparent prejudice, how everything base and cruel in the men armed with the awful power of the Inquisition poisonously blended itself with their unselfish zeal for the unity of the Church, which represented to them the salvation of souls, and how the evil ceased to be deadly only when it excluded the good. It is true that the Inquisition did apparently accomplish the purpose of its founders, and suppressed heresy in the countries where it had full sway. This will not seem wonderful to any one who acquaints himself with its unlimited means and its unscrupulous methods, nor will it appear contradictory to say that the Inquisition left the Church in those countries without the vitality which it still shows in lands where the Inquisition never existed. There is in the course of history something more than the suggestion that evil dies of the mortal sting which it inflicts, and that it defeats those who employ it, in accomplishing itself.

II.

It will be interesting to know how this happened with the evil known as the Inquisition, with that fulness of detail which we may expect in Mr. Lea's second and third volumes, announced to complete the work projected in his first. In the mean time some of the questions involved will present themselves to the reader of Zola's latest and perhaps awfulest book, *La Terre*. Filthy and repulsive as it is in its facts, it is a book not to be avoided by the student of civilization, but rather to be sought and seriously considered. It is certainly not a book for young people, and it is not a book for any one who cares merely for a story, or who finds himself by experience the worse for witnessing in literature the naked realities of lust and crime. This said, it is but fair to add that it legitimately addresses itself to scientific curiosity and humane interest. The scene passes in that France where the first stirring of a personal conscience once promised a brilliant race the spiritual good which triumphant persecution finally denied it; and it is not wholly gratuitous to suppose that we see in the peasants of *La Terre* effects of the old repressions which stifled religious thought among them, and bound all their hopes, desires, and ambitions to the fields they tilled. When the Revolution came, it came too late to undo the evil accomplished, and the immediate good that it did included another evil. It justly gave to the peasant the ownership of the land, but it implanted in him the most insatiable earth-hunger ever known in the world. This creature, this earth-fiend whom Zola paints, is superstitious, but cynically indifferent to religion, and apparently altogether unmoral; lustful and unchaste, but mostly saved from the prodigal vices by avarice that spares nothing, relents to no appeal, stops at no wrong, and aspires only to the possession of land, and more land, and ever more land. This is the prevailing type, varied and relieved by phases of simple, natural good in a few of the characters; and the Church, so potent against the ancestral heresy, struggles in vain against the modern obduracy, in the character of the excellent priest, who is the only virtuous person in the book. The story is a long riot of satyr-lewdness and satyr-violence, of infernal greed that ends in murder, of sordid jealousies and cruel hates; and since with all its literary power, its wonderful force of realization, it cannot remain valuable as literature, but must have other interest as a scientific study of a phase of French life under the Second Empire, it seems a great pity it should not have been fully documented. What are the sources, the proofs, of this tremendous charge against humanity, in those simple conditions, long fabled the most friendly to the simple virtues? This is the question which the reader, impatient if not incredulous of all this horror, asks himself when he has passed through it.

III.

He must ask it also at the end of that curious narrative drama of Tolstoï's, known to us as yet only in the French version of *La Puissance des Ténèbres*. This too deals with peasant life, and with much the same hideous shames and crimes as *La Terre*. The main difference—but it is a very great one—is that the Russian peasant, wicked as he is, is not so depraved as the French peasant; he has a conscience; he is capable of remorse, of repentance, of expiation. It is true that one of the *muzhiks*, to whose amendment the drama is addressed, and to a group of whom Tolstoï read it for their criticism, declared that the principal person, after accomplishing his purposes, would not have owned his crimes or wished to suffer for them as his one hope of escape from self-torment; but we may suppose this opinion the effect of restricted observation, and may safely trust the larger and deeper knowledge of the author. We should again, however, like to have the documentary proofs in the case, and should feel more hopeful of the good to be done among the muzhiks by the play if we felt sure that they would recognize it as a true picture. In the mean time they are not likely to know much about it; the censorship has forbid-

den its representation in Russia, and it remains for the consideration of such people of other countries as know how to read.

Whether much is done to help those whose life is depicted in fiction is a question which no one is yet qualified to answer, fiction has only so very recently assumed to paint life faithfully, and most critics still claim that it is best for it not to do so. It is said that the stories of Erckmann-Chatrian, by their fidelity to [1] the abominations and horrors of war, have had the effect of weakening the love of military glory in the French people; and the books of the pastor Bitzius, who [2] wrote fifty years ago—under the pseudonym of Jeremias Gotthelf—stories as intensely realistic as any of the present day, are claimed to have wrought a great reform in the manners and morals of the Bernese peasants, whom he photographed in their own dialects. But we suspect that fiction, like the other arts, can only do good of this kind indirectly; when it becomes hortatory, it is in danger of becoming dull, that is to say, suicidal.

IV.

The autobiography of the English painter Frith, who dealt so much with the [3] every-day life about him, and loved above everything else to deal with it, and was so devoutly if not passionately faithful to it in his work, is not without suggestion upon some of these points. It is a delightful book, as autobiographies are apt to be, with signal merits of simplicity and honesty, and manifold attractions of gossip about art and artists and the world of London around them. All forms of æsthetic life there are more closely related and touch fashionable life at more points than with us; the relations of art to taste or to patronage are more social; the experience of the painter is richer and more varied, and his talk has a wider range. Mr. Frith's has the range of a very long period, in which he has been part of what he tells. He keeps himself modestly enough in the background when it is best to do so; but he does not forget that it is his own life which he is writing, and that he has reason to suppose that the reader will like to know all about his opinions, his ideals, his endeavors, and his achievements, even his grievances and prejudices. His more characteristic pictures are well known through the popular reproductions, and the reader has more than the usual materials for judging between the artist and his critics in a quarrel which has been nearly life-long. Simply stated, the quarrel is that Mr. Frith believed he saw the dramatic, the poetic, the beautiful, the sublime, the eternal, in the contemporary life of the London streets, the railway stations, the sea-side resorts, the race-courses, and his critics maintained that he saw only the commonplace, the vulgar, the trivial, and the transitory. He won the day, with the public at least, and we think that the criticism of the future will be kinder to him than that of his own time. We think it will not, for instance, find good reason for accepting Hogarth's "Rake's Progress," and rejecting Frith's "Road to Ruin," so conscientiously studied and so tragically realized. We have only the literary quality of the work in mind; matters of technique we do not understand, and we gladly leave them to the art critics, who do not understand them either, if we may trust the artists. Mr. Frith declares that he never got help or hurt from them; that it was wholly idle to regard their printed opinions; and that when he really felt any doubt as to what he happened to be doing, he took counsel with some brother artist, who was often severe enough, but who was always intelligent, and who had the right point of view.

V.

The question whether he was right or whether he was wrong is part of a much vaster question. Undoubtedly his opinion is qualified by the resentment which a spirited, earnest, and successful man must feel under the application of criterions recognizably narrow and antipathetic; but it is intelligible also that he may be perfectly sincere, and even perfectly right. It is interesting, at any rate, to find Mr. August St. Gaudens, who has certainly[4] had no reason as yet to complain of critical unkindness, saying, in a recently printed interview: "Books on art are of no value. They are worse than useless, and should be left alone. The pencil, the brush, and the modelling-stick should take their place, and be the student's constant companions. I do not wish to be understood as discouraging general reading. On the contrary, the broadening of the mind obtained from a knowledge of miscellaneous literature is to be desired."

This accuses criticism upon more general and impersonal grounds than Mr. Frith's, but it is to the same purport, and it probably embodies the experience of every man who has done anything worth while in any of the arts. Criticism, apparently, is for the edification of the reader, and not for the instruction of the artist; but upon this point we should not like to speak very confidently without more documents. The Study is hospitably open to any author, sculptor, painter, or architect who wishes to contribute to the evidence from his own experience. Perhaps from a comparison of experiences something useful to criticism might be evolved. It needs help, at present, more than any of the arts, and is not much more fitted to deal with them than the Inquisition would be to deal with the problems of modern science.

VI.

How very fallible criticism is at the best, and under the most favorable conditions, may be conceived from the cruel error into which the Study itself—mirror of impartiality and balance of justice as it is—fell into lately concerning Octave Thanet's admirable group of sketches, *The Knitters in the Sun*. The reader will remember that we were able to convict that clever writer of lese-reality in an important point, and to deliver a very pretty lecture upon the "ways of God to man" in censuring her for romantically misrepresenting them. We were, as usual, perfectly right in our opinions, but we were wrong in our facts; we had overlooked a passage in the story reprehended which gave it a wholly different complexion, and conformed it to our own ideal. We must send the reader to the little book for the damning evidences of our peccability in full, and we can assure him that it is otherwise very well worth looking at.

We wish we could truthfully say that it gives us pleasure to make this correction. It does nothing of the kind; it is extremely distasteful, and nothing could oblige us to do it but the love of justice, and the hope of breaking down any small remnant of respect for criticism generally which might be left in the mind of our readers by the Study's past attacks upon it.

---

[1] Emile Erckmann and Alexandre Chatrian, joint authors.

[2] Albert Bitzius.

[3] William Powell Frith, My Autobiography and Reminiscences (London: Richard Bentley and Son, 1887).

[4] This should be Augustus (not August) St. Gaudens.

April, 1888

Editor's Study.

I.

AMONG the many efforts to philosophize the French Revolution, to find out its meaning and point its moral, Mr. Laurence Gronland's *Ça Ira* challenges attention. We may call him a dreamer, or we may call him an economist; we may class his *Co-operative Commonwealth* with Plato's Republic, or we may regard it as the divination of the political future from the conditions of the present and the past; but we must allow that the author is very much in earnest, and that the book is cogently addressed to the civic conscience. It is not in revery that he prophesies the total change of our polity, and the reconstruction of our society upon the broad principle that those who do not work shall not eat, and that no man who is willing to work shall starve. Mr. Gronland believes that this is implied by the very facts and forces that seem to imply the contrary. He believes, for instance, that the collection of all the productive and distributing industries into a few hands and in vast establishments—that trusts, pools, combines, and the like, are the unconscious agencies of socialism, or, as he prefers to call it, collectivism, and that alike by their uses and their abuses they are destined to hasten the downfall of the whole wage system, and to reconcile labor and capital in a state which shall employ both for the good of all.

For the historical proofs he goes back a great way, as the student of every question feels obliged to do in these times. He finds an imperfect and finally broken image of his coming state in the conditions of the Middle Ages, before money began to fructify and capital began to rule, and he does not regard the French Revolution as the effect of immediate causes, or as purely French in its origins; he does not treat it as a single sequence, running its course from the constitution of the National Assembly to the Eighteenth Brumaire. He holds that the popular revolution was accomplished in the triumph of the commoners over the king, the nobility, and the clergy in that Assembly; and that then the moneyed class began through the Girondists a counter-revolution, which should gather and keep the power in their hands; that the Jacobins crushed this capitalistic reaction; and that the Terror was the result, not of bad principles, but of bad leadership, of the supremacy of Robespierre and the fall of Danton; that the final plutocratic ascendency, which ended in the Eighteenth Brumaire, the Consulate, and the Empire, was the inauguration of conditions which survive to-day in the world-wide exploitation of labor by capitalized enterprises, and the re-enslavement of the masses under the wage system.

II.

The most interesting chapter of the book is the last, in which the "transition state" is regarded as extending from 1794 to the present time. This state is the same in all civilized countries; it is the expression of the power of capital and the subjugation of men. It is not peace, anywhere, and it cannot promise permanence. It is a state of war, in which the frequent battles between the ruling force and its subjects are alternated with truces, broken again by crises, by overproduction, by strikes. Each man is the rival of every other, till two or more agree to combine instead of competing, and then unite their energies in preying upon all the rest. This is the aspect which individualistic society wears to the regard of Mr. Gronland and other collectivists; and ugly as it is, we must all own that it is not wholly unfamiliar to any of us. Professor R. T. Ely, of Johns Hopkins University, in a most interesting and valuable tract on *Land, Labor, and Taxation*, goes so far as to say of it: "I am not sure that I would not agree with Mill when he says if he were obliged to make choice between existing economic society, without hope of further improvement, and communism, all the difficulties, great and small, real and imaginary, of communism would not for a moment deter him from accepting the latter alternative."

The boasted free play of energies, Mr. Gronland tells us, has resulted in the power of the strong over the weak, of the rich over the poor; and under the name of democracy we have a republic in which there is no equality, not even equality before the law. He proposes instead that we shall have a commonwealth in which it shall be the first business of government to provide that no one who is willing to work shall suffer, and that no one who is idle shall enjoy. He takes the trades-unions, with the mutual sacrifices of their members, as the norm of his interdependent society, and constructs an ideal state in which those who are lowest shall appoint their chiefs, and so upward till all interests are represented in the rule of the fit over the many, in which the tenure of office shall be fixed as it now is in the unions, by efficiency and good behavior. His co-operative commonwealth is the reconciliation of interests which now antagonize one another, the substitution of the ideal of duties for the ideal of rights, of equality for liberty. In his state we should have fewer laws but more law, less force but more justice, more self-sacrifice and less suffering. "But this," says Professor Ely, again, "is precisely the point.... With the best will, we cannot avoid the fear that in the socialistic state public opinion would exercise a tyranny now unknown—and even now its force is terrible, and in many respects baneful—which would repress as with an iron hand any divergence of belief or action from a low prescribed level."

We have reported the general intention of Mr. Gronland's *Co-operative Commonwealth*, because the theory of that work seems to give its chief value and significance to his present sketch of the French Revolution. What relates in *Ça Ira* to men and events will appear perfunctory, we think, to most readers; the author is really interested in tracing influences and tendencies which must inevitably result in the establishment of collectivism or the socialistic state. The French Revolution, interrupted and perverted as it was, he regards as the first great step in that direction, but he does not expect the last step from the French people. He believes that any effort to found the co-operative commonwealth in France would be defeated by the revengeful memories of the Commune, and by the treachery of the *bourgeoisie*, who would invite German intervention. In Germany there would be obstruction from Russia; but in Great Britain, where the study of social problems has made socialists of many scholars, clergymen, and economists, and in the United States, where the assemblage of production and distribution into the control of a few vast agencies has unconsciously prepared the way for collectivism, he looks for the first experiments in political co-operation. He believes it the duty of all to facilitate the peaceful solution of the problems before us, but he does not point out the measures to be actually taken

by a people accustomed to express their purpose in suffrage and legislation; and here is the point at which the interest of the average American reader must falter. If a philosopher cannot tell him just what to do, he is apt to lose faith in the philosophy, however just and beautiful it may appear. Even Professor Ely, who is not a collectivist, seems more explicit when he says, "Natural monopolies, in my opinion, such as railways, telegraph lines, gas-works, water-works, etc., should be owned and managed by central or local governments." Here is a platform which voters may stand upon or knock from under the feet of other voters; and we know nothing quite so direct in the programme of any collectivist organization.

Mr. Gronland, however, is a man to be read with respect for those qualities which we have indicated, and his work cannot be ignored by any one who wishes to acquaint himself with the hopes and motives of a very intelligent body of men. As represented by Mr. Gronland, they are not less friendly to their country and their kind than any other class of Americans. One may read his books without risk of offence to one's patriotism or humanity, whatever one concludes as to the wisdom or practicality of his teachings, and with great advantage to one's knowledge of a palpitant question. It is not the last word on socialism, but it is certainly the latest, that he says.

III.

Mr. Gronland is careful more than once to distinguish between collectivism, which means the fulfilment of common duties, and anarchism, which is the realization of individual rights; in this sense he would perhaps regard the present condition as anarchical. Neither does he expect his commonwealth from the confluence of separate communities, as the earlier socialists did, under the lead of Owen and Fourier. All that is now changed, and it is rather the wrath of the pools, the trusts, and the combines which is to befriend the good cause. These violently destroy competition, and afford the norm of production and distribution on a colossal scale, and by gathering the industries in a few hands will facilitate their possession by the state, when the time comes, without awakening popular opposition or regret. But formerly it was hoped that the communities and the phalanxes would afford the norm of the mutualistic state, and ardent sympathies and strenuous endeavors were generously contributed to their universal failure. Fifty or sixty years ago the regeneration of mankind was largely expected of enterprises which inaugurated the industrial millennium by antagonizing the existing industries, and by taking part, voluntarily or involuntarily, in the general system of competition. What was so largely attempted at that time is recalled by Mr. Adolphus Trollope in his very entertaining autobiography, *What I Remember*, where he speaks of Miss Fanny Wright's experiment in Alabama. She bought a great property there, and freed the slaves upon it, and founded a community with this and such other material as she could assemble. Her New Harmony evolved the usual discords on a rather larger scale than usual; and Mr. Trollope remembers to have heard of the foundress "marrying a French teacher of languages at the close of a course of lectures given by her against the institution of matrimony." She was, in fact, a woman who at that period largely filled the public eye (or perhaps it would be more exact to say the newspaper eye) by her originality of character and philosophy, which ranged from dress reform to reform in all its branches. Mr. Trollope's mother was amicably associated with her before the disastrous failure of her own enterprise at Cincinnati cost the whole country the long-resented severities of one of the earliest English books about it. Probably it was an honest enough book, and just enough; we are not so faultless now that we can believe the Western people of that remote time were wholly misrepresented in Mrs. Trollope's *Domestic Manners of the Americans*. The trouble was that the title of the book implied a study of the whole country, which Mrs. Trollope had certainly not made; and even of the Southwest (as it then was) the study was not accurate or impartial. Among the things that Mr. Trollope remembers there seems to be nothing that he recalls more fondly, or with a keener sense of its proper charm, than the life which his mother depicted as so grotesque, not to say offensive. To the young man's eyes it was simple, easy, and cordial; but there is everything in the point of view, and he explains that his mother's was that of a disappointed person who saw the people among whom she failed through the color of her disaster.

Mr. Trollope never mentions us but in a kindness which those who read his agreeable book will reciprocate almost in the measure of those who have personally made his agreeable acquaintance. It is the story of a life of hard work, like that of his brother, the greater novelist, but not of trials or exigencies, and it flows or pauses among the pleasantest places of the earth. The longest, quietest stretch of it is the period passed at Florence, which is here celebrated with much charming and valuable reminiscence of Landor, the Brownings, George Eliot, Powers, and other more or less Italianate English and American sojourners, and with very intelligent and friendly observation of the native life. It is this Italian part of the book which has the greatest value, and it would be a pity if it did not send many readers to all those works from Mr. Trollope's hand which concern Italy in fiction and history. His novels are good, clear, honest, pleasant dealings with contemporary Italy; his histories just as honest, good, and clear, if not so pleasant, inquiries into the past. His *Decade of Italian Women* we have not read, but we speak by the card when we praise *Paul the Pope and Paul the Friar*, and *Filippo Strozzi*, as books of singular importance to the student of that Italian civilization which has lessons for the whole world and all time. As for the *History of the Florentine Commonwealth*, when the ideas and events of that wonderful democracy come to be studied as they should, for the light they can throw upon just such problems—the relations of capital to labor, and the duties of the state to the citizen—as are so deeply concerning Christendom to-day, the excellence of the only work in English which gives them the true perspective will be recognized.

IV.

But this takes us rather far from Mr. Trollope's autobiography, as we must call it in spite of his deprecation of so large a name. We do not know that we have much more to say of it, except heartily to commend it to all lovers of the most delightful species of literature. The return to it, however, brings us also to Professor J. B. McMaster's *Life of Franklin* (in the "American Men of Letters" series) by a path less circuitous than the mind often traces in thinking from book to book. One cannot very well mention autobiography without mentioning Franklin, whose fragment in that sort remains the chief literary work of his life, and the perpetual pleasure of whoever likes to meet a man face to face in literature. The reader of Professor McMaster's very attractive volume will enjoy the curious story of this autobiography as it is given there, and will, we think, be glad to find Franklin portrayed with the freedom and candor which he used in writing of himself; the biography is in the spirit of the autobiography.

Franklin, who was in many if not most respects the greatest American of his time, has come down to ours with more reality than any of his contemporaries, and this has by no means hurt him in the popular regard. It could not be shown by the most enthusiastic whitewasher that Franklin's personal conduct was exemplary, and Professor McMaster is not a whitewasher. He is not tempted to paint Franklin as a hero or a saint, and Franklin was assuredly neither. But he was a very great man, and the objects to which he dedicated himself with an unfailing mixture of motive were such as concerned the immediate comfort of men, and the advancement of knowledge in even greater degree than they promoted Franklin's own advantage. He tore the lightning from the clouds, and the sceptre from tyrants; he also invented the Franklin stove, and gave America her first postal system. He was a great natural philosopher, a patriotic statesman, a skilful diplomatist, a master of English prose; he was likewise the father of a natural son whose mother he abandoned to absolute oblivion; he was a rather blackguardly newspaper man, a pitiless business rival, a pretty selfish liberal politician, and at times (occasionally the wrong times) a trivial humorist. The sum of him was the intellectual giant who towers through history over his contemporaries, indifferent to fame, almost cynically incredulous of ideals and beliefs sacred to most of us, but instrumental in promoting the moral and material welfare of the race; a hater of folly, idleness, and unthrift; and finally, one of the most truthful men who ever lived. It would be hard to idolize him or to overvalue him.

Professor McMaster studies his character without blinking any of its contrasting traits, and makes a book remarkable for its succinctness, its vividness, and its eminent readableness. This charm any reader of his former work must have expected him to impart, and he has imparted it throughout, but nowhere in such degree as in the chapter devoted to Franklin's nine years in France as the commissioner of the Colonies and the representative of the States. All the more remarkable because of the brilliant success of such a bit of characterization is the author's failure to penetrate the intention of Franklin's proposed paraphrase of the Book of Job. Instead of the accepted version, Franklin pretended that he would have us read: "And it being levee day in heaven, all God's nobility came to court to present themselves before Him; and Satan also appeared in the circle as one of the ministry. And God said unto Satan, You have been sometime absent; where were you? And Satan answered, I have been at my country-seat, and in different places visiting my friends. And God said, Well, what think you of Lord Job? You see he is my best friend, a perfectly honest man, full of respect for me, and avoiding everything that might offend me. And Satan answered, Does your Majesty imagine that his good conduct is the effect of personal attachment and affection?" Professor McMaster is at the trouble to parallel these with the corresponding passages from the King James version, and to show how their "force and beauty were wholly lost" upon Franklin. He does not seem to have seen in Franklin's paraphrase a ribald irony hardly to be matched out of the writings of Swift, and he gravely reprobates it as being "of all paraphrases of the Bible surely the worst." Gravely? Perhaps Professor McMaster also is ironical here. His acumen and cleverness elsewhere almost persuade one to think so.

V.

If Emerson was the consummate flower of Puritanism, Franklin was the fruiting of that other stock in New England civilization of which we do not take account when we think of it as wholly Puritanic. Mr. Matthew Arnold, who seems to hold Emerson and Franklin in equal esteem as the two greatest Americans, would hardly send those who "wished to live in the spirit" to the latter, though if he were advising any one where to go for the wisdom of this world, he could not give him a more useful address.

From time to time the novelists have attempted to catch this unpuritanic phase of New England character, which is at its highest and best in Franklin, and at its worst in Burr, and which is not nearly so tangible as the Puritanic phase. Once again, the effort which Hawthorne made in this direction is made by Mr. Marion [1] Wilcox, the author of *Gray, an Oldhaven Romance*, with more than usual literary felicity. It is made somewhat in Hawthorne's manner, and somewhat in the manner of the author of *Margaret*. Is- [2] rael Slyme is the person in whom the antitype of Puritanism is attempted, and he is drawn young, beautiful, and conscienceless, with a will of iron, and a mind strong and clear and disciplined. To a certain degree the story realizes him, but in spite of a murder, a betrayal and abandonment, a case of insanity, a mysterious and immortal stranger, and various abnormalities and eccentricities, he is not thrown into perfect relief. Yet the writing is so good, specific bits of observation are so uncommon and original, and the local color is here and there so well rendered, that one wonders how the author would have succeeded in the same direction with less tremendous means, and rather longs to have him try it some time. He might take a lesson from his own work in the delightful sketch of Señora Villena, where the lightest and slightest devices suffice to give us a living sense of a charming group of people, discreetly differenced and interestingly contrasted with witty and graceful sympathy. It is rare skill that catches these Spanish accents and temperaments, and a fortunate inspiration that relieves them against those of the native Oldhaveners among whom we find them. Their whims and loves and affections are touched with an art that makes each one of them an acquaintance. If one were to complain of anything, it must be of what we shall have to call an absence of background; the figures are projected against too thin an ether; the local how and why are not sufficiently given; you are too jauntily and scrappily informed about them; and you are left with a teasing sense of having been hurried away from by the author, when he ought to have staid and satisfied a legitimate curiosity in you.

VI.

The promise of better work to come in the good work here done also attends the reader of *Five Hundred Dollars, and Other Stories of New England Life*, against the author of which he can have no such grudge as Mr. Wilcox leaves him to. Perhaps C. H. W. had not the same [3] difficulty in reconciling his people with their environment; there is a Yankee homogeneity in nearly all of them, and they are at once conceivable in their time and place. Fisher-folk, sailors, small-villagers, and neighboring farmers are the stuff with which C. H. W. loves to deal, and with which he deals freshly, simply, and faithfully. It is all very good work, which has its defect mainly through the prepotent sense of humor which sometimes betrays the author into exaggeration. Yet to this sense we owe the delicious fun of St. Patrick, in which one minister finds himself done out of the material of his lecture by the too comprehensive prayer of the other who opens the meeting, and who weaves all the known facts of the saint's life into his supplication; and we owe to it also that most delightful story of *The New Minis-ter's Great Opportunity*, which he improved to the extent of sketching the advance of civilization during the hundred years lived by the hopelessly unhistoric subject of his funeral sermon. We must not be too stringent with it, remembering this; and we must acknowledge that when the author gives himself more soberly to such a piece of work, say, as Captain Pelham in *By the Sea*, he pictures with masterly ability and quite faultless skill a type of man extremely difficult to suggest, by reason of the negative qualities which prevail in him. It is a quiet success of which perhaps all will not feel the charm, the spare pathos, the delicate truth.

In his *Mr. Absalom Billingslea and Other Georgia Folk*, Mr. R. M. Johnston has a like advantage of homogeneity in his material, though nothing could well be more different from C. H. W.'s than his people and conditions. Mr. Johnston has the same temptation through his feeling for the grotesque, and we must own that he yields to it almost habitually. In fact it has become the medium through which the life of all his Georgia folk appears to him, and he works through it to a truth of feature and expression about which it is still the atmosphere. In this respect he differs from the younger school of Southern writers, who deal with their material more objectively. Yet the subjective method has its advantages, which it would be absurd to deny; and all of Mr. Johnston's work has a charm which his readers of nearly half a century will not cease to feel in his latest book. He is in fact one of the truest humorists of a country superabundant in humorists, and he has unfailingly the racy local flavor of the Southern humorist. *The Dukesborough Tales* long ago gave proof of this, and these Georgia Folk corroborate the evidence.

---

[1] This should be Marrion Wilcox.

[2] Margaret, by Sylvester Judd.

[3] "CHW" is Herman White Chaplin.

May, 1888

Editor's Study.

I.

THE second volume of Mr. Henry Lea's *History of the Inquisition of the Middle Ages* concerns the work of the Holy Office in Languedoc, France, Spain, Italy, the Slavonic countries, Germany, and Bohemia; and it traces, with the patience and temperance characteristic of his inquiry in the first volume, the growth and decline of that institution in the different states and the different conditions. It appears that the mediæval Inquisition was bad enough, but it is from the Spanish Inquisition, which succeeded it in Spain and her dependencies alone, that the popular impressions of inquisitorial atrocity are derived. The action of the former was shaped from Rome; it was not only directed against heresy, but it asserted a political pretension of the Holy See in the several countries; and wherever the local temporalities were sufficiently strong, or became so, the Inquisition of the Middle Ages submitted to their control, and finally lost its own potency in the sovereign will. This happened not only in Italy, Germany, and France, but in Spain itself, before bigotry became incarnated in the Spanish princes, and the lust of empire replaced the love of liberty in the Spanish people. Sadly enough, the mediæval Inquisition accomplished its aim thoroughly in Languedoc alone, where religious thought had first known freedom, and where civilization flowered earliest in the humanities, which then found a friendlier air beyond the Alps, in that Italy where the great poet was doubting whether to write his "Divine Comedy" in Provençal or Tuscan. This was partly because the Counts of Toulouse had not the force to maintain themselves against Rome, and partly because Catharism, the form of heresy commonest in Languedoc, was itself a belief which, as the world advanced, must cease to fortify its devotees against persecution. As Mr. Lea says: "The secret must be looked for in the hopeless pessimism of the faith itself. . . . Manes had robbed the elder Mazdeism of its vitality when he assigned to the evil principle complete domination over Nature and the visible universe, and when he adopted the Sankhya philosophy, which teaches that existence is an evil, while death is an emancipation for those who have earned spiritual immortality, and a mere renewal of the same hated existence for all who have not risen to the height of the austerest maceration. . . . The world was . . . . unconsciously preparing for the yet unknown future in which man was to regard nature not as an enemy, but as a teacher. Catharism had no possibility of development, and in that lay its doom."

It was doomed, and it was destroyed; but Mr. Lea never allows us to imagine that the guilt of the Church which destroyed the Catharists was the less because the error of Catharism was great, and because it had a truer faith and a saner philosophy. Even if the monstrous fables invented concerning the rites of the Catharists had been true, if they had really worshipped the deity with the obscene orgies attributed to them, still the system of persecution which wrung the confession of the enormities from accused heretics by torture was a far more damnable thing in the sight of God. It is possible that the inquisitors believed these lies; but as one of the things that were most apt to lead to the suspicion of heresy was a virtuous life, it is not probable that they believed them. In any case, however, persecution resulted in a type of character among Catholics which has been repeated in fainter lines among the zealots of every sect, and produced in its most impenetrable and inexorable form that bigotry which other Christians associate with the thought of Catholicism. This is an inevitable part of the retribution which the Catholic Church of to-day suffers for its past sins against human nature and the Divine mercy, in teaching that a heretic was by reason of his heresy destitute of those claims upon honor, love, and trust to which a righteous life entitled a believer, and that a good life in a heretic ought only to make him the more abhorrent, the more to be suspected and shunned.

II.

Of course it is impossible for unperverted human nature to receive and act upon these teachings; and the study of a case of perversion, which the Spanish novelist Perez Galdós makes in his recently translated romance of *Leon Roch*, is not the study of a character now common, we suppose, even in Spain. The fact that such talents as Galdós and Valdés are analyzing it so unsparingly, yet so justly, as they are doing, contains the promise of its disappearance, or at least its modification, in the course of time, and we may enjoy the pictures they draw with the reasonable hope that the original is never to be generally mischievous again. But we cannot hug ourselves upon the freedom of the Protestant faith from such forms of bigotry; it is the touch of poor foolish human nature in their heroines which makes them universally recognizable as portraits from life.

In *Leon Roch*, as in *Marta y Maria*, the name of the devotee is Maria, but in this case she is not an exalted sentimentalist seeking the fulfilment of her selfish pietistic dreams in a convent, but a loving wife whom her religious intolerance transforms into a monster of cruelty and folly.

The situation is simply that of a young scientific man, whom his great wealth has left to the unmolested study of science, till he marries the daughter of the insolvent and morally bankrupt house of Telleria. The Marquis and Marchioness of Telleria are a worthless couple, who have reproduced their qualities in a family of children amusingly self-satisfied, wasteful, and vicious, with a devotion to the offices of the Church unequalled but for their abandon to the corruptions of the world. The exceptions to their vices as well as their absurdities are Maria and her twin brother Luis Gonzaga, a young monk with whom she has passed her childhood in an atmosphere of the austerest bigotry, and whom she regards as a saint. Her husband, in the guilelessness of his gentle nature and the hopefulness of his tender heart, imagines that he is going to form Maria's character and make her over in his own ideal; but Maria's character is formed already, and she is made once for all. She looks upon her husband, who is a scientific agnostic, as an atheist; she always speaks of his attitude toward the Church as atheistical; and so far from lending herself to his plans for a union of aims and sympathies, she sets herself to save his soul in the manner advised by her spiritual director. Failing this, she relaxes him, as it were, to the secular arm; she upbraids him continually with his "atheism"; she spends half her time at church, and turns his house into a chapel of ease for her overflowing devotions; she schools herself to regard whatever is evidently good and kind and sweet and true in him as of

evil; she steels her heart to his love as against a snare of the devil. In the end he abandons her, after a vain attempt to compromise with her by giving up his scientific studies if she will give up her week-day devotions. She consents; but when her sainted brother comes home to die in her house, and shows by his perpetual aversion of the man who tenderly nurses and befriends him that he regards him as a lost and perilous wretch, she cannot keep faith with him. She does what she can to break her husband's heart, but, in her way, she loves him still; she loves him enough to be madly jealous, and when she hears that he has gone into the country, near the woman who had loved him in their childhood, she follows him to denounce him and reclaim him. He tells her that he no longer loves her, and her frenzy ends in a brain-fever of which she dies.

The excellent thing in the treatment of Maria's character is that her sincerity, deadly and pitiless as it is, is honored throughout, and the man whom she makes so entirely miserable never entirely loses his respect for it. She is the incarnation of the terrible spirit of bigotry, of Catholic bigotry, surviving in all its intensity into an age whose light shows the fashionable religiosity of her family comic. They are really a delightful group, with their several vices, their common willingness to live upon Leon, their patronizing deprecation of his "atheism," their frank denunciations of each other, and their collective resolutions to reform their extravagant and worldly life, which none of them ever begins to keep. Their friends of the aristocratic world are sketched with like mastery, and it is hard not to give one's heart to men drawn with such wonderful truth as the newly rich Marquis of Fúcar and his thorough scoundrel of a son-in-law, Federico Cimarra.

It is this worst of bad subjects whom Pepa Fúcar marries in her despair and rage when she hears of Leon's engagement to Maria. She pays for her rashness by a life of abject misery with him, but she never pretends that she has not brought her misery upon herself. She is one of those mixed characters who are beginning to get out of life into fiction; but no other sort seems to get into Galdós's book, and perhaps this is the reason why some of his most reprobate people have a hold upon our sympathies. Pepa, untrained, capricious, violent, and impassioned, has the brains and the heart to know Leon's rare goodness, and to be guided by it, when she would gladly have gone to ruin from her love of him. She is a modern woman, vivid, intuitive, brilliant, the truthfulness of whose portrait may be felt under these skies of ours—in which the sun is as high at midwinter as in Spain—no less than under her own, and she belongs to that order of women, rare in fiction, who, like Aurore Nancanou in Mr. Cable's *Grandissimes*, leave the reader with a sense of personal acquaintance. In fact, Galdós's people all do this in some degree, and the action in which they are concerned remains in the mind like something one has known in life.

We will not follow it in detail, or spoil the pleasure of those who like to come freshly to a story. It is one that satisfies the best feeling morally; the only lapses are artistic, and these are in the long letter with which the story opens, and the long speeches of the interview with which it practically closes. The letter, which is supposed to be Maria's, repenting to Leon her antenuptial jealousy of Pepa, is employed to introduce the situation and recount the preceding facts, much as the first dialogue of a play used to be; and perhaps the Spanish preach at each other as the persons of that interview do, but we doubt it. In these two places, however, the author seems to have deposited all that was mistaken and tedious in his method, and the conduct of the story between is as brilliant as perfect mastery of his material can make it. In fact, it is as much better than the conduct of most American and English stories as Spanish art is better than English art, than American art; though, after saying this, it seems too strong, and we should like to modify it by advising our novelists, if they would learn how to imitate nature, to go learn of the contemporary Spaniards—after they have learned all they can of the Russians.

III.

Which brings us, as usual, to Tolstoï, though not, unfortunately, to a novel of his, but only to his recently translated essay on Napoleon and the Russian campaign. We do not mean that every word of it is not worthy of the closest attention, both for the general theory of war involved and for the specific opinions from time to time advanced, but only that we would rather read a novel of Tolstoï's than an essay of his or of any one's. His notion of the Russian campaign is that it was in its details and final results the effect of a popular impulse blindly working to a divine end; one of those race movements from west to east, and from east to west again, by which, somehow and however terribly, mankind is advanced, and its conditions are ameliorated. The great man fades and dwindles in this conception, and has importance only as he embodies the common impulse; his will is accomplished only as a part of

it, and can never be accomplished against it, and the hero is no more emancipated from his duty to other men and his responsibility to God than the meanest of his human instruments. The infernal pretension that "genius," of whatever sort, in virtue of being "genius," is a law to itself in morals and politics, has the dynamite shaken out of it forever, and is tossed aside harmless into the general dustheap of obsolete superstitions. It is not strange, then, that the quiet, patient, tireless Koutouzof, waiting throughout for the stir of the great popular Russian impulse, should be the supreme figure of the campaign in Tolstoï's eyes, and not the dramatic, restless, wilful Napoleon, whose egoistic ambition was confounded in the calamity he had invoked.

"How was it that this old man," asks Tolstoï, in summing up his chapter on Koutouzof, "alone against many, divined with so much perspicacity the national import of events, and did not once contradict himself throughout the whole campaign? This power of insight had its source in the sentiment of the Russian people, which was carried by Koutouzof in his heart with undiminished vigor.... This sentiment and nothing else elevated Koutouzof to the height of human feeling....This simple, modest, and therefore truly grand figure was not cast in the ready-made factitious mould employed by history for the manufacture of European heroes. To the valet he is not a great man; the valet has his own conception of greatness."

Throughout, the words employed to characterize Koutouzof paint the portrait of Lincoln; and the student of men, who ought also to be their friend, may greatly interest and edify himself by comparing the passages relating to the former in Tolstoï's essay with the noble lines of the Commemoration Ode, in which Mr. Lowell has divined and imperishably fixed the touchingly homely yet majestic lineaments of the latter. Slowly but surely the stupid vanity, the cruel error, of the race is being enlightened, and we are learning that there is no greatness except that which lends itself with instinctive humility to the expression of the common-sense and the good-will of the masses of men. More and more the individual ceases in importance, and the time advances when no fortune and no grandeur shall seem desirable except such as all men can share, except such as gladly makes itself the servant of all, to help them, comfort them, enlighten them.

IV.

It is interesting to see in how many ways the prescience of this finds utterance. It illumines history; it shapes and colors all that is worth reading in fiction; it animates the highest poetry of our time, it redeems and ennobles its doubt.

One is sensible of it in the *Lyrics of the Ideal and the Real* which come to us from a poet of the West, of which the first and chiefest is the colloquy of "Pessim and Optim." These two voices speak of the becoming and of the being, here and hereafter, of our race, according to the differing natures intimated in their names, and the latter has the last word, employed to enforce the idea that heredity and immortality are one. It is a notion which hardly reassures the personal "dread of falling into naught," but it expresses unselfish trust and patience, and it has its suggestiveness. It is the poet's sweep of fancy, however, and the language which so strenuously follows its flight, which we wish to praise, rather than his philosophy of life and death. Here, for example, is a passage of luminous reach into heights and depths difficult for words to explore:

OPTIM.

"Ay, we are dreamed; and if ever the Dreamer
Wake from the sleep to remember the dream,
We of His waking shall thrill in the tremor,
Dawn with His memory, mingle and stream.

"What though He slumber through eon on eon?
When He has dreamed all the infinite full,
Dreamed all the worlds, and the lives there to be on,
Out to dreamed gravity's uttermost pull;

"Dreamed forth of matter and force interblended
(Storm-drifts of matter and torrents of force),
Cyclones of flame, globed, exploded, and rended—
Wide wild beginnings of Time's endless course;

"Dreamed out of chaos the suns in the spaces,
Dreamed down the suns to their white molten cores,
Dreamed off the worlds in their systemal places,
Over them dreaming the continent floors;

"Out of their pulps of fire dreaming the oceans,
Out of the rain from their heavens of steam,
And of their mad elemental commotions
Moulding the motions of life in His dream;

"Dreaming the marvellous atoms together
Into the miracles feeling and thought,
Hitching, with matter's mysterious tether,
Selfhood of sense to insensible naught;

"Dreaming the span of the measureless chasm
Yawning between the live and the dead—
Wonder of dreams in the organless plasm
Crawling to soul from the sea's oozy bed—

"Feeling to soul in the sea's vital foment,
Feeling to form and to faculties dim,
Till, at the touch of a consummate moment,
Loosed into freedom to rise and to swim—

"Swimming of dreams in the nightmare of waters!
Hydras, chimeras, and gorgons of sleep,
That by transitions of mutual slaughters
Play the dream-tragedy Life in the deep;

"When His long dream through the spawning and swarming
Sea-generations has passed into things
Creeping aland, and has risen transforming
Into the slow apparition of wings;

"When from the budding of nerves in the banded
Spirals of earth-crawling pleasure and pain
Upward has issued His dream and expanded
Into the glorified blooming of brain—

"Flower of all the world's forces and ages,
Top-bloom of matter exhaling the soul,
Opening volume whose unopened pages
Yet of God's being shall utter the whole—

"Here from His dream shall He start into waking—
Dream of the universe waking in Me—
Me as a shore where the great billows breaking
Leap out of silence in sounds of the sea....

"When, through heredity raised and perfected,
Faculties now in the germ shall have bloomed,
All the forgotten shall be recollected,
All that is buried shall be disentombed.

"Whatso has ever with being been gifted,
Since the first givings of being began,
Living again shall be gathered and lifted
Into the sovereign consciousness, Man."

In this we perceive the presence of a true poet, and we welcome him none the less cordially because it is the late-coming of one who has lingered long in the repute won him by a single charming lyric. Mr. Coates Kinney, whom we have been quoting, is the author of "Rain on the Roof," which perhaps more people have got by heart than will care to read his "Optim and Pessim"; but now he takes a vast stride forward, and places himself with the few who think in the electrical flushes known only to the passion of most men. Throughout this poem there is a grasp of not easily tangible matter which cannot fail to strike any reader, and which will bring to some the thrill imparted by mastery in an art which has of late seemed declining into clever artistry. In other poems of the present volume the author shows a kindred power, more or less; and in that addressed to Tennyson on his becoming "My Lord," there is a rise on a narrower base almost to the level of the first; but that alone is enough to merit all our praise; and we may fearlessly allow for much indifference and mediocrity besides.

V.

It is a pleasure to recognize the intellectual force of this mature mind, and it is with equal but different joy that one finds both promise and performance, fruit and flower, in an unmistakably youthful book. Mr. Madison J. Cawein is another Western poet (but of Kentucky, whereas Mr. Kinney is of Ohio), and there is much that is expressive of the new land as well as of the young life in his richly sensuous, boldly achieved pieces of color. In him, as in his elder, one is sensible (or seems so) of something different from the beautiful as literary New England or literary New York has conceived it. Here is a fresh strain; the effect of longer summers and wider horizons; the wine of the old English vine planted in another soil, and ripened by a sun of Italian fervor, has a sweetness and fire of its own. This native spirit is enveloped in flavors too cloying for the critical palate at times, but one can easily fancy the rapture it must have for a reader as young as the poet. How can any reader, in fact, refuse the charm that is in such a gorgeously decorative thing as this which the poet calls "The Ideal"? Its very excess is refluent of one's own youth.

"Thee have I seen in some waste Arden old,
  A white-browed maiden by a foaming stream,
With eyes profound and locks like threaded gold,
  And features like a dream.

"Upon thy wrist the jessied falcon fleet,
  A silver poniard chased with imageries
Hung at a buckled belt, while at thy feet
  The gasping heron dies.

"Have fancied thee in some quaint ruined keep,
  A maiden in chaste samite, and her mien
Like that of loved ones visiting our sleep,
  Or of a fairy queen.

"Or one in Avalon's deep-dingled bowers,
  On which old yellow stars and waneless moons
Look softly, while white downy-lippèd flowers
  Lisp faint and fragrant tunes.

"Where haze-like creatures with smooth houri forms
  Stoop through the curling clouds and float and smile,
While calm as hope in all her dreamy charms
  Sleeps the enchanted isle.

"And where cool heavy bow'rs unstirred entwine,
  Upon a headland breasting purple seas,
A crystal castle like a thought divine
  Rises in mysteries.

"And there a sorceress full beautiful
  Looks down the surgeless reaches of the deep,
And bubbling from her lily throat, songs lull
  The languid air to sleep.

"About her brow a diadem of spars,
  At her fair casement seated, fleecy white,
Heark'ning wild sirens choiring to the stars
  Through all the raven night.

"And when she bends above the glow-lit waves
  She sees the sea-king's templed city old,
Wrought from huge shells, and labyrinthine caves
  Ribbed red with rosy gold."

For a fitting pendant to this the reader should turn to "The Mermaid," or to "A Guinevere," or to both rather than neither. "Guinevere" is not to be encouraged in all respects, perhaps, but it has touches of passion unquestionably graphic.

"Am I happy? Ask the fire
  When it bursts its bounds and thrills
  Some mad hours as it wills
If those hours tire.

"See! the moon has risen white
  As this bursten lily here
  Rocking on the dusky mere
Like a silent light.

"I must go now. See! there fell,
  Molten into purple light,
  One wild star. Kiss me good-night;
And once more farewell."

We do not find that Mr. Cawein echoes any of the poets who are apt to reverberate in the pages of beginners. There is something surprisingly authentic in his verse; and if he reminds you of any one, it is of Keats, and that rather by his point of view than by anything in his conception or execution. What you definitely feel is that here is the same love of beauty in nature and in art, the same divine intoxication with the music of one's own heart and the employment of one's sense, as in the earlier poet.

[1] Leo Tolstoy, "The Physiology of War: Napoleon and the Russian Campaign," Huntington Smith, trans. (New York: T. Crowell, [c1888]).

June, 1888

Editor's Study.

I.

IN the case of a poet like Mr. Lowell, so worthy of honor and so secure of remembrance, there can be little profitable talk of defects or excellences, of better or worse, and little that is new of qualities and characteristics. Those who have read him know these already ; his place is established, and neither what he says now nor what any one else may say can much affect it. He is part of our literary history and of our political history ; no one treating of American civilization could fail to name him, to dwell upon his work ; not necessarily for what he has accomplished in it, but certainly for what it records and expresses. Voluntarily and involuntarily it is the record of an heroic cycle, a period which greatly believed, and achieved as greatly ; and the measure of his sympathies is to be found in that poetry which expresses the unselfish endeavor, the fearless humanity, of the long struggle against slavery, from the murder of Lovejoy to the murder of Lincoln. Reading his *Heartsease and Rue*, one is sometimes troubled with the fear that the poet fails of the import of conditions that he has himself so largely promoted. He has been so long the apostle of democracy that if we fancy him forgetting that the meaning of democracy is still before and not behind, we cannot escape a certain anxiety, a certain discomfort. But Mr. Lowell is right about some of our faults, and he has earned the right to tell us of them ; besides, *Heartsease and Rue* is not the whole of Mr. Lowell ; the poet in his historical entirety cannot reasonably be sought there.

What may be sought in almost every passage is the ripened richness of wording, which seems to us apter and finer at times than ever before. One comes again and again upon lines of a strenuous beauty rare in the verse of any time, and scarcely to be matched in that of ours ; and feels in their robust force the joy given only by thought without a syllable of waste verbiage on it. This poet had always the power of striking the nail on the head, but here he seems to need never to hit more than once ; and along with his truth of eye and power of hand there is

at times a caressing, melancholy tenderness, an exquisite kindness, which seems the refinement of all that showed itself sweetest in his nature earlier. Inevitably we fall into the vein of personality ; but *Heartsease and Rue* is a very personal book, and none but the unwise will impute its personality to it for a fault. Between an author and the public an intimacy tacitly establishes itself, which in time neither wishes any longer to ignore ; and with the poet it must come to some such effect as in this book, where the writer seems so often to be musing aloud. It breathes full Cambridge, and addresses itself directly and indirectly to the friends of the date and place of the greatest literary centre we have ever had ; but none of its charm need be lost upon the general reader for that reason. The business of a book is to acquaint us with the author's way of thinking and feeling, and both by its inclusions and its exclusions *Heartsease and Rue* acquaints us with Mr. Lowell's way of thinking and feeling almost beyond any other book of his. This is what greatly forms its value, which the fact that it imperfectly represents the range of his thinking and feeling does not at all affect.

It would be hard to say why we think one passage from the very Lowell-like poem on Agassiz is more Lowell-like than anything else in the book ; but we will venture to say so before trying to say why. For one thing, it appears to us a strain of sentiment peculiar to a poet often involved and withdrawn in his scholarship ; for he who of all our great poets has come closest to the common life, and has made most of it as material for his art, is at times furthest from it in a sort of literary distance. But here, in these verses, he draws near to the reader's heart in frank avowal of things usually blinked or glossed in spiritual hypocrisy.

" Truly this life is precious to the root,
  And good the feel of grass beneath the foot ;
  To lie in buttercups and clover bloom,
  Tenants in common with the bees,
  And watch the white clouds drift through gulfs
    of trees,
  Is better than long waiting in the tomb ;
  Only once more to feel the spring,

As the birds feel it when it bids them sing,
Only once more to see the moon
Through leaf-fringed abbey arches of the elms
Curve her mild sickle in the west,
Sweet with the breath of hay-cocks, were a boon
Worth any promise of soothsayer realms
Or casual hope of being elsewhere blest;
To take December by the beard
And crush the creaking snow with springy foot,
While overhead the North's dumb streamers
    shoot,
Till winter fawn upon the cheek endeared;
Then the long evening-ends
Lingered by cozy chimney-nooks,
With high companionship of books,
Or slippered talk of friends
And sweet habitual looks,
Is better than to stop the ears with dust.
Too soon the spectre comes to say 'Thou must.'"

This keen rapture with natural aspects, mixed with as fond a love of letters to one meaning of regret for the life that slips to uncertainty through all our hands, is a mood very characteristic of the poet's later work. No one else has known how to impart so fully the tender, sadly smiling, self-consciously helpless grief with which we see the days go when they begin to go swiftly. The strain is audible so often in *Heartsease and Rue* that it might be called the keynote of the book. With all the humor that plays through it, and sparkles into sunny fun at times, it is not a gay book; its cheer and its pensiveness are both autumnal; there is nothing of the dramatic make-believe of a young poet, of those spring days that prophesy the fall afar.

II.

Yet we are very far from believing that such a poet as Mr. Lowell was here moved by his own pathos or wit in the degree that a number of well-known novelists would persuade us in a late number of *The Critic* to believe authors moved by their work. These ladies and gentlemen, marshalled under the blended banners of Horace and Mr. Walter Besant, are free to proclaim that they have suffered to tears and exulted to laughter in the work of wringing their reader's heartstrings and tickling his risibles. They accept Mr. Besant's declaration that "it is a sign that one possesses imagination if one can laugh and cry over the fortunes of one's own puppets," as a right version of Horace's "Si vis me flere, dolendum est primum ipsi tibi," though it is really not so; and they allege in proof and justification of their own the anguish and hilarity of Dickens, of Thackeray, of George Eliot, in like moments. Not all of our fictionists, however, are of this emotional make. Some of them, like Mr. Boyesen, make a mock of the question as not serious; Dr. Eggleston does not believe any author worthy of note ever cried over his work when quite sober, and

thinks that if an author loses control of himself, he loses control of his subject; Mr. Robert Grant holds that the tearful and hilarious sort ought logically to die with a broken-hearted heroine or contract *delirium tremens* with a leading villain; Mr. Lathrop does not think it necessary for an author to be hysterical in order to be moved himself or to move others; Mr. Bishop "never knew but one author who wept and howled over his characters; he was not of the first magnitude, ... and these characters were of but the faintest doll-paper pattern."

Here seems to lie the whole trouble. Saving Mr. Besant's respect, it is *no* "sign that one possesses imagination" because he or she sobs or chuckles over his or her "puppets"; it is merely a sign that he or she possesses great sensibility, or is in a nervous condition, and ought to take a rest, or horseback exercise, or something. We do not go so far as to impeach his or her good sense. We once met a novelist who could only gauge the tears he shed over his characters by handkerchieffuls, yet he was a most estimable and charming person, an able business man, a good husband and father, an upright citizen, a loyal friend, and everything that one would wish to be on one's tombstone.

III.

We do not attempt to settle this interesting question, and we suppose it can be decided only by a fair count, after the returns are in. Not all of our novelists have been heard from yet; and there are several back counties from which no poll has been reported, while others are coming in very slowly by townships and precincts. For example, there is nothing at all from the authors of three of the most striking novels which we have read for some time; we mean Mr. Joseph Kirkland's *Zury*, Mrs. Kirke's *Queen Money*, and Mr. E. W. Bellamy's *Looking Backward*. Yet there are few passages in fiction more simply and truly touching than those in which Mr. Kirkland portrays the hard beginnings of pioneer life in Illinois, with the death of Zury's little sister, and later that of his mother. If the inquiry is important at all, it would be valuable to know whether a writer who could move the reader so strongly melted over his work; but there is no evidence in the case, and in its absence we venture to think that he did not. Throughout his story there is proof, in the clear conception and the strong handling, that he is not one to lose his head in any situation. He has made it his business to realize for us the character of a man whom early hardship nerved to the acquisition of wealth, and who gave his whole life, up to a certain point, to getting value together in lands, flocks, and herds, not because he loved money as the miser does, but because he enjoyed its chase as men do the pursuit of any ambition. This is the modern type, the American type, and Mr. Kirkland has the credit of first putting it in fiction, so far as we know. There is nothing fine, or we had better say refined, about Zury Prouder; he exults in his popular repute of the "meanest man in Spring County"; he is grasping and pitiless in acquisition; but there is and has always been a soft spot in his heart. When Mr. Kirkland tries to make this soft spot do duty for the regeneration of the man into a character adequate to some exigencies of the plot, his trouble begins; and to tell the truth, we do not think he altogether succeeds. The figure of the story whose evolution remains with the reader of the book as perfectly natural is Anne Sparrow, the pretty Lowell factory girl who comes out to be school-mistress in Zury Prouder's district. She is a type of New England woman to whom justice has not been done before, and justice was none the less her due because she is not the highest type. She is very handsome, in a red-headed, freckled way; she is refined to a certain degree by reading; she is ambitious and resolute and brave; she is very feminine, and nervous in one sort; she is right-principled; but it is only an inherited and rather superficial Puritanism in her that overlies a passionate and impulsive nature. The reader must go to the book for the part which Anne Sparrow plays in Mr. Kirkland's story; but we wish to speak of the admirable self-restraint with which he has respected her character, and never shown it for more or less than what it is—not yielded to the temptation of taking her quite out of the range of the reader's sympathy, or of gifting her with a delicate-mindedness beyond her right claim upon it; he is faithful to a conception of character in her which is a very strong one. We cannot say that any of the people in his fresh and native story are weakly conceived; on the contrary, they all have the air of life, and they are racy of their time and place. Those gaunt, sallow, weary, work-worn women, those tireless, rude, independent, and mutually helpful men, belong to a period now driven to the furthest frontier; their look and speech are caught here with a certainty that can come only of personal knowledge. But personal knowledge alone does not suffice in such a case, and we are to be glad of an artist with clear eyes and an honest hand in the author of *Zury*—one incapable of painting life other than he has found it.

IV.

A sense of the brilliant workmanship

throughout and of the dazzling successfulness of parts remains with the reader of *Queen Money* after he has perhaps closed the book with a grave misgiving as to what he can sincerely say in its praise. This seems certain: that no one among our novelists has a vivider touch or a finer skill in catching some aspects of worldliness than the author of this rather disappointing book. Her literary equipment is very uncommon; she can make people talk wittily, with the effect of having heard them talk so, and she can portray an order of æsthetico-fashionable folk so charmingly as to make you think you have seen just such persons in just such situations and conditions. But look a little closer, and you perceive something histrionic, solicited, operated, in the action and motives—a Cherbuliez quality, say. In *Queen Money* this is distinctly so when one of the young ladies proposes to rescue two foolish wives from their folly by winning for herself the young man they are letting their rival fancies stray after. We have often heard of young ladies doing this on the stage, but never off it; and we doubt if they ever do it in life. It is this error of putting probable people into theatrical postures, or rather of moving them by theatrical motives, which constitutes the defect of this author's singularly clever work. It does not disable it altogether; you remember that you were interested, you were surprised, you were amused, you were even touched; but the best meaning of a book is lost if it does not leave you with the sense that the things in it might have happened, has not shown you its people doing and suffering from things which you can conceive yourself capable of. The final effect of *Queen Money* is a regret, not for any one in it, but for the accomplished artist who, for the sake of a plot below her skill, seems to have wilfully denied you the privilege of taking all its lessons home to yourself.

V.

With a work in the region of pure romance, with a frank allegory, like Mr. Bellamy's *Looking Backward*, one can have no such quarrel as with one portraying realistic people with unreal motives. You concede the premises, as in a poem, and after that you can hold the author only to a poetic consistency; he has no allegiance to the waking world. You may say that this is not the time of day for romances, for allegories, but that does not affect the quality of the kind of work which the author has chosen to do. Besides, the extraordinary effect which Mr. Bellamy's present romance has had with the public may well give pause to the doctor of literary laws, and set him carefully to revising his most cherished opinions.

For here is a book which in the sugar-coated form of a dream has exhibited a dose of undiluted socialism, and which has been gulped by some of the most vigilant opponents of that theory without a suspicion of the poison they were taking into their systems. They have been shown the world as it is fancied to be a hundred years hence, when the state shall perform all the offices of manufacture, transportation, and distribution now abandoned to the chances of competition or combination, and they have accepted it as the portrait of a very charming condition of things, instead of shuddering at the spectacle in every fibre.

Mr. Bellamy's allegoric state of A.D. 2000 is constructed almost exactly upon the lines of Mr. Gronland's *Co-operative Commonwealth;* and it is supposed to come into being through the government acquisition of the vast trusts and monopolies, just as the collectivist author teaches. These grow, the larger absorbing the smaller, till the nation finally perceives their significance, and by a peaceful assertion of power possesses itself of them, and remains its own sole capitalist, producer, and distributor. The conditions which in Mr. Bellamy's book present themselves to a man of our time, carried far into the next century by a somewhat abnormal nap, are such as to make him heartily ashamed of our competitive civilization: but it is not our affair to reproduce the smiling picture. One cannot deny the charm of the author's art, which has made itself felt before now in *Dr. Heidenhoff's Process* and in *Miss Ludington's Sister.* The present story, compared with these, is no story, and the character-drawing is of the slightest; there are in fact only a number of personages who explain to the survivor of the nineteenth century the nature and extent of the economic change which has taken place. But there is a force of appeal in the book which keeps the attention, and which appears in the case of so many critics to have captivated the reason; and whether Mr. Bellamy is amusing himself or not with his conceit of the socialistic state as an accomplished fact, there can be no doubt that he is keenly alive to the defects of our present civilization. Here, for instance, are passages from the supposed narrator's view of our existing system as he looked back upon it after waking from his secular slumbers: "I cannot do better than to compare society as it then was to a prodigious coach which the masses of humanity were harnessed to, and dragging toilsomely along a very hilly and sandy road. The driver was hunger....The top was covered with passengers who never got down, even at the steepest ascents. These seats on top were very breezy and comfortable....For all that they were so easy, the seats were very insecure, and at every jolt of the coach persons were slipping out of them and falling to the ground, when they were instantly compelled to take hold of the rope and help to drag the coach on which they had before ridden so pleasantly....At times the desperate straining of the team, their agonized leaping and plunging under the pitiless lashing of hunger, the many who fainted at the rope and were trampled in the mire, made a very distressing spectacle, and often called forth highly creditable displays of feeling on the top of the coach. At such times the passengers would call down encouragingly to the toilers of the rope, exhorting them to patience, and holding out hopes of possible compensation in another world....If the passengers could only have felt assured that neither they nor their friends would ever fall from the top, it is probable that, beyond contributing to the funds for the liniments and bandages, they would have troubled themselves extremely little about those who dragged the coach."

The reverse of this state of things is that to which the narrator wakes up in the year 2000, when, in a condition of absolute equality produced by the people's management of their economic affairs as well as their political affairs, there is no longer idleness or want, riches or poverty, and all the luxuries and delights of life are enjoyed in common by those who earn them. We should not be dealing honestly with the possible readers of this alluring allegory if we did not again warn them that the author has, wittingly or unwittingly, presented in it an image of the future as the socialists have long dreamed it; but we can only concern ourselves incidentally with its political significance. What interests us in it from a literary point of view is the employment of a form once so much a favorite with writers who had some didactic aim in view, and often used with charming effect. In our own century, Miss Martineau employed it in a realistic guise to enforce her ideas of political economy; and within a recent period Mrs. Lynn Linton, in her story of *Joshua Davidson,* in which she gave Jesus the Son of David modern circumstance, has powerfully used a vehicle which, with Mr. Bellamy's present achievement before us, we cannot venture to pronounce outworn.

VI.

The reversions or counter-currents in the general tendency of a time are very curious, and are worthy tolerant study. They are always to be found; perhaps they form the exception that establishes the rule; at least they distinguish it. They give us performances which have an archaic charm, but it is seldom that they embody anything so robustly pertinent to actual interests as Mr. Bellamy's book. By-and-by, as we have before asked the reader to observe, things captivate for reasons unconnected with their inherent beauty. They become quaint, and this is reason enough for liking them, for returning to them, and in art for trying to do them again. The at-[4] tempt is made more or less frankly, but it is a misfortune of this sort of achievement that one involuntarily compares it with the first in its kind.

If one were to do this with the pretty book which Mr. and Mrs. Joseph Pennell have made about a tricycling tour in France, and called *Our Sentimental Journey*, because it was largely upon the lines of Sterne's, he might easily find it less important than its prototype, but he would also fail to do justice to its proper charm. It is a light and pleasant record in print and picture of things seen and suffered on a sufficiently adventurous little expedition. It appears that the tricycle affords fresh effects of landscape and figure to its riders, who, however, pay for this gain with a good many annoyances from the civilization and the weather. In the present case they bear them all courageously, and from Mrs. Pennell's story, very frank and ingenuous throughout, one learns a great deal that is new about both. The writing is not humorous exactly; it is sprightly; it is usually sympathetic, but when it is antipathetic it is very antipathetic indeed; it is always neatly intelligent, without the slightest tendency to sentiment; upon the whole it is not much like Sterne. In the pictures Mr. Pennell seems to be at his very best, and the sunny sweetness of his work is to be praised without qualification. The page, in fact, flashes to the eye in those gay, bright illustrations as with so many gleams of veritable sunshine; they impart precisely the sentiment of the glimpses of roads, fields, canals, cottages, peasants, garçons, gendarmes, chamber-maids, and soldiers which the artist himself caught, and of the different interiors with which his fortunes or misfortunes brought him acquainted. The reader perceives that we celebrate, as usual, only the literary quality in these pictures; again, as always in such cases, we leave their technical shortcomings, if they have any, to those who may deny themselves a good deal of pleasure in detecting them.

[1] Anonymous, "On the Writing of Novels," The Critic, 12 (March 24, 1888), 135.

[2] "Si vis me flere, dolendum est primum ipsi tibi." - If you want to see me weep, you must first be sad yourself.

[3] "Mrs. Kirke," author of Queen Money, is a misspelling of Ellen Warner Kirk.

[4] Criticism and Fiction, p. 118.

July, 1888

Editor's Study.

I.

IT has been interesting to note the effect of Matthew Arnold's death upon a people whom his criticism had just irritated against him. The sad event cut short many expressions of resentment, and even turned to kindness the more difficult mood of those who were disposed to laugh at him. It restored the perspective in which we had seen him before he came to us, and enabled us again to value his censure aright. Upon the whole, the impression which Americans had received from him personally was not one of great dignity, and though this was partly the result of that mischievous license of the reporters which he complained of, it was also partly due to something in his own mental make-up and attitude. He became, in a certain degree, one of our national jokes, and he suffered a slight with those who most deplored the injustice done him by this fate. Something of D'Oyly Carte, and association with the management of Mr. Oscar Wilde's mission and Messrs. Gilbert and Sullivan's comic operas; something of the ignominy of subjection to calls of "Louder!" at his half-heard lectures; something of the malicious pleasure men take in finding an arbiter of taste saying things in bad taste, and a wise person committing indiscretions, contributed to his lapse as a cult among us; but we must not deny that this happened also because we are an irreverent people, and find from time to time a pleasure in trampling on the idols we set up. Now, however, that is all past; death has made it impossible for us to rail or smile at the man whose presence could not always command our homage, and we can freely admit his greatness in literature and his good-will toward a perverse generation. Even while we perceive that his observation of our life wanted breadth and depth and finality, we must acknowledge that in its superficial way, and as far as it went, it was mainly just. We cannot deny that we are a loud and vain and boastful nation; that our reporter-ized press is often truculently reckless of privacy and decency; that our local nomenclature is beggarly in its poverty and horribly vulgar, and that tens of thousands of our places seem to have been named with less sense and less taste than dogs and horses are named; that our cabs and hotels are expensive; that a moderate income does not go so far here as in England; and that to the average person of culture we must be less entertaining than almost any other nation. We are not picturesque, and we are not splendid. Our towns, when they are tolerably named, are not varied in their characteristics, and our civilization, as a means of pleasure to polite people of limited means and of sympathies narrowed to their own class, with the historic ideals of beauty and grandeur, is very much of a failure. Mr. Arnold might have said with some truth that we have not even been equal to our political and economic opportunities; we cannot be particularly proud of our legislatures and administrations; the relations of capital and labor in our free democracy are about as full of violence as those in any European monarchy; we have wasted the public lands which we won largely by force and fraud, and we are the prey of many vast and corrupting monopolies. Perhaps any other Aryan race could have done as well as we have done with our liberties and resources; and if the future is still ours, the present is by no means without its danger and disgrace.

II.

Yet some good things we have done, some great things achieved, and among these is the abolition of that "distinction" which Mr. Arnold found wanting in our life. We have noticed a disposition among the critics of his criticism to dispute the fact, but it is his only stricture upon our conditions which we should gladly accept as true. If we have really got rid of distinction of the sort he seems to prize. we have made a great advance on the lines of our fundamental principles. If we understand it aright, distinction of the sort that shows itself in manner and bearing toward one's fellow-men is something that can exist only through their abeyance, not to say their abasement. Our whole civilization, if we have a civilization of our own, is founded upon the conviction that any such distinction is unjust and deleterious, and our whole political being is a protest against it. In every way our history has said that a game of that kind was not worth the candle, and that human nature was better in itself than any aristocratic extract or decoction from it. One of the truths which Americans have always held to be self-evident was that a man, if he was honest, was not only privileged, but was in duty bound, to look other men in the face, with eyes as nearly upon the same level as congenital differences would allow. The fear with most Americans to whom this truth is precious has been that our social structure was not responsive to our political ideal; that the snobbishness, more or less conscious, which alone makes distinction possible was at least microscopically present in our composition. But if an observer like Mr. Arnold, accustomed to distinction as it shows itself in European civilization, was unable to perceive it here—if he could find great ability, power, goodness, in our noted men, and every virtue except distinction, we may reasonably console ourselves with the hope that snobbishness is also absent from all Americans not corrupted by the evil communications of the Old World.

So far from feeling cast down by Mr. Arnold's failure to detect distinction in a nation which has produced such varied types of greatness in recent times as Lincoln, Longfellow, Grant, Emerson, John Brown, Mrs. Stowe, Hawthorne, not to name many others eminent in art and science and finance, we are disposed to a serene complacency by it. Here, we may say, with just self-gratulation, is positive proof that we have builded better than we knew, and that our conditions, which we have always said were the best in the world, have evolved a type of greatness in the presence of which the simplest and humblest is not abashed. Somehow, the idea that we call America has realized itself so far that we already have identification rather than distinction as the fact which strikes the foreign critic in our greatness. Our notable men, it seems, are notable for their likeness to their fellow-men, and not for their unlikeness; democracy has subtly but surely done its work; our professions of belief in equality have had their effect in our life; and whatever else we lack in homogeneity, we have in the involuntary recognition of their common humanity by our great men something that appears to be peculiarly American, and that we think more valuable than the involuntary assumption of superiority, than the

distinction possible to greatness, among peoples accustomed to cringe before greatness.

III.

We have come to this rather lately, and we fear we have not come to it so fully as Mr. Arnold would have the world believe. But we may see the progress we have made in the right direction by the study of our own past, and especially of that formative period when the men who invented American principles had not yet freed themselves from the influence of European traditions. We spoke in a recent Study of the character of Franklin,[2] and we think of him now as the most modern, the most American, among his contemporaries. Franklin had apparently none of the distinction which Mr. Arnold lately found lacking in us; he seems to have been a man who could no more impose upon the imagination of men used to abase themselves before birth, wealth, achievement, or mastery in any sort, as very many inferior men have done in all times, than Lincoln or Grant. But he was more modern, more American, than any of his contemporaries in this, though some of them were of more democratic ideals than he. His simple and plebeian past made it impossible for a man of his common-sense to assume any superiority of bearing, and the unconscious hauteur which comes of aristocratic breeding, and expresses itself at its best in distinction, was equally impossible to him. It was very possible, however, with other men as ardently and unselfishly patriotic and as virtuous as he, and distinction was not wanting to the men of the Republic's early days. Washington had it, and Hamilton; Jefferson tried hard not to have it; but Burr had it, and Hancock had it; and most of the great men whom New York contributed to that period of our history had it; and of course the Carolinians, as far as they were eminent. Above all, Gouverneur Morris had it, and he had it for the very reason that Franklin hadn't it, because he was well-born, because he was brought up in the heart of a rich, gay, patrician society, because all the foolish things which have been done since the world began to differentiate men from men socially had been done for him in the full measure of the Colonial possibilities.

In the brilliant sketch which Mr. Theodore Roosevelt has written of Morris's brilliant career (it is among the very best of Mr. Morse's "American Statesmen" series) the reader may study one of the most interesting characters of our history, with the advantages of a most suggestive, intelligent, and comprehensive authority, and it will be his own fault if he fails of that finer meaning of the book which is sometimes tacit even for the writer of it. The one thoroughly admirable thing in Morris, his prompt and unfailing patriotism, in which he was as American as his antitype, Franklin, remains the consolation of such as cannot admire his other qualities. These were the qualities of a brave, truthful, generous, impulsive, yet clear-headed aristocrat; and his greatness was limited chiefly by his want of sympathy with men outside of his own class. His services were given freely and fearlessly to his country; yet what he did for nationality, for democracy, was done somewhat from that curious inverted pride which is a common foible of the aristocratic temperament. In his long mission to France he saw too much of the nobility and too much of the mob for a man of his make to believe fully in either: he wrote of both with contemptuous sarcasm: but at home he was of those who distrusted the popular initiative, while foreseeing the future greatness of the country which that initiative could alone promote. In private life he was at least as blameless as Franklin, if that is not saying very much; he was not scrupulous about women, and he had those traits of a man of the world which all silly women admire, and some sensible women admire sillily. When a young man he lost a leg by an accident which his own coxcombry provoked, but he bore his misfortune through life with uncomplaining dignity and with bitter irony in about equal parts. His courage was cavalieresque, but he had an eighteenth century skeptical spirit, and he was neither saintly nor exactly heroic. In spite of his foibles, he was a man of great common-sense, and though he took himself seriously as a "gentleman," he did not take himself solemnly; he was too critical to be altogether disdainful. His political services were general rather than particular; as a statesman he forecast the material rather than the political future of the country, and the social future growing out of it; he would not have liked or trusted modern Americanism any more than Mr. Arnold, to whom, if he could have appeared, he would certainly have appeared distinguished. Distinction, in fact, is what one feels throughout in regard to Gouverneur Morris, and in the end one feels that if he had been less distinguished he would have been greater; he would have been a lesson and an incentive, which, with all the respect his qualities inspire, one can hardly say that he was. Did his distinction, that effect of waning traditions, that result of the misfortune of being born with all the advantages, keep him just short of the highest usefulness to his generation as well as ours? Probably Mr. Arnold would not think so; but all the same, as

a historical figure, he remains more decorative than structural; that is, the Revolution could have been without such a man as Morris infinitely easier than without such a man as Franklin. He was a brilliant finial, but the temple of our liberties in no wise rests upon him.

IV.

Far be it from us to say anything against the decorative in its place. It is something that we cannot afford to lose out of life; but somehow it must be had at less cost than hitherto, and we must not mistake it for anything vital. It is valuable, in a way it is even important, but it is not vital, and in our haste to be finer and politer than our critics will allow us to be, we ought not to seek it at the cost of anything vital, of anything that keeps men humble and simple and brotherly, the greatest with the meanest. Except as distinction can grow out of an absolutely unassuming attitude, and the first man among us appear distinguished from the rest only by his freedom from any manner of arrogation, we are much better without it. The distinction that abashes and dazzles, this is not for any people of self-respect to cultivate or desire; and we mean here precisely the best distinction that Mr. Arnold can mean. We do not mean the cheap and easy splendor of the vulgar aristocrat or plutocrat, but that far subtler effect in lives dedicated to aims above the common apprehension, and apart from the interests and objects of the mass of men; we mean the pride of great achievement in any sort, which in less fortunate conditions than ours betrays itself to the humiliation of meaner men. The possessor of any sort of distinction, however unconscious he may be of the fact, has somewhere in his soul, by heredity, or by the experience of his superiority, the spark of contempt for his fellow-men; and he is for that reason more deplorable than the commonest man whom his presence browbeats. If our civilization is so unfavorable to the expression of contempt that Mr. Arnold could find no distinction among our great men, then we may hope that in time it may be wholly quenched.

We are so far from taking his discovery ill of him that we cheerfully excuse to it his failure to detect the existence of literature and art among us. Comparisons are odious, as we found ourselves when Mr. Arnold compared Emerson to his disadvantage with several second-rate British classics, and we will not match painter with painter, architect with architect, sculptor with sculptor, poet with poet, to prove that our art and literature are at least as good as those of present England. In some points we might win and in others lose, but in any case it would be an idle game. What we should like to do, how-ever, is to persuade all artists intending greatness in any kind among us that the recognition of the fact pointed out by Mr. Arnold ought to be a source of inspiration to them, and not discourage-ment. We have been now some hun-dred years building up a state on the af-firmation of the essential equality of men in their rights and duties, and whether we have been right or been wrong the gods have taken us at our word, and have responded to us with a civilization in which there is no distinction perceptible to the eye that loves and values it. Such beauty and such grandeur as we have is common beauty, common grandeur, or the beauty and grandeur in which the qual-ity of solidarity so prevails that neither distinguishes itself to the disadvantage of anything else. It seems to us that these conditions invite the artist to the study and the appreciation of the common, and to the portrayal in every art of those finer and higher aspects which unite rather than sever humanity, if he would thrive in our new order of things. The talent that is robust enough to front the every-day world and catch the charm of its work-worn, care-worn, brave, kindly face, need not fear the encounter, though it seems terrible to the sort nurtured in the super-stition of the romantic, the bizarre, the he-roic, the distinguished, as the things alone worthy of painting or carving or writing. The arts must become democratic, and then we shall have the expression of America in art; and one reproach which Mr. Arnold is half right in making us shall have no justice in it. The implica- [4] tion of his censure was not so much that we had no literature or no art, as that we had nothing that was strictly American in either; but even in this he seems to have been speaking without the documents. Here and there a man has detached him-self from tradition, and has struck some-thing out of our life that is ours and no other's. Of late this has been done more and more in our fiction, which, if we were to come to those odious comparisons, we need not be afraid to parallel book for book with contemporary English fiction; and no one can look at Mr. St. Gaudens's head of Sherman in the Academy and fail to see how possible the like achievement is in sculpture—at least to a St. Gaudens. It has no distinction, in Mr. Arnold's sense, no more distinction than he would have found in the great soldier's actual pre-sence, but it seems to express the grandeur of a whole people, a free people, friendly, easy, frank, and very valiant.

VI.

There is a lovely prose poem of Tour- [5] guénief's, telling how he went into a church when a boy, and knelt down be-side a peasant. Suddenly it rushed into the boy's mind that this man was Jesus Christ, and for a while he could not look round at his companion for awe of his own hallucination; when he did so, there was only the plain, common man. Then it was borne in upon him that Christ was really like that poor peasant when he was on earth, and only a plain, common man. There is, indeed, no evidence that the founder of our religion struck his contemporaries as "distinguished," and there is considerable proof in the record of his doings and sayings that he would hardly have valued distinction in others.

We need not at least impute it to our-selves as a serious moral shortcoming if we are without it, and we may find some consolation in the fact that we have in a measure realized the Christian in the democratic ideal. There is something sweet, something luminous, in the reflec-tion that apparently there is in the or-dinary American the making of the ex-traordinary American; that the mass of our people were so near to such great men as Grant and Lincoln in sympathy and intelligence that they could not be awed from them to the distance that lends dis-tinction. It was the humane and benefi-cent effect of such grandeur as theirs that it did not seem distinguished, but so nat-ural that it was like the fulfilment of the average potentiality.

[1] Richard D'Oyly Carte was impresario of the Gilbert and Sullivan comic operas.

[2] See pp. 130b-131b.

[3] John Torrey Morse, ed., American Statesmen [first series] (Boston: Houghton, Mifflin [c1882]).

[4] Criticism and Fiction, pp. 138-140.

[5]Ivan Turgenev, <u>Poems in Prose</u> (Boston: Cupples, Upham, and Company, 1883).

August, 1888

Editor's Study.

I.

THE "Library of American Literature," which Mr. E. C. Stedman and
Miss E. M. Hutchinson have compiled,
promises to be one of the worthiest works
of the kind attempted; in fact, there is nothing quite of its kind in the same field.
This, in the three volumes already published, reaches from the earliest dates in Virginia and New England up and down the
thirteen Revolutionary colonies, and in
the seven to follow it will broaden over
our whole continent. No reviewer, not
even the omniscient presence of the Study,
can pretend to know this field so well as
the editors of the Library; and one has
one's conscience in proposing to say how
extremely faithful, thorough, and judicious the performance of their task has
been. Of the narratives of adventure by
the first explorers and settlers which so
largely compose the literature of the
seventeenth century one might have
something intelligent and authoritative
to say, but how easily one's innocence of
all the contemporaneous sermoning might
be abused! We cannot suffer ourselves
in praising this part of the selection to go
beyond recognition of an entirely satisfactory appearance. Heaven only knows
whether our editors have been truly representative or not in it, and the truth is
likely to remain in their keeping; no one
will have the hardihood to call upon them
for the proof that those old divines were
drier and tougher than the chosen mor-
sels show them.

Drier and tougher we will freely grant
they might very well be in the whole body
of their polemics and theology; but here
one feels a charm in their obsolete opinions as well as their archaic diction.
There is little savor of literature in them;
they were ponderously learned, they were
prodigiously devout, and awfully in earnest, but the graces did not hover about
their style. Even with the masters of it,
English prose was then still in the hippo-
potamic stage; the newspaper humorist
had not yet arisen to give it the gazelle-like
movement in which it now disports itself;
and the New England divines wrote as
they thought, heavily, intricately. Yet

they imparted to their sermons the sincerity of their daily lives, and perhaps it
is this which now interests and touches in
the passages given from their writings.
One is aware of it in the reluctant flow
of the periods of Thomas Shepard, John
Norton, John Eliot, James Noyes, and
the elder Mather; in the neat, clear simplicity of Thomas Hooker, and in the
searching and powerful appeals of Roger
Williams. The words of the last are full
of the sweetness and light of toleration,
that highest gift of the Divine Mercy to
mankind; and He who sends His rain
upon the just and the unjust, and had
lifted up His countenance and made it to
shine upon His servant, while all about
him those who would fain have been His
saints wandered in error more cruel and
dismal than the forests that blackened
their New England shores, endowed him
artistically beyond most of them. From
Williams the editors give the dialogue
on Persecution between Truth and Peace
from his *Bloody Tenant yet more
Bloody*, and from the same tract his warning to John Endicott. When we remember that in the whole world the claim of
the weaker to think differently from the
stronger was then punishable with the
stake and axe and gibbet, we can imagine
the astounding boldness of his doctrine,
and we can rightly value the courage and
the conscience of the man who went into
exile from exile rather than fail of the duty
laid upon him. He was not more conscientious or courageous than the mistaken
men whom he rebuked, but they were
many and he was one, not only against
them, but against the world. His words
have power and meaning for a generation
and a people who are still by no means
guiltless of the sin he rebukes, and who
have accepted toleration rather with their
tongues than with their hearts; and if
there had been nothing else written during the seventeenth century in America,
we should have a claim through his
words to a prime place in the literature of
thought and humanity.

Besides these, there is much in the selections from the old theologians that one

may read with pleasure to the historical sense at least. There is a very beautiful passage from Shepard in praise of his dead wife, which in its pathetic tenderness forms a truly dramatic contrast to the lurid gloom of his theology. The Puritans' impassioned belief in their pitiless and unjust God sometimes broke into a terrible poetry; but this is to be found oftener in their sermons than in their songs; these are of a dulness which not even the doctrine of predestination and election could ordinarily kindle to the heavenly flame. But one exception there certainly is, and that is Michael Wigglesworth's frightful conception of the "Day of Doom." His poem has scarcely won the fame that its imaginative qualities merit; or rather these have been eclipsed by the baleful power with which its error is enforced. But it is really a great poem, and altogether the most memorable thing that our Puritans did in poetry, with a sort of sweet, Chaucerian simplicity of phrase, and a curious tenderness working out from the heart tortured and perverted by its infernal doctrine. Once grant the doctrine, as we grant Dante his theological premises, and the fancies that follow from it have their proper literary charm, their pathos and their power. As a study of the human reason submitting itself to atrocious dogma, and operating by an insane logic to conclusions that defame the ideals of divine justice and mercy, it is also full of a dark fascination, which every reader of æsthetic sensibility must recognize.

II.

The writings of all those early New-Englanders have an Elizabethan raciness of diction which one tastes alike in the quaintness of Bradford's and Winslow's records of Plymouth, in the seriousness, sincerity, and credulity of Higginson, and in the ribaldry of the ungodly and unruly Thomas Morton of Merry Mount. One fond of tracing the origin of national traits and customs will find a pleasure in following to its far source in some of the New England and Virginia Englishmen of the seventeenth century the modern American fashion of booming a new country. The Rev. Francis Higginson does this in pleasing prose, and the good William Morrell in deadly verse, for Massachusetts Bay; John Smith blows the trumpet for Jamestown, and for all Virginia Colonel Norwood, in his *Voyages,* 2 sounds repeated blasts, while Master R. Rich praises the new land in as woful a ballad as any made to a mistress's eyebrow. Norwood has more than gleams of gayety, if one may not quite call it humor; his work has unquestionably literary quality, and we wish we could say as much for John Rolfe's wordy and scat-

tering apology for marrying Pocahontas; but that has chiefly the quality of a very disagreeable self-righteousness.

The most valuable fact about the earliest American literature, which is not yet American of course, is that it so fully reflects the life of the time and place—the objective life of daring and adventure and hardship, and the subjective life tormented and maddened by abominable beliefs, with its struggles to escape from them. In Virginia these are not felt; there is a delightful freedom from them; but for this very reason the literature of that colony has a more superficial character; it lacks the depth as well as the gloom which characterizes the sermons and memoirs of New England.

Whether life more influences literature, or literature life, is a question we need not stop to dispute about here; they probably have a perfect balance of interaction at all times; but what one might certainly infer from this anthology of the Puritan literature is the Puritan life. If there were no other records of the state, of the civilization, which produced these writings, the general complexion of that life might be inferred here, and this gives a historical importance to the compilation which might be easily underrated. It would be a mistake to suppose that the Puritan life in New England was all psalms and sermons; enough is given to show that it had its reliefs, and to let the reader perceive that these were something of the nature and the general pleasurable effect of dancing in chains.

III.

This seems to be true rather of a later period than that of the first settlement; and when the divinity of the time got in its full work there came a sort of intellectual decay, such as followed the prevalence of Jesuitism in southern Europe. The writers of the early years of the eighteenth century are not comparable for grasp and freshness of thought to those who preceded them. For Williams and Hooker we have Increase and Cotton Mather, with their deadly creed rotted into a yet deadlier credulity that naturalized the devils from the other world in this, and affirmed the bodies of the living as well as the souls of the dead to be their prey. The Puritan minister degenerated into the Puritan priest, and Cotton Mather celebrating his remarkable providences and the deeds of the New England witches is as essentially monkish as any mediæval zealot recording the miracles of the saints and the sufferings of the fathers of the desert. "But I pray what will you say to this? Margaret Rule would sometimes have her jaws forcibly pulled open, whereupon something invisible would be poured down her throat; we all saw her swallow, and yet we saw her try all she could, by spitting, coughing, and shrieking, that she might not swallow; but one time the by-standers saw something of that odd liquor on the outside of her neck; she cried out of it, as of scalding brimstone poured into her, and the whole house would immediately scent so hot of brimstone that we were scarce able to endure it—whereof there are scores of witnesses. ....The enchanted people talked much of a white spirit, from whence they received marvellous assistance in their miseries. What lately befell Mercy Short, from the communications of such a spirit, hath been the just wonder of us all; but by such a spirit was Margaret Rule now also visited. She says that she could never see his face, but that she had a frequent view of his bright, shining, and glorious garments; he stood by her bedside continually, heartening and comforting her, and counselling her to maintain her hope and faith in God, and never comply with the temptations of her adversaries."

Contrast these confessions of a gross and baseless superstition with the high and noble reasons of Roger Williams, and his appeals and warnings to the enemies of toleration, and you have some conception of the moral and intellectual lapse of New England. But we must not deny a charm of style in the relations of Mather. The language, if less sweet and fresh, is more flexible than before; the diction is simple and graphic. Modern spiritualism, so far as we can remember, has never expressed itself so attractively.

His literary skill was sufficiently recognized in his own time, when his superstition was not so offensive as it afterward became. The good Benjamin Tompson, in some verses prefixed to the *Magnalia Christi Americana*, demands:

"Is the bless'd Mather necromancer turned,
To raise his country's fathers' ashes urned?
Elisha's dust life to the dead imparts;
This prophet, by his more familiar arts,
Unseals our heroes' tombs and gives them air;
They rise, they walk, they talk, look wondrous fair;
Each of them in an orb of light doth shine,
In liveries of glory most divine."

To put one above Elisha is certainly not to rate him low; and the praise is a satirist's who lashed the luxury if not the vice of New England society, so soon did it begin to lose its simplicity, if not its innocence. The mutual admiration of the Bostonians, betrayed to the world by the most brilliant of their number in modern times, was of early date, and our editors give a poem by the Rev. John Norton in eulogy of Anne Bradstreet's poems which any literary lady of our time might be glad to merit:

"Her breast was a brave palace, a Broad-street"— the reader will note the merry conceit in the play upon Mistress Bradstreet's name—

"Where all heroic, ample thoughts did meet,
Where Nature such a tenement had ta'en
That others' souls, to hers, dwelt in a lane.
Beneath her feet pale envy bites her chain,
And poison malice whets her sting in vain"—

much as they did at that time in all the polite countries of Europe; we were not outdone in allegory anywhere, and perhaps our poetry was no worse than most, if not so good as some. It was always a little below our prose, which at the date of this eulogy began to be rich in narratives of captivity among the Indians, plain, unaffected, and sometimes extremely moving, with a breath of real piety in them that is sometimes as beautiful as tedious, and that is saying a good deal. At the same time Samuel Sewall was holding the mirror up to society in New England in his delightful diary. The [3] editors do well to give a long passage from it, and better still to copy into their Library the old judge's confession of his error in condemning the hapless persons accused of witchcraft—one of the most monumental things in human history, if we consider its heart-felt humility, and the circumstance of his standing up to take shame upon himself before the whole congregation while the Rev. Mr. Willard read it aloud.

IV.

After all, the Puritans lived their greatest things, and it would be less honor for them to have written them, as some other peoples have done, though the gain to literature might have been more. A tenderer love for their civilization than we can affect could not pretend that their literature was very entertaining, and it must be owned that some of the best and liveliest of it was not meant for print. We will not call Sewall's diary lively, though it is very good; but the editors quote from the journals of Madam Sarah Kemble Knight the account of her journey from Boston to New York in 1704, [4] which is both lively and good. It shows touch; and that such easy, vigorous writing should be in a private diary suggests at least a growing literary temperament among the Bostonians of the time. In Connecticut they were trying the metrical stops then fashionable in the mother country, and Roger Wolcott described a storm at sea as any poet of Grub Street might have done it:

"Here the ship captain in the midnight watch
Stamps on the deck and thunders up the hatch,
And to the mariners aloud he cries:
'Now all from safe recumbency arise!
All hands aloft, and stand well to your tack!
Engend'ring storms have clothed the world with black;
Big tempests threaten to undo the world:
Down topsail; let the mainsail soon be furled,'"

and so on. "Safe recumbency" was perhaps not just the phrase the captain used, but it is mighty fine, and we know there are many still who love the high literary way best; for the rest, one recognizes the true old sea-dog diction in the stirring appeal to the safely recumbent mariners.

The editors are obliged all through this early period of our literary history to extend the citizenship with a generosity worthy of the workers of a close campaign on the eve of election. They are able, on account of his long residence in Rhode Island, to naturalize George Berkeley among us, wholly to the gain of their readers. But the great powers of Jonathan Edwards were native here, and we can be rightfully proud of them beside any question of the use he put them to. He might almost be called the last, as he was certainly the greatest, of the Puritan theologues, and from his lofty narrowness the record broadens down to the genial and fruitful levels—immeasurable in some of their reaches, and everywhere habitable for human nature—of Ben Franklin. He is still one of the greatest literary Americans, and with the other writers and orators who made the Revolution and the nation he gave us a real literary epoch—partly without knowing it, being bent upon better things than literature. We need not catalogue these men; their names are on every school-boy's tongue from generation to generation; but we wish the reader to observe qualities in Francis Hopkinson, for instance, which are of the first literary importance. The editors give, among other things from him, a sketch called "Benedick the Married Man," which is in the right spirit of very much of the most American humor since. His verse is always very neat and clever, but this sketch of a Philadelphia merchant's journey to New York with his family is of a lively fidelity which the re-alism of a later time could not easily surpass. The most astonishing thing about it is that so accomplished a writer should have stooped so low as to touch a subject next his hand. There are people in our day who would have had him avoid it on that account.

V.

The third volume, which is mainly devoted to the Revolutionary period, is too rich in its variety to be treated specifically, or even to be touched at all points. It is, like the others, admirably expressive of the contemporary life and character, and with these it forms so really a library of American literature up to the beginning of our century that acquaintance with it would possess the reader fairly well with a sense of the nature and scope of that literature. A work done so judiciously cannot have been easy to do, and it probably has not excluded all the errors which might have been avoided; but we gladly leave their detection to others. In fact—we will whisper it in the reader's ear—we have not the material for a very critical examination of its shortcomings; and we have derived from this charming compilation a more comprehensive knowledge of the literary periods it embraces than we had before—we had almost said than we hope to have again. But that would not be quite true, for the impression of the work that remains is something delightful as concerns its matter, and something thoroughly respectful as concerns the editors' labors. In their brief introduction they give us at once the right point of view, and then they make haste to stand out of the way and let us enjoy a prospect of American literature which could hardly have been more complete, and which, whatever it leaves unshown, certainly seems to leave nothing unsuggested.

[1] Edmund Clarence Stedman and Ellen Mackay Hutchinson, eds., A Library of American Literature from the Earliest Settlement to the Present Time (New York: C. L. Webster & Company, 1889-1890).

[2] A Voyage to America, by Henry Norwood.

[3] Diary of Samuel Sewall. See note 1 above.

[4] Sarah Kemble Knight, The Private Journal kept by Madam Knight, on a Journey from Boston to New York, in the Year 1704. See note 1 above. This journal is excerpted from an earlier work titled The Journals of Madam Knight, and Rev. Mr. Buckingham.

September. 1888

Editor's Study.

I.

SO many books of verse have come to the Study lately that a department much more obstinate than this in its impressions might well question whether it was not mistaken in ever supposing a decline of poetry among us. Quantitatively, at least, we do not think the Study could maintain that opinion, and qualitatively there is a chance that possibly the Study may have been wrong, though that is a great deal to say. What is certain is that in these books, quite fortuitous in their arrival and desultory in their range, there is the presence more and more of what seems the color of an authentic life; or, if we may not quite say this, then there is the increasing absence of reflected life. We have before now spoken of the gradual silencing in the minor poets of the echoes from the great modern masters; and though this hush means the extinction of the voices that woke the echoes, it means something more than that too. Perhaps while they sounded at their grandest, it was not possible for any lesser note to lift itself except in tune with them; perhaps an interval of suspense in what has long seemed the highest poetry was necessary to the facultation of any new utterance. At its lowest the ebb is a prophecy of the flood, and the rising tide is the next thing in order, unless the moon forget her office upon the seas and the sensibilities.

The reader is not to imagine, however, that the tide is coming back with the fabled rush of its reflux on Labradoran coasts; there will be time enough apparently for every one who dislikes poetry to get out of the way before it touches high-water mark. But the fact remains that there seems really a stir again in forms supposed nearly lifeless, and that the impulse is from within rather than from without.

It must always be a surprise to the critic nurtured in the times of the great poets now quiet or quiescent not to find their influence in every young poet he takes up; but this is the surprise, not to say disappointment, we have suffered in the new books of verse before us. It is impossible not to name Tennyson here, and one hardly feels contemporary with these poets who have not only not tried to write like him (with all that sweet unconsciousness of imitation once so delightfully obvious), but who are apparently insensible if not ignorant of him. We do not find his mental attitudes in them, nor his turns of phrase, nor his pet words; it is all very strange; it is like another country, another language, another world; we are a little lost in it. He is even more extinct in them than Dickens, his only compeer as an influence, is in our fiction; for one still comes upon traces of that master now and then in apprentices of the art. It would be extremely interesting, if one could do it, to follow the decline of such a literary domination, and mark the moment of its final lapse; but the inquiry would be possible only to German thoroughness and German patience. Our airier criticism may yet make this sort of research its office; but in the mean time it can now only recognize the accomplished fact, and another fact equally important, that there is no reversion to still earlier types in the new writers who have cast off this influence. The poets who do not sing like Tennyson do not sing like Byron either, nor like Keats, nor Shelley, nor Wordsworth.

A literary influence seems to cease at a certain date, so that even the writers who once felt it strongly no longer feel it after that date. We were struck in reading Mr. Coates Kinney's powerful poem "Optim and Pessim," a few months ago, with the absence of Tennysonianism in the treatment of a theme akin to several that Tennyson treated with his greatest mastery; and this although Mr. Kinney was a mature writer at the time of Tennyson's supremacy as an influence. It would have been impossible, we are almost ready to say, for him to have written "Optim and Pessim" fifteen or twenty years ago and not have betrayed the Tennysonian control: we will not be quite positive, for in other poems Mr. Kinney seems to have escaped it in singular degree. But others of our poets, who at one time came under it devotedly, and wrote poems that Tennyson might perhaps have been willing to own, and certainly would have been puzzled to disclaim, have completely outgrown his influence in their later work; and they now no more write like Tennyson than Mr. Madison Cawein does, or Mr. Robert Burns Wilson, or Miss Lizette Woodworth Reese, or any of the new poets whose books have inspired these observations.

II.

But by all this we hope we have not been denying the enduring influence upon the language of such a poet as Tennyson; this will last always, though no one imitates his manner any more. English is a sweeter and suppler tongue for his having used it and governed it with his mastertouch; whoever, to the end of time, writes in it, will find it a mellower instrument because Tennyson's breath so long filled it. The new men have not escaped his influence in this sense; their phrase is lovelier and more elect because his exquisite sense of diction has ennobled and clarified the poetical vocabulary, leaving it impossible for them to be as crude or prosaic in their wording as they might have been without him. In this effect, however, Tennyson does not stand for himself alone, but for many tendencies, for the general tendency of English verse to a strictly poetic expression; his utterance is habitually what that of Wordsworth, of Keats, of Coleridge, of Shelley, was at its best.

We should like to know if our young poets read him as fondly as their literary uncles and aunts and elder brothers did, and we wish some of the journals that make a business of symposiums concerning questions of ethics and æsthetics would invite a general confession on this point. Who, in fact, is now the most influential poet? We interrogate the work of our young poets in vain; it gives back no certain sound; if it is imitative at all, it is eclectically, not specifically, imitative, and reverberates a synthesis of all the poetic moods of the century. We have spoken of Mr. Cawein's verse before, and we have to note in *The Triumph of Music, and Other Lyrics*, chiefly the ripening of qualities felt in his first volume: a love of nature in her recondite as well as obvious aspects, and a rich sympathy with all that is splendid and beautiful in the outer world. The spirit of his poetry feels itself akin with the arts that interpreted the old mythologies, and yet is at home with the least associated suggestions of the new land in which it is native, and in which it naturalizes the lovely things of old, as the spirit of Keats revived Greece under the gray English skies. Our words do not say it quite, and it is hard to choose from the book just the passages which shall characterize it; for a book is like a man's face, and one point of view

gives only one effect, and is not the whole of its meaning. But perhaps the reader will get some intimation of what we intend from this very aerially fancied, delicately worded little poem:

"THE DRYAD.

" I have seen her limpid eyes,
Large with gradual laughter, rise
Through wild roses' nettles,
Like twin blossoms grow and stare,
Then a hating, envious air
Whisked them into petals.

" I have seen her hardy cheek
Like a molten coral leak
Through the leafage shaded
Of thick Chickasaws; and then,
When I made more sure, again
To a red plum faded.

" Often on the ferny rocks
Dazzling rimples of loose locks
At me she hath shaken,
And I've followed; 'twas in vain;
They had trickled into rain
Sunlit on the braken.

" Once her full limbs flashed on me,
Naked where some royal tree
Powdered all the spaces
With wan sunlight and quaint shade;
Such a haunt romance hath made
For haunched satyr races.

" There, I wot, hid amorous Pan,
For a sudden pleading ran
Through the maze of myrtle,
Whiles a rapid violence tossed
All its flowerage; 'twas the lost
Cooings of a turtle."

Another mood utters itself here in no less choice and fortunate phrase, whose truth will be felt by any one who recalls a country usage in the South and older West, where a family's dead are often laid in a little plot of ground near the home of the living:

"THE FAMILY BURYING-GROUND.

" A wall of crumbling stones doth keep
Watch o'er long barrows where they sleep,
Old chronicled grave-stones of its dead,
On which oblivious mosses creep,
And lichens gray as lead.

" Warm days the lost cows as they pass
Rest here and browse the juicy grass
That springs about its sun-scorched stones;
Afar one hears their bells' deep brass
Waft melancholy tones.

" Here the wild morning-glory goes
A-rambling as the myrtle grows,
Wild morning-glories, pale as pain,
With holy urns that hint at woes,
The night hath filled with rain.

" Here are blackberries largest seen,
Rich, winy dark, whereon the lean
Black hornet sucks, noons sick with heat,
That bend not to the shadowed green
The heavy-bearded wheat.

" At dark, for its forgotten dead,
A requiem of no known wind said,
Through ghostly cedars moans and throbs,
While to thin starlight overhead
The shivering screech-owl sobs."

For the mere pleasure of it we light our page with these gorgeous dyes from the poet's study of an old garden:

" Bubble-like the hollyhocks
   Budded, burst, and flaunted wide
Gypsy beauty from their stocks;
   Morning-glories, bubble-dyed,
Swung in honey-hearted flocks.

" Tawny tiger-lilies flung
   Doublets slashed with crimson on;
Graceful girl slaves, fair and young,
   Like Circassians, in the sun
Alabaster lilies swung.

" Ah, the droning of the bee
   In his dusty pantaloons
Tumbling in the fleurs-de-lis;
   In the drowsy afternoons
Dreaming in the pink sweet-pea.

" Ah, the moaning wild-wood dove,
   With its throat of amethyst
Ruffled like a shining cove
   Which a wind to pearl hath kissed,
Moaning, moaning of its love.

" And the insects' gossip thin,
   From the summer hotness hid,
In the leafy shadows green;
   Then at eve the katydid
With its hard, unvaried din.

" Often from the whispering hills,
   Lorn within the golden dusk—
Gold with gold of daffodils—
   Thrilled into the garden's musk
The wild wail of whippoorwills.

" From the purple-tangled trees,
   Like the white, full heart of night,
Solemn with majestic peace,
   Swam the big moon, veined with light,
Like some gorgeous golden fleece."

Caprices, conceits if you will, and excesses, as in the case of this moon doing double metaphoric duty on such short notice, but all full of the security and courage of the born artist who dashes his color or his epithet on, and leaves it to approve itself to you or not as you choose. We cannot put down his book without copying one thing more from it, in which he touches a flying emotion that perpetually escapes the hold:

"DEFICIENCY.

" Ah, God! were I away, away,
   By woodland-belted hills,
There might be more in Thy bright day
   Than my poor spirit thrills.

" The elder coppice, banks of blooms,
   The spice-wood brush, the field
Of tumbled clover, and perfumes
   Hot, weedy pastures yield.

" The old rail-fence, whose angles hold
   Bright brier and sassafras,
Sweet priceless wild flowers, blue and gold,
   Starred through the moss and grass.

" The ragged bank path that winds unto
   Lone cow-behaunted nooks,
Through brambles, to the shade and dew
   Of rocks and woody brooks.

" To see the minnows turn and gleam
   White sparkling bellies, all
Shoot in gray schools adown the stream
   Let but a dead leaf fall.

" The buoyant pleasure and delight
   Of floating feathered seeds,
Capricious wanderers, soft and white,
   Born of silk-bearing weeds.

" Ah, God! were I away, away,
   Among wild woods and birds,
There were more soul within Thy day
   Than one might bless with words."

We will not dwell upon the fidelity with which all this sumptuousness and subtlety renders the thought and the thing in the poet's mind and eye. Here, whatever his future in other ways, is already a master of diction. By an affinition which we will let the reader trace, the poem last quoted brings us to one of the loveliest in Mr. Robert Burns Wilson's volume of *Life and Love*. Without representing his whole range, it intimates the tender pensiveness of most of his work.

"IN SEPTEMBER.

" The slanting sun shines softly on the hills
   Where lift the glittering domes of green and gold;
The hush of forest cities, tranced and still,
   Creeps out upon the gray and tangled wold.

" Half-heard, uncertain rustlings fill the air
   Among the trees and on the crisp, warm ground,
Which to the soul recall some joy or care,
   Made quick by feeling rather than by sound.

" The wild blackberry bushes' mottled green
   Glows with the touch of wine upon its leaves;
Her silken threads, that stretch their glossy sheen
   From stem to stem, the careful spider weaves.

" The mullein stalks, disconsolate and lean,
   Look idly on their shadows all the day—
Poor lingering ghosts that haunt the changing scene
   Where summer's silent feet have passed away.

" The loosened leaves fall circling far and near,
   Down to the silence of the woodland road,
And on the pool by which the unyoked steer
   Stands now, forgetful of the stinging goad.

" Along their homeward path the cattle graze
   Amid the cadence of their answering bells,
Soft silhouettes against the evening haze
   Which rises now from out the dreamy dells.

" The scarlet berries on the dogwood's stem
   Grow bright and deepen with a ruddier glow,
The shadows lengthen from the forest's hem,
   And soft the cooling airs begin to blow.

" Oh, wistful days of melancholy joy,
   That breathe in music tones of sweet despair,
Rich with the beauty that must yet destroy,
   Bright with the darkness, languishing but fair—

" Days when the spirit with the vision turns
   From cloud to cloud, from changing tree to tree,
From field to forest, and the full heart yearns
   For something—God knows what—that cannot be!

" Mayhap the rose is lovelier that it fades,
   The daisy fairer for the mower's scythe;
Perhaps it is the gloom of nightly shades
   That makes the songs of morning seem so blithe.

" Shall then the soul that knows not but to glean
   Its few short joys from thorns of biting pain
Be happier finding fields forever green
   And flowers that cannot die to bloom again?

" Perhaps—perhaps—and life is nothing more;
   Perhaps it is a dream that dies away,
Like echoes lost on some forgetful shore
   In endless silence of a twilight day."

This tranquil noting of natural aspects and question of their relation to human life recalls the softer and gentler English poetry that began to look about it and to rediscover this beautiful world after the long reign of convention in the last century; and in the little pang at the close, as well as the melancholy serenity of the whole picture, there is a touch of Leopardi, a poet with whom Mr. Wilson has no other affinity.

Both of the young poets whom we have quoted are Kentuckians, and in them the South makes again a very valid claim to recognition for the literary impulse which has already strikingly fulfilled itself in fiction. The claim is not weakened in the thin, prim, drab-colored little book which brings from Maryland the poems of Lizette Woodworth Reese. In these, as in those of Mr. Cawein and Mr. Wilson, we fancy properties distinctly Southern; and in all there is certainly the same tendency to close, loving, and vivid picture of nature. It might almost be called a landscape school of poetry, in the pieces of which the attitude of the poet mainly supplies the human interest. The charm of a delicate little painting like this below will be, for the sympathetic witness, largely in the suggestion of the environment that invited to the study for it:

"SUNSET.

"In the clear dusk, upon the fields below,
  The blossoming thorn-bush, white and spare and
    tall,
  Seems carved of ivory 'gainst the dark wall;
  Shut from the sunset, sharp the farm roofs
    show;
  But here, upon this height, the straggling hedge
  Burns in the wind, and is astir with bees;
  The little pool beneath the willow-trees,
  Yellow as topaz, flames from edge to edge;
  A line of light the desert highway glows.
  Odors like sounds down the rich air do pass,
  Spice from each bough, musk from the brier-
    rose
  Dropping its fine sweet petals on the grass;
  Swallows are whirring black against the blaze;
  I hear the creek laugh out from pebbly ways."

In the poems of all three of these writers, so keenly alive to every look and tone of nature, we imagine not only the spacious receptivity of youth, but the effect of a less dense and hurried life than ours at the North. They are unconsciously true to the more sparsely peopled Southern world in their converse with woods and fields and skies; and they record a social period in terms of value both to the lover of beauty and the student of literary history.

III.

It is interesting to pass from their work, so young and so sensuous, so meridional and in a good sense local, to that of Dr. Holmes in his latest group of verses, which he calls *Before the Curfew, and Other Poems*. The precision of form indicative of a close-wrought, highly polished intellectual life; the touch as firm as it is fine; the philosophic poise of mind; the inward and backward look; the question consoling itself with hope where faith would seem too arrogant; the gentle yet penetrating suggestiveness; the air of ripe learning, and all the discipline of social and literary culture, with that tenderness for the past, that half-compassionate interest in the present, which the years bring: how different it all is from the poetry of those young Southerners! What the books are alike in is the genuineness of their poetry; the same stream bubbles in the grass-grown spring and shines in the marble fount, sculptured and inscriptioned on every surface. But one is again struck with the deeply municipalized, personalized character of Dr. Holmes's verse. No poet ever more strictly identified himself with his native city than he. It is Boston throughout his book, in its public character; and then that inner Boston of classmates and friends which every Bostonian bears in his bosom. It is eminently a city of cherished friendships, and these speak constantly in the poems of occasion which half fill the volume; but it is friendship on its human or universal side that the Boston laureate celebrates.

There is no need to speak of his qualities, but it would be difficult to read these latest poems and not be sensible of the perfection of what we may call his instrumentation. Like the art of Longfellow, it seems only to have grown lovelier and finer with time, and more intimately responsive to the spirit whose music it transmits.

Dr. Holmes's poetry expresses New England on one side as Whittier's does on another, and Emerson's on yet another; and if we were to look for an embodiment in verse of New England womanhood, we do not know where we should find it so fully as in the *Poems of Rose Terry Cooke*. It is not complete; that could never be; but so far as it goes it is perfectly New England, and perfectly womanly. Mrs. Cooke's name is not new in our literature, and needs no special validation here; but of late years she has made herself known by her honest and strenuous dealing with New England in fiction to a generation too recent to remember when the ballad of "Rosalind" and the poem of "The Two Villages" imparted their pathos and solemnity to the young hearts of magazine readers. It is for this reason, as well as our regard for it otherwise, that we welcome a collection of her poetry; and we should be very sorry if it failed of wider welcome. It is, as we said, the expression of the *ewig Weibliche* as the New England civilization has influenced it: the passion deepened and silenced; the conscience piercing and relentless; the wide interest in the events of thought and of life; the high love of beauty and the higher love of truth; the tendency to self-question; and the revolt, within decorous bounds, from convention and tradition, which make that avatar of the *ewig Weibliche* a thing of perpetual fascination and occasional fear. There is little or nothing here of the Yankee humor which plays so richly through Mrs. Cooke's stories and sketches, and we are well enough content to have the humorist hushed in the poet. But there is great sweetness and tenderness and sympathy in response to widely varying appeals of life and letters. Something—we should not like to be asked what exactly—makes us think of Adelaide Anne Procter in Mrs. Cooke's poetry. Probably it is the fact that as contemporaries they both felt the wave of German influence which has now quite spent itself. The New England poet seems to have felt it more remotely than the kindred English talent, and her work, in choice of subject and in its versions, shows greater friendship with other literatures. Compared with that of our young Southern poets, her poetry addresses itself to the senses through the mind, while theirs seems to reach the senses first, like color.

IV.

The thing is not easy to say without seeming to slight the more intellectualized work; but if criticism has grown at all of late years, it has been in the direction of inclusion and of the appreciation of kinds. We no longer contend that if Pope was a poet, then Keats was none; we know they were both poets, and are a good deal richer for the knowledge. It would be easy to overrate the value of such poetry as that of those young Southerners, but it is not necessary to do this in order to prize it. In fact we shall like it all the better if we remember that its charm is from what they have in common, their youth, rather than from their separate qualities and intentions. They all have the stir of the impulse to appropriate the outside world by recognizing and naming its facts; they cannot rest till they have found a tint of phrase, a music of words, for each of its appealing sights and sounds, and thus made it, or seemed to make it, their own. It is winning, and touches the heart; but it is not the only poetry, though one likes to have them write as if it were.

On the other hand, we must not undervalue their work, as one might quite as easily do. If you look at it even casually you will find that it is nature, different in many things from that hitherto known to literature, which they are observing in such keenly felt detail. Traits of the outer world which are yet subtly to influence life appear in the verse which scarcely hints of the expression of social conditions; as in Mrs. Cooke's poems, and Dr. Holmes's, the external world is lost in the interest of associations, of experiences.

---

[1] ewig Weibliche - eternal femininity.

October , 1888

Editor's Study.

I.

IT is hardly worth while to attempt a full record of what has been done in fiction since the Study last gave its attention to that branch of literature. To note even the important events in it with the hope of doing justice to specific achievements is something beyond us. At best one can expect merely to appreciate with loose generality the work of new hands, and gratefully to welcome the increasing skill and power of some old ones.

Among these it seems to us that the touch of Mr. Henry James is of such excellent maturity in the short stories which he has lately printed that it would be futile to dispute his primacy in most literary respects. We mean his primacy not only among fabling Americans, but among all who are presently writing fiction. It is with an art richly and normally perfected from intentions evident in his earliest work that he now imparts to the reader his own fine sense of character and motive, and gives his conceptions a distinctness and definition really unapproached. There never was much 'prentice faltering in him; the danger was rather that in one so secure of his literary method from the first, a mere literary method might content to the end; but with a widening if not a deepening hold on life (all must admit that his hold has widened, whoever denies that it has deepened) this has clearly not contented him. No one has had more to say to his generation of certain typical phases than he, and he has had incomparably the best manner of saying it. Of course it can always be urged by certain mislikers of his—and he has them in force enough to witness the vast impression he has made—that these typical phases are not the important phases; but if they do this they must choose wholly to ignore such a novel as *The Princess Casamassima*. It is in a way discreditable to our time that a writer of such quality should ever have grudging welcome; the fact impeaches not only our intelligence, but our sense of the artistic. It will certainly amaze a future day that such things as his could be done in ours and meet only

a feeble and conditional acceptance from the "best" criticism, with something little short of ribald insult from the common cry of literary paragraphers. But happily the critics do not form an author's only readers; they are not even his judges. These are the editors of the magazines, which are now the real avenues to the public; and their recent unanimity in presenting simultaneously some of the best work of Mr. James's life in the way of short stories indicates the existence of an interest in all he does, which is doubtless the true measure of his popularity. With "The Aspern Papers" in *The Atlantic*, "The Liar" in *The Century*, "A London Life" in *Scribner's*, and "Louisa Pallant" and "Two Countries" in *Harper's*, pretty much all at once, the effect was like an artist's exhibition. One turned from one masterpiece to another, making his comparisons, and delighted to find that the stories helped rather than hurt one another, and that their accidental massing enhanced his pleasure in them.

II.

Masterpieces, we say, since the language does not hold their betters for a high perfection of literary execution at all points. "Louisa Pallant," for instance, is an unmixed pleasure if you delight in a well-taken point of view, and then a story that runs easily from the lips of the imagined narrator, characterizing him no less subtly than the persons of the tale, in English to the last degree informal and to the last degree refined. Just for attitude, just for light, firm touch, the piece is simply unsurpassed outside the same author's work. We speak now only of the literature, and leave the doubter to his struggle with the question whether a mother would have done all that about a daughter; and we will not attempt to decide whether the American wife in the "Two Countries" would have killed herself if her English husband had written a book against her native land. These were to us very minor points compared with the truthfulness of the supposed case and the supposed people, just as in "A London Life" it doesn't so much matter whether poor Laura mar-

157

ries or not as whether the portrait of Mr. Wendover is not almost too good to be felt by the public which reads in running, and whether some touch of Selina's precious badness may not be lost. There are depths under depths in the subtle penetrations of this story, the surprise of which should not be suffered to cheapen the more superficial but not less brilliant performance in "The Liar"; for there too is astonishing divination, and a clutch upon the unconscious motives which are scarcely more than impulses, instincts.

III.

To pass from these tales to such a novel as *The Man Behind* is to compass a distance as vast as that between the dense, highly organized European social life of to-day and the more crude materials of society as they existed in the great Middle West forty years ago. But in a genuine feeling for human nature Mr. Henry James and Mr. T. S. Denison, who publishes his own book as well as writes it, are not so far apart but that the Study can welcome them alike to the hospitality it rejoices to show all good work. The simple, the rude new-country life which most Americans of fifty have known, but which, with loss and gain, few Americans will know hereafter, is the setting of an action neither novel nor peculiarly ours. Men have so often tempted women to self-betrayal and then left them to their ruin, while they prospered on to riches and honors, that the fate of an ambitious farm-boy and backwoods girl could have no special claim upon the reader's interest if it were not for the local truth which the author is able to impart, or unable to withhold. We should like to say, if we might say it without offence, how it seems often the limited perspective which gives his work infinite pathos for those whose bounds have widened. His work has a real importance because of his apparent unconsciousness, because his ideals of worldly splendor address themselves simply to the intelligence of that wholesome majority of our people whose experience of more metropolitan glories is small or null. At the same time it has a truth to human nature in generals and in details which is uncommon—a greater truth to this always than to character in its more fluctuant shades and more flexible expressions. Such as it is, Mr. Denison's work has very distinct value, and the public, which is not suffering from over-production in that kind, ought to be glad of it, and want more of it.

IV.

Perhaps we can make clearer some points concerning Mr. Denison's work by contrasting it with Miss S. O. Jewett's in her late volume, *The King of Folly Island*, and other sketches. Here there is a knowledge of common life (we call it common, but it is not vulgar, like the life of most rich and fashionable people) not less intimate than his, and a kindness for it quite as great; but it is studied from the outside, and with the implication of a world of interests and experiences foreign to it. Of course Miss Jewett's lovely humor, so sweet and compassionate, goes for much in the tacit appeal, the mute aside, to the sympathetic reader for his appreciation of the several situations; but nothing is helplessly or involuntarily good in the effect; all was understood before and aimed at, and there is a beautiful mastery in the literature, which charms equally with the fine perception. From first to last both are so unfaltering in such a sketch as "Sister Wisby's Courtship" or "Miss Peck's Promotion" that one is tempted to call the result perfect, and take the consequences. At the same time the writer's authority is kept wholly out of sight; she is not sensibly in her story any more than a painter is in his picture. It is in this that her matured skill or her intuitive self-control shows to the disadvantage of a very clever writer like the author of *Tenting at Stony Beach*, who has herself too much in mind, and lets the reader see it. With the latter, humor occasionally degenerates into smartness; nevertheless it is for the most part very genuine humor, and it includes a lively sense of character both among the South Shore natives and the summer folks. The pretty girl of our civilization, who pushes into the canvas home of the tenters, is caught with much of Mr. James's neatness, while Marsh Yates, the "shif'less toot," and his beautiful, energetic wife, and Randy Rankin and her husband, are verities beyond his range.

V.

It is a pity that Miss Pool does not hold her hand altogether from caricature and melodrama; but it must be owned she does not. Still we are indebted to her for some types, if not some characters; and to Mr. Cable in his inter-related sketches called *Bonaventure* we owe the pleasure of some fresh characters in a romantic atmosphere where we could not have hoped for anything better than types. The book is no such book as *The Grandissimes;* let that be fairly understood before we praise it for qualities proper to its slighter texture. *The Grandissimes* is one of the great novels of our time, whereas *Bonaventure* is simply one of the gracefulest romances, in which high motive, generous purpose, and picturesque material answer for the powerful realities of the other. The facts of the case—the aspiration and the heroic self-sacrifice of the young creole school-master among the Acadians of Louisiana—are given by a species of indirection, a kind of tacking, which recalls Judd's method in his *Margaret*, a book which Mr. Cable could not have had in mind, but to which his work assimilates itself in the romantic atmosphere common to them both. It has its charm, but it also has a misty intangibility which baffles, which vexes. Nevertheless this too is the work of a master who gives us for the time what he thinks best, and who has not yet begun to deliver his whole message to a world where few of the prophets have both head and heart. We see in him a curious process of evolution, in which the citizen, the Christian, seems to threaten the artist; but out of which we trust to see them issue in indissoluble alliance for the performance of services to humanity higher than any yet attempted. It is the conscience of Mr. Cable that gives final value to all he does; it will avail him with readers similarly endowed against any provincial censure, and will not suffer him to slight any side of his most important work, or to forget that art is the clearest medium of truth.

It is a very delicate medium, however, and it breaks unless the ethical intention it is meant to carry is very carefully adjusted. One feels that something of this sort is the trouble with Mrs. Alice Wellington Rollins's book, which she calls *Uncle Tom's Tenement*. It is the work of an intellectual woman, and it is written with noble purpose from abundant knowledge; it interests, it touches, it stirs; but it is wanting in æsthetic solidarity, and one is sensible at last that, with all the fervor of its episodes, it must be judged on its economic side, if it is to be judged for what mainly occupied the writer. She has found that the tenement-house curse of New York has its origin primarily in the rapacity of the landlords, and secondarily in the savagery of the tenants; the former have accustomed the latter to squalor, till now they prefer it. The reform must begin in the consciences of the landlords, who ought to give their tenants improved tenements, and then the tenants ought to be educated up to their opportunities by surveillance and discipline. The abuses alleged are all undeniable and sickening enough; the extortions practised are atrocious; the abominations and indecencies unspeakable. If ever prosperity visits these miserable homes in the shape of better wages, it is seized and confiscated to the landlord's behoof in an increased rent. The disease is well studied, and the symptoms all clearly ascertained; the remedy proposed is more conscience in the landlords. But is there any hope of permanent cure while the conditions invite one human

creature to exploit another's necessity for his profit, or a bad man, under the same laws, may at any moment undo the work of a good one? This is the poignant question which the book seems to leave unanswered. It is so poignant that we are fain to turn from it to more strictly literary interests again, and try to forget it.

VI.

It was not because the censure of Mr. Cable was sectional or local that we were tempted just now to call it provincial, but because it was narrow-minded, the censure of people who would rather be flattered than appreciated; and in this sort the sum of our national censure of Mr. James is provincial. It is extraordinary that any one could read *The Reverberator* and not cry out in grateful recognition of its thorough Americanism; it makes one afraid that the author's patriotism has mistaken us, and that we are really a nation of snobs, who would rather be supposed to have fine manners than good qualities; or that we are stupid, and cannot perceive the delicate justice that rights us in spite of ourselves. But there is no mistake in his art, which, beginning with such a group of Americans as the Dossons and their friend the reporter of the society newspaper on the plane of their superficial vulgarity, ends with having touched into notice every generous and valuable point in them, and espoused their cause against that of the grander world. In the case of the obtuse Flack this effect is almost miraculous, in that of Mr. Dosson and his daughter Delia it is charming, and in that of Francie Dosson adorable. We leave the Probert group of Gallicized Americans to those who know them better, though Francie's lover Gaston goes to one's heart; but the Dossons are all true and verifiable in their inexpugnable innocence at any turn in the international world which Mr. James has discovered for us. Francie Dosson, with her beauty, her fineness, her goodness, and her helpless truth, is a marvellous expression of the best in American girlhood. She unwittingly does her lover's people an awful mischief, and to the end she remains half persuaded of Mr. Flack's theory that people really like to have their private affairs written up in the papers; but all the same she remains lovable, and Gaston loves her. "*Sie war liebenswürdig und er liebte sie.*" Mr. James makes you feel [2] once again that this settles it.

VII.

As for Flack, he is perfect, the very genius of society journalism. But apparently, however indigenous with us, his species is not confined to our own country in its origin, if we may believe Señor

Valdés in his latest novel, *El Cuarto Poder*, or *The Fourth Estate*, or the newspaper press mainly as it exists in the little seaport city of Sarrió, somewhere in northwestern Spain of to-day. Sinforoso Suarez is the resonant Spanish of the nature if not of the name of Flack, though with a mellifluousness and a malignity added which are foreign to Flack; for as a rule the American interviewer wishes his victim no harm, and does not ordinarily aim at fine writing, even when he achieves it. But, as in Mr. James's story, journalism is a subordinate interest of Señor Valdés's novel, which is mainly a picture of contemporary life in a Spanish town. The reader of these pages need be at no loss to conjecture our opinion of this author's work, and from the versions of his *Marquis of Peñalta* and his *Maximina* any English reader can test it for himself. We will only say that, without their unity, *El Cuarto Poder* is in other respects a greater work than either; its range is vaster, its tolerance as charming, its sympathy with all good things as pervasive, its humor delicious. Don Rosendo Bellinchón and the cigar girl whom he marries; their son Pablo, from boyhood to youth immoral, reckless, and cowardly; and their daughters Cecilia and Ventura, are, with Gonzalo de las Cuevas, the husband of Ventura, the principal persons, around whom are grouped the vividly painted *personnel* and circumstance of Sarrió. The novel is mainly the tragic story of Gonzalo, who abandons Cecilia and marries Ventura, and experiences through her ambition and treachery the truth of his uncle's saying, that God himself cannot help the man who breaks his word. But he is not a false person, only simply, helplessly true, and there grows up between him and Cecilia the sweetest and purest friendship ever imagined in fiction; it is most beautifully and courageously done; it consoles him in the worst affliction, but it cannot save him. Spanish aristocracy as it survives, intellectualized and agnosticized, into modern times is studied with irony that would be bitter, if Valdés could be bitter, in the Duque de Tornos, who seduces the ready Ventura; and a whole population of middle-class and plebeian figures live in the author's humorous sympathy.

Bellinchón himself is a character worthy of Cervantes, with his extravagancies and contradictions, and his wife, with her growth through sorrow into a refinement not otherwise possible to her simple goodness, is a lovely creation. It is impossible to touch the merit of the book at all points; it has in one romantic excess of self-sacrifice a single important fault; but it has that frankness, of which we must advise the intending reader, characteristic of Latin writers in treating Latin life; that is to say, Sarrió is not described as if it were Salem, Massachusetts.

VIII.

We are inclined to make much of the good fiction that comes to us from Spain, because we get no more from the only country that sends us better. But in default of a Russian novel, we are very glad of Stepniak's book on *The Russian Peasantry*, the facts of which throw such full and interesting light on the realistic fiction of Russia. Without this book many things must remain dark in Tourguénief and Tolstoï, and its details concerning the political, social, domestic, and religious life of the Russian people are of the greatest value in and for themselves. They testify to an immense intellectual and spiritual activity, and to a habit of self-government ineffaceable even by the most grinding despotism. Those stories of misery wring the heart, but they tell of so much good in the people, so much patience and strength, that they leave a hope of their future—a future which the now freest people may be glad to share if it brings fruition of the old Russian ideals of fraternity and the community of interests and benefits. Nothing could be more democratic than the Russian *mir;* each village is, as regards its economic affairs, a little indigenous republic, and the imported bureaucracy of the Czars has not yet crushed out its almost instinctive life. No peoples have more in common than the Americans and the Russians in the fine distribution of their autonomy; in fact the Russians are ultimately more democratic than we are; and they are apparently as fond of religious variety. The Frenchman who found us a nation of one gravy and a hundred religions could repeat his experience on as vast a scale among them as to the religions, though as to the gravies, he might not find any sauce more artistic than hunger.

One almost famishes as one reads of the Russian peasantry and their life-long craving for enough to eat, and has, by way of contrast, almost a sense of repletion in reading Mr. Pellew's book. He calls it *In Castle and Cabin; or, Talks in Ireland in* 1887; and this is what it literally is: talks with all kinds of people, gentle and simple, cleric and laic, about the Irish question. It is something more than this in its admirably clear Introduction, by which the reader is historically possessed of the situation, and in the author's careful and conscientious Conclusion, which largely leaves the reader to his own. But the main value of the book is that it affords the materials for judgment concerning the original situation, and the successive efforts to relieve it by legislation, and the strange practical complications resulting from these efforts. The whole business is a muddle of the most timid and conservative precedents and the boldest innovations; and the reader must share the author's misgiving whether home rule will right it all, though he will still feel that home rule ought to come. Mr. Pellew denies the analogy between Canada and Ireland, and affirms the necessity of a much closer union between Ireland and England, with an autonomy in the former much more strictly defined than Mr. Gladstone proposes. He thinks the Irish people will be content with this upon experiment, and after they have learned to trust English good-will as shown to them by acts of imperial administration which would be vigorously denounced as "paternalism" in this country. But with postal telegraphs and postal savings-banks England is already far gone in practical paternalism, and probably Mr. Pellew did not invent the suggestions he makes in that direction. Doubtless he heard them talked up by people opposed to granting full self-government to Ireland. He gives them without arrogance, without insistence, and with the same unprejudiced calm which characterizes his treatment of the position of the clergy, the plan of campaign, the boycott, the evictions, and all the other features of the situation.

We group with these excellent books another which we have read with equal interest, and that is Mr. William Eleroy Curtis's *Capitals of Spanish America*. The matter is very novel, and the author has somehow the art of delighting, a sort of charm like that of an easy talker. To be sure, he has the advantage of being able to astonish us by his account of the republics south of us; and astonishment is a thing which we all like to feel, and which readily attributes merit to the author of it. The book has given us unusual pleasure, and we fancy it could illumine as vast an ignorance as ours in many intelligent people. Till one reads Mr. Curtis one has no idea of the enormous advance in material prosperity which the Spanish American peoples have been making, with all their revolutions and earthquakes. Their republics are in most cases simple tyrannies, and yet the wills of their dictators have brought about a degree of liberty in some respects greater than certain free peoples enjoy. For example, there is one question which the President of Venezuela simplified by a message to his Congress beginning as follows: "I have taken upon myself the responsibility of declaring the Church of Venezuela independent of the Roman episcopate, and I ask that you further order that parish priests be elected by the people, the bishops by the rectors of parishes, and the archbishops by Congress, returning to the usage of the primitive Church founded by Jesus Christ and His apostles." Fancy such a consummation in Canada or—the United States! But Mr. Curtis's book is full of surprises, and even of edifications, for those of us who are able to learn respect for sister, or step-sister, republics almost as strange to us as so many imaginable commonwealths in the planet Mars.

---

[1] Magazine publications of the Henry James short stories referred to by Howells are as follows:
"The Aspern Papers," Atlantic Monthly, 61 (March, April, May, 1888), 296-315, 461-482, 577-594.

"The Liar," Century, 36 (n.s. 14) (May, June, 1888), 123-135, 213-223.

"A London Life," Scribner's Magazine, 3 (June, 1888), 671-688; 4 (July, August, September, 1888), 64-82, 238-249, 319-330.

"Louisa Pallant," Harper's Magazine, 76 (February, 1888), 336-355.

"Two Countries," Harper's Magazine, 77 (June, 1888), 83-116.

[2] Sie war liebenswurdig und er liebte sie. - She was lovable and he loved her.

[3]S. Stepniak is the pseudonym of Sergei Mikhailovich Kravchinski.

November, 1888

Editor's Study.

I.

AS this is a world of varied interests and many events, in which it is improbable that everything said in the Study is perfectly remembered, it may be well to remind the reader that we spoke a year or two ago of the first volume of Professor M. A. Canini's wonderful compendium, *Il Libro dell'Amore*. We then tried to give him some notion of the vast design and prodigious performance, and we have now to acquaint him with the fact that the second and third volumes of the work have been published, and that they are no less than the first worthy of admiration, even of veneration, if one likes to pay divine honors to transcendent learning, skill, and industry. The plan of translating into Italian the typical love poems of all times and languages is tirelessly carried forward with all the integrity and felicity of its inception; and the versions from the hand of the editor are accompanied as before with introductions full of the same *naïve* mingling of erudition and autobiography. There is so much of the latter, in fact, and the editor's trials and disappointments are so frankly confided, that it will hardly seem a violation of decorum to say that this colossal enterprise has been conducted by an old man busy with the duties of a learned professorship on a salary of fifty dollars a month. Here is hard living and high thinking for such as admire it; and there is food for another sentiment in the fact that in a land like ours, abounding in public and private libraries of all sorts, not a single copy has yet been sold of this work unique in literature. Such devotion as its author's is in the tradition of an elder scholarship, and is remote alike in time and in motive from the comfortable and practical endeavor of our day and race.

II.

Our insensibility to it in the fact alleged is nationally so discreditable that we are reluctant to urge another sin of omission upon the repentance of our readers. But it is perhaps a lighter one, and without seeming too reproachful we may quote the letter of a friend who writes to the Study from Stratford-on-Avon. "I have been visiting the Shakespeare Memorial here," he writes, "and noticing with delight the admirable beginning made of a complete Shakespearian library, as well as portrait and picture gallery. The memorial, with its fine theatre and beautiful gardens, only last week completed and open to the public, is really a noble enterprise, and one from which our countrymen are sure to reap constant advantage. When I tell you that notwithstanding all the interest shown in Stratford by Americans, and the appeal made by Minister Phelps in his speech in the Lyceum [1] Theatre in London to American Shakespearian authors and publishers for *American* editions and American Shakespeariana, there actually is shown in the library only three or four short shelves filled with some four or five of the recent complete editions—the Rolfe, Hudson, etc.—with [2,3] almost nothing in the way of separate plays, studies, notices of plays, programmes, etc., etc., you will, I am sure, agree with me in feeling that we in America owe a big debt to Stratford in this respect which we are altogether too indifferent about, especially in view of the bitter facts (to our friends here) that in New York alone there are fourteen copies of the First Folio, and not one in Stratford!

"Now pardon me if in the mingled emotions of American pride and mortification at this state of things I write to you, on the spur of the moment, and ask if there is not some quick, easy, and practicable way of setting the ball rolling in the way of *getting up a complete collection of American Shakespeariana* as a gift from Americans to the Stratford Memorial. It would be a much more significant and valuable gift than even fountains and statues, for this will, or ought ultimately to, become the centre for the study of Shakespeare, and the *library* is the true fountain for lovers of Shakespeare to furnish here."

III.

Our friend speaks with the zeal awakened by the sacred locality; but probably his appeal will not address itself to the same interest in people remote from it. Still, it ought to move at least the authors of unsuccessful essays and commentaries to contribute them to the Stratford Library. If the scheme of it included the unprinted MSS. of Shakespeare scholars, there would be no trouble in filling up those empty shelves till they groaned for another Omar.

The truth is—and from time to time the scribbling race had better face it—there is no very deep, no very wide, interest in even the greatest of authors.

"About the opening of the flower"

there are moments when Shakespeare seems essential to the young life; but he is not really so; and if the elder life will be honest it will own that he is not at all important to it. The proof of this is in the infrequency with which this prince of poets is not merely read but thought of. We single him out, a shining mark, not because we wish to abolish or supersede him —though many will read between these lines the same envious intent that moved us formerly to misbehave toward the fame of Thackeray and Dickens—but because we think it well to recognize the truth of a matter concerning which it is easy and sweet to gammon ourselves. Except the deceitfulness of riches, nothing perhaps is so illusory as the supposition of interest in literature and literary men on the part of other men. They are not altogether to blame for this; they are very little to blame for it, in fact, for it is only in the rarest instances that literature has come home to their business and bosoms. It is an amusement, a distraction, a decoration, taken up for a moment, an hour, a day, and then wholly dropped out of sight, out of mind, out of life. This may be inevitable, and forever inevitable; literature is an art like the rest; and we do not ask people to be vitally concerned about a picture, a statue, an opera, a building; but it sometimes seems as if it ought to be unlike the other arts, since if it would it could speak so frankly, so brotherly, so helpfully, to the mass of men. Heaven knows how it gets bewitched between the warm thought in the brain, the heart, and the cold word on the page; but some evil spell seems to befall it and annul it, to make it merely appreciable to the taste, the æsthetic pride, the intellectuality, of the reader. These are not his real life, and so it presently perishes out of him again, to be utterly forgotten, or recalled for the pleasure of the pleasure it gave, or recurred to in the hope of renewing an irrenewable experience.

IV.

These pessimistic, these corroding, reflections are not intended to have any immediate application, not even to Shake-speare, but to strike a wholesome misgiving into the cultivated person, and if possible to wound the tough vanity of the literary tribe, against which it may have been noticed we have a grudge. They are arrows shot into the air in the hope that they will come down somewhere and hurt somebody. Of course we are sensible of their illogicality in connection with the reproaches we have addressed our public for not buying *Il Libro dell' Amore;* and of course we are sensible that there is an increasing desire, if not effort, on the part of authors to come down to business with their readers, to befriend them, to serve them, as well as to amuse them. This is apparently the case with the author of *Robert Elsmere*, a novel that has won the attention of the English-speaking peoples in a very uncommon measure. It is a woman's book, with something of the perfervid feminine flutter in the emotional passages, but it is a thinking woman's book, and as a literary feat it is notable for its freedom from the prevailing foibles of English fiction; it is a return in manner to George Eliot, and to the same degree it is a return in spirit to Charles Kingsley. But it is not so ponderous nor so pendulous as George Eliot, whose words, sentences, paragraphs, chapters, and books were all apt to be over-lengthy; and it is not so straining and striving as Charles Kingsley; though this is not necessarily saying that it is as great as either, whatever its promise. There is no doubt but it is a very striking performance for a first essay in fiction, and that it has force of heart and mind in it. Briefly, it is the story of a high-natured young clergyman who finds himself one day without faith in the things he is teaching other people to believe, and who is constrained by honor and by honesty to renounce his office. He works back to a "reconception" of Christ through his work among the London poor; and the real tragedy of his life is that his wife, as noble and devoted as he, cannot follow him out of the Church. Here is a strong motive, and it is treated with dignity and truth. Occasionally a character weakens into a type, but for the most part it is men and women we meet, not allegories. The country scenes are affectionately felt, and an appreciable London is studied in novel and amusing aspects as well as to deeper effect. Saints are difficult to deal with in fiction; but Catharine, Robert Elsmere's wife, is a heroine who may be justly said not to get the better of the author. She is perhaps more real than her husband, and not being arrogant in her faith, the reader can thoroughly sympathize with her in ordeals which seem severer than his. After all, with a woman of that sort religion is a more vital matter than with a man of any sort, for with any sort of man it must be more an intellectual matter. In Mrs. Humphry Ward's novel the art is mostly equal to the strain an obvious purpose puts upon art. Without being cluttered, it gives a sense of the fulness of the English world, and it expresses that exaltation of English character which seems wholly compatible with British fussiness. The story abounds in minor characters, some of whom, like Catharine's younger sister Rose, are extremely well imagined. The veteran novel-reader will not always care to know what becomes of them, but he will like them while he is with them; and they will serve to give him the sense of society.

V.

In most American novels, vivid and graphic as the best of them are, the people are segregated if not sequestered, and the scene is sparsely populated. The effect may be in instinctive response to the vacancy of our social life, and we shall not make haste to blame it. There are few places, few occasions among us, in which a novelist can get a large number of polite people together, or at least keep them together. Unless he carries a snap-camera his picture of them has no probability; they affect one like the figures perfunctorily associated in such deadly old engravings as that of "Washington Irving and his Friends." Perhaps it is for this reason that we excel in small pieces with three or four figures, or in studies of rustic communities, where there is propinquity if not society. Our grasp of more urbane life is feeble; most attempts to assemble it in our pictures are failures, possibly because it is too transitory, too intangible in its nature with us, to be truthfully represented as really existent. At any rate, the strong novel with us has as yet dealt little with "society," and in Mrs. Margaret Deland's book, *John Ward, Preacher*, the scene is remote, as usual, from the "centres." Two or three small towns contribute figures enough to fill the stage, and it seems a like election of motives from different periods that supplies the character and action. We say seems, because we emancipated people of the seaboard had better not be too positive concerning the possible facts of faith and conscience among the strongly Calvinized minds of the Scotch-Irish Presbyterians of western Pennsylvania, among whom we suppose the story transacts itself. Helen Ward and her uncle, the rector, are modern folks, and so are all the minor personages, gentle and simple, in more or less graphic ways, but John Ward, the preacher, is a mind of the seventeenth century. This is not saying that there are not probably such survivals into our time, but the scheme loses verisi-

militude through Mrs. Deland's failure to accent Ward as an instance of atavism. He parts with his wife because she cannot believe in the everlasting punishment of sinners in the hell which seems to his darkened soul an essential to her salvation, and he breaks her heart and kills himself in this effort to reconcile her to his God. Suppose the case, and you accept with interest and sympathy the passages of life and character which follow from it. Some of these are of real power, and nearly all are of artistic merit. The people are not strongly localized; the cultivated have little to distinguish them from the ordinary educated New-Englanders of fiction; but the commoner sort have their own accent and complexion; they are treated with humor and humane tenderness; and Dr. Howe, the rector, is well managed. John Ward is got out upon the canvas mainly with the artist's help; he doesn't develop himself, and finally one asks one's self if the author has not asked too much in asking one to suppose the case. Still, we do not deny its possibility; it strikes us like one of those things that fascinate the author because they have really happened. There is want of unity, of coherence, in the book; but it is nevertheless an impressive book, and when it comes to dealing at close quarters with the impassioned and the grotesque, it is a greater book than *Robert Elsmere*. Mrs. Deland shows herself in it the poet we already knew her, and she reveals herself a humorist of a fine and high sort.

VI.

Humor at its best is indeed a kind of poetry, and we wish we could say that the reverse was true. But unhappily all poets are not humorists, though at first blush the author of a *Book of Day-Dreams* might seem a little ironical in offering to our hurried public a hundred sonnets upon the relations of the day-dreamer to his own soul. We do not say the public might not do very well to stop and listen to him, if the business upon which it is so eagerly bent is mainly the gambler's chance of each turning the luck of some one else to himself, by fair means if one may, and foul if one must: but that the public will not and cannot. The Study itself, whose affair it is to listen, has not quite had the patience to gather up Mr. Charles Leonard Moore's whole meaning from these hundred sonnets, but it has had a great deal of pleasure from several of them, and is aware of having had a real poet for its guest in the author of his delicately imaginative verse. Some proof of the fact may be offered to the reader in the first of the sonnets:

"Naked December I have curtained out,
  Its cobweb branches crossing the cold sky;

Dead am I to the hurrying flakes about,
  Dead and close-tombed in Eastern luxury.
But not the fire's rich rapture with itself,
  The carpet's glow, the painted air above,
The gleam of rich-clad volumes from the shelf,
  The stained chessmen or yon shadowy glove,
The mantel's romance of bronze-mailèd knights,
  The sometime showing frescoed pastoral,
The curtains closing me with these delights,
  Deep, deep, unfathomably out of call—
Not these, but dreams and reveries allowed,
Make me o'er all Time's empty triumphs proud."

And again in these, which, wanting the color of the first, have a farther reach and a more subtle suggestion:

"The action of the most heroic deed
  Is scarce distinguishable from a palsy fit;
Man in Life's stream is like a shaken reed,
  Silent for all the river's mouthing it;
Nothing does he reveal and nothing keep
  (Ranked ghost-like beckoner to the crinkling
      sedge)
Of the stream's purpose, flowing strong and deep
  Past his vague motions in its lapping edge.
I hear the foreign echoes from the street—
  Faint sounds of revel, traffic, conflict keen—
And think that man's reiterated feet
  Have gone such ways since e'er the world has
      been.
I wonder how each oft-used tone and glance
Retains its might and old significance."

"Soon is the echo and the shadow o'er,
  Soon, soon we lie with lid-encumbered eyes,
And the great fabrics that we reared before
  Crumble to make a dust to hide who dies.

Gone, and the empty and unstatued air
  Keeps not the mould or gesture of our limbs,
But with investiture and garb as fair
  Folds the next shape that to its circle swims.
Fools, so to paint our pageant grave with deeds,
  And make division with the elements.
Earth yields us splendid mansions for our needs,
  And only takes our lives to pay the rents.
Ah, but our dreams! Beyond earth's count they rise
In sage and hourly eternities."

We call this poetry, and whoever Mr. Moore may be now, we cannot believe that he is destined to be less hereafter. We commend the whole group of his sonnets to those large-leisured friends whom the Study likes to fancy present when it is doing its poor honors to a new poet.

We praise also that pretty book of Mrs. Rose Hawthorne Lathrop's, in which we find some things so distinctly good that we are willing to take her warrant for some others which we do not quite follow in all her intention. *Along the Shore*, she calls it, and in the first poem she strikes the note of impassioned pensiveness which imparts its character to nearly all the pieces in the book. Purely feminine the voice is, with an appealing, haunting quality that lingers, and that thrills to heart-break in such a piece as this:

FRANCIE.

"I loved a child as we should love
  Each other everywhere;
I cared more for his happiness
  Than I dreaded my own despair.

"An angel asked me to give him
  My whole heart's dearest cost;
And in adding mine to his treasures
  I knew they would never be lost.

"To his heart I gave the gold,
  Though little my own had known;
To his eyes what tenderness
  From youth in mine had grown.

"I gave him all my buoyant
  Hope for my future years;
I gave him whatever melody
  My voice had steeped in tears.

"Upon the shore of darkness
  His drifted body lies.
He is dead, and I stand beside him,
  With his beauty in my eyes.

"I am like those withered petals
  We see on a winter day
That gladly gave their color
  In the happy summer away.

"I am glad I lavished my worthiest
  To fashion his greater worth;
Since he will live in heaven,
  I shall lie content in the earth."

While we are about this work of distributing a month's immortality, we should be false to our office if we withheld it from William Ernest Henley, whose *Book of Verses* we have read with a grateful sense of his purpose to stand face to face with the painful facts of life, and read their poetry. His is the soul that finds nothing offensive in the miseries that are common to all men; nothing too shocking for all men to know if some men have to suffer it. Half the little book is called "In Hospital," and we will ask the reader to look with us at one of its passages, which, if he is the reader we take him to be, he will not shrink from because every day some brother must endure the reality.

CLINICAL.

"Hist?....
  Through the corridor's echoes
  Louder and nearer
  Comes a great shuffling of feet.
  Quick, every one of you,
  Straighten your quilts and be decent!
  Here's the Professor.

"In he comes first,
  With the bright look we know,
  From the broad white brows the kind eyes
  Soothing yet nerving you. Here, at his elbow,
  White-capped, white-aproned, the Nurse,
  Towel on arm, and her inkstand
  Fretful with quills.
  Here, in the ruck, anyhow,
  Surging along,
  Louts, duffers, exquisites, students, and prigs—
  Whiskers and foreheads, scarf-pins and spec-
      tacles—
  Hustle the class. And they ring themselves
  Round the first bed, where the Chief
  (His dressers and clerks at attention)
  Bends in inspection already.

"So shows the ring,
  Seen from behind, round a conjurer
  Doing his pitch in the street.
  High shoulders, low shoulders, broad shoulders,
      narrow ones,
  Round, square, and angular, serry and shove;
  While from within a voice,
  Gravely and weightily fluent,
  Sounds and then ceases; and suddenly
  (Look at the stress of the shoulders)
  Out of a quiver of silence,
  Over the hiss of the spray,
  Comes a low cry, and the sound
  Of breath intaken through teeth

Clinched in resolve. And the Master
Breaks from the crowd, and goes,
Wiping his hands,
To the next bed, with his pupils
Flocking and whispering behind him.

"Now one can see!
Case Number One
Sits (rather pale) with his bedclothes
Stripped up and showing his foot
(Alas for God's image!)
Swaddled in wet white lint
Brilliantly hideous with red."

From this to Mr. Moore's luxury of

day-dreaming it is a far cry. We do not know just what a far cry is, but Mr. Henley is an Englishman, and though we suppose not a fox-hunting one, he will know. The important thing, however, is that these antipodal talents are both very poets, and have the same claim through the same divine art—the art of John Keats, the art of Walt Whitman—to the world's attentive regard.

---

[1] "Minister Phelps" refers to Edward John Phelps, United States ambassador to Great Britain from 1885 to 1889.

[2] William Shakespeare, Shakespeare's Works, William James Rolfe, ed. (New York: Harper & Brothers, 1884).

[3] William Shakespeare, The Complete Works of William Shakespeare, Henry Norman Hudson, ed. (Boston: Ginn & Heath, 1880-81).

[4] Omar (c581-644), second Caliph of Islam, created its administrative system.

[5] Criticism and Fiction, pp. 130-131.

December, 1888

Editor's Study.

I.

IN the good old times, which are not so very remote chronologically, the heart oppressed by sympathy for want easily unburdened itself at the Christmas season in the elementary benevolence of gifts and alms; or if it was a literary heart it found the same comfort in prompting others to gifts and alms by kindly poems, by perfervent essays, and by tales, little or long, celebrating the bestowal of turkeys upon the turkeyless and geese upon the gooseless. Such remembrances of the destitute were preferably conveyed in hampers, with orders for coal, and in extreme cases with the accompaniment of nourishing wines. Pale, wistful little girls had much to do with them in giving and receiving, and apple-cheeked, chubby old gentlemen prevailed in the transaction; the reformation of deplorable habits and the amelioration of sordid and avaricious characters often followed; and inferably the wrong old world was set right, and went on its way afterward without wabbling. To be exact, matters happened in real life very much as they still do in comfortable comedies on the stage; or at least this is what was implied in the Christmas literature of that period of *Fifty Years Ago* which Mr. Walter Besant studies so delightfully in his book of the same name. A gentle superstition seems to have arisen to console the race for the formidable phase which the dismal science of political economy was then beginning to assume. It seemed destined at that moment to quit the cells of philosophy, and to descend upon the wings of Miss Martineau's allegories among the hovels of poverty, with the law of demand and supply under its arm, and a hamper full of stones admirably fashioned to resemble loaves, in response to the cry for bread which arose from those hapless homes. Something had to be done; the Muse bestirred herself, and produced the kind of Christmas literature which has appeased well-to-do people-of-heart for half a century. She need not really have been in so great anxiety; political economy exists, like other sciences, to learn from time to time that it is mistaken. It has come to recognize that circumstances alter cases; that conditions affect and annul infallible laws; that the supply often creates the demand; that the fact that two and two make four cannot be the last effect of mathematics. An unknown quantity lies beyond it still, and what if this lay behind it rather than before it?

II.

There seems arising in these times a new Christmas literature which boldly affirms that it lies behind, that science has ignored something, has left something out of the account, and that the forgotten factor is Christ himself. The new Christmas literature is not specifically adapted to the Christmas season; it is not expressed any more in kindly poems, perfervent essays, or tales, little or long, alone, but in books that have meaning for the whole year and for every moment of life, but that may be most profitably read and pondered now, when all the associations of the time ought to remind us of the Man who came to bring peace and good-will to men. The new Christmas literature does not necessarily deck itself with sprigs of holly, and bathe itself in pools of burning brandy on platters borne by the tinsel-crowned, bottle-nosed genius of the feast to the board smoking with bowls of wassail, while the upper servants carouse in their hall, and the scullions carry out the fragments of the second table to the dogs and the poor. But it remembers that the Son of Man came eating and drinking, and it does not frown upon honest revelry and innocent mirth, though it entreats each and every of us first to love his neighbor as himself, and to be mindful of him not only now, but throughout the year. Oddly enough, after a period of scientific exaltation, in which it seemed as if man might really live by the nebular hypothesis alone if he could but have a little help from the missing link, the new Christmas literature denies that there is anything of life everlasting in these things, and it reverts openly to the New Testament as the sole source of hope and comfort.

III.

The New Testament, in fact, is the direct inspiration of the new Christmas literature, as it was of the old, but in a far wider, higher, and more luminous sense, with implications infinitely more significant. This literature does not mock at gifts and alms for the holiday season or any other, but it warns us that they are provisional merely, expediential, temporary, and that the practice of charity in this form is not—inconsistent with the hardest selfishness. It appeals to no sentimental impulse, but confronts its readers with themselves, and with the problem which it grows less and less easy to shirk. Turkeys to the turkeyless, with celery and cranberries galore, and nourishing wines for the sick—yes, these are well, and very well; but ineffably better it is to take thought somehow in our social, our political, system to prevent some future year, decade, century, the destitution which we now relieve. This is what the new Christmas literature says to us, beginning with Lyof Tolstoï, that voice of one crying in the wilderness. The whole of his testimony is against the system by which a few men win wealth and miserably waste it in idleness and luxury, and the vast mass of men are overworked and underfed. From the volume called *What to Do*, dealing with the poor of Moscow, to the latest utterance from his seclusion—which he calls *Life*, and in which he rises to the question of how a man shall save his soul—he bears perpetual witness against the life that Christendom is now living—the life that seeks the phantom of personal happiness, and ignores the fact that there is and can be no happiness but in the sacrifice of self for others. Whatever we may say of his example, we cannot deny that his influence is increasingly vast, and that multitudes hear him who will never follow him to the work of the fields. His audience is, rather oddly, made up as yet chiefly of cultivated people, who have been surprised into the attitude of listening by the spectacle of a man noble, rich, brilliant, like Tolstoï, renouncing their world as of no worth. They hear him with heartache and trouble of mind, and many think it is a new prophet come to rebuke them; but Tolstoï himself constantly reminds them that it is Christ who has spoken the truth he tells, and bids them hear *Him*.

Christ and the life of Christ is at this moment inspiring the literature of the world as never before, and raising it up a witness against waste and want and war. It may confess Him, as in Tolstoï's work it does, or it may deny Him, but it cannot exclude Him: and in the degree that it ignores His spirit, modern literature is artistically inferior. In other words, all good literature is now Christmas literature. The old heathenish axiom of art for art's sake is as dead as great Pan himself, and the best art now tends to be art for humanity's sake. It does this sometimes unconsciously, and would be defiant of the supposition that it was working with an ethical purpose; but there is nothing so sanative as truth, and the literature that shows human nature as human wilfulness and error have made it is fulfilling a "mission" to men's souls, in spite of all theories and professions to the contrary. Yet the interesting and consoling fact about so many masters of our time is that they *are* conscious of a duty to man in their work, and they do it with a sense that it does not begin and end in themselves; that even art does not compass it all, and that to amuse or thrill their readers is no longer enough.

IV.

Art, indeed, is beginning to find out that if it does not make friends with Need it must perish. It perceives that to take itself from the many and leave them no joy in their work, and to give itself to the few whom it can bring no joy in their idleness, is an error that kills. This has long been the burden of Ruskin's message; and if we can believe William Morris, the common people have heard him gladly, and have felt the truth of what he says. "They see the prophet in him rather than the fantastic rhetorician, as more superfine audiences do;" and the men and women who do the hard work of the world have learned from him and from Morris that they have a right to pleasure in their toil, and that when justice is done them they will have it. In all ages poetry has affirmed something of this sort, but it remained for ours to perceive it and express it somehow in every form of literature. But this is only one phase of the devotion of the best literature of our time to the service of humanity. No book written with a low or cynical motive could succeed now, no matter how brilliantly written; and the work done in the past to the glorification of mere passion and power, to the deification of self, appears monstrous and hideous. The romantic spirit worshipped genius, worshipped heroism, but at its best, in such a man as Victor Hugo, this spirit recognized the supreme claim of the lowest humanity. Its error was to idealize the victims of society, to paint them impossibly virtuous and beautiful; but truth, which has succeeded to the highest mission of romance, paints these victims as they are, and bids the world consider them not because they are beautiful and virtuous, but because they are ugly and vicious, cruel, filthy, and only not altogether loathsome because the divine can never wholly die out of the human. The truth does not find these victims among the poor alone, among the hungry, the houseless, the ragged; but it also finds them among the rich, cursed with the aimlessness, the satiety, the despair of wealth, wasting their lives in a fool's paradise of shows and semblances, with nothing real but the misery that comes of insincerity and selfishness. ⌐[2]

V.

We need not remind the reader of the Study how little it cares for literature except as the language of life; and how always it is the Study's aim to include all accents rather than to exclude any. For this reason it does not find its Christmas literature in the master-works of modern thought alone, but in all expressions, the crudest and hastiest, which have tended at any time during the year to make one think less of one's self and more of others. It recalls a series of papers in a New York journal on the treatment of women servants in hotels which would be very good Christmas reading, and another series in a Chicago journal about the hardships of sewing-girls, which were full of matter appropriate to the holiday season. Some letters descriptive of life in the Pennsylvania coal mines which it remembers to have seen were equally calculated to call misery and hopeless poverty to mind at a time sacred to the gentler emotions. These sorrowful stories of wrong were all pregnant with the suggestion that turkeys and cranberries cannot by the utmost stretch of charity be sent to all the famine in the world, and that if they could, still one good dinner would not be enough for a whole year. A little candle on a Christmas tree may send its beams afar, but one good deed cannot penetrate all the darkness of the naughty world. Let us light the pretty tapers, and as many of them as possible, and let us do all the good deeds we can; but let us not forget the lesson of the new Christmas literature; let us realize that they are merely palliatives, and that infinitely deeper than their soothing can reach festers the plague that luxury and poverty, that waste and want, have bred together in the life-blood of society. Let us remember this, and take thought for its healing.

[1] Harriet Martineau.

[2] Criticism and Fiction, pp. 184-186.

January, 1889

Editor's Study.

I.

SUCH a book as *Face to Face with the Mexicans*, by Mrs. Fanny Chambers Gooch, has a value that only a quick, intelligent, sympathetic woman could give her study of a foreign people's life. Mrs. Gooch was seven years in Mexico, and made journeys and protracted sojourns in so many parts of the country that she may be said to have seen and known at least much that was best worth seeing and knowing in it. Her fullest observation relates to her experiences in the characteristic provincial city of Saltillo and in the metropolis; but with the key which her long residence in these places supplied she unlocks the door everywhere to our intimate acquaintance with neighbors whom we cannot afford to ignore. Her view is not only domestic and social—though it is largely that, thanks to her struggles with Mexican house-keeping and her hospitable acceptance among all classes—but she sketches the leading events and persons of Mexican history, she glances at the contemporary literature and art, she gives some notion of the folk-lore and folk-song, and she offers an instructive glimpse of the material conditions, of the politics and the religion, of the country. There is nothing absolute or final in her philosophy of the facts; but she is very candid, and her attitude toward the Mexicans is that of generous appreciation rather than censure, which, upon the whole, seems the best attitude one can take toward a strange civilization. If you begin by contemning it, you get no good even from the good in it, which is perhaps the reason why so few Englishmen have been improved in taste or temper by their visits to these States. But Mrs. Gooch began by being amused and pleased with Mexico; she was able to take the humorous view of the anomalies that presented themselves, and to console herself with their picturesqueness when their perplexity threatened to become unendurable. If she ended by accepting the customs of the country as pretty well adapted to the people who invented them, she reached a conclusion to which most of her readers will follow her.

II.

In fact a hardy spirit here and there may push beyond it, and ask what real advantage it will be to the Mexicans when we have got our civilization all sent down there by the daily express trains which we are running into their country. It is by no means a perfect civilization as we see it at home, and if it were not ours perhaps we should not like it very well ourselves in all respects. The dazzling hope of being one of the foremost, which every American cherishes, has hitherto blinded us to the fact that it abandons the hindmost to the fate attending the rear-guard of other civilizations; but the time has already come when this hope no longer wholly avails. Some observers of our national free fight have discovered of late that not all the combatants are on top; they notice with grave misgiving that a considerable number are apparently ground into the mire, and that there seem to be a great many broken bones brought away from the rush and scramble even by such as escape from it with its prizes. In its basis it does not differ from the civilization which the Mexicans have now; it is a question of quantity rather than kind, and it is for the Mexicans to say whether they will have more or less. The theory of our patriotic pride is that if they will have more they will become a rich and prosperous nation like ourselves, that they will develop their natural resources, and foster their unnatural ones. We do not stop to consider that the people who do the hard work of a nation, who really earn its living, seem by no means comfortable and happy in proportion to the national riches and prosperity; and it is doubtful whether we should be improving the condition of the Mexican masses by introducing the American trust, pool, combine, corner, and strike among them. We have built them some railroads with our capital; but should we be really befriending them if we succeeded in bestowing upon them the moral and financial chaos that we call our railroad system? Perhaps we do not make it any part of our business to pause for such inquiries; but here the Mexican's temperament favors his defence against our impatience. In his make-up to-morrow plays a much larger part than to-day; and if he accepts Americanism at all, it will be after long delay, not to say due reflection. In his poor way, however, he does seem to make his reflections; and he counts our hurry, our bluntness, our general gracelessness, against our civilization. The Mexicans, if we are to believe Mrs. Gooch, are, from highest to lowest, almost conscientiously well-mannered; to be sweetly polite, and to take time for being so, is what their children are taught from the first moments of intelligence; and she draws many charming pictures of the loving, courteous, devoted family life of which this is the ideal and the expression. Probably not more real good-heartedness is embodied in it than in our ruder ways; but, on the other hand, there is probably not less; and the Mexicans are so fixed in their belief that we are the worse for our lack of it that they like almost any other people better. The first care of a shrewd European is to guard against the chance of being taken for an American, if he desires even business success in Mexico; and in society Americans are apparently received only upon proof of their fitness, the burden of which rests with them. Once accepted, however, Mrs. Gooch would persuade us that they experience in the friendships they form a constancy known only to the romance of youth among ourselves, and this in spite of the historic grudge which the Mexicans as a people have against us. Their monuments, their memories, their literature even to their school-books, bear witness that we once did them a great wrong in the interest of the greatest wrong: that to perpetuate slavery we otherwise causelessly attacked them, and in a shameful war robbed them of provinces to which we had no more claim than any bully to the property of his neighbor.

III.

Mrs. Gooch does not paint all Mexican life rose-color. What splendor it has, and what opulence, it owes, as life everywhere owes its splendor and opulence, largely to the hopeless poverty of those that dig in fields and delve in mines and toil in mills, that hew the wood and draw the water. The system of peonage still exists, and the employer lawfully owns the 'employé he can keep in his debt. The political disturbances have abated and the economical disturbances have not yet begun, but only because labor is sunk in a deeper ignorance of its right to the pursuit of happiness than with some other nations, and they are sure to come. In the mean time there is wide-spread want, only not so grim as in the North,

because nature in that gentler climate forbids the worst of winter and famine. There is much good-will among the cultivated people toward modern ideas, there is religious toleration, and there is in large degree free education.

"The steam-ship and the railway and the thoughts that shake mankind"

are already the property of the Mexicans, who are only less shaken by them than we are because they do not think that sort of agitation good form. They have their passionate outbreaks, however, and in the nice conduct of a bull-fight they are even mortally exigent. They have adopted from us the horse-cars, which Latin people everywhere accept and cherish with a devotion unexcelled in Cambridge, Massachusetts; and the cities of Mexico are not less tramwayed than those of Italy.

But immutable under these superficial changes lie the immemorial customs of the country, from which there seems no appeal, so that *No es costumbre* is final against all suggestions of novelty. Mrs. Gooch is very amusing about it, but she does not allow the recollection of her sufferings from this inflexibility to render her insensible to the native sweetness and good-breeding which characterize the observance of the most inexorable *costumbres*. We get from her book, upon the whole, the impression that if civilized life ever ceases to be a battle and a game of chance, the Mexicans have qualities which will fit them to adorn it at least as much as ourselves.

IV.

Probably they have not much liberty and not much notion of it; we have rather more notion of liberty than liberty ourselves; and of equality they appear to have no conception. The division of classes is as sharp and deep as in Europe; and it would not be safe to argue from the exceptional success of an exceptional Aztec like Juarez, a parity of conditions and opportunities for the different races. It is the Spanish race, with its various grades, which gives the written and unwritten law to Mexico; though these have not prevailed to the extermination of the natives after our fashion. Nearly four millions in Mexico still speak their ancient tongues; but for the precise figures concerning them, and for many points which we have touched at second hand from the entertaining work of Mrs. Gooch —it is probably not so exact as it is graphic—the reader had better go to *The Mexican Guide* of Mr. Thomas A. Janvier. Not that we mean to confine him to the statistical side of that excellent little book; Mr. Janvier, whose agreeable quality has been abundantly shown elsewhere, is not able to deny a literary value to his performance where another might easily have done so. It seems sufficiently business-like in the matters with which a guide-book professionally deals; but we have not so much employed it in our stay-at-home travels for the choice of routes, hotels, restaurants, and the like, as for the supplementary light which it throws upon the fields of general interest traversed by Mrs. Gooch's narrative. It may be said that Mr. Janvier has a better perspective, and that the facts he gives have a juster historic proportion. For instance, he is able to give to the greatest fact of religious reform among our neighbors the proper interest, and to tell us that "the Church of Jesus in Mexico," with its Protestant bishop from the United States, was not an effect of our missions, but of a movement originating among native Roman Catholics, who wished to conform their worship to the ancient Mozarabic rite prevailing in Spain before the papal ascendency, and never wholly extinct, at least in Toledo, where it is still in use in three churches. A feeling for the picturesque and dramatic in his facts is tempered by an unfailing intelligence and by a wide knowledge of the situation; and what he has to say in the passages (always too brief) concerning the politics, literature, and religion of the country is said with authority as well as with taste and discrimination.

V.

His guide, and Mrs. Gooch's book, with Mr. W. H. Bishop's earlier volume of delightful papers on *Old Mexico*, and the chapters of his *Spanish American Republics* which Mr. W. E. Curtis gives to that country, ought efficiently to equip the Northern American who visits the antique land of the Aztecs either in fireside reverie or by Raymond excursion. They are all good in their way, and very good in its way is another book of travel, or of sojourn, which we have been reading. We mean *The Land Beyond the Forest*, as Transylvania interprets itself on the title-page of Mrs. E. Laszowska-Gerard's studies among the Saxons and Roumanians. She is an English woman whose Continental marriage and busy life beyond her own island have widened her horizons, and one accepts the kindness she shows the Roumanians and the dislike she feels for the Saxons as an effect of impartiality, if not perfect justice. The Saxons, whom the Hungarians invited into their eastern borders in the twelfth century, have all the unlovely virtues of thrift, caution, and economy, with some of the facilities of a less parsimonious civilization. Among them,

"the rude Carpathian boor
Against the houseless stranger shuts the door"

still, as in Goldsmith's time; and with an uncouthness of manner worthy of us at our worst they unite a practical ease of divorce unexcelled among us. In fact in one of their towns hardly more than the fabled twenty minutes for divorces which trains stopped for in Chicago are required of the anxious strangers who resort to its tribunals. But it ought to be added that in Klausenburg the ideas of the Unitarian Hungarians have prevailed to this extreme effect, though the Lutheran Saxons, if not so hospitable to aliens, are almost as kind to their own ill-matched couples. As formerly in Indiana, a girl marries in Saxon Transylvania with the mental reservation that, if she does not like the man, she can leave him; and parents who have succeeded in living together long enough to bring up a family instil this thought into their children. The Roumanians, on the other hand, who have inherited from the Eastern Empire the superstition that they are the ancient Romans, together with the Greek rite, have no divorce; but they have a great deal else which one may not talk of so freely. They also have charming manners, well adapted to win full justice from the foreigner who loves pretty ways and histrionic costumes. Mrs. Gerard gives us reasons for thinking that they have a national future, and facts for recognizing that they have a benighted and mostly squalid present, the result of a cruel past. Her studies of their folk-lore in all its kinds are most interesting, which is true of whatever she has to tell in the same sort of the Saxons; and they are done from a vantage-ground of comparative knowledge wanting in Mrs. Gooch's like chapters on the Mexicans. You have to supply this in her case, together with some Spanish grammar. To be sure, we must take Mrs. Gerard's Roumanian on trust. But both of these ladies have an abundance of very agreeable humor, which enables them to be tolerant, and gives a charm to their intelligence. Mrs. Gooch's account of her house-keeping in Saltillo, and her diversified experiences with the Mexican *mozo*, or man-of-all-work, and Mrs. Gerard's sketch of official society in Hermannstadt, where there were no young people, and the middle-aged husbands and wives spent their leisure in perfunctory flirtation, are alike delightful. All cannot hope to enjoy the advantages of Mrs. Gerard's intimate point of view, but we think her book is destined to open the countries of which she writes to the travel which has exhausted the color of southern Europe. They are lands of feudal romance and a classic tradition almost unexploited in modern experience.

Her amiable study brings vividly into the field of vision regions hitherto lost, and enriches the reader with an appreciable sense of conditions and aspects altogether novel.

VI.

This is one of the best offices of that curiously effective little book, *The Story of an African Farm*, which we have at last in an American edition. In tone and in treatment there is much in it to recall *The Story of a Country Town*. There is the same simple fidelity to conditions, and the same result in acquainting the reader with types of local life rather than with characters. Both books have an extraordinary pathos, the tragic elements prevail in both, and in both the authors are carried beyond self-control and beyond reality by the sufferings of their fictitious personages. For this reason what artistic virtue they have is in the management of the subordinate figures, and on the middle ground between a Teutonic vagueness of idealization and an English grossness of caricature, between Jean Paul Richter and Charles Dickens.

We try to touch their weak points without denying their strength. Elsewhere we have already had our say in praise of Mr. Howe's story, and now we [2] wish to own the singular charm we have in Miss Olive Schreiner's. She can be no longer known to the literary world as Ralph Iron, and her real name, with its implications of race qualities, is useful in any estimate or analysis of her book. Here is a flavor, here is a color, new in English, and very different from those of the contemporary English story-makers;

something that suggests a talent akin at its best to that of Björnstjerne Björnson, and that of Berthold Auerbach. It is more German than Norse, however, and it is curiously influenced by the colonial English conditions in which it has found expression at its worst. Its directness in touching facts and phases of South African life in a landscape as strange as they, with no apparent consciousness of their strangeness, is like the great Scandinavian's habit in his beautiful stories; but the sentiment is German, while the literosity in the poorer passages of the work is second-rate English. It is right to say that these passages are not so frequent as in any just sense to characterize the book. On the contrary, it makes a most distinct impression of originality and authenticity; and its courageous thinking in directions where most thinking is timid leaves the reader tingling with interesting question, and with the wish to have more of Olive Schreiner in fiction. What she has already done is to give us a conception of European life in a region so remote from ordinary European experience as to be without any but the vaguest associations. For the time being she naturalizes us to the Southern sky and the distant land among the Boers, the Kaffir serfs, the English emigrants, and adventurers; and we do not find the business of raising ostriches much odder than poultry farming. In the scenery which she paints, with its few monotonous features, even the vegetation assumes familiarity; and we reconcile ourselves to sympathy with the heroine's pretty reasonless anguish as a due effect of the prevailing magic, and suffer with her almost as much as the author intends.

---

[1] "No es costumbre." - It is not customary.

[2] For Howells' review of Howe's Story of a Country Town, see "Two Notable Novels," Century, 38 (n.s. 16) (August, 1884), 632-634.

February, 1889

Editor's Study.

I.

MR. WALT WHITMAN calls his latest book *November Boughs*, and in more ways than one it testifies and it appeals beyond the letter to the reader's interest. For the poet the long fight is over; he rests his cause with what he has done; and we think no one now would like to consider the result without respect, without deference, even if one cannot approach it with entire submission. It is time, certainly, while such a poet is still with us, to own that his literary intention was as generous as his spirit was bold, and that if he has not accomplished all he intended, he has been a force that is by no means spent. Apart from the social import of his first book ("without yielding an inch, the working-man and working-woman were to be in my pages from first to last"), he aimed in it at the emancipation of poetry from what he felt to be the trammels of rhyme and metre. He did not achieve this; but he produced a new kind in literature, which we may or may not allow to be poetry, but which we cannot deny is something eloquent, suggestive, moving, with a lawless, formless beauty of its own. He dealt literary conventionality one of those blows which eventually show as internal injuries, whatever the immediate effect seems to be. He made it possible for poetry hereafter to be more direct and natural than hitherto; the hearing which he has braved nearly half a century of contumely and mockery to win would now be granted on very different terms to a man of his greatness. This is always the way; and it is always the way that the reformer (perhaps in helpless confession of the weakness he shares with all humankind) champions some error which seems as dear to him as the truth he was born to proclaim. Walt Whitman was not the first to observe that we are all naked under our clothes, but he was one of the greatest, if not the first, to preach a gospel of nudity; not as one of his Quaker ancestry might have done for a witness against the spiritual nakedness of his hearers, but in celebration of the five senses and their equal origin with the three virtues of which the greatest is charity. His offence, if rank, is quantitatively small; a few lines at most; and it is one which the judicious pencil of the editor will some day remove for him, though for the present he "takes occasion to confirm those lines with the settled convictions and deliberate renewals of thirty years." We hope for that day, not only because it will give to all a kind in poetry which none can afford to ignore, and which his cherished lines bar to most of those who read most in our time and country, but because we think the five senses do not need any celebration. In that duality which every thoughtful person must have noticed composes him, we believe the universal experience is that the beast half from first to last is fully able to take care of itself. But it is a vast subject, and, as the poet says, "it does not stand by itself; the vitality of it is altogether in its relations, bearings, significance." In the mean while we can assure the reader that these *November Boughs* are as innocent as so many sprays of apple blossom, and that he may take the book home without misgiving.

We think he will find in reading it that the prose passages are, some of them, more poetic than the most poetic of the rhythmical passages. "Some War Memoranda," and "The Last of the War Cases"—notes made twenty-five years ago —are alive with a simple pathos and instinct with a love of truth which recall the best new Russian work, and which make the poet's psalms seem vague and thin as wandering smoke in comparison. Yet these have the beauty of undulant, sinuous, desultory smoke forms, and they sometimes take the light with a response of such color as dwells in autumn sunsets. The book is well named *November Boughs*: it is meditative and reminiscent, with a sober fragrance in it like the scent of fallen leaves in woods where the leaves that still linger overhead,

"Or few, or none, do shake against the cold — Bare ruined choirs where late the sweet birds sang."

It is the hymn of the runner resting after the race, and much the same as he chants always, whether the race has been lost or won.

II.

"To get the final lilt of songs;
To penetrate the inmost lore of poets ; to know
  the mighty ones—
Job, Homer, Æschylus, Dante, Shakespeare, Tennyson, Emerson;
To diagnose the shifting, delicate tints of love
  and pride and doubt; to truly understand,
To encompass these, the last keen faculty and
  entrance price,
Old age, and what it brings from all its past
  experiences"—

this is now the "good gray poet's" aspiration, and he throws it "out at the object,"
as Matthew Arnold says, with the syntac-
tical incompleteness of a sigh. It is the
mood and the manner of several other
lyrical passages in the book, and is more
important only because it bears incidentally upon the question lately asked by
Mr. Edmund Gosse, "Has America produced a poet?" Mr. Gosse says he asks it [1]
rather in compliance with an editorial
wish than from his own impulse, and certainly he asks it with all the grace and
gentleness inseparable from his literature.
In answering it negatively he confines
himself to poets no longer alive, and so no
longer susceptible to hurts of pride or
vanity. At the same time he intimates
that if it were a question of living poets it
could not be a question at all; or, if he
does not intimate this, he leaves the living
poets to infer it from the kindness of the
terms he uses toward them. He names
Chaucer, Spenser, Shakespeare, Milton,
Dryden, Pope, Gray, Burns, Wordsworth,
Coleridge, Byron, Shelley, and Keats as
the British worthiest; and he asks, "What
dead American is worthy to join the twelve,
and make an Anglo-Saxon's baker's
dozen?" He thinks none, and he gives
his reasons: perfectly good reasons for
those who are already of his opinion;
charming reasons for all; courteous reasons, respectful, even reverential reasons,
but carrying conviction to no contrary
mind. This is in the nature of things;
for as no one can say what poetry is, so no
one can say who is a poet. One may quite
easily defy Mr. Gosse to say what touch
in all Dryden thrills and lifts like many
touches in Emerson. One may challenge
him to prove the art of Pope finer than the
art of Longfellow, or bid him show where
and how Burns is better than Bryant. But
at the end of the ends the case is what it
was: he remains as unpersuaded as you
do. Still, as true Americans, and as the
most provincial people on the planet in
certain respects, we could not leave the
case as it was. One of the literary newspapers invited a symposium of American
authors to sit upon Mr. Gosse and his
reasons, and they all, or nearly all, declared that Emerson was worthy to be the
baker's-dozenth; there might be doubts
about Longfellow, or there might be
doubts about Bryant, but there could not

be any doubt about Emerson. The verdict was interesting as a proof that Emerson holds the first place in the critical esteem of those among us best fitted to judge
him; but it seems odd that at a feast
where there were so many living poets
(whose worthiness Mr. Gosse refused to
question) none was found ready to sacrifice
either his brother or himself, and so provide an immortal thirteenth on the spot.

Though why Mr. Gosse should have demanded a thirteenth of us, when he had
already counted up that number of undying fames, or why he should always
speak of his thirteen British worthiest
as twelve, we cannot understand, unless
he is in the habit of finding but nine fingers on his pair of hands. This might
well happen in Ireland, where the reck-
oner would begin by saying, "The two
thumbs is one," but not in the more logical isle. The only explanation is that
Mr. Gosse is himself too much of a poet
to be a great mathematician. But even
if Edward's one, and Elizabeth's two,
and Charles's two, and great Anna's one,
and the Georges seven made twelve, and [2]
not thirteen, as they certainly appear to do,
still, if we added another, we should have
that concern which none of us can escape
in sitting down thirteen at table. Why
should Mr. Gosse desire that thirteenth of
us? If we supplied it, what dire thing
equivalent to death might not happen in
the fields of asphodel? One shrinks from
conjecturing. One takes refuge in simple
addition, and insists that there would be
fourteen if we supplied the thirteenth.
Still there seems a risk, and we should
not be willing to convince Mr. Gosse with
Emerson, chosen by universal suffrage to
represent us among the immortals; for
perhaps seven and six do make twelve,
after all. He may have two, or three, or
five poets from us, and if he cannot find
them among those already dead, he may
choose them provisionally among the un-
questioned living; but one he may not
have; and for the greater number he must
wait the course of nature. There is no
disposition to a happy despatch in the
poets yet with us, and we cannot think of
any critic who would be willing to offer
them up, even for the national honor, and
from the impartial motives that always
actuate criticism.

III.

We ourselves would rather part with
two or three novelists, though we should
not like to take leave first of Dr. Eggleston, for he seems in his latest story to have
done his best work. It will be nothing
against *The Graysons* if it is not so popular as *The Hoosier School-master* and the
other earlier books; for it lacks the novelty which these had, and its very finish and
mastery must be against it with a public

which mainly loves crudity, and does not care to have its emotions truly and simply interpreted, but (under instruction from most critics) likes them served washy and mawkish. We hope that we are implying by this flattering characterization of the general taste that the texture of *The Graysons*, though the book is of every-day material and common homespun, is fine and close. The story deals with elements that lie about us like earth and water, motives underfoot like grass, overhead like leaves, every-day loves and hates, hopes and fears, crimes and sacrifices. Briefly, it tells of a poor young fellow in pioneer Illinois unjustly accused of killing his enemy, and it invites into the drama the great figure of Abraham Lincoln, then an awkward, sad-eyed country lawyer at the beginning of his career, who rights the innocent boy by his legal skill and his native cunning. The author uses a local tradition, and he uses it with skill; the historical grandeur of Lincoln suffers nothing in his hands; he is extremely well managed, and is duly subordinated in the reader's interest to Tom Grayson, whose life he saves. Grayson himself is not a personage who remains supremely endeared to the fancy for his artistic presentation; the whole group of those immediately concerned and the mere lookers-on are done with the same vivid accuracy, from the same affectionate and abundant knowledge. It is a book to be very glad of on all accounts; and it is a pleasure to praise it for qualities which one might sometimes fancy authors took pains to keep out of their books, as common honesty in dealing with human nature, a love of common beauty, a reverence for common truth.

IV.

But probably these are the very hardest qualities of all to get into a book, and the authors are not so much to blame for their absence. Most readers would not know them when they felt them, and would suppose themselves moved by something else; most critics would contemn them as vulgar and trivial. What they want is "passion," "imagination," "style," "virility"—they are great fellows for virility. We are afraid that the neatly studied selfishness of a small nature like the elder Thomas Grayson must pass for something very commonplace with them; we do not suppose they will be satisfied with a Lincoln who does not, as a young country lawyer, dramatically forecast the martyr President; a figure like big Bob McCord, in which the stalwart, shrewdly simple, rude, plebeian, good-natured, joking pioneer race is typified, must appear very unworthy of literature, inadequately moved, and wanting in heroic breadth and height.

But we take leave to like him for some of the reasons that we like the persons in Björnstjerne Björnson's drama of *Sigurd Slembe*, which we have just now in the English of Mr. W. M. Payne. It cannot have been an easy thing to put into English, for between the two tongues directness might readily get changed into bluntness, and simplicity into poverty, and those who cannot read Björnson's verse may well give thanks for Mr. Payne's English, as we do. It is mostly clear, unaffected, and unpretentious: one feels that it is faithful, and follows the poet's word without caracoling about in periphrasis, after the manner of those who believe in giving the "spirit" of an author. It is the more fortunate because the play is itself not a thing that could bear much expansion: an author who elsewhere makes his effect with a few massive strokes in narrow compass here disperses himself over a vast area of time and space. It is necessary to recognize this, but it is useless to blame it; he did his work in this way because he could not do it in another; and perhaps the very faltering and wandering in the conduct of the drama were requisite to the self-expression of the hero's halting, Hamlet-like character. In the thoroughly excellent critical preface with which Mr. Payne equips his version he tells us that the drama is founded upon historical fact, and deals with the life of an actual pretender to the throne of Norway, from the moment when he learns that he is the late king's natural son to the final hour when he falls into the hands of his enemies after a hopeless defeat. The poetic solution of the situation is Sigurd's reconciliation to failure and death, after a career of violent ambition, in which the burning sense of injustice yields from time to time before the doubt of means and ends abhorrent to his higher moods. It is the old lesson of self-renunciation, so hard to learn, so insistent in the human heart, so cogent in the human reason, the only sufficient and final and eternal answer to fate. The great Scandinavian critic Georg Brandes censures the author's anachronism in attributing nineteenth-century motives to twelfth-century men, but this is a defect such as inheres in all historic fiction, whether it feigns the past in paint or in print. That is one of the reasons why we think historic fiction ought not to be; but if it must be, we would not have it impoverish itself in the vain endeavor to be strictly true to the past. The main truth in *Sigurd Slembe* is the truth at all times, and we can afford to let the temporary truth go if we cannot have the higher on any other terms.

V.

In the picture of contemporary life we can have both, if the author is wise enough to see and honest enough to tell both. This is never easy, but it is what constitutes the greatness of Björnson in the dramas of his second period, when first he turned from such unmoralized idyls of peasant life as *Arne, Synnöve Solbakken, The Happy Boy*, and *The Fishermaiden*, and began to own his responsibility to the larger life about him in *The Bankrupt, The Editor, The King, The Glove*. In this range he deals with commercial dishonesty; with the abuses of journalism; with the monarchical principle, surviving, archaic and outgrown, into our day; and with the impudent and cynical pretension that there can be one standard of purity for men and another for women. But this range, wide as it is, by no means describes his literary and ethical activity. In *Flags in the City and Harbor* he studies the problem of transmitted and inherited crime; in *Captain Manzana*, the acutest divination of Italian character by any foreigner that we know of, he inquires the effect of the perpetual intrusion of civic interests upon individual and domestic life; and in *Dust* he confronts with their hypocrisy those who teach the belief of immortality as a pleasing mythology to their children, while they hold it with lax insincerity or not at all themselves.

But these books, again, are indicative of his line of work rather than the extent of it in literature. In politics he has led at least as large and fearless a life: he headed the uprising against the reactionary ideas of the King of Norway and Sweden which resulted in the perfect autonomy of Norway—a country where there is no longer a nobility, and where democratic principles prevail as thoroughly as in ours. In a sketch written by Professor Boyesen some years ago [3] there is a graphic little picture of Björnson addressing the peasants, from what we should call the stump, in his campaigns against the King. It is said that since his return to Norway from a long sojourn in Paris he has gone a step farther, and that his political radicalism has assumed the social and economic phase, apparently inevitable in the evolution of those who profoundly sympathize with the people. How thoroughly Björnson knows his own people the readers of this Magazine will be able to judge from the series of studies beginning in the present number; and we trust that the acquaintance it will enable them to make with the material and scenery of his literature will make them wish to know that too. As yet the American edition, with

the exception of *Sigurd*, embraces none of his dramas, and leaves us to desire an English version of the plays which we have mentioned, and which the reader will find more fully studied by Mr. Brandes and Professor Boyesen. Their frankness can hurt no one, and can help many in America as well as Norway, for the conditions with which they deal are common everywhere in the civilization ironically called Christendom.

We have more than once spoken of Björnson in treating of that great intellectual movement so imperfectly suggested by the name of realism. His place in it is a foremost one, though his realism is of the spiritual type, like that of the Russians, rather than the sensual type, like that of the French. It would be impossible for such a man to remain satisfied with things; he must have the reason of things, for he is, above all, a poet. He is as impatient of conventionality in literature as he is of any other form of tyranny; and he is one of the chief of those great Norsemen of our time who have led their poetry back not only to the life but to the language of the people, and have refreshed it from the never-failing springs of the common speech.

VI.

These poets did consciously what our humorists have done unconsciously to some extent, and what all our so-called "dialect" story-tellers will, we hope, continue to do. If the American we speak and write shall incidentally become as different in its vocabulary from the English of the scholasticists as the rehabilitated Norse is from the Danish, we do not think that will be cause for grief, but the contrary. From its grammatical simplicity and inflexibility our language on the imaginative and critical side is always in danger of becoming poverty-stricken; any one who employs it to depict or to characterize finds the phrases thumbed over and worn and blunted with incessant use, and experiences a joy in the bold locutions which these writers report from the lips of the people, where it is still alive. In fact it is in our humorists that the American spirit is most truly reflected; and if they are grotesque and extravagant, it is because most Americans are mostly so. We are not so much discouraged, therefore, when Mr. Gosse denies us a great poet, as we should be if he refused us a great humorist. But this we are sure that he would never think of doing; and in our security we are tempted to turn upon him and ask, "Has England produced a great humorist?" Looking over Mark Twain's *Library of American Humor*, in which our inextinguishable laughers are democratically distributed without reference to age, sex, or previous condition of servitude, we find such unassailable renowns as Hosea Biglow, John Phœnix, Artemus Ward, Mark Twain, Josh Billings, Uncle Remus, *The Burlington Hawkeye* man, *The Danbury News* man, and Messrs. Warner, Harte, Aldrich, Lanigan, and Bierce; and with these thirteen, counting as twelve, we confidently challenge England to produce the Anglo-Saxon baker's-dozenth.

But attending the symposium of Englishmen whom we expect to vote upon the matter, we are not willing to take leave of Mark Twain's compilation without some recognition of the pleasure we have had in it, apart from the gratification of our national pride. Its humorously hap-hazard arrangement is by no means unfavorable to a critical conception of the quantity and quality of our indigenous fun; and for those who like fun for its own sweet sake, the joke of coming upon something unexpected enhances the delight of whatever the thing happens to be. It happens very generally to be good; the book not only fairly represents our range, but it testifies to our accuracy of aim; it gives the best shots of our champions, and some wonderful practice on the part of our amateurs. It represents all periods and sections; and we need hardly say that as we Americans have begun to joke since most people found out that it was just as easy to be decently funny as not, there is nothing in it to make us ashamed of having laughed.

VII.

We are the less disposed to insist upon the comparison of American superiority with English inferiority in this sort because we think that any international comparison is increasingly apt to work injustice. The futility of it struck us especially in looking over those sketches of travel in the South which Mr. Charles Dudley Warner has now collected in a volume, and called *On Horseback*. Here the humor which penetrates and perfumes the whole record is something that springs from the common and life-long experience of American things. No foreigner could possibly taste it as we do, with our keen delight in it, though no intelligent person anywhere could fail to perceive that it was subtle and rare. No foreigner would be qualified to judge it, or to establish the author's place. That is for his own people to do, and it is for them to decree his standing. His comparative excellence in any international competition is a matter of no consequence; it is his positive excellence which they alone can know to the last touch, and which they alone can authoritatively declare.

So we take a little courage about our poets, whether they seem to be dead or whether they seem to be alive. If we are really a nation with a tradition and an ideal of our own, and with a civilization necessarily springing from our peculiar conditions and impossible from any others, then it is inalienably for us to say whether our poets are great or small.

---

[1] Edmund Gosse, "Has America Produced a Poet?" Forum, 6 (October, 1888), 176-186.

[2] British monarchs whose reigns coincided with the lives of the poets on Gosse's list. "Great Anna" apparently refers to Queen Anne, during whose reign Alexander Pope first published.

[3] Hjalmar Hjorth Boyeson, "Björnstjerne Björnson," American, 1 (1881), 23+, 59+.

[4]The list, then, is as follows:

Hosea Biglow - narrator of James Russell Lowell's Biglow Papers

John Phoenix - pseudonym of George Horatio Derby

Artemus Ward - pseudonym of Charles Farrar Browne

Mark Twain - pseudonym of Samuel Clemens

Josh Billings - pseudonym of Henry Wheeler Shaw

Uncle Remus - pseudonym of Joel Chandler Harris

The Burlington Hawk-Eye man - The Burlington Daily Hawk-Eye
of Burlington, Iowa for years during and after the
Civil War published humorous pieces on its front
page in a column called "The Hawk-Eye." The pieces
were unsigned, but presumably the work of the paper's
publisher, C. Dunham.

The Danbury News man - J. M. Bailey (See The Danbury News Man's
Almanac, and Other Tales (Boston: Shepard & Gill,
[1873]).)

Charles Dudley Warner

Bret Harte

Thomas Bailey Aldrich

George Thomas Lanigan

Ambrose Bierce

Editor's Study.

I.

"DIDST thou stand forth by my worthy friend and bear him company? Did thy soul suffer with him and rejoice with him, riding in his chariot of triumph, to the block, to the axe, to the crown, to the banner, to the bed and ivory throne of the Lord God, thy Redeemer?"

These glowing words were written by one Fifth Monarchy man to another who had followed Sir Harry Vane to Tower Hill the day when the great republican gave up his life for his faith in the people's right to rule themselves. The fortunate ecstatic had seen his leader lay his head on the block after his broken and insulted endeavor to read his defence before the crowd; and when the headsman asked him, "Will you raise your head again?" he had heard Vane answer, "Not till the final resurrection." It was the valorous close of a career which, whatever its errors had been, never wavered from that faith; the end of a man who had been true to the people against the first Charles, whom he would not have slain; against Oliver Cromwell, whom he rebuked for his usurpations; against Richard, whom he despised for "an idiot without courage, without sense — nay, without ambition"; against the second Charles, who divined that one holding him the servant not the master of the state was "too dangerous a man to let live," and who forswore himself in Vane's death.

The story of his life is told again with all fulness, and with luminous conscience and singular attractiveness, by Professor J. K. Hosmer, whose studies have peculiarly fitted him for the work; and it is told with the constant purpose of showing how early, how in the very dawn of our light here, English statesmanship began to feel and reflect that light. This *Life of Young Sir Henry Vane* is, in fact, the opening chapter of any modern history of the American Revolution, of the war for the Union. Unquestionably there is a spiritual, a moral sequence in all these events, though the reader may question how much or how little influence Vane's brief sojourn among the heroes, the zealots, the bigots, of New England had in

forming him to the shape of steadfast truth to the principle of popular sovereignty. It does not seem to us quite the school of such ideal love of liberty as his; but without doubt he might well have first imagined there the possibility of a state without a prince, of which our present greatness is the realization. Our pride would be willing to give conjecture the furthest reach in this direction, but Professor Hosmer himself does not suffer us to forget that Vane was acquainted with practical republicanism in Switzerland before he saw it in New England, and that he knew Geneva before he knew Boston. It is very likely he found the like social and religious conditions in both countries, in both cities; one does so still; and it is not very likely that Vane learned his subtlety, not to say his sinuosity in some things, on one continent altogether, and strengthened himself in the courage and the love of freedom, which nevertheless ruled his decisive actions, altogether on the other, as Professor Hosmer seems to think. The biographer may be right or he may be wrong about this; the important fact is that he honestly shows Vane in his defects as well as his virtues, and does not try to make him appear one of those monsters of perfection which history as well as fiction has so long foisted upon us. He lets us know that Vane's early life was worldly, that he was many times tempted by personal, not to say selfish, motives, and that at some times his conduct had an effect of duplicity; it is all the more edifying that he overcame himself in the main and in the end, and that he died a martyr to the principle which now, theoretically at least, governs the whole English-speaking world. He would very willingly not have died a martyr; when the King cast about for some means by which he could "honestly put him out of the way," and had him accused of treason, he fought hard for his life; he fought not only with truth and with right, but he met wrong with legal cunning, and injustice with subtlety. No man need think the worse of him for that, and every sensible man will be glad that this great soul is suffered to be seen with the passions and dispositions of the average little human soul. He did not die the less nobly and exemplarily on that account; he was not less a martyr because he would rather not have been one; and we have to thank his present biographer for making this very clear. He has a courage in portraying Vane's character throughout which is excellent; and a frankness in recording contemporary and subsequent opinion of him which goes far to turn even Carlyle's wrath to praise, and inclines the reader to the author's more patient and more generous mind. His chapter on how Vane has been judged is a triumph of impartiality, for which, indeed, there is a constant endeavor in his fascinating book.

It is all so interesting that we are not sorry for any of the excursions which the author makes to include the history of Vane's time, even where Vane is not actively a part of it. We could not so well understand him without that fulness of contemporary light; and besides, one is never tired reading of the English commonwealth which foreran the American commonwealth, and in its extinction long gave the enemies of both so much hope of our own downfall. That hope seems now finally defeated, or, if not quite defeated, then very thoroughly baffled. Our facts pretty effectually refute the criticisms upon our theories, and Professor Hosmer believes they will continue to do so as long as men of English race dominate our political and social life.

II.

Perhaps America will not cease to be America even when it ceases to be English. It is pleasant to indulge our race piety in the fancy that constitutional liberty was given to our keeping solely, but we cannot think it is altogether free from a taint of superstition. Mr. Walt Whitman, in his letter to the Spanish fellow-citizens who celebrated a few years ago the three-hundredth anniversary of the city of Santa Fe, said some things pertinent to this point: "We Americans have got really to learn our antecedents. . . . They will be found ampler than has been supposed, and in widely different sources. Thus far, impressed by New England writers and school-masters, we tacitly abandon ourselves to the notion that our United States have been fashioned from the British Islands only, and essentially form a second England only—which is a very great mistake. Many leading traits for our future national personality, and some of the best ones, will certainly prove to have originated from other than British stock."

It does not seem safe to claim a perpetuity of rôle for any race in the drama of humanity. Israel was the vessel consecrated to the reception of religious truth; but have the Jews now a genius for religion above other people? The Italian love for beauty, if we are to believe most of their modern art, has lapsed to tastelessness; but, on the other hand, they are among the foremost contemporary nations in the wise conduct of their political affairs. The French were long dedicated to gayety, then to glory; but they have apparently had enough of pleasure and of war. What has become of the impassioned and aggressive monotheism of Islam? and will knowledge of the one God be less in the Orient and the Levant when Christianity prevails there? It seems to us that there is much which is arbitrary in the ascription of this or that quality or function to this or that nation. It is like dividing the mind into faculties: the imaginative faculty, the reflective faculty, the critical faculty; as if either of these were something that could act alone. As far as the English race is concerned, it may almost be said that there is no such thing, the English are so mixed of British, Saxon, Dane, Norman. Professor Hosmer tells us that Vane himself derived from a far-off Celtic ancestor, the Welsh Howel ap Vane; and in his letters and speeches Vane is always citing classic examples, as if his soul had been nurtured in the love of popular supremacy upon

"The glory that was Greece,
And the grandeur that was Rome,"

rather than upon any English tradition.

No one has had greater influence in forming the citizens of this republic to their faith in themselves and in one another than Jefferson; yet Mr. Bryce in his new book says that Jefferson was one with Rousseau in supposing a natural elevation in average human nature and trusting to it. As Rousseau was the first one, he was probably *the* one, and through his foster-son was the father of American democracy, of that in us which more distinctively than anything else we can call Americanism—our faith in humanity, our love of equality. One cannot claim that Americans of English origin are alone the depositaries of this belief, this passion; and we rather doubt if either would perish though all Americans of English stock perished. The ideal America, which is the only real America, is not in the keeping of any one race; her destinies are too large for that custody; the English race is only one of many races with which her future rests. A man of quite different race, in fact, has conceived a loftier and nobler civic ideal than any Englishman has done; and Giuseppe Mazzini's commonwealth, in which duties shall have an equal recognition with rights, may be the form of our more civilized, our more Christian, future.

III.

But we had no intention of wandering from Professor Hosmer's delightful book into thistly byways of dissent; and we return to it if for no other purpose than to give ourselves the pleasure of praising the charming attitude of the author throughout. In some such way all history might be rewritten, to the great gain of those who are to read it hereafter. It is simple, familiar, personal, without being undignified; and it is especially effective when the author rehabilitates the old battle-fields by visiting them and vivifying their great moments against a background of actual observation. If this blending of travel and history, of past and present, is not quite new, then no one else has carried it on so large a scale to such harmonious perfection. It is a very different sort of thing from the romantic picturesqueness attempted formerly in minor historical narrations, which expired of its own offensiveness in the efforts of Mr. Hepworth Dixon. Professor Hosmer's serious theme is always first in his mind, and with more than the usual temptation to be emotional in the treatment of a figure whose qualities, great and little alike, appeal strongly to a sympathetic biographer, he does not sentimentalize him.

He has in his way as great a literary charm as Mr. John Fiske, whose collected papers on *A Critical Period in American History* we had been reading before we took up Professor Hosmer's book, with a sort of despair of finding again anything so easy and so good. The path by which he leads you through the story of our transition from a Confederation to a Union, from the end of the Revolutionary war to the adoption of the Constitution, is not inviting in the prospect, but he makes it blossom with interest at every step. There is a sort of poetic heat in Mr. Fiske's thinking which kindles life in the driest material, and even the facts of a period of provincial jealousies and bickerings between the authorities of the newly liberated colonies are not proof against it. Before the reader well knows he knows the whole situation; he assists, in fact, at a kind of dramatic representation of it, and with no more fatigue than if it had actually been put upon the scene before him; perhaps with not so much. It is true that till slavery enters, the events do not fuse; but when once that danger appears they take the tragic impress which they bore more or less sharply throughout our national life from 1787 till 1865. It was a proper effect of the intrigue that the compromise which alone made the Union possible should at last make it impossible, and that when it was reconstituted at Appo-

mattox, it was upon a basis in which that treacherous cement had no part.

Mr. Fiske likes as well as Professor Hosmer to turn the light of accomplished facts upon his subject, but he does not otherwise deal with them; and it would not be just to suppose that he lets the dramatic quality of the slavery question in the Constitutional Convention lure him from any of the others before it. Mr. Fiske in his work shows how weak and cold the sentiment of union became after the Revolution, when the pressure of a common danger was relaxed. The sentiment of local patriotism was not then tempered by humor as it is now, when the rivalry of Chicago and St. Louis is mainly expressed in question of the size of the shoes respectively worn by the ladies of those cities; it was something ignorant and morose—a real distrust between the people of New York and Connecticut, Pennsylvania and New Jersey, like that which twenty years ago divided the different provinces of Italy. It was then such a poor little country, hemmed in by hard circumstances, and bowed by heavy burdens; and the notion of a closer union and a veritable nationality was repugnant not only to the traditions, but the envies, the fears, almost the religions, of the different particles of the old Confederation, which existed only to invite foreign contempt and aggression. When one looks at the map of the continent as sketched by the friendly court of France in 1782, with a narrow strip of Atlantic coast for the United States, and all the rest for the savages, the English, and the Spaniards, one realizes a little the need felt by our statesmen in the five ensuing years for a union strong enough to assert itself against such misconceptions of our destiny.

IV.

Even after the "compromises of the Constitution" had given us the Union there was a willingness, not to say an eagerness, on the part of some European countries to run our politics for us. It is always polite to suppose that American readers know American history, and so we will say that those who have forgotten how much this was the case may refresh their recollection from the "Omitted Chapters of History," which Mr. M. D. Conway discloses in the *Life and Papers of Edmund Randolph*, our first Secretary of State under our first President. In Washington's time we had a French party and a British party in our politics, each more or less championed by the French minister and the British minister. Everybody who read the newspapers last summer remembers how Washington was obliged to send M. Genet his passports for taking part in our private affairs, and attempting the direction of public opinion among us in a measure which makes the Murchison letter of poor Lord Sackville appear a model of discreet impartiality. But not everybody remembers (we ourselves in the pressure of critical duties had almost forgotten) that his successor, M. Fauchet, quite as ill-advised [3] as to his proper functions, if not as imprudent as M. Genet, had power enough for evil to bring Randolph to political ruin, or at least to cause his withdrawal from Washington's cabinet. His enemies said the worst of him, and perhaps even believed that he had corruptly lent himself to the machinations of the French minister against England or the English party. Washington did not believe that at the worst he was worse than imprudent, by Mr. Conway's showing; but Mr. Conway thinks that Washington himself was perhaps not quite candid with the man he had so wholly trusted and esteemed; at any rate he finally suffered him to be sacrificed to the English party. The charge of a default brought against Randolph his biographer proves to be wholly unfounded. It is a pathetic story, told with ardor, and with recognition of the fact that the fathers of this republic were of the same clay as its sons; they had their prejudices and their animosities, and they knew quite as well as we how to make these do duty for principles and virtues. Among the rest Edmund Randolph's character may be studied for instruction in humanity, unselfish patriotism, and political instinct, and hardly found less than the greatest. He seems to come into a little sharper perspective in Mr. Fiske's account of the Constitutional Convention than he does in Mr. Conway's, but in both he appears a leading and controlling force for good and not for evil. He was of that older Virginian race who lived before the time when the cotton-gin began to illumine the minds and consciences of Southern statesmen, and he believed that slavery was wrong; he assented as reluctantly as any Northerner to its recognition in our polity; he expected its early extinction, and he abolished it as far as he could by offering his own slaves their freedom when he took them to Philadelphia: in Virginia he could not free them. In all the personal and private relations of life Mr. Conway paints him endearing and beautiful; but he would say that it was not through these that he wished to urge his claim to our regard, our reverence, our regret; that with the fresh evidences of public integrity which he has studied and which he presents so fully he demands attention for a statesman wronged in his own time and not righted in ours. The book is one which Americans disposed to know America as well as possible cannot ignore; and if one does not care for its

immediate object, it may be read and enjoyed for many spacious passages where the question of Randolph's defence does not enter—passages where we see the men of an earlier day swayed by the interests and passions of ours, and the past wearing the complexion of the present in that unity of motives which makes all ages contemporary.

V.

These books are all three extremely suggestive, and in some sort they supplement one another. It is the enlightened philosophy of American civilization, its origins and its destinies, which unites them even in the differing conclusions they might lead to upon particular points. A vaster than either in scope, and closer and finer in its observation of the field, is Mr. James Bryce's grand work on *The American Commonwealth*. Many Studies, in long concameration, would fail of room for justice to it at every point; and it may be as well to say a few things in this corner about it, and then release the reader to the book itself. If he is an American reader he will pass with comparative lightness over the first volume, in which Mr. Bryce studies with remarkable insight and frankness our duplex polity and its working in State and nation. This might, we could imagine, be the main interest for some Englishmen, but Americans will (erroneously in most cases) consider themselves sufficiently informed upon the subject already, and will hurry to such chapters of the second volume as those on the operation of public opinion in this republic; our popular fatalism; the real and supposed faults of our democracy; the position of women; religion; railroads; and in fact all that relates to the social and economic aspect of our national life and character. We shall not say that, with all his carefulness as to facts, Mr. Bryce is not sometimes (perhaps often) mistaken in his inferences; it could not be otherwise with any writer, native or foreign; but it is only fair to this most thorough and able man to say that he seems never mistaken through narrowness, wilfulness, or ungenerous prejudice. Prejudice he has, of course; this is merely allowing that he is a man born and nurtured in conditions different from ours. But his prejudices are usually in our favor, and we would not ourselves undertake to keep as perfect temper as he does, with all the shortcomings and excesses of this sufficiently faulty people. If the world should make up its opinion from Mr. Bryce's book, and condemn us, most Americans would have nothing to say, not only because they would not really care (which is true), but because no people were ever before studied with such conscientious earnestness, such large-minded friendliness. At no moment does he suggest the propriety of our making ourselves over. He knows we are what we are because we have not only willed it, but because we could not help it; he becomes himself fatalistic in his patience with the most fatalistic nation which has ever spread its rule over so measureless a space. For some sense of this we may commend the reader not only to his chapter on "The Fatalism of the Multitude" among us, but to his whole book; it colors nearly all his conclusions. Yet he recognizes that we never submit without a struggle, and that our fatalism is not a faith but a reason, the sane conviction that it is folly to fight the majority, at least on its own ground. He perceives that all the same we proceed to turn it into a minority, and that we are long-suffering to that end, and seize every occasion to it. We try a thing, and if it will not work we give it up, and try something else. That is our vitality; that is our difference from the Oriental fatalists. They yield because it is foreordained; we acquiesce because the other side had the most votes, which, if we are very much in earnest, we mean to have ourselves by-and-by. This accounts for our willingness to experiment in all directions, and for the readiness of a nation more individualized than any other to throw the doctrine of *laissez faire* overboard whenever it suits the public convenience.

At the end Mr. Bryce does not romance us. His last words, where he treats of our social and economic future, embody the thoughts of every enlightened American when he clears his head of the denser fumes of patriotism and allows himself to look our facts in the face. Mr. Bryce sees us for what we are when we have not dined off spread-eagle—a practical, patient, straightforward people, vulgarized as all commercial peoples must be by the war of interests, but lifting ourselves above them when there is supreme need; fatalistic, but not desperately fatalistic, because of failure and disappointment; hopefully fatalistic, on the contrary, because we have hitherto experienced prosperity and success.

---

[1] Richard Cromwell, who succeeded his father as lord protector in 1658.

[2] Santa Fe, New Mexico was founded early in 1610, and therefore could not have been celebrating its 300th anniversary in the 1880's as Howells implies. Whitman's letter was probably part of the "Tertio-Millenial Exposition," celebrating the 333rd anniversary of the advent of Europeans upon New Mexican soil. The festival began on July 2, 1883 after more than a year of preparation.

[3] Jean Fauchet headed a four member delegation that replaced Edmund Genet as minister plenipotentiary on February 22, 1794.

April, 1889

Editor's Study.

I.

THE agreeable essay on *Musical Instruments and their Homes*, by Mrs. Mary E. Brown and Mr. William Adams Brown, is one of the holiday books that ought to survive the holidays. It can please both those who think music a heavenly maid, and those who go no farther than to say they suppose there is no harm in her; who believe with the Chinese that concord of sweet sounds is the inspiration if not the soul of the universe, or with the Arabs that "singing and songs cause hypocrisy to grow in the heart like as water promoteth the growth of corn." Between these extreme doctrines there is a wide neutral ground where all others may comfortably linger in the enjoyment of the inquiry our authors make for us. It is confined to the musical instruments and the music of the Chinese and Japanese and Coreans; of the Siamese and Burmese; of the Hindoos, Arabs, and Persians; of the African and American tribes. The range is sufficiently vast, and there was obvious reason for studying primitive and barbaric music with the care given it, and for leaving the reader to deal himself with the subject in its less recondite branches; though the book, for what it is, is always so entertaining that there may be some danger of forgetting the labor and the learning which went to make it.

The story of music in China, where its dedication to the highest office tended to fix and petrify its forms, in some such fashion as happened with painting in the Byzantine civilization, and in Japan, where a finer artistic instinct secularized it, is something very much more than curious; and the contempt into which it fell among the Hindoos, as well as the abhorrence in which the Arabs held it, has instruction for those who have to do with any of the articulate and representative arts as well. The law of right rests even upon the fabric of sound that comes and goes in a breath; it cannot be defied without shame and ruin. All arts decay when they begin to exist for themselves alone, or merely for the pleasure they can give, since truth beyond and beside them must be their incentive. But it is not apparently the wish of the authors that the consciousness of this should weigh heavily upon their readers. They sketch pleasantly the history of music in its less familiar evolution, and their wide reading has laid many sources under contribution for anecdote and instance. As for Mr. Brown's illustrations, they form a sort of orchestral accompaniment to the text, and are interesting to study with reference to the different national conditions and character; for they lead to continual conjecture of the causes of the grace and ugliness of the instruments, their picturesqueness and grotesqueness. Why should the *soung*, the boat-shaped harp, the most beautiful of all the barbaric instruments, have been the invention of the Burmese, a people who developed such a fantastic conception of the art that their law condemned whoever sang a new song before their king to death? This was treason; but their famous minstrel Moung Thaw Byaw several times forgot himself, and vexed his prince with music he had never heard before. When he was led out to die he invariably captivated his executioners with his art, and they spared his life, adopting the simple and natural device of executing an inferior musician in his place, in order to observe the letter of the law. The king was always sorry before long that Moung Thaw Byaw had been put to death, and always delighted when he turned up alive and well at the next royal feast.

II.

The story may be romantic; in any case it seems one made to the hand of Mr. William Gilbert; and it is a pity that he or some one else should not turn it to account in comic opera. Perhaps the author of *Vagrom Verse* will think of it. There is a dry wit and a dry wisdom in much of Mr. C. H. Webb's rhyme which would give one hopes of his handling such a theme successfully; but at present we should like the reader to see two or three of the things he has already done, such for instance as

THE VISIT.

Wearing a suit of simple gray,
I called upon a friend one day.

He straight unlocked his cedar room:
My senses swam with the perfume.

From shelves that hung at wondrous height
He took down wear that dimmed my sight:

Breeches that buckled at the knee—
"Smallclothes," but much too large for me—

Laced doublets, and cross-gartered hose:
It was a wondrous wealth of clothes.

But 'twas not meant that I should share:
They were not shown for me to wear.

'Twas only meant that I should see
How very fine a man was he.

And while he walked in brave array,
I sat there in my simple gray:

Think you that when I left his door,
I went much richer than before?

Another poem, in another strain, not less wise, and of a higher truth, is this which he calls

REVENGE.

Revenge is a naked sword;
 It has neither hilt nor guard.
Wouldst thou wield this brand of the Lord?
 Is thy grasp, then, firm and hard?

But the closer thy clutch of the blade,
 The deadlier blow thou wouldst deal,
Deeper wound in thy hand is made—
 It is thy blood reddens the steel.

And when thou has dealt the blow—
 When the blade from thy hand has flown—
Instead of the heart of the foe,
 Thou mayst find it sheathed in thine own!

Other pieces yet give a sense of qualities which John Paul's repute of joker will not always allow him to indulge; but it is best to be honest from time to time, and we will own that not all of Mr. Webb's things are so good as those we have quoted. Out of the more strictly humorous sort we should like to give "Love's Ante-crematory Farewell," which is delightfully mock pathetic and ghastly funny; and for a sort of grim suggestiveness the humanely manly lines entitled "Colored People allowed in this Car."

III.

But we remember that the Study has architectural limits; besides, there is a poet on our list toward whom we feel something of the high and sacred self-satisfaction of discoverer, and of whom we are in some haste to speak. That is to say, we do not remember to have seen any recognition of Mr. Lampman's poetry which brings us from the cold Canadian fields much of the charm already recognized here in Mr. Cawein's Kentucky verse. The poets are not otherwise alike, except in their intimate friendship with Nature; but Mr. Lampman has always, like Mr. Cawein, the right word on his lips; if this word is not usually so full of color, it is sometimes of even finer meaning; and some things with him are thought out in regions to which Mr. Cawein's impulses of feeling have not yet

carried him, as in the very wise and noble sonnet which he calls

THE TRUTH.

Friend, though thy soul should burn thee, yet be still.
 Thoughts were not meant for strife, nor tongues
  for swords.
He that sees clear is gentlest of his words,
And that's not truth that hath the heart to kill.
The whole world's thought shall not one truth fulfil.
 Dull in our age, and passionate in youth,
 No mind of man hath found the perfect truth;
Nor shalt thou find it; therefore, friend, be still.

Watch and be still, nor hearken to the fool,
The babbler of consistency and rule:
Wisest is he who, never quite secure,
 Changes his thoughts for better day by day:
To-morrow some new light will shine, be sure,
 And thou shalt see thy thought another way.

There are other sonnets as wise and as noble as this in a book which the reader worthy of it will like to turn to again and again. Mr. Lampman—it is Mr. Archibald Lampman, and those who cannot find his book elsewhere can get it of his publishers, J. Durie and Sons, Ottawa—calls his volume *Among the Millet and other Poems*, and it is mainly descriptive; but descriptive after a new fashion, most delicately pictorial and subtly thoughtful, with a high courage for the unhackneyed features and aspects of the great life around us. We quote for example two sonnets out of five to "The Frogs":

All the day long, wherever pools might be
 Among the golden meadows, where the air
 Stood in a dream, as it were moored there
Forever in a noontide reverie,
Or where the birds made riot of their glee
 In the still woods, and the hot sun shone down,
 Crossed with warm lucent shadows on the brown
Leaf-paven pools, that bubbled dreamily,

Or far away in whispering river meads
 And watery marshes where the brooding noon,
 Full with the wonder of its own sweet boon,
Nestled and slept among the noiseless reeds,
 Ye sat and murmured, motionless as they,
 With eyes that dreamed beyond the night and
  day.

And when day passed, and over heaven's height,
 Thin with the many stars and cool with dew,
 The fingers of the deep hours slowly drew
The wonder of the ever-healing night,
No grief or loneliness or rapt delight
 Or weight of silence ever brought to you
 Slumber or rest; only your voices grew
More high and solemn; slowly with hushed flight
Ye saw the echoing hours go by, long-drawn,
 Nor ever stirred, watching with fathomless eyes,
 And with your countless clear antiphonies
Filling the earth and heaven, even till dawn,
 Last-risen, found you with its first pale gleam,
 Still with soft throats unaltered in your dream.

A score of pieces and of passages tempt us to repetition from the poet's page; and here is a poem which we must give, with an italic insistence, after the old manner, upon bits that seem to us blest with uncommon fortune of touch where all is excellently good.

HEAT.

From plains that reel to southward, dim,
  The road runs by me white and bare;
Up the steep hill it seems to swim
  Beyond, and melt into the glare.
Upward half-way, or it may be
  Nearer the summit, slowly steals
A hay-cart, moving dustily
  With idly clacking wheels.

By his cart's side the wagoner
  Is slouching slowly at his ease,
Half-hidden in the windless blur
  Of white dust puffing to his knees.
This wagon on the height above,
  From sky to sky on either hand,
Is the sole thing that seems to move
  In all the heat-held land.

Beyond me in the fields the sun
  Soaks in the grass and hath his will;
I count the marguerites one by one;
  Even the buttercups are still.
On the brook yonder not a breath
  Disturbs the spider or the midge.
The water-bugs draw close beneath
  The cool gloom of the bridge.

Where the far elm-tree shadows flood
  Dark patches in the burning grass,
The cows, each with her peaceful cud,
  Lie waiting for the heat to pass.
From somewhere on the slope near by
  Into the pale depth of the noon
A wandering thrush slides leisurely
  His thin revolving tune.

In intervals of dreams I hear
  The cricket from the droughty ground;
The grasshoppers spin into mine ear
  A small innumerable sound.
I lift mine eyes sometimes to gaze:
  The burning sky-line blinds my sight:
The woods far off are blue with haze:
  The hills are drenched in light.

And yet to me not this or that
  Is always sharp or always sweet;
In the sloped shadow of my hat
  I lean at rest, and drain the heat;
Nay more, I think some blessèd power
  Hath brought me wandering idly here:
In the full furnace of this hour
  My thoughts grow keen and clear.

We only hint the riches of this poet's book; every page of it has some charm of phrase, some exquisite divination of beauty, some happily suggested truth. It is no part of our business to guess his future; but if he shall do no more than he has already done, we believe that his fame can only await the knowledge of work very uncommon in any time.

IV.

We praise him without prejudice to another poet, whose *Old and New World Lyrics* we have been reading. Mr. Clinton Scollard has a name already known to the readers of the magazines, and it is his second volume of verse which has given us pleasure. We fancy him at his highest in the well-conscienced poem which he calls "A Dream of Peace"; but a little thing which we find admirable for the thought cut in it has the clear beauty of a fine intaglio:

IN SOLITUDE.

Sometimes at lonely dead of night
  Weird sounds assail the ear,
And in our hearts is cold affright
  To think a ghost is near.

Why should we feel swift through us thrill
  A sense of awe and dread?
It is the living work us ill,
  And not the peaceful dead!

Then here is something that in its reach of association, as well as in its felicities of forms and colors, intimates the mood of a book which, of course, it does not wholly represent:

A WINTER TWILIGHT.

The silent snow-flakes glance and gleam
  Adown the chilly Northern air;
The West has thrown its dying beam
  Athwart the forest gray and bare.

And now a gradual dimness veils
  The wintry landscape near and far,
And while the windy daylight pales,
  Out-glimmers clear a single star.

Lulled by the sound of tinkling strings
  Where nimble fingers weave their spell,
I quite forget the North that stings
  Without the cozy oriel.

And on the wings of music borne,
  Aglow with floods of gold, I see
The blue of skies that rarely mourn
  Arch o'er the slopes of Italy.

The melody seems wafted down
  From laurelled heights where roses blow,
That shimmer like an emerald crown
  Above embowered Bellaggio.

A molten sapphire Como lies,
  And opal sails across it skim;
Green stair on stair the mountains rise,
  And cut the calm horizon's rim.

All dims as dies the rapturing strain;
  Once more the deepening dusk I see;
Then strike the silent chords again,
  That I may dream of Italy!

A like grace of sentiment, a like feeling for form, and a music as refined and sweet, characterize Mr. Frank Dempster Sherman's *Madrigals and Catches*. It is useless to blink the fact that both he and Mr. Scollard have been influenced by the agreeable masters of the modern English school of rondeau and triolet makers; which is no more than saying they are both people of their own time. Where they seem to differ from these masters, and where all our younger American poets (we gladly count Mr. Lampman as an American poet) differ from the English, is in their purer sympathy with Nature. They do not flirt with her; they love her ardently, tenderly; and their delight is to watch her moods, to paint her beauty in all its ever new surprises, to catch her tones, to echo her lightest whisper. Mr. Sherman, who is much taken with the pretty airs of the love-making time of life, and courts a young, well-dressed, harmlessly knowing, carelessly conscious, stylish Muse, is still best in some such landscape, sensitively faithful and in all points fortunate, as this:

DAWN AND DUSK.

I.

Slender strips of crimson sky
Near the dim horizon lie,
Shot across with golden bars
Reaching to the fading stars;
Soft the balmy west wind blows
Wide the portals of the rose;
Smell of dewy pine and fir,
Lisping leaves and vines astir;
On the borders of the dark
Gayly sings the meadow-lark,
Bidding all the birds assemble—
Hark, the welkin seems to tremble!
Suddenly the sunny gleams
Break the poppy-fettered dreams—
  Dreams of Pan, with two feet cloven,
Piping to the nymph and faun,
  Who, with wreaths of ivy woven,
Nimbly dance to greet the dawn.

II.

Shifting shadows indistinct;
Leaves and branches, crossed and linked,
Cling like children, and embrace,
Frightened at the moon's pale face.
In the gloomy wood begins
Noise of insect violins;
Swarms of fire-flies flash their lamps
In their atmospheric camps,
And the sad-voiced whippoorwill
Echoes back from hill to hill,
Liquid clear above the crickets
Chirping in the thorny thickets.
Weary eyelids, eyes that weep,
Wait the magic touch of sleep;
  While the dew, in silence falling,
Fills the air with scent of musk,
  And this lonely night-bird, calling,
Drops a note down through the dusk.

Something more of the seventeenth century, however, than we find in the others is in him, and is of an affinity, perhaps not openly traceable, with the gay spirit of the *Old Songs* which Mr. E. A. Abbey and Mr. Alfred Parsons offered us at Christmas-time with pictures familiar to all the readers of this Magazine. It seemed to us that these illustrations were sometimes the last effect that the joint arts which produced them could ever give in that way. To single one out of the whole group, could any chance of luck or could any touch of skill surpass that vision of young happiness, so perfect in its black and white that the color of a joyful flush almost comes as you look upon the cheek of Jenny going arm in arm "With Jockey to the Fair" in a rapture, a panting breathlessness of love and hope, which art has caught and kept forever?

V.

Such illustration as that of Messrs. Abbey and Parsons brings more to these old songs than it finds in them, as the best art of the modern theatre does to the old comedies, but there are times when song can in like manner enrich the sister art. Will not one of the loveliest pictures in the world have a lovelier meaning hereafter for all who look upon Murillo's "Immaculate Conception" with this beautiful sonnet in mind?

Whence is the spell, O fair and free from guile,
  Thou with the young moon shod! that binds my
    brain?
Is thine that orb of fable which did wane,
Darkening o'er sad Ortygia's templed isle—
Beautiful Artemis, hid from earth awhile,
  And on the pale monk's vigil risen again,
  A wonder in the starry sky of Spain?
Comes the Myth back, Madonna, in thy smile?
  Yea! thou dost teach that the Divine may be
The same to passing creeds and ages given;
And how the Greek hath dreamed or churchman
    striven,
  What reck we, who with eyes tear-blinded see
Thee standing loveliest in the open heaven?—
  Ave Maria, only heaven and thee!

These elect words are the words of a poet whom the inexorable conditions of life made a journalist; whose delicate fibre, the material expression of his fine spirit, gave way under the stress of the burdens put upon it; who passed through years of pain and struggle back to the possibility of work, but never again to health; who found the light of religion on his stony path, and kept his heart alive in that; who realized in a passionate ideal of self-renunciation the peace that passes understanding.

The story of David Gray the reader will find told with tenderness and truth in the volume of his *Letters, Poems, and Selected Writings*, edited, with a biographical memoir, by J. N. Larned. They form the tribute to his memory which his friends in Buffalo thought his most fitting monument, and their tone of reverent affection, kept modest by the biographer's instinct and by his sense of what the poet's own manly reserve would have suffered from any exuberance, is that of the regard in which he was held by the whole city of his adoption. In singular measure he was the literary pride of a singularly generous and appreciative community; but the sober reticence with which Mr. Larned has expressed the fact liberates his genius and character to the admiration of all who anywhere care for a lofty purpose consecrated through suffering, and kept with steadfast unselfishness. We have given Gray's best poem, but, good as it is, it is not the best part of him. That can best be known to such as follow the career of the young Scotch lad, whom his family carried with them from Edinburgh to the backwoods of Wisconsin, and who kept alive there a glowing and growing passion for poetry, forbidden to find "an earthly close" by the duties and ambitions that brought him later to Buffalo, and made him the leading journalist of his city. There is something exceedingly touching, exceedingly sweet and charming, in the records of the early life of the ardent youth, especially of his literary friendship with the boy on the next farm, which kept his heart fresh so long afterward in the drought of streets and newspapers. But Gray's whole life was a life of friendships; men spoke of him with a sort of tremble of tenderness; those who knew him knew it a privilege. When the light of the other world began to invade the twilight of this, and to show him many of its pleasures and its objects futile, vain, even harmful, which had once seemed otherwise, the most mundane of his acquaintance, while they wondered and grieved at his withdrawal into what seemed a strict asceticism, had nothing but reverence for his sincerity, his aspiration, his endeavor for heaven on earth. His end came amidst the horrors of a railroad accident, but the scene of tumult was made as serene to him

" As a sick man's room when he taketh respose
  An hour before death."

And none who had known David Gray but felt that he had left something of his peace with them when the grave closed over his long, unrepining patience. These volumes bear witness to the excellent work which he could do, and still more might have done, in literature; but we feel that we are recognizing their highest office when we welcome them as an intimation of the fineness and richness of his life.

---

[1] "John Paul" is the pseudonym of Charles Henry Webb. Using that name he contributed the "John Paul letters" to the New York Tribune in 1873. They were collected and published in 1874 as John Paul's Book.

Editor's Study.

I.

A PAPER on Sir Walter Scott, dealing [1] with him in the way of reminiscence and anecdote, has been introduced to the readers of one of our magazines with a page of rather abstract eulogy by a gentleman eminent for his services to the cause of education, from whom one cannot learn without concern that to go back to the fiction of Scott "from Flaubert and Daudet and Tolstoï is like listening to the song of the lark after the shrieking passion of the midnight piano-forte"— how lurid the poor domestic piano-forte appears in this figure!—"nay, it is like coming out of the glare and heat and reeking vapor of a palace ball into a grove in the first light and music and breezes of the morning."

Our own intimacy with the midnight piano-forte is small, and with the lark even less; but when it comes to the "glare and heat and reeking vapor of a palace ball," we are at home. Nothing was more familiar to our gilded youth than this atmosphere; and we clearly recall the soothing effect upon our fevered senses of the "first light and music and breezes of the morning." It is true we did not come out into them; the reigning prince (sometimes he was an emperor, but usually a plain, simple, unostentatious king) always made us stay the remnant of the night with him; but before flinging ourselves upon the silken shake-down that our host had invariably made up for us in his own room it was our custom to lift the window for some moments of those delicious sights and sounds. Perhaps it was only the unfinished window of Aladdin's palace; no matter; the recollection of it enables us to know what one means when one talks of coming out of a palace ball. We dare say all palaces are much alike in the "glare and heat and reeking vapor" of their balls; and we suppose any friend of the romantic will be ready to count our imagined experience of palaces and their balls for something as good as the reality. But we are by no means so sure that we agree with the writer in question in the application of a figure that has

stirred our fancy to such extraordinary feats; and we have some grave misgivings as to whether the unqualified acceptance of Scott would prove with readers the "blessing not merely to their minds, but also to their hearts and souls," which he promises.

There is, to begin with, that falsification of historic perspective which Scott never scrupled at when it served the purpose of his romance, and which never fails to confuse the young readers to whom his books have now mostly fallen. Then there are his mediæval ideals, [1] his blind Jacobitism, his intense devotion to aristocracy and royalty; his acquiescence in the division of men into noble and ignoble, patrician and plebeian, sovereign and subject, as if it were the law of God; for all which, indeed, he is not to blame as if he were one of our contemporaries, though any Amer- [2] ican would be very culpable if he did not warn his children against them when he put Scott's books into their hands. We will not defend Daudet from complicity with the midnight piano-forte, for we are not always satisfied of the singleness of Daudet's intention or the effect of his books; and then, he is hardly a realist; but Flaubert's *Madame Bovary* is one impassioned cry of the austerest morality, far above the conception of the art of Scott's time; and when we come to Tolstoï there is no comparison of the masters in any kind. Beside that most Christian of the moralists Scott is the spirit of the world incarnate, and of the feudal world at that; and beside that conscientious and perfect artist he is a prentice artificer. In the beginning of any art even the most gifted worker must be crude in his methods, and we ought to keep this fact always in mind when we turn from the purblind worshippers of Scott to Scott himself, and recognize that he often wrote a style cumbrous and diffuse; that he was tediously analytical where the modern novelist is dramatic, and evolved his characters by means of long-winded explanation and commentary; that, except in the case of his lower-class personages, he made them talk as seldom man and never woman talked; that he was tiresomely descriptive; that on the simplest occasions he went about half a mile to express a thought that could be uttered in ten paces across lots; and that he trusted his readers' intuitions so little that he was apt to rub in his appeals to them. He was probably right: the generation which he wrote for *was* duller than this; slow-witted, æsthetically untrained, and in maturity not so apprehensive of an artistic intuition as the children of to-day. All this is not saying Scott was not a great man; he *was* a great man, and a very great novelist as compared with the novelists who went before him. He can still amuse young people, but they ought to be instructed how false and how mistaken he often is. As for [3] the man who teaches us that all war, private and public, is a sin; who bids us beware of our passions; who strives unceasingly to free us from the enmities and hates in which we poor worms sting one another to death; who preaches, first and last and always, peace and purity and pardon — we urge his censor to some further study of him. He will find no word of Tolstoï's that contravenes the Sermon on the Mount; this inapproachable artist has no need of anything factitious for his effects, because they are those of truth; and he has never constructed an ideal of chivalry for us to worship, because humanity is good enough for him. One might learn from Scott to be a gentleman, but Tolstoï teaches us to be good men. Unless one hears the shrieking passion of the midnight piano-forte and tastes the reeking vapor of the palace ball in the four gospels, we do not really understand how one should perceive them in the ethics of Tolstoï. His censor is apparently not very clear about the whole matter, however, or he would know that the motives of Victor Hugo and Scott are not alike, and that, in all their books can teach, it is Tolstoï and Manzoni who are of the same tradition, and not Scott and Manzoni. If Tolstoï had not written, we could almost agree with the gentleman we have so cordially disagreed with, and might rank *I Promessi Sposi* as highly as he does; but the Italian's work falls below the Russian's because Manzoni wrote in the infancy of his art and Tolstoï has written in its maturity. The Russian is the more perfect master for that reason, but they are equal and coeval in the inspiration of their work. Both are penetrated with the beauty of Christianity, and both are filled with the same pity for the oppressed, the poor, the lowly, the same abhorrence of violence and pride; both are alike

"Dowered with the hate of hate, the scorn of scorn,
 The love of love."

II.

Their tradition, with a strange mixture of the realistic and the romantic in attitude, is perceptible in George Meredith's story of *Beauchamp's Career*, where, as in the work of Tolstoï and Manzoni, one is aware of being helped to a clearer vision of life by the novelist. *Beauchamp's Career* is not a new book, not even new in the American edition which embodies the author's work to our public; but in the Study it is never too late to speak of any book; and we wish to acknowledge what seems to us its great worth in the kind we have hinted. We offer our tribute to it the more eagerly because we have not hitherto found Mr. Meredith easy to read, and in acknowledging the greatness of his power in this instance have had to silence some prepossessions or some principles: we will call them principles. Realistic the book certainly is not, unless we stretch that elastic term to cover a case in which the inner truth burns through an outside of sufficiently conventional English-novel material; squires, lords, and ladies, country-house sojourning, Parliamentary election, dining, poaching, yachting, and all; with the Gallic background of an unhappy marriage and love of the elderly French neighbor's wife. Out of this collection of antiquated properties a great, fresh, and noble ideal of conduct evolves itself in the character of Beauchamp, the valiant young aristocrat turned democrat, and in the supreme, culminating episode of the flogging of Dr. Shrapnel, the all but socialistic radical, by Beauchamp's uncle and benefactor, Romfrey. In fact this episode, with Romfrey's final self-humiliation before the man he has brutally and mistakenly outraged, is the meaning, is the true business, of the book. In his ethical attitude here, in his perception of the bearing of all the facts upon the morals of his reader, and in his truth to the truth that the forgiveness of the wronged man is heavenly far above the patrician pride of the gentleman who disgraced him so that he must seem to forgive through fear, the author allies himself with the greatest master of fiction, and touches a point reached hitherto only when Tolstoï's Karenin sees that he cannot forgive with dignity and yet forgives. Higher praise we cannot give him on that side, which is to us the really important side; but to those who care for the minor qualities of George Meredith's work we commend study of that certain splendid massiveness of effect in it from a narrative so often apparently wandering and capricious, and a style so wilful. His progress toward a given end is by a thousand sinuosities, deflections, halts, impulses, but he seems to get there, as our slang is, all at once, and to possess you of the situation by a light gathered from all points upon it. We cannot well say how it is done; we are not sure that we altogether like it; we are only sure that it is the work of a master, about whom, in detail, we might have our reserves; whom we might call Carlylese in some moments, some manners, if he did not otherwise give as deep an impression of originality as he gives of strength; whom we should certainly accuse of letting his people all talk too like one another, and too like their author.

III.

One's reserves one nearly always has, and in coming to praise even such powerful work as Henrick Ibsen's dramas (of which the reader may now get three in English in the cheap and pretty Camelot 4 editions) one must own that there is often more of type than of character in his personages, and that the reality of the action is sometimes strained to an allegorical thinness. Nevertheless the effect is not much less than tremendous, especially in that play called *Ghosts*, where the sins of the father are visibly visited upon the son. Life is made a little difficult by the contemplation of the far-reaching suggestion of this simple action: it appears that you are not only to live rightly for your own sake, but for your children's sake, in whom your vices and evils will walk the earth long after you are under it. This was hinted by the prophets aforetime, science has since affirmed it, and again the poets are burning it into the tough human consciousness. We have already spoken of Björnson in his dealing with the same problem, and now one may learn how forcibly his great fellow-laureate handles it. Ibsen's other subjects are *The Pillars of Society*, in which we see how the precious superstructure which we are so zealous to "save" from time to time is propped upon an inwardly rotten respectability; and *The Enemy of Society*, who tries to 5 set right a dangerous evil in his little town, and has his windows broken by his more public-spirited fellow-citizens for his trouble, and stands outcast and alone where he had been idolized before. All three of the plays are bitter with the most caustic irony, which is all the more mordant because it is so just. The literary quality is peculiar. The action opens so tamely, so flatly, that it seems to you impossible to go on with a thing like that; but at the same moment you find yourself in the grip of a curiosity which intensifies to the most poignant interest, and holds you spell-bound to the end.

These dramas are played in Europe. We fancy them offered to the fat optimism that goes to our theatres only to be "amused"; but what our average audiences would have to say of them we will not fancy. Nothing, though, need prevent the reader from setting up a scene for them in his own imagination; and if he likes to know something of the man who wrote them, and who lives in willing exile from the narrow social conditions of home, we commend him to the essay of Georg Brandes (published by 6 Putnams), and to the interesting paper of Mr. Edmund Gosse in the *Fortnightly* 7 for February.

IV.

When we come to speak of American fiction after such work, it is with no shame for some literary aspects of it, but with a distinct sense of its want of reach in other ways. Fine artists we have among us, and right-minded as far as they go; and we must not forget this when it seems as if all the women had taken to writing hysterical improprieties, and some of the men were trying to be at least as hysterical in despair of being as improper. If we kept to the complexion of a certain school—which sadly needs a school-master—we might very well be despondent; but, after all, that school is not representative of our conditions or our intentions. We need not be very 8 specific about it in order to justify the pride and hope we have in the wholly different work of Miss Murfree. Was there something said here once in censure of some of her artistic motives, of points in her literary method? Let us say now, then, that *The Despot of Broomsedge Cove* is a book which we have no wish to censure upon those grounds, if any others. Whether of conscious purpose or through involuntary evolution, she has here wrought free of the faults which existed in her earlier work, and has deepened her hold upon the reader's interest while throwing aside all the romantic devices with which she once appealed to it. There is a fine solidity in this new story, which is at no point weakened by the attribution of improbable motive. The scene is, as usual, in the Tennessee mountains; the persons are our old friends the mountaineers; but the characters are new, the situations are fresh, and the action has a pristine vigor. The whole effect is that of rugged strength; but there are passages, episodes, incidents, of surpassing delicacy and beauty, and of a truth that delights and uplifts. The meeting of the hero and heroine while they take shelter from a shower under a way-side tree is one of these: it is simply perfect in its fidelity to nature and to their characters and social traditions. So far as we recall, no fact or trait in the people is overstrained for the purpose of an effect; an admirable verity gives you the sense of its presence throughout. The Despot is imagined in the spirit of this; he is a poet who supposes himself a sort of prophetic agent of the Almighty because he is so filled with the splendid and awful beauty of the Bible; and the study of Marcella Strobe, good, shrewd, earthly, limited to fact by her affections and ambitions, but generous and fine all the same, is even more subtle. Her father and her grandmother—especially the latter, who is the *bouffe* element of the piece—are triumphs of a skill which we seldom find at fault in this book, with its large group of finely differentiated figures.

V.

Of this art, and of the art of several other American women now writing fiction, we were thinking with patriotic self-satisfaction as we read an English story, recently much praised by English criticism. We mean *A Village Tragedy*, by Mrs. Margaret Wood: a story of intense pathos, and certainly of very great force as a social study, relieved by genuine humor and full of excellent character, but, beside kindred American work, showing certain vices from which our writers are as free as the Russians or the French. It would not be very easy to specify these aberrations of art, of taste, but perhaps they may be summed up as consciousness of the reader, or the confidential attitude. We do not think of any English novelist, high or low, except Thomas Hardy, who guards himself from them, who writes, as the novelist always should write, with an eye single to his story, and as if there were no such thing as a reader in the world. If *our* reader will think of Miss Jewett's work, or Miss Wilkins's, or Miss Murfree's, when he comes to Mrs. Wood's tragedy he will see what we mean; but we suppose he will finally so lose himself in it that he will end by thinking us unjust. When Mrs. Wood loses herself in it she proves us so, and we may as well own that our strictures do not apply to the last half of her book. There the consciousness falls from her; the lines, at first tentative and timid, become large and bold, and an impression of the misery, forever hopeless in our present conditions, is left as deep in the heart as if one had personally witnessed it. *A Village Tragedy* is that of a poor girl whom her uncle adopts from her home in the London slums, and whom his harshness drives to the love of a simple, honest, ignorant ploughboy, her faithful husband in all but the marriage rite. His violent death before this can be accomplished leaves her to drown herself and abandon their babe to the workhouse, from which the father came, and from which it was his dying wish to save it. Given away in this sort, the story

seems cheap enough; but that is far from the feeling which its grim outlines and its varied detail of incident and character will impart to the reader. A sense of the inevitable repetition of such tragedies as long as the needless poverty of our civilization exists will haunt him after the features and incidents of the story begin to fade.

VI.

Something of the same fault which we have regretted in Mrs. Wood's otherwise excellent work seems to be the trouble with Mr. Kirkland's story of *The MacVeys*. We make bold to speak of it because we liked his *Zury* so very much, and said so. He wrought himself in that book a wide margin on which he could fail a little without ruinous disaster; and he has failed a little in *The MacVeys*. He continues for us the acquaintance of Anne Sparrow and her children, in the stress of social misgiving, as it comes upon them all, concerning the paternity of the children, and Anne's own sense of loyalty when a fine fellow, ignorant of her past, falls in love with her. The situation is good, and new enough; Anne's character was worth tracing through it; but having taken the people of *Zury* up again, the author should have guarded himself from consciousness of the reader's interest in them. It is here that he fails; the creatures of his imagination are not more projected from him than before; they are less so; he is even a little fond with them; and the inevitable result is that his caresses react upon the reader. The characters affect one somewhat as spoiled children.

It is difficult to touch a mistake of this sort without seeming to bear on; but what we mean is that Mr. Kirkland does not keep that distance both from his characters and from his readers that an artist best succeeds by keeping, and is on rather too intimate terms with both. Perhaps this comes about through a sense that the same actors again address the same audience; but it is nevertheless a pity, though it is not inconsistent with some excellent performance otherwise in the book, which at times deals so ably with the painful problem in hand.

Another book by another author who can afford to be sometimes at less than her best is Mrs. Rose Terry Cooke's *Steadfast*, of which the opening chapters seem to us almost the best we have had from her hand. At any rate, we do not well see how the reality of those chapters could be surpassed. They stamp with the distinctness of shadows cast in electric light the sorrow and despair which fall upon the home of the simple country doctor when his widow and his daughter sit down in it after his death; and they portray with the same vivid touch the beautiful constancy of the young minister who marries the wreck of the self-devoted girl he had loved too well in her bloom and loveliness to forsake when they had left her forever. We wish to accent our praise of these passages, because the story is afterward not so simple, as we think, in motive, and not so strong in effect. It interests, however, in dealing with some of those antipuritanical or reactionary phases of New England character which are nowhere, perhaps, presented so sharply, so unsparingly, as in Mrs. Elizabeth Stoddard's very uncommon stories, *The Morgesons, Two Men, Temple House*. These stories, recently reprinted, but written many years before realism was named, are not unlike some more modern pieces of realism in concentrating their fierce light upon certain characters, certain traits, and in failing to indicate the general conditions in which these are exceptional, and the moods which often subdue even their exceptionality. But they are bold impulses in the direction of truth, and must be more and more valued in any study of the evolution of American realism. They have fine moments, and are written with a disrespect for the conventional view of New England nature which consoles. It would be very interesting to see what sort of work in fiction Mrs. Stoddard would do to-day.

A writer who, like her, began to be a name while our names were far fewer than now, is Mr. Edward House, whose new novel, *Yone Santo*, we have been reading with rather more satisfaction as a study of Japanese life and character than as a story. It is written from the inside, as regards these, and it presents us a type of most pathetic loveliness in the person of the heroine. If the race whose artistic gift has enriched and modified the taste of the whole world within the last decade can indeed produce such women as *Yone Santo*, its destinies can be best left in the keeping of its mothers and daughters; for our civilization has little to teach them, by example at least, in goodness, patience, self-sacrifice, and all noble ideals.

VII.

We leave ourselves too little room to speak fully of Sidney Luska's new volumes, in which are printed his magazine story, *A Latin Quarter Courtship*, and a fresh novelette, *Grandison Mather*. His pseudonym is now the transparent disguise of Mr. Henry Harland, who makes in these later books a frank advance on the realistic lines while keeping enough of the romantic thaumaturgy to please the reader of his earlier fiction. Both books have the charm which can come only from a wholesome and generous talent dealing with the perennial interest of young love. They are very sweet; they are pure and fine. Perhaps the character in *A Latin Quarter Courtship* is a little more delicately touched; after a year the young lady doctor and the very American painter in Paris survive in our thought as figures treated with subtle art to an effect of delightful humor; but nothing can be more attractive than such a study of new married life as the author makes in *Grandison Mather*. The scene is in New York, and the history is that of a young literary man who marries a lovely girl, loses his fortune through the rascality of his agent, and retrieves himself through his own powers and the inspiration of her faith and affection. Their adversity will have thrills and pangs enough for the reader, who will make acquaintance through them with the facts of a literary struggle as they really are; there are times for holding the breath, times of poignant defeat and disappointment, when one must look at the last page to reassure one's self. Mr. Harland is a born story-teller; he attracts you from the first word, and goes on to the end with a cumulative interest. He has moreover a sense of his responsibility to something better than your curiosity, and nothing that is good is sacrificed to any mere literary end in his work. The praise seems negative, but it has its positive side too; for the finest work of our day teaches that to be morally false is to be æsthetically false. It is a pleasure to recognize this quality in one of our most promising talents, and to welcome these two charming books, not only as entertaining, but as truly representative. Nothing is more normal than the aspects of life with which they concern themselves, and as long as there are "two young lovers lately wed" anywhere in the world, their history will take people out of themselves in a transport which even care and sorrow can feel. We could say nothing friendlier of Mr. Harland's work than that when we return from it to ourselves, it is with the sense of having actually met his characters, and of feeling the happier and kindlier for their acquaintance.

---

[1] Sir Leslie Stephen, "Leslie Stephen on Scott," The Critic, 13 (September 1, 1888), 107.

[2] *Criticism and Fiction*, p. 22.

[3] *Criticism and Fiction*, pp. 21-22.

[4] Henrik Ibsen, *The Pillars of Society, and Other Plays*, Havelock Ellis, ed., in *The Camelot Classics*, Ernest Rhys, ed. (London: W. Scott, 1886-91).

[5] Most modern editions translate Ibsen's title *An Enemy of the People*, but in the Camelot Edition which Howells was using (see note 4 above), the play is called *An Enemy of Society*, and this is how Howells refers to it.

[6] Georg Morris Cohen Brandes, *Henrik Ibsen* (New York: B. Blom, [1964]). This is a reprint of Brandes' three essays on Ibsen, written in 1867, 1882, and 1898, respectively. The third, of course, was written after Howells' reference. The first two were published separately in Brandes' *Aesthetiske Studier* (Kjøbenhavn, 1888).

[7] Edmund Gosse, "Ibsen's Social Dramas," *Fortnightly Review*, 51 (January 1, 1889), 107-121.

[8] *Criticism and Fiction*, pp. 129-130.

Editor's Study.

I.

ONE of the great newspapers the other day invited the prominent American authors to speak their minds upon a point in the theory and practice of fiction which had already vexed some of them. It was the question of how much or how little the American novel ought to deal with certain facts of life which are not usually talked of before young people, and especially young ladies. Of course the question was not decided, and we forget just how far the balance inclined in favor of a larger freedom in the matter. But it certainly inclined that way; one or two writers of the sex which is somehow supposed to have purity in its keeping (as if purity were a thing that did not practically concern the other sex, preoccupied with serious affairs) gave it a rather vigorous tilt to that side. In view of this fact it would not be the part of prudence to make an effort to dress the balance; and indeed we do not know that we were going to make any such effort. But there are some things to say, around and about the subject, which we should like to have some one else say, and which we may ourselves possibly be safe in suggesting.

II.

One of the first of these is the fact, generally lost sight of by those who censure the Anglo-Saxon novel for its prudishness, that it is really not such a prude after all; and that if it is sometimes apparently anxious to avoid those experiences of life not spoken of before young people, this may be an appearance only. Sometimes a novel which has this shuffling air, this effect of truckling to propriety, might defend itself, if it could speak for itself, by saying that such experiences happened not to come within its scheme, and that, so far from maiming or mutilating itself in ignoring them, it was all the more faithfully representative of the tone of modern life in dealing with love that was chaste, and with passion so honest that it could be openly spoken of before the tenderest bud at dinner. It might say that the guilty intrigue, the betrayal, the extreme flirtation even, was the exceptional thing in life, and unless the scheme of the story necessarily involved it, that it would be bad art to lug it in, and as bad taste as to introduce such topics in a mixed company. It could say very justly that the novel in our civilization now always addresses a mixed company, and that the vast majority of the company are ladies, and that very many, if not most, of these ladies are young girls. If the novel were written for men and for married women alone, as in continental Europe, it might be altogether different. But the simple fact is that it is not written for them alone among us, and it is a question of writing, under cover of our universal acceptance, things for young girls to read which you would be put out-of-doors for saying to them, or of frankly giving notice of your intention, and so cutting yourself off from the pleasure—and it is a very high and sweet one —of appealing to these vivid, responsive intelligences, which are none the less brilliant and admirable because they are innocent.

III.

One day a novelist who liked, after the manner of other men, to repine at his hard fate, complained to his friend, a critic, that he was tired of the restriction he had put upon himself in this regard; for it is a mistake, as can be readily shown, to suppose that others impose it. "See how free those French fellows are!" he rebelled. "Shall we always be shut up to our tradition of decency?"

"Do you think it's much worse than being shut up to their tradition of indecency?" said his friend.

Then that novelist began to reflect, and he remembered how sick the invariable motive of the French novel made him. He perceived finally that, convention for convention, ours was not only more tolerable, but on the whole was truer to life, not only to its complexion, but also to its texture. No one will pretend that there is not vicious love beneath the surface of our society; if he did, the fetid explosions of the divorce trials would refute him;

but if he pretended that it was in any just sense characteristic of our society, he could be still more easily refuted. Yet it exists, and it is unquestionably the material of tragedy, the stuff from which intense effects are wrought. The question, after owning this fact, is whether these intense effects are not rather cheap effects. We incline to think they are, and we will try to say why we think so, if we may do so without offence. The material itself, the mere mention of it, has an instant fascination; it arrests, it detains, till the last word is said, and while there is anything to be hinted. This is what makes a love intrigue of some sort all but essential to the popularity of any fiction. Without such an intrigue the intellectual equipment of the author must be of the highest, and then he will succeed only with the highest class of readers. But any author who will deal with a guilty love intrigue holds all readers in his hand, the highest with the lowest, as long as he hints the slightest hope of the smallest potential naughtiness. He need not at all be a great author; he may be a very shabby wretch, if he has but the courage or the trick of that sort of thing. The critics will call him "virile" and "passionate"; decent people will be ashamed to have been limed by him; but the low average will only ask another chance of flocking into his net. If he happens to be an able writer, his really fine and costly work will be unheeded, and the lure to the appetite will be chiefly remembered. There may be other qualities which make reputations for other men, but in his case they will count for nothing. He pays this penalty for his success in that kind; and every one pays some such penalty who deals with some such material. It attaches in like manner to the triumphs of the writers who now almost form a school among us, and who may be said to have established themselves in an easy popularity simply by the study of exotic shivers and fervors. They may find their account in the popularity, or they may not; there is no question of the popularity.

IV.

But we do not mean to imply that their case covers the whole ground. So far as it goes, though, it ought to stop the mouths of those who complain that fiction is enslaved to propriety among us. It appears that of a certain kind of impropriety it is free to give us all it will, and more. But this is not what serious men and women writing fiction mean when they rebel against the limitations of their art in our civilization. They have no desire to deal with nakedness, as painters and sculptors freely do in the worship of beauty; or with certain facts of life, as

the stage does, in the service of sensation. But they ask why, when the conventions of the plastic and histrionic arts liberate their followers to the portrayal of almost any phase of the physical or of the emotional nature, an American novelist may not write a story on the lines of *Anna Karenina* or *Madame Bovary*. *Sappho* they put aside, and from Zola's work they avert their eyes. They do not condemn him or Daudet, necessarily, or accuse their motives; they leave them out of the question; they do not want to do that kind of thing. But they do sometimes wish to do another kind, to touch one of the most serious and sorrowful problems of life in the spirit of Tolstoï and Flaubert, and they ask why they may not. At one time, they remind us, the Anglo-Saxon novelist did deal with such problems—De Foe in his spirit, Richardson in his, Goldsmith in his. At what moment did our fiction lose this privilege? In what fatal hour did the Young Girl arise and seal the lips of Fiction, with a touch of her finger, to some of the most vital interests of life?

Whether we wished to oppose them in their aspiration for greater freedom, or whether we wished to encourage them, we should begin to answer them by saying that the Young Girl had never done anything of the kind. The manners of the novel have been improving with those of its readers; that is all. Gentlemen no longer swear or lie drunk under the table, or abduct young ladies and shut them up in lonely country houses, or so habitually set about the ruin of their neighbors' wives, as they once did. Generally, people now call a spade an agricultural implement; they have not grown decent without having also grown a little squeamish, but they have grown comparatively decent; there is no doubt about that. They require of a novelist whom they respect unquestionable proof of his seriousness, if he proposes to deal with certain phases of life; they require a sort of scientific decorum. He can no longer expect to be received on the ground of entertainment only; he assumes a higher function, something like that of a physician or a priest, and they expect him to be bound by laws as sacred as those of such professions; they hold him solemnly pledged not to betray them or abuse their confidence. If he will accept the conditions, they give him their confidence, and he may then treat to his greater honor, and not at all to his disadvantage, of such experiences, such relations of men and women as George Eliot treats in *Adam Bede*, in *Daniel Deronda*, in *Romola*, in almost all her books; such as Hawthorne treats in the *Scarlet Letter;* such as Dickens treats in *David Copperfield;* such as

Thackeray treats in *Pendennis*, and glances at in every one of his fictions; such as Mrs. Gaskell treats in *Ruth Barton*; such as most of the masters of English fiction have at some time treated more or less openly. It is quite false or quite mistaken to suppose that our novels have left untouched these most important realities of life. They have only not made them their stock in trade; they have kept a true perspective in regard to them; they have relegated them in their pictures of life to the space and place they occupy in life itself, as we know it in England and America. They have kept a correct proportion, knowing perfectly well that unless the novel is to be a map, with everything scrupulously laid down in it, a faithful record of life in far the greater extent could be made to the exclusion of guilty love and all its circumstances and consequences.

We justify them in this view not only because we hate what is cheap and meretricious, and hold in peculiar loathing the cant of the critics who require "passion" as something in itself admirable and desirable in a novel, but because we prize fidelity in the historian of feeling and character. Most of these critics who demand "passion" would seem to have no conception of any passion but one. Yet there are several other passions: the passion of grief, the passion of avarice, the passion of pity, the passion of ambition, the passion of hate, the passion of envy, the passion of devotion, the passion of friendship; and all these have a greater part in the drama of life than the passion of love, and infinitely greater than the passion of guilty love. Wittingly or unwittingly, English fiction and American fiction have recognized this truth, not fully, not in the measure it merits, but in greater degree than most other fiction.

V.

Who can deny that it would be incomparably stronger, incomparably truer, if once it could tear off the habit which enslaves it to the celebration chiefly of a single passion, in one phase or another, and could frankly dedicate itself to the service of all the passions, all the interests, all the facts? Every novelist who has thought about his art knows that it would, and we think that upon reflection he must doubt whether his sphere would be greatly enlarged if he were allowed to treat freely the darker aspects of the favorite passion. But, as we have shown, the privilege, the right to do this is already perfectly recognized. This is proved again by the fact that serious criticism recognizes as master-works (we will not push the question of supremacy) the two great novels which above all others have

moved the world by their study of guilty love. If by any chance, if by some prodigious miracle, any American should now arise to treat it on the level of *Anna Karenina* and *Madame Bovary*, he would be absolutely sure of success, and of fame and gratitude as great as those books have won for their authors.

But what editor of what American magazine would print such a story?

Certainly we do not think any one would; and here our novelist must again submit to conditions. If he wishes to publish such a story (supposing him to have once written it), he must publish it as a book. A book is something by itself, responsible for its character, which becomes quickly known, and it does not necessarily penetrate to every member of the household. The father or the mother may say to the child, "I would rather you wouldn't read that book"; if the child cannot be trusted, the book may be locked up. But with the magazine and its serial the affair is different. Between the editor of a reputable English or American magazine and the families which receive it there is a tacit agreement that he will print nothing which a father may not read to his daughter, or safely leave her to read herself. After all, it is a matter of business; and the insurgent novelist should consider the situation with coolness and common-sense. The editor did not create the situation; but it exists, and he could not even attempt to change it without many sorts of disaster. He respects it, therefore, with the good faith of an honest man. Even when he is himself a novelist, with ardor for his art and impatience of the limitations put upon it, he interposes his veto, as Thackeray did in the case of Trollope when Trollope approached the forbidden ground.

It does not avail to say that the daily papers teem with facts far fouler and deadlier than any which fiction could imagine. That is true, but it is true also that the sex which reads the most novels reads the fewest newspapers; and, besides, the reporter does not command the novelist's skill to fix impressions in a young girl's mind or to suggest conjecture. All this is very trite; it seems scarcely worth saying; and it appears pathetically useless to answer in the only possible way the complaint of the novelist that in the present state of the book trade it is almost impossible to get an audience for an American novel. That seems very likely, but, dear friend, your misfortune begins far back of the magazine editor. If you did not belong to a nation which would rather steal its reading than buy it, you would be protected by an international copyright law, and then you might defy the magazines and appeal to the public in a book with a fair hope of getting some return for your labor on it. But you *do* belong to a nation that would rather steal its reading than buy it, and so you must meet the conditions of the only literary form with which stolen literature cannot compete. The American magazine much more than holds its own against anything we can rob the English of. Perhaps it is a little despotic, a little arbitrary; but unquestionably its favor is essential to success, and its conditions are not such narrow ones. You cannot deal with Tolstoï's and Flaubert's subjects in the absolute artistic freedom of Tolstoï and Flaubert; since De Foe, that is unknown among us; but if you deal with them in the manner of George Eliot, of Thackeray, of Dickens, of society, you may deal with them even in the magazines. There is no other restriction upon you. All the horrors and miseries and tortures are open to you; your pages may drop blood; sometimes it may happen that the editor will even exact such strong material from you. But probably he will require nothing but the observance of the convention in question; and if you do not yourself prefer bloodshed he will leave you free to use all sweet and peaceable means of interesting his readers.

Believe us, it is no narrow field he throws open to you, with that little sign to keep off the grass up at one point only. Its vastness is still almost unexplored, and whole regions in it are unknown to the fictionist. Dig anywhere, and do but dig deep enough, and you strike riches; or, if you are of the mind to range, the gentler climes, the softer temperatures, the serener skies, are all free to you, and are so little visited that the chance of novelty is greater among them. [1]

---

[1] *Criticism and Fiction*, pp. 147-162.

Editor's Study.

I.

THE paper of Mr. Brander Matthews on the "Dramatic Outlook in America,"[1] which was printed in the May number of this Magazine, touches certain aspects of the situation which we should have been glad to have it dwell upon more fully; for Mr. Matthews is one of the very few people among us authorized by knowledge and experience to treat of a matter so many are willing to handle without either. His wide acquaintance with dramatic literature affords him the right critical perspective, and his ventures as a playwright enable him to conceive of the subject from the theatrical point of view, and to represent those claims of the stage which literary men are sometimes disposed to contemn. It is important when such a man concludes that if Americans are ever to write plays it must be with the advice and instruction, if not the active co-operation, of the theatre.

We believe that good plays were never otherwise written in any age or any country, and that if at any time or anywhere the drama seemed the creation of poets writing independently of the theatre, this was an illusion which very slight question would dispel. Shakespeare, Goethe, Schiller, Goldoni, Molière, Lope, to mention only the greatest in their kind, wrote their plays in the theatre or in constant rapport with it, and from their intimacy with actors and acting learned how to make their words "speak to the eye," as Mr. Harrigan has fortunately phrased it; and so far as we yet have a drama, it has been produced on the same terms, and on these terms only.

II.

The author and actor named has already been recognized in these pages as an artist working on the lines of a natural and scientific development of drama from local origins, and we recur to his work now because we believe that the American drama, like the American novel, will be more and more a series of sketches, of anecdotes, of suggestions, with less and less allegiance to any hard and fast intrigue. In this view of the matter we take heart of hope from the very despair of Mr. A. M. Palmer, who has lately written so frankly of the present state of the[2] drama amongst us, and who sees no future in such work as Mr. Harrigan's or Mr. Denman Thompson's because it lacks this allegiance. Mr. Palmer, like Mr. Matthews, is certainly authorized to speak on the subject; he is a manager of long experience, of unquestionable taste, and of uncommon literary sense; whatever he says must be received with deference. Yet here, we venture to suggest, he is not quite in touch with the most modern spirit. Because the drama has been in times past and in other conditions the creature, the prisoner, of plot, it by no means follows that it must continue so; on the contrary, it seems to us that its liberation follows; and of this we see signs in the very home of the highly intrigued drama, where construction has been carried to the last point, and where it appears to have broken down at last under its own inflexibility. In Paris itself during the past winter the two greatest dramatic events were the production at the Théâtre Libre of Tolstoï's *Powers of Darkness* and Goncourt's *Germinie Lacerteux*, mere series of impressions, with nothing of the close texture of the old-fashioned French play of artifice. In fact, if we go back of these, what is *Hamlet* even but "a prolongation of sketches," studying now one phase and now another of the same irresolute temperament, without necessary sequence and without final unity of effect?

III.

Mr. Palmer thinks that Mr. Harrigan's work and Mr. Thompson's work will not take a place in a national drama, because their plays were contrived for themselves and not for the general stage, and that they will pass away with their authors. He says one has produced "a prolongation of variety sketches," and the other "an entertainment." He does full justice to the charming qualities of both, but he denies that either has written a play; he holds by the old theory of what a play ought to be, and refuses to acknowledge as such any dramatic representation that does not conform to it. His position is interesting, and we wish to state it with entire respect, though we can in no wise agree with him, if the name of play is to stand for what is alone dramatically worthy. Whether Mr. Harrigan's work or Mr. Thompson's work can claim a place in a national drama or not, we feel pretty sure that we shall never have a national drama till our playwrights approach social and psychological problems in the spirit of their liberal art, and deal with them as simply, freely, and faithfully as those authors deal with the humble life of New York and New England. We believe, moreover, that a national drama can arise with us only as it has arisen with other peoples: that is, out of some such wilding native growths as these authors are cultivating.

IV.

Up to this time the only contributions which we have made to the stock of histrionic character are the Darky as the minstrels evolved him, the Yankee, and the low-down New-Yorker in his various phases. These are in their sort the American masks, as much ours as Pantalone was Venetian, or Policinello was Neapolitan, or Stenterello is now Florentine; they are inalienably and unmistakably ours. Strictly speaking, we have nothing else on the stage that is our own, excepting the continental type of Colonel Sellers. Of the others, the Darky mask is obsolescent, if not obsolete, through the operation of historical events. Slavery gave him to art, but the conditions that characterized him so sharply are past, and he is no longer distinctly representative. He survives, however, in the scenes of Mr. Harrigan, who studies him as one variety of the low-down New-Yorker, together with the German, the Irishman, the Chinaman, the Italian of our streets. Mr. Palmer says that none of these is native American, which is true; and he implies that they cannot therefore have a place in a national drama, which is not true, to our thinking. Our civilization has differentiated them from all others of their kind, and they are naturalized, if not native. Mr. Harrigan likes to portray them; that is his taste, his preference; but his art is applicable to the most indigenous of our citizens, and when it is employed by some one whose taste, whose preference, is in their direction, we can only hope that it may be with his excellent fidelity and refined perception. We use our adjectives consciously, and in spite of a rankling disappointment with his last play, as a whole. In *Waddy Googan* the effort to work out a plot of the sort supposed essential to a play warped him from his true function as a painter of life, and merged in the coarse colors

of a melodrama the delightful *nuances* with which he realizes character both in his writing and his acting. His art is essentially sympathetic and delicate, and we hope he will yet have the courage to discard altogether the traditional allegiance to intrigue, and in some framework as simple as that of *The Old Homestead* frankly commit himself to a "prolongation of sketches." People may or may not call it a play: we are sure it will be a charming piece of dramatic art.

V.

We like to speak of Mr. Harrigan and Mr. Thompson together, because we find them in their different ways working to the same effect of refinement and truth. Mr. Thompson has taken the old mask of Yankee life as Mr. Harrigan took the old mask of New York life, and through his study of nature has produced a series of pictures as true to Swanzy, New Hampshire, as Mr. Harrigan's work is true to the Bowery, to Mott Street, and to Mulberry Bend. We must congratulate him upon having worked with even greater contempt of the dramatic superstitions, and made his "entertainment" a play almost without a plot. There is a succession of natural situations in which the simple characters develop themselves; the scene follows the boy who left his home, after the bank robbery, from Swanzy to New York and back to the country again; nobody, if we remember rightly, is married, and certainly nobody killed; the interest centres upon the love of an old Yankee farmer for his son, and this is sufficient to hold all hearts, while the faithfulness, the courageous sincerity, in the study of this old farmer's nature and circumstance sparkle into humor as wholesome and genuine as the pathos. Of course the piece has its defects, its moments of weakness, when the humor lapses into burlesque and the pathos approaches bathos; but these moments are comparatively rare; and it is little short of astonishing to find a veteran manager and actor inviting Nature into the theatre and making her at home there with a cordiality which she has seldom known in that place. Mr. Thompson has not only gone back into his own early life for the truth about the country, but he has used his larger and later experience to verify the facts of the city. The hackneyed conception of the case, as cruel and vulgar as it is false, would have shown Joshua Whitcomb's old friend, grown rich and grand in New York, ashamed of the farmer when he comes to visit him. The truer art of Mr. Thompson makes him glad of every rustic quaintness that recalls the days when they were barefoot boys together in Swanzy. The scene which follows, when the millionaire and the farmer sit down together and begin to talk over those days, and to clap each other on the back, and nudge each other in the side, and to laugh and laugh, is one of the most beautifully veracious we remember on the stage, and it is played with a naturalness that enriches the spectator like some happy experience of his own. We could not praise it too much; in conception and execution it is a masterpiece. Its homeliness may not appeal to those whose sensibilities have been coarsened by the world, but we should confidently trust it to move any man who had kept his boyhood uncontaminate in his heart, and the finer the spirit the more deeply should we expect this lovely piece of art to move it. Many other passages approach it in excellence; the play abounds in delightful touches; and is faithful, so far as it goes, both to country and to city. Joshua Whitcomb talking to the tramp before his door, and Joshua Whitcomb furtively peering into the faces of the passers before Grace Church for the face of his son, are different aspects, alike true, of the same wholesome, natural, and winning character; but we do not know that they are better or more charming than others of other characters in the piece. These were in fact so well imagined and so well played that we doubt whether the piece will necessarily cease to be given when Mr. Thompson ceases to take the leading part. To be sure, we cannot suppose any one else playing, or rather *being*, Joshua Whitcomb with his exquisite perfection. There is not a false note in the old Yankee's personality from first to last; every fibre of the actor's body, as well as every faculty of his mind, seems attuned to its expression; the illusion is without a flaw, and the sense of what is truly fine and good within the rustic simplicity is unbrokenly imparted. It is a surpassingly subtle study; and yet we can imagine the character in the hands of a less accomplished artist without ruinous detriment to the piece. It is by no means a one-part piece; one has as great pleasure at moments in the old fellow who comes in and stumps round in a belated effort to court Joshua's sister as in Joshua himself. This old-maid sister and her Irish help, Rickety Ann from the poor-house and the whistling hobbledyhoy farm boy, the tramp and Joshua's millionaire friend in New York— they are all conceived in the same delightful sincerity, and they are all played with the same honest art, insomuch that you can hardly resist the inference that the actor would not fail to hold the mirror up to nature so often if the author oftener gave him the mirror to hold up. But we have before now paid our duty to the general excellence of the acting on our stage; it

is indefinitely better than the material it usually has to deal with; and in the high level kept by the players in *The Old Homestead* we see what pleasure the theatre might give us if we had a drama worthy of it. We cannot leave speaking of this piece without reminding the reader of the adequacy of its setting, especially the New England landscape which forms the background for the scenes of the first act, and the night view of Grace Church in the second. As mere accessories, inarticulately appealing to the imagination, the choral outburst from the church and the procession of the Salvation Army before it are finely thrilling; when those girls lift their tambourines and face about as they beat them, and their wild hymn rises, you cannot refuse to share their exaltation.

VI.

In fact, on a wider plane than any one else has yet attempted, Mr. Thompson gives us in this piece a representation of American life. Of course it is mere suggestion, mere intimation in places, but at its sketchiest it is true, and that is the great matter. Where it is most satisfyingly full, however, is in its proof that the simpler phases of our life still make the strongest appeal to all. It is the old homestead in the country which has remained the ideal of a nation tossed in a wilder rush of interests and ambitions than ever tempted men before; the heart yearns forward or backward to it, "a home of ancient peace," amidst the turmoil and the strife. The existence of this sentiment foreordains the success of any piece of art which deals with it, and other playwrights have not been slow to take a hint from Mr. Thompson's work. So far, indeed, as we now have any drama, outside of Mr. Harrigan's work, it mainly deals with New England country life. We do not forget the excellent work of Mr. Gillette and Mr. Bronson Howard on other lines, but we think our words indicate the prevailing tendency. If we have any school, it is the school which is developing the old American mask of Yankee character; but we shall not go so far as to boast that we have a school in speaking of the work of Mr. Neil Burgess and Mr. Charles H. Hoyt in this direction. It is not on the level of Mr. Thompson's work, and any recognition of its amusing qualities should frankly include some such confession at the outset. We do not know who gets Mr. Burgess's pieces together; perhaps he does it himself; but *The County Fair*, as well as *Vim*, is contrived to throw into constant relief the character of a bustling Yankee housekeeper. So far as they concern her they are deliciously true, and as they concern very little else, we need not criti-

³

cise them. If we remember rightly, the scheme of *Vim* was a little broader than that of *The County Fair;* it included not only Tryphena Puffy, but another real character in her slow, taciturn, evasive husband, who had his own deliberate way in spite of all her volubility, energy, and rapidity. *The County Fair* includes no character but that of a like ineffectively bustling housewife. In both cases Mr. Burgess is homicidally funny; but it is an easy matter to kill people with laughing, and yet not win their admiration. Mr. Burgess does win it, because he is an accomplished artist. He helps himself out with vastly more farce than Mr. Thompson uses; but for the most part Tryphena Puffy and her analogue (we really forget the name in *The County Fair*, but it does not matter; the character is so much the same) are rendered with an accuracy, a closeness, quite worthy to be spoken of in the same breath with the characterization of Joshua Whitcomb. When Mr. Burgess begins to talk, you want him to go on forever; every most satisfying accent makes you hunger for more. All of us know Tryphena Puffy; we remember her from childhood, or we have summer-boarded with her, or our lot is still cast with her in the country; we instantly recognize the type, and if Mr. Burgess will allow us to spend the evening in her company we can ask nothing better of him. When she sits down with her knitting and begins to rock, and asks, "Who'd you see at the post-office?—anybody 't I know?" it is enough. The drama can do no more, and in fact it does very little more than show this phase and that of her peremptory, kindly, shrewd, trusting nature; it really is not of the slightest consequence otherwise, and need not be.

VII.

In Mr. Hoyt's play of *A Midnight Bell* we have something more structural; a plot that rather unfortunately recalls *The Old Homestead* in its bank robbery and its irrelevantly whistling and singing overgrown boy. It lacks both in character and incident the sweetness of Mr. Thompson's pastoral; the fun is harsher, and the serious passages are without tenderness; a spirit of caricature and exaggeration prevails. There is a villain, a bad, black-hearted villain, whose very walk is full of wickedness, and who is so obviously the real bank robber from the beginning that you resent the self-sacrifice of the good nephew, who proclaims himself the thief to divert suspicion from the good uncle, rather more than you commonly resent the self-sacrifice of the stage hero; no one outside of that simple community could have sus-

pected any other than that villain with that abandoned walk and those truculent side whiskers and that deadly manner. It is perhaps too much to ask Mr. Hoyt to recast his work for our comfort; but we really think he missed a charming and novel effect in failing to make the dismissal of the minister for protecting the school-mistress the pivotal fact of his drama. All the action could have moved naturally and probably about that fact, and the elimination of the villain and the robbery would have been gain incalculable. The minister and the school-mistress are both well imagined, and at times the school-mistress is well realized; but Mr. Hoyt's work seems to suffer from the keeping of a company trained to the performance of his riotous farces. One perfectly charming moment it has, when the little girl speaks her piece at the school examination; this is extremely pretty. The piece shows familiarity with country life and love of it; at times it is very amusing; but because it is never more than amusing, and when most amusing not half so amusing as Mr. Hoyt's riotous farces, we prefer the riotous farces. These are full of actuality, and in all their exaggeration there is truth to our characteristics and conditions. *The Rag Baby, A Tin Soldier, A Hole in the Ground, The Brass Monkey*—they are not achievements of high art, but they are genuinely funny, and for the most part harmlessly so, wholesomely so. Sometimes you are a little ashamed to have laughed, but they never make you hang your head in despair, as some serious American dramas do—dramas which have kept the stage for hundreds of nights. They are the work of a real humorist, a comic talent perfectly sensible of their limitations, and willing to transcend them, as we see in such an effort as *A Midnight Bell*.

VIII.

It is impossible not to wish Mr. Hoyt well when you read those little prefaces to his comedies in the play-bills, in which he confides to the spectator his own modest estimate of them; and the desire to prophesy greater things for him is almost irresistible. But perhaps it is best to modify our predictions to the opinion that his development lies rather in the line of *The Rag Baby* than in that of *A Midnight Bell*. The purely comic is by no means a bad thing nor a low thing; and again we wish to put forward our heresy that for a play a plot of close texture is no more necessary than for a novel; that for either, in dealing with modern life, it would be an anachronism. We will not disparage the endeavor of other dramatists to give us plays of the sort to which Mr. Palmer would confine the name; we will even ask the reader to abate somewhat from the praises we have been bestowing so freely upon the work of Messrs. Thompson, Harrigan, Burgess, and Hoyt; we do not at all pretend that they have produced a great drama. But we do pretend that in such prolongations of sketches as they have given they have made the right beginning of an American drama. With the exception of Mr. Hoyt, they are all actors and managers, and they build their plays on their own stages. We believe Mr. Hoyt has his company, and is in effect a manager. They absolutely control the conditions under which they appear to the public, as no other sort of dramatist could hope to do; and if literary men are ever to reach the public on equal terms it must be by some such means. In our time, as in all times, the dramatic poet should be part of the theatre. All managers are not dramatic poets, nor all dramatic poets managers; but the apparent enmity between them is needless, and they must work to-

gether in amity and mutual respect before we can have American plays in such quantity and quality as will satisfy even American play-goers. This is saying with Mr. Matthews that co-operation is the solution of the problem, and it is perhaps not saying more. But we have gone a long way roundabout to say it, and that is something. It is something also to have differed so distinctly with Mr. Palmer on one point that we can self-respectfully agree with him on others, and especially upon the absence of a public taste in regard to the drama. This taste, he reminds us, exists only in countries where "dramatic art has for centuries been fostered by the people, and oftentimes protected and patronized by intelligent governments." Perhaps we may yet, when the people really come to their own, have a municipal theatre in every city and town, sustained by a tax, where the best dramas may be seen for a tenth of the price one now pays to see the worst.

[1] Brander Matthews, "The Dramatic Outlook in America," Harper's Magazine, 78 (May, 1889), 924-930.

[2] G. E. Montgomery, "A. M. Palmer and His Theatre," American Magazine, 9 (1885), 1+.

[3] Neil Burgess is the sole author of Vim, and collaborated with Charles Barnard in writing The County Fair.

August , 1889

Editor's Study.

I.

THE hospitality of our English tongue to people born to the comparative inarticulateness of other speech is something very pleasing, if not personally creditable, to each of us with whom English is natural, and who do not refuse to share its advantages with those poor aliens. Perhaps we could not refuse them if we would, but this ought not to take from the nobleness of our actual behavior in the matter; and for our own part we will not deny ourselves the satisfaction of a host in calling attention to the happy facility in English of such a Norseman as Mr. H. H. Boyesen. None has shown it greater love or deserved a warmer welcome to it than this American novelist, whom we will hardly allow to have ever been anything else. He might, indeed, have been more American than any of us; for if his ancestors could have endured New England, after they discovered it, and had not abandoned the potentiality of Boston to the hardier sensibilities of its future Puritan founders, we might now be writing this Study in very choice Norwegian, which would have been the language of the country. But since it all happened differently, we feel that we acquire merit through Mr. Boyesen's excellent use of English in his *Vagabond Tales*. As all the world knows, it is by no means his first essay in it; he began to write English almost as soon after coming to America as an Irishman begins to vote; and the Study might easily grow autobiographical in recalling the days when he became a contributor and it was still an editor. His earliest contribution to the *Atlantic Monthly* of those days was that pretty Norwegian idyl, *Gunnar*, whose charming freshness and poetic simplicity are not yet surpassed in American literature; and all that he wrote was reminiscent of his Northern father-land: the slim birch lightened and whispered and the tall fir darkled and sighed in his page; the *loor* called from the *saeter*, and the Hardangar fiddle in the hall followed the strophe and the antistrophe of the *stev* that was both sung and danced; the Necken gleamed beside the torrents leaping to the fiord, and in the thicket shone the golden braids of the Hulder, dreamily whisking her heifer tail to keep away the mosquitoes. We do this sort of thing but once, if we do it at all; and Mr. Boyesen's work became rapidly less Norse, rapidly less romantic; but he did not cease to be a poet in becoming more and more an American. His study of Schiller and Goethe is now a text-book in our colleges; and his scholarly repute has kept pace with his fame as a novelist; as a professor in a leading university, and as lecturer and critic, his name appeals to the recognition of many who might not fully know him as a magazinist. But to one who has watched his career among us nothing is more interesting than his development in fiction, which has been so strictly obedient to the laws of his origin and environment. He was in the prime of youth when he became naturalized to our language and our life, and he seems to have felt the same keen joy in the one as an instrument that he felt in the other as material. With *Gunnar* he put the purely Norse world behind him, and dealt with the facts of ours in the terms which he caught from our lips. But, for all his avidity in this, he did not rashly abandon the ground where he no longer wholly dwelt; and even in these Vagabond Tales, more or less recent, he is still dealing with Norse character in the process of transformation into American character. Nearly all the stories begin in Norway and end in our Northwest; the light of the midnight sun lingers on them, and invests their persons with a romantic grace; but no one can read them rightly without feeling that the line of the author's growth is in the direction of a perfect realism, which need not be ever less poetical because it is ever more conscientious. A great deal of humor tempers his conception even of the heroic; and here the author himself seems to be translated, so entirely does he throw himself into the American attitude toward the extraordinary, the unexpected. Of the English which he writes so wonderfully the worst that any one could say is that it is too American; and we have no wish to say this. Between book English and spoken English, we prefer the spoken; and we would rather have Mr. Boyesen over-vernacular than pedantic: he would be closer to the life. When he shall give us a novel of American life, spacious in design and full of the results of his varied acquaintance with our civilization, there is a chance that he may give us the American novel for which criticism has so long panted; or, failing that, we feel sure that he will give us in English and in fiction a work of thoroughness and grasp not easily outrivalled by that of any to the manner born.

II.

In the mean time we praise these tales not only for the style which the author has made recognizably his own in an alien language, and for the fresh tint which his Norse associations now and again give a word, a phrase, grown faded to us from use, but also for the pleasant novelty of their *personnel*. These people are not the men and women whom we know in other Scandinavian fiction. Scandinavian they indeed are, but the American situation has differenced them from other Scandinavians, and we get them in the same sort of relief effect which the European situation lends to Mr. Henry James's Americans. We have spoken already of *A London Life*, which while it was still a serial seemed to us so extraordinarily good in prospect. In retrospect it is even better (in the volume of stories which it names); and we invite the reader to notice the sharp severity of moral outline in the American personages against the London background. Good and bad alike, they have carried with them into foreign atmosphere the unsparing definition which all objects wear in ours; when they are not grotesquely intense they are pathetically intense in the strange environment. It is an effect which we notice in one another abroad, and which makes us wonder where in the world all the odd Americans in Europe come from. But we suspect that it is the very accuracy with which Mr. James reproduces it that makes some of us so angry with him for what we call his caricatures of his countrymen, and especially his country-women. They are really not caricatures: a caricature of any sort would be impossible to his delicate art: they are exact portraits, and not the less perfectly realized because they seem so pitiless. One cannot accuse him of drawing the English people in *The Liar* with unnatural tenderness; yet the worst of them has a softer psychological outline than that charming, that thoroughly good American girl, Laura Wing, in *A London Life*, whose most tremulous uncertainties are all so distinct. That group of varied Bostonians on *The Patagonia* is something to make one shiver; each seems thrusting a rectangular elbow into one's ribs from a personality as clear cut as the sculpture of long self-consciousness could make it; yet they are only on the way to Europe, and have, as it were, their Back Bay and their South End still about them. They will not show a keener contour against the vague English light when they arrive; it will do its best to mellow their edges; but it will not succeed; and because they will block themselves out in it as sharply as they would against their native sky, they will seem the caricatures which they really are not.

III.

No one but a fine artist like Mr. James would have felt their peculiarity, or had the courage to recognize it in his work; but he must pay the penalty of being true, which attends that sort of conduct pretty unfailingly. He could make himself much more acceptable to his generation if he would treat his negatives a little, and flatter away those hard edges in the process which we believe the photographers call vignetting. But since there is small hope of his making this patriotic sacrifice, we will take what comfort we can from the thought that there must be a compensating advantage spiritually in the definiteness which makes us appear odd socially, even in our own eyes, when we see our pictures. We fancy, for instance, that the virtues of such a man as Emerson could have acquired their edge in no other environment than ours, and that a certain degree of rigidity was a condition of their effectiveness. The important study of *Emerson in Concord*, by his son, Dr. Edward W. Emerson, will hardly change this impression, which was left by Mr. Cabot's biography, [2] and we do not suppose it is intended to change it. The author only wished to present Emerson with more fulness in his relations to his family and his fellow-villagers, and his very agreeable book has at least thrown a more abundant light upon him there. In view of the result, it is well to remember that there was once an American public which regarded this great man, with his really planetary distinctness, as something vague and nebulous. Perhaps it never quite got at him; perfect simplicity, entire sincerity, is baffling; people do not know quite what to make of it; and we have a feeling, whether we get it from Dr. Emerson's book or not, that his father came much nearer to his townsmen than they came to him. With most of them he must usually have seemed to mean more or less than he meant; few of them could have been so merely compact of goodness and truth as to conceive of a character, a life, an intention, which was nothing but the love of goodness and truth. They were all fond of him and proud of him; but for the right local estimate of Emerson, for the light of the store, the hotel office, the barn, and the hay field, we must probably always wait: these centres of village thought are not inarticulate, but they are unliterary. The domestic circle is much more expressive, and what Emerson was to his family, with his seriousness, his tenderness, his lofty ideals of conduct, his rather Spartan severity with weakness in which there was an alloy of selfishness, his spare, fine humor, his pure courage and immaculate veracity in every phase of being, we have no reason for not knowing from his son's memoir.

Yet, after all, there are not many details, not many instances, in it. The father standing beside the coffin of his first-born, and saying, "That boy! that boy!" the wise disciplinarian sending the fretful child from the table out into the air to regain the lost balance of its nerves from the serenity of nature; the impartial lover of fun inextinguishably laughing over the tomcat parody of his *Brahma;* the philanthropist patient with the vagaries of all friends of humanity, but inflexibly resolute to talk only in the yard with the reformer who would not take off his hat in the house; the lover of nature abandoning the garden to other spades and hoes, and doing his own work as he wandered through the woods; the heir of Puritan good sense and decorum forbidding the children cards in the morning and battledoor and shuttlecock on Sunday: these are the small facts we recall at hap-hazard, without referring to the book, and they are perhaps such as will remain in the minds of most readers. For the rest, the author imparts the sense of a tranquil and joyous religion, of a steadfast faith in good as the only reality, and in life as necessarily continuous from the implications of all experience. This survived for Emerson after all creeds had fallen dead with him—this and the reverent affection for tradition in which belief was embalmed. Some misguided persons who held that the disciples had practised a fraud by stealing the body of Jesus from the tomb and reporting that He had risen, seemed to Emerson to have pulled up lilies and planted skunk-cabbages in their places; and throughout his life he honored the worship and respected the religious sentiment of others, though he was perfectly explicit concerning his own opinions when necessary. The devout spirit did not hesitate to repudiate the church when it faltered, as the good citizen made haste to advise his townsmen to seek all occasions for breaking the law where it bade them enslave a man.

IV.

In fine, freedom in all things was his ideal, and this meant with him freedom to seek the good, the only real. Yet because Emerson supremely loved the untrammelled use of his own being he never would bind himself even to the cause of the abolitionists, though sometimes he asked leave to sit on the platform with their speakers, when there seemed unusual danger of violence to them. He held that the scheme of his life included their work, and undoubtedly he was right, just as undoubtedly he must have seemed deficient to some true and noble friends of the slave in refusing their label. On an indefinitely loftier level we feel that Mr. William M. Salter, in one of the essays of his recent work on *Ethical Religion,* fails of the measure of Christ in His merely human character of reformer when he notes that He did not utter Himself against slavery or the oppressions of His day. It seems to us that He who bade us love one another, and be last if we would be first, and do unto others as we would that they should do unto us, began the beginning of the end of slavery, and of every social wrong beside: His ideal of life once conceived, it became finally impossible for one man to hold another in bondage. The process was long, terribly long, and it will not be completed till every man's toil is paid according to its worth, and not according to his necessity. Then we shall have the Christendom which has never yet existed on earth, and still in that era of unexampled freedom and justice we shall fall short of fulfilling Christ's ideal of equality and fraternity, which indeed no society except that of the early Christians or the early Quakers has ever even attempted to realize.

But leaving apart all question of its negations, and taking it solely on its affirmative side, where it deals with civic, social, personal duty, Mr. Salter's book is consoling and inspiring. He reasons of such important matters as: what is a moral action; is there anything absolute in morality; the social ideal; the rights of labor; personal morality; the supremacy of ethics; and he reasons earnestly, ably, interestingly always. Still we cannot perceive that he treats these important matters and others in any other than the Christian manner, except that he seems to confine motive more to the life here and now. When he says, "Morality is this going out of one's self and living in, living for, something larger," he is presenting, in other words, Tolstoï's declaration that there is no such thing as personal happiness, no bliss but forgetting ourselves and remembering others, no life but in its loss for goodness' sake. But Tolstoï is repeating this truth with reference to its origin in Christ and its effect in eternity; and so we find greater support in it than when the same ideal of conduct seems to restrict itself to time and space.

But, after all, however, it is well to have an ideal of conduct so humane preached for any reason. Mr. Salter's question of the ethical finality of Christ's precept and example is thoroughly reverent, and no Christian need be troubled at any man's endeavor to imagine something beyond them in their kind. Our author is still centrally within their lines when he establishes his system of ethics on the ground of self-sacrifice, and preaches justice. We do not, for instance, see how any Christian can read his lecture on the Rights of Labor without a thrill of assent or a throe of conviction, according as he has or has not been himself a doer of the Word. In fact the Word as a rule of life has never yet governed the world that calls itself Christian; but at last men are longing to embody it in their social and political ideals, with an impulse that animates every humane thinker, whether he calls himself Christian or not.

V.

One may refuse to recognize this impulse; one may deny that it is in any greater degree shaping life than ever before, but no one who has the current of literature under his eye can fail to note it there. People are thinking and feeling generously, if not living justly, in our time; it is a day of anxiety to be saved from the curse that is on selfishness, of eager question how others shall be helped, of bold denial that the conditions in which we would fain have rested are sacred or immutable. Especially in America, where the race has gained a height never reached before, the eminence enables more men than ever before to see how even here vast masses of men are sunk in misery that must grow every day more hopeless, or embroiled in a struggle for mere life that must end in enslaving and imbruting them. With heart-sickness and shame one reads in Mr. Lee Meriwether's book, *The Tramp at Home*, that in this country, this continent, superabounding in every element of wealth, a New England factory family earns but a hundred dollars more than a factory family in worn-out Italy, and with the closest economy saves no more —that is, saves nothing. That seems an insufficient result from all the protection we have given labor through capital; and it is plain from the facts of Mr. Meriwether's entertaining, rather helter-skelter, book that we are as far from

having solved the problem as the most perplexed people of the Old World.

Mr. Meriwether, as special agent of the United States Department of Labor, wandered up and down, and back and forth, over our hemisphere, from Brooklyn to San Francisco, from Texas to Oregon; and as if the trouble revealed—the overwork and underpay, the oppression and revolt, the strikes and the lock-outs in the factories, the foundries, the mines, the farms, the shops, the offices—within our vast borders were not enough, he gives us a glimpse of sailor slavery in a voyage to the Sandwich Islands, where, as he says, the people are "being civilized into poverty." He does not suffer us always to have this terrible question before us; he is amusingly discursive, as "full of anecdote" as the hero of *Engaged*, and surprisingly light-hearted in his stories of first and second hand adventure. But he comes back to business at last, and in a final chapter disposes of organization, education, co-operation, temperance, and economy and industry, as all mere temporary expedients, and recommends free-trade and a graduated land tax as the solution of the labor question.

VI.

Mrs. Helen Campbell, on the other hand, concludes her book, *Prisoners of Poverty Abroad* (it is mainly a study of the condition of working-women in London and Paris), with the opinion that the sole hope of labor in the future is some sort of socialism. To this end she regards the land tax and free-trade as steps perhaps necessary to be taken, but not a solution. "The co-operative commonwealth must come; and when it has come . . . . when the spirit of brotherhood rules once for all, the city of God has in very truth descended from the heavens, and men have at last found their own inheritance."

Mrs. Campbell, apparently, finds the prisoners of poverty abroad in no more hopeless captivity than those at home, whose sorrowful durance she told us of in a former book. The needle-women of New York are allied to those of London in the dismal conditions of their lives rather than to those of Paris; they have less sunshine and society than the French wage-slave-women, and far less than the Italian, who can work so much out-doors, even with the sewing-machine, in their fortunate climate. But everywhere the story is the same; competition has reduced the pay to the line of mere subsistence; the large commerce has devoured the small; there is absolutely no hope of better things, not even the hope of exile; for greed has seized even the waste places, and, as Mr. Meriwether shows, has shut out by fraud the labor willing to exchange home and friends for the mere chance of life elsewhere. The national domain of the United States, the immeasurable lands of Australia, New Zealand, and South Africa, to which the starving working-men of the Old World could once escape, are occupied or pre-empted, and on an area almost as vast as that of civilization the powers that be are confronted with the danger that threatened England before Chartism found vent in emigration. Fifty years ago Carlyle wrote to one of his brothers: "Millions (a frightful word, but a true one)—millions of mortals are toiling this day, in our British Isles, without prospect of rest, save in speedy death, to whom, for their utmost toiling, food and shelter are too high a blessing. When one reads of the Lancashire factories and little children laboring for sixteen hours a day, inhaling at every breath a quantity of cotton fuzz, falling asleep over their wheels, and roused again by the lash of thongs over their backs or the slap of 'billy-rollers' over their little crowns; and then again of Irish Whitefeet, driven out of their potato patches and mud-hovels, and obliged to take the hill side as broken men—one pauses, with a kind of amazed horror, to ask if this be earth, the place of hope, or Tophet, where hope never comes."

In Ireland, after fifty-six years, the situation is quite the same; but the system of hopeless labor has now been carried over the whole earth, and the hours of work have been fixed in India at the old figure, with all the old blessings of the cotton manufacture as they were enjoyed in England before the law interfered with the sacred inspirations of self-interest.

Carlyle then looked to America for relief; but America must soon begin looking somewhere herself for relief. The planet Mars is known to be adapted to human life; the day is longer than ours, and more work could be got out of people. Both capital and labor would probably prosper there—labor through capital, of course—but awaiting the clearer knowledge of that globe which a more pressing necessity will doubtless achieve, we can commend the last volumes of *Carlyle's Letters* which Professor Norton has given us for the light which they casually throw upon some terrestrial aspects between the years 1832 and 1836. It is not always the clear beam which Emerson's mind cast about it; sometimes it is smoky with passion and foul with prejudice, and sometimes it is a flicker sad and faint enough from the sickness which was always apt to cloud it. But it reveals Carlyle himself more and more distinctly, and in phases of greater lovableness. The reader of *Emerson in Concord* may profitably compare the two men in the familiar relations in which these letters and that study reveal them. With much more talk to that effect Carlyle was far less a stoic than his "American friend" (as he several times calls Emerson here), and so far from making a silent fight against the belittling influences of ill health, he rather invites his demon of indigestion to utterance. He was not a simpler or sincerer nature than Emerson, but more primitive; and he remains to the end without Emerson's large perspective. Both men are tenderly true to kin and home; but in the fidelity of Carlyle there is something aggressive, a glimpse of the mail he wore against his world in defence of poor and humble beginnings, which a man need not quite yet put on in America. Or, perhaps he perceived that these lowest things were really the highest, and burned with indignation that others should not see it.

[1] Hjalmar Hjorth Boyeson, Gunnar: A Norse Romance, Atlantic Monthly, 32 (July-December, 1873), 13-26, 166-179, 320-332, 426-436, 513-526, 681-691.

[2] James Elliot Cabot, A Memoir of Ralph Waldo Emerson (Boston and New York: Houghton, Mifflin and Company, 1887). (Howells reviews this book in the "Study," pp. 118a-119b.)

[3] Criticism and Fiction, pp. 183-184.

September , 1889

Editor's Study.

I.

The Rose of Flame and Other Poems of Love, by Anne Reeve Aldrich, is a little book which must sometimes, we are afraid, make the friendly critic rather sorry for the really gifted woman who has had the courage to write it; or perhaps we had better say the daring to print it. In the fifty or sixty little pieces, which it is made up of, she perpetually, not to say monotonously, dramatizes the love which has been betrayed to ruin, and the long unending

> "ricordarsi del tempo felice
> Neila miseria."

But her experience must have been fortunate, if she has found her readers always able to seize the dramatic intention. We cannot ourselves praise her taste without reserve; we have our misgivings as to the final usefulness, which is to say the lasting beauty, of much of what she has written. Many women must have thought such things, felt such things as she expresses; and yet there is somewhere a limit, an end, to the open saying of such things as one thinks and feels. We are not inclined to draw the line very fast, or draw it very close; but we suggest that there are risks in not drawing it at all. Yet this said we are bound to recognize the truth, the power, of Miss Aldrich's verse at its best; and we should think it really a dishonest neglect of critical duty if, in regretting much of her work, we failed to draw attention to the subtle perception, the impassioned solemnity of such a poem as this:

NEW EDEN.

In that first Eden, Love gave birth to Shame,
  And died of horror at its loathsome child.
Let us slay Shame, and bury it to-day—
  Yea, hide it in this second Eden wild,
This dim, strange place where, for aught we two
    know,
No man hath stepped since first God made it so.
    *   *   *   *   *   *   *
Look on this tangled snare of undergrowth,
  These low-branched trees that darken all be-
    low ;
Drink in the hot scent of this noontide air,
  And hear, far off, some distant river flow,
Lamenting ever till it finds the sea.
New Life, new World, what's Shame to thee and
    me ?

Let us slay Shame; we shall forget his grave
  Locked in the rapture of our lone embrace.
Yet what if there should rise, as once of old,
  New wonder of this new, yet ancient place,
An angel, with a whirling sword of flame,
To drive us forth forever in God's name!

Then for the art to catch and the skill to impart the sadness of fate, and the mystic helplessness of being, this piece called *A Song of Life* may well bear witness in its author's favor:

Did I seek life? Not so; its weight was laid
    upon me;
And yet of my burden sore I may not set my-
    self free.
Two love, and lo, at love's call, a hapless soul
    must wake;
Like a slave it is called to the world, to bear
    life, for their love's sake.

Did I seek love? Not so; Love led me along
    by the hand.
Love beguiled me with songs and caresses, while
    I took no note of the land.
And lo, I stood in a quicksand; but Love had
    wings, and he fled.
Ah fool, for a mortal to venture where only a god
    may tread !

Such words as these could not have come from a shallow heart or a narrow brain; bitter and rebellious as they are, they are profoundly appealing, they embody a reality that no one can gainsay, and that is none the less a truth because it is not the only truth about life. The ability to write poetry like this accuses much of the author's verse of mere sensuousness in the rapture and the regret it records; and it may be hopefully left to condemn to her the error and excess which we often feel in her book.

II.

In like manner, we are willing to deliver over to his own judgment some passages of Mr. Cawein's *Accolon of Gaul*. He did not invent the facts; they are in the old legends out of which Tennyson mined the *Idyls of the King;* but the younger poet might well have studied from the master the science of assay which rejected the baser particles of the ore imbedding them. It is because these passages are well done that one feels it the greater pity they should have been done;

they mar, if they do not spoil the beauty
of the poem, which abounds in splendors
such as the rich fancy of Mr. Cawein
loves. We have before now tried to
make the reader feel his lyric quality,
and now we have to recognize his power to tell a story not only with pictorial sumptuousness but with dramatic
strength. There is "passion" galore in
it; that we have reproachfully intimated;
but there is character too; and the poet
knows how to lead on to a supreme moment, as when Queen Morgane has sent
her lover Accolon to kill Arthur, and
having murdered her husband Urience,
against his return, hears

> "a grind of steeds,
> Arms, jingling stirrups, voices loud that cursed·
> Fierce in the northern court. To her athirst
> For him her lover, war and power it spoke,
> Him victor and so King; and then awoke
> A yearning to behold, to quit the dead.
> So a wild spectre down wide stairs she fled,
> Burst on a glare of links and glittering mail,
> That shrunk her eyes and made her senses quail.
> To her a bulk of iron, bearded fierce,
> Down from a steaming steed, into her ears,
> 'This from the King, a boon!' laughed harsh and
>   hoarse;
> Two henchmen beckoned, who pitched sheer with
>   force,
> Loud clanging at her feet, hacked, hewn, and red,
> Crusted with blood, a knight in armor—dead;
> Even Accolon, tossed with a mocking scoff,
> 'This from the King!'—phantoms in fog rode off."

With pictures, with colors, this poem
and the others that go with it to make up
the book, abound, perhaps superabound.
In one of his securest and loveliest lines,
Mr. Edgar Fawcett speaks of a butterfly
whose wing is a "turmoil of rich dyes,"
and the phrase would fit much of Mr.
Cawein's work; too often he seems like
the painter Monticelli, to have given you
his palette instead of a picture. But having said this we are rather sorry, for we
are not aware of being the poorer for this
young poet's opulence; and one rather
likes to see his appetite for splendor glut
itself; the time will doubtless come when
he will feed sparely enough. In the mean
while, it is as if we had another Keats, or
as if that fine, sensitive spirit had come
again in a Kentuckian avatar, with all its
tremulous hunger for beauty. We had
marked a good many passages for quotation in the *Accolon*, such as—

> "some frail lady white
> As if of watery moonbeams, filmy dight,
> Who waves diaphanous beauty on some cliff
> *That drowsing purrs with moon-drenched pines*";
and
> "A forest vista, *where faint herds of deer
> Stalked like soft shadows*";

or these lines from the poem *To the Rain
Crow:*

> "Oft from some dusty locust that thick weaves
>   With crescent pulse-pods its thin foliage gray,
> *Thou, o'er the shambling lane which past the sheaves
> Of sun-tanned oats winds, red with rutty clay,*

One league of rude rail-fence, some panting day,
  When each parched meadow quivering vapor
    grieves,
Nature's Astrologist, dost promise rain....
And thou.... contented art
  In thy prediction, fall'n within the hour;
*While fuss the brown bees homeward from the
    heart
Of honey-filtering bloom;* beneath the cart
  Droop pompous barn-yard cocks damped by
    the shower;
And deep-eyed August, bonnetless, a beech
Hugs in dishevelled beauty, safe from reach
    On starry moss and flower."

Or this sonnet, from four on *Loveliness:*

> "Oft do we meet the Oread whose eyes
>   Are dew-drops where twin heavens shine con-
>   fessed;
> She, all the maiden modesty's surprise
> Blushing her temples—to deep loins and breast
> Tempestuous, brown bewildering tresses press-
>   ed—
> Stands one scared moment's moiety, in wise
> Of some delicious dream, *then shrinks distressed*,
> *Like some weak wind*, that haply heard, is gone
> In rapport with shy Silence to make sound;
> So like storm sunlight, bares clean limbs to bound,
> A thistle's flashing to a woody rise,
> A graceful glimmer, up the ferny lawn."

But this picturesqueness, this daring for
a phrase, ending sometimes in luminous
felicity and sometimes in teasing obscurity, but always leaving the sense of a
vivid and gracious intention, is the very
texture of Mr. Cawein's verse, and it is not
so different from what we have tried to
make the reader know of him before. His
exuberance will tame itself in time; he
will learn temperance and self-denial,
which are as good in the worship of the
beautiful as in other things. But he gives
now with both hands, and we are rather
disposed to enjoy the spectacle of his profusion. At least it shows that he has
something to give.

III.

Or, at the end of the ends, and if we
must come very low in our defence of one
we own a favorite with us, he is at the
worst not writing from a theory, which
seems to be what works Mr. William
Sharp an injury in his *Romantic Ballads
and Poems of Phantasy.* Mr. Sharp believes that "there is a romantic revival
imminent in our poetic literature," as "in
pure fiction the era of romance as opposed
to pseudo-realism is about to begin, if the
tide be not already well on the flow," and
he appears to have set himself rather consciously to take it in the direction of fortune. Or perhaps it is his preface coming
before his poems that gives this impression; very possibly the poems were written first, and the preface imagined from
them. In any case, he thinks much may
be done with "the weird, the supernatural," and he is hard upon those whose ballads are of blue china and the like rather
than of white ladyes and the like. He
may be right; the children still tell ghost

stories; but we remind the reader that romanticism was the expression of a world-mood; it was not merely literary and voluntary; it grew naturally out of the political, social, and even economical conditions at the close of the eighteenth century. It was a development of civilization, and not simply a revulsion from the classicistic literary fashions which it replaced, or it could not have gone so deep in the lives of men as it did. In its day it was noble and beautiful; it lifted and widened the minds of people; it afforded them a refuge in an ideal world from the failure and defeat of this. To assume that we can have it back on any such terms as Mr. Sharp imagines seems to belittle a world-mood to a study-mood, a closet-mood; to narrow its meaning, to take it from humanity and give it to the humanities. Romanticism belonged to a disappointed and bewildered age, which turned its face from the future, and dreamed out a faery realm in the past; and we cannot have its spirit back because this is the age of hopeful striving, when we have really a glimpse of what the earth may be when Christianity becomes a life in the equality and fraternity of the race, and when the recognition of all the facts in the honest daylight about us is the service which humanity demands of the humanities, in order that what is crooked may be made straight, and that what is wrong may be set right. The humanities are working through realism to this end, not consciously, for that is not the way of art, but instinctively; and they will not work to that other end, because, so far as it was anywise beautiful or useful, it was once for all accomplished by the romanticists of the romanticistic period.

So it seems to us, but we may be wrong. What we are sure of is that in reacquainting ourselves with the weird and the supernatural, as they are seriously addressed to the reader's sensation in Mr. Sharp's ballads, we have failed to experience that agreeable condition of goose-flesh which we knew in our romantic youth, and which we understand to be the intentional and exemplary state of the neo-romanticist of whatever age. Mr. Sharp's *Weird of Michael Scott*, the wizard who accidentally burns up his own soul, which he happens to find outside his body, is a Weird that leaves us quite cold, though we own to have experienced rather a fine thrill in reading the poem of the Willis Dancers, those youths and maids who have died unloved, and whose spirits meet in phantasmal wooing above the churchyard mould. The suggestive theme is treated with delicate insight, and with a tenderness which gains nothing when it attempts to express "passion."

IV.

Perhaps we do scanty justice to Mr. Sharp's poetry in our dissent from his theory; one of the evils of having very firm convictions is that you want to deny all merit to people who have different ones. Mr. Sharp is by no means a narrow-minded critic, and he has a word of warning for those who think the importance of a work of art lies in the subject rather than the treatment; he reminds them that noble or ignoble is in the mind of the artist, not in the material he works in. He is so reasonable in this that we would like to call his notice, and that of others who are nowadays asking a good deal of the imagination, to a passage concerning the true nature and office of that mental attribute. The passage is from Isaac Taylor's *Physical Theory of another Life*, and is in explanation of his preference of analysis for his attempted exploration of the unknown. "Plainly," he says, "it is not the imagination that can render us aid in conceiving of a new and different mode of existence, *since this faculty is but the mirror of the world around it, and must draw all its materials from things actually known.* It may exalt, refine, ennoble, enrich what it finds, and it may shed over all the splendor of an effulgence such as earth never actually sees; yet it must end where it began, in compounding elements and in recombining forms furnished to its hand; *and if ever it goes or seems to go beyond these limits, the product is grotesque or absurd, not beautiful; there is no grace or charm in that which trenches upon the actual forms of nature.*"

It seems to us we have here a reason why a generation like the present, so rich in the experience of the past as to have really ascertained two or three æsthetic principles, should not revert in its poetry and fiction to the inspirations of romanticism, which belonged to the childhood and the second-childhood of the world, when people believed in the grotesque creatures of their own imaginations, and then when they made-believe in them. The whole affair seems very simple and plain. All the machinery of romanticism, so far as it involves the superstitions, helpless or voluntary, of either epoch, is grown finally ramshackle; and for our own part, we cannot see why it is any more reverend than an idol which has become a doll, or any more capable of resuscitation in the awe or the sentiment of grown people. Nobody, we suppose, would ask us to go back and believe in, or make-believe in, the knights and ladies, pages and squires, hinds and minstrels, of romance,

as at all like the real ones who once existed; and it is rather hard to be asked to
toy again with the wizards and the phantoms, the weirds and the wraiths, that
never existed. Once we believed in them,
and once we made-believe in them. Is not
that enough? Or are we to make-believe
again? How tiresome! Why not go back
and do pastorals a third time? Or is there
some law of the mind that suffers one reversion of this sort, but forbids two?

V.

But while we could never consent to let
Mr. Sharp reromanticize imaginative literature by any exhortation or endeavor, we
are very sensible of the gracious service
he has done American poetry in his collection of *American Sonnets*. We do
not know that we should ever have
thought so well of our compatriotic sonnet without his work in its behalf. Out
of some two hundred and fifty sonnets,
there are really none bad, and some are of
prime excellence. Here and there a poet
is made memorable by a single sonnet,
who would have been otherwise quite unknown, or would have been forgotten;
and in several cases it happens that a
poet is seen to be at his best in the sonnet, whom we might else have hardly
thought it of. But we know too well the
jealous and vengeful nature of sonneteers
to venture upon any comparison of their
work; and from like motives of prudence
we refrain from specifying our favorites
among the living poets represented in
Mr. Sharp's excellent collection. It is
safe, however, to thank him for a sense
of Longfellow's greatness in this kind,
and for his cordial recognition of the
mastery of several other of our poets in it.
His collection is of singular worth, to our
thinking, because we cannot think (for
the present at least) of any memorable
sonneteer who has been forgotten in it;
though we might easily be wrong in this.
Sometimes it seems to us that Mr. Sharp
fails to include the best sonnet of this or
that poet—he likes to call poets "bards"—
but he has fairly represented the quality
of each. A noticeable feature of the
whole is the fact that one of our greatest
poets is not in it, because he had not used
a form so popular with our younger if
not wiser poets. Holmes is there in one
sonnet; Whittier in three; Lowell in five:
none of them at their best, or second best;
but Emerson is not there at all. One can
easily fancy that he, who rejoiced in compactness, must have found a conventional form like the sonnet too irksome; and
it is hard to understand just why fourteen
lines of rhymed decasyllabic verse should
prove so perfect a vehicle for the thoughts
and creations of so many poets in every
tongue. The structure of the American

sonnet is varied as to the rhyme; but
there is a general tendency to the Pe-
trarchan order; Bryant is almost alone
with Sidney Lanier in writing the Shakespearian sonnet. Mr. Aldrich, who has
done his most serious work in the sonnet,
is one of the most scrupulous in respecting the Italian form, but not more so than
some others: Mr. Fawcett, for instance,
who also is perhaps at his best in his sonnets; and Mr. Gilder, of whom the same
might be said. There remains to be made
a strict analysis of the sonnet form, and an
inquiry into the secret of its convenience,
which it doubtless would not surprise, but
which would be very interesting. It is a
form of extraordinary vitality, and survives in our time as vigorous as it arose
in that of whatever remote Italian invented it.

VI.

But we find ourselves recalled from the
pleasure of praising Mr. Sharp's American
Sonnets to our grievance with him concerning a romantic revival, by Dr. S. Weir
Mitchell's suggestive treatment of the old
superstition of the elixir of life in his new
poem, *The Cup of Youth*. Here the
poet evolves from the subject qualities
which appeal in the highest degree to the
imagination without overtaxing your
modern capacity by asking you to suppose his own acceptance of the superstition; whereas, if we understand the neo-
romanticists aright, he should have pretended to make himself a party to it.
Uberto, the inventor of the elixir in *The
Cup of Youth*, might have really drunk
it off, and in his return to youth abandoned to loveless old age the wife who
had devoted her life to him. But this
would have been a fruitless effect in
the reader's mind; it would have been
recognized, and then it would have
ceased. As it is, the group of people
sketched remain living in our thoughts:
the selfish seeker after the secret of renewed existence, defeated and mocked in
the very moment when he was to have
triumphed, by the girl who spills the draft
and avenges the poor old wife, and then
finds her own punishment in the rejection
and disavowal of her deed, to which the
wife's pity of her pitiless husband's suffering moves her. Here are real motives
that go far deeper than any make-belief
could reach; they touch that feeling for
all the actors in the little drama which
the wise view of any human situation
must evoke, and which plays from one to
another in equal interest. Here is the
truly imaginative treatment of a romantic theme; that is, the scientific treatment,
which can alone dignify it. What was
vital in it is suggested; the mere husk is
still left for the fancy of any neo-romanticist to batten on. In some such sort Dr.

Holmes has dealt with recondite phases of our common nature, and has given them the last charm for the imagination by refusing to deal with them in the spirit of make-belief, by keeping himself an impartial spectator. In the same sort Hawthorne himself achieved his highest effects; and with that delicate smile of his cast a final discredit on the superstition he had been playing with. But no such tricksy gleam remains upon the tragedy which our poem has sketched: the picture at the close perpetuates a moment of poignant pathos.

---

[1] "Ricordarsi del tempo felice/ Nella miseria." – To remember happy times/ In misery.

Editor's Study.

I.

MR. HENRY CABOT LODGE'S life of Washington is almost the most important in Mr. Morse's series of American Statesmen, whose lives have been [1] written with so much ability under the eye of an editor who has chosen their biographers with so much tact. We say almost, because we like to inculcate temperance of expression rather than because we can think, off-hand at least, of any other that surpasses it in the series; and if we cannot say it is the last, we can say it is certainly the latest word concerning a man about whom the words are not likely ever to have an end. It is the novel treatment, and in a very good sense, the original treatment, of material often treated before, but never to an effect so fresh in the portrayal of Washington as an American.

This effect, which remains with the charm of surprise from the reading of the book, is the note struck at the beginning, and the note struck at the end. In the first place, Mr. Lodge had to reclaim Washington from Fable-land, and in the last place from England; and it was much easier to do the one than the other. In fact, although the Weems con- [2] ception of Washington as saint and hero is still the popular conception, and perhaps must always be the elementary conception of his character—for in the patience and power of Washington there really was much that was saintly and much that was heroic—still, there is a large and growing minority who find comfort and profit in imagining him a man of like material if not like make with themselves. Such people, if they do not delight, do not grieve to know that he swore in moments of great exasperation; they are not sorry to realize that he was quite a man of his place and his period; that though he came to deplore slavery, he held slaves all his life; that though he was a thorough republican, he was not socially a democrat; that though he was temperate, he was not prohibitory; that he was a home-bred provincial of the eighteenth century, though when occasion came, he turned out to be the first of the continentals. Yet it is among this minority that

a superstition concerning Washington far more injurious than that of the majority has arisen. The people who could not accept the Washington of Weems seem to have been willing to believe that one of the most thorough Americans who ever lived was an English country gentleman born by some accident out of his native country; and as if we had been so rich in great Americans since his time, have consented to expropriate us of his matchless glory in behalf of a country and a system which he gave his conscience, his wisdom, and his power to overthrow on our continent: which his instincts and his principles alike taught him to condemn. If profane swearing in the Elysian Fields were imaginable, one might well fancy Washington's shade permitting itself a few dozen round oaths in reception of the first gentleman who ventured to confront him among the asphodel with such a notion of his nationality. But we do not think this misconception of the great Virginian can long survive the light which Mr. Lodge lets in upon it. The whole tenor of his book is against it; and in the last chapter, to which we particularly commend the reader, he studies it with a masterly analysis which leaves it no longer any claim even to be discussed.

The wonder that it should ever have been seriously regarded, however, remains; for if any Englishman of the eighteenth century or of any century were like Washington, it would not be so strange. But none with whom he has been compared is really the least comparable with him either in grandeur or in texture. American he was, by nature, by tradition, by education, with such traits, such difference of qualities as the New World could alone give a man of the Old World race; or, if we must liken him to some European, it cannot be to any Englishman, for England's occasions were never such as to produce such a man; but to the great Dutchman, William the Silent, who indeed strikingly resembled [3] him in some points. Their civilizations were so distinct that in all transmitted traits, and probably in all civic ideals they were unlike, but in certain individual characteristics they were alike; both had so wide a hold upon the faith and the love of their countrymen that they embodied in themselves and prolonged in their wills the often-flagging revolutions that they led; both knew how to turn defeat to the account of victory, and to give retreat the value of pursuit; both had infinite patience, infinite tact; both were incorruptibly unselfish, and concentrated the ardor of all their passions in a love of the public good. In reading the story of our revolt against England as Mr. Lodge tells it, one is reminded again and again of the revolt of the Netherlands against Spain; it is a war of principles in both cases, and in no other case does the far-spread popular impulse seem to have been so steadily centred in one mind, and so wisely directed from it. His latest biographer, who is no hero-worshipper, does justice to those properties of leadership in Washington which more and more made the guidance of the Revolution his, almost as if he had been the first to imagine it, to invent it; the heat of his passionate nature was the force that fused all interests and welded all wills in the endeavor for independence. As one realizes this, one realizes in its full proportions the unselfishness of Washington in leaving to its own destiny the nationality that, far more willingly than we can otherwise understand, would have kept him its master. He had above all else the genius of republicanism, the faith proved by fire in the adequacy of a people to themselves, which after a hundred years was revived in Lincoln. Yet we must be careful, if we would be just, not to regard even Lincoln as the peer of Washington; for Washington was all that Lincoln was in this, with a vast breadth of military power and achievement beside and beyond. Both men centred in themselves the national love, but Washington was as the father where Lincoln was the brother of his country.

Something of this Mr. Lodge makes one feel more distinctly than one has felt it before, without removing Washington beyond the range of human experience. In fact, the great value of his study is that it presents us a purely human, as well as a thoroughly American Washington. He is both, even to the point of liking and sometimes making a joke, though we are hardly prepared to flaunt him as the first of American humorists in the face of the nation bereft of him as an eighteenth-century squire. We are afraid that the laughing mood was rare with him, though it was none the less genuine for that, as Mr. Lodge is able to show. He is not able to conceal that he is sometimes an unconscious humorist, who makes us smile at the stately phrase, the lace and the ruffles, in which his generation loved to clothe its thoughts. He was a thoroughly eighteenth-century person in that and in his manners, not to mention some of his morals, but an eighteenth-century American, with a love of English rather than French models; we still have our little preferences, and Washington did not know French. If he had been in France, he might have given the revolution there a watch-word, as Franklin did, or learnt many from it, as Jefferson did; but no doubt it was well for us that he staid at home and read the *Spectator* rather than the Encyclopedists.

II.

He is not much more old-fashioned than Mr. John Fiske when the humor takes him to talk of " a " Cæsar, " a " Cicero, " a " Socrates, and other people who ordinarily get on in his pages quite well without their indefinite articles. The little rhetorical touch will not often qualify the pleasure of reading *The Beginnings of New England*. The book is written with all the charm of Mr. Fiske's clear style, vast knowledge, and right perspective: in his treatment it is a part of the history of the human race. It is not a contribution of fresh facts; it is an attractive arrangement, rather, of well-known compositions, and performs for the historians the office performed by Mr. Fiske's metaphysical essays for Darwin and Spencer. It sets in memorable light things otherwise easily forgotten, and assembles to an effect of excellent unity traits and phases of the past from widely scattered sources. The book may be fairly called a portrait of Puritan New England, less flattered than Palfrey's, and considerably [4] more flattered than Mr. Brooks Adams's. [5] Of that bold, powerful sketch, in which no rugosity of the original was spared, Mr. Fiske frankly takes cognizance, and his conception of the Puritan theocracy is more than once tacitly shaped by *The Emancipation of Massachusetts*, which must hereafter influence all students, or at least challenge them and give them pause. Yet Mr. Fiske writes with tolerance of a polity which Mr. Adams wrote of with abhorrence, and he willingly turns its good points to the light. He is perhaps moved to this by his admiration of the character of the Puritan people, who were so much wiser and better than the Puritan rulers. "It was the simple truth," he says, "that was spoken by William Stoughton when he said in his election sermon of 1688: 'God sifted a whole nation that he might send choice grain into the wilderness.'"

Whether this is indeed the simple truth might of course be questioned. Mr. Fiske gives it the weight of his authority, but we are struck rather with its modesty than its truth, and we would suggest that among the chaff left in England after God had sifted the nation there was the stuff of the great rebellion and the commonwealth, to say nothing of the seed which blossomed in the splendor of Virginian statesmanship on our own soil, and fruited in the lives of the great men from the Middle States who did at least as much as any New-Englanders to shape our polity. Mr. Fiske at other times recognizes the comparative worth of New England on a juster scale. At such times he has the right humorous sense of a people who, like so many others in history, thought themselves peculiarly pleasant and important to Providence, and especially admitted to the confidence of the Almighty. But he could not have given us this book about them, so full of sympathetic appreciation, if he had not sometimes taken them on their own terms. Their sense of their worth was well-founded, and their intensely individualizing faith gave them qualities of personal valor and endurance conspicuous in both our revolutions: the revolution against England when the generalship came from the South, and the revolution against Slavery when the generalship came from the West. As Mr. Lodge reminds us, Washington testified to the very qualities in the common New England soldiers which availed every Union leader in our last war; and we should be the last to depreciate a tendency which democratized intelligence, fidelity, and responsibility. The only mistake in regard to such a tendency which could be made would be the mistake of supposing it confined to any section of the American people, and this Mr. Fiske sufficiently guards us against. It is in fact quite as much the sense of his constant good faith, his sincerity, his honesty, as the grace of his literature which gives him his wide and ever-widening hold upon the public.

III.

The opening essay of Mr. Fiske's volume on the Roman Idea and English Idea, which forms the philosophical basis of the others, might serve equally well as the introduction to Mr. Theodore Roosevelt's *Winning of the West*. In a far wider field, and with circumstance more varied and picturesque, the English Idea of nation building, as opposed to the Roman Idea, realized itself in the occupation of the vast region between the Lakes and the Gulf, the Ohio and the Mississippi. As in New England, the English Idea had rather to pervade than to prevail; but at one point it came in contact, if not in conflict, with the Roman Idea, in the West, as it never did in the East: when the

American backwoodsmen possessed themselves of the French towns in Illinois. These towns were British posts, and were taken for that reason, but, as throughout Canada, the military conquest had left the *habitans* to their Latin polity, and it was the Americans and not the English who endowed them with the rights of self-government. The gift was sufficiently alarming to these simple children of despotism, and when they perceived that they were really abandoned to all the embarrassments of freedom as embraced by the English Idea, they petitioned Congress for somebody to come and order them about in the good old way of the French king's and then the English king's officers.

Mr. Roosevelt tastes the humor of the situation with a sense whose lack would have fatally disabled him for studying the early history of the Great West; so often was the grotesque interwoven with the heroic in its annals. To those of like mind, as most Americans are, the qualification is natural and agreeable; and we think one distinct charm of a thoroughly charming book is the constant play of the small through the large, the personal through the general, the individual through the national, which he allows us to see at all times, not only in the aggregate, but often in the same man. His work is in very uncommon and very delightful degree anecdotical: it must be so in the narration of a story which is seldom occupied with massive events, but is always alive with the innumerable adventure of the pioneers and hunters who singly, or in bodies heroically and pathetically small, carried the English Idea into the wilderness and dispossessed the English, who had lost it, and their savage allies. Yet the narration embodies these details in a whole of weighty effect, and at the end we have been beguiled and delighted to the sense of the making of a great state, with the differences from the East and the South which the West still shows. The Watauga commonwealth in Tennessee, the settlement of Kentucky, the conquest of Illinois, and the occupation of the intermediate territory, are the main features of a race movement romantic in high degree, and yet soberly matter-of-fact in tendency, and marked by characteristics peculiarly its own. The subjection of the Indians then really began, and then their power was broken forever. They were beaten by white men with their own arts, in their own way, on their own ground; but they did not yield without exerting to the utmost the warlike qualities which distinguished them above all other savages; which Mr. Parkman was first among our historians to appreciate, and which Mr. Lodge, Mr. Fiske, and Mr. Roosevelt in their kindred studies constantly recognize. It remained for Mr.

Roosevelt, however, to make us feel this more than any other, and while doing full justice to the courage and sagacity of the Indians, to estimate in all its enormity the crime of the British ministers in turning the ferocity of such allies loose upon the American frontiers. He rightly says that this act, which involved unspeakable atrocities perpetrated against helpless women and children as well as armed men, must be forever a disgrace to the English name; and he follows its consequences in many a scene of misery and horror which now seems incredible of the English if not of the Indians.

He closes his narrative with the close of the Revolution, though it would seem that its proper climax was in St. Clair's defeat and the victory of Anthony Wayne, which involved the final great struggle with the Indians. The reader may in some sort supplement Mr. Roosevelt's work, so far as these episodes are concerned, by the vivid sketch of the effect of St. Clair's defeat on Washington, in Mr. Lodge's biography. Washington was himself one of the greatest Indian fighters, and in feeling and forecast was by no means the least of the Westerners. In fact, the early West was characterized by the South and the southernmost of the Northern colonies, in a measure to which our casual thought hardly does justice. New England had little or nothing to do with it; and Mr. Roosevelt makes us understand how some traits which seem those of Puritanic civilization were really derived from the Scotch-Irish Presbyterians, who were the earliest prophets and teachers in the West, as well as sturdy fighters and sober citizens. He has rather a peculiar liking for those bleak Calvinists, and rather a peculiar misliking for the Quakers. As for the Moravians, who were so successful in Christianizing the Indians, and who founded the little towns on the Muskingum, where their inoffensive converts were finally massacred by the Americans, he can only say of the peaceful doctrine they taught, that "No greater wrong can ever be done than to put a good man at the mercy of a bad man, while telling him not to defend himself or his fellows; in no way can the success of evil be made quicker or surer." Another moralist, however, in whom the Moravians seem to have trusted, said: "Resist not evil: but whosoever shall smite thee on thy right cheek, turn to him the other also.... Love your enemies, bless them which curse you, do good to them which hate you." Between these authorities, in the abstract, we will not venture to decide; but in the particular case of the Moravian Indians, some past study of the facts emboldens us to say that at no moment of their most pathetic history, either when they were harried out

of Connecticut, or forbidden to enter New York, or hardly suffered to linger on the Pennsylvanian border, would war have availed them. It was in virtue of literally doing the word of Christ that they existed at all; that they softened for a while the stony hearts of the pioneers, and for a while won from the savages themselves toleration beyond the white settlements; and their doom finally came at a time and in a form when if every man among them had been eager to fight, the bloodiest valor would not have averted it.

IV.

An interesting contrast to the spirit of many who deal speculatively with the question of labor is that of its latest historian, Mr. C. Osborne Ward, Librarian of the United States Department of Labor, whose very important *History of the Ancient Working-People* will hardly fail to impress the reader. It is by no means a faultless book; it is in some literary aspects a very faulty one; the author has occasionally a vehemence of diction that carries him beyond any lexicon known to us; one cannot always agree with his philosophy or accept his conclusions; but without doubt his work is one of vast and conscientious research, and opens a prospect of ancient society scarcely less than astonishing. It was already known how that society was universally founded upon slavery; from many sources it could be known how atrocious that slavery was, and how in Greece and in Rome its victims were maddened to desperate revolt, and maintained themselves in long, wide-spread, and heroic struggles, to fall again into subjection, and, if possible, into more hideous misery. But Mr. Ward makes us understand how largely these slaves were the countrymen and the kinsmen of their masters, he acquaints us with the details of their sufferings, and shows us how these were necessarily involved by the civilization and the religion of the Greeks and Romans. Both had to pass away before the slave could hope for freedom; it was from Jesus Christ that he first learned not only that he was a man, but that he was a human being, with a soul like the brother who owned and tortured and slew him, and that his naked and branded and dishonored body was the temple of the Almighty, the Ever-living; it was through the crucifixion of Christ that the ignoble punishment which the heathen state reserved for the servile outcast and the base mechanical became a sacrament.

Mr. Ward tells us that beginning his work with the obscure resentment of Christianity which too many friends of labor feel, he came to see at last that the founder of Christianity was the first wise friend that labor ever had, and that in his counsel of peaceful means is the only hope that labor yet has. He recounts, with sympathy that thrills and fidelity that agonizes, the story of the servile wars in the ancient republics, in which neither the fortitude of the slaves nor the splendid generalship of their leaders availed, and which all ended in disaster, celebrated by their triumphant masters with cruelty that brought the count of slaves crucified after the suppression of their several rebellions to a million in all. It is with poetic justice rather than with scientific accuracy that Mr. Ward speaks of these revolts as strikes; but he is strictly right in warning the working-men of our own day against violent attempts at redressing their wrongs. "So long as labor still obstinately refuses to vote and insists upon rebellion, continues to choose the irascible rather than the diplomatic, how can it be otherwise hoped or expected than that history will repeat itself?"

We have no great objection to Mr. Ward's poetic justice in the use of terms, for the servile tradition continues, whether the workman is owned, or whether he is underpaid; the difference between the coal-miner in Pennsylvania and the silver-miner in Attica is probably not such as would fill the coal-miner with pride if he could realize it; and in Greece and Rome, the conditions of the slaves and the free laborers whom they supplanted, tended perilously nearer and nearer to each other: a trifling act, a trifling debt, made them quickly convertible, in spite of all the societies and guilds and unions which the freemen had formed for their protection. But the study of these organizations in Mr. Ward's book is none the less interesting because of the sense of their immediate futility which besets the reader. It is a branch of historical inquiry worth all the pains Mr. Ward has bestowed upon it, not only in the antipathetic and mutilated classic histories, but in the results of antiquarian research before his own, and those yet more recondite documents, the tablets and mural inscriptions in which "the short and simple annals of the poor" survive from those far-off days to ours. It is well for us to see how unbroken is the tradition of the working-man's efforts at self-help, and to learn that the organizations which most people vaguely suppose to have arisen in the Middle Ages had their origin in the dawn of time, before "dignified" history first deigned to ignore them. Their story under

"The glory that was Greece,
And the grandeur that was Rome,"

was pretty much what it is under the creature comfort that is America: they served a social rather than an economical purpose, and their grudgingly permitted existence was hedged about with conspiracy laws that reduced their action in any special exigency of the working-man to something almost burlesque. This, too, is an important fact, and it by no means invalidates Mr. Ward's work in developing their extent in the ancient civilizations. The idea of the brotherhood of men which they embodied was that which Christ erected into a religion, and which remains for the working-men to erect, when they will, into a polity.

It would be natural for a writer who had bestowed so much study upon them to exaggerate their proportions, and we should not be surprised if Mr. Ward were found to have done this. But we are not prepared to say that he has done it, while we are quite ready to commend his book, with all its errors of taste, to the gentle reader. The gentler the reader, the better for his book, we should fancy; for there are traits of it that will appeal most keenly to the greatest refinement, if the refinement be genuine. Such refinement will not object even to the typographical rudeness of the book, which in these days of dandified print and binding has the appearance of having been got up in some poor little country newspaper office.

---

[1] See note 3, p. 146.

[2] Mason Locke Weems, The Life of George Washington, 6th ed. (Philadelphia: Printed for the author, 1809). (The "6th edition" is an extensive revision of an earlier work called A History of the Life and Death, Virtues and Exploits of General George Washington.)

[3] William I, Prince of Orange (1533-1584).

[4]John Gorham Palfrey, A Compendious History of New England from the Discovery by Europeans to the First General Congress of the Anglo-American Colonies (Boston: J. R. Osgood and Company, 1884). (This is a collection of two earlier volumes published in 1872 and 1873, respectively.)

[5]The Emancipation of Massachusetts, by Brooks Adams.

November, 1889

Editor's Study.

I.

HOW a better fashion can ever change for a worse; how the ugly can come to be preferred to the beautiful; in other words, how an art can decay, is a question which has often been approached, if not actually debated in this place. We do not know that we expect to debate it now; in the hurry of month after month, when the toe of September comes so near the heel of August, and March galls the kibe of February, the time never seems to arrive when the Study can really sweep and garnish itself, and quiet down to a season of serene inquiry upon such a point. At best it appears able only to cast some fitful gleams upon it, and then have its windows broken by all the little wanton boys of newspaper criticism, who like to throw stones at the light wherever they see it. The cost the Study is at in the mere matter of putty and glass, after one of their outbreaks, is such as would discourage a less virtuous apartment; but with the good conscience we have, and the faith we cherish that these *gamins* may yet grow up to be ashamed of themselves, we cheerfully pay the expense, and trim the lamp anew, and set it again where those who care may come to it. If they are not a great many, they are all the closer friends, perhaps, for being few; and it is in a kind of familiar intimacy that we turn to them with a question like that we have suggested. It has been coming up in our mind lately with regard to English fiction and its form, or rather its formlessness. How, for instance, could people who had once known the simple verity, the refined perfection of Miss Austen, enjoy anything less refined and less perfect?

With her example before them, why should not English novelists have gone on writing simply, honestly, artistically, ever after? One would think it must have been impossible for them to do otherwise, if one did not remember, say, the lamentable behavior of the people who support Mr. Jefferson, and their theatricality in the very presence of his beautiful naturalness. It is very difficult, that simplicity, and nothing is so hard as to be honest, as the reader, if he has ever hap-

pened to try it, must know. "The big bow-wow I can do myself, like any one going," said Scott, but he owned that the exquisite touch of Miss Austen was denied him; and it seems certainly to have been denied in greater or less measure to all her successors. But though reading and writing come by nature, as Dogberry justly said, a taste in them may be cultivated, or once cultivated, it may be preserved; and why was it not so among those poor islanders? One does not ask such things in order to be at the pains of answering them one's self, but with the hope that some one else will take the trouble to do so, and we propose to be rather a silent partner in the enterprise, which we shall leave mainly to Señor Armando Palacio Valdés.

II.

This delightful author will, however, only be able to answer our question indirectly from the essay on fiction with which he prefaces his last novel, and we shall have some little labor in fitting his saws to our instances. It is an essay which we wish every one intending to read, or even to write, a novel, might acquaint himself with; and we hope it will not be very long before we shall have it in English, together with the charming story of *The Sister of San Sulpizio*, which follows it. In the mean time we must go to the Spanish for some of the best and clearest things which have been said of the art of fiction in a time when nearly all who practise it have turned to talk about it.

Señor Valdés is a realist, but a realist according to his own conception of realism; and he has some words of just censure for the French naturalists, whom he finds unnecessarily, and suspects of being sometimes even mercenarily, nasty. He sees the wide difference that passes between this naturalism and the realism of the English and Spanish; and he goes somewhat further than we should go in condemning it. "The French naturalism represents only a moment, and an insignificant part of life.... It is characterized by sadness and narrowness. The prototype of this literature is the *Madame*

Bovary of Flaubert. I am an admirer of this novelist, and especially of this novel; but often in thinking of it I have said, How dreary would literature be if it were no more than this! There is something antipathetic and gloomy and limited in it, as there is in modern French life;" but this seems to us exactly the best possible reason for its being. We believe with Señor Valdés that "no literature can live long without joy," not because of its mistaken æsthetics, however, but because no civilization can live long without joy. The expression of French life will change when French life changes; and French naturalism is better at its worst than French unnaturalism at its best. "No one," as Señor Valdés truly says, "can rise from the perusal of a naturalistic book.... without a vivid desire to escape" from the wretched world depicted in it, "and a purpose, more or less vague, of helping to better the lot and morally elevate the abject beings who figure in it. Naturalistic art, then, is not immoral in itself, for then it would not merit the name of art; for though it is not the business of art to preach morality, still I think that, resting on a divine and spiritual principle, like the idea of the beautiful, it is perforce moral. I hold much more immoral other books which, under a glamour of something spiritual and beautiful and sublime, portray the vices in which we are allied to the beasts. Such, for example, are the works of Octave Feuillet, Arséne Houssaye, Georges Ohnet, and other contemporary novelists much in vogue among the higher classes of society."

III.

But what is this idea of the beautiful which art rests upon, and so becomes moral? "The man of our time," says Señor Valdés, "wishes to know everything and enjoy everything; he turns the objective of a powerful equatorial toward the heavenly spaces where gravitate the infinitude of the stars, just as he applies the microscope to the infinitude of the smallest insects; for their laws are identical. His experience, united with intuition, has convinced him that in nature there is neither great nor small; all is equal. All is equally grand, all is equally just, all is equally beautiful, because all is equally divine," as the Study has before now perhaps sufficiently insisted. But beauty, Señor Valdés explains, exists in the human spirit, and is the beautiful effect which it receives from the true meaning of things; it does not matter what the things are, and it is the function of the artist who feels this effect to impart it to others. We may add that there is no joy in art except this perception of the meaning of things and its

communication; when you have felt it, and told it in a poem, a symphony, a novel, a statue, a picture, an edifice, you have fulfilled the purpose for which you were born an artist.

The reflection of exterior nature in the individual spirit, Señor Valdés believes to be the fundamental of art. "To say, then, that the artist must not copy but create is nonsense, because he can in no wise copy, and in no wise create. He who sets deliberately about modifying nature, shows that he has not felt her beauty, and therefore cannot make others feel it. The puerile desire which some artists without genius manifest to go about selecting in nature, *not what seems to them beautiful, but what they think will seem beautiful to others,* and rejecting what may displease them, ordinarily produces cold and insipid works. For, instead of exploring the illimitable fields of reality, they cling to the forms invented by other artists who have succeeded, *and they make statues of statues, poems of poems, novels of novels.* It is entirely false that the great romantic, symbolic, or classic poets modified nature; such as they have expressed her they felt her; and in this view they are as much realists as ourselves. In like manner if in the realistic tide that now bears us on there are some spirits who feel nature in another way, in the romantic way, or the classic way, they would not falsify her in expressing her so. Only those falsify her who, without feeling classic wise or romantic wise, set about being classic or romantic, wearisomely reproducing the models of former ages; and equally those who without sharing the sentiment of realism, which now prevails, force themselves to be realists merely to follow the fashion."

The pseudo-realists, in fact, are the worse offenders, to our thinking, for they sin against the living; whereas those who continue to celebrate the heroic adventures of Puss in Boots and the hairbreadth escapes of Tom Thumb, under various aliases, only cast disrespect upon the immortals, who have passed beyond these noises. ⌐[2]

IV.

The ingenious English magazinist who has of late been retroactively fending the works of Tolstoï and Dostoyevsky from the last days of that saint of romance, George Sand, as too apt to inspire melancholy reflections in a lady of her life and literature, and who cannot rejoice enough that her dying hours were cheered by the writings of that reverend father in God, Alexander Dumas, *père,* would hardly be pleased, we suppose, with all the ideas of Señor Valdés concerning the novel, its nature, and its function, in modern life. "The princi-⌐

pal cause," the Spaniard says, "of the decadence of contemporary literature is found, to my thinking, in the vice which has been very graphically called *effectism*, or the itch of awaking at all cost in the reader vivid and violent emotions, which shall do credit to the invention and originality of the writer. This vice has its roots in human nature itself, and more particularly in that of the artist; he has always something feminine in him, which tempts him to coquet with the reader, and display qualities that he thinks will astonish him, as women laugh for no reason, to show their teeth when they have them white and small and even, or lift their dresses to show their feet when there is no mud in the street. . . . What many writers nowadays wish, is to produce an effect, grand and immediate, to play the part of *geniuses*. For this they have learned that it is only necessary to write exaggerated works in any sort, since the vulgar do not ask that they shall be quietly made to think and feel, but that they shall be startled; and among the vulgar of course I include the great part of those who write literary criticism, and who constitute the worst vulgar, since they teach what they do not know. . . . There are many persons who suppose that the highest proof an artist can give of his fantasy is the invention of a complicated plot, spiced with perils, surprises, and suspenses; and that anything else is the sign of a poor and tepid imagination. And not only people who seem cultivated, but are not so, suppose this, but there are sensible persons, and even sagacious and intelligent critics, who sometimes allow themselves to be hoodwinked by the dramatic mystery and the surprising and fantastic scenes of a novel. They own it is all false; but they admire the imagination, what they call the 'power' of the author. Very well; all I have to say is that the 'power' to dazzle with strange incidents, to entertain with complicated plots and impossible characters, now belongs to some hundreds of writers in Europe; while there are not much above a dozen who know how to interest with the ordinary events of life, and with the portrayal of characters truly human. If the former is a talent, it must be owned that it is much commoner than the latter. . . . If we are to rate novelists according to their fecundity, or the riches of their invention, we must put Alexander Dumas above Cervantes," says Señor Valdés; but we must never forget that Dumas brought distraction if not peace to the death-bed of a woman who would probably have been unpleasantly agitated by those Russian authors who are apt to appeal to the imagination through the conscience.

"Cervantes," Señor Valdés goes on to say, "wrote a novel with the simplest plot, without belying much or little the natural and logical course of events. This novel, which was called *Don Quixote*, is perhaps the greatest work of human wit. Very well, the same Cervantes, mischievously influenced afterward by the ideas of the vulgar, who were then what they are now and always will be, attempted to please them by a work giving a lively proof of his inventive talent, and wrote the *Persiles and Sigismunda*, where the strange incidents, the vivid complications, the surprises, the pathetic scenes, succeed one another so rapidly and constantly that it really fatigues you. . . . But in spite of this flood of invention, imagine," says Señor Valdés, "the place that Cervantes would now occupy in the heaven of art, if he had never written *Don Quixote*," but only *Persiles and Sigismunda*!

From the point of view of modern English criticism, which likes to be melted, and horrified, and astonished, and blood-curdled, and goose-fleshed, no less than to be "chippered up" in fiction, Señor Valdés were indeed incorrigible. Not only does he despise the novel of complicated plot, and everywhere prefer *Don Quixote* to *Persiles and Sigismunda*, but he has a lively contempt for another class of novels much in favor with the gentilities of all countries. He calls their writers "novelists of the world," and he says that more than any others they have the rage of *effectism*. "They do not seek to produce effect by novelty and invention in plot. . . . they seek it in character. For this end they begin by deliberately falsifying human feelings, giving them a paradoxical appearance completely inadmissible . . . Love that disguises itself as hate, incomparable energy under the cloak of weakness, virginal innocence under the aspect of malice and impudence, wit masquerading as folly, etc., etc. By this means they hope to make an effect of which they are incapable through the direct, frank, and conscientious study of character." He mentions Octave Feuillet as the greatest offender in this sort among the French, and Bulwer among the English; but Dickens is full of it (Boffin in *Our Mutual Friend* will suffice for all example), and the present loathsome artistic squalor of the English drama is witness of the result of *effectism* when allowed full play.

V.

But what, then, if he is not pleased with Dumas, who was sovereign for George Sand in sickness, and is good enough for the ingenious English magazinist in health, or with the *effectists* who delight genteel people at all the theatres, and in most of the romances, what, we ask, will satisfy this extremely difficult Spanish gentleman? He would pretend, very little. Give him simple, life-like character; that is all he wants. "For me, the only condition of character is that it be human, and that is enough. If I wished to know what was human, I should study humanity."

But, Señor Valdés, Señor Valdés! Do not you know that this small condition of yours implies in its fulfilment hardly less than the gift of the whole earth, with a little gold fence round it? You merely ask that the character portrayed in fiction be human; and you suggest that the novelist should study humanity if he would know whether his personages are human. This appears to us the cruelest irony, the most sarcastic affectation of humility. If you had asked that character in fiction be superhuman, or subterhuman, or preter-human, or intrahuman, and had bidden the novelist go, not to humanity, but the humanities, for the proof of his excellence, it would have been all very easy. The books are full of those "creations," of every pattern, of all ages, of both sexes; and it is so much handier to get at books than to get at men; and when you have portrayed "passion" instead of feeling, and used "power" instead of common-sense, and shown yourself a "genius" instead of an artist, the applause is so prompt and the glory so cheap, that really anything else seems wickedly wasteful of one's time. One may not make one's reader enjoy or suffer nobly, but one may give him the kind of pleasure that arises from conjuring, or from a puppetshow, or a modern stage play, and leave him, if he is an old fool, in the sort of stupor that comes from hitting the pipe; or if he is a young fool, half crazed with the spectacle of qualities and impulses like his own in an apotheosis of achievement and fruition far beyond any earthly experience. If one is a very great master in that kind, one may survive to be the death-bed comfort of a woman who is supposed to have needed medicining of a narcotic kind from a past of inedifying experiences, and even to be the admiration of an ingenious English magazinist who thinks fiction ought to do the office of hyoscyamus or bromide of potassium.

But apparently Señor Valdés would not think this any great artistic result. Like Emerson, he believes that "the foolish man wonders at the unusual, but the wise man at the usual," that "the perception of the worth of the vulgar is fruitful in discoveries." Like Emerson, he "asks, not for the great, the remote, the romantic"; he "embraces the common," he "sits at the feet of the familiar and the low." Or, in his own words, "Things that appear ugliest in reality to the spec-tator who is not an artist, are transformed into beauty and poetry when the spirit of the artist possesses itself of them. We all take part every day in a thousand domestic scenes, every day we see a thousand pictures in life, that do not make any impression upon us, or if they make any it is one of repugnance; but let the novelist come, and without betraying the truth, but painting them as they appear to his vision, he produces a most interesting work, whose perusal enchants us. That which in life left us indifferent, or repelled us, in art delights us. Why? Simply because the artist has made us see the idea that resides in it. Let not the novelists, then, endeavor to add anything to reality, to turn it and twist it, to restrict it. Since nature has endowed them with this precious gift of discovering ideas in things, their work will be beautiful if they paint these as they appear. But if the reality does not impress them, in vain will they strive to make their work impress others."

VI.

Which brings us again, after this long way about, to the divine Jane and her novels, and that troublesome question about them. She was great and they were beautiful because she and they were honest, and dealt with nature nearly a hundred years ago, as realism deals with it to-day. Realism is nothing more and nothing less than the truthful treatment of material, and Jane Austen was the first and the last of the English novelists to treat material with entire truthfulness. Because she did this, she remains the most artistic of the English novelists, and alone worthy to be matched with the great Scandinavian and Slavic and Latin artists. It is not a question of intellect, or not wholly that. The English have mind enough; but they have not taste enough; or rather their taste has been perverted by their false criticism, which is based upon personal preference, and not upon principle; which instructs a man to think that what he likes is good, instead of teaching him first to distinguish what is good before he likes it. The art of fiction, as Jane Austen knew it, declined from her through Scott, and Bulwer, and Dickens, and Charlotte Brontë, and Thackeray, and even George Eliot, because the mania of romanticism had seized upon all Europe, and these great writers could not escape the taint of their time; but it has shown few signs of recovery in England, because English criticism, in the presence of the Continental masterpieces, has continued provincial and special and personal, and has expressed a love and a hate which had to do with the quality of the artist rather than the character of his work. It was inevitable that in their time the English romanticists should treat, as Señor Valdés says, "the barbarous customs of the Middle Ages, softening and disfiguring them, as Walter Scott and his kind did"; that they should "devote themselves to falsifying nature, refining and subtilizing sentiment, and modifying psychology after their own fancy," like Bulwer and Dickens, as well as like Rousseau and Madame de Staël, not to mention Balzac, the worst of all that sort at his worst. This was the natural course of the disease; but it really seems as if it were their criticism that was to blame for the rest: not, indeed, for the performance of this writer or that, for criticism can never affect the actual doing of a thing; but for the esteem in which this writer or that is held through the perpetuation of false ideals. The only observer of English middle-class life since Jane Austen worthy to be named with her was not George Eliot, who was first ethical and then artistic, who transcended her in everything but the form and method most essential to art, and there fell hopelessly below her. It was Anthony Trollope who was most like her in simple honesty and instinctive truth, as unphilosophized as the light of common day; but he was so warped from a wholesome ideal as to wish at times to be like the caricaturist Thackeray, and to stand about in his scene, talking it over with

his hands in his pockets, interrupting the action, and spoiling the illusion in which alone the truth of art resides. Mainly, his instinct was too much for his ideal, and with a low view of life in its civic relations and a thoroughly *bourgeois* soul, he yet produced works whose beauty is surpassed only by the effect of a more poetic writer in the novels of Thomas Hardy. Yet if a vote of English criticism even at this late day, when all continental Europe has the light of æsthetic truth, could be taken, the majority against these artists would be overwhelmingly in favor of a writer who had so little artistic sensibility, that he never hesitated on any occasion great or small, to make a foray among his characters, and catch them up to show them to the reader and tell him how beautiful or ugly they were; and cry out over their amazing properties.

Doubtless the ideal of those poor islanders will be finally changed. If the truth could become a *fad* it would be accepted by all their "smart people," but truth is something rather too large for that; and we must await the gradual advance of civilization among them. Then they will see that their criticism has misled them; and that it is to this false guide they owe, not precisely the decline of fiction among them, but its continued debasement as an art. [3]

[1] Armando Palacio Valdes, La Hermana San Sulpicio, 2 tom. (Madrid: N.P., 1889). The critical comments that Howells refers to are from the author's preface. The English translation appeared the year following this review under the title Sister Saint Sulpice, Nathan Haskell Dole, trans. (New York: T. Y. Crowell & Co., [1890]).

[2] Criticism and Fiction, pp. 57-64.

[3] Criticism and Fiction, pp. 65-77.

December , 1889

Editor's Study.

I.

TO most of the best and wisest people of the North American continent, who are one in their expectance of the great annual number of this Magazine, these presents will bring our greeting equally for Thanksgiving and for Christmas. It is a feeble image of the effective union of these holidays, the one universal and the other provincial, the one Puritan and the other Christian, in the reverence and affection of our people, of which there has been sufficient illustration in the history of the country, ever since the Roundheads landed at Plymouth and the Cavaliers at Jamestown. They were not then exactly Roundheads as yet, and not exactly Cavaliers; but the future of that severalty was in them, as well as more remotely the future of a final coparcenary. Roughly speaking, the Virginians established Christmas in the heathen wilderness, and the New-Englanders invented Thanksgiving there; though we have no doubt that a great deal might be said to show that neither did either. It is a point that we should yield more readily to compulsion than to persuasion, and for our actual convenience we shall regard it as incontrovertible; for it is important, if not essential, to the fancy we should like to indulge of a gradual fusion of the literature proper to Christmas and the literature proper to Thanksgiving in a literature appropriate to both; and without the Roundheads and the Cavaliers to go back to, our fancy would experience a difficulty comparable to that of the elephant which the world once rested upon if the fundamental turtle had been taken from under its feet. The state of that elephant would have been awkward; he would not have known what to do; and our fancy would now be very much at a loss without its Roundheads and its Cavaliers: perhaps without them it could not be indulged at all.

II.

We have not the documents at hand, and we cannot attempt to prove with accuracy just how thoroughly the festival of Thanksgiving has penetrated the South. Before the war, this festival was finding a slowly increasing observance in the North; it was carried westward by the New-Englanders wherever they went, and there began to be a pretty general proclamation of Thanksgiving by the different Governors, without any very widespread attention from the people invited to keep the day. It was an affair of families, of neighborhoods; and perhaps a turkey-shoot was the most prevalent expression of the rustic piety outside of New England. But after the war Thanksgiving was officially nationalized, and the Presidents relieved the Governors of the duty of annually proclaiming it. While reconstruction was still imperfect, and the different races at the South had not yet reached their present condition of ideal harmony, the black race may have seized upon Thanksgiving Day as a symbol of their liberation at the hands of its Northern inventors, and revered it accordingly. But of this we are not satisfactorily advised; and we will not insist upon it as a conjecture. Probably such a conjecture must encounter the fact of an ethnical conservatism in the black race, who would cling to the elder festival of Christmas with that fondness for the things of custom which is one of their most engaging traits. What is certain, however, is the diffusion of Christmas throughout the North, not only in those parts characterized by the South and the Middle States, but in the vast regions colored by the New England civilization, and in the remotest fastnesses of New England itself, triply guarded against it once by the pumpkin, the codfish, and the bean. It is not much more than a yesterday in our national past since this beloved holiday, the most sacred and the dearest to the heart of humanity, was abhorred on those bleak shores as part and parcel of the Romish mummery which the Puritans had banished together with the mass-priests and all their works; since the good Sewall, cast down by the first rumor of its return under the protection of prelacy, walked out on Christmas morning in Boston, fearful of some sign of its presence,

"And somewhat grimly smiled"

to see the farmers coming in from their snow-choked hills with their sled-loads of firewood, as bitterly bent on their money's worth that day as on any common Tuesday or Thursday of them all. No doubt the sacred feast had been abused to evil; and Christmas had to come again, refined and purified, before it could meet the acceptance it now has not only in the hearts but in the minds of men. The outward signs of rejoicing remain much the same as of old—the holly, the mistletoe, the yule-log; even the mince-pie and the wassail-bowl and the plum-pudding are with us as before; but the mirth is decenter, and something more of the true meaning of the day is yearly expressed in its observance.

III.

It would be very interesting, if there were any means of doing it, to take account of the changing tone of the various Christmas homilies, from doctrinal to vital, from ideal to real; but the accumulation of any such statistics must be for some larger room than the Study. Here there is only space for a guess, a question, a hasty conclusion or two; and these are preferably concerned with the less serious aspects of the subject in hand. We may venture upon the suggestion that Thanksgiving with its direct relation to recent and obvious fact has characterized Christmas feeling and thinking, as these have imparted something of their significance to the modern holiday; but we can offer no proof of its correctness. That there has been an unconscious unification of the two feasts in certain material aspects, every one knows. The Thanksgiving turkey has driven the Christmas goose from all tables; and in turn the mince-pie of Christmas shares the honor of completing the Thanksgiving indigestion with the pumpkin-pie which once monopolized the work. We fancy that the visiting Englishman would note for his book or his article about us almost no difference between the fare of the American Thanksgiving and the fare of the Americanized Christmas. He would find on either day almost the same religious observance by all sects (including even that of the mass-priests), and the same social and domestic rejoicing. Perhaps in New England he would see something more of family reunions on Thanksgiving; but we should not like to promise him this; for with the softening of our manners, the children of the same household find it more and more pleasant to come together on both days, or at least to meet on either at their convenience; and the kindly influence has penetrated the ice and granite even of the old Puritan stronghold.

IV.

This reflection brings us back to our starting-point: a point which the philosophical thinker always reaches with surprise that he has got safely round to it again, and with pride in proportion to the vastness of the compass he has fetched. As at the beginning, we are animated by the hope of a fusion of Thanksgiving literature and of Christmas literature; and our imagination pleases itself with the fond anticipation of a time when the two sorts may be used convertibly. We think every editor will agree with us that some such combine, or rather pooling of issues, is desirable; for as both literatures deal preferably with the uncommon and the unexpected, it is plain that there must soon come a moment of absolute dearth in their material unless it is more carefully husbanded than it has been. In a world where explorers have penetrated almost every secret of physical geography, and inquirers have pierced every dark continent and shady corner of human nature, the chance of bringing a prodigal home to Thanksgiving from some unknown sea, or of reforming a stony-hearted miser through the influence of a Christmas dinner, with any decent degree of probability, is growing so small that it must be more sparingly taken in the future, if any hold is to be kept upon even the easy credulity of the average story-reader.

The two kinds, or rather varieties of story have a different origin, as we all know; and yet they are, more remotely, of the same religious, social, and domestic tradition. We have transplanted the Christmas story from England, while the Thanksgiving story is native to our air; but both are of Anglo-Saxon growth. Their difference is from a difference of environment; and the Christmas story when naturalized among us becomes almost identical in motive, incident, and treatment with the Thanksgiving story. If we were to generalize a distinction between them, we should say that the one dealt more with marvels and the other more with morals; and yet the critic should beware of speaking too confidently on this point. It is certain, however, that the Christmas season is meteorologically more favorable to the effective return of persons long supposed lost at sea, or from a prodigal life, or from a darkened mind. The longer, denser, and colder nights are better adapted to the apparition of ghosts, and to all manner of signs and portents; while they seem to present a wider field for the active intervention of angels in behalf of orphans and outcasts. The dreams of elderly sleepers at this time are apt to be such as will effect

229

a lasting change in them when they awake, turning them from the hard, cruel, and grasping habits of a lifetime, and reconciling them to their sons, daughters, and nephews, who have thwarted them in marriage; or softening them to their meek, uncomplaining wives, whose hearts they have trampled upon in their reckless pursuit of wealth; and generally disposing them to a distribution of hampers among the sick and poor, and to a friendly reception of chubby gentlemen with charity subscription papers. Ships readily drive upon rocks in the early twilight, and offer exciting difficulties of salvage; and the heavy snows gather thickly round the steps of wanderers who lie down to die in them, preparatory to their discovery and rescue by their immediate relatives. The midnight weather is also very suitable to encounter with murderers and burglars; and the contrast of its freezing gloom with the light and cheer in-doors promotes the gayeties which merge, at all well-regulated country houses, in love and marriage. In the region of pure character, no moment could be so available for flinging off the mask of frivolity, or imbecility, or savagery, which one has worn for ten or twenty long years, say, for the purpose of foiling some villain, and surprising the reader, and helping the author out with his plot. Persons abroad in the Alps, or Apennines, or Pyrenees, or anywhere seeking shelter in the huts of shepherds or the dens of smugglers, find no time like it for lying in a feigned slumber, and listening to the whispered machinations of their suspicious-looking entertainers, and then suddenly starting up and fighting their way out; or else springing from the real sleep into which they have sunk exhausted, and finding it broad day, and the good peasants whom they had so unjustly doubted, waiting breakfast for them. We need not point out the superior advantages of the Christmas season for anything one has a mind to do with the French Revolution, or the Arctic explorations, or the Indian Mutiny, or the horrors of Siberian exile; there is no time so good for the use of this material; and ghosts on shipboard are notoriously fond of Christmas Eve. In our own logging camps the man who has gone into the woods for the winter, after quarrelling with his wife, then hears her sad, appealing voice, and is moved to good resolutions as at no other period of the year; and in the mining regions, first in California and later in Colorado, the hardened reprobate, dying in his boots, smells his mother's dough-nuts, and breathes his last in a soliloquized vision of the old home, and the little brother, or sister, or the old father, coming to meet him from heaven; while his rude companions listen round

him, and dry their eyes on the butts of their revolvers.

It has to be very grim, all that, to be truly effective; and here, already, we have a touch in the Americanized Christmas story of the moralistic quality of the American Thanksgiving story. This was seldom written, at first, for the mere entertainment of the reader; it was meant to entertain him, of course; but it was meant to edify him, too, and to improve him; and some such intention is still present in it. We rather think that it deals more probably with character to this end than its English cousin, the Christmas story does. It is not so improbable that a man should leave off being a drunkard on Thanksgiving, as that he should leave off being a curmudgeon on Christmas; that he should conquer his appetite as that he should instantly change his nature, by good resolutions. He would be very likely, indeed, to break his resolutions in either case, but not so likely in the one as in the other.

Generically, the Thanksgiving story is cheerfuler in its drama and simpler in its persons than the Christmas story. Rarely has it dealt with the supernatural, either the apparition of ghosts or the intervention of angels. The weather being so much milder at the close of November than it is a month later, very little can be done with the elements; though on the coast a northeasterly storm has been, and can be, very usefully employed. The Thanksgiving story is more restricted in its range; the scene is still mostly in New England, and the characters are of New England extraction, who come home from the West usually, or New York, for the event of the little drama, whatever it may be. It may be the reconciliation of kinsfolk who have quarrelled; or the union of lovers long estranged; or husbands and wives who have had hard words and parted; or mothers who had thought their sons dead in California and find themselves agreeably disappointed in their return; or fathers who for old times' sake receive back their erring and conveniently dying daughters. The notes are not many which this simple music sounds, but they have a Sabbath tone, mostly, and win the listener to kindlier thoughts and better moods. The art is at its highest in some strong sketch of Mrs. Rose Terry Cooke's, or some perfectly satisfying study of Miss Jewett's, or some graphic situation of Miss Wilkins's; and then it is a very fine art. But mostly it is poor and rude enough, and makes openly, shamelessly, sickeningly, for the reader's emotions, as well as his morals. It is inclined to be rather descriptive. The turkey, the pumpkin, the corn field, figure accessorily throughout; and the leafless woods are blue and cold against the evening sky behind the low hip-roofed old-fashioned homestead. The parlance is usually in the Yankee dialect and its Western modifications.

V.

The Thanksgiving story is mostly confined in scene to the country; it does not seem possible to do much with it in town; and it is a serious question whether with its geographical and topical limitations it can hold its own against the Christmas story; and whether it would not be well for authors to consider a combination with its elder rival. As we have represented, the Christmas numbers of the magazines come out before Thanksgiving Day, and the two feasts are so near together in point of time that they could be easily covered by the sentiment of even a brief narrative. Under the agglutinated style of A Thanksgiving-Christmas Story, fiction appropriate to both could be produced, and both could be employed naturally and probably in the transaction of its affairs and the development of its characters. The plot for such a story could easily be made to include a total-abstinence pledge and family reunion at Thanksgiving, and an apparition and spiritual regeneration over a bowl of punch at Christmas.

Not all Thanksgiving-Christmas stories need be of this pattern precisely; we wish to suggest merely one way of doing them. Perhaps when our writers really come to the work, they will find sufficient inspiration in its novelty, to turn to human life and observe how it is really affected on these holidays, and be tempted to present some of its actualities. This would be a great thing to do, and would come home to readers with surprise.

---

[1] *Criticism and Fiction*, pp. 163-170.

January, 1890

Editor's Study.

I.

FROM time to time the Study has done its poor endeavors for a more courteous behavior on the part of literary criticism. If it has not taught this so much by practice as by precept, that is the misfortune of much other instruction; but it is not wholly disabling; and in view of Mr. Philip Gilbert Hamerton's recent essays comparing the *French and English*, the Study has the courage to go even further and commend the spirit of comity in international criticism which his book is such an admirable example of. It was on the point of our pen to write that it was an altogether novel thing in its kind; but we remembered *English Traits* in time, and we remembered Mr. Bryce's *American Commonwealth*. Mr. Hamerton's comparison is not so full of insight as the first, for it is no offence to say Mr. Hamerton is not Emerson; and it is not so comprehensive as the last. But it abounds in opinions agreeably reasoned from the uncommon experience of an Englishman who has spent the greater part of his life in France; and one cannot read it without a various edification. On such points as education, politics, religion, virtues, custom, society, it will give us Americans, who dutifully derive our ideas of the French from the English, frequent occasion to revise our convictions, and some occasion to disown them. Certain of them we may be ashamed of by its help, and perhaps we shall learn from it to achieve the difficult moral feat of respecting national merits different from our own, or of another complexion. In Mr. Hamerton's picture the typical Frenchman does not appear the cynical, sensual, sanguinary personage we evolve from history and romance; but a character, for the most part, rather anxious about the appearances, especially in women; soberminded, frugal, domestic; narrow and sceptical as to things out of France, and devoted to the admiration of all things French; conservative, prudent to selfishness; faithful rather than generous; not very hospitable however social; a creature of well-controlled passions and impulses, and of a life as pure as that of most Englishmen.

We have to reproduce Mr. Hamerton's careful picture in the spirit of the daily newspaper reproductions of art; but we believe we are not false to the whole effect. In all respects his study is highly interesting, and it is at no time, apparently, prejudiced or caricatured. The reader may learn from it to know justly a Catholic and Celtic civilization in most of those points where we most misjudge it; and begin to conceive of a political state in which the dominant republicanism is not good form, and which is advancing toward socialism without making any recognizable impression on good society. In a country where there are no legal titles, the most inexorable aristocracy reigns in undisputed supremacy over a world which fortune, talent, office, distinction cannot enter, of their own right, even as subjects.

The matter of the book is all very important; much of it is very new, and the manner of the book is even more extraordinary. It is at no time supercilious, patronizing, or insolent; it generalizes from facts, not prepossessions; it does not accuse from conjecture; it does not heap contempt upon what appears anomalous because it is strange; throughout it is gentlemanly. One begins to fear that Mr. Hamerton is really denationalized, so different is his behavior toward the people of an alien country from that of nearly all other Englishmen.

The chapter on Purity will most surprise Anglo-Saxon readers; but the chapter on Caste is of even more interest, and it is of almost unique value both in temper and in substance, for it describes without caricature, in a democratic commonwealth, and on the verge of the twentieth century, an ideal of life entirely stupid, useless, and satisfied, and quite that which Mark Twain has been portraying in his wonder-story of *A Connecticut Yankee at the Court of King Arthur*. Mr. Hamerton's French noble of the year 1890 is the same man essentially as any of that group of knights of the Round Table, who struck Mr. Clemens's delightful hero as white Indians. In his circle, achievement, ability, virtue, would find itself at the same disadvantage, without birth, as in that of Sir Launcelot. When you contemplate him in Mr. Hamerton's clear, passionless page, you feel that after all the Terror was perhaps too brief, and you find yourself sympathizing with all Mr. Clemens's robust approval of the Revolution.

II.

Mr. Clemens, we call him, rather than Mark Twain, because we feel that in this book our arch-humorist imparts more of his personal quality than in anything else he has done. Here he is to the full the humorist, as we know him; but he is very much more, and his strong, indignant, often infuriate hate of injustice, and his love of equality, burn hot through the manifold adventures and experiences of the tale. What he thought about prescriptive right and wrong, we had partly learned in *The Prince and the Pauper*, and in *Huckleberry Finn*, but it is this last book which gives his whole mind. The elastic scheme of the romance allows it to play freely back and forward between the sixth century and the nineteenth century; and often while it is working the reader up to a blasting contempt of monarchy and aristocracy in King Arthur's time, the dates are magically shifted under him, and he is confronted with exactly the same principles in Queen Victoria's time. The delicious satire, the marvellous wit, the wild, free, fantastic humor are the colors of the tapestry, while the texture is a humanity that lives in every fibre. At every moment the scene amuses, but it is all the time an object-lesson in democracy. It makes us glad of our republic and our epoch; but it does not flatter us into a fond content with them; there are passages in which we see that the noble of Arthur's day, who battened on the blood and sweat of his bondmen, is one in essence with the capitalist of Mr. Harrison's [2] day who grows rich on the labor of his underpaid wagemen. Our incomparable humorist, whose sarcasm is so pitiless to the greedy and superstitious clerics of Britain, is in fact of the same spirit and intention as those bishops who, true to their office, wrote the other day from New York to all their churches in the land: "It is a fallacy in social economics, as well as in Christian thinking, to look upon the labor of men and women and children as a commercial commodity, to be bought and sold as an inanimate and irresponsible thing . . . . The heart and soul of a man cannot be bought or hired in any market, and to act as if they were not needed in the doing of the world's vast work is as unchristian as it is unwise."

Mr. Clemens's glimpses of monastic life in Arthur's realm are true enough; and if they are not the whole truth of the matter, one may easily get it in some such book as Mr. Brace's *Gesta Christi*, where the full light of history is thrown upon the transformation of the world, if not the church, under the influence of Christianity. In the mean time, if any one feels that the justice done the churchmen of King Arthur's time is too much of one kind, let him turn to that heart-breaking scene where the brave monk stands with the mother and her babe on the scaffold, and execrates the hideous law which puts her to death for stealing enough to keep her from starving. It is one of many passages in the story where our civilization of to-day sees itself mirrored in the cruel barbarism of the past, the same in principle, and only softened in custom. With shocks of consciousness, one recognizes in such episodes that the laws are still made for the few against the many, and that the preservation of things, not men, is still the ideal of legislation. But we do not wish to leave the reader with the notion that Mr. Clemens's work is otherwise than obliquely serious. Upon the face of it you have a story no more openly didactic than *Don Quixote*, which we found ourselves more than once thinking of, as we read, though always with the sense of the kindlier and truer heart of our time. Never once, we believe, has Mark Twain been funny at the cost of the weak, the unfriended, the helpless; and this is rather more than you can say of Cid Hamet ben Engeli. But the two writers are of the same humorous largeness; and when the Connecticut man rides out at dawn, in a suit of Arthurian armor, and gradually heats up under the mounting sun in what he calls that stove; and a fly gets between the bars of his visor; and he cannot reach his handkerchief in his helmet to wipe the sweat from his streaming face; and at last when he cannot bear it any longer, and dismounts at the side of a brook, and makes the distressed damsel who has been riding behind him take off his helmet, and fill it with water, and pour gallon after gallon down the collar of his wrought-iron cutaway, you have a situation of as huge a grotesqueness as any that Cervantes conceived.

The distressed damsel is the Lady Corisande; he calls her Sandy, and he is troubled in mind at riding about the country with her in that way; for he is not only very doubtful that there is nothing in the castle where she says there are certain princesses imprisoned and persecuted by certain giants, but he feels that it is not quite nice: he is engaged to a young lady in East Hartford, and he finds Sandy a fearful bore at first, though in the end he loves and marries her, finding that he hopelessly antedates the East Hartford young lady by thirteen centuries. How he gets into King Arthur's realm, the author concerns himself as little as any of us do with the mechanism of our dreams. In fact the whole story has the lawless operation of a dream; none of its prodigies are accounted for; they take themselves for granted, and neither explain nor justify themselves. Here he is, that Connecticut man, foreman of one of the shops in Colt's pistol factory, and full to the throat of the invention and the self-satisfaction of the nineteenth century, at the court of the mythic Arthur. He is promptly recognized as a being of extraordinary powers, and becomes the king's right-hand man, with the title of The Boss; but as he has apparently no lineage or blazon, he has no social standing, and the meanest noble has precedence of him, just as would happen in England to-day. The reader may faintly fancy the consequences flowing from this situation, which he will find so vividly fancied for him in the book; but they are simply irreportable. The scheme confesses allegiance to nothing; the incidents, the facts follow as they will. The Boss cannot rest from introducing the apparatus of our time, and he tries to impart its spirit, with a thousand most astonishing effects. He starts a daily paper in Camelot; he torpedoes a holy well; he blows up a party of insolent knights with a dynamite bomb; when he and the king disguise themselves as peasants, in order to learn the real life of the people, and are taken and sold for slaves, and then sent to the gallows for the murder of their master, Launcelot arrives to their rescue with five hundred knights on bicycles. It all ends with the Boss's proclamation of the Republic after Arthur's death, and his destruction of the whole chivalry of England by electricity.

We can give no proper notion of the measureless play of an imagination which has a gigantic jollity in its feats, together with the tenderest sympathy. There are incidents in this wonder-book which wring the heart for what has been of cruelty and wrong in the past, and leave it burning with shame and hate for the conditions which are of like effect in the present. It is one of its magical properties that the fantastic fable of Arthur's far-off time is also too often the sad truth of ours; and the magician who makes us feel in it that we have just begun to know his power, teaches equality and fraternity in every phase of his phantasmagory.

He leaves, to be sure, little of the romance of the olden time, but no one is more alive to the simple, mostly tragic poetry of it : and we do not remember any book which imparts so clear a sense of what was truly heroic in it. With all his scorn of kingcraft, and all his ireful contempt of caste, no one yet has been fairer to the nobility of character which they cost so much too much to develop. The mainly ridiculous Arthur of Mr. Clemens has his moments of being as fine and high as the Arthur of Lord Tennyson; and the keener light which shows his knights and ladies in their childlike simplicity and their innocent coarseness throws all their best qualities into relief. This book is in its last effect the most matter-of-fact narrative, for it is always true to human nature, the only truth possible, the only truth essential, to fiction. The humor of the conception and of the performance is simply immense; but more than ever Mr. Clemens's humor seems the sunny break of his intense conviction. We must all recognize him here as first of those who laugh, not merely because his fun is unrivalled, but because there is a force of right feeling and clear thinking in it that never got into fun before, except in *The Bigelow Papers*. Throughout, the text in all its circumstance and meaning is supplemented by the illustrations of an artist who has entered into the wrath and the pathos as well as the fun of the thing, and made them his own. [3]

III.

This kind of humor, the American kind, the kind employed in the service of democracy, of humanity, began with us a long time ago; in fact Franklin may be said to have torn it with the lightning from the skies. Some time, some such critic as Mr. T. S. Perry (if we ever have another such) will study its evolution in the century of our literature and civilization; but no one need deny himself meanwhile the pleasure we feel in Mr. Clemens's book as its highest development. His keen-tempered irony is something that we can well imagine Franklin enjoying, if he is really the Franklin Mr. J. T. Morse divines him in the life he has lately contributed to his series of *American Statesmen*. The book is mainly a study of Franklin's political and diplomatic career; and it is of such an intelligence, temperance, and good sense as to make Mr. Morse's reluctance to add another life of Franklin to those we had already seem the only mistaken thing in it. We cannot call his use of familiar material less than novel, or his progress in the dry and dusty paths to which he tries to confine himself other than charming; though we are always glad when he turns aside to give us a glimpse of the more personal Franklin. To be sure, the official Franklin was personal far beyond most officials: his sagacity and self-knowledge, and most of all, his humor, put the interest of a delightful character into the details of his public acts. Mr. Morse's feeling for this side of the man who was not asked to write the Declaration of Independence because, as Mr. Parton suggests, he would [4] probably have made a joke in it, is so pleasant that we wish he would add to his present volume another which should be chiefly devoted to that. We would allow him to keep all the excuses he makes for not doing it if only he would do it, especially the excuses which recognize the worth of Mr. Parton's work. Mr. Morse conceives of Franklin in his modernity with peculiar if not unique success; and judges him with something of the tolerant, friendly patience with which Franklin judges others: perhaps Franklin inspires him to do this; but above all he is cognizant of the pervading humor in much that Franklin said and much that Franklin did.

IV.

A very pretty instance of that humor we have happened upon in a book which we wish to speak of presently for other reasons, and which gives some passages from Franklin's pen about our Indians. They are mostly anecdotes, quoted or told again; but they are all touched with the light of Franklin's wise smile, and they form not so much an image of the red savagery as an ironical reflex of the white civility. We doubt very much whether the school-boys who are to use Harper's Fifth Reader will find anything better in it, either in matter or manner, though the book is suggestive of all that we have been doing in literature since those passages were written.

It was a happy thought, since our school-boys are, or are to be, Americans, to give them a literary text-book which is made up wholly from American writers, the latest as well as the earliest. Some few selections seem to have got in without sufficient warranty; but it would be ungracious to specify them, and not practicable to specify all the rest which are there by right. We meet a good many old friends, and some old enemies, in its pages: Halleck's Marco Bozzaris, Patrick Henry's great speech, Wirt's magniloquent sketch of the Blind Preacher and his sermon, Paulding's John Bull and Brother Jonathan, Willis's Absalom, Drake's American Flag: the names echo [5] against the Study walls from the school-house windows forty years away, with the pathos of young voices long lost in age or death. But for the greater part the pieces are from authors grown classic since these, and from yet others growing classic as fast as they can. We like the evident disposition of the editor to avoid fragmentary selections: literature more than elocution has been regarded; in some cases the selections are five or six pages in length, and give the whole of certain sketches, studies, and essays. It seems to us that the poetry has not been so fortunately chosen as the prose, but it is apparent that there has been a wish to do justice to the whole body of American poetry, and the feet of clay have not been forgotten any more than the members fashioned of more precious stuff.

V.

The holiday season is upon us with its illustrated books, and again we are reminded of the fact that there seems a demand for inferior quality in all of the arts which superior quality cannot supply. Certain sorts of intelligences, which famish upon excellence, pasture with delight upon what is less than excellent. The appetite of youth, indiscriminating and uncultivated, remains the taste through life of a vast multitude of people who never mature æsthetically. These cannot get the good of what is wholly good; they can only get the good of what is partly good; and no doubt it is their need that accounts for the existence of mediocre artists and mediocre works in every kind. In the divine economy there are many romancers for one Tolstoï, many poetasters for one Tennyson, many lifelong apprentices in architecture, sculpture, painting, for one master; for one Mark Twain a thousand newspaper funny men; for one Posnett, with the wide light of his *Comparative Literature*, for one Hamerton, with his conscientious impartiality, so gentle and so dignified, an innumerable cry of small, offensive, critical insects with the whole power of their being pointed to a poisonous sting. This is wisely ordered, for those who are able to enjoy and profit by what is first-rate are few indeed compared with those who are able to enjoy and profit by what is second-rate, third-rate, fourth-rate. No doubt the majority will shift, in the course of ages; but it will be many long winters yet before the rule of holiday publications, say, will be the present exceptional if not singular volume of illustrations which Messrs. Abbey and Parsons call *A Quiet Life*. If that delicate grace of theirs, that quaint and airy humor, that touch which gives character and meaning and beauty and repose to every line, shall find a few thousand out of our sixty or seventy millions to prize it aright, it will fare surprisingly well. But there cannot be any question of the success, almost as wide as Christmas itself, which will attend the efforts of secondary, of tertiary art, though these shall make the flesh of the judicious creep, and set their teeth on edge.

In one of his lectures, Mr. William

Morris asks his hearer to go through the streets of any city and consider the windows of the shops, how they are heaped with cheap and vulgar and tawdry and foolish gimcracks, which men's lives have been worn out in making, and other men's lives in selling, and yet other men's lives in getting money to waste upon, and which are finally to be cast out of our houses and swept into our dust-bins. He instances the demand for these as one of the cruel sham-needs which the exigencies of competition have created, and he looks forward to the co-operative society of the future for the redemption of art; to the order in which excellence and not commercial success shall be the aim of artistic endeavor. His position is interesting, but we think he hardly takes account of the æsthetic immaturity to which crudity is nutritive. We must allow the children, the old children, as well as the young ones, their pleasure in what is inferior and mediocre. We may say, if we will, that they would better have nothing than what they enjoy; but possibly we should not be right. Before we censure them too strenuously for liking what we know to be not good, we must ask ourselves whether it is not good for them. Toys they must have, and cakes and ale, and ginger hot in the mouth; their weak intelligence, their gross appetites crave them. Some of us like to see life in literature as it is; but far more like to see it in circus dress, with spangled tights, riding three barebacked horses at once, hanging by its instep from trapezes, and suffering massive paving-stones to be burst asunder on its stomach with sledge-hammers. Again we say, as we have always said, that there is no great harm in that: let the little children have their fairies; let the big children have their heroes. When the Study opens its windows and sees the cattle on a thousand hills, how contentedly they munch away at the grass, and how even the poor thistle has its admirer, it is not minded to insist that there shall be nothing but choice and delicate fruits in the world. At such, or like, moments it discerns a use not only for mere fodder in all the arts, but for the criticism which commends it, and cries out over it as if it were a banquet for the gods. It is sadly aware that those honest oxen, those amiable sheep, those worthy donkeys must starve at the tables it would spread for them; and it recognizes the necessity for other purveyors, humbly if reluctantly.

The inferior unquestionably has its place in the realm of art. If there were nothing but masterpieces there would be no masterpieces; and there must be inferior kinds as well as inferior performances in good kinds. There is a chromo appetite in human nature which legitimately demands satisfaction, and which is probably the cultivated form of an appetite still more primitive. The true criticism will not regard it with contempt, but will endeavor patiently to convert it to a taste for better things. But in this educative work criticism must never for an instant lose sight of the fact that a chromo is a chromo, and that all the joy in it of all the ignorant cannot change it into a work of fine art.

[1] English Traits, by Ralph Waldo Emerson.

[2] Benjamin Harrison was U.S. President at the time of the writing.

[3] This should read The Biglow Papers, by James Russell Lowell.

[4] James Parton, Life and Times of Benjamin Franklin (New York: Mason Brothers; Boston: Mason and Hamlin; [etc.], [etc.], 1864).

[5] Contributors to the reader are: Fitz-Greene Halleck, Patrick Henry, William Wirt, James Kirke Paulding, Nathaniel Parker Willis, Joseph Rodman Drake.

February, 1890

Editor's Study.

I.

AN excellent thing in the beautiful edition of *Boswell's Life of Johnson*, which Messrs. Harper and Brothers have lately published, is the lightness of each of the stately six volumes. We would by no means ignore the editorial labors of Mr. George Birbeck Hill; these are worthy of the highest praise, from the first prefatory passage, all through the army of footnotes, to the last line of the most satisfying of indexes; and as for the chief of biographers, he has lived his way through the stupid disdain of generations of critics to a station far beyond the acclaim of any: the first of Interviewers survives in the immortality of his Interviewed, a perpetual example of triumphant self-sacrifice, to all his kind. Delightful the book is, wherever you open it, and astonishing to any he that will consider how it is the work of a commonplace man about a writer singularly uninspired in his poetry, obtuse in his sense of beauty and of art, mistaken in his political economy, narrow and intolerant in his religion, mechanical in his morality, servile in his theories of society; one who is no longer read now in his unwieldy and pedantic prose, and has been wholly superseded even as a lexicographer, but who is present here in the largeness of his heart, vastly and simply human; no poet, no critic, no philosopher, no *savant*, by the fine modern tests, but somehow immensely a man: a warm, huge bulk, living, breathing, not to say snoring, and simply biographied to undying fame. But all this, or the like of it, has been very much said before, and we were going to speak of that purely material property of the book, which we have already hinted at; for we think it cannot be too highly commended. For our own part we hope for a time when no new book will be made larger than a volume of the Tauchnitz editions, or rather when every author worth reading shall be published in some such convenient form. Then the proud, who love to see large octavos and duodecimos in vain bindings on their shelves, may have their fancy's fill, while to every sincere lover of literature shall be given his little light bookling, to be read abed, or lounged

with in an easy-chair, or to be unpocketed for a taste of its sweetness in city car or cab, or upon still country by-paths. No book too heavy to hold in one hand has any right to exist, to the exclusion of the same work in the ideal form; and we would have that form the original shape of publication; those who want books to furnish their libraries, not their minds, might wait. As it is now, half a dozen vested interests conspire to give the lover of literature his love first in a guise that makes it a burden. Certain works of science and of art, whose primary appeal is not literary, might take the shape their authors judged fittest; but there is no reason except the commercial reason why fiction, poetry, travel, biography, history, should not always be offered us first as we have suggested. Most duodecimo books, even, are too thick and too heavy, though generally the weight is from the quality, not the quantity, of the paper used; so that the royal octavos of this new edition of *Boswell's Johnson* are no more fatiguing to the wrist than half the duodecimo novels that issue from the press. A new book of the kinds we have mentioned should be heavier than a metropolitan Sunday newspaper, which it hardly exceeds in the number of its words, only by the weight of a very thin, flexible cloth binding. This might be as gay and costly, or as simple and cheap, as the taste and the purse of the purchaser allowed; but in an age when all things become more and more perceptibly transitory, the first appeal of a book should not be made from covers bespeaking perpetuity. That should be for the library edition, to come later, if at all. The ideal book should open easily, and stay open till the reader shuts it; and it should slip easily into a man's breast pocket or a lady's shopping bag. In Plato's Republic (or if it was not there perhaps it was in Mr. Bellamy's *Looking Backward* commonwealth) all new books were physically adapted to the strength of the delicate and ailing people—mostly delicate and ailing women—who have always done most of the reading in the world; and the library editions were awarded as prizes to the winners in the Olympian games, who generally could not spell, but who had the muscle to handle those athletic volumes, which snapped shut like steel-traps when you tried to open them, and were bound in thick, heavy, brutal boards, as unyielding as plate-armor.

II.

We mentioned the Tauchnitz form as ideal, but it is not the only ideal. There is another size and shape equally amiable: not a little quarto, but narrower and taller, like that which contains Mr. E. Hughes's essays on *Some Aspects of Humanity.* This volume comes to us from England, and it opens readily, and willingly remains open in the manner that makes English books better than ours; but the covers are thick, and overweight it. Otherwise it is worthy of the pleasant literature which fills it. The author's name is new to us, and some things in his work give the notion of youth, but it is carefully thought and excellently said, in kinds which will probably gain him wider recognition on our side of the ocean than his own. There are only seven essays in the little book, and they are not all of the same quality, though they are all worth reading. "Waste in the Under-World," is one that we think will enlighten and comfort many who despair of the meaning of things; and so will "Patient People"; but in every one the altruism which is the inspiration of good literature in our day is working. The essayist says that "human life under any aspect must spurn a treatment which is all of sight, and not at all of faith," and perhaps this is the key-note of his book. It prevails in the essays of a more metaphysical cast, and it strongly qualifies two of the most important, in which he deals with "Present-day Novels" and "The Heirship of the Novel." In the latter he regards the novel as "an epitome of life, appealing to the sympathies *of* all who live *for* all who live," and he tries to make us realize "the greatness of its mission as a humanizing influence." How far beyond the English ideal of fiction he has wrought is apparent not only in this essay, but in the other, which he devotes to a study of the difference between English and American fiction. The first he defines as working from within outwardly, and the second from without inwardly. The definition is very surprisingly accurate; and the critic's discovery of this fundamental difference is carried into particulars with a distinctness which is as unfailing as the courtesy he has in recognizing the present superiority of American work. He seems to think, however, that the English principle is the better, though why he should think so he does not make so clear. It

appears a belated and rather voluntary effect of patriotism, disappointing in a philosopher of his degree; but it does not keep him from very explicit justice to the best characteristics of our fiction. "The American novelist is distinguished for the intellectual grip which he has of his characters. . . . He penetrates below the crust, and he recognizes no necessity of the crust to anticipate what is beneath. . . . He utterly discards heroics; he often even discards anything like a plot. . . . His story proper is often no more than a natural predicament. . . . It is no stage view we have of his characters, but one behind the scenes. . . . We are brought into contact with no strained virtues, illumined by strained lights upon strained heights of situation. . . . Whenever he appeals to the emotions it would seem to be with an appeal to the intellect too. . . . because he weaves his story of the finer, less self-evident though common threads of human nature, seldom calling into play the grosser and more powerful strain. . . . Everywhere in his pages we come across acquaintances *undisguised.* . . . The characters in an American novel are never unapproachable to the reader. . . . The naturalness, with the every-day atmosphere which surrounds it, is one great charm of the American novel. . . . It is throughout examinative, discursory, even more—quizzical. Its characters are undergoing, at the hands of the author, calm, interested observation. . . . He is never caught identifying himself with them; he must preserve impartiality at all costs. . . . but. . . . the touch of nature is always felt, the feeling of kinship always follows. . . . The strength of the American novel is its optimistic faith. . . . If out of this persistent hopefulness it can evolve for men a new order of trustfulness, a tenet that between man and man there should be less suspicion, more confidence, since *human nature sanctions it,* its mission will have been more than an æsthetic, it will have been a moral one." [2]

III.

Mr. Hughes distinguishes very nicely the differing methods of the American novelist and the French novelist; he finds ours the more intellectual, the more critical, in its aloofness, and he says that the Frenchman identifies himself so closely with his material that his hands infect his book with the sensual taint of his characters. This is not always so, and not necessarily so, as one may learn from the little collection of tales which Mr. Jonathan Sturges has so limpidly Englished of late from the French of De Maupassant, with the title of *The Odd Number.* [3] They are extremely clever stories, and illustrative of the French sense of art in all things, so fine that it attains even the pathetic in these little pieces. "The Diamond Necklace," "A Piece of String," are of a heart-breaking pathos, and there is a sadness of tone in all; the material is what our "critics" call "commonplace," and there is the greatest simplicity in the handling. Those who know the author's larger work, with its brutal freedom, and its tremendous plunge into abysses which our modest fiction hardly approaches the brink of, will be sensible of a certain slightness of fibre in these tales. But they are masterly, and it is most important to have them, if only to realize that in the work of some of our own tellers of short stories we have something cleverer in the same kind than that of the cleverest Frenchman going. In a degree we have inherited the vice of over-explanatory fullness from the English, who seem to address their fiction to the æsthetically idiotic; but such a sketch, for instance, as Miss Jewett's "Going to Shrewsbury" has the [4] virtue of the best continental work and something more: humor of the delicious sort of which Americans seem to have the secret.

Very much of all that Mr. Hughes says of our novels applies with peculiar force to an American novel which we have just been reading with great respect for its conscientious art, and with the satisfaction which comes from promise fulfilled in any writer. Mr. G. P. Lathrop's book is called *Would You Kill Him?* in a lurid taste which we could not sufficiently deplore; but our censure would hardly go beyond the title-page. The power which he gave proof of in *An Echo of Passion* is here an intensified force grappling successfully with a more complex problem, and keeping in the light of common day an action whose springs are in the darkest fastnesses of the soul. It is not Holsclaw's killing of Vail, with all its consequence in his conscience and his life, which forms the most original phase of the tragedy: the predicament in that homicide is one that has declared itself heretofore in fiction as well as in fact. But the domestic situation from which it is evolved is something that the novelist has not dealt with before, so far as we know, perhaps because it is one almost peculiar to American life. The study of the "maiden vampire" Lily Britton, whom the folly of Alice Holsclaw suffers to insinuate herself into her conjugal life, and to be not only her witness but her partisan in the things in which she should have no witness and no partisan, is singularly perfect; so fine, so just, so careful, indeed, that it establishes the truth in a probability at no point contestable. The helplessness of the husband and the wife in the clutch of this wretched creature, who is stupidly obstructive

rather than malignant in her helpless lust of power, is exquisitely portrayed. She destroys their perfect intimacy without knowing herself why, and interposes her aimless and senseless authority where their love should be the sole law; till at last the wife can see her duty only in rebellion against her husband, and Holsclaw is driven to the homicide which he commits. We leave the processes, subtle yet distinct, to the reader of the book, who will find them all breathlessly interesting; but we must praise the ethical insight as well as the artistic mastery with which the most difficult implications of the affair are touched. Mr. Lathrop releases Holsclaw from no necessary burden of guilt; he recognizes always that he is a free agent; but we think that the reader will have a sense of Lily Britton's more than equal complicity, if not final responsibility, in the deed of a man she had "wrought upon and perplexed in the extreme."

IV.

As for the minor morals of the work, they seem to us exceedingly well handled, with passages of most uncommon vigor, and with forays of the imagination into regions little explored. If we mention the use in the tragedy of the wandering wreck which the steamer runs into at the moment Holsclaw kills Vail, it is less to note the thrilling effectiveness of that incident than to recognize the courage and truth with which the author forbears to relieve the whole catastrophe by allowing Vail to be found alive on the wreck, as a weaker, or an earlier, novelist would have consented to do. We have indeed a fiction here intensely interesting and powerful in very unusual direction and degree, but of a thoroughly modern and most American type. So, in another region, is *A Little Journey in the World* thoroughly modern and most American. It is thoroughly modern and most American in spite of a manner in which a writer like Mr. C. D. Warner, with such lovely manners of his own, chooses to remind us of an author who from his nature, no less than from his epoch and environment, could not have conceived of experience so fine and high as fit matter for a novel. Thackeray was an Englishman of a time now left very remote by the advance of humanity through science in ethics and æsthetics; and questions are questions now which were none in his day. The particular question with which Mr. Warner deals is almost peculiar to our American civilization, or at least it has a peculiar poignancy for us. It is the question of a beautiful, conscientious, cultivated, sympathetic New England girl decaying through the temptations of wealth into a rich leader of society, brilliant, magnificent, joyless, sordid, hard, buying a little rest for her soul by charities which she has· no heart in, and risking the next world, not to win but to *lose* the happiness of this. It is a great tragedy, followed tenderly, pityingly, but most faithfully, from the first moment when her husband begins to bribe her acquiescence in the gains of a railroad wrecker by gifts of his booty for the good objects she loves, till the time has come when she has ceased to love them, when they bore, when they weary, when they stupefy her, and she can talk of the "ingratitude" of the poor.

We will not repeat the story which Mr. Warner has told so well, with indeed a slight strain of the autobiographical machinery to operate experiences beyond the narrator's observation, but always with an unerring sense of the importance and significance of the situation. This sense, expressed in the winning irony, the delicate satire, the sunny wit and the friendly humor which he has taught us to expect of him, employs all his gifts of insight and all his graces of style to the end which no writer who thinks can now shun. In view of the dangers which threaten to transform us from a democracy to a plutocracy, dazzling us with its dollars to a betrayal of the best hopes and highest aims of the race, the types he has struck of men who win money ruthlessly, almost helplessly, through the vastness of the opportunity, are each a startling homily. We have met most of them in the newspapers already, but it was for the novelist to present them in the full presence of their cynical humor, their vulgar *bonhomie*, their laughing, kindly, loose-jointed immorality, which would as lief do a good action as not, and has nothing mean about it. This sort of enemies of the commonwealth Mr. Warner has portrayed for us with the same delicate touch which has given us his pathetic heroine; and in this story he has placed himself with the few literary men, destined to be more, for whom literature does not suffice as an end, but who regard it consciously or unconsciously as a means, and who give their work enrichingly back to the life from which its materials came.

V.

You go with no sense of violent transition from such a book as Mr. Warner's to such a book as Professor Richard T. Ely's, on *Social Aspects of Christianity*, though one is a novelist and the other is a political economist. Perhaps this is because as political economist and as novelist they are both men of a new fashion. Mr. Warner, who once had his misgivings about the photographic school in fiction, and then deprecated the novel of pur-

pose as a sort of social science tract, has ended by writing a social science tract illustrated with photographs; and we cannot praise him too much for the good work he has done in it. One could hardly have expected that he would be contented to write a romance of the silly old fashion, when once he came to the work, and in this novel he has been true to all the claims of the strong motive which inspired it. If he does not leave his reader palpitating in a sensuous sympathy with two young people who have succeeded in getting married after everything the author has done to prevent them, it is probably because experiment has taught him that it is *not* the first business of the novel to be entertaining, and that it is better to make his reader think than to make him thrill. He has proved himself one of those who can carry the interest beyond the fifth act, as a French critic said of Tolstoï, and make it seem as really an affair of practical import as any of the matters discussed by Professor Ely. It is no more surprising that a novelist should do this than that an associate professor of political economy in one of our leading universities should be preaching primitive Christianity, and counselling the members of the churches to brotherly love as a token and a proof of their faith, with the severe morality of a socialist of the first century. This remarkable political economist denies that self-interest should be the ruling principle of life, and that all things shall be added unto us if we seek first the kingdom of Mammon and his unrighteousness. He is terribly unsparing in his recurrence to chapter and verse; he will not allow us a moment's rest in the spoil of the stranger and the poor. He believes that Christ really meant the young man of great possessions to give up his worldly goods when he said so, and that He taught a political economy in no wise impossible or mistaken. Himself a church member, he accuses the churches of alienating the poor by forsaking their cause in the interest of the rich; by saying smooth things to capital and rough things to labor; by refusing to second the working-men's endeavors to enforce the Sunday laws that they might rest, while strenuous in closing libraries and galleries against them on the Sabbath. He tells the church that its work is primarily to make justice and peace and love at home upon the earth, and secondarily to save souls for heaven thereby. He calls in witness such words as those in which we are told the Last Judgment shall be delivered to teach that the first duty of all is to the least of the brethren. Then, going from generals to particulars, he declares that by usury the Bible meant the interest on one's money, by which so many of our worthiest people now live in great satisfaction; and that in lending to the needy we ought not only to forbear to take greater usury of them because of their necessity, but that we ought to take none at all.

One sees what confusion the practice of such precepts would bring about in the world; and the saddest reflection arising from the perusal of books like Mr. Warner's and Professor Ely's is not that the facts dealt with do exist, but that they *must* exist in the present frame of things. The legal right of one man to luxury through the misery of another is unquestionable; and it is comically, it is tragically, futile to tell people not to get gain, and take advantage, when even the wayfaring man can see that these are the very conditions of success, and of mere bread and meat, in society constituted as it is. The trouble seems to be the trouble apprehended long ago from putting new wine into old bottles. Something came into the world once that was then and will be forever irreconcilable with the world as the world was and is: we will say a heaven-descended conscience, or we will say the Church, or we will say Christianity. This something has improved the world at points; it has abolished the exposure of infants, gladiatorial shows, slavery, private war, piracy, the slaughter of prisoners; but after all civilization has remained pagan, though it has been ever so obliging in calling itself Christian. Its ideals are pagan; its practices are pagan; as any one may see who will go to an evening party, or a battle, or a grain or stock exchange. The confusion in the minds of reformers comes from finding so many Christians in pagan society, and so many society pagans in the Christian church, and they break out into vain censure of appearances which are the inevitable expression of the very constitution of things.

VI.

It all makes one a little tired to think how long it has been going on, this criticism of the old bottle. *Social Aspects of Christianity* was written as far back as the time of Edward III.; only then it was called *The Vision of Piers Plowman ;* and William Langland looked with all of Professor Ely's "soreness of heart upon the sufferings of poor country folk, and upon the wantonness of the monks, and the extravagance of the rich, and the hatefulness of the proud."

We read these words from a very pleasant book, written by an author who was one of our first delights in literature; and to whom we gladly pay our debt of gratitude. It is the Ik Marvel of forty years ago, who now talks of *English Lands, Letters, and Kings* with the same light grace that charmed us then in *Reveries of a Bachelor* and *Dream Life,* after long silences fitfully broken but twice or thrice since. Mr. Donald G. Mitchell rambles over fields with which we are comfortably accustomed to think ourselves familiar, but which we shall most of us know better, and which some of us possibly may know only, from having been through them with him. His essays, or talks, are about English literature from its first beginnings to

"The spacious times of great Elizabeth";

and in his modest preface he expresses his reluctance to offer the public his generalities in these days of specialists. It is indeed true that he nowhere drinks so deep of the springs of literary history as not to leave a sip or two for those who come after; but then neither does he roil their sweet waters and leave them turbid for his having been at them. Kindly and reverently, with a real love of literature, he recalls the masters of the past, and casts upon their work the light of social and political conditions without which it cannot be seen aright. His criticism, which is as much of the men as of their books, is always intelligent and always gentle, and it is often very keen and fine. It is the companionship of a cultivated and sympathetic host which you enjoy in his book, and he delicately contrives not to let you feel at once all the obligations you are under to him.

---

[1] Christian Bernhard von Tauchnitz published this series of books under the title Collection of British and American Authors (Leipzig: Tauchnitz, 1841) before the International Copyright Agreement.

[2] Criticism and Fiction, pp. 121-123.

[3] Guy de Maupassant, The Odd Number: Thirteen Tales, Jonathan Sturges, trans., Introduction by Henry James (New York: Harper & Brothers, 1889). See also p. 310b.

[4] Sarah Orne Jewett.

[5] Ik Marvel is the pseudonym of Donald Grant Mitchell.

March, 1890

Editor's Study.

I.

A SUGGESTIVE contribution to recent magazine literature is the Hon. E. J. Phelps's paper on "The Age of Words." [1] Mr. Phelps, though four years our minister at the Court of St. James, is so little vitiated by the maxims of diplomacy that he does not, even in an age of words, employ language to conceal thought, but what he thinks of certain rather important matters, he lets us know plainly in what he says. Perhaps the subject of his essay is not quite new; we all know how the age of words was discountenanced by Thomas Carlyle in a great many octavos; and from time to time we have heard from other voluble people that there is too much talking. Mr. Phelps makes the same complaint; but we are not sure that he makes it very much more reasonably. It seems to us that there is not more talking than is needed, but that the wrong people do the talking.

Mr. Phelps has so lately arrived home from a foreign country that he may be supposed not yet to have adjusted his perceptions to conditions in which speech is so generally silvern, so habitually worth eighty cents on the dollar, as ours. Even where he prolongs a strain often heard in the organ harmonies of this Study, and laments that the reading of fiction should form the only reading of so many people, we fancy that he is suffering from the recollection of English novels rather than from an immediate experience of our own. He has unmistakably in mind the decaying literature of the British Isles, when he says that "the everlasting repetition .... of the story of the imaginary courtship and marriage of fictitious and impossible young men and women; and when all conceivable incidents that could attend this happy narrative are used up, and the exhausted imagination of the narrator refuses any further supply, then in their place an endless flow of commonplace and vapid conversation, tending to the same matrimonial result, until it is clear that the parties, if they were real, would talk themselves to death—this is the staple of what is now called fiction." We cordially agree with Mr. Phelps that these are the character-istics of the vastly greater number of English novels; and we believe with him, that for "the large class who derive their ideas of life and the world from this source, ... and enter upon married life with ideas and expectations so false and theories so absurd, nothing but disappointment and unhappiness can follow."

Nevertheless, we think that if Mr. Phelps had been writing more directly from the documents he would not have denounced these traits and these effects as peculiar to the modern novel, even the modern English novel, purposeless and flabby and false as it mostly is. If he had cared to look a little into the history of fiction he would have learned that formerly the novel of the highest grade presented ideals which are now chiefly to be found in the novel of the lowest grade; and that the modern novel of the realistic or intellectual school has for its supreme aim the exact portrayal of the motives as well as the facts of life. It is because the English novelists and their imitators mainly hold by the romantic tradition that they are so mischievous, or when not mischievous, so extremely debilitating. If Mr. Phelps would acquaint himself with the great novelists of the Continent, he would see that fiction was never before so constant to the final inspiration and object of the noblest of the arts.

II.

We did not mean, however, to dispute so long concerning this point, though in an age of words it might be allowable to do so. What we were really trying to get at, with a much more damaging purpose, was Mr. Phelps's apparent misconception of the nature, and the ends and aims of the literary life. We are all the more eager to demolish this, because it seems to be the misconception of many other worthy people who, in an age of words, are apt to let their talking outrun their thinking; and if we seem at times to be personal, in the application of the truth which is in us, we beg to assure the sufferers beforehand that we shall only be so illustratively. We shall by no means hold Mr. Phelps chiefly accountable for words that, in an age of them, happen to have come out of the point of his pen, for they are words that have the air of having met the eye before, not just in their present order, perhaps, but certainly to their present effect. "Book-making," says he, "has become a trade. Profit is its chief end. The day of studious and self-denying lives, devoted to study and thought, and regardless of gain, are almost gone by," he says; and though we could have wished here a little closer agreement between his verb and its nominative, we are not going yet to gainsay him. "Literature is no longer cultivated upon a little oatmeal; nor for its own sake upon any fare. Men do not write because they are charged with a message to humanity that has been mellowed and tempered by long reflection, by communion with nature and the higher influences of the soul. . . . Reputation depends on good management much more than on merit. Not so were the enduring achievements of the human intellect brought forth. They were not the product of any age of words. They were chiefly out of the great silences, when thought was mightier than speech, when words were fit but few. There has been noise always in the world, no doubt, and it has died away for the most part into everlasting stillness. It is only the silences that have become vocal, whose voices remain and will remain."

This is what Mr. Phelps says (with some regrettable duplication of his relative pronouns at last), and we will not deny that his utterances are such as would carry conviction to any party of gentlemen after dinner. The Study can imagine itself so full of Veuve Cliquecot, or Moët et Chandon, or the Grand Vin Sec, as to applaud them to the echo. But in the cold light of the next morning, amid the throbs of a retributive headache, we think it would ask itself, How is the parturition of an achievement possible? How can thought be mightier than speech; or what superior potency is there in merely thinking without speaking? When was thought mightier than speech, and how did the fact become known? How can a silence become vocal, and how can a voice remain? The Study would puzzle over these figurative expressions which seemed so brilliant and so convincing last night; but if it found no truth in them we suspect it would not rest satisfied with its discovery. We are afraid it would want to ask Mr. Phelps how and when book-making became a mere trade, and just at what moment authors began to be recreant to their high calling; it would demand the proof that literary reputation now depends more on good management than on merit. We do not believe that he would have his wit-

nesses in court; and we are quite sure he would not be ready with evidence that the great achievements came out of the great silences. There was a great silence in English literature between Chaucer and Spenser, and the enduring achievement that came out of it was the immortal poetry of one Gower, whose first name we [2] cannot remember. Did Shakespeare's plays come out of a great silence? No, but amidst the "melodious burst" of such minstrelsy as Beaumont and Fletcher's, Marlowe's, Greene's, Drayton's, Webster's, Jonson's, and the like. Did the "Divine Comedy" come out of a great silence? Petrarch and Boccaccio were the contemporaries of Dante. Did *Don Quixote* come out of a great silence? Cervantes wrote while Calderon and Lope and the other masters of the Spanish drama were making their "noises" about him. Did "Faust" come out of a great silence? Schiller was the friend and fellow-townsman of Goethe, and all Germany was "flooded over with eddying song" from a score of throats. Did Longfellow sing "to one clear harp in divers tones" in a great silence? Emerson, Whittier, Holmes, Lowell, Poe, Bryant, formed such a choir about him as we may not hear again in centuries. Perhaps the thoughts of all these great men would have been mightier if they had never been put into words; though we do not think so.

III.

But what is merely an affair of literary history may be safely left to take care of itself. It is the question of a decadence in the motives and aims of the literary life which we think deserves some little serious consideration, and we are quite ready to affirm that these motives and aims have never been higher. Possibly Mr. Phelps may be able to name some "bella età dell' oro" when they were not essentially what they are now; but we do not believe it. They never were different, and in the nature of things they never can be different, for they are now, as always, the motives and the aims of a self-devoted love of literary art. Of all the men and women now practising this noble art, however unfitly and ineffectually, we believe there is not one who has taken it up except for the love of it. They may often have been deceived in the hope of that just reward of their toil which all men look forward to, but they are not writers for the love of gain, at the worst, but writers for the love of letters; otherwise they would have been railroad men, and stock-brokers, and dry-goods merchants, and liquor sellers, and corner grocers, and lawyers: few of them are so poor of wit as not to be able to succeed in callings which men make money by.

The fact that some literary men earn

enough to live comfortably has nothing to do with the question whether profit is the chief end of authorship or not. They have a right to live comfortably by their art, just as a physician or a minister has a right to live comfortably by his unselfish calling. In the mean time, we say that Mr. James, for example, writes his novels from the love of letters and the hope of recognition and the need of living, just as Fielding and Richardson and Scott and Thackeray and George Eliot and Trollope wrote their novels, and as Boccaccio and Cervantes and Goethe wrote theirs. On their level, which is by no means a low one, Mr. Bronson Howard, Mr. Denman Thompson, and Mr. Edward Harrigan give us their different plays from exactly the same love of the drama and of fame, and the same reasonable hope of pecuniary return that governed Euripides and Aristophanes, Shakespeare and Molière. The fruition of that hope does not make it their chief end; it is the last and the least of the ends they work for. Mr. McMaster and Mr. Fiske write their histories from the same motives that inspired Thucydides and Tacitus; and if Mr. Phelps really believes that the day of studious and self-denying lives is gone by, we will instance that of Mr. Francis Parkman, whose great and beautiful work in history has certainly not been carried on as a paying enterprise.

Let us clear our minds of cant, if possible, and own that there never was a time when literature was indifferent to the butcher's bill. Money is no fit reward for it, we allow, and we can conceive of a state of things in which the hope of it would not enter; but in the economic chaos of competitive society, there is no other way for authors to live. What we cannot conceive of is the age of the great silences, when authors kept their mighty thoughts to themselves, "regardless of gain," till they could not help "bringing forth enduring achievements," and we do not believe it ever existed outside of rhetoric hard up for a rounded period.

IV.

"Povera e nuda vai, Filosofia," **3**

says Petrarch; but we venture to think, Never willingly, poor girl! Philosophy, like other ladies, likes to be in the fashion, and we do not blame her. Neither does Mr. Phelps, we suspect, at the bottom of his heart. She may be

"Clad in the beauty of a thousand stars,"

but that pretty costume will not keep her from the cold in our climate, and there never was a time or a place in the world, since the love of her began, that it was not with her lovers as it is now. Never did they forego more for her sake; for in

our conditions, where the prizes of material success are so great, it is bitterer than ever to take the second premiums.

Of all the silly superstitions that have survived out of the credulous past, none is sillier than the notion that literature ought to work for nothing and find itself. The most prosperous writer in our country probably gets no more for his work than tens of thousands of lawyers and doctors each receive; but in a civilization where every office rendered to the commonwealth is paid for, where every conceivable service from man to man has its wage, it is felt that the author if paid at all ought to be underpaid; that he is the only laborer unworthy of his hire. We will allow that if you take the word of literary men about one another they are mostly unworthy of their hire; in their jealousies and envies they have themselves much to blame for the common feeling concerning them. But, after all, how many authors among us keep their carriages, or have three kinds of wine at table, out of their disgraceful gains? Mr. Phelps says that book-making has become a trade, and that profit is its chief end. For the present we will not deny this, but we warn all those intending to go into the business with a view to profit as the chief end, that there is not much money for the amount of work in it. In spite of Mr. Phelps's confidence, however, there is probably no man or woman in the country intending to go into it with that view. Those who love literature have at least wit enough to know that they will never become rich by it; and that probably they will always remain poor. They know that if by some rare fortune a man writes a book of permanent pecuniary value, his grateful country will, after forty-two years, anticipate his wish to become a public benefactor, and will confiscate his property in it, throwing it open to any of his fellow-citizens who may like to steal it. Nevertheless, literary men do hope to live by literature, because they pursue it as their happiness, and because it is often impracticable to borrow and always disagreeable to starve; but they know they have not the right to expect much more; and they are willing, as such men and women in all times have been willing, to lead those "studious and self-denying lives" which Mr. Phelps says are now almost things of the past; though he would not have said so, we think, if he had looked about him in a university town like New Haven, where there is probably as much devotion to the humanities "regardless of gain" as ever there was among the same number of scholars anywhere in the world. If he cannot find such lives at Yale, we assure him he can find them at Harvard, at Johns Hopkins, at Cornell, at Ann Arbor, at Dartmouth. Or, if the humanities must be subdivided, we believe that he will find very much the same devotion to their art in the people who write our magazine poetry and fiction and criticism; and among those who write the newspaper articles; and even among those who write the interviews and the police reports. In no other industry could the same talent be so poorly paid; and we may safely say that from this point of view they are all "regardless of gain," high and low, great and small. No author believes that any reputation he achieves will "depend on good management much more than on merit." He understands that without a good deal of some kind of merit, he can achieve no reputation; and that what seems mere trash is somehow much more than trash if it wins even a passing popularity for its author. He may envy its author, but he will be slow to declare it absolutely wanting in the right to be.

V.

This literary man will also have other hesitations where Mr. Phelps appears to have none. He will not defy us to say where "our poets, our dramatists, our historians, our essayists, our philosophers, our really capable critics" are, nor will he brave us to name many "living writers who have contributed anything that will live in after-time, or whose names will be likely to be remembered when they have been dead fifty years." As to these last he will understand that immortality is becoming always more and more difficult, and that there are many people writing now who would easily survive their death fifty years if they were living in any century before this. He will know that taste is now so advanced, and literary skill so diffused, and the literary sense so highly developed, that two-thirds of the British Classics in poetry and fiction would be rejected by a conscientious editor, not because they were wanting in sensation, as Mr. Phelps seems to think, but because they were wanting in form, or wanting in truth, or wanting in art, or wanting in humanity, or wanting in common decency. "The past literature of our language is splendid and unsurpassed," he tells us; but this is true only in a restricted sense. It is splendid in certain names, which again are splendid in certain lights; but, like all other literatures, it has vast masses and spaces of dulness in it; and it is surpassed by several other literatures in easily namable characteristics. It is indeed of mighty bulk; but if it were thoroughly winnowed by modern criticism it would show, like the discourse of Gratiano, a grain of wheat in a bushel of chaff.

VI.

As for our present dearth of writers, it seems to us the effect of imagination disheartening itself to make a point, rather than a fact of literary history. We are always in a period of transition, and, if we are to confine the question to America, we should say that in the article of poets, though we have now passed the time in which our great cycle of poets flourished, we still have Holmes, Whittier, Lowell, Whitman, Trowbridge, and Stoddard among us; that Stedman and Aldrich are in the prime of their power; and when you come to younger poets, we have a group whose work is as distinguished and as distinctive in promise as that of almost any group of the past, which finally gave us a splendid and unsurpassed literature. If we mention only Messrs. John Boyle O'Reilly, G. P. Lathrop, R. W. Gilder, James Whitcomb Riley, H. H. Boyesen, J. Madison Cawein, the Canadian Lampman, H. C. Bunner, Edgar Fawcett, Maurice Thompson, it is because their names come to mind as we write, and not because there are not also others who if they had done in another time what they have done in ours would easily have achieved a place in the British Classics. Our dramatists are yet mainly to come, but the work of some now writing is upon the only lines that give a foundation of enduring solidity, the lines of the truth which is also beauty; and several have achieved very remarkable success by work that has an authentic and native excellence. We cannot be supposed poor in historians when Mr. Parkman, the greatest historian whom America has produced, (we wish he had a better taste in fiction!) is still weaving that web of glowing colors in which the picturesque past of our continent magically reappears. We need not dwell upon the monumental labors of Mr. Herbert Bancroft and his coadjutors in the annals of the Pacific coast; but surely we may be proud of Messrs. McMaster and Fiske, in their several ways; and Mr. Henry Adams has just given us two volumes of American history which are not less important than any ever written. The scientific spirit, blent with a fervor and force of his own, characterizes the studies of Mr. Roosevelt in pioneer history; and at this moment Messrs. Hay and Nicolay, in their life of Lincoln, are completing[4] a historical work sufficient in magnitude and thoroughness to command the admiration of any age or country. We only touch a few facts of the case, and what shall we say to a gentleman who asks for our essayists in the presence of Messrs. Higginson, Curtis, and Warner, Burroughs, Scudder, and Woodberry, whose culture, whose grace, whose humor is shared in degree by clever magazinists not to be named for number? As for philosophers, the Study has not so much knowledge of them as it could desire; but it has supposed that Mr. John Fiske had a European reputation in that sort, that Professor William James and Professor Josiah Royce were men of the first quality as metaphysicians, and that there were able thinkers and writers in the different departments of philosophy at several American universities besides Harvard. Perhaps there are some at Yale.

Capable critics are always rather rare birds. But we had imagined that Mr. Lowell was rather a capable critic; Mr. Stedman is a critic of very great capability; and we will mention Mr. T. S. Perry, as the author of a study of *English Literature in the Eighteenth Century*, which in learning, insight, and a breadth and depth of critical science is of a sort simply impossible to the crude conceptions of earlier criticism—as far beyond that as antiseptic surgery is beyond the old methods. In all our periodicals, quarterly, monthly, weekly, and daily, men are writing criticism which is really capable, which is mostly honest and impartial, and considering their cruel trade, humane. They have as yet too little grasp of principles; their perspective is often bad, and their taste is sometimes not good. But generally they have right feeling and that love of literature without which no one writes even criticism. Under the chastening influences of the Study, we hope that they will more and more realize that their function is not to legislate for literature, but to observe and register

its facts. In the mean time, they are, on the whole, producing an average of better criticism than we have had in the past.

VII.

In fine, we say in all seriousness, that in this new country, drunk with prosperity and besotted as it is with material ideals, the literary standard is as high as ever it was in the world; and that the literary performance is of an excellence which is only not conspicuous because it is so general. If any one doubts it, let him compare an average piece of fiction in the *Atlantic Monthly*, or the *Century*, or *Scribner's*, or *Harper's* with an average piece of fiction in *Blackwood's*, or *Fraser's*, or *Tinsley's* of fifty years ago; or an average essay in one of our periodicals with an average essay of the best English time; or an average poem of our day with an average poem of the "splendid and unsurpassed literature of the past"; or an average review in the Sunday papers with the "really capable criticism" of the heyday of English reviewing.

It is easy to cry down the present in favor of the past; but we think Mr. Phelps, if he had "mellowed and tempered" his "message to humanity" by somewhat larger reflection, would not have been quite so ready to pronounce this an age of words in any ill sense. We have ourselves the belief that it is the age of words because it is also the age of thoughts, and that the ages of great silences were epochs in which men's tongues were still because their lives were dull and their heads were empty, and they mostly did not know how to read and write.

[1] Edward John Phelps, "The Age of Words," Scribner's Magazine, 6 (December, 1889), 760-768. Reprinted in Orations and Essays of Edward John Phelps, J. G. McCullough, ed. (New York: Harper and Brothers Publishers, 1901), pp. 455-476.

[2] See p. 264a for correction. (It is John Skelton, not John Gower, who wrote between Chaucer's time and Spenser's.)

[3] "Povera e nuda vai, Filosofia," - Go poor and naked, Philosophy.

[4] John Milton Hay and John George Nicolay, Abraham Lincoln: A History (New York: Century, 1890).

Editor's Study.

I.

TO realize God in the minds of men as He has always somehow been realized in their hearts; to possess the intellect of the precious truth of Him in place of its ever-worthless question of Him; to bring Him home to us in terms sensible to our knowledge as the power, the goodness which works in us hitherto and evermore, a very present helper against ourselves; to discover Him to us as the service of the meanest, as sacrifice, as suffering, as meekness, as the love within the law: this has been the effort of the author whose book, called *God in His World*, comes to us without an author's name. It is a book which may chance to meet the worst fate, and fall from the vague curiosity which people feel about the matters it deals with, to the indifference which they also feel; but we do not believe this is likely to happen. To the Jews a stumbling-block and to the Greeks foolishness, such a book must be. It will probably be buffeted about between Jew and Greek as a piece of obstructive and ridiculous mysticism; but it will not be so with those who come to it with singleness and directness, without dogmatic or sophistical preoccupation; or as they would to a poem. A poem, in fact, the book is, and in great measure one should keep one's self in the mood in which one reads a poem, if one would get the good of it. At times, the appeal which it addresses to the reason through the affection may fail to reach it; something seems left, at times, to apprehensions almost as subtle as those which seize a musician's intention; and the poetic quality is always there in the most intellectual moments. Certain conditions must be made for the right enjoyment of the literary form of the book; and the reader must indulge the author in his archaic present tense, which we confess goes sometimes to make his inner seriousness mere quaintness outwardly.

But we should give a wrong notion of an important book if we left the reader to suppose something wholly or mainly rhapsodical from what we have been saying. The rhapsody in it is the emotion breaking psalm-like from the intense conviction; and the poetry is the flower of the involuntary growth of a life into the light. The work differs from all other modern interpretations in having no structural endeavor in it. The author would gladly have you of his thinking; but after the passages of his impressive introduction, he wholly drops the office of controversy. His book is a growth, not a building; a tree, not a temple. You shall sit in its shelter, and eat of its fruit, and welcome; but there is nowhere that you shall be locked in, and be kept, if you would rather be going your way. Yet it abounds in evidences of a learning, and of a wide knowledge of what others have found in search of truth; it is clearly the work of a scholar as well as the work of a poet; of a scholar who is always too much a poet to be saddened or broken by his acquirements; and whose intuitions have not been put to death that his analytic powers might flourish in abnormal activity.

Christ, and His life and His words, are the first and last authorities for the truth with this poet; but he finds that measure of the truth which every generous mind must find in all the prophets and all the religions. The early Aryan beliefs and the Vedic hymns; the Hellenic development of faith and its mysteries; and the decay of these in the hard fixity of the Roman civility, are passages of the race-history that take new meaning under the light he throws upon them, and that fitly lead up to the spacious moment when the cross was lifted in supreme significance on Calvary. The author deals attractively with the facts of empires and civilizations which embody the revelations, but he never forgets that the revelations are the great matter, and that their eternal, not their occasional, effect is that to be verified. His studies, therefore, even of the beginnings of Christianity have this look to the ends of Christianity, and in recognizing the socialistic republic which sprang up among his followers from the precept and example of Jesus, he makes us see that it arose not from any civic ideal, but from that unselfish love of the neighbor without which we can never again have the kingdom of heaven on earth.

But the correspondence of the Word to Nature, and the divine traits in Nature and in Christ, are the things on which he lays weight, that he may make us feel how the creative care for the creature—

"La somma sapienza è il primo amore"— **2**

forever incarnates itself in the universe, and unites the divine with the human whenever one man desires unselfishly to befriend another.

We touch at a few points the meaning of the book as it expresses itself to us. It seems to us a book that will have more and more meaning for those whom life has prepared for it, by loss, by trouble, by despair. We should not suppose it would convert or convince any one who was of another way of thinking; perhaps it would repel and confirm such a one in his own thinking; very likely he would feel no need of it; and we fancy the author would be the last to blame him for his aversion, or to be vexed by it. Experience, the whole of what we have known up to a certain time, not the process of logic, is what prepares us for the reception or rejection of this postulate or that; the heart must be touched before the brain can be reached; but to those who have shuddered in the void and darkness of sorrow, this book, which has its foible as well as its strength, but which is so earnest and brotherly, will bring hope, and may bring faith in a God who is always in His world, very near at hand, and so approachable that whenever we go wholly out of ourselves we can find Him, not only in every wretchedest fellow-being, but in the meanest thing He has made.

II.

"Gods,
To quench, not hurl the thunder-bolt; to stay,
Not spread the plague, the famine; Gods indeed,
To send the noon into the night, and break
The sunless halls of Hades into Heaven"—

this is the prescience of the Divine to succeed the old terror, the old caprice, which lifts the lament of Demeter for Persephone out of despair at last, in that great new poem which Tennyson has given the world; and this is the faith which breathes in the book we have been speaking of, and which stirs in every human soul, however mutely. One must feel the presence of this larger hope in nearly all the poems of the laureate's volume; one might say that it formed the dominant note of its most noble music. The highest reach of Tennyson's poetry was always in its impassioned spirituality; the human tragedy, or the human comedy, rising so high above its mortal source as to catch the light of Heaven, and flash into supernal meaning. "Demeter and Persephone," "Vastness," "Forlorn," "The Leper's Bride," "Romney's Re-

morse," "Parnassus," "By an Evolutionist": one is aware of the same quality in them all, which will not let doubt remain doubt, and still less despair remain despair, but transmutes them into a trust of the goodness over all, the mercy that endureth forever, the wisdom that knoweth our frame, that remembereth we are dust. It is a natural piety that supremely befits the aged poet, and that gives dignity to all he says, and that can help those who have always loved his song because this piety has always been its inner voice. If this were the last work Tennyson should give us, it seems to us such work as he might well be willing to let be his last. Every life is a fragment; it is broken off always and never rounded to a close; something in it is still left unfinished. But in most unusual degree the poems of this volume summarize the qualities of all Tennyson's poetry. The opening strain of the lament for his son's death that recalls "In Memoriam"; the "Demeter and Persephone," which belongs with that group of classic pieces which "Ulysses" was perhaps the first of; "Owd Roä," with its reminiscence of the "Northern Farmer"; "The Ring," and "Romney's Remorse," which bring back all he has done in drama and idyl; "The Throstle," with the lyrical gush of a score of matchless songs in it; even the stanzas on the "Jubilee of Queen Victoria," with their fresh proof of how well and ill a great poet can sing when he sings officially: they all suggest, without repetition, the turns, the accents, endeared by life-long association, the earlier manner and the later manner, the divers tones and the one clear harp. It is as if the poet said to the world, "Here is a thing I think you will like, if you liked 'Morte d'Arthur'"; or "The Miller's Daughter"; or "The Two Voices"; or "The Talking Oak," or this or that; and then sang something that put the world in mind of any or all of these without being either again. The world, enamored of that perfect voice, which seems to have grown in no wise thin with years, could listen forever, glad of any strain that recalled any other. Once he does give us, in "The Progress of Spring," a song really of that old time which was the young time, and we listen with a pleasure mixed with wonder that he could have withheld so lovely a thing so long in any manner of doubt of it. There is a lesson of the highest value, however, in this reticence, this patience, though we marvel at it; and we could well commend it to poets who cannot keep back any part of their youth till they are elderly men. Yet, perhaps we should be the losers; there is a simultaneity in moods which keep poet and reader in rapport, and now or never is a good motto for both. We would rather have

Tennyson remind us of his youth in his age than give us of it. In what he does now the art is mellower, the thought richer than in what he did then, beautiful as all that was. But if some younger readers of his verse cannot agree that he is better now than when he was young like them, no one can deny his supreme mastery in his kind,

"As he stands on the heights of his life with a glimpse of a height that is higher."

III.

It is giving one's self as queer a sensation as one well could in all literature to go from Tennyson's "Demeter" to Browning's "Asolando": from that crystal lucidity to this opaline blur of mists and lights; from those clear parables and allegories to these riddles and conundrums; from those lines and phrases distinct, direct, errless in point and aim, to these crabbed interrupted interruptions, parentheses, interjections, backings and fillings, crisscrossings, gasps, hiccoughs; from that bass-relief in polished marble to this mosaic turmoil of a thousand fragments. The old exasperation with the man's freakish wilfulness, the old worship of his strength, mingles with the old wonder at his flashes of divination and the range of that self-knowledge which is the knowledge of others; and as you read you feel that this poet too has epitomized his work, and left his last book as a witness of his whole intent in poetry. It is forever too late to criticise or characterize it, even if he had not always been doing that himself. At any time, no doubt, it was ridiculous to attempt the censor's idle office upon him, though many fools and wise have done it; and all that one can say now is, This was the make of the man. These facts, these features of his poetry may be faults or they may be virtues, but they are certainly the literary expressions of traits in the man himself, and his poetry is no more to be extricated from them, or was ever to have been, than the man was ever to have been extricated from his characteristics. The question is, how much or how little was there of the man; in this smoky splendor, this turbid fume intershot with flame, how great is the flame that gives off so great fume? Time will come soon enough with his chemic tests; he comes dreadfully soon; and long before Browning is dust the world will know how much of him was thought, and how much mere thrill, impulse, guess, vagary. But even when this is known, the form in which the truth is wrapt will remain, and those whom it stupefied and those whom it enraptured will keep their quarrel over it and one who found all dimensions of grandeur in "The Ring and the Book,"

and none but flatness in "The Inn Album," will be of his divided mind about the poet of both. What is certain is that Browning appears never to have been more thoroughly Browning than he was when writing the pieces that go to make up his last book. It has the effect of being thrown down at the feet of Time, or perhaps flung at his head: a defiance, a gage of battle, a challenge to him to do his worst on one who was so intensely, immensely, immutably himself. In nothing is it little; for good or bad it is huge; the very wilfulness is vast; and whatever the poet intended by this or that, there is no question but he intended his meaning to come to the reader in this or that form. It might not be so very strange if after all the most valuable thing that Browning was found to have done for poetry was to take from it the literary pose and diction, and make it take the attitude and speak the dialect of life.

IV.

The attitude and dialect of life are what chiefly delight us in the achievement of a Western poet and humorist who calls himself "Ironquill"; but it is a life which [3] would have been inconceivable to Browning, perhaps, though we are not sure he would have disliked it if he could have imagined it. We who have somewhat known it, here in the New World, recognize in the poetry of "Ironquill" the natural carriage of the-man-let-loose, and the natural language of his let-looseness; though we hasten to reassure the reader that this language which we have called the dialect of life is not a more or less factitious Southwestern parlance, but the ordinary more or less newspaperized English of our day. What gives it especial quality and truth in the verse of "Ironquill" is his humor and his poetry.

"I'll wear Arcturus for a bosom pin,"

is the bold menace or promise of his title-page, and he goes far to keep it. He can be colossally fatiguing as well as colossally amusing; but he can be nothing on a small scale; and his fun is of a coolness and grimness which seem the play of surface moods in a Titan. Of the whole range of it we can give no just idea by quotation, and we think we can best prepare the way for some of it by copying one of his serious pieces; for the fooling of a fool is not very funny, and we all like to be assured that the fooling we enjoy is that of a man who is not a fool.

FEAR YE HIM.
I fear Him not, nor yet do I defy.
Much could He harm me cared He but to try.

Much could He frighten me, much do me ill,
Much terrify me, but—He never will.

The soul of justice must itself be just:
Who trembles most betrays the most distrust.

So plunging in life's current deep and broad,
I take my chances,—*ignorant*—unawed.

Now we think we may safely intrust the reader with a fable which "Ironquill" calls

ZEPHYR ET CANINE.

Once a Kansas zephyr strayed
Where a brass-eyed bird-pup played,
And that foolish canine bayed
    At that zephyr in a gay,
    Semi-idiotic way.
Then that zephyr in about
    Half a jiffy took that pup,
    Tipped him over wrong side up,
Then it turned him inside out,
    And it calmly journeyed thence
    With a barn and string of fence.

When communities turn loose
Social forces that produce
    The disorders of a gale,
Act upon the well-known law:
Face the breeze but close your jaw.
    It's a rule that will not fail.
If you bay it in a gay,
Self-sufficient sort of way,
    It will land you, without doubt,
    Upside down and inside out.

This poet is a sort of reversed Omar Khayyam; that is, his darkest hour has the rosy tint of dawn in it: his fatalism is Occidental, not Oriental.

WHIST.

Hour after hour the cards were fairly shuffled,
    And fairly dealt, but still I got no hand;
The morning came, but I with mind unruffled,
    Did simply say, "I do not understand."

Life is a game of whist. From unseen sources
    The cards are shuffled and the hands are dealt.
Blind are our efforts to control the forces
    That, though unseen, are no less strongly felt.

I do not like the way the cards are shuffled,
    But still I like the game and want to play;
And through the long, long night will I, unruffled,
    Play what I get, until the break of day.

The secret of America is here; and one gladly allows a man who can be so wise his horse-play with the mystery of nature:

On the shores of Yellow Paint,
    After winter, cold and chill,
When the spring-time strikes its focus,
By what magic hocus-pocus
Come the primrose and the crocus
    On the meadow and the hill?
Whyfore buds the hamamellis?
Whyfore twining up the trellis,
Whyfore from the painted lattice,
Does the columbine peep at us?
    If you'll answer this, I'll fill
You with ardent spirits gratis.

But only "Ironquill," taken in his whole book, can give any just notion of his own let-looseness; and as the book is probably not to be found at the polite Eastern book-stores, we will whisper the reader that he can get it of the Kellam Book and Stationery Company, Topeka, Kansas. When he has got it he may learn how tiresome the author can be in some of his pieces, and how unutterably delightful in others. We will mention among those which have given us the most redundant satisfaction, "Hic Jones," "A Romance," "Neutralia," and "The Medicine Man"; and from this last we will copy a passage in taking leave of the poet. It is a physician who speaks, after prolonged failure to find practice in Kansas:

"There is something in this country that I do not understand;
Working, scheming, trade and business, lively lawsuits, labor, land. . . .
Day by day a man keeps working just as happy as a clam,
If he only has the cash to buy a lawsuit and a ham.
Only yesterday I saw a man I thought would surely die;
He had got a compound, comminuted fracture of the thigh.
Aching but a half an hour or so, the leg declined to swell,
He poured cold water on it, and the next day it was well.
Then he worked six hours that afternoon, and ere the sun went down,
He got into a lawsuit with the fattest man in town.

Now and here I pack my little trunk. By vum! I wouldn't stay
In climates where a man gets old, dries up, and blows away." . . .
Shortly after this a mule-train from the westward coming slow,
Camped beside the raging Paint Creek, with the doctor on the go.
An old army mule that evening, after supper, just for fun,
Kicked and broke the doctor's arms and legs, and all his ribs but one.
This old mule would make a hero for a romance or a song;
When the drums beat and the bugles sounded battle loud and long,
He enlisted in the army, and he helped to pull a train
Up the mountains, down the valleys, through the sunshine and the rain;
And right well he served his country, for he knew where duty lay;
He could live for weeks on end-gates, when they wouldn't give him hay. . . .
Lightning struck him, cannon shot him, but he never failed or flunked;
Danger left him as it found him, undiscouraged, undefunct;
And in all my army service I have never seen a mule
With a keener comprehension of the educated fool.
He would spot a man instanter if he overheard him speak
About Darwin, Herbert Spencer, Correlation, Force, or Greek.
He would work and watch in silence, and look sheepish day by day,
One eye closed in meditation, till that man got in his way;
Then that person's friends were lucky if they did not have to make
A collection of their comrade with a basket and a rake.

V.

From far New Zealand comes a little volume of *Themes and Variations*, by Mrs. J. Glenny Wilson, who does not write so well at all times as she does now and then. But it is both a poet and a painter that can make such a picture as this:

High in her little rose‑clad room, niched in the
    winding stair,
My lady sits and looks abroad on the wind's
    thoroughfare. . . .
The circling landscape underneath glows through
    its misty veil;
The thunder-cloud against the wind beats up, a
    blackening sail.
The sea, that shone like silver scales, fades, tar-
    nished by its breath;
The shaking poplar turns her face as in a wind of
    death.
Still half the fields return the sun, still laughs the
    running wheat:
The bird sings on,—one sheet of flame! And
    now the thunders meet!

Mrs. Wilson is sometimes so good that one wonders why she should not always be very good. She varies not only from poem to poem, but from verse to verse, as if the piece came from a genuine but inadequate impulse of feeling, of fancy. For good or for ill one feels no such inequality in the poems severally or wholly that make up Mrs. Louise Chandler Moulton's new volume of poetry, which she calls *In the Garden of Dreams*, but is sensible of a constant firmness of artistic motive increasing to such mastery as has been sought in her faithful work from the beginning. This is not saying that we like it all; it is often too stressfully subjective, perhaps even generally so; but when one comes to such a sonnet as this, one must be slow to deny that the writer could fail of the highest effect she aimed at:

SISTER SORROW.

I found her walking in a lonely place,
    Where shadows lingered and the day was low;
    She trod a devious path with footsteps slow,
And by the waning light I scanned her face,
And in its loveliness beheld the trace
    Old tears had left and woes of long ago;
    Then knew she I was kin to her; and so
Stretched forth her chill, soft hand with welcom-
    ing grace.
Now I walk with her thro' her realm of shade;
    I hear gay music sound, and laughter ring,
    And voices call me that I knew of old,
But of their mocking mirth I am afraid:
    Led through the dusk by her to whom I cling,
    May I not reach some blessedness untold?

Among the things that Mr. Walter Learned has (not always) said so gracefully, so lightly, so charmingly, so sincerely, in *Between Whiles*, there is none said so wisely, justly, kindly, as this, which he supposes himself to have written on a fly-leaf of *Manon Lescaut:*

To you whose temperate pulses flow
With measured beat, serene and slow,
The even tenor of whose way
Is undisturbed by passion's sway,
The tale of wayward love may seem
The record of a fevered dream.
And yet we too have that within
To make us what our kind have been.
A love more strong, a wish more faint,
Makes one a monster, one a saint;
And even love, by difference nice,
Becomes a virtue or a vice.
The brier that o'er the garden wall
Trails its sweet blossoms till they fall

Across the dusty road, and then
Are trodden under foot of men,
Is sister to the decorous rose
Within the garden's well-kept close,
Whose pinioned branches may not roam
Out and beyond their latticed home.
There's many a life of sweet content
Whose virtue is environment.
They erred, they fell; and yet 'tis true
They held the mirror up to you.

VI.

If we were master to strike any such bargain with fame we would not give being the author of one of Mr. Aldrich's beautiful sonnets to be the author of many "Wyndham Towers," however skilfully architected, and finely fretted over with prithees and sooths, anons and wots, beshrews and bethoughts. Yet we could cull many passages from the poem to show it was a fine poem; and no one need deny it is so because he likes another piece of the poet's work better. At the same time it does not seem to us always wrought with his happiest fortune. Such a line as

" Poet, soldier, courtier, 'twas the mode,"

makes us uncomfortable, and such a fancy as

    "A dark, inexplicable blight
Had touched her, thinned her, till of that sweet
    earth
Scarce more was left than would have served to
    grow
A lily"

makes us more than uncomfortable.
  In another place the poet says,

"Off shore a buoy gleams like a dolphin's back
Dripping with brine, and guards a sunken reef,"

which is altogether fresh and lovely. But he adds,

" Whose sharp incisors have gnawed many a keel,"

and that is not lovely, however fresh. Yet to what end do we make our little strictures? If we know at all the heart of authorship, those incisors are the very last thing the poet would give up. But here is a magnificent painting of his that there can be no possible dispute about with any who love nature or art:

Black lay the earth in primal blackness wrapt
Ere the great miracle once more was wrought.
A chill wind freshened in the pallid East
And brought new smell of freshly blossomed foam,
And stirred the leaves and branch-hung nests of
    birds.
And the slow dawn with purple laced the sky
Where sky and sea lay sharply edge to edge.
The purple melted, changed to violet,
And that to every delicate, sea-shell tinge,
Blush-pink, deep cinnabar; then no change was,
Save that the air had in it sense of wings,
Till suddenly the heavens were all aflame,
And it was morning.

[1][Henry Mills Alden], God In His World: An Interpretation (New York: Harper & Brothers, 1890).

[2]"La somma sapienza e il primo amore" - The highest wisdom is the first love.

[3][Eugene Fitch Ware], Rhymes of Ironquill (Topeka, Kans.: T. J. Kellam, 1885).

[4]Manon Lescaut, Historie de Chevalier Des Grieux et de Manon Lescaut [by A. F. Prevost d'Exiles] (N.P., 1753).

May, 1890

Editor's Study.

I.

ONE of the most curiously interesting books we have read for a long time is Mr. Carl Lumholtz's account of his life among the cannibals in Australia. It is curious and interesting not only for the novel matter of it, but for the manner too, which is to the last degree simple and informal. Whatever it may have been in the original Norwegian, the narrative is quite without what we call "style" in its English; but we do not mean by this that it is without charm. In fact, it has a very great charm, which seems to reside in the author's wish to realize without literary parade of any sort the facts of an experience almost unique. In a field that offered unrivalled opportunities for pictoriality he has been content to give his adventures and record his discoveries with the accurate drawing and faithful coloring of a scientific illustration; they have in this way a value that they could have won in no other; and they reflect with admirable distinctness the training and temperament of the author. As member of the Royal Academy of Sciences, he went out to Australia, partly at the cost of the University of Christiania, for the purpose of studying the native life, and making collections for the zoological museum of that institution. He found two new marsupials, one a tree-dwelling kangaroo; and he made other important contributions to natural history; but to the general reader the attraction of the book will be the close-at-hand investigations of the savage habits and customs which Mr. Lumholtz could not have helped carrying on in the pursuit of his scientific inquiries.

Upon the whole, life among the northern Australians could hardly be desirable on any terms, and on their own it seems not acceptable. Their religion is a fear, their existence a series of escapes from starvation and homicide, their morality a mere tribal obligation to the most elementary fealties, their polity an ultimation of the principle that might makes right within the tribe as well as without: a despotism of the strong hand tempered by cunning. In the society of these children of

nature certain persons skilled in Devil-devil, as they call the invocation of their supreme demon, and certain old ladies accomplished in catering to their simple appetite for human flesh are the ruling influences. They are all cannibals, as opportunity offers; and in default of enemies to eat, they will sometimes eat their friends; they will even eat their children, though this is exceptional. Otherwise, they live mostly upon poisonous roots, which have to be carefully prepared; upon worms and grubs; upon snakes and lizards; and upon such birds and beasts as they can kill, though they are not good hunters and are poorly weaponed for the chase. They go naked, and almost houseless; a shelter of boughs is their conception of a house. After four years among them, and the bestowal of inestimable benefits in tobacco, Mr. Lumholtz could not flatter himself that he had ever succeeded in appealing to any sentiment but fear in them; they did not kill him because they imagined him an adept in Devil-devil, and because they were afraid of the Baby of the Gun, as they called his revolver; but they would not have eaten him, because they had found that upon the whole white men did not agree with them. In spite of their fears they had accesses of treachery in which they longed so much to kill him that it was never safe to let them get behind him; and apparently no kindness could win them to affection. On such conditions life began to be for him at moments the poor possession that it seemed to them; and he experienced a deep despondency mixed with indifference, from which he had to pull him together with a strong effort of the will at last, in order to escape from the psychical miasm of their most miserable existence. They were children, and bad children, with no lovable traits that he could discover, and cruel and filthy in their ignorance. In spite of their abominable customs and their squalid conditions, the life of the open air and of the woods and hills is so wholesome that fine physical types are not rare; and in this fact there might be some hope for the race, if it met the least justice in contact with the whites. But on the frontiers, says Mr. Lumholtz, "any savage discovered by the white men runs the risk of being shot. Poison was laid in the way of the blacks once when I was in Queensland. . . . A squatter . . . . shot all the men on his run because they were cattle-killers, the women because they gave birth to cattle-killers, and the children because they would in time become cattle-killers." The blacks show the curious readiness of our own Indians to merge the tribal fealty in an allegiance to government when employed as police, and are murderously destructive when used against their own race, as they commonly are in Australia. Mr. Lumholtz feels that their complete extinction is only a question of time; and little as he could like them, he denounces with abhorrence the atrocious injustice with which they are treated by the English law as well as the English lawlessness.

II.

Our race, in fact, has not been the slowest to murder, at any time, and has gone more than half-way, usually, to meet the most homicidal savages on their own ground. Even where its gifts in bloodshedding have not been called out by contact with an inferior race, it has contrived to kill within its own ethnical limits in a measure which would not discredit barbarians who hold man-slaying in honor. The reader will find interesting illustrations of this trait in Mr. Reuben Davis's otherwise very interesting *Recollections of Mississippi and Mississippians.* A red stream trickles through half the course of these pleasant memoirs, which does not become vivider when it broadens into the current of the great rebellion, though undoubtedly it deepens. Among the "polished and accomplished" gentlemen whom Mr. Davis remembers almost without number in his long and eventful life, the use of the knife, the pistol, and the rifle seems to have been the prompt resort in differences of opinion; and so far from condemning it, the venerable author records his own experience in that method of controversy as frankly as if it were the usage of good society everywhere. Very early in his career in Mississippi he attacked with a pocket-knife another gentleman who insulted him at an evening party, upon some question "as to the precedence of claim upon the attention of one of the ladies"; and after he became a leading member of the bar, he resented an adverse ruling by trying to cut the throat of the court, while the court beat him over the head with a hammer. Grotesque as this seems, however, the ferocity depicted with no sense of its difference from the impulses of polished and accomplished gentlemen everywhere was not inconsistent with much that was really noble and fine. The men who got drunk, and swore like pirates, and slashed one another with knives, were neither liars nor thieves; a sincere and fervent piety gave a religious cast to the intellectual life; there was some old-fashioned love of literature, especially poetry; there was a high ideal of womanhood, which the good and beautiful women inspired by their daily lives; and there was a sense of real fraternity in the unstinted hospitality and the eager helpfulness of the whole people. But in doing justice to the good traits of such an anomalous civility, we must not forget that it was founded upon the cruel and corrupting barbarism of slavery, and that it was essentially abominable in being essentially aristocratic. The ease with which Mr. Davis secured the acquittal of gentlemen who had killed other gentlemen is not more remarkable than the difficulty he had in saving from the gallows a poor man who slew a rich libertine for attempting the virtue of his wife. In his case justice was disposed to be inexorable; and the low-down homicide had a narrow escape.

III.

Those interested in the study of conditions will find somewhat to their taste concerning our Southwestern populations at a still earlier day in the first volume of Mr. Henry Adams's history of the United States during the second administration of Thomas Jefferson, which is so largely occupied with the famous conspiracy of Aaron Burr. The clear light which the historian throws upon this plot to dismember the Union gives an oft-told tale the charm of novelty, and must set it before most readers for the first time, we fancy, with all its amazing suggestions of opéra bouffe. It seems to have been such a conspiracy as might have been carried on in the rarefied air of the Grand Duchy of Gerolstein. The chief conspirator, who has been Vice-President of the republic he proposes to mutilate, is in league with the General-in-Chief of its army, who has been for twenty years in the pay of the Spanish King for little secret services rendered him from time to time. They both treat their plot with such frankness, and write and talk so loosely about it with the eminent politicians and leading citizens in complicity, that nearly everybody in the West and Southwest knows something of it, and one distinguished jurist keeps the Chief Magistrate of the republic constantly informed of it by letters, which the Chief Magistrate constantly ignores. The affair runs prosperously along. The person who is going to dissolve the Union, as a little preliminary to becoming Emperor of Mexico, collects men and arms, and sets sail down the Mississippi in pursuance of his purpose. By this time his fellow-conspirator, the General, has made up his mind to have him shot as soon as he falls into his fraternal hands; but the intending Emperor is arrested at another point. He is a man of approved courage in battle and duel, but he now falls into the greatest terror. At the same time the Chief Magistrate of the republic has roused himself, and he moves heaven and earth to have the conspirator convicted of treason and hanged; but in this he is frustrated by the Chief Justice of the Supreme Court of the republic, who is the Chief Magistrate's enemy. The *primo tenore* escapes, and the whole ends happily, the curtain coming down upon the chorus of lawyers, judges, generals, and conspirators joining in lively song and dance business.

Not quite this, perhaps; but something extremely like it. But what we meant, when we turned from Mr. Davis to Mr. Adams, was that the phase of later life which Mr. Davis describes is foreshadowed, or rather foreshown, in the earlier phases studied by Mr. Adams with a far keener eye and with a perfect perspective. There can be no doubt of the historian's consciousness of the loose social structure, the weak sense of collective interest, the intense and exaggerated individualism fostered by the exigencies and opportunities of pioneer existence, which evolved the civilization Mr. Davis is so proud of. At the same time he treats it with that sort of fine toleration, that delicate and penetrating justice of his, which give a kind of æsthetic beauty to his criticisms of communities and men. His truth is unsparing but it is not unkind, and with a humorous perception of whatever was ridiculous in the situation, he is always alive to whatever was important and finally significant. Jefferson is probably not the kind of man Mr. Adams would admire, and yet how unfailingly he lets his reader see when and where Jefferson was admirable! He could not have been charmed with that period of our national adolescence, and yet how faithfully he turns all its good points to the light!

One rises from his book with one's pride of country and faith in human nature (when it is good-natured human nature, especially) rather refreshed than otherwise; for one says to one's self, If that poor little nation which we were then, and those raw, ignorant, often conceited, headstrong, turbulent people, could struggle past so many perils without and within, what may we not hope for, having come to our present pitch of wisdom, refinement, and power? It was indeed the day of small things with us under Jefferson's second administration. The mighty republic of to-day was then nearly always cooling its heels in the antechambers of monarchy. Majesties and ministers bid it about at pleasure, and between Napoleon and Pitt its habitual diet was an humble-pie which we certainly should not stomach for a moment now. At home the ties that bound the States together were so frail that the only wonder is Burr did not carry out his plot with triumphant success. It is Mr. Adams who seems the first to have studied the sources of his failure in traits of folly, recklessness, and fantasticality which have not heretofore had their due representation in any study of a man reputed wicked indeed but not weak or unwise in his own way: that is, the way of the transgressor.

IV.

After all, Jefferson may have been quite well aware what he was about in his lax treatment of Burr's conspiracy. Perhaps he knew the man enough to feel easy and almost indifferent while a man of his make was plotting the end of a republic and the future of an empire, and believed that he could be safely trusted to bring himself to naught if he were given time enough. Perhaps he understood the nature of the Western people too, and perceived that, although they held their allegiance loosely, they were not fools, and were not likely to be led into treason by conspirators so *bouffe* as Burr and Wilkinson. It is a charitable theory, which the kindness Mr. Adams leaves one feeling for Jefferson rather inclines one to; and it is not inconsistent with Jefferson's final wish to have Burr hanged. At any rate we can use a leniency of conjecture in the case which would have been impossible to many of Jefferson's contemporaries. These could keep no terms with him either in their thoughts or their words, and one satiric poet of the time addressed him some metrical reproaches which are amusing enough now:

" And thou, the scorn of every patriot's name,
Thy country's ruin and thy council's shame!
Poor servile thing! derision of the brave!
Who erst from Tarleton fled to Carter's Cave;
Thou who, when menaced by perfidious Gaul,
Didst prostrate to her whisker'd minion fall;
And when our cash her empty bags supplied,
Didst meanly strive the foul disgrace to hide;
Go, wretch, resign the Presidential chair,
Disclose thy secret measures, foul or fair.
Go search with curious eye for horrid frogs
'Mid the wild waste of Louisianian bogs;
Or where Ohio rolls his turbid stream,
Dig for huge bones, thy glory and thy theme.
Go scan, Philosophist, thy Sally's charms,
And sink supinely in her sable arms;
But quit to abler hands the helm of State."

We have become so tolerant of scientific inquiry that we should not at present consider it so very loathly or unworthy to search for "horrid frogs," or to dig for "huge bones," if the ends of knowledge were to be served; to scan one's Sally's charms might still be objectionable. But apparently these acts were all classed together as vices and follies in the minds of Jefferson's enemies when William Cullen Bryant hurled his burning heroics in the teeth of the dastard head of the republic. The poet was, to be sure, only sixteen years old at the time he demanded Jefferson's resignation, [2] but he seems to have been as mature in his thinking as many other Federalists of his day. He came afterward to be a champion of Jeffersonian democracy when there came to be a Jeffersonian democracy, and as occasion served his inimical brother journalists waked these slumbering strings of his lyre. They found it a good joke to set them vibrating in the newspapers, but probably their music did not trouble Mr. Bryant much.

He was not a man of much humor, but he had the greatest common-sense, the utmost singleness of purpose, and the purest integrity; all his long life long, he had the wish, as he had the singular happiness, to dedicate his eminent powers to the right. The story of such a life could not be told too often, and we have to thank Mr. John Bigelow for newly telling it again in one of the most agreeable volumes of Mr. Warner's "American Men of Letters" series. It is in some sort the story of American literature, which came to be pretty much what it is in the course of Mr. Bryant's life of eighty-four years, or at least had assumed, before he died, its main characteristics. But we do not think a dispassionate estimate of his work would claim for him that primacy which the warmth of Mr. Bigelow's personal affection awards him. Mr. Bryant was a great journalist, a statesman-like and incorruptible politician, and as truly a poet as any that has lived; but he was not the foremost American man of letters, and while Irving, Emerson, Hawthorne, Longfellow, Lowell, Holmes, Whittier, and Poe were his contemporaries he could not have been first among his peers. He was in a few things their superior, in many their equal, in others distinctly their inferior. No one, we believe not Mr. Bigelow himself, would think of matching him with Irving for grace and gayety of spirit; with Emerson for reach of thought and electrical beauty of phrase; with Hawthorne for imagination; with Longfellow for breadth of culture and sympathetic loveliness of art; with Lowell for the flower-like delicacy of feeling that in his robust and vigorous poetry makes you think of a tree in blossom; with Holmes

for wit and nimbleness of mind; with Whittier for impassioned humanity breaking into song; with Poe for weird fancy and artistic sense. Yet Bryant was a very great man; and though he never embodied to his country or to the world at large the fact of our literary importance as any of these others did, he was thoroughly and magnificently American. During the latter part of his life he was somewhat cheapened to hasty criticism by the flattery, the adoration, of a not very intellectual metropolis; but this was an effect which could not outlast his life, and we may now see him in the true proportions of his grandeur. He gave proofs of greatness in his boyhood by a poem which for lofty eloquence is unexcelled in our literature, and there was an early maturity in all he did which was wholly unlike prematurity. He never reverted afterward to the shallower sources of inspiration, as precocious talent is fatally apt to do, but he kept to the end the high level which he attained so soon. The achievement of his prime was all the more astonishing because there was nothing hurried or heated in his nature; on most occasions and to most people he was a cold man, of unready and reluctant expression as regarded his feelings. But this was largely the effect of a self-control that he studied, and of a scrupulous regard for the truth, which often makes people of the Puritanic strain silent till they can be sure of the truth. He had depths of tenderness for those he knew, and he was ideally faithful to his friends as long as they were faithful to the right. Even when they were not very wise, as sometimes happens with one's friends, he stood by them as closely as their folly would allow. An instance of this constancy appears in his management of the difficulty with Irving which the zeal of his friend Leggett involved him in. Bryant had asked Irving's good offices in the republication of his poems in England, and Irving had gladly given them at some trouble to himself; but he had consented, in the interest of the book, to change a few words in one of the lines which the English publisher thought might offend the English public. It was a generous mistake, and Irving paid for it in being held up to patriotic scorn as a toady and a snob by Mr. Leggett, who was the near friend of Mr. Bryant, and had been his partner. Irving could not help protesting in a letter to Leggett's paper, expressing with perfect dignity and good temper his sense of injury, and his surprise that it should come from a friend of Bryant's. Leggett could only affirm the fact that Bryant had nothing to do with his onslaught, and on his part Bryant could only express his regret that Irving had been wounded, while he forbore to inflict upon Leggett the snub which he richly deserved. The affair ended with a letter of the most gracious sweetness from Irving; but it is doubtful if such a hurt can ever be perfectly healed; and the reader remains with a sense of the cruelty of Bryant's position, and with something like a wish that he had relieved himself from it at the expense of Leggett.

Still, constancy is a virtue, and in this case its exercise was magnanimous. As for that hidden tenderness in a man who was all New England in his emotional make, there is a most touching revelation of it in the unfinished poem found among Bryant's papers after his death. It is to his wife, to whom while she lived he never failed to "repeat and take her judgment upon" every poem he wrote, and it thrills with such heartache as only such sorrow can know:

"The morn hath not the glory that it wore,
    Nor doth the day so beautifully die,
Since I can call thee to my side no more,
    To gaze upon the sky.

"Here where I sit alone is sometimes heard,
    From the great world, a whisper of my name,
Joined haply to some kind, commending word
    Of those whose praise is fame;

"And then as if I thought thou still wert nigh,
    I turn me, half forgetting thou art dead,
To read the gentle gladness in thine eye,
    That once I might have read.

"I turn, but see thee not; before my eyes
    The image of a hill-side mound appears,
Where all of thee that passed not to the skies
    Was laid, with bitter tears.

"And I, whose thoughts go back to happier days
    That fled with thee, would gladly now resign
All that the world can give of fame or praise,
    For one sweet look of thine.

"Thus, ever, when I read of generous deeds,
    Such words as thou didst once delight to hear,
My heart is wrung with anguish as it bleeds
    To think thou art not near."

A fragment, and we do not give it all, but enough to leave us loving a man whom we cannot cease to admire and revere.

---

[1] Karl Sofus Lumholtz, Among Cannibals (London: J. Murray, 1889).

[2] Bryant, born in 1794, could not have been sixteen years old while Jefferson was President (1801-1809). In fact, Bryant wrote the poem, "The Embargo," in February of 1808, before his fourteenth birthday. For an explanation of the circumstances surrounding the writing of the poem see The Poetical Works of William Cullen Bryant, Henry C. Sturges, ed. (New York and London: D. Appleton and Company, 1916), p. xxxvi. For the full text of the poem see The Embargo, Introduction and Notes by Thomas O. Mabbott (Gainesville, Fla.: Scholars' Facsimiles & Reprints, 1955).

June, 1890

Editor's Study.

I.

IN spite of the vigilance of our dramatic criticism, which has shown such unwearied perseverance in undervaluing whatever was native or novel in the efforts of our playwrights, we really seem to be pretty well on our way toward the promise of an American comedy. We do not like to put the case more strongly than this, because even yet we have moments when we can scarcely credit the fact, the disparity between the opposing forces is so great.

On the one side, we have long had a large body of gentlemen trained to a profound misconception of their office, and deeply grounded in a traditional ignorance of the essence and nature of the drama, writing every night about the theatres, and more and more believing in themselves and their ideal of what a play ought to be, without reference to what life was. The criticisms which they have thus produced between church-yard-yawning and cock-crowing, with the advantages of a foreman behind and a night editor before, hurrying them up for their copy, have been such as must surprise the sympathetic witness by their uniform confidence and severity; but they have not in great measure carried, even to the most generous compassion, the evidences of fitness for the censorship assumed. These gentlemen have sometimes been able to tell us what good acting is, for they have seen a great deal of acting; but here their usefulness has too often ended; not certainly by their fault, for no man can be justly blamed for not telling more than he knows. Many of them know what a French play is, for they have seen enough adaptations of French plays to have learned to admire their extremely neat carpentry, and their carefully adjusted and brilliantly varnished sections, which can be carried to any climate, and put together and taken apart as often as you like, without making them less representative of anything that ever was in the world. They have been struck with the ingenious regularity of the design in these contrivances; they have seen how smoothly they worked, and they have formed such

dramatic theories as they have from dramas in which situation links into situation, and effect into effect, upon lines of such admirable rigidity that it is all as unerring as making up a train of cars with the Miller Coupler and Buffer. But it would be wrong to say that many of these gentlemen apparently know anything of the contemporary Italian drama, Spanish drama, Russian drama, German drama, Norwegian drama; and it would be still more unjust to accuse them, upon the proofs their work has given, of knowing anything of the true functions of any drama, or caring at all for the life which all drama should represent.

On the other hand, opposed to this powerful body of critical gentlemen, whose discipline is so perfect that they often seem to think as one man, and sometimes even as no man at all, we have had a straggling force of playwrights and managers, disheartened by a sense of their own want of conformity to the critical ideal, and by a guilty consciousness of preferring the realities they have seen and known in America to the artificialities which exist in the Miller Coupler and Buffer pattern of French drama. These poor fellows have not only been weakened by a knowledge of their inferiority in numbers and discipline to the critics (who count about a hundred to every manager, and a thousand to every playwright), but they have had a fear that there was something low and vulgar in their wish to see American life in the theatre as they have seen it in the street, and the counting-house, and the drawing-room, as they have even seen it in the novel. They have been so much unnerved by this misgiving that they have not yet ventured to be quite true to life, but have only ventured, so far, to offer us a compromise with unreality, which we can praise at most for the truth which could not well be kept out of it.

II.

We say kept out of it; but this may be an appearance only, and it may be that there is all the truth present that there could be got in. The new American play is still too much of the old Miller Coupler and Buffer pattern. We think we discern in it the evidences of a tripartite distrust, which we hope and believe it will outlive; but as yet we should say that the playwright fears the manager, the manager fears the public, and the public fears itself, and ventures to like what it enjoys only with the youthful diffidence which our public has concerning everything but its material greatness. Then this nascent drama of ours, is retarded in its development by a fact necessarily present in all evolution. The men whose skill and training would enable them to give it an early maturity are themselves in a process of evolution, which they will probably never complete, because they have not fully the courage of their convictions. Their work will remain after them, for younger men to finish—a fact always interesting in any history of the æsthetic arts, but a little pathetic to witness in the course of its realization. The very men who are now doing our best work will hardly live to do the still better work they are making possible. But the future is not our affair, and we are not going merely to find fault with the present. On the contrary, we fancy that we shall be blamed for praising it too much, and that those who hope nothing may have some reason to reproach us for hoping anything. But such is the uncritical nature of the Study that when anything has given it a pleasure it cannot help being grateful. If it is too grateful, the balance can always be trimmed with the reluctances of those who think it a weakness to own they have been pleased, and a sign of superiority to withhold their thanks. The gentlemen who mostly write the dramatic criticisms, in fact, prove their right to condemn a new play in nothing so much as in allowing its defects to hide its merits, and in magnifying these as the trophies of their own victory over the playwright. A grudging and sneering concession of something funny here and pretty there, of something that touched, something that thrilled, in what was after all not a play, because a true play always has a Miller Coupler and Buffer at each end of every act, goes a great way with our simple-hearted public, which likes hash because it prefers to know what it is eating. With shame we confess we do not know how to practise this fine reticence in praise, this elegant profusion in censure, but we always try our best to hint our little reserves concerning matters before us; and if we have been too lavish in our recognition of the high perfection of our dramatic criticism, we will try to be blind to some of the more obvious inadequacies of our dramatic literature.

III.

We could note enough of these in Mr. James A. Herne's drama of *Drifting Apart*. It did not seem to us well to represent the events in two acts of a serious play as occurring in a dream; but there was much in the simplicity and naturalness of the action which consoled us for this mechanical contrivance. Other things were not simple and not natural: the death of the starving child, affecting as it was at the time, was a forced note, with that falsetto ring which the death of children on the stage always has, though the little creature who played the scene played it so wonderfully; but the passages between the desperate mother and the wretched father, whose drunken dream prefigures the potential future shown in these acts, are of a most truthful pathos, and are interpreted with that perfect apprehension of the dramatist's meaning which is by no means the sole advantage that comes from acting one's own play. Mr. and Mrs. Herne, who take respectively the parts of husband and wife in a drama which they must have largely constructed together, are both artists of rare quality. Mrs. Herne has the flashes of power that transcend any effect of her husband's exquisite art; but this art is so patient, so beautiful, so unerring, that upon the whole we must praise him most. It never falters, never wanders; it is always tenderly sympathetic. In those dream passages it has a sort of dumb passion that powerfully moves, and in the lighter moments of the opening and closing acts it delights with a humorous playfulness which never forgets itself to farce. It perfectly fits the plain and simple story of the Gloucester fisherman, whose tempter overcomes him on Christmas Eve, and who returns home drunk to his wife and mother, and falls into a heavy sleep, and forecasts all the calamity of the two ensuing acts in his nightmare; but one readily believes that it would be equal to the highest demand upon it, speaking even after the manner of dramatic critics. We ourselves think that no more delicate effect could be achieved than that it makes in the homeliest scenes of the play; and if we speak of that passage in which the man talks out to the two women in the kitchen from the little room adjoining, where he is putting on his best clothes for Christmas, and whimsically scolds them for not being able to find his things, and intersperses his complaints with bits of gossip and philosophy and drolling, it is without the least hope of persuading artificial people of the value of such an episode, but with full confidence that no genuine person can witness it without feeling its charm.

IV.

The play has its weak points, as we

have hinted. The author has by no means broken with tradition; he is apt to get the stage to help him out at times when nature seems reluctant in serving his purpose; but upon the whole he has produced a play fresh in motive, pure in tone, high in purpose, and very simple and honest in method. He is one of whom much better things may be reasonably expected, and we do not think he will disappoint even a great expectation. Born and bred to the theatre, he brings an intimate knowledge of its possibilities to his twofold interpretation of life as a dramatist and as an actor. He has that double equipment in art which, from Shakespeare down, has given the finest results.

Another play of the general make and manner of the *County Fair* and the *Old Homestead* was *Old Jed Prouty*, which we can praise with the usual reserves. Like these, and like *Drifting Apart*, it is of the New England school. The scene is frankly laid in Bucksport, Maine, and the excellent local color in the piece might well have been the effect of a summer's sojourn in the place, whose racy charm a keen-eyed, humorous actor would be sure to feel. It is such an actor who writes and plays the leading part in the piece, and who seems, when he wished to go beyond character-sketching in his drama, to have called in the services of a professional playwright with a very unnatural father and a highly foreclosable mortgage in stock. Consequently the literary structure of the drama is upon the old familiar lines, while the characters are fresh and genuine. The opening scenes in the Bucksport hotel are delightfully done, with such figures of landlord, hostler, table-girl, house-keeper, drummer, farmer, teamster, and loafer as we all know. These people are admirably realized in dress, and parlance, and manner; and some of the finer traits in them are subtly felt. Up to the end of the first act, the thing is not a caricature. After that the less said the better. It is as if at this point the observation of the author gave out, and his invention began; and all the rest is very sorrowful mirth, with occasional gleams of sense and truth in it all, which at least forbid us to despair of him.

V.

When you go from such a play as this to such a play as *Shenandoah*, you are in another air. Nothing there is accidental or unconscious; nothing is built better than the author knew, and nothing worse. What happens is what he meant to happen; no room was left for chance by the skilful and workman-like development of the whole. We will say at once that the piece gave us a very great pleasure. It has charm, from the first moment to the

last, and it has passages of nobility and beauty, with effects that ravish the sense and kindle the fancy, by the legitimate realization of facts that cannot be put into dialogue or action. Those bugle calls of unseen cavalry, and the signalling by night with the shifting lanterns on the eve of battle, are descriptive phrases of the highest value, employed with admirable knowledge and art. It was a brave stroke, too, of the imagination to pour half a battle, with all its unblinked tragedy of blood and dust and wounds and death, across the stage; and from first to last the drama has a largeness in its vistas which suits the grandeur of the mighty war living still in our pride and grief, and present in all the words and thoughts of the people in Mr. Howard's scene. We could hardly overstate the success with which the ample design of the author has been fulfilled in his work. It is indeed a splendid passage of the war, and it suggests the whole course of the war, from the firing upon Sumter at Charleston to the review of the triumphant Union forces at Washington. The swiftly moving history is expressed from the patriotic point of view in such terms and characters as do justice to the high motives and unselfish heroism on both sides. There are several of perfectly novel effect in the large group of interesting personages, but among these none is so vivid and charming as that gay, soldierly, very winningly girlish daughter of the Union General, who dances on the horse-block before the rebel mansion where she is visiting while the Northern troops file by; and none more delightful than the veteran Irish corporal who never appears but to bring light and laughter into the scene. The hero is a very good fellow, and likable far beyond the wont of heroes; and there is a very fair to middling villain, who has not less than the usual motive for his villany. The General who is the father of that charming girl is natural and American from first to last too, and upon the whole the average of reality in motive, incident, and personality is very high indeed. For our own selfish pleasure we could have wished to have no pursued and doubted wife in the piece. We believe that the pursuit of wives by villains is so very uncommon in our society as to be scarcely representative or typical; where there is any pursuit of the kind, the energy and initiative of our women would rather imply that it is the pursuit of villains by wives. But we are bound to own that the pursuit in Mr. Howard's play is wholly unjustified by anything in the behavior of the wife.

VI.

We cannot say so much for the wife

who is pursued in the highly amusing comedy of *The Senator.* She seems to us a lady of the very questionable sort who are saved in the theatre by the ingenuity of friends, but who would hardly be thought worth saving out of it. In fact, we should like to ask the designers of these uncertain wives whether they really think a woman who is willing and ready to run away from her husband with another man has not already lost her virtue, and has not committed that sin in her heart from which she is melodramatically saved. If they could once arrive at the truth on this point, perhaps they could be persuaded to forbear the further employment of a character in the American drama who does not characterize American society, and who is as loathsome at every moment and in every mood as she is anomalous. In Mr. Lloyd's play, which is the last we shall have from the talent so early lost in death, this foolish person is very tiresome, and very, very untrue to conditions and to human nature. But perhaps we owe her rather to Mr. Lloyd's collaborator, [1] Mr. Rosenfeld. We are sure we owe the Senator himself, with his pure-blood Americanism in every phrase and act, to Mr. Lloyd; for he is full of the life that vivified a like character in Mr. Lloyd's former play, *For Congress.* There is a patch on the clear humanity of his motive, however, that came out of the rag-bag of worn-out dramatic invention; for neither of the collaborators got from any experience of life the notion that Senator Rivers would push through the Denman claim so as to make Mabel Denman, whom he loves, rich enough to become the wife of Count von Strahl. That is a kind of rubbish which we permit ourselves the pleasure of calling *rot.* It is as thoroughly false as the soul of a wife who has to be saved from shame by a *coup de théâtre;* and is worthy of the authors of *The Charity Ball,* who seem to have got near-[2] ly their whole play out of the rag-bag. In *The Senator,* the susceptible young widow, Mrs. Hilary, is a pleasing invention, colored to life, and probably actuated throughout; she is almost as good as the Senator himself, who is immensely American. The Chinese Minister is a good bit of refined farce; the claimant Denman is excellent; and the daughter of the Secretary of State (husband of the mechanically virtuous wife) is very well fancied indeed, but perhaps pushed a little far in the direction of hoydenish burlesque.

We noticed in both of these agreeable plays, however, a good deal of suspended or retentive love-making, which did not seem altogether called for. People came to the very point of saying they loved other people, who were so visibly wishing to be loved that it seemed wholly unnecessary for the lovers to stop and turn away with a despairing sigh. Yet this was just what they did, especially the two laconic lovers, who stepped severally into each play out of the Robertsonian comedy. In both cases they are very coolly brave; they are soldiers afraid of nothing in the world but the young women who are so obviously anxious to be made love to; and they are so alike in their experience that they have to make exactly the same answer to the same question. Each tells how he met a deadly enemy. "Oh, what did you do?" quaver the two young women. "I killed him," reply the two young men, in quite these words, at Proctor's Theatre on Twenty-third Street, and at the Star Theatre on the corner of Broadway and Thirteenth. It is a curious case of telepathy, which might not have occurred, if the young men had been drawn from life, and not from the Robertsonian comedy. [3]

VII.

We cannot praise the realism of these young men, and we do not think it adds greatly to the effect of reality in *The Senator* and *The Charity Ball* to give some of the characters the names of well-known families, to say nothing of the questionable taste of doing it. As far as *The Charity Ball* is concerned, we doubt if anything could give it reality. It is very strongly localized, but it seems to us false in motive almost from first to last. There are moments when you say, "Now it cannot help being a little natural!" but it mostly does. It has an appearance of being very jovial and very tender, very lofty and very lurid, very angelic and very diabolical; but it never is really so. The humor is coarse, the fun hoydenish and rowdyish, the sentiment is mawkish; seldom in any octave is a true note struck. Yet here is a piece dealing at close quarters with the actualities of New York life, by authors who have apparently the best will in the world to be perfectly faithful to it. What is the trouble? Apparently that they have never looked directly at human nature, which is the same here and everywhere, but always indirectly through melodrama and romantic fiction.

The piece, like all the other pieces we have been speaking of, was extremely well played, and we wish once more to bear our testimony to the very high grade of acting in our theatres. We have not only a wonderfully equipped dramatic criticism ready to exact a classic excellence from the nascent American drama, but a school of acting well fitted to interpret its finest inspirations. We cannot indeed truly say that the average of acting we saw at the American theatres was so high as that we found one night at the German theatre, where we went to hear a play that made all our American plays seem playthings. This was *Die Ehre*, a piece by the young dramatist Sudermann, [4] who has dared to put more truth into it than has been put into any other modern play except, perhaps, *La Morte Civile*. It [5] is simply the story of a young man whom a patronizing benevolence has educated above the station of his family, but who comes loyally back to his father and mother and sisters from the prosperity that has dawned upon him in India, to live with them and be one of them. He finds the elder sister married to a brutal workman, the younger mistress to the son of his patron. He appeals to her and the parents against the wicked life that none of them have been ashamed of; and they have promised to go back with him to India, when the patron comes in and makes good the wrong his son has done with a handsome check. They are of the poor who can be bought, he of the rich who think money can pay anything. The son is defeated, and fairly driven from his home by his kindred, who fawn upon the patron, and turn from cursing to flattering the guilty girl who has brought them so much money with her dishonor. It is a horrible scene, but as you witness it you realize the horrible truth back of it, that poverty when it is dire must sell itself, and that wealth when it is corrupted with the sense of its power can feel no harm in buying. The piece arraigns existing society, not in set terms, but tacitly, by inexorable truth to its facts. It is weakened by a *deus ex machina* who appears from time to time, and at last carries the young man back to India with the patron's daughter for his bride; but even this folly cannot obscure its awful lesson, or silence its appeal to the social conscience.

---

[1] David Demarest Lloyd (1851-1889), and Sydney Rosenfeld (1855-1931).

[2] The Charity Ball, [by David Belasco and Henry Churchill De Mille].

[3] Thomas William Robertson (1829-1871), English comic playwright.

[4] Hermann Sudermann (1857-1928).

[5] La Morte Civile, by Paolo Giacometti.

July, 1890

Editor's Study.

I.

WE have often admired the noble disdain with which we have seen an editor treat a correspondent asking him to retract some mistaken statement, or correct some injurious error. In these cases a correspondent is seldom able to lout so low, or to pitch his prayer in such a bated key, that the editor will not somehow spurn him with his foot, or deal him a box on the ear for his impudence. This behavior we have conceived to be the right way of maintaining the dignity of the press; it has seemed to us even more effective than the contemptuous silence of other editors who refuse to print any appeal from themselves to themselves; for it carries with it the terrors of a public disgrace, and may well be supposed to act deterrently. We confess that we have always envied it, and in the beginning we intended to practise it; but we early found that the Study was of such a defective make that it was useless to attempt the highest journalistic methods in it. The consequence has been that from time to time the presiding Genius of the Study (we make the little concession of the word Genius to the amiability of the superstitious who believe in such a thing) has found itself publicly eating humble-pie, owning itself wrong, trying to repair harms done, and otherwise dishonoring the calling of a censor. Strange to say this genius (whom we can allow a large G only in the first instance) has not only thriven upon the repulsive diet, but has formed a morbid appetite for humble-pie, and eats it with avidity; so that the Study is perhaps the only tribunal of the kind which is not merely willing but eager to be convicted of flaws of judgment, sins of ignorance, and inaccuracies of expression.

Some such explanation seems needed to account for the publication of the following note from a fellow-critic, which we print without suppressing any of those caressing expressions which we like, but which we do not exact from correspondents seeking to set us right.

II.

"DEAR MR. STUDY,—I wish I had your facile felicity of expression; then could I review friends' books without giving offence to my friend or my conscience. But when you say (re *Garden of Dreams*), 'One must be slow to deny that the writer could fail of the highest effect she aimed at,' I fancy your phrase reverses your thought. 'Slow to assume' she could fail would be praise; 'slow to deny' she could fail is derogatory.

"*Enemy.* 'She could fail.'

"*Friend.* 'I deny that she could fail.'

"*Half-friend.* 'I am slow to deny,' etc.

"I was tempted to exploit this in my literary column—good jokes against the Study are so scarce—but I thought I'd do as I'd be done by for once."

We suppress the real name of the writer, who would probably be mobbed by those lewd fellows of the baser sort, to whom his reluctance to break the Study's windows when he had a chance will seem a cowardly treason; and we are very glad of his letter in the interest of Mrs. Moulton's charming volume. We thought when we wrote the sinuous sentence he has quoted that we were praising her work by that graceful indirection which a real literary person likes to use, and now we see that we were doing nothing of the kind. Even if we had said what we meant we should not have been praising it enough; but we had to be reticent so as to show a critic's natural, and in fact, unavoidable superiority to a poet. We thank our correspondent for his correction, and we commend his letter as a model to all intending petitioners for justice at our hands. We will do justice upon any appeal, but we will do it a great deal more promptly and handsomely if there is mingled with the appeal a little judicious recognition of those virtues inherent in the Study, which, knowing it as we do, we should be the last to deny.

III.

The next piece of humble-pie is rather more difficult to manage. Not only is the keen edge of appetite blunted by the earlier refection, but it seems to us that a rather stronger relish of humiliation lurks in the following letter, and that there is a tang of irony in the smooth flavors of its most deprecatory expressions, though this may be merely our fancy. In spite of it, if the reader will watch, he shall see how manfully we will swallow it.

"DEAR SIR,—Pardon the liberty I take in addressing you, but my excuse is simply that I have been much interested in your Editor's [2] Study for March, and I am a little puzzled to know what Gower you refer to as coming between Chaucer and Spenser. I thought John Gower, the poet, a contemporary of Chaucer. Was it not Chaucer who gave him the name of the 'Moral' Gower, because of the moral tone of his poem in French, the one of his writings of which no known copy exists?

"Is there another Gower you have in mind? I feel that you must be right in the matter, and yet I do not see just how you are. Again apologizing for writing you, I am,
Respectfully yours,
—— ——."

There! But we wish to say, before leaving a subject that would be so distasteful to a less disciplined spirit than the Study's, that our correspondent is right in every particular, and particularly right in holding that though we were apparently so mistaken in our literary history, we must be correct upon general principles; in other words, that we were infallible. We hoped that we might easily establish, for the sake of the "great silence" between Chaucer and Spenser which Mr. Phelps would find so vocal in thought, that there really was another Gower, as our correspondent suggests. But upon referring to a friend who owns a copy of Chambers's *Encyclopædia of English Literature*, and getting him to refer to that, we learned that there really was no other Gower. We then instantly perceived that as it was impossible for us to have been wrong in our position, we were the victim of a gross typographical error; and that we had not written Gower at all, but Skelton. Of course it was impossible that we should not have written Skelton, for with Pope's couplet in our mind,

"Chaucer's worst ribaldry is learned by rote,
And heads of houses beastly Skelton quote,"

it was inevitable, by any orderly psychological process, that we should fail to write Skelton after writing Chaucer. In fact, what we did write was "beastly Skelton," as could be readily proved by referring to our manuscript, if we had not instantly destroyed it upon making up our mind to this assertion.

IV.

We turn without reluctance from this correspondent to another, who, while owning us impeccable, convicts us of a sin of omission. This sort of sin is far less heinous than a sin of commission, and the delinquent may deal with it much less heroically. For some such

reason we shall not be half so strenuous in denying that we said anything of the sort attributed to us; we will even admit that we did not go as far as we meant to go in the very direction our correspondent takes.

"As a rule," she begins, and we cannot praise her beginning too highly, "you always say just what I would like to say if I only knew how. But for once you have disappointed me. In speaking of the *Odd Number* [3] volume of Maupassant's stories you say, '"The Diamond Necklace" and "The Piece of String" are of heart-breaking pathos,' meaning thereby they are imbued with that sadness of life seemingly hopeless, because answering no comprehensible purpose or fulfilling any adequate design. The review was evidently of a cursory character, which can alone explain a lack of quick responsiveness to the fine subjectivity of this work. The stories are of course caviare to the general, and on the face altogether pessimistic. Of those above-mentioned, the life's sacrifice in one was apparently useless; the death in the other a sort of moral murder; the impression received of the remainder being likewise depressing. The technique of each is perfect in itself, in its faultless simplicity and analytical candor; and this is what is seen and admired, and this is what the Study calls '*extremely clever.*' But hidden in this ingenious mechanism is a tiny, vital spark, which, when found, sheds a psychological light over the whole. It shows us we are not mere victims of the dooming mysteries of life; we are not placed here to suffer for some enigmatical cause to be revealed in the hereafter, if indeed it may ever be revealed at all. But it teaches that while a wilful insistence for the false leads to moral degeneration or ruin, yet we also often find ourselves the subjects of undeserved calamity. The apparent injustice of this, Maupassant solves as did the old philosopher:

'If I and mine are of the gods neglected,
There's reason for their rigor.'

He also teaches it is good to follow the strongest law of our being if it satisfies the higher part of us, no matter as to the outward form it may take on. It shows that most tragedies of common occurrence may be traced to the often obscure source of an 'overmastering passion' of some sort. Indeed it is doubtful if these lessons could be conveyed as effectively other than in this clear searching light of every-day life. For all these meanings and many much deeper does the little spark reveal, and is to the plot what the soul is to the body."

This seems very penetrating and just criticism, not so well expressed, of course, as if the Study had uttered, rather than adopted it; but showing that ethical and æsthetic refinement which the habitual reader of the Study is pretty sure to share with it sooner or later. It will reach the professional critics last of all; but even in them, the Study sometimes already fancies the gleam of a reflected light. In the mean time, it has many gratifying proofs that its readers think; and it does not insist that they shall always think with it. On the contrary, it is quite willing they shall think beyond it if they can, though we promise them they will find this difficult, as in the case of a correspondent who has lately written us, asking our influence against the use of criminal incidents in fiction. A coarse diet, our friend perceives, the crude-minded must have in literature, as we suggested a few months ago; but need it be poisonous? Why not hold out a wisp of sweeter grass to the donkey that likes thistles, and keep beckoning? Or, if an author must portray evil, should he not be most careful, most religiously careful to leave no doubt as to his own feeling in regard to the implications of the problem he handles, since " if we are interested in the work of an author, we are jealous of his personal integrity"? Unquestionably he should, for if he fails to do so, he does a moral mischief which no artistic virtue can atone for. The blind faith with which a young reader especially trusts the direction of his sympathies, almost his conscience, to the imagination of a great "genius," is something that no writer can abuse without being an infinitely greater scoundrel than "genius." Our correspondent has hinted the pathos of a case whose perils the Study has more than once declared, both directly and indirectly, when it has pleaded with the band of intellectual giants who are now writing our novels to use the minor means of interesting their readers, to employ the *milde Macht*, which, if it does not always cure, is not so apt to kill. How many times has not this apartment rung with entreaties to be simple, to be rational, to be cleanly, to be decent, to be natural, addressed to the prodigious forces which too often revel in blood and tears, filth and crime, shame and vice, in order to enable the average novel-reader to pass an agreeable half-hour?

V.

These entreaties have not been without their effect, if we may trust the kind expressions of another correspondent (like the last three quoted, of the letter-writing sex), upon American novelists, and secondarily upon English readers, who are being here and there led to recognize the superiority of our fiction over their own.

"On opening HARPER'S MAGAZINE this evening," she writes us from a large provincial city in England, "and turning to the Editor's Study, I was much struck, in reading the remarks on 'The Age of Words,' by the fact that the comparative value of American and English modern novels as literature has been occupying my thoughts a good deal lately.... It will perhaps be not altogether unpleasant to the editor of HARPER'S to hear my opinion, as it is also the opinion of several sensible but

not 'literary' girl friends, with whom I have occasionally discussed modern novels.

"A number of years ago I became a member of a magazine club. We got thirteen magazines monthly, and as I am a terribly greedy reader there was scarcely an article and certainly not a story in one of the magazines unread by me. The magazines were *Contemporary, Nineteenth Century*, HARPER'S, *Atlantic Monthly, Scribner's, Cornhill, Blackwood's, Temple Bar, Chambers's, Argosy, Magazine of Art, Longman's*, and *English Illustrated*.... In this range of reading the novels which have impressed me most during the last five or six years have been American. Their great charm was their exceeding naturalness. The characters in each of them seem to stand out in my memory as the figures stand out in some of Millet's landscapes. In many of the modern English novels, after six months it is difficult to recall the characters; they seem to get hazy, and mixed up with the surroundings. .... With most of the clever modern English novelists the characters are made subservient to the ideas that the author wishes to promulgate.... Or he gives you just a string of incidents, often highly improbable; and at the end the heroine is rewarded by marrying a wealthy man, if she does not become a great heiress herself. The description of the dress or dresses, furniture and bric-à-brac, is simply tiresome, and it is pretty bad reading for the general public, who are already enough given to think more of a person's surroundings and circumstances than of the person himself. I cannot say that I have read many American novels, or that I know American novelists so well as English, but those I have read lately in HARPER'S and *Scribner's*, although there have been beautiful surroundings, beautiful dress, and *heaps of money*—so that everybody can go to Europe!—these are only *by the way*. The stories are written to show character, and how the circumstances and surroundings influence the character.

"In regard to short stories, Americans are before the English. The short stories in most English magazines I never remember after I read, but in the American magazines I remember a number, and all good.

"In HARPER'S MAGAZINE the reviews on books are always worth reading, although they occasionally differ from some English reviews. Mark Twain's new book has been severely criticised here; it was called *irreverent*. I confess I did not feel the irreverence; but perhaps HARPER'S is *Americanizing* me, as I very much enjoyed reading *A Yankee at the Court of King Arthur*, and read bits aloud to any one I can get to listen."

VI.

Nothing but the most inflexible devotion to justice, to justice presenting itself in the peculiarly winning form of justice to ourselves, could have prevailed upon us to print some passages in the closing paragraph of this very suggestive letter. But from time to time it is necessary to sacrifice modesty in the cause of truth, and we cheerfully "give publicity," as the editors say, to our correspondent's recognition of the value of our reviews. They do indeed occasionally "differ from some English reviews," and we have had moments when we fancied that their value largely resided in this difference. But we will not insist upon a point possibly offensive to the patriotism of a correspondent so agreeable; and we hope it will not be displeasing to her if we own that we think HARPER'S *is* Americanizing her, and at such a rate that nothing but the absence of woman suffrage among us could keep her from voting at the next Presidential election. There is something very charming in the ingenuous daring, the ingenuous misgiving expressed in her opinion; it must have cost something in face of tradition and convention to arrive at beliefs so little conformable to the teachings of all the critical authorities of her island.

All? Perhaps not all. Here is Mr. Grant Allen, in a late contribution to that new English journal, *The Speaker*, saying very much the same things as our fair correspondent, and he is one of those critical authorities. He makes bold to declare that the present taste in fiction among his fellow-countrymen is a "recrudescence," and that it is in America [5] the true principle is honored, and the character novel of the great English novelists is developing with traits peculiar to our conditions, while it is falling into almost entire neglect at home. He blames somewhat the weekly instalment plan of publication for the present state of things in England, with the demand for a constant quiver of sensation which it must supply; but he is aware that this is not the whole trouble, and he frankly attributes the greater part of it to the decay of the critical faculty among the critics. He might not agree with us that it is the want of humanity in English criticism that disables it; and by this we do not mean a want of kindness to any given author under review, but a want of sympathy with race interests. We think it quite impossible for criticism in sympathy only with class interests, growing out of class education, and admitting only class claims to the finer regard and respect of readers, to do justice to the American school of fiction.

"The modern American novel," as Mr. Allen truly says, "is built upon principles all its own, which entirely preclude the possibility of introducing those abrupt changes, sensational episodes, improbable coincidences, which to our contemporary English romance are indispensable ingredients. It is the real Realism, the natural Naturalism; it depends for its effects upon the faithful, almost photographic delineation of actual life, with its motives, its impulses, its springs of action laid bare to the eye, but with no unnatural straining after the intenser and coarser emotions of blood and fire, no intentional effort to drag in murder, crime, or fierce interludes of passion, without adequate reason. If these things belong by nature to the particular drama, as it rises spontaneous in the author's brain, fall into their places they will and may; but the drama won't certainly go out of its fixed path to look for them. Such a conception of the nature of romance stands to the conception of the current English novel precisely as the modern landscape of truthful transcript from nature stands to the Claudesque and Poussinesque landscape of impossible composition and pseudo-classical idyl." [6]

It would be hard to give a more exact and vivid statement of the artistic intention in the American novel, but we feel that Mr. Allen leaves a very important, a very essential matter untouched, and that is the American novelist's inherent, if not instinctive perception of equality: equality running through motive, passion, principle, incident, character, and commanding with the same force his interest in the meanest and the noblest, through the mere virtue of their humanity. Without this perception English romance wallows in sensation, and English criticism flowers in the vulgarity of the *Saturday Review*. Without this we have here in America our imitators of that romance and that criticism: poor provincials who actually object to meeting certain people in literature because they do not meet such people in society!

It is mostly these Little Peddlingtonians, trying so hard to be Little Londoners, who do the crying out for the "ideal" among us: for the thing that they think ought to be, rather than the thing that is, as if they, peradventure, knew what ought to be better than God who made what is! Their noise is at times so confusing that one almost asks one's self if they have not some reason. But presently from somewhere comes a clear note, like a great dispersing light, and then we know that they have none, and can have none. Such a note came lately in a letter of Mr. Lowell's, written thirty years ago to Mrs. Stowe, and now printed in her biography: [7]

"My advice is to follow your own instincts—to stick to nature, and to avoid what people commonly call the 'Ideal,' for that, and beauty, and pathos, and success, all lie in the simply natural. We all preach it, from Wordsworth down; and we all, from Wordsworth down, don't practise it. Don't I feel it every day in this weary editorial mill of mine, that there are ten thousand people who can write 'ideal' things for one who can see, and feel, and reproduce nature and character! Ten thousand, did I say? Nay, ten million. What made Shakespeare so great? Nothing but eyes and—faith in them."

This is anticipating by a long stretch of time the principles laid down by Señor Valdés in the prologue of his last story. [8] But it is advice that may be advantageously offered still, even to American novelists, some of whom are more or less frightened from their propriety by those "infants crying in the night" for the moon: not of course the real moon, all uncomfortably cratered over with extinct volcanoes, and unpleasantly cold, but the ideal moon, the toy moon of the poets, the silvery orb of the love-sick swain. Señor Valdés set the figure of those who could write novels of effectism at some hundreds, to ten or twelve living authors who could write novels of character; but Mr. Lowell makes it ten million to one; and we do not think he is more than two or three million out of the way, if that.

---

[1] In the Garden of Dreams, by Louise Chandler Moulton. See p. 251a.

[2] See p. 243b.

[3] See pp. 237b-238a.

[4] Jean François Millet (1814-1875) was a French painter of the Barbizon school.

[5] Criticism and Fiction, p. 107.

[6] Claude Lorrain and Nicolas Poussin, 17th century French painters.

[7] Howells quotes an excerpt from a longer letter to Harriet Beecher Stowe from James Russell Lowell, in which he praised Mrs. Stowe's story "The Minister's Wooing." Howells' source was: Charles Edward Stowe, Life of Harriet Beecher Stowe (Boston and New York: Houghton, Mifflin and Company, 1890), pp. 333-336.

[8] See note 1, p. 226.

Editor's Study.

I.

CANON FARRAR'S article on literary criticism in a recent number of the *Forum* is something very much to the liking of this Study. We should not say that it was the last word about the matter; we shall try to have a later word or two about it ourselves; but upon the whole it is almost the best word we have seen, up to the present time. It can be of great value to the readers if not to the writers of literary criticism. These, in fact, are so often delivered over to the evils of their own hearts that it may be hard for any saving message to reach them; but if they could take home some of the things that Canon Farrar says to them and of them, we might all live in a sweeter and clearer atmosphere. He tells them, as the Study has often told them before, in almost the same terms, that "they are in no sense the legislators of literature, barely even its judges and police "; and he reminds them of Mr. Ruskin's saying that "a bad critic is probably the most mischievous person in the world," though a sense of their relative proportion to the whole of life, would perhaps acquit the worst of them from this extreme of culpability. A bad critic is as bad a thing as can be, but, after all, his mischief does not carry very far. Otherwise it would be mainly the conventional books and not the original books which would survive; for the censor who imagines himself a law-giver can give law only to the imitative, and never to the creative mind. Criticism has condemned whatever was, from time to time, fresh and vital in literature; it has always fought the new good thing in behalf of the old good thing; it has invariably fostered and encouraged the tame, the trite, the negative. Yet upon the whole it is the native, the novel, the positive that have survived in literature. Whereas, if bad criticism were the most mischievous thing in the world, in the full implication of the words, it must have been the tame, the trite, the negative, that survived.

II.

Bad criticism is mischievous enough, however; and we think that nearly all current criticism as practised among the English and Americans is bad, is falsely principled, and is conditioned in evil. It is falsely principled because it is unprincipled, or without principles; and it is conditioned in evil because it is almost wholly anonymous.

At the best its opinions are not conclusions from certain easily verifiable principles, but are effects from the worship of certain models. They are in so far quite worthless, for it is the very nature of things that the original mind cannot conform to models; it has its norm within itself; it can work only in its own way, and by its self-given laws. Criticism does not inquire whether a work is true to life, but tacitly or explicitly compares it with models, and tests it by them. If literary art travelled by any such road as criticism would have it go, it would travel in a vicious circle, and would arrive only at the point of departure. Yet this is the course that criticism must always prescribe, when it attempts to give laws. Being itself artificial it cannot conceive of the original except as the abnormal. It must altogether reconceive its office before it can be of use to literature. It must reduce this to the business of observing, recording, and comparing; to analyzing the material before it, and then synthetizing its impressions. Even then, it is not too much to say that literature as an art could get on perfectly well without it. Just as many good novels, poems, plays, essays, sketches, would be written if there were no such thing as criticism in the literary world, and no more bad ones.

III.

But it will be long before criticism ceases to imagine itself a controlling force, to give itself airs of sovereignty, and to issue decrees. As it exists it is mostly a mischief, though not the greatest mischief; but it may be greatly ameliorated in character and softened in manner by the total abolition of anonymity. We have no hesitation in saying that anonymous criticism is almost wholly an abuse, and we do not confine our meaning here to literary criticism. Now that nearly every aspect and nook and corner of life is searched by print, it is intolerably oppressive that any department of current literature, or of the phase of literature we call journalism, should be anonymous. Every editorial, every smallest piece of reporting, that involves a personal matter, should be signed by the writer, who should be personally responsible for his words. In a free country where no one can suffer for his opinions, no one has a right to make another suffer by them more condemnation than his individual name can carry. Thanks to the interviewer, the society reporter, and the special correspondent, the superstitious awe in which print has been held is fast vanishing; but print still bears too great authority. If each piece of it were signed by the author, its false advantage would be dissipated.

We believe that journalists generally have far more conscience in dealing with events than they are credited with; but we are afraid that they have also less. This was some time a paradox, but the situation it suggests would pass with the temptations and privileges hedging in the man who shoots from the dark at a man in the light. There ought not to be any such thing as journalistic authority which can continue in equal force through all the changes of *personnel* in the journalistic management, and can be handed on from a just and upright man to a mean and cruel and vindictive man, and still carry to the reader the weight of a great journal's name. If every interview were signed, so that the public might understand that it was relying upon the accuracy and honesty of this or that reporter, and not upon the good faith of the journal whose management can have no means of verifying the interview, the interviewer would cease to represent anything but himself, and if he were held directly and personally responsible, it would be much to the health of his own soul, and the advantage of the public. As it is, he is supposed to represent the journal which employs him, and the management is from time to time obliged to endorse him or disclaim him. He is called, in his own language, the *Times* representative, or the *Sun* representative, or the *World* representative; but as a matter of fact he represents nothing but himself. He can represent nothing else; and no writer of leading articles in any journal can represent anything more. Journalistic entity is a baleful fiction, a mask which ought to be torn from the features of the Browns, Joneses, and Robinsons who usually wear it. No danger would attend these champions of the common good in a free state, if their visors were lifted, beyond what attends each of us in

our every-day affairs, which we conduct in person with a due regard to law and the decencies of society. These forbid us to injure others, or to affront them by insolent or arrogant behavior, such as we witness every day in anonymous journalism.

IV.

We speak of journalism in this connection because journalism is criticism, the criticism of life, and therefore intimately associated with the criticism of letters. Literary criticism is only life criticism dealing with the finished product instead of the raw material; and generally its manners are as bad when it is employed in the one way as when it is employed in the other. Except for the constant spectacle of its ferocity, incompetency, and dishonesty, one could not credit the fact. We think it would be safe to say that in no other relation of life is so much brutality permitted by civilized society as in the criticism of literature and the arts. Canon Farrar is quite right in reproaching literary criticism with the uncandor of judging an author without reference to his aims; with pursuing certain writers from spite and prejudice, and mere habit; with misrepresenting a book by quoting a phrase or passage apart from the context; with magnifying misprints and careless expressions into important faults; with abusing an author for his opinions; with base and personal motives. Every writer of experience knows that certain critical journals will condemn his work without regard to its quality, even if it has never been his fortune to learn as one author did from a repentant reviewer that in a journal pretending to literary taste his books were given out for review with the caution, "Remember that the *Clarion* is *opposed* to Soandso's books." Any author is in good luck if he escapes without personal abuse; contempt and impertinence as an author no one will escape. If the Study were disposed to be autobiographical it might instance its own fate during the five years of its existence, in which it has practised the invariable courtesy toward persons which is possible with those who treat of methods and principles, and has every month been assailed with personal offense from the whole cry of anonymous criticism; so that in some moments of extreme dismay it has been almost disposed to regard itself as perhaps really an enemy of mankind. But its final conclusion appears to be that anonymous criticism is this enemy, and that the man, or even the young lady, who is given a gun, and told to shoot at some passer from behind a hedge, is placed in circumstances of temptation almost too strong for human nature.

V.

As we have already intimated, we doubt the more lasting effects of unjust criticism. It is no part of our belief that Keats's fame was long delayed by it; or Wordsworth's, or Browning's. Something unwonted, unexpected, in the quality of each delayed his recognition; each was not only a poet, he was a revolution, a new order of things, to which the critical perceptions and habitudes had painfully to adjust themselves. But we have no question of the gross and stupid injustice with which these great men were used, and of the barbarization of the public mind by the sight of wrong inflicted with impunity. This savage condition still persists in the toleration of anonymous criticism, an abuse that ought to be as extinct as the torture of witnesses. It is hard enough to treat a fellow-author with respect even when one has to address him, name to name, upon the same level, in the open; swooping down upon him in the dark, panoplied in the authority of a great journal, it is impossible. One must then treat him as prey, and strike him into the mire preparatory to tearing him limb from limb.

Every now and then some idealist comes forward and declares that you should say nothing in criticism of a man's book which you would not say of it to his face. But we are afraid this is asking too much. We are afraid it would put an end to all criticism; and that if it were practised literature would be left to purify itself. We have no doubt literature would do this; but in such a state of things there would be no provision for the critics. We ought not to destroy critics, we ought to reform them, or rather transform them, or turn them from the arrogant assumption of authority to a realization of their true function in the civilized state. They are no worse at heart, probably, than many others, and there are probably good husbands and tender fathers, loving daughters and careful mothers among them. We venture to suppose this because we have read that Monsieur de Paris is an excellent person in all the relations of private life, and is extremely anxious to conceal his dreadful occupation from those dear to him. ⌋ [3]

If we could credit the average critic with so high a motive we should not perhaps insist so strenuously upon the abolition of anonymity. But we greatly fear that the concealment of the name in the critic's case is from no such honorable desire of obscurity, and that he wears a mask chiefly that he may the more securely give pain and more of it. So we believe he had better leave it off, and learn to deal face to face with the author he censures. If anonymity is nothing worse than absurd, it is too absurd for endurance, and it ends in placing the journal which practises it in all sorts of ridiculous positions. We see the proof of this constantly in the glaring inconsistencies of which the party newspapers convict one another. With the changes of *personnel* which death, sickness, and other chances bring about in every newspaper come changes of opinion which a wary antagonist easily makes his prey. If Brown had signed his article, Jones who succeeds him could easily say to the rival accusing him of inconsistency that it was Brown who wrote that compromising article, and that he declines to be answerable for it. Whereas now the newspaper which Brown formerly represented and which Jones represents at present is put to open shame by the variance of these gentlemen's opinions. The same lamentable effect is predicable of a literary journal, and in fact there is a very signal instance of this apparent inconsistency in the London *Saturday Review*. This journal, which is now the great champion of Thackeray's posthumous renown, defending it against all comers as something too precious, too sacred for question, and maintaining his art to be not only insurpassable but inapproachable by any art of later date, was in its own pungent youth so afflicting to that great man that he habitually spoke of it as the *Superfine Review*. The epithet never seemed to us of a killing quality, but it is historical of the offense he suffered from the sniffs and sneers which represented the high disdain of the *Review* for the democratic feeling fostered in his novels. Now if Brown had signed those immortal sniffs and sneers with his name, Jones, who at present worships at the shrine of Thackeray in the same review, would not be bringing a contrite publication to confusion with all who esteem consistency a jewel.

VI.

If we leave all such disaster out of the question, and consider the matter in the interest of common-sense and common decency, we shall have hardly less reason for urging the abolition of critical anonymity. ⌐ It is evident to any student of human nature that the critic who is obliged to sign his review will be more careful of an author's feelings than he would if he could intangibly and invisibly deal with him as the representative of a great journal. He will not like personally to make a butcherly appearance even before the public which laughs at his amusing cruelties; and he will be loath to have his name connected with those perversions and misstatements of an author's meaning in which the critic now indulges without danger of being turned out of honest company. He will be in some degree forced to be fair and just with a book he dislikes; he will not wish to misrepresent it when his sin can be traced directly to him in person; he will not be willing to voice the prejudice of a journal which is "opposed to the books" of this or that author; and the journal itself, when it is no longer responsible for the behavior of its critic, may find it interesting and profitable to give to an author his innings when he feels wronged by a reviewer and desires to right himself; it may even be eager to offer him the opportunity. We shall then perhaps frequently witness the spectacle of authors turning upon their reviewers, and improving their manners and morals by confronting them in public with the errors they may now commit with impunity. Many an author smarts under injuries and indignities which he might resent to the advantage of literature and civilization if he were not afraid of being browbeaten by the journal whose nameless critic has outraged him. ⌐|4

In fact we look forward to the time when it will be regarded as monstrous and dishonorable for a review to keep an anonymous critic; and it will be no more permissible than for a gentleman to keep a masked bravo in his pay. The temptation for a critic to cut fantastic tricks before high heaven in the full light of day is great enough, and for his own sake he should be stripped of the shelter of the dark. Even then it will be long before the evolution is complete, and we have the gentle, dispassionate, scientific student of current literature in place of the arrogant, bullying, blundering pedant, who has come down to our time from the heyday of the brutal English reviewers. In his present state he is much ameliorated, much softened; but he still has the wrong idea of his office, and imagines that he can direct literature, not realizing that literature cannot be instructed how to grow, or not knowing that it is a plant which springs from the nature of a people, and draws its forces from their life. If it has any root at all, its root is in their character, and it takes form from their will and taste. ⌐|5 Persuaded of this, we have welcomed every excellence in literary art among us that seemed to promise a difference from the literary art of the English, as a token of authenticity, and an evidence of native vigor. Nothing, we have felt, could come from what was like that art in ours, but only from what was unlike it; but the sense of this has not penetrated the great mass of our critics, or indeed gone much beyond the precincts of the Study. For our own part we have found

in the work of the poor funny man or the lowly paragrapher of the daily press more to give us hope of the future of American literature than in some very careful and studied efforts of culture; and now and then we read some reporter's sketch of a fire, or the eviction of a delinquent tenant, or the behavior of working-men on a strike, that seems to us more important than several current romances of the ideal. But, as we said before, these opinions are not shared by many. The poor funny man and the lowly paragrapher would, we fear, be among the foremost to reject them with scorn; for it is still the prevailing superstition that literature is something that is put into life, not something that comes out of it.

<h2 style="text-align:center">VII.</h2>

We have several times before now besought the literary critics of our country to disabuse themselves of the mischievous notion that they are essential to the progress of literature in the way they have vainly imagined. They cannot reform or purify or direct it; but they can render the reading public an acceptable service by observing the traits of our growing literature, by recognizing and registering its facts, and by classifying and comparing books as they appear. Canon Farrar confesses that with the best will in the world to profit by the many criticisms of his books, he has never profited in the least by any of them; and this is almost the universal experience of authors. It is not always the fault of the critics. They sometimes deal honestly and fairly by a book, and not so often they deal adequately. But in making a book, if it is at all a good book, the author has learned all that is knowable about it, and every strong point and every weak point in it, far more accurately than any one else can possibly learn them. He has learned to do better than good for the future; but if his book is bad, he cannot be taught anything about it from the outside. It will perish; and if he has not the root of literature in him, he will perish as an author with it. ⌐|6

So it is not in the interest of authorship that we urge criticism to throw off its mask, but in the interest of the reading public which is corrupted by the almost inevitable savagery and dishonesty of the anonymous critic, and in the interest of his own soul constantly imperilled by the temptation of these sins of pride, of prejudice, of cruelty which he may safely indulge in the dark.

If we could once make our brother censors, and especially our sister censors, and more especially those of the sharp tongue and the ready wit, realize how sweet and fit it is to write no more and no other about a book than one can put one's name to, we should be rendering them a great service. We should not ask them to forbear everything they would not say of it in the author's presence. That may come yet, to the infinite gain of the critic's manners. But for the present we would ask them to stand fairly out in the light, and deliver their judgment for what it is worth, as that of this or that man or woman, and not advance upon the quaking author in the obscurity, bearing the doom decreed by a powerful review or influential journal. The editor cannot rightfully lend its authority to criticism he has not verified, and he has no right to lend it to an anonymous critic. Still less has he the right to deprive the reviewer of the praise that should come to him personally from a well-written, well-felt, and, above all, well-mannered criticism, and claim the advantage of it wholly for his publication. The only advantage which the publication ought to enjoy, is the credit of employing an able, modest, and courteous critic; and all else should belong to the critic, the honor and the cumulative repute, which would naturally remain with his name, and follow it to any other publication using him wiselier, and paying him better.

---

[1] F. W. Farrar, "Literary Criticism," Forum, 9 (May, 1890), 277-291.

[2] Howells was himself "house critic" at Atlantic Monthly for a period in the 1870's.

[3] Criticism and Fiction, pp. 45-52 (abridged).

[4] Criticism and Fiction, pp. 52-53.

[5] Criticism and Fiction, p. 55.

[6] Criticism and Fiction, pp. 56-57.

September, 1890

Editor's Study.

I.

IN the twenty years that have passed since Mr. John Hay gave us the poems presently reprinted with others in a volume enlarged to nearly twice the size of his first venture, the reading world has been of many moods. At present it is certainly no longer of the mood in which it received with acclaim the heroic tales and dramatic measures of the Pacific slope, and fondly accepted them as divination, if not revelation. It is a world where nothing is lasting, nothing is final; where judgments are often reversed, and more errors are made than are acknowledged. One of these errors was to confound Mr. Hay's work in "dialect" balladry with that of other poets, who were so creative that they created even the vernacular employed by their rude sons of the soil. Mr. Hay never could justly claim to have done this; he must be content with the slighter praise that belongs to the observer of life, and can have no higher honor than comes from having imagined characters; he did not imagine dialects. Perhaps it is for this reason, however it brings his "genius" in question, that the Pike County Ballads are still enjoyable, now when our faith in the self-sacrifice of steam-boat engineers and martyr stage-drivers has somewhat lapsed, and we find it difficult to believe even in the altruism of the greatest millionaires.

In "Little Breeches," and "The Pledge at Spunky Point," and "The Mystery of Gilgal," as in the gay lyrics and sketches of life indefinitely alien to Pike County, the wit is always the stream of Western humor, springing from the same source in the heart of America. The poems are interestingly biographical of a writer whose Americanism is of a quality as unmistakable in other things as in his wit, and who has had the advantage to have been in touch with the world outside America at many points without leaving any part of himself in its grasp. That basal good-nature on which our national being rests underlies the poetry of the whole book, and its airiest wit is alive with the trust in men which is the practical religion of these States. Something faithful, true-hearted, generous, is never far off, even from passages that promise, or threaten, to be quite sophisticated and cynical. There is kindness in the shrewdest irony, and no final bitterness in the laughter. As to the more serious pieces, it seems to us that there has never been a better or braver word said for Liberty than in the poem of that name; and that the great meaning of Christianity illumines with its tenderest and loveliest light the beautiful lines on Mount Tabor. There is so much that is so good in the pieces of a religious cast in the volume that we are inclined to commend them especially to the reader, and especially to the reader who has hitherto known the poet on his most obvious side. Among those of a different cast, "A Triumph of Order" is something that makes the heart bleed still as if the boy-communist had just been shot in Paris. For the poetic effect that may be embodied in the very plainest and barest phrase, "Miles Keogh's Horse" is a masterpiece; and "Sister St. Luke," in another kind, is a picture perfectly painted of features whose delicate spirit could not have been easily caught:

> "She lived shut in by flowers and trees,
> And shade of gentle bigotries.
>
> .   .   .   .
>
> *But in her small, dull Paradise,*
> Safe housed from rapture or surprise,
> Nor day nor night had power to fright
> The peace of God that filled her eyes."

That is admirable; and admirable in its way is the handling of the legend of "The happiest of all lovers," Ernest of Edelsheim—

> "His true love was a serpent
> Only half the time."

In a kindred sort "The Enchanted Shirt" is excellent; in another sort and of a lofty level is "Guy of the Temple," with its fine mystical passion, and its hour of that religious ardor long lost to the world except in such poems as this and Tennyson's idyls. As for those "Distiches," which appear to be the latest minting of

273

the poet's treasure, they are pieces of fine gold, so sharply and cleanly struck, and of such a clear brilliancy and ringing truth, that they are like so many Greek coins.

II.

It is difficult to say what manner of poet a certain poet is; to be quite modest, it is impossible; and yet, like the question of the first cause and the last end, it is always tempting endeavor. As for Mr. Hay's work one feels as if he were saying in this or that instance of it, "Here is what I could do in a given direction if I chose." We wish he had chosen to do more in one kind or another, but perhaps this is only an impulse of the baffled critical faculty which prefers something distinctively ranged, finally classified. But again perhaps a wiser criticism than ours (we imagine it with considerable effort and reluctance) will be more and more content with each artist for just what it finds him, if it finds him good; and if it must still place and label him will say of such a poet as Mr. Hay: "Ah, yes! An unclassifiable. This is nice. Put him with the class of the unclassifiables."

We fancy him in company there with another American who is chiefly recognizable as American because he is not recognizable as anything else, and who must be called a novelist because there is yet no name for the literary kind he has invented, and so none for the inventor. The fatuity of the story as a story is something that must early impress the story-teller who does not live in the stone age of fiction and criticism. To spin a yarn for the yarn's sake, that is an ideal worthy of a nineteenth-century Englishman, doting in forgetfulness of the English masters and grovelling in ignorance of the Continental masters; but wholly impossible to an American of Mr. Henry James's modernity. To him it must seem like the lies swapped between men after the ladies have left the table and they are sinking deeper and deeper into their cups and growing dimmer and dimmer behind their cigars. To such a mind as his the story could never have value except as a means; it could not exist for him as an end; it could be used only illustratively; it could be the frame, not possibly the picture. But in the mean time the kind of thing he wished to do, and began to do, and has always done, amidst a stupid clamor, which still lasts, that it was not a story (of *course*, it was not a story!), had to be called a novel; and the wretched victim of the novel-habit (only a little less intellectually degraded than the still more miserable slave of the theatre-habit), who wished neither to perceive nor to reflect, but only to be acted upon by plot and incident, was lost in an endless trouble about it. Here was

a thing called a novel, written with extraordinary charm; interesting by the vigor and vivacity with which phases and situations and persons were handled in it; inviting him to the intimacy of characters divined with creative insight; making him witness of motives and emotions and experiences of the finest import; and then suddenly requiring him to be man enough to cope with the question itself; not solving it for him by a marriage or a murder, and not spoon-victualling him with a moral minced small and then thinned with milk and water, and familiarly flavored with sentimentality or religiosity. We can imagine the sort of shame with which such a writer, so original and so clear-sighted, may sometimes have been tempted by the outcry of the nurslings of fable, to give them of the diet on which they had been pampered to imbecility; or to call together his characters for a sort of round-up in the last chapter. [1]

The round-up was once the necessary close of every novel, as it is of every season on a Western cattle ranch; and each personage was summoned to be distinctly branded with his appropriate destiny, so that the reader need be in no doubt about him evermore. The formality received its most typical observance in *The Vicar of Wakefield*, perhaps, where the modern lover of that loveliest prospect of eighteenth-century life is amused by the conscientiousness with which fate is distributed, and vice punished and virtue rewarded. It is most distinctly honored in the breach in that charming prospect of nineteenth-century life, *The Tragic Muse*, a novel which marks the farthest departure from the old ideal of the novel. No one is obviously led to the altar; no one is relaxed to the secular arm and burnt at the stake. Vice is disposed of with a gay shrug; virtue is rewarded by innuendo. All this leaves us pleasantly thinking of all that has happened before, and asking, Was Gabriel Nash vice? Was Mrs. Dallow virtue? Or was neither either? In the nineteenth century, especially now toward the close of it, one is never quite sure about vice and virtue: they fade wonderfully into and out of each other; they mix, and seem to stay mixed, at least around the edges.

Mr. James owns that he is himself puzzled by the extreme actuality of his facts; fate is still in solution, destiny is not precipitated; the people are still going uncertainly on as we find people going on in the world about us all the time. But that does not prevent our being satisfied with the study of each as we find it in the atelier of a master. Why in the world should it? What can it possibly matter that Nick Dormer and Mrs. Dormer are not certainly married, or that Biddy Dormer and Sherringham certainly are? The marriage or the non-marriage cannot throw any new light on their characters; and the question never was what they were going to do, but what they were. This is the question that is most sufficiently if not distinctly answered. They never wholly emerge from the background which is a condition of their form and color; and it is childish, it is Central African, to demand that they shall do so. It is still more Central African to demand such a thing in the case of such a wonderful creature as Gabriel Nash, whose very essence is elusiveness; the lightest, slightest, airiest film of personality whose insubstantiality was ever caught by art; and yet so strictly of his time, his country, his kind. He is one sort of modern Englishman; you are as sure of that as you are of the histrionic type, the histrionic character, realized in the magnificent full-length of Miriam Rooth. *There* is mastery for you! There is the woman of the theatre, destined to the stage from her cradle: touched by family, by society, by love, by friendship, but never swayed for a moment from her destiny, such as it is, the tinsel glory of triumphing for a hundred nights in the same part. An honest creature, most thoroughly honest in heart and act, and most herself when her whole nature is straining toward the realization of some one else; vulgar, sublime; ready to make any sacrifice for her art, to "toil terribly," to suffer everything for it, but perfectly aware of its limitations at its best, while she provisionally contents herself with its second-best, she is by all odds so much more perfectly presented in *The Tragic Muse* than any other like woman in fiction, that she seems the only woman of the kind ever presented in fiction.

As we think back over our year's pleasure in the story (for we will own we read it serially as it was first printed), we [2] have rather a dismaying sense of its manifold excellence; dismaying, that is, for a reviewer still haunted by the ghost of the duty of cataloguing a book's merits. While this ghost walks the Study, we call to mind that admirable old French actress of whom Miriam gets her first lessons; we call to mind Mrs. Rooth, with her tawdry scruples; Lady Dormer, with her honest English selfishness; Mrs. Dallow, with her awful good sense and narrow high life and relentless will; Nick's lovely sister Biddy and unlovely sister Grace; Nick himself, with his self-devotion to his indefinite future; Sherringham, so good and brave and sensible and martyred; Dashwood, the born man of the theatre, as Miriam is the born woman; and we find nothing caricatured or overcharged, nothing feebly touched or falsely stated. As for the literature, what grace, what strength! The style is a sweetness on the tongue, a music in the ear. The whole picture of life is a vision of London aspects such as no Englishman has yet been able to give: so fine, so broad, so absolute, so freed from all necessities of reserve or falsity.

III.

Its modernity, its recognition of the very latest facts of society and art, and of that queer flirtation between them that can never be a marriage, is one of the very most valuable, most delightful things about the book. Modernity, indeed, is always somehow a charming thing when you get it skilfully expressed in a picture or a story, or in some such piece of personal history as Baroness Deichmann's translation of Baroness Stackelberg's life of Carmen Sylva, the Queen of Roumania. When you think of the [3] figure that royalty once cut in the awed imaginations of men, wrapped round with mists of twilight, it is sufficiently striking to have it electric-lighted, even to its intimate life and its recondite emotions, by such a memoir as this. Happily, the Queen of Roumania, if a poet of less effect than feeling, is a person whose life is as noble and beautiful as that of most women in the humbler walks of love and duty, and bears knowing as well. We are aware that this is saying a good deal for a queen; but we think it may be safely hazarded. We think the great attraction, the great use of the book is that it shows how little a princess of forty or fifty descents is characterized by lineage, and how little a good and gifted woman is embellished by royalty. You discover that she was like any number of other impulsive, cultivated, gifted girls, and is like any number of other self-sacrificing, heroic women, tried by love, by sorrow— the wives of lawyers, doctors, ministers, mechanics, and laborers. Her father and mother were excellent people, and there was talent in the family; but her training was no better, one might almost say it was no other, for it could not well be any other, than such as most intelligent and conscientious people now give their daughters in ethics and æsthetics; though perhaps the average American girl, from being a Protestant all her life, might have some misgiving in adapting herself to the Greek religion as soon as she became Queen of Roumania. But we are not sure that Carmen Sylva did not do wiselier in bringing herself close by all possible means to the hearts of the people she desired to love and has greatly befriended: it is hard for a sovereign to be of any real use, with all the advantages.

IV.

Her life, like the curious autobiography of *A Japanese Boy*, which has lately come to our hand, testifies to the fact of human equality, and there is something of the same pleasure in knowing her one of us all, that there is in recognizing the Japanese boy's identity in essentials with the American boy. We wish to make Shinkichi Shigemi, who seems to be still at school in New Haven, Connecticut, our compliment on the excellent simplicity with which he has told the story of his child life in the little seaport of Imabari; and we can cordially commend it to the youth of our schools, our colleges, our newspapers, our magazines, our pulpits, for that virtue. It is really very delightful, that simplicity; and we hope Shinkichi Shigemi will not lose it, when he is able to free his English of all color of a foreign idiom. He tells us of his schools, tasks, plays, punishments; his home life, in kitchen and parlor; the village life outside; the theatres, the manners and customs of the people; his relations and neighbors; the family sports and amusements; the holidays, and the religious rites and feasts. It is all very queer, outwardly; but inwardly the life is like our own, with the same affections, the same emotions, the same ambitions, the same ideals of rectitude and kindness and purity. We value the book not only for the pleasure, the sincere and graphic life-pictures given in it, but for the contribution to man's knowledge of himself which it makes. It will help to clear away the delusion that the quality, the essence of human nature is varied by condition, or creed, or climate, or color; and to teach the truth of our solidarity which we are so long a-learning.

V.

It is easy to go from such a book as this boy's autobiography to such a book as Balzac's *Sons of the Soil*, lately issued in the admirable series of American translations of his novels, for with all the vast changes otherwise, one does not change the atmosphere of reality. We should say, if we did not pride ourselves upon the Study's caution and infallibility, that this book was almost the most modern of Balzac's novels: in motive and in method it is up with the latest discoveries in study, the newest fashions in art. It is so very "actual" in all these things that one rather wonders, in reading it, why Zola was at the trouble to write *La Terre*, since there already existed this report of rural France not very different in tenor or effect from that which he has given, and very much decenter in terms, and much less romantic in spirit. When we think of the two books together, it is apparent that the later novelist could not have taught the earlier master anything of realism; in this book, written in what seems his clearest and most fortunate moment, Balzac shows himself wellnigh the foremost artist of our time, and inexpressibly ahead of his own. If he could always have freed himself so wholly from the mists of romanticism which he was all his life struggling out of, he could have been one of the foremost artists of every time. But it is well that the past leaves something for the future to do, that all the facts are not accomplished. No doubt it is well also that there should be a reversion to the earlier types of thinking and feeling, to earlier ways of looking at human nature, and we do not refuse the pleasure offered us by Mr. Lafcadio Hearn because we find our pleasure chiefly in Tolstoï and James and Galdós and Valdés, and Thomas Hardy and Balzac at his best. In Mr. Hearn the public has learned to know an artist of those who think in color; and perhaps one doubts whether it might not be better for him to paint his sketches than to write them. As a painter he is of the most modern school: an impressionist who puts on pure color, and loves to render light in its fiercest and brightest and gayest tints; it is as a fictionist that he seems a reversion. His story of *Youma*, which we should perhaps more fitly call a poem, is an illustration of both facts in its dealing with tropical landscapes and natures, and its motivation of the chief character. Youma does the old sublimity-act of perishing before her lover's eyes with her master's child in her arms, and refusing to be saved from the flames that have made a holocaust of the white refugees. The scene is in Martinique, where the slaves have risen at the rumor of a new revolution in France and turned upon their owners; the situation is powerfully suggested, and the race differences and dissonances finely accorded in all the shades of black and white. Those who know Mr. Hearn's writing need not be assured that the local color is luxuriously given, that the descriptions are rapturous. Here is a man born to do the work he is doing, and one must not too coldly question whether he is not overdoing it. That is really a matter for him to settle himself with his readers at large; criticism cannot do more than note his characteristics; it cannot teach him anything, or mend him, or mar him. What it can be certain of and grateful for is the fact that in the great array of mediocrity and passivity, here is a positive talent that vividly distinguishes itself from all others, and joys in its life and strength. The love of doing the things that he does is evident in all his work; and it is this that in *Youma* charms and recompenses and promises.

It is the sign manual of the poet; the impress of authority and right.

VI.

The qualities of mind for which Mr. John Morley praised the author of *Castle and Cabin*, Mr. George Pellew's book on [6] Ireland, when he spoke of him as a judicial thinker and observer of a rare type, are evident in Mr. Pellew's *Life of John Jay*, the latest of the "American Statesmen Series." The clear intellect, the just spirit, the conscientious question are all present in this biography as they are in everything that Mr. Pellew has done. It was impossible to make a hero of John Jay, after the high romantic fashion, and no one could have detested such a hero more than Jay, unless it were Mr. Pellew; but there was material in the first Chief Justice for the portrait of a simple great man: a great man of the English ideal. The strange thing about Jay, however, was that he had nothing English in him; not a drop of English blood, but was of French and Dutch descent, and had none of that sentimental kindliness for England which gave many of our Revolutionaries pause, and long kept them reluctant to break wholly with the mother country. When he dedicated himself to the American cause it was with no backward look, from the moment he began to deal with its local enemies in New York till the time when he stood out against King George's ministers and refused to open negotiations for peace before the independence of the United States had been acknowledged.

Mr. Pellew makes clear the importance of such a character to people feeling their way to full political consciousness, as ours were then; and the services that Jay did the nation in many ways are part of its history. The sacrifices he made can be best appreciated on reading the early chapters descriptive of the training he had received for a career of tranquil prosperity and that domestic quiet to which the last chapter portrays his return in such sincere satisfaction. He was a man tenderly attached to wife and home and friends; but he gave up all for country. Here and there are touching words of affection and regret that show how much it cost him; but the sense of his cheerful and manly adequacy to every test of duty remains chiefly with the reader of this life of him.

Jay was an aristocrat by birth, training, and doubtless, as Mr. Lowell has described the condition, "a Tory in his nerves," but from first to last he was the stoutest of rebels, the hardest-headed of republicans, the truest and warmest lover of liberty, and not liberty for the whites alone, but for the blacks too. He saw the faults of Liberty, but he loved her none the less, and when it came to a question of final political responsibility, he was willing to trust her younger and plainer sister Equality. Simplicity he loved too as the best expression of a republican's self-respect, and he wished to realize it in his family life as well as in his public words. The character is one that bears study at every point, and we have not got us so much wisdom yet but that it will still yield us a little instruction.

---

[1] *Criticism and Fiction*, pp. 118-120.

[2] Henry James, *The Tragic Muse*, *Atlantic Monthly*, 63 (January, 1889), 1-20 through 65 (May, 1890), 588-604.

[3] Natalie von Stackelberg, *The Life of Carmen Sylva, Queen of Roumania*, Baroness Deichmann, trans. (London: Kegan Paul & Co., 1890).

[4] Honoré de Balzac, *The Works of Honoré de Balzac*, Introduction by George Saintsbury (18 vols. New York: Harper, N.D.).

[5] *Criticism and Fiction*, pp. 117-118.

[6] See pp. 160b-161a for Howells' review.

Editor's Study.

I.

A FRESH instance of the fatuity of the historical novel as far as the portrayal of character goes, is Mr. Harold Frederic's story, *In the Valley*. We do not mean to say that it is not very well written, and all that; it is uncommonly well written, and the whole *mise en scène* has verity and importance, for the valley of the Hudson, at the moment before the Revolution broke out, is new to romance, and it is certainly picturesque. But after we have owned the excellence of the staging in every respect, and the conscience with which the carpenter (as the theatrical folks say) has done his work, we are at the end of our praises. The people affect us like persons of our generation made up for the parts; well trained, well costumed, but actors, and almost amateurs. They have the quality that makes the histrionics of amateurs endurable; they are ladies and gentlemen; the worst, the wickedest of them is a lady or gentleman behind the scene. [1]

We make the freer to say these things of Mr. Frederic's historical romance because it gives us the occasion to do grateful homage to his novels of contemporary life, which we have hitherto let go by. Perhaps because the Study is getting a little old (it is now doting in its fifth or sixth year), it does not fling its doors eagerly open at the alarm of every new poet or novelist; but sometimes this is a loss to it, as we will allow with our characteristic readiness to confess ourselves wrong. It is a loss not to have known till now two books so robust, so sound, so honest as *Seth's Brother's Wife* and *The Lawton Girl*. They have to do with country, village, and minor city life in central New York, and they touch it at a great many points, both on the surface and below it. The metaphysics and ethics of the books are very good; the soul and its affairs are decidedly not left out of the account; and Mr. Frederic shows himself acquainted with the deeps as well as the shallows of human nature. But what seem to us the newest and best things in his story of *Seth's Brother's Wife* are his dramatic studies of local politics and politicians. These are rendered as we find

them in the field of actualities, and as the newspapers, from which Mr. Frederic seems to have got his training for literature, know them. The Boss of Jay County, with his simple instinct of ruling and his invulnerability to bribes, is an example of Mr. Frederic's fidelity to conditions not much understood by people out of politics, which are managed by ambition rather than by money, as a general thing. Next to this in value is the truth, almost as novel, with which farm life, inside and out, is painted: it is so true that as you read you can almost smell the earthy scent of the shut-up country parlors; and the sordid dulness of those joyless existences lies heavy on the heart. The vigor with which the type of rustic murderer is worked out in the hired man Martin excuses the resort to the grand means for evolving character, which Mr. Frederic is rather apt to permit himself when they are not necessary. He shows a prentice touch in this more than in anything else, in both books; but in *The Lawton Girl* the characterization of the cheap young reprobate Horace Boyce is masterly; and the elder scoundrel, Judge Wendover, who uses him, is quite as satisfyingly good. In its way, the portrait of Mrs. Minster's respectability and mere wealthiness is excellent; and the decayed soldier in General Boyce is finely done.

II.

It is a pathetic fact that with such artistic and important books in our reach, the great mass of us prefer to read the Rider Haggards and Rudyard Kiplings of the day, but it cannot be denied. Of these two the new fad is better than the old fad; but he seems a fad all the same: the whim of effete Philistinism (which now seems the æsthetic condition of the English), conscious of the dry-rot of its conventionality, and casting about for cure in anything that is wild and strange and unlike itself. Some qualities [2] in Mr. Kipling's tales promise a future for him; but there is little in the knowingness and swagger of his performance that is not to be deplored with many tears; it is really so far away from the thing that ought to be. The thing that ought to be will be vainly asked, however, of the English of Smaller Britain, or of any part of the English race which her bad taste can deprave. We must turn to the more artistic peoples for it, to the Continental writers whose superiority in fiction has often been celebrated here. If the reader will take *The House by the Medlar-Tree*, as the American version of Giovanni Verga's *I Malavoglia* is called, and will examine a little its structure and material, he will understand what we mean. We have seldom read a book in which the facts, the characters, and conditions were so frankly left to find their own way to the reader's appreciation, were so little operated or explained. It is very simple life that the story is concerned with, but the fine shades and delicate tones are here as in the most complex life. They are let appear, not made appear; but there is nothing dim or uncertain in their appearance. The whole little fishing village lives in plain day, with all the traits that make it modern Italian in full sight. It is in that transitional state which every place is everywhere in, and the revolutionary priest who represents the past and the revolutionary apothecary who represents the future are the forces that the whole world knows in the various guises of science and religion, as well as delightful personalities. There is sorrow and suffering enough, and deep heart-breaking tragedy, as well as noble duteousness and tender passion in the tale, but all is delicately and modestly touched by a master-hand. Let any one contrast the episode of Mena Malavoglia's self-sacrificing love, or that of her sister's ruin, or of her grandfather's heroically simple honesty, or of her mother's long grief and death, with one of Mr. Kipling's jaunty, hat-cocked-on-one-side, wink-tipping sketches, and he will find the difference between painting and printing in colors.

III.

Or, perhaps he will not; it depends very much upon what sort of reader he is. But it is certain that his preference will class and define him, and that if he should prefer the Kipling sketches, he had better get some sackcloth and ashes and put them on, for he may be sure that his taste is defective. The conviction need not lastingly affect his spirits: bad taste is a bad thing, but it is not sinful. Ruskin observed long ago that the best people he had ever seen knew nothing and cared nothing about art; and Tolstoï noticed among the literati of St. Petersburg that those who had the true theory of fiction were no better men than those who had the false theory. This was one of the things, in fact, that made him despair of all forms of æsthetic cultivation as a means of grace. The moral superiority of good art of any kind is in its truth, but we can have truth without any art whatever. It is well to keep both of these points in mind, the one that we may be good artists, and the other that we may be modest about it. There is danger to man, who is first of all a moral being, in setting up merely an æsthetic standard of excellence, and endeavoring for that, or in making the good of life consist of æsthetic enjoyment, which is really only one remove from sensual enjoyment. It is doubtless his keen perception of this that makes Tolstoï say those bitter things about music, or the worship of music, in *The Kreutzer Sonata*.

We suppose we must accept the sayings in that powerful book as Tolstoï's personal opinions, and not as the frenzied expressions of the murderer in whose mouth the story is dramatized, since Tolstoï owns them his in the deplorable reply he has made to the censors of his story. It is doubly a pity he made any such reply, because it detracts from the impressiveness of the tale, and because it dwarfs a great and good man for the moment to the measure of a fanatic. It does not, indeed, undo the truth of much that is said in the book; it does not undo the good for which the name of Tolstoï has come to stand with all who have hearkened to his counsel; but it does hurt both, and it puts a weapon in the hands of those who hate him. When a man like Poschdanieff, who has lived in the vice that the world permits men, marries and finds himself disappointed in marriage to the extreme of jealousy and murder, every one who looks into his heart, and finds there an actual or a potential Poschdanieff, must feel the inexorable truth of the story. Such a man, the natural product of our falsely principled civilization, could find nothing but misery in marriage; every one sees that, feels that. But when presently the author of the story comes and tells us that marriage itself is sin, and not merely the pollution in which the Poschdanieff nature steeps marriage, one must listen reverently, because it is Tolstoï who speaks, but one must shake one's head.

Tolstoï alleges the celibacy of Christ for the supreme example to all Christians; but if Christ discountenanced marriage, why was he present at the wedding feast of Cana? If we were to recommend either the novel or the author's gloss of it for the truth it could teach, it must be the novel; for that is true to Poschdanieff, and the other seems to us untrue to Tolstoï; the one is evil crazed, and the other is good gone wild.

IV.

Of Tolstoï there are some good things said in the *Views and Reviews* of Mr. W. E. Henley, whose very honest and vigorous verse we once had the pleasure of praising. More than most English critics he has had the gift to see beyond his own skies, and the field of his vision has included that portentous planet which to some has seemed a star of blessed promise, and to some a malignant comet, but whose splendor none can deny. Mr. Henley comes near summing up the whole of Tolstoï's art, the greatest art that ever was, when he says, "He is one to the just and the unjust alike, and he is no more angry with the wicked than he is partial to the good." When he adds, "He is the great optimist, and his work is wholesome and encouraging in direct ratio to the vastness of his talent and the perfection of his method," he has stated another truth almost as important concerning him, which nothing but Tolstoï's late manifesto could make any one question.

Nearly all the things, in fact, that Mr. Henley says of Tolstoï are good, but not quite all. He is more accurate when he generalizes than when he distinguishes; he notes that "only in the highest and lowest expressions of society is unsophisticated nature to be found," and he adds that Tolstoï loves to portray only these extremes, forgetting that *The Death of Ivan Illitch*, which he so justly praises, is simply a study of the mortal sickness and last end of a snob, a purely middle-class person, with the Philistine worldling's ideal of appearing rich and great when he was neither. If it were the study of an unsophisticated nature it would be false and meaningless.

It would not be so very unfair to say that a vivid generalization, with a tendency to the brilliant epigram in which that sort of thing culminates, was Mr. Henley's strong point in all these interesting little essays; and that when he attempts to refine and exemplify he weakens. He makes the most satisfying phrases, as, for instance, where he remarks that George Meredith is "not content to be a plain Jupiter; his lightnings are less to him than his fireworks," but when he specifies he is not so fortunate. The paper on Thackeray is the best, all round; but there Mr. Henley's dislike of Thackeray, whom he dislikes for almost the opposite reasons that he dislikes George Eliot, commits him to certain injustices. In fact he is continually beset and often overcome by the peculiar temptations of the literary judgment-seat. It appears that when one sits in judgment upon the works of another, one is apt to be arrogant and extreme and cruel, to say biting and burning things, and to bully the prisoner at the bar in the spirit of the French criminal courts, where the judge helps the prosecution to bring the accused to conviction. It is a curious spectacle, and not gratifying, we think, to the better feelings of our poor fallen nature. We do not mean to say that Mr. Henley's sessions gratify the worst of these feelings; but after reading three or four of his criticisms, and believing ourselves ready to call his little book a very agreeable little book, we were finally unable to do so; not because it was not brilliant and amusing, but because it was critical; and we presently found ourselves questioning the Study, if it were so very much better, or if being of a like critical make, it were not in like manner essentially regrettable.

This doubt rendered us very uncomfortable until it occurred to us to assert our difference if not our superiority by making a mock of those ideals of the passionate and the heroic which Mr. Henley shares with his fellow-islanders, and constantly seeks to find realized in the authors he admires. The love of these, we recovered our self-esteem in reflecting, is what keeps him from being really fine, with all his wit, and from being true, with all his honesty. It is such a crude and unwholesome thing, so deaf and blind to all the most delicate and important facts of art and life, so insensible to the subtle values in either that its presence or absence makes the whole difference, and enables one who is not obsessed by it to thank Heaven that he is not as that other man is.

When we had made up our minds to say this, or something like it, or worse, if possible, we were ready to admit that, leaving this out of the question, Mr. Henley's book was a book worth reading; that the farther off from his own time and place he wrote, the better he wrote; and that where his mistaken ideals were not concerned, he was often both just and generous.

V.

He speaks, indeed, of "the shadow-land of the American novel," and that seems a little unkind; but we do not believe the American novelist need suffer greatly from it, if he understands it aright. Probably in this phrase Mr. Henley meant to be unkind; but it ought to suggest to the philosophical mind some reflections upon the interesting variation of the same race by change of habitat and conditions, which may bring us consolation. There can be little question that many refinements of thought and spirit which every American is sensible of in the fiction of this continent, are necessarily lost upon our good kin beyond seas, whose thumb-fingered apprehension requires something gross and palpable for its assurance of reality. This is not their fault, and we are not sure that it is wholly their misfortune: they are made so as not to miss what they do not find, and they are simply content without those subtleties of life and character which it gives us so keen a pleasure to have noted in literature. If they perceive them at all it is as something vague and diaphanous, something that filmily wavers before their sense and teases them, much as the beings of an invisible world might mock one of our material frame by intimations of their presence. It is with reason, therefore, on the part of an Englishman, that Mr. Henley complains of our fiction as a shadow-land, though we find more and more in it the faithful report of our life, its motives and emotions, and all the comparatively etherealized passions and ideals that influence it.

In fact, the American who chooses to enjoy his birthright to the full, lives in a world wholly different from the Englishman's, and speaks (too often through his nose) another language: he breathes a rarefied and nimble air full of shining possibilities and radiant promises which the fog-and-soot-clogged lungs of those less-favored islanders struggle in vain to fill themselves with. But he ought to be modest in his advantage, and patient with the coughing and panting of his cousin who complains of finding himself in an exhausted receiver on plunging into one of our novels. To be quite just to the poor fellow, we have had some such experience as that ourselves in the atmosphere of some of our more attenuated romances.

But we have just been reading a book with perfect comfort and much exhilaration, whose scenes we are afraid the average Englishman would gasp in. Nothing happens; that is, nobody murders or debauches anybody else; there is no arson or pillage of any sort; there is not a ghost, or a ravening beast, or a hair-breadth escape, or a shipwreck, or a monster of self-sacrifice, or a lady five thousand years old in the whole course of the story; "no promenade, no band of music, nossing!" as Mr. Du Maurier's Frenchman [3] said of the meet for a fox-hunt. Yet it is alive with the keenest interest for those who enjoy the study of individual traits and general conditions as they make themselves known to American experience. A little less apparent partiality [4] for the right side; a little less apparent dislike of the wrong side, would have been better, we think, because we think it is no part of the author's business to be other than the colorless medium through which the reader clearly sees the right and wrong. But although *Miss Brooks* is Miss White's first novel, it is so full of such [5] very good performance that it will not do to treat it as if it were disabled by the

openness of its sympathies and antipathies, or to regard it as merely a promise of better things. Some of the best things are already here. As a character, Miss Brooks is a very high achievement. In her nobleness and her narrowness alike, she is perfectly divined; she is a New-Englander, a Bostonian, of that perfectly cultivated, virtuous, self-satisfied, imaginationless, impenetrably ignorant type, which fills the most charitable witness with despair, and seems to leave him no expression for his feelings but gnashing of the teeth. She is a person who is capable of any sacrifice for what she thinks right; but as her Bostonian criterions have taught her infallibly to know what is right, you feel the fact only a little surcharged when she sacrifices her lover, who has lost his money and has to go and live in Texas, to the duty of remaining in Boston, and being true to its ideals and ties. The rupture of their engagement is a foregone conclusion from its beginning; it is the reason of the story's being; and the novel is nothing more than the gradual evolution of this result. It is for this reason that we think its eventlessness would try the nerves of an Englishman so, used as he is to the robustious suspenses and athletic catastrophes of his native fiction. It is only the American who can taste to its last flavor the delicate pleasure the book purveys, and we suspect that a Bostonian who had come to regard himself objectively is the sort of American who would most delight in it. Such a Bostonian would best appreciate the skill with which the traits of such a good-familied, perfectly circumstanced Boston old maid as Miss McLinton are accented.

It is a phase of Boston, not all Boston, that the book shows, but it seems to us that the given phase has not been better shown. Miss White has at once placed herself with the few who can see truly and record simply; that is, with the artists. As you read, you feel that the head and the heart of the author are right; she loves what is good and kind and high wherever she finds it; but we think she looks a little too much for it toward the West. The West is representative of nothing permanent, but there is still the equality of newness there, and some generous and noble characteristics persist there that are lost to older civilizations. Yet essentially there is nothing grander in getting money than in possessing it; the same economic conditions will accrete the aristocrat and evolve the snob in the West that have produced them in the East; and West and East together, unless something happens to wean us from the love of money for the sake of power and station, we shall go the gait of Europe, whose political tradition we have broken with, but whose social and economical ideals we have clung to and still cling to.

[1] _Criticism and Fiction_, p. 117.

[2] _Criticism and Fiction_, p. 107.

[3] George Du Maurier (1834-96), grandfather of Daphne Du Maurier.

[4] _Criticism and Fiction_, pp. 125-127.

[5] Eliza Orne White.

November, 1890

Editor's Study.

I.

THOSE of our fellow-Aryans who have been reposing like ourselves in the comfortable belief that our race all came from a definitely described area on the plains of Asia, where its rude nonage was nurtured upon sun myths and mare's milk till it mustered strength enough to over-run Europe and supplant the primeval peoples of that continent, will be considerably shaken up by Mr. Isaac Taylor's book on the *Origin of the Aryans*. Perhaps they will be altogether shaken out of their firmest prepossessions, and will end by thinking with him that the European Aryans did not come from Asia at all, but in their several varieties were themselves the first inhabitants of the regions they now occupy; and so far from having overrun Europe from Asia, have done all their overrunning in precisely the opposite direction. Mr. Taylor, whose whole book is extremely interesting, arrives at his conclusions from a study of the facts of archæology. The inventors of the theory which he rejects, and which may be distinguished for convenience as the philological theory of the origin of the Aryans, relied almost wholly upon philology; but Mr. Taylor admits the philological evidences only where they agree with those of archæology. A conquering people often adopts the language of the vanquished, but almost never the shape of their skulls; and it is from the prehistoric skulls and their measurements that Mr. Taylor prefers to read the race of the people who did their thinking in them. Oddly enough, it appears from these in some cases that peoples of the race we call Aryan were not the puissant, always conquering invaders we have too eagerly supposed them: they were the autochthons, whom another race sometimes subjugated if not dispossessed; they were the earliest, and not the later Europeans.

II.

These conclusions are not those alone of the eminent English scholar who writes this essay on the origin of the Aryans, but are held in common with many, or indeed most, of the ablest continental students of the subject. If we understand Mr. Taylor aright, no modern-minded inquirer now accepts the theory of our race origin which was so confidently assumed and so fully accepted such a very few years ago. In view of this fact it is interesting to recur to the bold and sweeping question of the philological theory made by Mr. J. W. De Forest in a paper printed in the *Atlantic Monthly*, some time in the later seventies. Mr. De Forest based his question of that theory not upon the archæological facts accumulated by Mr. Taylor and the later scientific students, but upon the historical evidences to the contrary, and urged its total want of probability in all respects as sufficient reason for discarding it. His very entertaining and really important paper embodied the conjectures and the convictions of a keen and independent thinker, which are now gratifyingly confirmed by the investigations of scholars, but which could then have no weight with a race enamored of primordial sun myths and mare's milk, and disposed to have little patience with the bold agnostic who said there was no real proof of the invasion of Europe by the Asiatic herdsmen, but many proofs that the invasive movements of the peoples had usually been from west to east, and not from east to west. It is pleasant, however, to know that Mr. Taylor, to whose knowledge Mr. De Forest's paper has been brought since the publication of his own essay, has recognized its interest and value, and expressed his regret that it had hitherto escaped his notice and the notice of the German scholars. It was merely a logical forecast of conclusions which these *savants* have since ascertained in the scientific way, but it is worth while to remind the reader of its existence, and it is pleasant to know of Mr. Taylor's hearty acknowledgment of its importance.

III.

We have given his own theory in the barest outline, and we are aware that we have imparted little notion of the charm his book has apart from its value as a contribution to knowledge. It is a little late to recommend it as an agreeable and wholesome substitute for the great mass of summer reading among the Aryan peoples; but if some even of the ladies of that race would take it up in the first revulsion of sober thought on their return from their various leisures and vacations, they might fortify themselves for the pleasures and duties of the winter by an acquaintance with the life of the ladies of the prehistoric period. These ladies, who are for the most part only craniologically known to our time, probably assisted in the philological development of neolithic culture, but they seem to have led a less positive life than the men of our race, and archæology exhumes few traces of their usefulness. It is very likely, however, that the kitchen-middens, or bone and shell mounds of prehistoric Denmark, are monuments of their first house-keeping, when the highest dreams of domestic sanitation did not go beyond the simple act of throwing the broken victuals out into a heap beside the door of the dwelling. If this conjecture is as true as it is bold, then it is owing to the primitive efforts of woman in what the enemies of her rights insist is her heaven-appointed sphere, that the archæologist of the present is able to peruse the history of the remote past of our race. He indeed delves in the forgotten graves and determines from the size and shape of the skulls he finds whether the people who possessed the land were Aryans or not, but it is in the "relic-beds" near their long-vanished dwellings that he reads their slow, far-off approaches to our present polite condition. In these beds, resting one upon another, he finds not only the weapons and implements fashioned by men, and determines from their material the period which they belonged to, but he finds the bones of the animals which they used to feed on, and which the deft and dainty touch of woman prepared for her liege lord on his return from the chase, or the round-up of his prehistoric cattle. If these are the bones of wild animals, he knows that the people who dined on them were less advanced; and if they are the bones of domesticated creatures, that they were more so. In northern Italy he finds acorns, hazel-nuts, and cherry-stones, which primitive woman gathered for primitive man's simple desserts; or else primitive man knew the reason why. It is not to be supposed that primitive man altogether idolized primitive woman; or if he did he made his divinity pay for any failure to come up to his expectations, as primitive man does yet. She probably managed to get round him in various ways, but he had usually been at considerable pains or expense to secure her, first by going hunting for her, and bringing her in like game, and in a later age by trading for her, or buying her. Then she not only cooked for him, but sewed the skins he wore with bone needles, while he was away in the woods or pastures, or was lying round the house, fashioning flints into arrow points and spear heads, and swapping myths with the other men, and so laying the foundations of the romantic fiction, which survives in all its neolithic ingenuousness to our own day.

We say she, but we grieve to explain that the word must be taken in a plural sense, for the neolithic Aryan was generally a polygamist. His polygamy is another feature of his social life which survived till a late period in North America, (whither a branch of the race had migrated), either through the ease and frequency of divorce, or through the direct re-establishment of the institution among the inhabitants of a whole province. The custom of human sacrifice, which Mr. Taylor tells us "prevailed among the Celts in Cæsar's time, and among all the Teuton tribes," persisted to the close of the nineteenth century among the American Aryans, who began about that time to put men to death by electricity, as archæology has proved. In the relic-beds of the neoelectric period, portions of baked skulls and fragments of the metallic chairs of sacrifice were found, and the philological evidences lead to the belief that the victims were offered up to appease and propitiate the goddess Society, much worshipped in that day.

IV.

The whole chapter on neolithic culture in Mr. Taylor's book is delightful reading, and presents a most interesting example of the methods of the scientific spirit in reconstructing a probable and credible image of a past condition from its refuse heaps and immemorial charnels. As one reads, it is difficult to realize that these dismal sources of information supply nearly all the materials which the historian of the prehistoric times employs. The philological evidences he uses sparingly, and with much misgiving where the graves and the kitchen-middens and relic-beds do not corroborate them. Some of those accepted are rather picturesque, as the proof that the primitive Aryans were a pastoral people, from the fact that their only names for colors were those of the usual colors of cows: green and blue were unknown to them. They had names for only two seasons, summer and winter; the name for autumn was invented last, when the Aryans began to gather harvests, and ceased to be a purely pastoral people. Marriage was their only social institution, and the relations which result from it have names which are believed to be primitive, as father, son, daughter, sister, son-in-law and step-mother, "though they are wanting in one or more of the Aryan languages." The names for mother, brother, and father-in-law are alone "found in every branch of Aryan speech. .... The last is of especial value, as it affords a conclusive indication of the institution of marriage, and of orderly family arrangement among the undivided Aryans." Among the other "recent results of philological research, limited and corrected as they have now been by archæological discovery," are the facts that the Aryans had no property in land, but only in cattle; that they believed in a future life, but had no gods, worshipping "in some vague way the powers of nature." They had devised a decimal system from the five fingers, and could count up to a hundred. They had a name for a month, but not for a year; and the week was "not a primitive conception, the months being divided into half-months by the light half and dark half of the moon."

To the general reader nothing is more interesting, more edifying, in a study of this kind, than the curious proofs it presents of the survival of primitive customs and the reversion to them in the most recent times. The state tenure of land, which so many now regard as the true relation of a people to the soil, was practically realized among the earliest Aryans; the single-tax man of our day derives from the primeval herdsman of the remotest past; and he survives side by side with the monopolist of the syndicate variety, the latest, most precious flower of civilization.

The lake-dwellers of Switzerland advanced successively from the condition of wild huntsmen, feeding upon the game they killed, to that of shepherds and quasi-husbandmen, domesticating first the ox, then the goat, then the sheep, then the pig, last the horse. Among the neoelectric Aryans of North America those conditions were found existing chronologically side by side: the cattle king of the great plains cow-boyed his innumerable herds in the far West, while in the vast middle region of the continent the more advanced and enlightened husbandman counted his pigs (the pig came later than the ox) by millions, and supported the prosperity of the second city of the hemisphere by their multitude. At the same time a branch of the race, still in what may be called the goat epoch, pastured its domestic animals upon the tomato cans and scrap-iron in the rocky acclivities of upper New York. These goatherds dwelt in habitations little better than those of the neolithic Aryans of Britain, who lived in "pits carried down .... to a depth of from seven to ten feet," roofed with "interlaced boughs coated with clay," and

"entered by tunnels."

"The taste for fish and the art of fishing seem to have been developed at a comparatively late period," and so it is not so surprising to find both the taste and the art so widely diffused among the neoelectric Aryans of this continent. Their kitchen-middens were as rich in fish bones as those of prehistoric Denmark; whole highways were faced with oyster-shells; and there is philological proof that the recurrence of the first moon with the letter r in its name, when oysters began to be eaten after the summer fast, was a time of national rejoicing.

One of the facts which the philological theorists were surest of was that the horse was brought with them into Europe by the first Aryan immigrants from Asia. But, as Mr. Taylor shows that the Aryans did not come from Asia, it is easy to suppose that they did not bring the horse with them from Asia. "The Latin name *equus* is common to all the Aryan languages....But recent archæological discoveries have....shown that the common name must have referred to the wild horse which roamed in immense herds over Europe, and formed the chief food of the palæolithic hunters." In view of this fact the movement among a branch of the palæoelectric Gauls to return to the horse as a food is one of the most striking cases of reversion known in the life of the race. It is to be paralleled perhaps only by another reversion, but in this case it is a reversion to the primitive dress rather than diet. Scraps of linen fabrics are abundant, Mr. Taylor says, in the Swiss pile-dwellings, but "there is no sign of any garments having been fitted to the figure. The first trace of any such advance in the art of tailoring is afforded by the word 'breeks,' which, as proved by the old Irish *bracæ*, must, at the period when the Celts still inhabited central Europe, have been borrowed from the Celts by the Teutons and Slaves. No distinction seems to have been made in early times between the dress of the women and the men," and in the latest moment of the neoelectric epoch we find a distinct return, in the divided skirt of the Americans and Britons, to the epicene *bracæ* of the Celts of three or four thousand years earlier: the first tailor-made suits worn by the ladies of our race.

V.

The chapter on Neolithic Culture, which we have here been synopsizing and commentating, is by all odds the most attractive in Mr. Taylor's book; but we are by no means sure that it is the most important. Perhaps the chapter on Aryan Mythology is even more important; for if it does not deal so constructively with the matter in hand, its critical value to those who are still in the darkness of the old philological superstition must be almost incalculable. This belief embodies the doctrine that the Aryans possessed a very full if not perfect system of mythology, which they held in common from a common source. But Mr. Taylor altogether denies this. "It has been shown," he says, "that the primitive Aryans were not, as was formerly supposed, a semi-civilized race who, in the bronze period, some fifteen centuries B.C., migrated from Asia into Europe, but rather that they were the descendants of the neolithic people who occupied Europe for unnumbered ages. Can it be supposed that these rude barbarians, clad in skins, ignorant of agriculture and metals, unable to count above a hundred, who practised human sacrifice, were capable of elaborating a complex and beautiful mythology? or if they invented it is it likely that the names and adventures of dawn maidens and solar heroes could have been handed down orally in recognizable form through so many millenniums during which the art of writing was unknown?"

Mr. Taylor is rather of opinion that such myths as the Aryans can be really proved to have held in common were such as travelled from people to people by hearsay, and were not independently derived from the same remote source as the comparative mythologists assume. "Religious myths, like folk tales and popular fables, have an astonishing faculty for migration.... In any case it is clear that the conclusions which were in vogue thirty years ago as to the nature and extent of the primitive Aryan mythology are based upon assumptions as unwarranted as the theories of the successive migrations of the Aryan nations from the East."

It is not practicable to follow Mr. Taylor through the facts and reasons by which he comes to these conclusions, and we will not ask our reader to take our word that they are convincing. It will be better for him to go to the book for them, where they are open to all. The author recognizes himself that "the work of the last ten years has been mainly destructive," but at least the ground has been cleared for the true theories. "The whilom tyranny of the Sanscritists is happily overpast, and it is seen that hasty philological deductions require to be systematically checked by the conclusions of prehistoric archæology, craniology, anthropology, geology, and common-sense." The last is the qualification which most of us will think we can bring to bear upon Mr. Taylor's essay, and no one can read so far as these closing words of it without being gratefully sensible of the author's own willingness to employ it. In some sort it seems a pity to have the old theory of our origin overthrown. It was very simple, very intelligible, very portable. Any one could grasp the notion that the whole Aryan race came first from a certain spot in central Asia, and spread itself all over Europe, carrying to the different localities a common language and religion and civilization, which in the course of ages became just enough varied to require the scholarship of their polished descendants for their exploration back to the common source. This done, the affair was ended. Besides being so complete, the old theory flattered our race vanity with the attribution of antiquity and prowess and strangeness. We were a very old family, we came from far, and we possessed the land of the vanquished.

VI.

But perhaps it is right that all these comfortable considerations should be surrendered for the sake of the truth. Even in matters of fact the truth is desirable, and in science a fact is almost as valuable as a conjecture. You may have to go farther, and wait longer for it, but it seems to be better worth having.

In contemplating such a complete overturning of a long-established doctrine as Mr. Taylor offers us the spectacle of, one is reminded how much of science is still conjectural in other directions. The atomic theory is still a theory, the nebular hypothesis still a hypothesis; the missing link in the Darwinian chain is missing still. The bases of knowledge are not the rocks of fact in all cases, but are often the shifting sands of speculation; one respects, admires, the zeal and courage of the adventurers among them, but prefers to wait before going in on the ground-floor at the first proclamation of solidity. Better than science seems the scientific spirit, and after many theories and hypotheses have fallen to ruin this will remain. It is the spirit which denies nothing in wishing to prove all things; which neither grovels nor persecutes, and seeks only the truth. There was one little time not so very long ago when it seemed as if the votaries of this pure spirit were willing to erect a scientific papacy, with the Survival of the Fittest in its Vatican. But that evil moment passed, and the moral world, the world redeemed by the supreme sacrifice and suffering of every martyr, was relieved from its menace. It cannot be denied that a certain brutalization resulted from the mistaken application of that ideal. It appeared from this that the physically fittest was alone meant to survive; but a more enlightened conception modified this, and now we know that what is altogether fittest will survive.

The lesson of all this seems to be that we need not hastily surrender any long-cherished beliefs at the behest of science, which one day affirms and another denies. With science as with revelation, it is the spirit which giveth life, and the letter which kills. Yesterday we all came from Asia; this morning we perceive that we were immemorially European; to-morrow afternoon we may have dropped from the clouds. But the very errors of science teach wisdom, and the effect of the rising and falling waters of theory is to

> " carve out
> Free space for every human doubt
> That the whole mind may orb about "

in the untrammelled search for truth.

> " To swim on sunshine measureless as wind "

is what this genius of inquiry enables the soul to do in a world where the first speech that rises to the lips is in question of its mysteries. But to enjoy this precious privilege no one need abandon any belief that truly comforts or shelters him. Some dogmas indeed we must hold passively, till science has ceased to change her mind, and declares finally and forever that the world is round and moves. Till she does this in each case, and none of her votaries question her decision, we may keep our creeds intact, even those of us who find consolation and moral support in a personal devil.

---

[1] [John William De Forest], "The Cradle of the Human Race," *Atlantic Monthly*, 41 (February, 1878), 145-157.

December, 1890

Editor's Study.

I.

THE Study could scarcely believe its windows.

It knew that this was the witching Christmas-time, when, if ever, the literary spirit begins to see visions, with morals hanging to them like the tails of kites; and to dream dreams of a sovereign efficacy in reforming vicious lives.

But the Study was so strongly principled against things of this sort that it was not willing to suppose itself the scene of even the most edifying hallucination. It rubbed its large French plate panes to a crystal clearness, sacrificing the beautiful frost-work on them without scruple, and peered eagerly into the street, emptied of all business by the holiday.

II.

The change which had passed upon the world was tacit, but no less millennial. It was plainly obvious that the old order was succeeded by the new; that the former imperfect republic of the United States of America had given place to the ideal commonwealth, the Synthetized Sympathies of Altruria. The spectacle was all the more interesting because this was clearly the first Christmas since the establishment of the new status.

The Study at once perceived that what it beheld from its windows was politically only a partial expression of the general condition; that the Synthetized Sympathies formed a province of the Federation of the World, represented by a delegation eager to sacrifice their selfish interests in the Parliament of Man, but was not by any means the centre of things. The fact was not flattering to the Study's patriotic pride, but upon reflection the Study was aware of a supreme joy in not having its patriotic pride flattered.

Every aspect of "this new world which was the old" attracted the Study, but being a literary Study, and not a political or economical Study, its interest was soon centred in the literary phases of the millennial epoch. These were of every possible character, and their variety was so great that it was instantly evident how hopeless it would be to note them all.

But one thing that struck the Study with peculiar force was the apparent reconciliation of all the principles once supposed antagonistic, the substitution of emulation for rivalry, the harmonization of personal ambitions in a sweet accord of achievement for the common good. It was not exactly the weather for floral displays, but among the festive processions which poured into the public square under the Study's windows was one of Dramatic Critics wreathed with rose-buds, and led in flowery chains by a laughing band of Playwrights, who had captured these rugged natures, and had then persuaded them to see that they could themselves hope to live only by uniting with the playwrights in the endeavor for the beautiful. The critics had been taught to realize that if they kept on killing off the playwrights at the old rate they would soon have no plays to write about, and must themselves starve to death. The playwrights had first appealed to their instinct of self-preservation, and had then convinced their reason that they had no hope but in recognizing and fostering the good in our infant drama, and that one critic who perceived this was much greater than the aggregate of many who could not.

From time to time the procession paused to allow the critics and playwrights to clasp hands and publicly avow a lasting friendship. After them came in long file the Literary Critics, accompanied each by the poet, novelist, historian, or essayist whom he had most deeply injured, and to whom he was linked by a band of violets. The Study understood that these flowers were chosen by the critics themselves, out of all the products of the vegetable kingdom, as best expressive of the critics' modest and shrinking character. They paced with downcast eyes, and were every few steps openly overcome by the honor of walking in those fragrant bands with Creative Authors. These encouraged and supported them, and when the critics would have gone down before them and acknowledged their inferiority and unworthiness, the Creative Authors would not suffer it, but consoled them with the assurance that they too had their uses in the literary world, in noting and classifying its phenomena, and that their former arrogance and presumption would not be counted against them, now they were truly penitent. Each of the critics bore his name and that of the journal he wrote for distinctly inscribed on a badge worn over his heart.

Suddenly, on the flank of this friendly troop of authors and critics, there appeared at no great distance two figures. The first was that of an extremely decrepit old man, dressed to a fantastic youthfulness, with his hair and beard washed to a saffron tint that was not in the least golden. His costume was out of the rag-bag of all epochs, and on his head he wore a wreath of paper flowers.

The other was armed as to his head in a huge helmet like that of the *secutor* who fights with the *retiarius* in the Roman arena, and his face was completely hidden; his body was covered with a suit of scale armor, as the Study at first imagined; to learn later that the scales were a natural expression of the wearer's serpentine nature. Instead of a sword he carried a repeating rifle in his hand, and from time to time he dropped a panel of tall fence from his shoulder to the ground, and crouching behind it fired at some author in the procession.

Horrified at this outrage, which no one seemed inclined to interfere with, the Study threw up one of its windows, and called to a boy who was passing on the pavement below: he proved to be the very boy whom Old Scrooge sent to buy the turkey when he woke from his fearful dream and found it was nothing but a dream.

"Our good boy," said the Study, finding the vocative of the editorial plural absurd, but clinging to it with its well-known fondness for tradition—"Our good boy, will you tell us what is the meaning of that abominable person's behavior in firing into the procession? Is he a Pinkerton man, and does he mistake it for a parade of strikers? Who is he, anyway, and that grotesque simulacrum with him?"

"Those fellows?" asked the boy. "Oh! the one in front is the Last of the Romanticists, telling the same old story; and the other is the Anonymous Critic, firing blank-cartridges at authors. It's Christmas, you know, and they let the poor old fellows out to amuse themselves."

"Is that all?" said the Study, immensely relieved. "Well, we see no objection to that. But what is that curious structure there in the centre of the place?"

The Study now indicated a monumental object which had for the first time caught its notice. At first glance it was not easy to determine the character of

this pile, but upon closer scrutiny it turned out to be a mighty heap of books of all sizes and shapes, but mostly those cheap paper editions of foreign authors with which we have become familiarized and perhaps corrupted a little.

The boy looked up at the open Study window, and said, "Well, it would take a little time to explain, and I'd have to wait for the procession of the Visiting Authors, anyway." He seemed anxious to be gone; but the Study, piqued by that phrase Visiting Authors, implored him to stop a moment longer.

"Why that's Mount Restitution," said the boy, and he started on.

The Study called after him, "We will give you a quarter if you will tell us just what you mean."

"Oh, no!" said the boy coming back. "You can't work that old racket on me, if I *am* a boy. If you want me to tell you willingly, you've got to let *me* give *you* something first."

"Oh," said the Study, considerably mystified. "Is that the new order of things? Well?" But it had hardly got the word out before it was aware of having a quarter thrown in through its open window upon its tessellated marble floor.

"Now," said the boy, "as it's bitter cold, and I'm on an errand that I sha'n't get anything for if I don't hurry, I shall be glad to stop here at great personal inconvenience and explain this little matter; though where you've been, not to know all about it already, *I* can't make out. You remember when the last international copyright bill failed because Congress decided that our people must have cheap books, by fair means or foul?"

"Yes," the Study assented with a pang of shame; and it controlled an impulse to shut its window, and curtain itself from the light of day.

"You know Congress did this repeatedly, time after time?"

"Alas, yes!" sighed the Study.

"Well, the last time people began to understand that if it was a sin and a shame to take the work of foreign authors from them, and not pay them anything for it, Congress had made it the *national* sin and shame. It was no use pretending any longer that it was the wicked publishers did it, and howling 'pirate' after them. If there was any pirate about it, the pirate was the whole American people, for they had said through Congress, over and over again, that it was right to take the work of foreign authors, or if it was not right, then it was cheap, and they were going to do it anyway."

"We see," groaned the Study. "Go on."

"But the last time the new arrangement to have the whole people vote on every bill of general interest that passed

Congress had come in—"

"*New* arrangement!" cried the Study. "Why, Switzerland had it away back in the nineteenth century."

"Well, we didn't get it till toward the end of the twentieth," said the boy.

"Why, it *is* the twentieth century!" the Study reflected, taking note of the fact for the first time.

"I should think so," said the boy. He spoke throughout this interview in the crowing treble of typical boys with a sarcastic turn of mind, and we need not say that the Study employed the falsetto affected by all amiable old gentlemen in the Christmas stories.

"Well, as soon as they could get the international copyright bill submitted to the people, it was unanimously adopted. The pirates themselves voted for it; even the Congressmen did. They said they had been laboring under a misapprehension. The first Fourth of July after that was the greatest Fourth that ever was. The people said they had declared their independence of Great Britain over again when they would not take English books without paying for them."

"Wasn't that rather fine?" the Study suggested.

"Yes, it was," said the boy. "And then they passed a joint resolution to build this monument to commemorate international copyright. Somebody thought it would be a good thing to build it of pirated editions, so as to show how big the wrong had been, and to keep the people in mind of it, and prevent anything like it from ever happening again. It's pretty high, isn't it?"

The pile seemed to swell and soar as the Study gazed. "It is, indeed. We should think that in favorable states of the atmosphere it could be seen from the planet Mars. It's grand," the Study added, with a curious patriotic pride in such a colossal witness of the national wrongdoing. "We don't suppose there was ever anything like it in the world before. But what has it to do with the Visiting Authors?"

"Oh, I forgot," answered the boy, who was starting off. "It was decided by a Popular Impulse—"

"Popular Impulse?" queried the Study, with an instant perception of the capital letters.

"That's what they call a national decision that needn't be put to a vote. And it was decided by a Popular Impulse that the foreign authors should visit us every Christmas morning, and get their annual royalty from the Treasury of the Synthetized Sympathies."

"We should have thought the publishers would have paid them!" said the Study.

"So they do, for their new books," answered the boy. "But the royalty from the S. S. Treasury is a voluntary restitution by our whole people of the money kept from them in the past. It's purely an affair of honor. There's no law about it. A law can't be retroactive, you know."

"No," the Study admitted. "But how do our native authors like the new status?"

"Oh, *they* like it. As soon as we began to pay the foreigners it shut out the worthless foreign books, and when our authors were freed from that sort of competition, they began to get rich. They all keep their carriages now; they keep them at home. You won't see them driving in them. They've gone half-way to meet the Visiting Authors."

"Half-way?" gasped the Study.

"Yes. Submarine pneumatic tube, you know. The visitors have to be home for breakfast."

"Oh! Yes, yes!" said the Study, ashamed to betray its ignorance.

III.

The Study now observed that the authors and critics had all disappeared from the square, and that the Last of the Romanticists and the Anonymous Critic were poking about in its emptiness in a forlorn and aimless manner. The Romanticist sank down on the curb-stone and fell asleep with his head dropped between his knees; his paper-flower wreath tumbled into the gutter. The Anonymous Critic removed his helmet and revealed his death's-head; he took out a black buccaneer's flag from the helmet and wiped the perspiration from his skull. "Hot work," he said, looking round for the boy.

But even the boy had vanished; and now the square was given up to a series of allegorical interludes. The first of these was the Identification of the Real and the Ideal. The two principles appeared hand in hand, like Tweedledum and Tweedledee in *Through the Looking-glass*, and at once began their great transformation act, by passing into and out of each other with such lightning-like rapidity that they were soon no longer distinguishable. The moment this result had been accomplished, an electric transparency appeared above the consolidation with the legend, *Which is which?* The Romanticist continued to sleep audibly, and the Anonymous Critic said, "Give it up." Then the Real and the Ideal bowed together, and separately withdrew.

The True and The Beautiful now entered the square together, and performed their famous *pas seul à deux*. This was not so difficult as it seems when put in words; for The True and The Beautiful are one and the same; only The True is the one, and The Beautiful is the same. They faced the Study windows first as The True, and after performing their dance in that character, wheeled half round and appeared as The Beautiful, in the manner of the person who used to dance as the soldier and the sailor on the stage. Over their head flashed out the words, "Beauty is truth, truth beauty."

The Anonymous Critic read the legend aloud, and then murmured vindictively, "Keats! I did for *him* pretty thoroughly, anyway."

"Oh, no!" the Study retorted. "You did your worst, but after all you didn't kill Keats. You hurt him, but he took you very philosophically, at a time when you were very much more regarded than you are now."

It is the nature of the Anonymous Critic not to be able to bear the slightest contradiction. He raised his weapon and immediately fired a blank-cartridge at the Study windows, putting on his helmet at the same time to avoid recognition. The report woke the Last of the Romanticists, who scrambled to his feet, exclaiming, "Saved, saved! They are saved at last!"

"Who are saved?" asked the Study, with unbroken windows.

"The good old-fashioned hero and heroine. Didn't you hear the minute-gun at sea? He arrived with his raft just as her bark was sinking. He fired one shot, and the miscreant relaxed his hold from her fainting form, and fell a corpse at her feet. The sharp clap of thunder, preceded by a blinding flash, revealed the path they had lost, and they stood at the castle gate. The retainers joined in a shout that made the welkin ring, and the brave cow-boy rode into their midst with the swooning châtelaine on him, while the Saracens and Apaches discharged a shower of arrows, and then fled in all directions. That shot, which proclaimed the suicide of the gambler, in order to give his body for food to the starving companions he had fleeced in the snow-bound Sierras, was the death-knell of the commonplace. Here they come, dying for each other! Ah, that is something *like*! What abundant action! What nobility of motive! What incessant self-sacrifice! No analysis *there*!"

The Study could never understand exactly how it was managed, but in the antics of the fantastic couple who now appeared it was somehow expressed that the youth was perpetually winning the maiden by deeds of the greatest courage and the most unnecessary and preposterous goodness, while the maiden enacted the rôle of the slave at once of duty and of love. When she was not wildly throwing herself into her lover's arms, she was

letting him marry another girl, though she knew it would make him unhappy, because she believed the other girl wanted him.

"Ah," sighed the Anonymous Critic, "*there* is profound knowledge of the heart for you! What poetry! What passion!"

Nevertheless he had the air of being extremely bored by the spectacle before him. Several times he took aim at the hero and heroine, and he would probably have fired, if the Visiting Authors had not suddenly appeared upon the scene, attended by their friends, the native authors of Altruria. The Study looked round for the explanatory boy, but he was nowhere to be seen. However, it perceived that he was not necessary to an understanding of the simple affair before it. "Only," it soliloquized, "it's a pity he should have given us this quarter for almost nothing."

Of course it could not be expected that the foreign authors, who were mostly English, should all take their repayment from the S. S. Treasury graciously. They said, with the frankness of their nation where disagreeable things are concerned, some very disagreeable things, and they thought they ought to have interest on the moneys so long withheld. The Altrurian authors could not deny the justice of their claim, while they regretted its spirit. Some of them sent home and sold their carriages, in order to satisfy it; they never used their carriages, anyway, to avoid wounding the susceptibilities of the lawyers, doctors, brokers, and merchants who had none. But not all the foreign authors received their back royalties so greedily; some of them accepted the restitution as cordially as it was offered; and it was affecting to see the surprise mingled with pleasure in the countenances of the widows and orphans of certain authors who had died without the sight of this supreme act of national atonement. They had not expected to be included in the restitution, but the agents of the S. S. Treasury (all chosen by emulative examination, and regardless of party ties) held that a debt of honor must be paid to the remotest heirs of the creditor, and these widows and orphans received their just share. Some of them were enriched beyond the dreams of avarice, but there were other cases in which authors who had supposed themselves plundered by the extensive sales in this country, were disappointed by the showing from their publishers' books. These, however, were consoled by the appearance of the pirates in a state of total bankruptcy.

The whole ceremony of restitution had taken place in less time than we have employed to describe it, and the Visiting Authors had gone home to breakfast. There was a sort of simultaneity about all the occurrences in Altruria that struck the Study very agreeably; no sooner was a good thing thought of than it was done. This was especially the case with the proposition to fire the pile of pirated editions, in order to light the Visiting Authors on their way back through the submarine pneumatic tube.

The Creative Authors and the Critics embraced in the genial glow, and a Congressman, who had been one of the bitterest opponents of international copyright, arose and said that he wished to signalize a change of heart he had undergone, by proposing Perpetual Copyright. He said that he did not see why a man should not have as lasting property in something he had actually created, like a book, as in something he had simply come by in the way of trade, perhaps honestly, perhaps dishonestly. During his arguments, which were unanswerable, the Creative Authors remained modestly silent, but when he sat down, the Critics burst into such a roar of applause that the Study awoke.

Of course it had been dreaming. It was Christmas-time, when allegorical visions are almost unavoidable.

---

¹Howells' The Shadow of a Dream was published June 7, 1890, about three months before the writing of this installment. A Traveler from Altruria was not published until May 28, 1894.

January, 1891

Editor's Study.

I.

Following the Guidon, by Mrs. Elizabeth B. Custer, and *Campaigning with Crook*, by Captain Charles King, are two recent books which are almost as distinctly related as if the second had been written to succeed the first; but of course their relation is purely accidental. As a matter of fact Mrs. Custer's book is the revision of old scenes in the twilight of pathetic memory, and Captain King's is a compilation of sketches written for a Milwaukee newspaper some years after the Indian campaign of 1876; but it happens that this campaign was undertaken after that which closed so tragically with the death of General Custer, and the historical sequence from one volume to the other is unbroken. One cannot read either without feeling afresh the grotesque and cruel absurdity of our Indian policy. This is especially apparent in Captain King's vivid sketch of the encounter of our troops with the Cheyennes who had left their reservation to join the Sioux butchers of Custer and his men. The Cheyennes were surprised in their advance, and after a sharp fight they were turned back. But as soon as the United States forces had driven these idiotic murderers within the lines of their reservation, where the United States authorities had provisioned and armed them for their foray, the United States forces were unable to follow and punish them, because they were then again under the protection of the United States authorities. Nothing could be more maddeningly ridiculous than such a situation, and it is no wonder that a thrill of indignation runs through Captain King's whole story of Crook's campaign. The narrative tingles with an outraged sense of the fatuity of respecting their tribal condition, and regarding them at once as wards and enemies. This anomaly seems at last to be reaching an end; but such books as these two make one impatient for the time when it will be little less than incredible that the Indians should have ever been treated otherwise than in severalty.

II.

Another effect of these volumes, which in such singular degree acquaint us with the intimate life of our army, is the lesson in conduct which they teach. Mrs. Custer's book imparts the more fully the charm of that life, on the side of its brotherly devotion and kindliness, its community of feeling and interest, and solidarity of ideal. Her picture is lit up with abundance of amusing incident, and of hardship and inconvenience gayly borne. There is the play, all through it, of the humor that every American knows more or less how to smooth and soften insoluble difficulties with, and that her hero, who is forever the nation's hero, used up to the very moment of charging an enemy. No one can know General Custer as he ought to be known to every grateful American, without this witness to his *bonhomie*, his cheery good sense, his love of a harmless laugh; and the sketch of Mrs. Custer's experience in shanty and tent and bivouac, ought to endear him to all women. It is with delicate mastery that she portrays the details of a situation which was always rude, and sometimes squalid in details, and makes you feel how perfectly delightful it was to the heart and soul even of a house-keeper in all that really makes life worth while. The jest with which the general, re-enforced by his brother the colonel, tenderly laughed away a thousand fears and anxieties that beset the young wife in the camp and on the march, and turned all present danger and perplexity into matter of future merriment, is intimated with a fine intelligence that can be known only at first-hand. The delightful record is all the more winning because of the shadow which coming events cast upon it; the lightest and gladdest incident is touched with a pathetic meaning. But the immediate significance of it is that life is happy and worthy in proportion to its cares and trials, if these are genuine, and are not the factitious cares and trials of

> "luxury straining her low thought
> To form unreal wants."

Women delicately bred and accustomed to all the elegancies and flatteries of society, welcomed cheerfully if not eagerly the rough sincerities of an existence stripped to the barest necessities or the simplest adequacies, and gladly shared the hard heroic condition of men whose ideal was duty. In the army, with its vague and few and distant rewards, there may be and there are rivalries in devotion and daring, but there is no competition for place and money as there is in civil life; and yet the soldiers' ideal being duty, the performance of duty seems sufficient. It is a state of things which can suggest much to those who are fond of baffling the hope of better things in us with the assertion that it is contrary to human nature to act from any but interested and selfish motives. Human nature is a great mystery, and we have not yet begun to solve it; but it appears that a number of men drawn at random from society, and trained to a belief in duty as the chief good, will keep on not only living it but dying it. We civilians talk much, we almost talk solely, of our rights, but in the army it seems that men talk chiefly of their duties, when they talk at all, and never of their rights. These things are true of all ranks; the ideal is the same from the private to the general, and it seems to correct all the mistaken tendencies of the time before they became soldiers.

If, as Ruskin has fancied, the army should ever serve us as the norm of the civil state, and we should come to have "soldiers of the ploughshare as well as soldiers of the sword," it might not be long before we should be told that it was against human nature to act selfishly, and that to be recreant to the general welfare in any aim or deed was to be guilty of conduct unbecoming a citizen and a gentleman. However this may be, it is certain and it is significant that those who have attempted to dream out a future brighter than this present have always had something like a military organization in their eyes; but these visionaries have somehow beheld little of the gayety and enjoyment which are quite as compatible with the performance of duties as with the assertion of rights. Here again Captain King's book, and still more Mrs. Custer's book, can teach us something, and can make us see the sort of jovial and kindly intimacy into which people are thrown who are bound by common obligations to self-sacrifice, and how much fun can be got out of giving up one's own comforts and interests. It is not only the dying for one's country— that is, for all the unknown brotherhood —which is sweet and fit; it is also the endurance of a thousand little discomforts, inconveniences, and perplexities, which we groan over and swear at when we bear them for ourselves, but which Crook's men and Custer's men joked over and laughed at when they bore them for others.

III.

The sense of this important and suggestive fact is what gives their highest charm to Mr. Rudyard Kipling's studies of English army life in India; those, we mean, that are not records of the robust flirtations in which battered cantonment coquettes lead tender subalterns captive. In one of the later sketches, where he deals with the honors paid a literary man, a noted novelist, by some young army men among whom accident throws him, the different simplicity of the military and the literary life, the young officers' subtle perception of the old author's subtlety, and their mutual respect and kindliness, are valuable facts delicately and truly felt. What strikes and most mystifies the author in these young soldiers, who are so very young as to seem almost boys to him, is their devotion to duty unmixed with fear or selfishness of any sort; and the hope that it suggests to the reader is the same that so often arises in him from the facts of Mrs. Custer's book and Captain King's book: the hope of a final perfectibility of human nature in the direction where it has appeared so hopeless that those who have ventured even to ask if it might not be bettered have worn the character of dangerous agitators to the eye of after-dinner economists.

A kindred spirit, the spirit of men expected to do their duty because it is their duty, and not because it is the means to success or the way to glory, is what gives meaning to that vivid allegory of Indian service which Mr. Kipling calls "The Galley-Slave." It seems to us on the whole the strongest and best poem in his volume of *Departmental Ditties and Other Verses*, with its intense colors of feeling, and dazzling successes of phrase and rhythm, though there are two fine sonnets depictive of the summer's stressful presence and winter's coming in India, and there are some passages of serious beauty in certain of the ironies and satires of the local economic and social conditions.

There is no allegory about "The Grave of the Hundred Dead," but a grim, naked, ugly truth to what Tolstoï calls "the spirit of the army" turned demon in the breasts of the native soldiery; and we commend the piece to those who would know more of the poet's picturesque force. It is like a painting of Verestchagin's.

IV.

The strange *Poems of Emily Dickinson* we think will form something like an intrinsic experience with the understanding reader of them. They have been edited by Mrs. Mabel Loomis Todd, who was a personal friend of the poet, and by Colonel T. W. Higginson, who was long her epistolary and literary acquaintance, but only met her twice. Few people met her so often, as the reader will learn from Colonel Higginson's interesting preface, for her life was mainly spent in her father's house at Amherst, Massachusetts; she seldom passed its doors, and never, for many years, passed the gates of its grounds. There is no hint of what turned her life in upon itself, and probably this was its natural evolution, or involution, from tendencies inherent in the New England, or the Puritan, spirit. We are told that once a year she met the local world at a reception in her father's house; we do not know that there is any harm in adding, that she did not always literally meet it, but sometimes sat with her face averted from the company in another room. One of her few friends was Helen Hunt Jackson, whom she suffered to send one of her poems to be included in the volume of anonymous pieces which Messrs. Roberts Brothers once published with the title of *A Masque of Poets*. Whether the anonymity flattered her love of obscurity or not, it is certain that her darkling presence in this book was the occasion of her holding for many years a correspondence with its publishers. She wrote them, as the fancy took her, comments on their new books, and always enclosed a scrap of her verse, though without making any reference to it. She never intended or allowed anything more from her pen to be printed in her lifetime; but it was evident that she wished her poetry finally to meet the eyes of that world which she had herself always shrunk from. She could not have made such poetry without knowing its rarity, its singular worth; and no doubt it was a radiant happiness in the twilight of her hidden, silent life.

The editors have discharged their delicate duty toward it with unimpeachable discretion, and Colonel Higginson has said so many apt things of her work in his introduction, that one who cannot differ with him must be vexed a little to be left so little to say. He speaks of her "curious indifference to all conventional rules of verse," but he adds that "when a thought takes one's breath away, a lesson on grammar seems an impertinence." He notes "the quality suggestive of the poetry of William Blake" in her, but he leaves us the chance to say that it is a Blake who had read Emerson who had read Blake. The fantasy is as often Blakian as the philosophy is Emersonian; but after feeling this again and again, one is ready to declare that the utterance of this most singular and authentic spirit would have been the same if there had never been an Emerson or a Blake in the world. She sometimes suggests Heine as much as either of these; all three in fact are spir-

itually present in some of the pieces; yet it is hardly probable that she had read Heine, or if she had, would not have abhorred him.

Here is something that seems compact of both Emerson and Blake, with a touch of Heine too:

I taste a liquor never brewed,
From tankards scooped in pearl;
Not all the vats upon the Rhine
Yield such an alcohol!

Inebriate of air am I,
And debauchee of dew,
Reeling, through endless summer days,
From inns of molten blue.

When landlords turn the drunken bee
Out of the foxglove's door,
When butterflies renounce their drams,
I shall but drink the more!

Till seraphs swing their snowy hats,
And saints to windows run,
To see the little tippler
Leaning against the sun!

But we believe it is only seeming; we believe these things are as wholly her own as this:

The bustle in a house
The morning after death
Is solemnest of industries
Enacted upon earth,—

The sweeping up the heart,
And putting love away
We shall not want to use again
Until eternity.

Such things could have come only from a woman's heart to which the experiences in a New England town have brought more knowledge of death than of life. Terribly unsparing many of these strange poems are, but true as the grave and certain as mortality. The associations of house-keeping in the following poem have a force that drags us almost into the presence of the poor, cold, quiet thing:

"TROUBLED ABOUT MANY THINGS."
How many times these low feet staggered,
Only the soldered mouth can tell;
Try! can you stir the awful rivet?
Try! can you lift the hasps of steel?

Stroke the cool forehead, hot so often,
Lift, if you can, the listless hair;
Handle the adamantine fingers
Never a thimble more shall wear.

Buzz the dull flies on the chamber window;
Brave shines the sun through the freckled pane;
Fearless the cobweb swings from the ceiling—
Indolent housewife, in daisies lain!

Then in this, which has no name—how could any phrase nominate its weird witchery aright?—there is the flight of an eerie fancy that leaves all experience behind:

I died for beauty, but was scarce
Adjusted in the tomb,
When one who died for truth was lain
In an adjoining room.

He questioned softly why I failed.
"For beauty," I replied.
"And I for truth,—the two are one;
We brethren are," he said.

And so, as kinsmen met a night,
We talked between the rooms,
Until the moss had reached our lips,
And covered up our names.

All that Puritan longing for sincerity, for veracious conduct, which in some good New England women's natures is almost a hysterical shriek, makes its exultant grim assertion in these lines:

REAL.

I like a look of agony,
Because I know it's true;
Men do not sham convulsion,
Nor simulate a throe.

The eyes glaze once, and that is death.
Impossible to feign
The beads upon the forehead
By homely anguish strung.

These mortuary pieces have a fascination above any others in the book; but in the stanzas below there is a still, solemn, rapt movement of the thought and music together that is of exquisite charm:

New feet within my garden go,
New fingers stir the sod;
A troubadour upon the elm
Betrays the solitude.

New children play upon the green,
New weary sleep below;
And still the pensive spring returns,
And still the punctual snow!

This is a song that sings itself; and this is another such, but thrilling with the music of a different passion:

SUSPENSE.

Elysium is as far as to
The very nearest room,
If in that room a friend await
Felicity or doom.

What fortitude the soul contains,
That it can so endure
The accent of a coming foot,
The opening of a door!

The last poem is from the group which the editors have named "Love"; the other groups from which we have been quoting are "Nature," and "Time and Eternity"; but the love poems are of the same piercingly introspective cast as those differently named. The same force of imagination is in them; in them, as in the rest, touch often becomes clutch. In them love walks on heights he seldom treads, and it is the heart of full womanhood that speaks in the words of this nun-like New England life.

Few of the poems in the book are long, but none of the short, quick impulses of intense feeling or poignant thought can be called fragments. They are each a compassed whole, a sharply finished point, and there is evidence, circumstantial and direct, that the author spared no pains in

the perfect expression of her ideals. Nothing, for example, could be added that would say more than she has said in four lines:

Presentiment is that long shadow on the lawn
Indicative that suns go down;
The notice to the startled grass
That darkness is about to pass.

Occasionally, the outside of the poem, so to speak, is left so rough, so rude, that the art seems to have faltered. But there is apparent to reflection the fact that the artist meant just this harsh exterior to remain, and that no grace of smoothness could have imparted her intention as it does. It is the soul of an abrupt, exalted New England woman that speaks in such brokenness. The range of all the poems is of the loftiest; and sometimes there is a kind of swelling lift, an almost boastful rise of feeling, which is really the spring of faith in them:

I never saw a moor,
I never saw the sea;
Yet know I how the heather looks,
And what a wave must be.

I never spoke with God,
Nor visited in heaven;
Yet certain am I of the spot
As if the chart were given.

There is a noble tenderness, too, in some of the pieces; a quaintness that does not discord with the highest solemnity:

I shall know why, when time is over,
And I have ceased to wonder why;
Christ will explain each separate anguish
In the fair school-room of the sky.

He will tell me what Peter promised,
And I, for wonder at his woe,
I shall forget the drop of anguish
That scalds me now, that scalds me now.

The companionship of human nature with inanimate nature is very close in certain of the poems; and we have never known the invisible and intangible ties binding all creation in one, so nearly touched as in them.

V.

If nothing else had come out of our life but this strange poetry we should feel that in the work of Emily Dickinson America, or New England rather, had made a distinctive addition to the literature of the world, and could not be left out of any record of it; and the interesting and important thing is that this poetry is as characteristic of our life as our business enterprise, our political turmoil, our demagogism, our millionairism. "Listen!" says Mr. James McNeill Whistler in that "Ten o'Clock" lecture of his which must have made his hearers feel very much lectured indeed, not to say browbeaten, —"Listen! There never was an artistic period. There never was an art-loving nation." But there were moments and there were persons to whom art was dear, and Emily Dickinson was one of these persons, one of these moments in a national life, and she could as well happen in Amherst, Mass., as in Athens, Att.

Some such thing we understand Mr. Whistler to teach us in those dazzling fireworks of his which scale the heavens as stars, and come down javelins on the heads and breasts of his enemies. Art arose because some artist was born with the need of beautifying the useful, and other men used the beautiful things he created while they were off killing and tilling, because there were no others to use when they got back: they *had* to drink out of decorated cups and dwell in noble palaces.

The explanation is very simple and in a way satisfying; and we commend that lecture of Mr. Whistler's above anything else in the queer volume he calls *The Gentle Art of Making Enemies*. This art scarcely deserved so much study as is there given it. To make enemies is perfectly easy; the difficult thing is to keep them; the first you know they are no longer hating you, they are not even thinking of you. That seems to deprive Mr. Whistler's controversial sarcasms of importance; to leave them faded, as they were already ephemeral. Any author can test the fact in his own case. Read a bitter censure of your book the morning it is printed, and the world is filled with it forever; read it next month, and there never was anything of it.

---

[1] Vasili Vasilievich Vereshchagin (1842-1904) was a Russian genre and battle painter.

[2] George Parsons Lathrop, ed., A Masque of Poets (Boston: Roberts Brothers, 1878).

February, 1891

Editor's Study.

I.

IF Messrs. Nicolay and Hay needed any justification or defence for the proportions which the biography of Abraham Lincoln took in their hands, they [1] could find it in the words of that other greatest American, who said, "He is the true history of the American people in his time." But they do not need these [2] words of Emerson to account for the growth of their work to the ten generous volumes which seem at last to have compassed it, and no more. The narrative is a continually expanding stream which leaves its source at the dim beginning of our annals, and winds its way with broader and broader glimpses of all the bordering facts and conditions till it swells into the sea of national life, and becomes for a time the main which all tributary streams enter and are lost in. But if it had been from the opening to the closing passage simply and strictly the story of Abraham Lincoln, what he said and did, what he thought and was, we should not have censured it for its length, or found it too much. It is his life, his character, his personality, which gives a final charm to the masses and details of fact wherever they seem little, or loosely, or not at all, related to him, and the outcome if not the progress of the history is biographical. Its persons are made to live in the reader's thoughts; their experiences become part of him; it achieves by the simplest means the result which history mostly fails of, insomuch that if we cannot say that we wish history might always be written like it, we are quite ready to say that we would on no account have had this history written otherwise. The authors were most familiarly, if not most intimately associated with the man from whose story their names cannot hereafter be dissociated; and it is as if they had instinctively told it as he would have wished it told. It is informal to the last degree, but never undignified; it is plain, but never common; and it is in style and in method as far as can be from all other histories of our time. We are not so conversant with Mr. Nicolay's manner as

with Mr. Hay's, but we have seldom been able to assure ourselves that this or that episode was from one or other of the joint authors. Their sacrifice to their task has been complete; they have not merely not wished to distinguish themselves in it, but they have not tried to distinguish themselves from each other. Every part of the immense accumulation of material has been assimilated by the two writers, but the form of its reproduction is so impersonal that it seems as if the facts had made their own record, as if the Nation and the Man had here told their own story in their own way. It does not lessen, it heightens the illusion that the matter often utters itself in divers tones of never unkindly irony: that is the surface mood of America, it was the surface mood of Lincoln, and it does not discord with the deeply underlying earnest in the theme. But nothing of the effect which is so satisfyingly appropriate can be accidental; it must be the result of long-studied and well-counselled intention; and we can be glad of the greatest biography of Lincoln not only as the most important work yet accomplished in American history, but as one of the noblest achievements of literary art: the art which is never noble, but always trivial and base when it is sundered from the service of truth and humanity.

II.

Looking back over the whole course of the narrative, the most interesting thing to note is how gradually yet inevitably Lincoln grew to a national proportion, until at his death he stood so completely for his country that without him it may be said that his country would have had no adequate expression. If America means anything at all, it means the sufficiency of the common, the insufficiency of the uncommon. It is the affirmation in political terms of the Christian ideal, which when we shall affirm it in economical and social terms will make us the perfect state; and Lincoln was the earliest, if he is not yet the only American, to realize in his office the divine purport of the mandate, " Is any first among you? Let him be your servant." He had a just ambition, and a just pride in duty well done, and a just hope of gratitude and recognition; but all these motives sank into abeyance, and may be said not to have governed his action, which was ruled simply by the desire to serve to his best ability the people who had set him over them. If it were not for the record, this long tale of what he bore and did, his patience with every manner of wilfulness and weakness, vanity and arrogance, wickedness and stupidity, would be incredible. His one desire to get the best out of himself, seems to have taught him how to get the best out of others, and he cast no man aside while there was even the hope of any good in him. There is no more signal example of this fact than his treatment of McClellan; and we might almost say that in no other passages of his history is the character of Lincoln made so fully known as in those which give the tragedy of that immeasurable disappointment. A color of his magnanimous patience characterizes the judgment of his historians; they do justice to McClellan's good qualities and his finally unimpeachable patriotism; and they recognize that what Lincoln was hopelessly contending with in the man was not a vice or a crime, but an incurable temperament.

Very possibly the situation has been portrayed before, but we have not been given so perfect a sense, before, of the attitude which Lincoln kept throughout the war, between his people and his generals, until Grant came to his relief. In the mirror which is now held up to that great, unhappy time we see Lincoln, diffident of his own skill in war craft, urging the military leaders on in the way which was the right way, and continually thwarted by their delay, their error, or their disobedience, while keeping back their civil censors, and bearing with superhuman patience their blame for not satisfying the longing for action that was rending his own heart. It is a wonderful spectacle in the plain daylight now thrown upon it, but not more wonderful than the less dramatic spectacle of Lincoln's position in his own political household, with the rivalries of Seward and Chase in latent or overt contention about him. When both of these really great statesmen and really unselfish patriots one day resigned, and Lincoln prevailed on them both to come back into the cabinet, he found relief in the humorous sarcasm, "I can ride easy now; I've got a pumpkin in each end of the bag."

III.

The humor of Lincoln was, like that of most great humorists, the break of an intense and profound seriousness. Its sunny flash caught the eye more than the solemn depths from which it rose, and his biographers make something like a protest against the exaggerated popular estimate of it. This is very well, but it will not avail. There is a sort of tricksy caprice, a whim like a woman's, which fixes the popular estimate of all things, and which no reasoning can change. It is this, apparently, which has chosen the Gettysburg Address to pre-eminent fame out of all the beautiful and perfect things that Lincoln has written and said. Something in the supreme occasion, in the matchless worth of the main thoughts, and in the very quality of haste evident in it, consecrates it to the first place in the memory of the people, and it would be both perilous and futile to attempt to replace it with any other words even of the same man. What surprises, what astonishes, one in a critical examination of his words at all times, almost from the first use he makes of written words, is his artistic sense of them. Here, indeed, is something like the operation of genius, of the thing that we are so many of us eager to substitute for consciousness. It is as if Lincoln were so deeply concerned with what he was thinking that he did not know how electly he was saying it. But we believe it would be a mistake to suppose this; we believe that this man, without any scholarly training, had schooled himself, had trained himself, to the study of expression, till he felt through all his consciousness the beauty of simplicity, that last and farthest grace, and till it became his second nature to use the right word in the right place, so that he could not have erred without the pain the artist knows when any vocable rings false.

Literary men are somewhat beclouded by the traditions of the shop, in their view of literature. They think it is somehow peculiarly the affair, the product of literary men; and it is good and very wholesome for them to realize that it is by no means entirely so, or perhaps more than partly so. It is not literary men who give it even its most delicate or penetrating subtlety; and there are many other sorts of men who endue it with nobleness and strength. We were thinking as we read many passages quoted in this life of Lincoln from jurists and statesmen, and mere politicians, what a high level of literature was struck by these other sorts of men whenever they had something important to say; and more than ever we rebelled against the notion that good literature is solely the effect of literary culture. In fact his learning may sometimes cumber a man, and make him clumsy and diffuse, and it is always tempting him to mistake the outward shape for the vital inward structure, and to prize what has been put on more than what has come out. Perhaps the fact that the culture, the learning of other men is in unliterary directions is what gives them the advantage of literary men when it comes to literary expression; though this seems pushing conjecture into paradox. What is certain is that the literature of those other men, as we find it quoted in these volumes, is something that gives the reader the pleasure which any fine art imparts. Even the terms in which the Dred Scott decision was rendered are very noble and simple. That decision is not better literature than the dissenting opinions, but it is remarkable for being no worse; it has a kind of state that charms as much as its misreading of history shocks; and it is not without a touch of pathos for "the unfortunate race" whose cruel destiny it finds implicated in its cruel past. But for the most part the pro-slavery men wrote worse and spoke worse, in the artistic sense, than the antislavery men; perhaps the habit of declaring wrong right, in defiance of reason, resulted in an intellectual decay which inevitably expressed itself in bombast and swagger. At any rate that seems to have become for a time the type of the literature of the South, where since the hard necessity of affirming the heavenly origin of slavery has passed, the work in literature has been so wholesome and important.

Of course it will not do to carry too far the theory of a strict relation between ethics and æsthetics, and to deny that a thing artistically good can come out of a thing morally bad. It might be proved; it seems very probable; but it is not indispensable to an appreciation of the excellence of Lincoln's way of saying things. Any study of any writer will establish the proposition that right-mindedness is the condition of clear-mindedness, that no man can hope to muddle others without first muddling himself; and it never was the wish of Lincoln to do either. Reason charmed him. It is beautiful to see how from the first he sought only to have a lucid vision of the thing before him; how he never failed to accept, to exalt any truth that he clearly discerned. But he had to find out the truth for himself; he reasoned to it; he could not take it ready-reasoned from another, no matter how great, how wise. It was this trait that made him one of the most consistent statesmen who ever lived, and kept him honest from the log cabin to the White House. It is this that gives a perfect solidarity to his whole history, and makes it not less important in its study of his obscure beginnings than in its reflection of his life when it encom-

passed the nation's. He had faults and foibles which are not blinked by his biographers; he was not far ahead of his time at any time, and he was always of his place, in the Mississippi flat-boat and in the ship of state. But his face was always and everywhere toward the light. This is perhaps the sum of what his biographers make you feel concerning him, and you might justly say that you knew this already.

IV.

The fact that almost everything about Lincoln was known already must have added immensely to the difficulties of their task. No man ever lived whose character, whose history, whose heart has been more thoroughly explored. The inmost recesses of his most intimate experiences have been laid bare to the curiosity as well as to the sympathy of the world, and his public acts have been subjected to a scrutiny whose intensity has left no motive unsearched. The make of the man in every regard has been portrayed till his image and superscription are ineffaceably stamped upon the thoughts of the generation that knew him in life; and whatever mystery may hereafter gather about him in the ages of an undying fame, the strong, deep lines will always show clear to the eye that scans them. The work of his biographers, then, has been largely a synthesis of impressions, and a dignified and temperate criticism of portraitures which distort or misrepresent him in this point or that, but are none of them wholly unlike. In fact Lincoln was so like all other men, was so essentially human, that if any honest man conceives clearly of himself he cannot altogether misconceive Lincoln. He was so simple, so modest, so good, that he seems a riddle to the sophisticated, and perhaps until the world wholly changes its ideals of distinction and majesty this plainest great man who ever lived must remain a mystery with those who require distance in their great men. He was every one's neighbor, the friendliest, the faithfulest; and he solved in his life the question of how one may continue a hero to one's valet simply by not having any valet, or even thinking of any human being in that relation to him.

V.

It is because we feel that he could only have gained from it that we wish these biographers who knew him so near at hand, had somewhere synthetized their personal impressions of him, and confided to us the last possible word that could be said of his private life. It is true that scattered throughout their biography there are glimpses of what we desire to be fully shown, but without some massing of these details there is a sense of incompleteness. Perhaps we shall finally have added to this monumental work the studies of Lincoln's daily life in the White House which one of the authors is now publishing; if so, there would be nothing left to desire in the materials they supply for a judgment of the man. **3**

As to the general structure of the history, it seems to us admirably fitted to the materials. There were certain interests that must be treated throughout the whole narrative, and there were certain others that could be regarded as episodes, and set aside after the course of the story had been stayed long enough to do them justice. The French invasion of Mexico was distinctly one of these; and the Vallandigham farce another; and such characters as those of John Brown and Stonewall Jackson could be considered in a single chapter, and thereafter let alone. It is true that Brown had a historical importance which Jackson never had; Brown was of the course of events, but he was a reversionary type like Jackson, who was historically a mere anecdote, curious but not important. What makes him chiefly interesting is that psychologically he was so much of John Brown's make. Our authors study his character in the biographies written by his friends, and their account of Andersonville is wisely drawn entirely from Confederate sources. In fact, considering the many matters of impassioned opinion involved by their subject, the relation of our authors to men and events is remarkably judicial. There is never any question of what their own mind is, but they have a resolute fairness toward those who are of another mind. An eminent example of this is to be found in their scrutiny of the career and character of Stephen A. Douglas, the early rival of Lincoln—an able, selfish, unscrupulous, but not finally dishonest or unpatriotic partisan. Another example of it is in their treatment of the peace party at the North. **4**

But we wish especially to persuade intending readers of the work from slighting the chapters and volumes relating to the origin and development of Lincoln, in the belief that they are comparatively unimportant. They are comparatively most important. They establish the perspective through which only he can be seen aright on the great scene of national history. That part of the work is done with perhaps even greater solidity and dignity than the later passages, which are suffused with a greater warmth of feeling. It is of course merely truistic to say that we cannot understand the man Lincoln became without knowing the man he was; but we are willing to say this in urging every part of his history upon the reader. We wish that it could be known

to every citizen of the republic, and especially to its Southern citizens, the young men coming forward to rule the heritage which in the nature of things they must be only too apt to idealize their mistaken fathers for having tried to throw away. It is the history of this great error couched in terms which ought not to offend, and which can greatly instruct them.

VI.

People who like a strong novel, with intense yet real feeling in it, and the suggestion of earnest thinking, cannot do better than turn to the one which we read between chapters of the Lincoln history, not to shorten it, but to eke it out in length of time. This novel was the last of Björnstjerne Björnson's, which he calls *In God's Ways*, and which has to do with the several walks of a physician and of a minister in them. Norway is a little country and America is a big one, but the spiritual conditions are much the same; the type of pharisaism is the protestant type in both, and the questions involved fit either civilization. They are questions of conscience, and they are dealt with in the lives of people who when they answer them mistakenly do not answer them wickedly, and who when they answer them rightly are not supposed to acquire merit with their Maker for doing so: they remain all very fallible people the same, just as all but a very few of us should if we were in their places. The conclusion of the whole matter is expressed in the words of Pastor Tuft, after his reconciliation with Dr. Kallem, whom he and his wife (Kallem's sister) have so cruelly misunderstood, "There where good people walk, those are God's ways."

The words are spoken in response to the declaration Kallem feels bound to make, "But I do not share your faith," and they surrender the claim to judge another for his opinions and to punish him for them, which we all like to urge. Kallem's opinions are of various heterodox sorts: they permit him to marry a woman divorced from her first husband, and to revere her memory as that of a saint after his sister's not unnatural unkindness has followed her to her death with eager acceptance of all the neighborhood lies against her. Tuft's orthodoxy cannot yield to the necessity for a merely mechanical falsehood with a patient of Kallem's, who must be kept in ignorance of an amputation performed upon him, and whose death the pastor becomes accessory to in owning the truth about his case. We must leave the reader to follow the story through the evolution of its entirely human characters, and the passages of a drama which has moments of breathless interest; but we can assure him he will not be trifled with or defrauded by any trick of the trade in any part of the action. We ask him to note how probably, and yet how unexpectedly, the different men and women grow out of the children whose life is first presented to us. That is a very great thing, and very uncommon; it is only Tolstoï, that other giant of the North, who has known how to do it as well; and certainly even Tolstoï has not known better how to indicate the compensation of error and virtue in the same person. Any one who loves truth must feel a thrill of delight in the variety of the conceptions in this book, and of more than delight, of fervent gratitude. Such things console mightily; they give hope of a final perfection in art through the artist's simple devotion to truth. If any reader of these pages is at present skulking about with the guilty consciousness of having read Maupassant's *Notre Cœur*, we suggest to him that he can make that loathsome experience useful by comparing the Norwegian novel with the French novel, and observing how the Frenchman grovels into mere romanticism, and is false even to the fashionable filth he studies, while Björn-

son never fails of reality in the high level his imagination keeps.

It is interesting, at the moment Maupassant offers us his picture of high life in Paris, and fails to persuade us that it is a portrait of life anywhere, to find the Spanish novelist Valdés painting the aristocracy of Madrid with such vigorous strokes as vivify the scenes of his *Espuma*. The book, which we hope to take up again, is translated in English under the name of *Scum*, and this version of the word, which is a bit violent, is not inapt. It recognizes, once for all, that it is the top of aristocratic and plutocratic "society" in all countries which is really the scum, and not those poor plebeian dregs which mostly boil about the bottom of the caldron and never get to the surface at all. What Valdés's feeling about the "best" people of his country is, the reader of his former novels pretty well knows; but here it is stated in terms coextensive with his book; and the book is important because it is a part of that expression of contemporary thought about contemporary things now informing fiction in all countries but England.

---

[1] See p. 245b, and note 3, p. 246.

[2] Ralph Waldo Emerson, "Abraham Lincoln; Remarks at the funeral services held in Concord, Mass., April 19, 1865," in Emerson's Complete Works, XI (Boston: Houghton, Mifflin and Company, 1884), pp. 305-315.

[3] John Hay, "Life in the White House in the Time of Lincoln," Century, 41 (n.s. 19) (November, 1890), 33-37.

[4] Clement Laird Vallandigham - leader in the House of Representatives of the "Copperheads," Democrats opposed to Civil War policies. He defied an order from General Burnside and was tried and convicted. Lincoln commuted the sentence and banished him to the Confederacy. He returned to Ohio in 1864 and conducted a speaking campaign against Lincoln.

March, 1891

Editor's Study.

I.

IF ever there was a lovable time in the history of English literature, it seems to have been the time of Charles Lamb and his friends; yet no doubt the time had its hatefulness, and it is only a small literary group that one's heart may really warm to. Perhaps it is only Lamb himself: it will not do to inquire too curiously about anything. But Lamb one may always make sure of loving: not for his weaknesses and errors, which were small part of him, but for his good sense and kindness, which make him seem rather the best and wisest, as well as the delightfulest, of his contemporaries. The fact that he has been unsparingly sentimentalized, not only for his tragical experiences, his sacrifices and his sorrows, but for what his poor mad sister called his smokiness and drinkiness, without being rendered loathsome, is proof that he was too largely sound and sage to be made the prey of his weaker-minded worshippers. He had a robust, inward strength, like Keats, which has defended him from the worst endeavors of literary mawkishness, while his fortunes and his circumstances have moved the tenderness of all comers but Carlyle, who no doubt caught one aspect of him truly enough. We are never tired hearing of him; we are glad of every chance of his intimacy; and such a book as Dr. B.E. Martin's *In the Footprints of Charles Lamb* will come like a personal favor to each of his lovers. It is in novel wise another life of Lamb, and in tracing him from place to place, from house to house, from his first home to his last, it sees almost as much of him as most other biographies; and the point of view is such as shows him not merely at his best, but at his truest, which *was* his best, too. Dr. Martin tells us that in looking over the mass of literature about Lamb he noted the want of "what might be called a topographical biography of the man," and he has supplied this in terms such as only diligent study and genuine affection for the subject could inspire. There is a great deal of variety in the narrative, for its events are the different removals of Lamb, and Lamb lived in many houses: always

very plain and simple ones, and usually very little ones. Where they were, or where they are, Dr. Martin lets us see, with glimpses of their neighborhoods and interiors, and such account of Lamb's sojourn in each as serves to make it for the time a living home.

We do not remember to have read anything so full and definite concerning the tragedy which shaped and colored Lamb's whole career as the explicit story told here of his mother's death at the hands of his insane sister; and we find it easy to agree with Dr. Martin that there was no longer any reason for withholding any part of it. There long ago ceased to be any for blinking Lamb's own foibles. It is in its frank and philosophic treatment of these, and of his whole character, that this charming study of localities is lifted so far above the level of gossip and anecdote as to seem a new species in its kind. It is so suggestive of further work in the same direction that we hope Dr. Martin may deal in like manner with other literary figures in the places he knows so well.

II.

The book addresses itself from an American to Americans with peculiar force, for we fancy that the English do not yet rank Lamb so high as we do, or care so tenderly for him. This is to be accounted for by other facts as well as by the fact that his humor seems as little English in character as Heine's wit seems German. Lamb, by his intimate relations with such low radicals as Hunt and Hazlitt, in the time of the English reaction against the French Revolution, suffered some such disadvantage with his home public as a friend of abolitionists would have suffered sixty years ago, or a friend of socialists would suffer among us now. He had long to be explained and tolerated; very likely there was a time when he appeared "dangerous"; so fine a spirit must always have been apprehended gingerly by the Philistine world; and his associates whom we now see transfigured in the rosy sunset light must have looked very different in the hard noonday to their contemporaries. Yet they seem, as we began by saying, a lovable group of men; and one has a sort of grief in the dudgeon with which the kind-hearted Walter Scott resents the kind-heartedness of one of them. "Mr. Barry Cornwall writes to condole with me," he records in his *Journal*, shortly [1] after the death of his wife. "I think our acquaintance scarcely warranted this; but it is well meant, and modestly done," and we wish that the good romancer had taken it as well as it was meant. His feeling about it limits him, and breaks the flow of the reader's sympathy as nothing else in his diary does. The volumes of his *Journal* now given to the world are indeed such as must endear him more than ever to those who take him on his own faery ground; and they are in the last degree interesting. Of course the material was very freely used by Lockhart in his *Life*, [2] but here, in its continuous course, it has a fresh value, and it forms a sort of monograph upon the most momentous passage of Scott's career. Almost from the first we see the great and finally overwhelming disaster looming up; and the rest is the story of the long fight he made to ward off the financial ruin brought upon him by others. It is all very pathetic, though the struggle seems so needless, first through what appears to be the bad management of Scott's associates, and then through his own fatal devotion to a mistaken ideal of happiness. He really enslaved himself to the property he owned, and dedicated incessant toil to its preservation; his exertion was also to save from loss the creditors whose interests he had not himself imperilled; but the impression which the reader of his *Journal* keeps is of labor by night and day for the sake of the home created at Abbotsford: not that real home which a man may have anywhere, but the unreal home, the merely material home in which Scott had suffered his fancy to bind his heart up. He became the victim of his self-imposed conditions, and he worked himself to death that he might live at Abbotsford. His endeavor was by no means selfish; a thousand generous purposes were implied in it; this is what makes the spectacle so touching. But it is not alone touching; it is consoling; and one need not refuse to be comforted by the thought that Scott liked hard work, and that probably his greatest happiness in a most unhappy time was when he could lose himself in his work. It was not wholly an unhappy time; it was a time of prodigious literary triumphs and of pecuniary rewards past all modern paralleling. Think of forty-five thousand dollars cash in hand for *Woodstock*, which he wrote in three months! Other gains of his were upon

the same scale, and then the sum grows till one wonders at the ruin that could engulf it all. But there were long reliefs to the work, even. The *Journal* is a record of many travels, distractions, pleasures, and is a sort of object-lesson to any student of the art of representing life in its evidence of the fact that tragedy is not incessantly tragedy. Scott had accumulated sorrows and disasters of many kinds upon his money troubles; yet he often escapes from them all, from his grief for his wife's death, from his wearing fear for his little sick grandson's life. It is not gay, but it is not altogether dismal, either; and he sets it all down with equal courage, and almost equal fulness. He has a certain misbehavior of the bile which employs his pen a good deal, and there are such excursions as a recurrent rheumatism may afford the mind. There is also some mention from time to time of political as well as social matters; such an inveterate Tory cannot escape self-question in view of the fact that most of his wisest and best friends are Whigs. There are glimpses of right feeling about the labor problem, then already beginning to haunt men's thoughts; where his Toryism is not concerned, the poor have Scott's kindness. His was, in fact, one of the kindest hearts in the world, as well as the greatest heads; but his sympathies were limited in time and space. He was an early nineteenth-century North Briton; he had little outlook beyond his place and period.

In the *Journal* there is not much about his literary methods, and nothing of his theories. Perhaps he had none of these. He wished to tell a taking and keeping story, and he had little artistic scruple about ways and means; the great matter, so far as the *Journal* witnesses, was to get so many sheets a day done; but it is not safe to infer that his delight in writing was less than that of his public in reading; they were of a piece, and all romantic together in their ideals.

The paucity of literary "impression" in the *Journal* is somewhat compensated in the full and careful notes of Mr. David Douglas, the editor, who has always thrown a pleasant light upon matters where Scott is slight and cursory. Mr. Douglas's work is throughout faithfully and admirably done, and it adds greatly to the comfort and pleasure of the reader of the fascinating volumes of the *Journal*. With its help one comes to know distinctly the persons and places whom the author leaves in the vague of familiar allusion; and not the least service it renders is that of setting in the full light of circumstance certain passages and events that might have left one thinking less tenderly and reverently of Scott than one could have desired. The sins of omission, in the interest of a purely heroic conception, that is to say a false conception of him, have been few or none: one is allowed to see that it is not always his superhuman toil that Sampson Agonistes is sinking under, but that imprudences of diet have something to do with his sufferings, and that more than once he is prostrated by careless exposure to the weather without a great-coat or an umbrella.

III.

As to the overwork of the brain which we fondly wish to imagine the sole cause of Scott's breaking up, it was inevitable. Scott himself suggested that to caution him against it was like saying to the kettle over the fire, "Don't boil." Given the conditions, he could not do other than he did; he was over the fire and he must boil. The question is not of the consequences but of the conditions, whether they were necessary or not; and a like question of all conditions which lamentable consequences follow is becoming more and more the mood of the philosophic spectator. Such a spectator, we think, would by no means permit himself the virtuous self-satisfaction which we have seen some critics enjoy in censuring Mr. Ward McAllister's amusing volume, [3] *Society as I have Found It.* The spiritual squalor of the status which this volume reveals is the inevitable consequence of conditions which incite men to a rivalry in money getting and women to a rivalry in money spending, and do not really incite them to anything else with at all the same strenuousness. The contempt in which aristocracies have always held commercialized society is natural, and it is natural that such a society should always try to escape from itself by reverting to the ideals of aristocracy; this was the way of commercialized society in Venice and in Florence; but it is none the more dignified in New York for that reason. It is always and everywhere amusing to see a plutocracy trying to turn into an aristocracy, and this is what Mr. McAllister shows us, with no apparent sense of its comicality. These men who have had no ideal but to get more and more money, these women who have no ideal but to spend more and more, are necessarily ridiculous in the transformation act; but it is not Mr. McAllister who has made them so; he has merely shown them so. He did not create society; it created him; and if he is deplorable, society is to blame for him. If society had known how to do something besides dress and dine and dance, we have no doubt he would have said so; that is, he would have written a different book. But you cannot make

something out of nothing.

For our own part we would on no account have missed having his book; it is worth a thousand satires of the sort that "lash" and "scathe" society without taking account of conditions, and that conjure it to elevate itself by laying hold, as it were, of the legs of its trousers. His book is a contribution, if not to literature, then certainly to autobiography, whose delightful store it enriches after its own fashion; a fashion which prevailingly suggests that of the imaginary autobiographer Barry Lyndon in a certain provinciality which persists through all his experience of the world; his knowledge widens, but his point of view never changes; his ideal was formed very early. It would be absurd to make fun of him, and would partake of that bad-heartedness which he never shows in a book abounding in every manner of solecism. Upon the whole it seems better than the society that inspired it; and Mr. McAllister himself is superior to his circumstance. It is in reflecting upon these facts that the reader can get good from the book, and we heartily commend it to the reader's consideration in this light.

IV.

It does not follow because this is so, that "society" as Mr. McAllister found it represents the civilization of New York. There are several people in this city interested in the arts and sciences, and in polite literature. Whether they are in "society" or not, we do not know; but we think very likely not. One mostly meets them in their pictures and in their books; and it seems a pity Mr. McAllister never saw any of them. We think he would have liked them; a man whose own brother went about all his life with Milton under his arm at least could not have despised them. But it is useless to blame him for not having seen them. Again we insist that he is an effect, not a cause, and if you do not admire him, your quarrel is not with him but with "society" and the conditions of "society." Morally and mentally he is like the rest of it, and he is better than the spirit of "society," more kindly, more refined, really more educated, though we suppose that some of the four hundred must know when to sign their letters "Yours sincerely" and when "Yours truly."

At the moment his autobiography was "put upon the market," if we may color our phraseology from that of the plutocracy he celebrates, another autobiography appeared: that of a man whose name Mr. McAllister may have noticed on the playbills, and whom he may have made up a theatre party to see, some time. This autobiographer must also inspire the reader with kindness, but of another quality and of even greater quantity than that which springs from regarding Mr. McAllister as the irresponsible creature of conditions. We are all that, in some measure, and once more we protest that if he is not wholly admirable, he is not chiefly to blame; but we wish he could realize how much better and finer it is to be one Joseph Jefferson than all the four hundred of any best society, though we have no right to suppose him the only man insensible to the most incomparable art of our time, or, we imagine, of any. How much of his charm as an actor Jefferson is able to translate into literature will be the question with every one who turns to the story of his life; and we confess that its measure in the first chapters is a very little bit disappointing. The manner, there, especially in some facetious passages, is too intentionally funny; but as it goes on the manner sobers and mellows; and the humorist, as all humorists are apt to be, is at his best when he is at his most serious. Actors always talk delightfully of their art, and what Jefferson has to say of it, now and again, is said with the clearest subtlety. He gives you the same kind of pleasure when he analyzes his Rip Van Winkle that you get from seeing him play the character. It is measurably so when he speaks of another actor's art, and something more is gained then by the infusion of the man's sweet nature in the generous praise he gives his compeers, living or dead. He makes you love him the more in loving them; and it can be said that there is not a harsh or selfish criticism in his book, though he frees his mind at all times about people he has met on and off the stage. The world beyond the foot-lights is getting better and better known as one inhabited by a race peculiarly kind-hearted and finely impulsed; and Mr. Jefferson's book will make us like it more and respect it more. Out of all the multitude of portraits he paints, none are so winning and typical as those of his father and mother: both genuine artists, but so differently devoted to their art; one all light-hearted hopefulness and natural goodness, the other an anxious conscience, carrying into the theatre the high motives and ideals that governed her life. Such people, and the other people like them who abound in this friendly book, are the real people of the theatre, too long defamed, too long romanced out of all likeness to themselves; and one of the greatest services it can do the world outside is to make them truly known.

Actors' autobiographies are always interesting. Their varied lives abound in every sort of incident, and Mr. Jefferson's

has been peculiarly rich in experience, in both America and Europe, and amidst

"The long wash of Australasian seas."

Its unity is in a dedication of all its endeavors to an art which he has dignified and refined to an ideal delicacy and a beautiful reality never surpassed, to our thinking. We believe those who have seen his Rip Van Winkle have seen the perfection of that art; and the charm of that exquisite impersonation, the charm of a humor forever touching and blending with pathos, is the charm of his own personality, of his life, his book.

Many of the people who figure in his reminiscences are to be met again in Mr. Laurence Hutton's very agreeable volume, *Curiosities of the American Stage*, whose quality is already known to our readers through the papers reprinted in it from these pages. The most important chapter is that on the Native American Drama, with its subdivisions of Indian, Revolutionary, Frontier, Character, Local New York, and Society Drama. This is good work in a region little explored, work not merely historical, but critical, in the liberal spirit of modern criticism, which inquires whether a thing is good of its time as well as good of its kind. In fact the whole book may be regarded as a historical criticism of our theatre, dramatically and histrionically considered, and the persons and characters sketched in the various studies of the Stage Negro, the American Burlesque, the American Hamlets, are all in the sort of illustrations to the general theme. The book is both valuable and entertaining, and with an informality that is occasionally scrappy, is still of a final effect to which such an impression would be unjust.

V.

Another autobiography which we wish to commend is that of Chester Harding, one of our old masters, whom his extraordinary gifts and works have won a place in art not to be contested. He called it his Egotistography, when it was first published, but now that it is newly reprinted, with an introduction by his daughter, it is more soberly entitled *A Sketch of Chester Harding, Artist, drawn by his own Hand*. Of all careers his was one of the most marvellous: a man of as simple origin, almost, as Lincoln, coming to his artistic consciousness long after he had come to manhood (and then through the stress of poverty and by a species of fortuity), he mingled with the best society of two worlds, and died unspotted by either, a modest giant physically and intellectually. "Nature," Washington Allston wrote of him to a friend, "not only made him a painter but a gentleman; and you know her too well not to know that she does her work better than any Schools." Yet Nature has not made all of us masters or gentlemen, any more than she has made us six feet three and endowed us with the strength of oxen, as she did in Harding's case. So we can still be schooled a little to our advantage; and we can learn from Harding himself that it is well to assist Nature, even when she seems disposed to do all the work herself. He never failed to lend her a helping hand, and as one reads the plain and diffident story of his life, it sometimes seems as if Harding had done the most of the work by taking thought and taking pains.

Apparently there are always opportunities waiting for the right men, in every direction, and sometimes they wait so long that we get to thinking they are not there till the right man comes along and seizes one of them, or it seizes him. No doubt there had always been a chance for some one to do the eminently good work which Mr. G. W. Smalley has long been doing in his *London Letters* to reconcile journalism and literature in a sisterly embrace; but now that much of his *Tribune* [5] correspondence has been collected in two substantial volumes, we see with the clearness of retrospective prophecy the fact that he has done it for the first time. We do not know that we like all the qualities of Mr. Smalley's mind; we suspect that we do not; he has certain conventionalities of ideal which we are sure we do not like; much of his boldest thinking seems done on the safest lines; but the fact of his artistic handling of contemporaneous history remains unaffected by these considerations. His point of view is his own, and is taken with intelligence if not always without prejudice; his style is always clear and often brilliant; his manner is always interesting; he knows his London as few know it, and he has not forgotten his America. Those who recur to his work of many years in the volumes which form a fit monument to his skill and industry, will, we think, be impressed by a sense of their slowly accumulated debt to his full and easy affluence, and those who first make his acquaintance in them will be much more than instructed; they will be most agreeably and continually attracted by the literary charm of work which is primarily newspaper work. Much of it, perhaps all of it, was done in the days before the correspondents of our great journals cabled their letters home, but it was, quite the same, written with the pressure of the journalist's anxiety to be, above everything, timely in it. Under these circumstances the graces are not usually invited, or at least induced to come; but apparently Mr. Smalley always knew how to secure the presence of some of the "smartest" of them. His work is that of a man of the world, and its excellences are of one origin with its limitations. Such a man is not likely to think outside of the circles in which he moves; but within them he is very likely to think aptly, quickly, and symmetrically. As Mr. Smalley thinks, so he writes.

[1] Sir Walter Scott, The Journal of Sir Walter Scott, [David Douglas, ed.] (New York: Harper & Brothers, 1890).

[2] John Gibson Lockhart, Memoirs of the Life of Sir Walter Scott (Edinburgh: R. Cadell, 1845).

[3] Samuel Ward McAllister established "The 400" of New York society in 1892.

[4] Joseph Jefferson (1829-1905) was an American traveling actor; known for his portrayal of Asa Trenchard in Our American Cousin, he later adapted "Rip Van Winkle" to the stage with Dion Boucicault.

[5] George Washburn Smalley (1833-1916) was the European correspondent of the New York Tribune from 1867 to 1895.

Editor's Study.

I.

THE effect of all æsthetic endeavor, we suppose, is a disappointment after a compromise. One concedes everything, as one fancies, to one's material: he conditions himself in absolute submission, with the hope of final mastery; and he finds in the end that the ungrateful material has refused to keep terms with him, or to give more than a warped and twisted expression to his ideal. This, at any rate, seems continually the hard fate of him who has to do with the wretched trade of reviewing, especially favorable reviewing, which is the only branch of the business the Study really cares to practise. The critical kodak has not yet been invented; there is no little instrument that promises to do the rest in reviewing if you press the button; and in the mean time there is the chance of giving only a glimpse of the work that comes before one. One aspect is seized, and a moment only of that; a few traits are grouped about this general look of an author: a nose here, a mouth there, an eye or two, a chin; and then the whole must be intrusted to the intelligence of the reader, with the suggestion that he had better go to the book for a right conception of it.

That is what we should like to urge him with unusual warmth to do in the case of Mr. T. S. Perry's *History of Greek Literature.* This writer is one whose attitude toward his subject is of equal value with his treatment of the matter, and neither is easy to be had at second hand. His attitude, particularly, is difficult of report; for it seems at first sight as if it could not suffice for any long or thorough effort, and one is tempted to misrepresent it a little in order to offer a just notion of its efficacy. It is only after one has one's self read his work that one perceives the wisdom with which his point of view was taken, and the entire success with which it has been kept. He gives us a history of Greek literature as temperate as the spirit of Greek literature, and he does this simply by bringing to the study of it a mind as open to its facts as if it had never been studied before. His book is perhaps the most unliterary history of any literature ever written, and this in spite of a style that often recalls the lecture-room with its thuses and hences, its howevers and notwithstandings; and it addresses itself to the common-sense of the reader with a force that carries knowledge with it, and a serenity unruffled by the vindictive controversy which has raged all over the ground it covers. Its mood reflects the unliterary character of Greek literature itself, which, as Mr. Perry conceives it, was the most absolute expression of a people's life ever known. His effort throughout is to impart this sense of it, to make the reader understand that these poets, dramatists, orators, philosophers, who disastrously became the means of artificializing all subsequent writers, were themselves perfectly natural persons, who had no models but the human life about them, and who wrought by the simplest and readiest means. Their models are indeed still accessible to every artist who will use them, and every one who achieves anything in literature does use them; but it has hitherto been too largely the business of scholarship to persuade us that it is not life we should imitate, but the men who imitated life.

II.

Perhaps, though, that hitherto carries us too far; perhaps Mr. Perry is not the first to point the true moral of Greek literature; he would himself be apt to deny that any man was ever the first to do anything; but we think there can be no doubt he is the first to point it so keenly and so often. His book was written a little too soon to take due note of the support which scientific inquiry has brought to the claim of the Greeks that they sprang from the soil of Greece; but at every point it witnesses to their originality in literature, and again and again it contrasts their unliterary literature with the literary literature of the Romans, who were nothing if not imitative. Modern literature, so far as the old-fashioned scholarship could misguide it, has imitated the Roman imitators of the Greeks, so that we have not even had the advantage of aping at first hand; and we are only just beginning to feel the true influence of the Greeks, which is always toward the study of nature. Wherever one of us succeeds in representing life, he is seen to have done something Greek: that is, something true, something free, something beautiful, something novel, something temperate. This is what Mr. Perry's work teaches, and it is what no one can help seeing, unless he perversely shuts his eyes to it. The illimitable perspective which it opens is one in which alone the grandeur and magnificence of the Greek achievement in literature can be seen, and it can be fairly said at least, that no man writing of that achievement in the old way, as something whose glory could be felt chiefly if not only by the learned, has ever done it greater reverence than he who commends it to all the unlearned as something that it needs merely common-sense to appreciate. This history, then, without waiving for it any of those claims to learning which we leave others to pronounce upon, is one which we wish gratefully to celebrate as popular in the best way. In it once more the Greeks are at our doors, and it is our fault if we refuse to know them.

Starting from Homer and coming down to Heliodorus, the story of the greatest intellectual achievement of our race ends, as it began, with a novelist; but between the novelist who wrote in verse and the novelist who wrote in prose, there stretches a period of time twice as long as that since the first lispings of the English tongue made themselves heard in literature. Because so little has been left by the rage of superstition and the malice of conquest that any diligent reader can hope to possess himself of the whole of Greek literature in a comparatively little time, we are apt to forget how stupendous even in quantity that literature once was. But Mr. Perry's treatment of it is somehow favorable to a just conception of it from this side, as well as from others, and no reader can leave him without an enlarged as well as an enlightened sense of its magnitude in every way. Its decay is a very melancholy story, which he tells as clearly and charmingly as the tale of its manifold triumphs. We all know more or less of Homer and Hesiod, of Simonides and Pindar, of Æschylus and Sophocles and Euripides and Aristophanes, of Herodotus and Thucydides and Xenophon, of Isocrates and Demosthenes, of Socrates and Plato and Aristotle; these names represent to us "the glory that was Greece" in epic and lyric poetry, in tragedy and comedy, in history, in oratory, in philosophy. But at this point the Muse of literary history, who is perhaps the genteelest of all the Muses, usually rests; and it is with difficulty that one gets her to come down through the Alexandrian school, where the piping of eclogues and of pastorals was heard amidst the droning of grammarians and schoolmen, to those last Byzantine days when the great modern literary form, the novel, arose from the dust of all that long detrition, and Chariton of Aphrodisias made it possible for Rider Haggard to be. But it is Mr. Perry's passion (if the word is not unjust to a writer who is so conscientiously dispassionate) to seek not miracles of creation, but evidences of growth in the phase of human history he deals with. The beginnings of Greek literature are prehistoric, but its endings are known, and he finds its death instinct with the life of modern literature.

III.

It is our misfortune that the vices and follies of its dotage descended to us in undue measure. The Greeks who have most influenced modern literature, and especially our criticism, were not the great Athenians, but the little Alexandrians. In fact, literary criticism was hardly known to Athens, while it was the breath in the nostrils of Alexandria; and wherever at any time literature has become the affair of scholarship rather than humanity, the cart has been put before the horse in the true Alexandrian manner; and often there is no horse at all. The chapters which Mr. Perry devotes to that school are of the greatest interest and value, for there we are shown the earliest known processes of the schoolmen who have spread literature as a veil between us and Nature, instead of holding it up as a mirror to her. It was not that the Greek civilization failed to give masters in the different kinds, or the new kinds as long as any force of it remained. Polybius, writing at the verge of our era, conceived of history in something like the modern universal sense; Plutarch much later sounded the true note of biography; Lucian imagined satire which sufficed by simply stating a detestable thing, or letting it state itself. The epigrams of the Anthology were composed at a comparatively recent period; and the pastoral poets, who, if they used Nature consciously and decoratively, still loved her, arose and flourished. But none of these masters influenced after-time in at all the same degree as the schools did, with their grammarians and critics, their editors and commentators, their imitators and disciples, their translators and adapters. This is what Mr. Perry makes you feel, and he makes you see the reason for it in the community of childishness where the faltering of the superannuated ancient met that of the infant modern.

But we must not give the notion that he devotes himself mainly, or even largely to a study of Greek literature in its decay. The luminous effect of the closing chapters, where he deals with it, is a final concentration of the clear light which he throws upon the whole history of that literature; and of course he bestows his greatest attention upon its greatest epochs. From first to last he gives you, by precept and example, a conception of its relation to the life of the wonderful people it sprang from, and he handles his material with an ease and lightness which make no draft upon the reader's energies, and perhaps therefore all the more perfectly secure his sympathies. The manner is to the last degree plain and simple, so plain and simple that those who have been used to associating power with flourish may not always feel the virtue of it. This sort of readers will be apt to miss some of those subtle points of irony in which the author advances his personal feeling about this matter and that. They will miss some delicious touches of a peculiarly shy humor; but none of these we think will be lost to the judicious, who will perhaps grieve a little that Mr. Perry does not often let them know whose versions of the extracts they are reading, and is sometimes mechanically so inadvertent that he leaves them to find out for themselves which of the several authors mentioned together the several extracts are from. But one cannot really go wrong, though now and then it may be a trifle troublesome to find the way. The work is at every moment addressed to the reader's highest intelligence, but he need not be a learned, or even a "cultivated" person in order to appreciate the matter and the manner. Manner is the word rather than style which we should use in speaking of the artistic side of the performance; and we fancy that Mr. Perry would be one of the last to care for praise of his style. His personal quality in fact is so elusive that the suffusion of one's material with one's self, which we call a man's style, the individual color, so to speak, is not often present. We might say that it is chiefly noticeable by its absence; but there is a manner which no man keeps out of his work, and which is the outward expression of his mental attitude. With Mr. Perry this is unpretentious and unaffected, an expression of democratic sincerity as attractive as it is uncommon.

IV.

Something of the same motive that governs us to the frank avowal of our pleasure in him, makes it easy for us at all times to recognize the worth of what is our own in literature, and to shun at least the kind of provinciality which ignores it. This kind seems to us upon the whole a worse kind than the kind that boasts our own because it is our own; and we have lately seen with satisfaction some reluc-

tance in our criticism to accept the short stories of Maupassant as the best work of the sort that has been done. It seems to us not at all true that they are the best at all times, or so good at the best as the work of certain of our own writers; they are not so richly imagined, so finely wrought. They have for us the charm of strangeness, the fascination of coming from far, and they are undoubtedly done admirably, with perfect knowledge of technique, and that feeling for art which would make a Frenchman Greek if such a thing were possible. But their average seems not so good as that of Miss S. O. Jewett's little stories, which are as delicately constructed upon as true a method, and which abound with every grace of Maupassant's best, and are penetrated with the aroma of a humor which he never knew. If the reader cares to take her latest volume, *Strangers and Wayfarers*, and compare "A Winter Courtship," or "Mr. Teaby's Quest," or "Going to Shrewsbury," or "By the Morning Boat," or "In Dark New England Days," with any of the thirteen tales of Maupassant in the first of the Odd Number Series, we think he will see the truth of what we say. We think a comparison of these sketches with those of any other French writer will be as much to their advantage. Even the *Tales by François Coppée*, which form the latest issue of the same series, delicate and finished as they are, with that air of elegant unfinish, do not rival Miss Jewett's New England studies. It is not only the delightful mood in which these little masterpieces are imagined, but the perfect artistic restraint, the truly Greek temperance, giving all without one touch too much, which render them exquisite, make them really perfect in their way; and we hope it is with a joy in their beauty far above the chauvinistic exultation of knowing them ours, that we perceive we have nothing to learn of the French in this sort, but perhaps something to teach them.

V.

Another woman's work, but a Spanish woman's this time, has lately been giving us much the kind of pleasure we feel in Miss Jewett's art. The woman is Emilia Pardo Bazán, and the work is the story she calls *Morriña*, meaning homesickness, we believe, in the Galician dialect. It is about a mother and her son, and the servant-girl who comes to live with them in Madrid, because they are all from the same province, and she is homesick in that strange world, and longs for the sound of her own speech, and hungers for her own kind of people. She is of a simple, affectionate nature, impassioned beyond our cold comprehension, and in the shelter of that friendly home, where from the first she is treated more like a daughter of the house than like a servant, it is not long before she falls in love with the son. The expected happens, and it all ends with the poor girl's death by her own hand. The range of life is wider than our fiction commonly permits itself; but it is not wider than that of George Eliot's fiction, and the tragedy is pathetic beyond any reporting. The three principal figures have their setting of other characters, friends, neighbors, spectators, who give the scene the interest of large life, but these three transact the drama, which is very simple, and of a sort of fatal eventlessness in its march to the inevitable close. In the mean time their several characters are expressed in colors of conduct and in shades of behavior, always distinct, but nowhere insisted upon; you know them as if you had lived with them. A wrong is done and suffered, but somehow no one seems more to blame than another, and the imagined fact has the same value as a piece of what goes on in the world about us. The girl's nature has a most appealing charm, with the shadow of her origin thrown forward upon her— she is the daughter of a priest; but perhaps the connoisseur would say that the young man, just growing out of his mother's control and with the indefinite lines of boyishness not yet hardened in maturity, with his kindness and his selfishness of inexperienced youth, was better done, as he was certainly harder to do.

Some one ought to put the book into English, and some one probably will. Señora Bazán, who refuses to use her title of countess, with an indifference which we Anglo-Saxons cannot understand, is best known by her pamphlet on realism, *La Cuestion Palpitante*, written when the controversy was hottest, and taking the boldest ground in favor of the sincere art which now prevails everywhere but in England, where they still like to read novels of adventure as crude as the Greek romances. The chapter of this robust and vigorous, not to say athletic essay which relates to English fiction is curiously intelligent, and is interesting in its perception that all the English masters but Scott were realists, so far as they knew how, as well as in its recognition of George Eliot as the first novelist of her time.

VI.

The whole essay is redolent of the Spanish humor, which is so like our own, and yet has its peculiar perfume. This humor is what forms the atmosphere of Valdés's novels, and keeps his satire kindly even when his contempt is strongest, as in that last novel of his, which his trans-lator calls *Scum*, and which deals with society as Valdés "found it" in Madrid. Certain points of resemblance are to be found in "good" society the world over, nowadays, and one of these is its decorous religiosity. It appears that wherever people so far experience the favor of Heaven as to have nothing to do but to dress handsomely and to fare sumptuously, they are as punctilious in their devotions as they are in any of their social duties. Nothing could be more edifying than the Spanish novelist's study of the "smart set" of Madrid as he pictures them at a select service in the oratory of a devout lady of their number. They seem certainly to be more vicious than any smart set among ourselves, or at least differently vicious, but they vary little in their theory of life. If they worship God they do not forget their duty to Mammon, and money is to the fore among them as it is among us. One of their leaders is Clementina, the heroine, if the book can be said to have a heroine, who is the daughter of the Duke of Raquena, a robber baron of the stock exchange, an adventurer in Cuba, ennobled for his unscrupulous rapacity in accumulating money, after he returns to Spain. He is a great financier, as such people are with us, sometimes; he knows how to get up "corners" and to "squeeze" those he traps into them, quite as if he were an oil or wheat operator. He is the owner of some great quicksilver mines, and one of the most striking passages of the book is the account of the visit he pays these mines with a party of the "best" people of Madrid in his train of private cars. They are all hanging upon him in the hope that he will somehow make them rich, but some of the women are shocked at the life, or the death in life, of the miners, who are sufferers from mercurial poisoning, and who go shaking about like decrepit paralytics. The duke tells the ladies that the notion of mercurial poisoning is nonsense, and if the men would leave off drinking they would be well enough; just as one of our own millionaires has told us that the great cause of poverty is "intemperance." The duke's assurance comforts the ladies, and they have a banquet in one of the upper levels of the mine, while all round and under them the haggard miners are digging their own graves. Their gayety is a little chilled by the ironies of the young physician of the company, who takes a less optimistic view of the case than the good duke, though his life is spent among the miners and devoted to them. This physician is a socialist; and it is a curious sign of the times that the socialists should be making their way, in fiction at least, as the friends rather than the enemies of the race.

Tolstoï's latest book, *The Fruits of Culture*, which it is somehow natural to speak of after this novel of Valdés's, will certainly not offend in the way of the *Kreutzer Sonata*, though we fancy it will hardly interest as much. This time he has given us a drama, a comedy in which the vanity and emptiness of idle rich people's lives are pictured with the fidelity which is so much more terrible than satire. They are shown as given over to fads, where they have any interest apart from their real business of eating and drinking, and dressing and undressing. The truth which he specially brings out is one that he has shown before whenever he has revealed the contempt in which all people who work for a living cannot help holding those who do not work for a living, even when they envy them. The little group of peasants who come up from the country to buy land of Leonid Fedorovitch are not awed by him or his wife, though they are bewildered by them, especially when she drives them from her presence and has the place where they stood disinfected, because she has heard that they are from a district where she has heard there is diphtheria. They go quietly into the kitchen, where the servants invite them, and where they all join in laughing at their masters. Each of us who keeps a servant also keeps a critic, and a very scornful one, whose imagination he does not impress with his superiority in the least, and who knows him as he is for a more or less ridiculous dependent, if we are to believe Tolstoï.

The only way is to try not to believe him, but to believe Mr. McAllister, when he draws an affecting picture of "an old family servant" who joined the other grooms and coachmen in drinking up the champagne at a Newport picnic before the ladies and gentlemen could get at it, and who was bowed down with grief and shame when his "master" convicted him of peculiar wickedness in that quality. Perhaps the wily Irishman was really overcome with the contrition that "an old family servant" ought to feel, and was not laughing inwardly at his "master." Let us try to think so, for the credit of the human race, which is a good deal concerned in the matter. The romantic notion of the servant is altogether prettier, and much more comfortable to the master, and more particularly to the mistress; but it is not put forward by Valdés any more than by Tolstoï. The picture that the Spaniard draws of the contempt that the menials of rich people feel for them is much the same as that which the Russian offers; and there is something terrible in the mockery and contumely with which the "old family servants" of the Duke of Raquena use him in the imbecility which is his last phase. To be sure Thackeray had long ago shown the relation of master and man in its true light in that catastrophe where Morgan turns upon Major Pendennis at last with a ferocious explosion of the accumulated hatred of years. [3]

[1] See. for example, the review of Maupassant's "Notre Coeur" in Nation, 51 (October 16, 1890), 309.

[2] Guy de Maupassant, The Odd Number: Thirteen Tales, Jonathan Sturges, trans., Introduction by Henry James (New York: Harper and Brothers, 1889). See pp. 238b-239a for Howells' review of this volume.

[3] Howells refers to Thackery's novel Pendennis.

Editor's Study.

WHOEVER turns over the accumulation of verse in the little volumes which every few months begin to heap the reviewer's table, must be troubled, if he has a feeling heart, by something futile, something fatuous in their manner of approaching the public. There is hardly any one of them which has not something good in it, and even very good: some fine line, some fine stanza, some whole poem that is fine; but it is seldom that the entire book is good, though now and then this happens, too. It seems as if some better way of reaching the reader with what is really good in each might be imagined; and we have been wondering if the poets could not have a sort of spring and fall exhibitions, as the painters have. There might be a hanging committee, or a literary tribunal answering to it, which could decide upon the different pieces of verse to be presented to the public; there could be something equivalent to the line for the worthier efforts, and the poorer could be in some sort skyed. We have not thought it out very clearly; but we are sure that in Mr. Bellamy's commonwealth, when we get it, there will be no such ruinous and wasteful form of publication for poetry as we now have in these volumes of competitive verse. These represent individualism carried to its logical extreme of anarchism, and in its presence one feels that almost any form of collectivism would be better. Perhaps government control is what we need; perhaps a nationalistic production and distribution of poetry. We are certain that an immense saving of ink and paper could be at once effected if the theories of socialism could be realized in this region. Of course, it might come hard upon the poets at first, and there would probably be single cases of great suffering; but the gain to the public would be incalculable, simply incalculable.

I.

We are not saying all this of all the volumes of verse before us; and we shall conceal as artfully as we can which one of them we mean our remarks to apply to. Certainly Mr. Frank Dempster Sherman must by this time have made friends too formidable in number to suffer any such suggestion in regard to his work; and we do not know that we wish to offer it. The qualities which have made him liked before are mostly present in his last collection, which he calls *Lyrics for a Lute:* the grace, the nicely studied form, the well-attuned measures singing themselves to pleasant and gentle thoughts. A love of nature, a love of letters, a nimble fancy, are what we note as before in his truly conscientious and more and more artistic work; and it seems to us that we could not more fairly indicate the temperament of his book than by giving from it the poem he calls

MOTHS.

Ghosts of departed wingèd things,
    What memories are those
That tempt you, with your damask wings,
    Here where my candle glows?

Vainly you hover, circling oft
    The tongue of yellow flame:
A tiger by caresses soft
    You vainly seek to tame.

Here is no hope for you: nay, here
    Death lurks within the light,
To leap upon you flying near,
    And sweep you from the night.

Moon-butterflies, back to your blooms
    Born of the dew and stars!
Hence, ghosts, and find again your glooms
    Hidden by shadow bars.

Quick—speed across the dusky blue,
    Lest, in a sudden breath,
This tawny tiger wake, and you
    Endure a second death!

II.

In Miss Edith M. Thomas's elegiac poem, *The Inverted Torch*, we are aware of the technical refinements that have characterized her work from the beginning; and there is the same close and true friendship with nature that she has always shown; but the sorrow which has inspired her here has richly and abundantly supplied the human interest whose absence has sometimes seemed a defect of her landscape studies. It is a mother whom her music mourns, and it is a bro-

313

ken union of profound sympathies and interests which it laments in strains of noble sadness.

Hath God new realms of lovely life for thee
  In some white star, the soul of eve or morn,
  Whose full and throbbing lustre makes forlorn
Us who not yet across the void shall flee?
But why remote should now thy pleasures be,
  When yet thy joy in nature was unworn,
  Whether shot forth the tender blade of corn,
Or the wild tempest scourged the winter's tree?
Seeker and seer of beauty in each phase
  Of year on year through which the dear earth
    runs,
  Far be the Heaven of change-desiring ones;
Be thine not so; but love thou still to gaze
  On morning dews that wed with golden suns,
And happy deaths of stainless summer days.

Whether this is only the longing of the stricken spirit, or whether it is the glimpse of the truth which mortal eyes shall never wholly see, it is beautiful and consoling; and we can praise the whole poem for passages that will not leave the reader uncomforted. It will do its high office all the more perfectly because it never assumes to do other than pour out a natural grief, and a heart-break submissive even when impatient.

I once besought thee that thou wouldst return,
  And, spirit, clothe thyself in symboled speech
  That, though unheard, might still my spirit reach,
And arm to vanquish Death's negation stern.
        .   .   .   .
Thine answer came, with sad prevision keen:
  "Look not for this, but think, if it could be,
How many myriads gone had comfort seen.
  From the all-binding law not one goes free;
It is for us as it for all has been."

III.

Mr. Henry Austin's enemy seems to be haste, unless we misjudge the disabling cause in so many of his *Vagabond Verses.* One certainly feels like saying here that the picture would have been better if the painter had taken more pains; at least the defects are not such as more pains would make worse. There is vigorous thinking enough throughout, and manly feeling; but somehow the poet has not staid to tell all, or to say it in the best way. One is vexed, when one reads a poem so well wrought as "Mastodon-Saurus," that all the rest are not so; but the fact is, none of the rest are so; though everywhere there are good bits, along with a lot of indifferent bits, of quite worthless bits. Everywhere are the proofs of how much better the poet could do if he would, as, for instance, this "Fragment":

Shadow of smoke upon running water,
  How it symbols the life of man:
Pain his mother, Sorrow his daughter,
  Work his wife, since the world began!
Nay, how filmy our present vision!
  Deeper gaze through the river's run:
From dark trance into bright transition
  Dances Life, like a mote i' the sun.

IV.

We might very well make Mr. James Whitcomb Riley much the same reproaches we have made Mr. Austin if we could find it in our heart to make him any at all. But his *Rhymes of Childhood* take themselves quite out of the category of ordinary verse, and refuse to be judged by the usual criterions. The fact is, our Hoosier poet has found lodgment in people's love, which is a much safer place for any poet than their admiration. What he has said of very common aspects of life has endeared him; you feel, in reading his verse, that here is one of the honestest souls that ever uttered itself in that way, and that he is true to what we all know because he has known it, and not because he has just verified it by close observation. At times he is so very homely in material or phase that the thin academic skin creeps on the critical body, but the shiver checked, you perceive how good the thing is. It is the case with very many things in these *Rhymes of Childhood*, where you see that he is trying to express the child type in a child character. We do not know exactly why we should pass all these rhymes over to give the following descriptive piece, one of many in the book that addresses itself to the reader in grown-up language.

A SUDDEN SHOWER.

Barefooted boys scud up the street,
  Or skurry under sheltering sheds;
And school-girl faces pale and sweet,
  Gleam from the shawls about their heads.
Doors bang; and mother voices call
  From alien homes; and rusty gates
Are slammed; and high above it all
  The thunder grim reverberates.
And then abrupt, the rain, the rain! . . . .
  The earth lies gasping; and the eyes
Behind the streaming window-panes
  Smile at the trouble of the skies.
The highway smokes, sharp echoes ring;
  The cattle bawl and cow-bells clank;
And into town comes galloping
  The farmer's horse, with steaming flank.
The swallow dips beneath the eaves,
  And flirts his plumes and folds his wings;
And under the cataba leaves
  The caterpillar curls and clings.
The bumblebee is pelted down
  The wet stem of the hollyhock;
And sullenly in spattered brown
  The cricket leaps the garden walk.
Within, the baby claps his hands
  And crows with rapture strange and vague;
Without, beneath the rose-bush stands
  A dripping rooster on one leg.

Is not this excellent? There is not a false touch in it; that pelted-down bumblebee is worth his weight in gold; but then, so is the dripping rooster, for that matter.

V.

Mr. Eugene Field's *Little Book of West-*

ern Verse has much in common with Mr. Riley's work; but it appears to us rather less native and rather more conscious. Mr. Field has tried his clever hand in a good many ways, and the book consists largely, perhaps too largely, of proofs of what he can do in each; if there had been more unity of direction he might have gone farther. We confess to the same misgiving about the pieces in mining-camp "dialect" that we feel concerning the pieces in archaic English; they seem to us written by a somewhat remote and exterior witness. But when it comes to such a bit of characterization as "Little Mack," the Western journalist, who "runs"

The smartest, likeliest paper that is printed
    anywhere;
    And best of all, the paragraphs are pointed
    like a tack,
And that's because they emanate
    From "Little Mack,"

we have no question whatever of the point of view and the accurate intelligence of the performance. Not that Mr. Field does not do other kinds of things very well: the poems that relate to children are full of unaffected tenderness, and have now and then a keen pathos that comes from the heart and goes to it; and here is a poem whose charm we should not know just how to formulate, though we are sure all our readers will feel it:

HI-SPY.

Strange that the city thoroughfare,
    Noisy and bustling all the day,
Should with the night renounce its care
    And lend itself to children's play!
Oh, girls are girls, and boys are boys,
    And have been so since Abel's birth,
And shall be so till dolls and toys
    Are with the children swept from earth.
The self-same sport that crowns the day
    Of many a Syrian shepherd's son,
Beguiles the little lads at play
    By night in stately Babylon.
I hear their voices in the street,
    Yet 'tis so different from then!
Come, brother, from your winding-sheet,
    And let us two be boys again!

VI.

We believe that the piece we like best in Mr. Aldrich's new volume, *The Sister's Tragedy and Other Poems*, is the little rhyme he calls

MEMORY.

My mind lets go a thousand things,
Like dates of wars and deaths of kings,
And yet recalls the very hour—
'Twas noon by yonder village tower,
And on the last blue noon of May—
The wind came briskly up this way,
Crisping the brook beside the road;
Then, pausing here, set down its load
Of pine scents and shook listlessly
Two petals from that wild-rose tree.

Very simple, is not it, and very slight? but oh, young gentlemen and ladies intending verse, how difficult to do! To convey a sentiment, a mere emotion like this, wants the master-hand; any 'prentice touch would break the airy vase, and spill its delicate sweet. Then, here is something else that is almost as fine, that we like almost as well:

A MOOD.

A blight, a gloom, I know not what, has crept
    upon my gladness—
Some vague, remote, ancestral touch of sorrow or
    of madness;
A fear that is not fear, a pain that has not pain's
    insistence;
A sense of longing and of loss, in some foregone
    existence;
A subtle hurt that never pen has writ nor tongue
    has spoken—
Such hurt perchance as Nature feels when a
    blossomed bough is broken.

One does not lecture upon things like these; if they do not say themselves to the reader, you shall seek in vain to say them. But we would have the reader observe how wisely and how much the poet forbears in these exquisite portraits of mere feeling; how skilfully he escapes saying the fatal word that would have enforced and spoiled them. It is not for this place or this voice to limit the function of a poet like Mr. Aldrich; but we may say that he could not give us too many of these things for our pleasure; others may have other things of his, which it seems to us other people might do, and in which we fancy him striving disproportionately to the effect attained; but for ourselves we should have been glad if his whole book had been made up of moods and memories such as these.

VII.

Rose Brake is the name of a little volume of poems by Danske Dandridge, one of those Scandinavians, we think, like Mr. Boyesen, who naturalize so easily among us, and use our English as if they were born to it. Mrs. Dandridge has an ear for its finest music and repeats its most native strains to words of her own, that bring a Northern fancy into the song, and express some qualities that have the charm of another way of feeling life and nature. There are, for us at least, overmany fairies in her scheme; but we know that "the woods are full of them" in Norway and Denmark, and we tolerate them here in the hope that by-and-by they will settle down into law-abiding citizens and people her future books with somewhat more of the honest mortality we are more used to. Dryads we get on with better, and we decidedly like that one in Mrs. Dandridge's book who saw a young man one day in the forest:

> He smiled and sighed, and so was gone.
> 'Twas then I learned I was alone!
> When young birds chirp themselves to sleep,
> I sometimes wish that I could weep;
> I sit me down upon a stone
> And feel that I am all alone;
> I rest my cheek upon my hand
> And sigh, but nothing understand;
> I sing—my songs are very sad;
> I wish I ne'er had seen the lad!
> Ah me, I feel what must be pain;
> Would I might see the lad again!

But here is a poem we like still better, perhaps because it is all human, and wholly American:

INDIAN-SUMMER.

> Yes, the sweet summer lingers still;
> The hazes loiter on the hill;
> The year, a spendthrift growing old,
> Is scattering his lavish gold
>   For a last pleasure.
> The robins flock, but do not go;
> We share the word with footsteps slow,
>   In sober leisure,
> Or sit beneath the chestnut-tree,
> Our hands in silent company.
> Not yet, dear friend, we part not yet;
> Full soon the last warm sun will set;
> The crickets cease to stir the grass;
>   The gold and amber fade away;
> The scarlet from the landscape pass,
>   And all the sky be sodden gray;
> Too soon, alas! the frost must fall
>   And blight the asters on the hill,
> The golden-rod, the gentians, all,
>   And we must feel the parting chill.
> But oh, not yet, not yet we part:
> The summer strains us to her heart;
> The world is all a golden smile,
> And we may love a little while;
> The summer dies and hearts forget,
> And we must part—not yet, not yet!

VIII.

The only advantage of a sin of omission over the other kind, is that it may be sometimes repaired, if one has the proper humility; and we hope we bring a due sense of our deficiency in having failed hitherto to recognize the very rare and beautiful quality of Mr. William Watson's poetry to the pleasure of recognizing it now. We might forgive ourselves for overlooking it because it is so small in quantity, but we will not alloy our penitence with excuses; it shall be pure, and so perhaps avail the more. The poet's slight volume, spare almost as the glance of the "swart star" itself, is called *Wordsworth's Grave and Other Poems,* and it was published in London long enough ago last year to have become a cult in Boston. In its seventy-five pages there is very little that is not very good, though of course some things in it are very much better than others. For instance, no man could always keep the level of such a poem as this which we find among the short pieces Mr. Watson calls epigrams, with the true Greek sense of the word in mind:

BYRON THE VOLUPTUARY.

> Too avid of earth's bliss, he was of those
>   Whom Delight flies because they give her chase.
> Only the odor of her wild hair blows
>   Back in their faces hungering for her face.

We do not give this exquisite intaglio as Mr. Watson's finest work, though many might be glad to count it their best, and we should not care in any wise to limit him in our praise, if we could. A poet who could write either of the epigrams that follow, would be only too apt to transcend it:

AFTER READING "TAMBURLAINE THE GREAT."

> Your Marlowe's page I close, my Shakespeare's ope.
>   How welcome, after drum and trumpet's din,
> The continuity, the long slow slope
>   And vast curves of the gradual violin!

SHELLEY AND HARRIET WESTBROOK.

> A star looked down from heaven and loved a
>   flower
> Grown in earth's garden—loved it for an hour:
> Let eyes which trace his orbit in the spheres
> Refuse not, to a ruined rose-bud, tears.

It is all very literary, this, in interest, but not in feeling, where it is so simple, nor in manner, where it is so frank. As natural a strain, evoked with as free a hand, runs through the poet's whole work. The poems on Wordsworth are of the same spirit, and they impart in most musical and entrancing numbers a criticism of such high worth that it seems the only worthy criticism of Wordsworth till one remembers what Mr. Lowell has said of him. We do not know that even that [2] master has brought out as Mr. Watson's verse does the central truth, the divine secret, of Wordsworth's power:

> Not Milton's keen, translunar music thine;
>   Not Shakespeare's cloudless, boundless human
>   view;
> Not Shelley's flush of rose on peaks divine;
>   Nor yet the wizard twilight Coleridge knew.
> What hadst thou that could make so large amends
>   For all thou hadst not and thy peers possessed?
> Motion and fire, swift means to radiant ends?—
>   *Thou hadst for weary feet the gift of rest.*
>
> From Shelley's dazzling glow or thunderous haze,
>   From Byron's tempest anger, tempest mirth,
> Men turned to thee and found—not blast and blaze,
>   Tumult of tottering heavens, but peace on earth.
>
> Nor peace that grows by Lethe, scentless flower,
>   There in white, languors to decline and cease;
> But peace, whose names are also rapture, power,
>   Clear sight, and love: for these are parts of peace.

The poet strikes this note of fine appreciation again and again; such appreciation as might have satisfied the largest demand of a spirit which had known itself so misconceived and misunderstood as Wordsworth was so long.

He felt the charm of childhood, grace of youth,
  Grandeur of age, insisting to be sung.
The impassioned argument was simple truth,
  Half wondering at its own melodious tongue.

Impassioned? Ay, to the heart's ecstatic core!
  But far removed were clangor, storm, and feud;
For plenteous health was his, exceeding store
  Of joy, *and an impassioned quietude.*

But these literary characterizations, penetrated as they are with the keenest and loveliest feeling, by no means give the range of a poet whom we are so glad to know. He permits himself to think and to speak robustly about contemporary politics, and his English patriotism is qualified with a humanity far above and beyond it. For proof of this, look among several splendid sonnets he calls *Ver Tenebrosum;* but for evidence of his imaginative reach and force, let us give the striking poem which he names

THE MOCK SELF.

Few friends are mine, though many wights there be
Who, meeting oft a phantasm that makes claim
To be myself, and hath my face and name,
And whose thin fraud I wink at privily,
Account this light impostor very me.
What boots it undeceive them, and proclaim
Myself myself, and whelm this cheat with shame?
I care not, so he leave my true self free,
Impose not on me also; but alas!
I too, at fault, bewildered, sometimes take
Him for myself, and far from mine own sight,
Torpid, indifferent, doth mine own self pass;
And yet anon leaps suddenly awake,
And spurns the gibbering mime into the night.

Greater subtlety than this, in plainer or more strenuous terms, we should not know where to find at a moment's notice.

---

[1] The "commonwealth" is that described by Edward Bellamy in Looking Backward. See pp. 140b-141b.

[2] James Russell Lowell, "Wordsworth," in The Writings of James Russell Lowell in Prose and Poetry, VI (Boston and New York: Houghton, Mifflin and Company, 1886), pp. 99-114.

June, 1891

Editor's Study.

I.

WE believe the new edition of Mr. Lowell's works is the first to bring his writings in the different kinds together with anything like completeness. It has a greater completeness, he confesses in one of his prefaces, than he likes; he reprints some of his earlier pieces because, "owing to the unjust distinction made by the law between literary and other property," they will be reprinted by some one. The reader will scarcely share his sense of hardship in this; though the law that limits an author's control of his writings is none the less unfair and impudently sophistical.

The "early indiscretions,"as Mr. Lowell calls them, help to swell the bulk of his poems to four volumes; then there are four volumes of literary essays; a volume of literary and political addresses, and a volume of political essays. The revision of the work in either of these sorts is apparently very cursory, and the changes of the slightest. Doubtless something of temperament, something of habit, and something of instinct have prevailed with him to leave the pieces as he wrote them, in the shape that the glowing metal first took as it lost the heat of his mind. Of all our literary men he has wrought most in the tradition of the ideal poet: the form with him has been part of the inspiration, and it is said that whenever he has changed the form, in more critical moments, he has afterward changed it back in moments more critical still. The result is proof of the fact that the imagination is no bad critic, or that the old-fashioned division of the mind into the imaginative and the critical faculties, as if it were built in water-tight compartments, is altogether fantastic. The two operate inseparably together, the difference between Mr. Lowell's method and that of some others being simply that the imagination is more active with him in the vision, and with them in the revision. He has little or nothing to say about his work, now that all is done. There are two pages of prefatory note for the four volumes of poems; two for the four volumes of literary essays; none at all for the other things. But the work con-tinually talks about itself, especially the prose, where the scholarly ease, the intellectual intimacy, the impersonal familiarity, win the reader and endear the writer. We cannot always be up to the high humors of the Muse; some of us cannot follow her on the ethereal tops; but no one is averse to an arm-chair by the fire, a lamp at the elbow, and a book in the hand of a friend who reads all literature into and out of it. The essays are full of those confidences which such safety from the world and the weather invites to; and perhaps one who should declare that the real Lowell was to be found in them would not merit instant death. There are several real Lowells, the culprit might urge; and he could hedge, with no great loss of consistency, in owning that there was one in every kind of literature that our author has attempted. In fact, the sense of genuineness, of sincerity in all things, of impatience with affectation of any sort, is the sense that remains with the reader. Sometimes there is compression and abruptness, but there is never superfluity; there might often have been more with great advantage, there could not have been less without loss. There are certain expressions, especially in the poetry, that seem driven too far, or forced a little too violently to the service they are made to do; the thought overloads the phrase; but there is nowhere weakness or emptiness. As time goes on from the earlier to the later work, both in the verse and in the prose, these faults, if they are faults, disappear, and there is a mellow richness in it all, a harmony in the thought and the word, a fusion of all harsh splendors into one clear serenity. In the performance of every writer, of every artist, there are at times turns of good fortune, and these may occur in his earliest as well as his latest performance. But it is when his felicity becomes characteristic, when his prosperity is habitual, that he is approved a master.

II.

Any one wishing to make that study of Mr. Lowell's books which these strait limits will not allow would find such a pleasure in the inquiry as only the peculiar combination of qualities in him can give. His complexity is very simple, when once you have the key to it, and the final agreement between his contradictions is perfect. He is one who is always talking or singing about the ideal, but no one ever loved better to feel the honest earth under his feet. He likes to imagine flight; he approves of flying, admires, advises it; but he understands very well that, in matters of art, legs were made before wings; and that a steady pace carries one to the ends of the knowable world.

No realist ever felt reality more keenly than he, or strove more faithfully, more triumphantly, to get the light of its homely, heavenly countenance into literature. He is, of all things, a scholar; but he is naturally at such war with pedantry that he seems tempted at times to snub scholarship, and trust himself wholly to that basal common-sense which he loves in common men. His thought flows as naturally in the parlance that he caught from the lips of the wagoners and ploughmen of the rustic village Cambridge once was as in "the language of Shakespeare and Milton"; there are passages of the *Biglow Papers* that match the finest in the *Commemoration Ode*, or the *Agassiz*. In the last analysis Hosea Biglow and Sir Launfal are of the same make; the same heart, the same soul is in them both. No author more frequently reminds the reader that though God made us in His own image, He made us out of the dust of the earth, and his abiding sense of humanity as Divinity imagined it keeps his lightest laughter sweet. He makes merry with men's foibles, but he never makes a mock of them as some other great humorists do, disheartening and corrupting with the cynicism that likens folly with wisdom and evil with good, and finds all one. There is, so far as we remember, not one touch of cynicism in all that he has written; and for this reason, as a satirist he stands not only foremost but alone in our language. The sense of his pre-eminence in this sort is so strong at times as to make one forget his excellence in others; and it is well once in a way to consider the variety of his achievement in the works that testify to it. In fact, when one has said satirist, the word seems to minimize, or at least to misstate his *Biglow Papers*. He is there such a satirist, or in such a way, as Cervantes was: his humor does not merely criticise, it creates. Hosea Biglow, Birdofreedom Sawin, and Homer Wilbur are enduring and delightful types because they came from the real people out-of-doors, who always seem commonplace to the casual or unsympathetic eye. We said create, when we meant discover, or divine; and we do not suppose that the most powerful "genius" after training

itself into condition by the most assiduous intellectual athletics could create such types. With God all things are possible, but men are limited, and in literature the recognizable figures are those whose likeness we have seen before, in ourselves, in others. It is such figures that outlast all conditions, and that embody and perpetuate them to the imagination of aftertime. The Spain of Cervantes is conceivable to us from the characters he found there, and the New England of the Mexican War and the Secession has nowhere graven itself in literature so distinctly and enduringly as in the verse of our great humorist.

III.

Mr. Lowell is always a humorist, as we were trying to say, if a humorist is one who beyond other men sees both sides of every question and is haunted by the consciousness of the absurdity that lurks in all aspects of human affairs. You are aware of this all-round perception in him, whatever matter he is handling, and of its complete accord with reverence and honor where these are due. In this he is like some man of the great Elizabethan group; there is the freshness and largeness of those days in his diction, and that near neighborhood of heart and mind in his work which enabled them to leave the warmth of a living touch on any theme they handled. He views men and things with an impassioned reason; or, as the common phrase has it, he *feels* what he says. This is true not only of his literary opinions, but it is true, as well, of his judgments of public questions, which he always regarded with a vision almost prophetic in its scope. He is never a very good hater; his enemy too often amuses him for that; he is conscious that he might be some such man as his enemy in his enemy's place; and that his enemy is probably not such a bad fellow as he would like to make himself out. But if he is not a good hater (a stupid kind of creature, in spite of Dr. Johnson), he is one of the best and wisest lovers that ever were. It is not easy to see the virtues of a friend; but Mr. Lowell has this gift, and he uses it for us again and again in those poems which celebrate this one or that one he loves. The characterizations in the *Fable for Critics* are witnesses of the fact both as to friends and foes; and in those of the *Agassiz* the persons are sketched with an accuracy and truth which only a generous affection could have inspired. The climate of Cambridge, which is in some respects less agreeable than could be wished, seems always to have been favorable to the cultivation of the manly kindness that flowers so often in Mr. Lowell's verse. The harmony of his contradictions is nowhere more apparent than in what may be called his poems of friendship. The sympathies that are made to go round all humanity are said to be found rather thin at times for the wear and tear of everyday use; and the philanthropist, by some observers, has been accounted an inadequate neighbor. But it is certainly not so in Mr. Lowell's case. He gave himself wholly to a cause, the cause of freedom, at one period of his life; but men never became Man to him, not even black men; in spite of his explicit preference for types, he seems always to have liked characters a little better.

The student of his life will find nothing more important in it than the antislavery passage, which it would be a gross misconception to think of as an episode. It seemed to close with the end of slavery, for he was not of those who belabor a dead dog, to give him a realizing sense that there is a punishment after death. But the spirit that moved him, against tradition and association and interest, to take the side of the weak and the poor, has really been the guiding motive of his life. As he is above all things, however, a humorist, he does not fail to see the verge where the sublime touches the ridiculous, and he makes laughter his weapon against the wrong, and his defence, in the last resort, against the right even in himself; for nothing is so apt to "work like madness in the brain" as a sense of absolute and perfect right. He never, apparently, had this; he always saw the other side, with that circumvision of the humorist which forbids any prophet strictly to follow the slant of his own nose. If the ingredients had been less kindly mixed in him, the world might have had another humorist like Swift, or like Heine; that is, if there had been less heart or less conscience in him. But as there was so much heart and so much conscience we had Lowell; we had not the *Tale of a Tub*, or *Atta Troll*, but the *Biglow Papers*, and [2] all that smiling translucence which everywhere breaks through his phrase.

Probably no one, at the bottom of his soul, ever disliked convention more than he; yet every now and then he has a conscience even about convention, and especially in his later writings you find him taking a brace, and bringing himself up in behalf of the established, because it is the established. Yet give his conscience a little more time, and it works him back to his original attitude, as when, after due respect to the old, the historic in English affairs, expressed in this or that dedication of bust or statue, he finds himself saying to an English audience that democracy is the hope and the social salvation of the race.

To the short-sighted there may seem a prevalence of whimsicality in his intellectual temperament, as there so often is in its literary expression; but it will not seem so to those whose perception can compass the whole truth as to human motive. It is not always high noon or midnight with any man but a madman: the sane all have their small hours and their little halves and quarters of hours; and the fractions and subdivisions rather abound in Mr. Lowell.

He is true Elizabethan in his fondness for a quip, a quirk; and he will sometimes stay large discourse to have his smile at a vagrant humor flitting over the surface of his thought. Solemn persons may find this a trial, but no wise person will; for all who have lived with their eyes open have seen life itself as desultory and capricious at the most momentous junctures. Besides, to the mind of the humorist, especially if he be a great poet, no idea presents itself simply, but with a rich variety of color, and with endless implications. Some sense of this he cannot help imparting: the difference of humor and poetry from dulness and prose obliges him. But perhaps because dulness and prose have their rightful place in the world, there will always be some misgiving, some dispute, about Mr. Lowell's attitude in these matters. He is not a man whom all men can agree about. Some who nurtured themselves upon his heroic moods, his utterances for freedom and humanity, censure him for having faltered from his faith in humanity because he has not kept repeating it like a creed. But if any doubter will look at his work as a whole, we do not think he can fail to disabuse himself of his errors, unless they are wilful. Of course it concerns him rather than the author to do this: the poet, humorist, critic, publicist, who is as apt to be all of these together as one at a time, is safe enough from his mistake. The spirit of Mr. Lowell's work is one and the same from first to last, and in an unfailing sincerity it has the only valuable, the only possible consistency.

IV.

Of constructive satire such as his we have had little or nothing since his time; perhaps he is the last of a great line; but other sorts we seem not likely to lack. In fact we are at present developing a rather novel variety: the satire that accrues to a thing from the worship of its admirers. We have lately seen how damaging Mr. McAllister could make himself [3] to the best society of New York by his devout portrayal of it, and now another devotee of fashion is trying to play the part of iconoclast with the ideal of gentleman. *Gentlemen* is what he calls his book, which comes to us with all the graces of Mr. De Vinne's press; and he assumes to tell whatever is worth knowing about the art of being a gentleman, in dress, manners, morals, and mind. The treatise has not the charm of Castiglione's *Court-ier*, and yet it is delightful reading, in its way, which tries hard not to be the way of other behavior books. It is not easy to avoid this; if we can believe the unknown author of *Gentlemen*, he abhors nothing so much as vulgarity; yet he begins his instructions in dress by saying, "With judgment and economy one can be something of a dresser."

When he passes to graver matters, to customs and conduct, he tells us that "a body-coat should never be removed in the presence of ladies," unless a gentleman is pressed to appear in his shirt sleeves without a dissenting voice; and he should not "remain to a meal" unless he has made at least five calls in the house where he is asked. When seated beside a lady on a sofa he must not cross his legs; and "the conversation should be of a sensible topic, or if amusing, it should be at least interesting." "Unless you can do it gracefully, do not execute a dance, or attempt to imitate stage performers;" and at dinner, never rise before your host or hostess. In waltzing, "place your right hand at the lady's back below the lower ends of the shoulder-blades"; and never on any occasion "bite the lips, or pick the teeth, as both distort the face. Never use the eyes in a flirtatious manner, as it is very poor taste, and shows conceit."

The intending gentleman is not left without sound advice on more serious points; he is urged not "to take advantage of being alone with a lady in a carriage to address her in any way too familiar to be polite"; he must kiss no one but his betrothed, or his wife, or his blood-relations, not even a very old friend. But in making an offer of marriage, "when the lady replies affirmatively, immediately clasp her in your arms." This must always be done, and the most impetuous lover must not forget it.

V.

Such is the manner and such the matter of the latest advice to *Gentlemen*. We had our doubts, in reading it, whether the author was not laughing in the sleeve of that body-coat which nothing would induce him to remove in the presence of ladies; but on the whole we incline to think he is not joking. To turn from this great world of *Gentlemen*, to the small, lowly sphere where Miss Wilkins's humble folk have their being, is a vast change, but there is a kind of consolation in it. Here at least are real interests, passions, ambitions; and yonder there do not seem to be any. The scenes of *A New England Nun and Other Stories* are laid in that land of little village houses which the author of *A Humble Romance* has made her own. The record never strays beyond;

there is hardly a person in the dramas who does not work for a living; the tragedies and comedies are those of the simplest and commonest people, who speak a crabbed Yankee through their noses, and whose dress and address would be alike shocking to *Gentlemen*. Still they may be borne with, at least in the hands of an artist such as Miss Wilkins has shown herself to be. We are not sure that there is anything better in this volume than in her first; we note the same powers, the same weaknesses; the never-erring eye, the sometimes mistaken fancy. The figures are drawn with the same exquisitely satisfying veracity; but about half the time we doubt whether they would do what they are shown doing. We have a lurking fear at moments that Miss Wilkins would like to write entirely romantic stories about these honest people of hers; but her own love of truth and her perfect knowledge of such life as theirs forbid her actually to do this. There is apparently a conflict of purposes in her sketches which gives her art an undecided effect, or a divided effect, as in certain of them where we make the acquaintance of her characters in their village of little houses, and lose it in the No Man's Land of exaggerated action and conventional emotion. In the interest of her art, which is so perfectly satisfying in the service of reality, it could almost be wished that she might once write a thoroughly romantic story, and wreak in it all the impulses she has in that direction. Then perhaps she might return to the right exercise of a gift which is one of the most precious in fiction. But perhaps this could not happen; perhaps the Study is itself romantic in imagining such a thing. It may be that we shall always have to content ourselves with now a story of the real and unreal mixed, and now one of unmixed reality, such as Miss Wilkins alone can give us. At any rate her future is not in the keeping of criticism, to shape or to direct. Who can forecast the course of such a talent? Not even the talent itself; and what we must be grateful for is what it has already given us in the two volumes of tales, which are as good in their way as anything ever done amongst us; that is, among any people. In form they instinctively approach that of the best work everywhere in the fine detail of the handling; but in spirit they are distinctively ours. The humor is American, and they are almost all humorously imagined, with a sort of direct reference to the facts of the usual rustic American experience. The life of the human heart, its affections, its hopes, its fears, however these mask themselves from low to high, or high to low, is always the same, in every time and land; but in each it has a special physiognomy. What our artist has done is to catch the American look of life, so that if her miniatures remain to other ages they shall know just the expression of that vast average of Americans who do the hard work of the country, and live narrowly on their small earnings and savings. If there is no gayety in that look, it is because the face of hard work is always sober, and because the consciousness of merciless fortuities and inexorable responsibilities comes early and stays late with our people.

---

[1] James Russell Lowell, The Writings of James Russell Lowell in Prose and Poetry (Boston and New York: Houghton, Mifflin and Company, 1886).

[2] Tale of a Tub, by Jonathan Swift; Atta Troll, by Heinrich Heine.

[3] See pp. 305a-306a, and note 3 on p. 307.

July , 1891

Editor's Study.

I.

WE suppose it would be rather damaging to Professor William James
with other scientists to show that in his
volumes on *The Principles of Psychology*
he writes with a poetic sense of his facts,
and with an artistic pleasure in their
presentation. We must content ourselves
with a far less positive recognition of the
charming spirit, the delightful manner,
and the flavorous and characteristic style
of the work. There are moments when
he brings to the intellectual strain of the
subject the relief of a humorous touch;
when he gives the overtaxed faculties a
little vacation, and invites the sympathies
of the reader to a share in the inquiry.
It has so long been the custom to call a
certain friendly and consciously fallible
attitude "human" that we are reluctant
to proclaim his relation to his theme as
distinctly "human," yet the epithet comes
unbidden to the pen in attempting to label his performance. After all, it is perhaps as well to use it; perhaps it is as
well to admit frankly that the treatise
has often those graces and attractions
which we have hinted at. There are many
other times when it has none of them,
and when the author's attitude is so severely scientific, so pitilessly exigent of
the reader's co-operation, so remorselessly
indifferent to his mental repose, as to be
distinctly inhuman. But it must be said
of Professor James that he has not only
not tried to deny his theme the æsthetic
and ethical interest it inherently has for
every one having a mind, or thinking he
has one, but has been willing to heighten
it. In this way it must be admitted that
he has come dangerously near writing a
"popular" book. It is not exactly "summer reading"; the two vast volumes, ag-
gregating some fourteen hundred octavo
pages, would not go easily into the pocket
or the hand-bag; they will probably not
be found in competition with the fiction
of the news stands; we could not imagine
their being "lapped out" by the train-
boy. But there is no doubt that several of
the chapters, such as those on Habit, The
Consciousness of Self, Memory, Imagination, Instinct, Will, and Hypnotism, can
appeal successfully to people of average

culture; and that throughout the work
there are passages which may be read
aloud to the tenderest female, so lightly
and agreeably are some of the most difficult problems of the soul handled in
them. We say soul, but we really mean
mind, for although psychology took its
name from being the "science of the human soul," it has now decided that the
question of the soul is really no part of its
business: the mind only—its attributes,
conditions, phenomena—is dealt with; the
soul is left out of the account.

Not that as to the existence or the destiny of such a constituent of human nature this science denies anything. On the
contrary, in Professor James's work there
is a perceptible sympathy and regard for
the theories of it; but the inquiry is not
with them. The field is vast enough, and
the way obscure enough without them:
and one impression that remains to the
unscientific reader of Professor James's
work is that it has not yet been explored,
or mapped except at a few points. With
one's self always at hand, with one's fel-
low-creatures swarming upon one, with
all human history behind one, a collection of "infinitely repellent particles" of
fact is the sum of psychological industry. The talk is not only about, but
round about, the human mind, which it
penetrates here and there and wins a
glimpse of unsayable things. The fascination of the quest forever remains,
and it is this fascination which Professor
James permits his reader to share. It
could not be said that he has a philosophical system to establish; his philosophical
system is his method of collating and
presenting discoveries made, and suggesting conclusions from them, and he is always so frank, so tolerant, that you feel
he would willingly consider a different
inference, if you made it, and would be
gladly interested in it. Nothing could be
more winning than the informality of his
discourse; it captivates the average human being to find that the study of his
mind is not necessarily allied to a frigid
decorum. Those who know the rich and
cordial properties of the philosophical
writings of Henry James the elder, will

find a kindred heartiness in the speculations of his son, and will be directly at home with him. The ground, of course. is absolutely different; nothing seems further from psychology than theology.

The book is so full of proofs of what we have been trying to say that it seems absurd to cast in the line at one place rather than another, but perhaps the chapter on Will is more abundantly illustrative than some others, though we do not know that such a passage as the following is one of the most illustrative in it: "Men do not differ so much in their mere feelings and conceptions. Their notions of possibility and their ideals are not as far apart as might be argued from their different fates. No class of them have better sentiments or feel more constantly the difference between the higher and the lower path in life than the hopeless failures, the sentimentalists, the drunkards, the schemers, the 'dead-beats,' whose life is one long contradiction between knowledge and action, and who, with full command of theory, never get to holding their limp characters upright. No one eats of the fruit of the tree of knowledge as they do; as far as moral insight goes, in comparison with them, the orderly and prosperous Philistines whom they scandalize are suckling babes. And yet their moral knowledge, always there, grumbling and rumbling in the background— discerning, commenting, protesting, longing, half resolving—never wholly resolves, never gets its voice out of the minor into the major key, or its speech out of the subjunctive into the imperative mood, never breaks the spell, never takes the helm into its own hands. In such characters as Restif and Rousseau, it would seem as if the lower motives had all the impulsive efficacy in their hands. The more ideal motives exist alongside of them in profusion; and the consciousness of inward hollowness that accrues from habitually seeing the better only to do the worse, is one of the saddest feelings one can bear with him through this vale of tears."

It will have been perceived from this how much the moral aspect of the facts ascertained interests the writer, who feels their value not only as a moralist but as an artist; he cannot help stating his mind about them picturesquely. This must commend him to the general reader, who, although he may, and probably will, forget about the dark underlying premises of the luminous conclusions that delight him, cannot fail to be greatly stimulated and strengthened by the whole philosophy of the book. It would be hard for us, at least, to find a more important piece of writing in its way than the chapter on Habit; it is something for

the young to read with fear and hope, the old with self-pity or self-gratulation, and every one with recognition of the fact that in most things that tell for good or ill, and much or little in life, we are creatures of our own making. It would be well for the reader to review this chapter in the light of that on the Will, where the notion of free-will is more fully dealt with. In fact the will of the weak man is *not* free; but the will of the strong man, the man who has *got the habit* of preferring sense to nonsense and "virtue" to "vice," is a *freed* will, which one might very well spend all one's energies in achieving. It is this preference which at last becomes the man, and remains permanent throughout those astounding changes which every one finds in himself from time to time. "Every thought we have of a given fact," Mr. James says, "is, strictly speaking, unique, and only bears a resemblance of kind with our other thoughts of the same fact. When the identical fact recurs, we *must* think of it in a fresh manner, see it under a somewhat different angle, apprehend it in different relations from those in which it last appeared. And the thought by which we cognize it is the thought of it-in-these-relations, a thought suffused with the consciousness of all that dim content. Often we are ourselves struck at the strange differences in our successive views of the same thing. We wonder how we ever could have opined as we did last month about a certain matter. We have outgrown the possibility of that state of mind, we know not how. From one year to another we see things in new lights. What was unreal has grown real, and what was exciting is insipid. The friends we used to care the world for are shrunken to shadows; the women, once so divine, the stars, the woods, and the waters, how now so dull and common; the young girls that brought an aura of infinity, at present hardly distinguishable existences; the pictures so empty; and as for the books, what *was* there to find so mysteriously significant in Goethe, or in John Mill so full of weight? Instead of all this, more zestful than ever is the work, the work; and fuller and deeper the import of common duties and of common goods."

We can safely leave to the reader the implications of this admirable thought. If Psychology in this work is treated philosophically rather than scientifically, there can be no question but it is treated profoundly and subtly, and with a never-failing, absolute devotion to the truth. This fidelity is as signal in it as the generosity of the feeling, the elevation of the thought, the sweetness of the humanity which characterize it. If the book does not establish a theory, if it confesses the tentative, adolescent quality of a science which is as old as the race, and as young as the latest human consciousness, it is all the same a rare contribution to knowledge, and a treasury of suggestion which any cultivated intelligence can profit by. It is necessarily inconclusive in many ways, and very likely Psychology can never be a science as some other sciences are, but must always remain a philosophy. If this is so, it can change its mind with less confusion to the unlearned than they feel when they are told that all they have been taught by the highest scientific authorities is mistaken. It can so continue the possession of all who love wisdom, however far off, however wanting in the self-knowledge where all wisdom centres.

II.

What a work like Mr. James's (if there is another like it) does for the unscienced reader is to give him the habit of looking at his mental qualities and ingredients as materials of personality with which his conscience can the more hopefully deal, the more distinctly they are ascertained. It comes to an ethical effect, to suggestion for the ideal social life, with only rather more direct instruction than astronomy has. Kant felt the moral law within him one in meaning with the starry heavens above him; and in a book of sonnets, by a poet new to us, which we have lately been reading with singular pleasure, there is a like recognition of the unity of things which we can perpetually know better, but never wholly know.

The book is a series of poems by Mrs. A. M. Richards, called "Letter and Spirit," which all appeal with a serious and delicate beauty of their own. They are a fragment, the author tells us, of a design "giving expression to each of the manifold aspects of an unchanging and unchangeable truth," and they lead the thought on and on with a charm distinctly their own. We should not know just how to impart a sense of it in words of ours, and we are tempted to quote one of the poems, warning the reader at the same time that this sonnet, which hints the charm, does not suggest the range and scope of the others.

"I who am young, let me not crave too much
  The burden of content, not too much strain
The shining mirage of Desire to touch;
  Fruition's rest is full of nameless pain.
And yet, O End! O Rest! if there be such
In all the world, come in the mighty reign
Of autumn on this silent inland plain;
Come to a spirit toiling overmuch.
  I, who am old, let not my heart annul
With futile hope the gain of suffering years,
  Nor make the fine gold of their wisdom dull
With youth's sweet passion of unfruitful tears.
And yet, in this fair spring, with nature's tongue
I cry aloud: Would God I too were young!"

III.

Possibly there is something in the momentary mood of the world, the set of the wind from that particular quarter where it now is, that draws music of like spiritual quality from Æolian harps "of divers tones," and carries the same strain of feeling from poet to poet. There is no break in it between the sonnets we have been speaking of and most of the poems in Dr. Weir Mitchell's last volume of verse, though of course in externals there is any imaginable difference you like. In "A Psalm of Deaths" and the accompanying poems there is the same reverence, the same patience, the same resignation and abeyance in the presence of those large questions that seem to tempt only to baffle us, as we find in Mrs. Richards's beautiful sonnets. The feeling is audible in the solemn strains "Of Those Remembered," "Of One Dead," "Pained unto Death," "A Canticle of Time," "How the Poet for an Hour was King," and most musically of all in "A Psalm of the Waters." It is as old as the first man who asked himself "What for?" but we do not remember to have found it anywhere more sweetly or fully expressed, or with a more winning pensiveness:—

"Is it I who interpret
The cry of the masterful northwind,
The hum of the rain in the hemlocks,
As chorals of joy or of sadness,
To match the mere moods of my being?
Alas for the doubt and the wonder!
Alas for the strange incompleteness
That limits with boundaries solemn
The questioning soul! Yet forever
I know that these choristers ancient
Have touch of my heart; and also, too,
That never was love in its fulness
Told all the great sum of its loving!
I know, too, the years, that remorseless
Have hurt me with sorrow, bring ever
More near for my help the quick healing,
The infinite comfort of nature;
For surely the childhood that enters
This heaven of wood and of water
Is won with grayhairs in the nearing
That home ever open to childhood.
And you, you my brothers, who suffer
In serfdom of labor and sorrow,
What gain have your wounds, that forever
Man bridges with semblance of knowledge
The depths he can never illumine?
Or binds for his service the lightning,
Or prisons Neptune of the waters?
What help has it brought to the weeper?
How lessened the toil of the weary?
Alas! since at evening, deserted,
Job sat in his desolate anguish,
The world has grown wise, but the mourner
Still weeps and will weep; and what helping
He hath from his God or his fellows
Eludes the grave sentinel reason,
Steals in at the heart's lowly portal,
And helps, but will never be questioned."

IV.

We think that in his novel *The Mammon of Unrighteousness* Mr. H. H. Boyesen has kept all the promises and fulfilled all the hopes of his early fiction; but we doubt if those who first make the acquaintance of the author in its pages will feel all its greatness. Here is a novel that in breadth and depth has few equals as a study of American life, of American life psychically, socially, politically, in types drawn from a wide range of our conditions in city and country. Yet it is the work of a man born strange to our life, and coming to it with the disability of another language and another tradition. He was indeed in the perfect plasticity of his youth when he confronted it, and he had that love for its freedom and largeness, as well as that humorous sense of its grotesqueness, which fitted him to receive a keener impression of it than he perhaps knew at the time; but when Mr. Boyesen published his story of *Gunnar*, some twenty years ago, he was so intensely Norse that it did not seem as if he could ever be anything else. That lovely idyl of Norwegian peasant life was an outgrowth of the tremendous literary upheaval in Norway that shattered all the old literary ideals, and sent the poets and novelists of that little, mighty land back to the people to study their language at its source on their lips, and to purify and strengthen their diction for the expression of those conceptions in ethics and æsthetics which the names of Björnson and Ibsen now stand for. But the author of *Gunnar* began at once to take the stamp of his American environment, and to reproduce it in tales of more or less imperfect effect, but always of definite intention, until now he has given us a fiction which has few equals for truth and fulness among American novels.

Of course he has not got America all in. America will never all be got in till the great American novel is conceived in an encyclopedical form, with a force of novelists apportioned upon the basis of our Congressional representation, and working under one editorial direction. In the mean time, *The Mammon of Unrighteousness* may stand for an American novel of the first rank; and it is just to both sides of the national character, which so deep and sharp a line of cleavage divides that, looking at one, you are always inclined to deny that there is any other. No people ever presented as we do the beauty of the ideal and the ugliness of the material; but there are very few observers who see us in both. We are founded, cast, shaped in the ideal, yet most of our uses are frankly and brutally material. We are cynically selfish, we are magnanimously generous; the antagonism felt in each is expressed on a continually widening scale from the citizen up through the town meeting to the government of the whole republic. These facts of our civilization Mr. Boyesen does not represent in a single personality, however, but in two brothers, one of whom says, "I mean to be true to myself," and the other, "I mean to succeed." The allegory ends with their declarations, and the drama begins. These types are also characters, and it is with their fortunes as living men that the novel mainly concerns itself. It is from the outset boldly realistic; and it is at the same time poetical, as realism alone can be, since realism alone has the courage to look life squarely in the face and try to report the expression of its divinely imagined lineaments. If it cannot do this perfectly, that is because all art is imperfect; but the rudest endeavor at verity is better than the most finished pretence that there is something better than verity. To give what you think you ought to have seen in life rather than what you did see is a preposterous immodesty of which realism, with all its faults, has not been guilty; and Mr. Boyesen's errors are certainly not in this offensive direction. He will be blamed by those who cannot bear the real look of life; or who are so used to having the negative "touched," that a human face, as any mirror reflects it, is shocking to them. We can fancy such people troubled at this and dismayed at that in his story; not because it passes the limits of that strait decorum which Anglo-Saxon fiction has, we think rightly enough, set itself; but because within these limits it is faithful to every one's experience of one's fellow men and women. To such people the Rev. Mr. Robbins, with his simple-hearted love of smoking, and his perhaps culpable tolerance of very old Madeira, will seem a minister who ought not to appear in fiction, not because self-indulgent ministers are not known to them, but because they ought not to be known, because they ought somehow to be hushed up, and the defects of their virtues concealed. Kate Van Schaak, who makes the self-seeking Horace Larkin break his engagement with the minister's daughter, her cousin, and who matches her "family" with his "success" in the end, will be as little to their liking, not because she is untrue, but because she is true to the well-ancestored, rich, dull respectability from which she springs. For a like reason, her New York environment will have an effect of caricature for such readers, not because if they are in New York society they have not seen it, but because they have not seen it so depicted in literature. The society of the college town where the scene is laid is the society of a college town, but not of a college town as it should be in a novel professing to give an impression of it. "Let them paint them nude," says the Philistine in the Salon, "but let them put clothes on them." That is all that some people require of the novelist, and they rather prefer that he should put old clothes on them.

It must be confessed that the persons of Mr. Boyesen's book cannot respond satisfactorily to this demand, neither Horace Larkin whose egoistic fortunes are followed on one hand, nor Aleck Larkin whose adventures in the endeavor to be true to his convictions occupy the other half of the story. Evil is a tendency and good is a tendency, but in each there are eddies and counter-currents which such fiction as Mr. Boyesen's takes account of; but in most human beings neither tendency is so powerful as to be dramatically traceable. Vast groups of us remain stationary, and to the artist's eye are as bodies of still water, lessening from quiet ponds down to mere moral puddles. These reflect the sky and the surrounding objects, and give a light, a gleam here and there, to his picture, which would be less true without them; but they are hardly drawn into the course of events, and Mr. Boyesen's story loiters among them at times, though there is a tide of interest in it that finally leaves them far behind.

We confess that there are passages of it that we care less for than others. The complications of Obed Larkin's marriages seem to us an adventitious element of the composition, and though they are skilfully handled, affect us as an importation from an elder era of fiction than the rest

of the book belongs to. They involve the presentation of some admirable figures, and they effect the union of the good hero and good heroine, with some delightful and some sorrowful episodes of their semi-Bohemian life in New York, but they leave us wishing and believing that all this could have happened without them. On the whole, what we may call the Aleck Larkin side of the book is less important and less life-like than the Horace Larkin side; and if we were to choose something representative from it we should choose some passage of the egoist's career. When it comes to the choice, however, there is so much that is so good, that is subtle and penetrating in suggestion, that is fine and close and strong in execution, that we are embarrassed. Horace in politics, in law, in New York society, in the presence of the killing sorrow that he has brought upon the poor girl he has jilted, in his miserable success, is always himself, not with that mechanical singleness which a weaker art conceives, but with that mixture of motive yielding to the prevalent tendency of his character which it is the expression and the proof of mastery in an artist to render. In this novel, which we may truly call a great novel, Mr. Boyesen has given many such proofs. Hardly any figure that he touches is wanting in them, and those which he has devoted himself more especially to studying have a relief, a vitality, an existence which we recall like that of people we have met in the world.

---

[1] Nicolas Edme Restif de la Bretonne (1734-1806) was the French author of some 250 novels based upon his own immoderate life.

August, 1891

Editor's Study.

I.

NOT very long ago the Study had occasion to go to the news-stand in a metropolitan station, and get a book for a young lady who wished to be amused on the railroad journey she was about to make. Of course the only kind of book that is supposed to amuse young ladies, or old ones, for that matter, is a novel; and the Study found the news-stand so plentifully provided with novels that it asked itself whether they were not also supposed to amuse men of different ages. There seemed at first blush no difficulty in making a choice, but at each successive blush it became more and more difficult. The novels which so abounded at that news-stand were, upon closer inspection, such as might be supposed to amuse men of different ages, but if they were to amuse ladies of any age, they could hardly edify them; and whatever is to be said of the reading of men, men all feel that the reading of ladies ought to be edifying, or, at least, ought not to be offensive or deleterious. The news-stand had a very pretty look; it was decorative; for we have now got to making the cheap books very attractive, fashioning the outside of them after that of the French novels, and illustrating the covers in colors, not so artistically quite as the French do it, but not inartistically either. The trouble was not with the outside, however; if that had been the whole question the Study could easily have chosen, though there was upon the whole rather more kissing and embracing going on in colors than was quite in taste; where there was not this, the ladies portrayed had eyes too wide, too wise, too wandering, and corsages too low, or skirts too high; the gentlemen were too wickedly lurid in their *blasé* looks, and wore dress suits that seemed to be made up from the same piece as the scarlet garb of Mephistopheles, and afterward dyed black; their beards were cut to a point that seemed to take hold on hell; or else their mustaches were waxed to the last effect of wantonness and wickedness.

Some of these romances were translations from Continental tongues; there were, of course, the reprints of English novels of much innocenter aspect, but these looked dull; and the native American fiction was modelled outwardly, and too probably inwardly, upon that of the Latin tongue. It grieves us to add that a good many of these home products were the work of a sex whose influence is supposed to be altogether elevating and purifying. In the end, after lingering long and anxiously over this store of unwholesome sweets, the timid and fastidious Study ended by buying no novel at all. It bought several magazines, of the kind whose name is an absolute warrant of decency, to say the least; those novels all finally looked doubtful, if not indecent.

II.

Then, is there a decay in the morality of our fiction? It is always pleasant to think that there is a decay in things; it almost proves that there is no decay in one's self; but really, we are disposed, without claiming undue credit for the opinion, to say that there is a moral decay in our fiction. It is more artistic, or perhaps we had better say *chic*, than it was; but it is not so sound, we feel quite sure. Eighteen or twenty years ago, the news-stand in question would have been covered with novels vilely printed and repulsively bound, but certainly healthier in matter, if not so *chic* in manner. The people who do these nasty-looking contemporary things—authors, artisans, artists—have got touch; they are clever; and yet there are plenty of people who have got touch, who are clever, and who are not doing nasty-looking things. We all know them; it is needless to name them; but apparently the news-stand believes the public does not want them, at least in book form. You can get them in the magazines—in HARPER'S, in *Scribner's*, in the *Century*, in the *Atlantic;* and so, if you are as wise, or as scrupulous, as the Study, you will buy the young lady some magazines; for the news-stand will not let you have a choice of nice-looking things otherwise. It will show you five or six of them, but generally not more, and generally such nice-looking things as are dull-looking, or as everybody has read before.

Whom, then, does the literary nastiness of the news-stand accuse, with its decayed fiction? The public taste, or the taste of the panderer who purveys it? The panderer is probably a person of no taste whatever, good, bad, or indifferent, and at least as innocent as the ladies who write so many of his nasty-looking novels. All that we can be charitably sure of is that there is a mistake somewhere, from which the patrons of the news-stand are the final sufferers, and that the moral decay of our fiction is not only undeniable, but is unfortunately insisted upon, made evident, typical, representative, by the misunderstanding of those who suppose that others, most others, like taint.

III.

Some such error long disabled the theatre from offering pleasures which might be enjoyed with self-respect. But it is interestingly noticeable that of late the theatre has been somewhat better advised, and at the moment the news-stand has begun to topple on the edge of the pit, the drama has been trying to climb out of it. The theatre is still very coarse, very shameless, but we think it has really some impulses to purge and live cleanly, which ought to be encouraged by all who know its vast influence. As we have often said, it addresses the weaker intelligences, and not the cultivated, except on rare occasions. But apparently the news-stand also addresses the weaker intelligences, and the acted fiction has been growing morally better while the printed fiction has been growing morally worse, till now there is much less to choose between them than there once was.

This nascent reform of the stage (if it is not too hopeful to call it so) began, we think, when our playwrights turned to real life with a tentative question whether there might not be something there that was worth the attention of the drama. It began, as we pointed out several years ago, to the high disdain and the hysterical displeasure of critics who are just now beginning to recognize the fact with all the zest of discoverers, in the work of Mr. Denman Thompson, who put the rustic Yankee of the fields in the place of the rustic Yankee of the coulisses on the stage; in the work of Mr. Edward Harrigan, who gave us New York low life (it may be really higher, of course, than the life of people who do not work for their living; but we have to use the conventional terms) that we knew; in the excellent but more literary work of Mr. Bronson Howard; in the simplest sketches of the variety actors who studied their types from nature; and, further back yet, in the negro minstrelsy which is our sole in-

digenous drama. It has gone on through the work of the schools each of the gentlemen named has founded, until now there is a considerable range of fairly amusing plays of American authorship which may be seen without shame, or too great loss of self-respect.

They have their defects; we always say that; they are still primitive; they are none of them masterpieces; but remembering what went before them and passed for dramas, they are surprisingly good, and they all have moments of satisfying felicity. We ought to include in our praise of them another drama of American make which is very right in one direction, and is to be honored for the courage with which it holds it. The authorship of *Beau Brummel* has been the subject of some unseemly dispute, and so we will not call it Mr. Clyde Fitch's play, though we think Mr. Fitch bore himself with the greater gentleness and dignity in the controversy; but whether it is Mr. Fitch's, or whether it is Mr. Mansfield's, we feel quite sure it has not a moment of nature in it. From first to last the feeling is as maudlin as the history is false, and the art is obvious and hackneyed. It always crowds the theatres with those weaker intelligences who mostly resort there, and with the gentilities, who like to see lords and ladies on the stage, and princes of the blood. It is ill acted, except for Mr. Mansfield's carefully architected performance; the lords and ladies are not gentlemen and gentlewomen; the prince is portrayed in a manner to make every one but the gentilities bless God that he was born a republican; and yet the play has a great and saving virtue: it has quiet.

This quiet is the one true touch in it; and it is so true that it imparts a color of veracity to the whole, which the spectator has to look at twice to find a reflected light. It teaches in unanswerable terms that the strongest emotions may be expressed without the least noise, and that the lover of the drama may be made to understand the purport of a play without being hit on the head; and all this in spite of the purely counterfeit character of the particular transaction. The strong emotions of Beau Brummel are bogus, or rather they spring from sources of unreality that invalidate them; but they are a good imitation; and the important fact is that the perfect quiet of the action conveys them. Of course it is a one-man piece, and Mr. Mansfield pervades and dominates every part of it. The conception of it is arch-romantical, but the execution is as realistic as possible, and this constitutes its strength. Otherwise it is as flabby and formless as a jelly-fish cast up on the sand.

IV.

The fact is, the two kinds do not mingle well, but for a while yet we must have the romantic and the realistic mixed in the theatre. That is quite inevitable; and it is strictly in accordance with the law of evolution. The stage, in working free of romanticism, must carry some rags and tags of it forward in the true way; that has been the case always in the rise from a higher to a lower form; the man on a trapeze recalls the ancestral monkey who swung by his tail from the forest tree; and the realist cannot all at once forget the romanticist. Perhaps not till the next generation shall we have the very realist; which puzzles the groundlings, romantically expectant of miracles that shall clear away all trace of romanticism in an instant. At any rate the stage has not yet got beyond its past, as was evident enough in two plays which were unquestionably the most striking of all that were given in the last theatrical season.

V.

One of these was an English play, by Mr. Arthur Jones, whose work we have not had the pleasure of seeing before, but which we shall always take some trouble to see again. It had the good fortune to be in the hands of Mr. E. S. Willard, an actor of charming talent, trained to artistic excellence of the rarest if not the highest order. He had great natural sweetness of manner, and a refinement that was thoroughly kind and winning, and he contrived to impart the sense of this to the characters he played. In two plays of Mr. Jones's he had the leading part, and in one he saved a shapeless mass of romantic rubbish called *The Middleman* from offence by the truthful beauty of his work in its one real character. In *Judah*, the other play, his skill was not so essential to the piece, and there the dramatist stood upon his own feet. He stood squarely and solidly on them. It was a play of great merit, and of a kind that is so uncommon as to be almost unique. It dealt with a theme as modern as that of the faith-cure, and presented a psychic half-consciously deceiving her patients at the bidding of her wholly-conscious rascal of a father. In the small Welsh town where she goes to save the dying child of the local magnate, the ardent young minister, Judah Llewellyn, falls in love with her; and when she puts herself in the hands of some hard-headed scientific people, and is really starving in the fast that has hitherto been feigned, he abets her in

getting food. She is accused of the cheat, and then Judah, with lie upon lie, carries her through against her accusers. She is saved; the sick girl lives; but Judah remains in his sin, till he makes the supreme effort in which he confesses and obliges her to confess too. They are forgiven, and they resolve to begin life anew there where the worst of them is known.

Any one can see how strong the situation is, and how heroic the end. It is relieved with delightful humor in the scientific characters, and in its lighter as well as its graver qualities it is unspeakably in advance of the old-fashioned stage-play. It really gives one great hopes.

So does Mr. James A. Herne's *Margaret Fleming*, which is the other play we wished to speak of. It is not so good, all round, as the Englishman's play, but it is in places far deeper and greater, and it is ours; it is American to the finger-nails. Briefly, it is the story of a man who is false to his wife. He is a common, average sensual man; but she is a very uncommon woman. In the end, after cruel suffering, she forgives him; but she no more forgets than a man would forget a wife's infidelity. He is impossible to her; the last scene closes with his recognition and acceptance of the fact; and they go their different ways through life, friends, but lovers no more.

The power of this story, as presented in Mr. Herne's every-day phrase, and in the naked simplicity of Mrs. Herne's acting of the wife's part, was terrific. It clutched the heart. It was common; it was pitilessly plain; it was ugly; but it was true, and it was irresistible. At times the wife preached, and that was bad; there were passages of the grossest romanticism in the piece, and yet it was a piece of great realism in its whole effect. This effect, in Boston, where it was produced, was most extraordinary. Probably no other new play ever drew such audiences there, in the concert hall where it took refuge after being denied a chance at all the theatres. Literature, fashion, religion, delegated their representatives to see it, and none saw it without profound impression, so that it became the talk of the whole city wherever cultivated people met.

It would be rash to prophesy its future, but not Mr. Herne's. It is evident that in him we have not only an actor of the most advanced type (he did a refuse Yankee in the play deliciously), but a dramatist of remarkable and almost unequalled performance. We have spoken of his work in both kinds before. We could not now speak of it too hopefully.

[1] The controversy about the play's authorship arose because Richard Mansfield, an actor always in search of a role to display his talents, had envisioned a play based upon the life of George Bryan Brummel, and had established a significant part of the play's structure. Mansfield commissioned the young unknown playwright, Clyde Fitch, to do the actual writing. See Paul Wilstach, <u>Richard Mansfield: The Man and The Actor</u> (Charles Scribner's Sons, 1908), pp. 200-201.

September, 1891

Editor's Study.

I.

AN interesting phase of fiction, at present, is the material prosperity of the short story, which seems to have followed its artistic excellence among us with uncommon obedience to a law that ought always to prevail. Until of late the publisher has been able to say to the author dazzled and perhaps deceived by his magazine success with short stories, and fondly intending to make a book of them, "Yes. But collections of short stories don't sell. The public won't have them. I don't know why; but it won't."

This was never quite true of the short stories of Mr. Bret Harte, or of Miss Sarah O. Jewett, or of Mr. Aldrich; but it was too true of the short stories of most other writers. For some reason or for none, the very people who liked an author's short stories in the magazine, could not bear them, or would not buy them, when he put several of them together in a volume. They then became obnoxious, or at least undesirable; somewhat as human beings, agreeable enough as long as they are singly domiciled in one's block, become a positive detriment to the neighborhood when gathered together in a boarding-house. A novel not half so good by the same author would formerly outsell his collection of short stories five times over. Perhaps it would still outsell the stories; we rather think it would; but not in that proportion. The hour of the short story in book form has struck, apparently; for with all our love and veneration for publishers, we have never regarded them as martyrs to literature, and we do not believe they would now be issuing so many volumes of short stories if these volumes did not pay. Publishers, with all their virtues, are as distinctly made a little lower than the angels as any class of mortals we know. They are, in fact, a tentative and timid kind, never quite happy except in full view of the main chance; and just at this moment this chance seems to wear the diversified physiognomy of the collected short stories. We do not know how it has happened; we should not at all undertake to say; but it is probably attributable to a number of causes. It may be the prodigious popularity of Mr. Kipling which has broken down all prejudices against the form of his success. The vogue that Maupassant's tales in the original or in versions have enjoyed may have had something to do with it. Possibly the critical recognition of the American supremacy in this sort has helped. But however it has come about, it is certain that the result has come, and the publishers are fearlessly adventuring volumes of short stories on every hand; and not only short stories by authors of established repute, but by new writers, who would certainly not have found this way to the public some time ago.

The change by no means indicates that the pleasure in large fiction is dying out. This remains of as ample gorge as ever. But it does mean that a quite reasonless reluctance has given way; and that a young writer can now hope to come under the fire of criticism much sooner than before. This may not be altogether a blessing; it has its penalties inherent in the defective nature of criticism, or the critics; but undoubtedly it gives the young author definition and fixity in the reader's knowledge. It enables him to continue a short-story writer if he likes; or it prepares the public not to be surprised at him if he turns out a novelist.

II.

These are advantages, and we must not be impatient of any writer who continues a short-story writer when he might freely become a novelist. Now that a writer can profitably do so, he may prefer to grow his fiction on the dwarf stock; he may plausibly contend that this was the original stock, and that the *novella* was a short story many ages before its name was appropriated by the standard variety, the duodecimo American, or the three-volume English; that Boccaccio was a world-wide celebrity five centuries before George Eliot was known to be a woman. To be sure, we might come back at him with the Greek romancers; we might ask him what he had to say to the interminable tales of Heliodorus and Longus, and the rest; and then not let him say.

But no such controversy is necessary to the enjoyment of the half-dozen volumes of short stories at hand, and we gladly postpone it till we have nothing to talk about. At present we have only too much to talk about in a book so robust and terribly serious as Mr. Hamlin Garland's volume called *Main-Travelled Roads*. That is what they call the highways in the part of the West that Mr. Garland comes from and writes about; and these stories are full of the bitter and burning dust, the foul and trampled slush of the common avenues of life: the life of the men who hopelessly and cheerlessly make the wealth that enriches the alien and the idler, and impoverishes the producer. If any one is still at a loss to account for that uprising of the farmers in the West, which is the translation of the Peasants' War into modern and republican terms, let him read *Main-Travelled Roads* and he will begin to understand, unless, indeed, Mr. Garland is painting the exceptional rather than the average. The stories are full of those gaunt, grim, sordid, pathetic, ferocious figures, whom our satirists find so easy to caricature as Hayseeds, and whose blind groping for fairer conditions is so grotesque to the newspapers and so menacing to the politicians. They feel that something is wrong, and they know that the wrong is not theirs. The type caught in Mr. Garland's book is not pretty; it is ugly and often ridiculous; but it is heart-breaking in its rude despair. The story of a farm mortgage as it is told in the powerful sketch "Under the Lion's Paw" is a lesson in political economy, as well as a tragedy of the darkest cast. "The Return of the Private" is a satire of the keenest edge, as well as a tender and mournful idyl of the unknown soldier who comes back after the war with no blare of welcoming trumpets or flash of streaming flags, but foot-sore, heart-sore, with no stake in the country he has helped to make safe and rich but the poor man's chance to snatch an uncertain subsistence from the furrows he left for the battle-field. "Up the Coulé," however, is the story which most pitilessly of all accuses our vaunted conditions, wherein every man has the chance to rise above his brother and make himself richer than his fellows. It shows us once for all what the risen man may be, and portrays in his good-natured selfishness and indifference that favorite ideal of our system. The successful brother comes back to the old farmstead, prosperous, handsome, well dressed, and full of patronizing sentiment for his boyhood days there, and he cannot understand why his brother, whom hard work and corroding mortgages have eaten all the joy out of, gives him a grudging and surly welcome.

It is a tremendous situation, and it is the allegory of the whole world's civilization: the upper dog and the under dog are everywhere, and the under dog nowhere likes it.

But the allegorical effects are not the primary intent of Mr. Garland's work: it is a work of art, first of all, and we think of fine art; though the material will strike many gentilities as coarse and common. In one of the stories, "Among the Corn Rows," there is a good deal of burly, broad-shouldered humor of a fresh and native kind; in "Mrs. Ripley's Trip" is a delicate touch, like that of Miss Wilkins; but Mr. Garland's touches are his own, here and elsewhere. He has a certain harshness and bluntness, an indifference to the more delicate charms of style; and he has still to learn that though the thistle is full of an unrecognized poetry, the rose has a poetry too, that even overpraise cannot spoil. But he has a fine courage to leave a fact with the reader, ungarnished and unvarnished, which is almost the rarest trait in an Anglo-Saxon writer, so infantile and feeble is the custom of our art; and this attains tragical sublimity in the opening sketch, "A Branch Road," where the lover who has quarrelled with his betrothed comes back to find her mismated and miserable, such a farm wife as Mr. Garland has alone dared to draw, and tempts the broken-hearted drudge away from her loveless home. It is all morally wrong, but the author leaves you to say that yourself. He knows that his business was with those two people, their passions and their probabilities. He shows them such as [1] the newspapers know them.

III.

Such as the newspapers know them are many characters in Mr. R. H. Davis's rapid and graphic sketch of "Gallegher," which lends its name to his volume of stories and studies. It is an excellent piece of work, in which the journalistic types are admirably ascertained, and the strong material is fitly subordinated to the interest of the treatment of persons and circumstances. He knows that the important thing is the character of the office-boy Gallegher, and not the incidents that develop it; and it is much in the writer's favor that with a pen so facile, and a public so cheaply amused as ours, he keeps himself well in hand, and remembers that the merit of a story is in the art of the telling. He does this, and respects himself even when his readers mostly would not care to have him respect them. We do not say that he has altogether freed himself from the bonds of romanticistic superstition, and does not sometimes portray the thing less as it is than as he thinks his reader would like it to be; but he gives abundant evidence of the artistic conscience which no gentleman should be without. Literature is still first with him; but he loves the look of life, and he cannot be patient to see it through print, or to seek in it those poses and expressions which literature has already appropriated. In some of his slighter sketches, such as those relating to the amiable swell Van Bibber, we find qualities that almost inspire us to prophesy, and which certainly enable us to congratulate a vivid talent upon its performance. This, perhaps, is better than to talk of its promise; and there is really so much substance of things done in Mr. Davis's book that we have no occasion to draw upon his future in praising him. At all times he suggests the presence of a fine humanity in his thought, without which there cannot be the finest art in our time. What we could desire this brilliant writer, if we had our wishing-cap on, would be a perfect unconsciousness of his reader's presence, and an entire willingness to trust others with his facts as simply as providence confided them to him. This is difficult, but it is the first thing to be desired.

IV.

It is what we should like to urge even more strenuously upon the author of *Flute and Violin, and other Kentucky Tales and Romances.* The gods do not often deal so handsomely by a mortal as they did by Mr. James Lane Allen in putting such material as "King Solomon of Kentucky" in his hands, and he has not shown himself insensible of the value of their gift. His error is in the other direction; he is but too anxious the reader should know its value. But this aside, his work, of a finish now slightly archaic, gives value to it. Those local physiognomies and accents are delightfully caught; it is all very Southern, and nicely differentiated in its Kentucky Southernness from the like meridional character in Virginian or Louisianian life. What Mr. Johnson, of the *Dukesborough Tales,* has done for Georgia, Mr. Allen has done for Kentucky, and if Mr. Allen has been too literary in the doing, that is a mistake which may hereafter be corrected with a little thought. When from time to time he breaks a pane in his library window, he lets in voices and odors that entrance the soul with the sense of a new world. This is true not only in regard to the case of the white vagrant, King Solomon, who is bid off at sheriff's sale by the free negress, but it is still more eminently true of the beautiful and touching sketch, "Two Gentlemen of Kentucky." One is white and has been master, and the other is black and has

been slave; but both are gentlemen, and at heart they are brothers and equals. There is no sentimentality in the tenderness with which they are portrayed; and there is prevalent that note of newness which Mr. Henry James hails so gladly in Mr. Rudyard Kipling's work.

V.

The resolute introduction to the volume of stories by this writer called *Mine Own People* is largely Mr. James's word to the unconverted. It is admirable criticism, like all the criticism he writes; and if Mr. Kipling had done no more than make such a friend, such a lover, he might well feel himself a most successful man; the thing is not done every day. Several of the sketches in the present volume have been printed before. We are glad to find among them that study of contrasted authorship and soldiership called "A Conference of the Powers," which we have praised already, as an instance of the closer and finer work Mr. Kipling is able to do. Here are also "The Courting of Dinah Shadd" and "The Incarnation of Krishna Mulvaney," both of his more obstreperous note; and here in "Bimi," the homicidal ape, and "Moti Guj," the eccentric elephant, we have two curiously subtle studies of beast life, in which the author seems fairly to have penetrated the realm of lower consciousness, and to have understood the inarticulate moods of the brutes we call dumb. "The Man who Was" and "At the End of the Passage" are proofs of the singular imaginative force which perhaps gives Mr. Kipling his longest reach, if not his deepest hold. The book, in fine, represents him well; and either because we have become used, or the fact is so, we find it less noisy, less cockahoop, than other collections from his pen. At the worst, it is never dull; and in the light of Mr. James's generous appreciation, its best points turn themselves to the light, and shine with a brilliancy that provokes the interest anew.

VI.

Un-English, we should say his work was in spirit and matter. No man of English blood, who had not mainly spent his life out of England, could have arrived at Mr. Kipling's comprehension of strange peoples. He is American in this sympathy of his; we are almost of a mind to claim his bad qualities; but we will stop short of that. He is intensely modern, conscious, and nervous; an interplanetary space seems to separate his mood and ours from that of the mid-insular English world where Mr. Thomas Hardy found his *Group of Noble Dames.* We know that these last-century ladies are of our race and language; but if any one desires a psychological exercise of the most intimate and interesting kind, we advise the American reader of Mr. Hardy's delightful tales to make a study of their heroines in the light of his own Puritanized conscience. He may have long given up being guided by it himself, but it will serve him as a measure of the morality of a world never refined by a closely individualized religion.

These noble dames have the frank indifference of beautiful pagans where their passions are concerned. Their caste, as Mr. Grant Allen has pointed out, is a savage survival; and still finds its pleasure in the barbarous sports of the chase, and in games of chance; and perhaps they are unmoral in virtue of being aristocrats. But it is apparently not altogether a matter of caste. Time and place have much to do with the type of easy-going self-will embodied in all of them. In their life dutiolatry is unknown; they do not torment themselves with any problem but that of getting the man they want on such terms as they must. The questions that wear modern heroines to a thread are strange to them; when they suffer it is from self-indulgence, not from self-reproach; and they live mostly to a good old age after becoming mothers of large families of children. They have in all a sort of peasant simplicity; and they are not in manners or morals what an American woman with self-righteous self-consciousness would call "ladies." But they are very charming, in a way; and certainly very appreciably human in the pictures Mr. Hardy has drawn of them, with an art which has not at least obviously concerned itself with their souls. It is to us always a delightful art; we have often joyfully praised it, and we do not know that it has ever shown itself finer than in the perfect relief, the absolute verity, it has given to *A Group of Noble Dames.*

VII.

The heroine of Miss Fanny Murfree's *Felicia* is not the ideal contrast to these ladies we could find in our fiction, but she will serve the purpose of any one who likes to pursue the line of inquiry which we have suggested. But it would be a pity not to know her for other reasons. She is most truthfully, simply, and accurately studied, and the situation is given with rare distinctness. It is briefly that of a society girl (as society goes in a Western city) who leaves her paternal home of restricted ideals and sympathies to share the wandering life of her husband, a successful opera-singer. He is good and faithful, but his heart is in his work, for which he has great gifts. She tries to see his art as he does, and to conform her life to his; but she cannot, and this forms their tragedy. Nothing could exceed the quiet skill with which their several limitations are indicated; it is a war not so much of temperaments as of ideals. The histrionic world and its people are excellently treated, with a justice at once large and fine; and the world of dull bourgeois respectability which has cast the heroine off is not caricatured. In fact the whole story is extremely well managed, and is wrought out with a delicate sense of proportion, and an insight from which we may hope still greater things.

---

[1] This section was reprinted as the Introduction to a later edition of Garland's volume: Hamlin Garland, Main-Travelled Roads, Introduction by W. D. Howells and Decorations by H. T. Carpenter (Cambridge, Eng. and Chicago: Stone and Kimball, 1893). Howells changed the paragraphing in the reprinted version, and changed "Up the Coulé" to "Up the Coolly."

[2] The author of Dukesborough Tales is Richard Malcolm Johnston, not Johnson.

Editor's Study.

I.

MRS. OLIPHANT'S life of her kinsman Laurence Oliphant, and Mrs. [1] Sutherland Orr's life of Robert Browning, [2] are two books dealing with matters of such importance that they ought to have the character of human events; but they somehow fail of it. Why they fail of it might be easier to say than how they should have achieved it. They are both very entertaining books, and both very intelligent books, up to a certain point, and after that the authors seem either not to understand the men whose stories they are telling, or not to care for the edification of their readers. In Mrs. Oliphant this is the effect of her limitations, apparently; her agreeable talent could go so far and no farther; but with Mrs. Orr the shortcoming seems a bound voluntarily set.

II.

That is, Mrs. Orr impresses the observer as having chosen to interpret Browning, in his life and in his work, only to a given degree, which she had fixed in her mind before she began; to make you his acquaintance, but not his intimate. It is always possible that the fault is in him, and not in her theory of the way she should write his personal history: some men have no intimacy to impart or to be imparted; they are either of natures so recluse that they cannot be got at, or so simple that a bare statement is all there is of them. It is incredibly all in the case of a man like Browning, and though it may really be all, the world which he perplexed and piqued so much will not be satisfied that it is so by one assurance. The world will insist that it is only the more obvious self of Browning that has been set before it; that within this plain letter there must be a spirit to be expounded; and Mrs. Orr will always suffer from the charge of inadequacy, and of not being that prophetess which she never set up to be, which she clearly refuses to be.

It is rather hard, and we shall not be the foremost to urge it. We certainly find her philosophization of Browning scanty, but that it is inadequate we are not so sure. We fancy that though a darkling soul, he was not very complex.

He belonged to the order of great men who are constituted like common men; the stuff is finer, but it is put together in much the same way. He was of strictly citizen stock; he had not the romance of a low original like Keats or Burns, nor the glamour of high birth like Byron or Shelley. He had not the charm of anything bohemian; he was of the class that handles money; and though his own family had minds above money, their lives were of a clerkly conventionality: the Bank of England could tolerate nothing else. He was not a Jew, Mrs. Orr takes the pains to prove against conjecture to that effect, and he had no picturesque quarrel with conditions as Heine had. After a deeply domesticated youth, he indulged the one dramatic impulse of his life; he ran away with the gifted sufferer whom he lured from her sick-room to be his wife. He settled quietly in Italy, where his pleasant sojourn was often broken with pleasant journeys; and after her death he came back to great social acceptance in England, to be the cult of intellectual countesses, and the desired guest at dinners. Nothing could be more commonplace. The vein of poetry, running rich and full to the last through his life, was his love for his wife, whom he passionately believed his superior; but he had many æsthetic friendships, chiefly with women, and he was a man of warm and constant affections. He seems never to have hated anything so much as modern spiritism, and, for a moment, Mr. Edward Fitzgerald. But both these hates were the nether side of his faithful and beautiful love of his wife, whom he believed to have been deluded by mediums in her life, and insulted in her death by Fitzgerald.

There are few lives, even literary lives, so uneventful as Browning's. He had no struggle with poverty, as most authors have; and he suffered no persecution for opinion's sake, as many great ones have. At the most he had to endure the long indifference of the public, which did not even condemn his work, which simply ignored it. This was no doubt enough, for Browning must always have known that he was Browning, and a poet worthy fame. But still it was not misery, it was not sorrow; material comfort stayed him in it; he had the means to wait; he neither hungered, nor tasted *il pane altrui*. A certain placid security from the worst is reflected in his letters, which are almost unfailingly unimportant, as far as Mrs. Orr quotes them. What light and lift comes into the story of his life is rather from Mrs. Browning's letters; but these again are not of the letters that reveal the inner life: they have perhaps no expression of more intense feeling than that which she experienced when Browning shaved his beard.

III.

These facts derogate nothing from the greatness of the two extraordinary poets in question. They were so fortunately circumstanced that they could give themselves to poetry without care or anxiety for most things that break the heart and distract the mind in most poets. The nightingale can sing even without a thorn in his breast, and we should be the last to wish one always planted there. We are quite able to accept Browning's greatness while fully recognizing the simplicity of his nature, and the uneventful quiet of his career. We do not find his external ease and his happy domesticities inconsistent with greatness. We do not deny that "the camomile the more it is trodden the faster it grows," but we know that there are plants that do not require this harsh culture. From that prospered life of Browning's came the deepest if not the loftiest voice of our time, clothing itself in terms which will always be the clearer the more simply they are taken, and worth carefully listening to when of darkest meaning. At the end, if we remain a little dissatisfied with Mrs. Orr, we do not see why we should be so with Browning; and perhaps we are not justly so with her. Perhaps there was really no more of Browning, outside of his poems, than she has suggested if not shown. This would not be wonderful. Why should we ask a man to live as well as to write his poetry? That seems unreasonable, emotional, romantic; and when we have said romantic we have said enough.

IV.

In fact, we are disposed to praise Mrs. Orr's book for a certain self-respectful manliness which we find, or which we fancy we find in it. Possibly it is to this restraint that we owe a bareness in the lines of her characterization; she is so afraid of sentimentalizing her subject that she may withhold some colors of feeling which would have helped us know him better. In that case it is the defect of a virtue; and it is a defect which we cannot blame in Mrs. Oliphant's study of her surprising kinsman's career.

Surprising, very surprising, he always is to her; but whether he will be so to a people of other horizons may be doubted. Hers are strictly pinned down to the social, political, and spiritual state of her native island. All the world beyond is strange, vague, and somewhat regrettable, or at least not very nice. There is nothing severe or even unkind in her attitude toward the outside universe, and nothing perhaps worse than the consciousness that it is outside. That flutter of chimney-corner sensibilities throughout the book does not exclude any deserving portion of the human race; the exclusion of the vastly greater part of it was accomplished by an all-wise, loyal British Providence before the flutter began. This of course is saying it too large, but the like of this is the like of the work; and it would be hard to tell whether Mrs. Oliphant is more amusing when she is devoutly printing Sovereign with a capital letter, as one should print, say, Deity, or when she is taking her mind in both hands and trying to lift and broaden it to a conception of the curious psychical and geographical immensities beyond the British Isles, where Laurence Oliphant chiefly periculated. Her success in this endeavor is not commensurate with her good will. After all we get from her no impression of an America like the America we are accustomed to, and we suppose the poor Syrians and Cingalese would be equally confounded by her ideas of them. This inability to imagine other people she shares with all the English-born; but it is too bad that she should not have informed herself a little concerning the philosophy of Swedenborg before she identified it [3] with the doctrine of Mr. Harris, and attributed to the Swedish seer the notion of a dual, father-and-mother Godhead.

Still, these are minor offences, and we are not alleging them in disqualification of the book as the biography of Laurence Oliphant. Oddly enough it does, reversibly, and by reason of its very limitations, tangibly present him; but we should think it portrayed him more conceivably to us barbarians than to the elect whom it directly addresses. We, from our point of view, can see, as they can, what a winning and lovable creature he always was, and how true and unspoiled at heart he remained in spite of the adoration of his home and the flattery of his world; and we can see also that, though a good man and a gifted man, he was never at all a great man. He was a newspaper man, and not a newspaper man of the first quality, but of the second—the journalist who holds the middle ground between the reporter and the writer of leaders, and makes the best sort of special correspondent. When it came to fiction, to literary art. he was the victim of a tendency to exaggerate, to caricature, which kept him in the ranks of the second-rate novelists, and which leaves his work immemorable. If we may judge from his comments on America, he was, like all Englishmen, an astigmatic observer of alien people; and his forecasts of events prove him to have been a hasty and inadequate student of political conditions. Much talk is made of his diplomatic services, but these were always rendered in subordinate capacities, and he cannot be even charitably regarded as a first-rate man in that kind. What was beautiful and what was great in him was his steady perception, through all the glamour of worldly success, that the life of the spirit was the only real life, and any other was vanity of vanities. He came to this early, and he never lost it; if he was not one of the finest artists or wisest statesmen, he had the sense of universal proportion that set him far above literature and politics; he felt how cheaply the world is pleased and governed. His just perspective showed the monstrous irrelevance of most human endeavor, and he longed to turn aside from all our self-seeking ways, and find the one thing needful. When Mr. Thomas L. Harris appeared upon the horizon, with his assumption of confidential relations with God, Oliphant seems to have asked no other proof of his claim than the invitation to a life of absolute self-sacrifice which the prophet gave him. He embraced this life, and if he had embraced it in the interest of the poor and suffering, it would have given him the liberty and rest which he luminously desired; but he does not seem to have seen for many wasted years that he had taken up the cross for no real end, and that he had found only slavery and sore labor in his self-sacrifice.

V.

It is all a very melancholy story, and most pitiable where his mother and wife come into it, and make themselves the bondwomen of the prophet, at Brocton, New York; but we are unable to find it so surprising as it appears to his biographer. We can quite dispense with any hypnotic hypothesis in explaining the case. Such people were the natural prey of such a man, who, after all, was doubtless self-deceived before deceiving, and not at all out of the order of Providence. The Oliphants might have known that particular kind of tree by its fruits, but they seem not to have asked for fruits, but contentedly to have gathered thistles, Lady Oliphant to the last, and Laurence Oliphant and his wife till even

an infatuation so gross as theirs could no longer ignore the facts.

Yet the test is so simple, so accessible in such a case, that it seems to us the dupes inculpated themselves and helped to breed self-deceit in their oppressor when they failed to apply it. People have only to ask themselves what good to others their self-sacrifice is doing, and then, if they see any good, the gentlest born may honorably serve in the lowliest use; the lady may wash dishes and mend laborers' clothes; the gentleman may fitly chop wood and clean stables. It was not the rude toil imposed upon the Oliphants by their prophet which degraded the Oliphants; it was their voluntary subjection to a bondage that meant nothing. The mere work itself was creditable to them, and would be so to any well-born idler that did it. There is no difference of quality in men and women which warrants the wiser and stronger in devoting the weaker to the repulsive drudgery of the world. It is an insult to the reason to maintain that by virtue of more fortunate birth and happier circumstance one man should be exempt from labors which all may fairly share; but the constant implication that it was shocking to set such nice people as the Oliphants hoeing and digging and washing and ironing exasperates the intelligent reader throughout this part of their story. What is really shocking is that they wasted their energies for the prosperity of a delusion, and failed to see that their prophet did not even propose any general good to the suffering world from which he withdrew them. It was shocking that Oliphant should not see this, but should willingly submit his wife and mother to the same barren bondage whose yoke he took upon himself from no better motive than the desire we all have to escape from ourselves. They followed him for their love of him, but his was a selfish self-sacrifice, and it cannot be said that he had his reward altogether unjustly. Perhaps the mystical Harris might say in his own defence that he was not without injury when a man so gifted as Oliphant slavishly did his bidding; and that Oliphant's infatuation had helped to confirm him in his own. Here, at any rate, is a very pretty suggestion for a psychological story, which we make over to any deserving writer in want of a plot. To the general reader we commend a comparison of the self-sacrifice of Oliphant at Brocton with the self-sacrifice of Oliphant in Syria. At Haifa he devoted his wife's energies and his own to the poor people about them, and so approached the source of all good in the happiest and usefulest days of his life. At Brocton he devoted them to Harris, by whose grace he hoped somehow to achieve the intimacy of the Almighty, with a result of abject misery and sterile suffering. Oliphant's yearning for self‑forgetfulness was without merit and without fruition, till he began to forget himself for the sake of the plain and simple good he could do the least of his brethren; then his riddle was read.

It is easy for others to see his error, and it seems strange that he should have tried so long to gather grapes of thorns; but this sort of vintage is very common, and it ought not to be strange to any observer. The world yields no other harvest to those who live its life, and it is doubtful whether diplomacy, for instance, with its tricks and masks, is not a worse slavery than that which Oliphant embraced at the behest of Harris. It looks like lamentable waste when a gifted and accomplished man turns and does the work of a peasant, but it may be questioned whether most gifts and most accomplishments are not put to worse use in what we call civilization. Oliphant did not find rest unto his soul at Brocton, because his life there did not go beyond itself and reach out to the life of others, and so was not the Christ life but the Antichrist life. No doubt he at first felt a brute bliss in the utter self‑surrender demanded of his self‑weary soul; no doubt he tasted the bliss of non‑being, of death in life; but his experience is the allegory of every spirit which seeks good in oblivion, and not oblivion in good.

VI.

It must often occur to the reader of Miss Bacon's delightful book about *Japanese Girls and Women* to ask why in the world we should want to change the creeds and customs which have resulted in such lovely types of character as she portrays. Apparently we have nothing to teach the most artistic of peoples in the beauty of behavior or the graces of spirit. It would be hard to say how Christianity‑in‑name, as we mostly have it, could improve the conduct or character of the Japanese women, who seem always to have been very good Christians without knowing it, if we are to believe Miss Bacon. Perhaps the answer to the conundrum is that Christianity is not primarily a purifying force, but is first an enlightening force; that its ideal is virtue, not innocence; Gethsemane, not Eden. The harmlessness of the dove will not avail without the wisdom of the serpent; the impulse of our faith is towards consciousness, knowledge. No doubt this is what the Japanese feel in it; probably it is what makes them willing to change their civilization for ours. They really seem a race of better and sweeter nature than ourselves; unless their witnesses

misreport them they are gentler, kinder, even truer, than we are naturally. But something seems lacking to them, and they look towards us for it; they fancy spiritual possibilities on the plane which we tell them is above theirs. The fine perfection of their art is a stunted beauty; it has never the infinite reach of the Greek; the loveliness of their lives is childlike; it has not the celestial aspiration of the Hebrew; and no doubt they feel this as clearly as they perceive the difference between us and our ideals. We are ourselves mostly so obtuse to this difference that we suppose our women, if not our men, to conform to the ideal of goodness and softness. At least we are always telling them they do; we think they are lovely; at any rate a pretty woman of our race is by no means terrible to us; but they affect the Japanese, used to the meek beauty of their maidens and matrons, very differently. They do not see the charm we feel in "the fair, curling hair, the round, blue eyes, the erect, slim‑waisted, large‑hipped figures of many foreign beauties,—the rapid, long, clean‑stepping walk, and the air of almost masculine strength and independence, which belong especially to English and American women.... Blue eyes, set into deep sockets, with the bridge of the nose rising as a barrier between them, impart a fierce grotesqueness to the face that the untravelled Japanese seldom admire. The very babies will scream with horror at first sight of a blue‑eyed, light‑haired foreigner, and it is only after considerable familiarity with such persons that they can be induced to show anything but the wildest fright in their presence. Foreigners," Miss Bacon tells us, " who have lived a good deal among the Japanese find their standards unconsciously changing, and see, to their own surprise, that their countrywomen look ungainly, fierce, aggressive, and awkward among the small, mild, shrinking, and graceful Japanese ladies." The Japanese, who think our women's manners no better than their looks, severely criticise the deportment of such of their own girls as are educated in our missionary schools, and even "to a foreigner who has lived almost entirely among Japanese ladies of pure Japanese education, the manners of these girls were brusque and awkward."

VII.

It would be unjust to Miss Bacon's important and conscientious study of the life of Japanese women to leave the reader with the impression that it is confined to sketches of their manners, or that in her admiration of their character she ignores the wrong and hardship of their conditions. From these conditions come the sweet children, the lovely maidens, the true wives, the tender mothers who, as Miss Bacon teaches us, abound in Japan; but she teaches us that what they are they are in spite of their conditions, and makes us feel how lavishly kind nature must have been to their race. There is no mistaking the meaning of her attractively written, well philosophized observations of their life, and it would be a very perverse Study indeed that would darken counsel with any pretence that their conditions ought not to be changed. But our own are yet so far from perfect that we could wish that charming and gifted people, when the change comes, something better and wiser than our status. It does not seem too much to hope in their behalf; it is not incredible that if they are left to work out their own salvation they may achieve one yet that will not involve so much social and moral damnation as ours, and that if they finally receive Christianity it will be in the form of a life as well as a creed.

In the mean time they remain perpetually fascinating not only in the close and special scrutiny of such books as Miss Bacon's, but in such intelligent and agreeable sketches as Miss Scidmore's *Jinrikisha Days*, which we may commend as one of the most attractive volumes of foreign sojourn we have seen for a long time. Even in the snapshots of Miss Bisland, who has been kodaking the globe in *A Flying Trip Round the World*, these favored children of the Graces, if not the Muses, impart their witchery to the hastiest blue-print glimpses of their life. They are a moment only, however, in her course, which describes itself in all manner of vivid and graphic lines. Miss Bisland has, in fact, written such an instantaneous book as can well give us hopes of what the newspaper of the future may be in the hands of artists.

[1] Margaret Oliphant, Memoir of the Life of Laurence Oliphant and of Alice Oliphant, his Wife (New York: Harper & Brothers, 1891).

[2] Alexandra Sutherland Orr, Life and Letters of Robert Browning (London: Smith, Elder, & Co., 1891).

[3] Emanuel Swedenborg (1688-1772), Swedish theologian, and Thomas Lake Harris (1823-1906), founder of Brotherhood of the New Life.

November, 1891

Editor's Study.

I.

FROM time to time there comes a voice across the sea, asking us in varied terms of reproach and entreaty, why we have not a national literature. As we understand this voice, a national literature would be something very becoming and useful to us as a people, and it would be no more than is due the friendly expectation of the English witnesses of our destitution, who have denied from the beginning that we ever could have a national literature; and proved it. The reasons which they still address to our guilty consciousness in demanding a national literature of us are such and so many that the American who reads their appeals must be a very hardened offender if he does not at once inwardly resolve to do all he can to have one. For our own part, we scarcely know how to keep our patience with the writers who have as yet failed to supply us with it. We are personally acquainted with a dozen Americans who could any one of them give us a national literature, if he would take the pains. In fact, we know of some Englishmen who could produce a very fair national literature for us. All they would have to do would be to write differently from those American authors whose works have failed to embody a national literature, and then they would create for us a literature of unmistakable nationality. But with a literature of their own to maintain, it is too much to ask this of them, and we should not hope for help from English writers, except in the form of advice and censure. We ought to be very glad to have so much, but whether we are glad or not we are likely to have it, for there is nothing mean about Englishmen when it comes to advice and censure; and if we cannot get them to make a national literature for us, we had better learn from them how to make it ourselves.

II.

We do not understand the observers of our literary poverty to deny that in certain qualities and colors we have already something national in literature. Perhaps if they were to extend the field of their knowledge a little in the direction of their speculations they might discover that we had something more positive than these colors and qualities; but it never was necessary for an Englishman to know anything of American affairs before writing about them. Here and there an Englishman, like Mr. Bryce, takes the trouble to inform himself, but we do not fancy he is the more acceptable or edifying to his countrymen on that account; and the fact remains that he really need not do it. In treating of American literature the English critic's great qualification is that he should be master of the fact that Mr. Walt Whitman is the only American who writes like Mr. Walt Whitman. It must be owned that the English critic works this single qualification very hard; he makes it go a long way; but we do not blame him for his thrifty use of it; and we should be sorry to quarrel with the simple economy of the inference that we have not a national literature in the proportion that we do not write like Mr. Whitman. If this will serve the turn of the English writer with the English public, why should he be at any greater pains in the matter?

Usually the English writer is not at any greater pains, and the extravagance of knowing something more than what is necessary to such an inference is rare. Even Mr. Watts, who has lately exposed our literary lack to the world in *The Nineteenth Century*, and Mr. Quiller-Couch, who has blamed our literary indifference to the working-man in *The Speaker*, do not go much beyond this inference in their philosophization of our case. Yet, if we were to allow ourselves to bandy words with our betters, we think we might make a suggestion in the interest of general criticism which would perhaps advantage them.

III.

In the first place we should like to invite observation to the fact that for all æsthetic purposes the American people are not a nation, but a condition. They are the old, well-known Anglo-Saxon race, affected and modified by the infusion of other strains, but not essentially changed by these, and not very different from the English at home except in their political environment, and the vastness of the scale of their development. Their literature, so far as they have produced any, is American-English literature, just as the English literature is English-European, and it is as absurd to ask them to have a literature wholly their own as to ask them to have a language wholly their own. In fact, we have noted that where our language does differ from that of the mother English, or grandmother English, the critics who wish us to have a national literature are not particularly pleased. They call our differences Americanisms, and they are afraid of their becoming the language of the whole race.

They ought to be very careful, then, not to chide us too severely for our lack of a national literature. If ever we should turn to and have one, there might be a serious risk of its becoming the literature of the whole race. There is no great danger of an event so mortifying at present, and we merely intimate its possibility as a warning to our critics not to press us too hard. If things should ever come to that pass, we notify them that not only will the American parlance become the English language, but it will be spelled according to Noah Webster. The "traveller" will have to limp along on one *l*, and the man of "honour" will no longer point with the pride of long descent to the Norman-French *u* in his last syllable.

IV.

In the mean time we wish to ask our critics if they have not been looking for American literature in the wrong place; or, to use an American expression which is almost a literature in itself, whether they have not been barking up the wrong tree. It appears to us that at this stage of the proceedings there is no such thing as nationality in the highest literary expression; but there is a universality, a humanity, which is very much better. There is no doubt, judging from the enterprising character of our people in other respects, that if we had not come upon the scene so very late in the day we should have had a literature of the most positive nationality in form as well as spirit. It is our misfortune rather than our fault to have arrived when all the literary forms were invented. There remained nothing for us to do but to invent literary formlessness, and this, we understand, is what

the English admire Mr. Whitman for doing; it is apparently what they ask of us all. But there is a curious want of variety in formlessness; the elements are monotonous; it is their combinations that are infinitely interesting; and Mr. Whitman seems to have exhausted the resources of formlessness. We cannot go on in his way without servile imitation; the best we can do, since we cannot be national in form, is to be national in spirit and in ideal, and we rather think that in many good ways we are unmistakably so. This is evident from the comparison of any American author with any English author; the difference of qualities is at once apparent; and what more of nationality there might be would, we believe, come of error. There may once have been a time in the history of literature when nationality was supremely desirable: the nationality which expressed itself in the appropriation of forms; but in our time this is not possible, and if it were we think it would be a vice, and we are, above all, virtuous. The great and good things in literature nowadays are not the national features, but the universal features. For instance, the most national fiction at present is the English, and it is the poorest, except the German, which is not at all; while the Russian and the Spanish, the Norwegian and the Italian, the French and the American, which are all so much better, are distinguished by what they have in common rather than by what they have in severalty. The English, who have not felt the great world-movement towards life and truth, are national; those others who have felt it are universal; and perhaps the English critics could be more profitably employed in noting how much the American fiction resembles the Continental fiction than in deploring its want of that peculiarity which renders their own a little droll just now.

Besides, it seems to us that even if we were still in the dark ages when nationality seemed a valuable and admirable thing in itself, they would not find it in our literature in the way they have taken. In any research of the kind we think that the question is not whether this thing or that thing in an author is American or not, but whether upon the whole the author's work is such as would have been produced by a man of any other race or environment. We do not believe that any American writer of recognized power would fail to be found national, if he were tried by this test; and we are not sure but the general use of such a test would result in the discovery of an American literature commensurate in weight and bulk with the emotions of the warmest patriot. The distinctive character of a man's face resides in that complex called his looks; and the nationality of a literature is embodied in its general aspect, not in its particular features. A literature which had none of these would be remarkable for their absence, and if it were produced by one people more than any other would be the expression of their nationality, and as recognizable from its negativity as if it abounded in positive traits.

We do not know, however, that our censors reproach our literature for a want of positivity. Their complaint seems rather to be that it is inadequate to a people who are otherwise so prodigious and original. It strikes them that it is but a small and feeble voice to be the utterance of such a lusty giant; they are listening for a roar, and they hear something very like a squeak, as we understand them. This disappoints them, to say nothing worse; but perhaps it is only our voice changing, and perhaps it would not sound like a squeak if it came from a less formidable body, say San Marino, or Andorra, or even Switzerland. We ought to consider this and take comfort from the possibility, while we taste the tacit flattery in their expectation of a roar from us; from a smaller republic our comparatively slight note could very well pass for a roar, and from a younger one for a mature utterance.

What it is, it is; and it is very probably the natural expression of our civilization, strange as the fact may appear. Our critics evidently think that the writers of a nation can make its literature what they like; but this is a fallacy: they can only make it what the nation likes, involuntarily following the law of environment.

It has been noted that our literature has always been distinguished by two tendencies, apparently opposite, but probably parallel: one a tendency toward an elegance refined and polished, both in thought and phrase, almost to tenuity; the other a tendency to grotesqueness, wild and extravagant, to the point of anarchy. The first has resulted in that delicate poetry which is distinctively American, and in that fiction which has made itself recognized as ours, wherever it is liked or disliked. The last has found its outcome in our peculiar species of humor, which no one can mistake for any other, not even for the English imitations of it. Our literature has these tendencies because the nation has them, and because in some measure each and every American has them. It would take too long to say just how and why; but our censors may rest assured that in this anomalous fact exists the real nationality of our litera-

ture. They themselves have a half perception of the truth when they accept and advance Walt Whitman as the representative of our literature. With a supreme passion for beauty, and impatient of all the trammels and disguises of art, he is eager to seize and embrace its very self. For the most part the effort is a failure; the divine loveliness eludes him, and leaves only a "muddy vesture of decay" in his grasp. He attains success often enough to make good his claim to the admiration the English yield him, and he misses it often enough to keep the more intelligent American observer in doubt. We understand better than they how and why Walt Whitman is; we perceive that he is now and again on the way to the way we should all like to find; but we know his way is not the way. At the same time we have to own that he is expressive of that national life which finds itself young and new in a world full of old conventions and decrepit ideals, and that he is suggestive if not representative of America. But he is no more so than the most carefully polished writer among us. He illustrates the prevalence of one of our moods, as Longfellow, say, illustrates the other. No one but an American could have written the poetry of Whitman; no one but an American could have written the poetry of Longfellow. The work of both is a part of that American literature which also embraces the work of Mark Twain and of Lowell, of Artemus Ward and of Whittier, of Bret Harte and of Emerson, of G. W. Cable and of Henry James, of Miss Murfree and of O. W. Holmes, of Whitcomb Riley and of T. B. Aldrich.

V.

The great difficulty with America is that she has come to her consciousness at a moment when she feels that she ought to be mature and full-grown, the Pallas among the peoples, with the wisdom of a perfectly trained owl at her bidding. It will not do to be crude when the farthest frontier has all the modern improvements, and the future is penetrated at every point by the glare of an electric. If we are simple we must know it; if we are original, it must be with intention and a full sense of originality. In these circumstances we think we have done not so badly in literature. If we listen to our censors, in generals we shall probably do still better. But we do not think we shall do better by heeding them in details. We would not have any considerable body of our writers set about writing novels and poems concerning the life of toil, which Mr. Quiller-Couch says we have neglected; because in the first place Mr.

Quiller-Couch seems to speak from rather a wide-spread ignorance of the facts; and because in the last place the American public does not like to read about the life of toil; and one of the conditions of producing an American literature is that it shall acceptably address itself to the American public. Nearly all the Americans are in their own persons, or have been in those of their fathers or grandfathers, partakers of the life of toil; and anything about it in literature is to them as coal is to Newcastle, or corn-bread to a Kentuckian. They have had enough of it. What they want is something select, something that treats of high life, like those English novels which have chiefly nourished us; or something that will teach us how to escape the life of toil by a great stroke of business, or by a splendid marriage. What we like to read about is the life of noblemen or millionaires; that is our romance; and if our writers were to begin telling us on any extended scale of how mill hands, or miners, or farmers, or iron-puddlers really live, we should very soon let them know that we did not care to meet such vulgar and commonplace people. Our well-to-do classes are at present engaged in keeping their eyes fast shut to the facts of the life of toil, and in making believe that the same causes will not produce the same effects here as in Europe; and they would feel it an impiety if they were shown the contrary. Our finest gentilities do not care anything about our literature; they have no more concern in it than they have in our politics. As for the people who are still sunk in the life of toil, they know enough of it already, and far more than literature could ever tell them. They know that in a nation which honors toil, the toiler is socially nothing, and that he is going from bad to worse quite as if the body politic had no interest in him. What they would like would be some heroic workman who superhumanly triumphs over his environment and marries the boss's daughter, and lives idle and respected ever after. Almost any class of readers would like a hero of that mould; but no class, and least of all his fellows, would like the life of a workman shown in literature as it really is, and his condition painted as hopeless as the condition of ninety-nine workmen out of every hundred is. The life of toil will do very well for nations which do not honor toil, to read about; but there is something in the very reverence we have for it that renders the notion of it repulsive to us. This is very curious; we do not attempt to explain it; but we can promise the foreign observer that he need not look for American literature in that direction. The life of toil! It is a little too personal to people who are trying to be ladies and gentlemen of elegant leisure as fast as they can. If we have had to dig, or if we are many of us still digging, that is reason enough why we do not want the spade brought into the parlor.

VI.

In literature it is very much as it is in love: people desire their opposites. We need not go farther than the English of our day for illustration. A people refined to the last degree of sensibility, instinctively delicate, subtle in perception, peculiarly gracious and hospitable in their mental attitude, their delight is to read of rude adventure; of high crimes and misdemeanors of all kinds; of battle, murder, and sudden death; of direful toil and penury; and their fiction responds to this demand of their taste. On the other hand, the Americans, whose lives are passed in the midst of miseries and hardships, such as the English like to dream of, are fond of tales and poems treating of aristocratic refinement and of motives and actions attenuated almost to effeminacy by the highest civilization; and their literature, as Mr. Quiller-Couch has seen, is of a patrician character, which is scarcely to be surpassed, if equalled, in its hauteur and disdain.

Perhaps his impression of this trait of our literature is derived from too slight an acquaintance with it. We know it is rather hard to ask a critic to examine the premises of his conclusions, but it seems to us that this might sometimes lead to a change of opinion in our English witnesses. The authors whom Mr. Quiller-Couch specifically alleges in proof of his charge of a high, Pooh-Bah indifference to the claims of common humanity upon their literature have rather appeared to us to have a sneaking affection for the plebeian life we Americans have all sprung from, and to have slyly celebrated it in some of their works. But we do not insist upon this, because, for one thing, if it were a fact, it would disable the theory which we have just been at some pains to build up concerning American literature. So we do not urge it, and upon the whole we prefer to withdraw from a position too hastily taken. It is tenable, but it is not desirable to hold it.

VII.

It is interesting to have the adequacy of American literature inquired into and its traits scrutinized just at this time when there is the hope, if not the promise, of a change in its conditions. It seems now as if American literature were to have, for the first time, a fair chance with the American people. Until now it has been cramped and crowded out by the great mass of English literature which our people found it so cheap to borrow without the consent of its owners. At last this species of forced loan can no longer be levied; and the English "book honestly come by" is to be our competitor in the future. Perhaps the American people, who have not before really deserved a great literature, will hereafter have one commensurate with their tardy virtue.

It may be that we shall presently see our English brethren, who have long observed our inadequacy from afar, bringing over their literary plants, and turning out a literature proportionate to the grandeur of the republic on our own soil. Our breweries are already largely in the hands of English syndicates; why should not our literature be so? Nobody apparently knows the defects of our literature so well as the English, and it stands to reason that they will be able to remedy them. We are sure that we should welcome some such transfer of their industry, subject, of course, to the law against contract labor. Superannuated poets and decaying novelists would be excluded by the statutes against assisted emigrants; but young authors and authoresses, with fresh, new ideas of what a true American literature ought to be, and the critics who have guided and instructed them, would always be welcome to the citizenship of the republic; and we should be only too glad to have them show us by example how we ought to write here.

---

[1] Howells has apparently misstated his reference. The article by Watts to which he refers is as follows: Theodore Watts, "The Future of American Literature," Fortnightly Review, 55 (o.s.) (June 1, 1891), 910-926.

[2] Arthur Quiller-Couch, The Speaker, 4 (August 1, 1891), 143-144.

December , 1891

Editor's Study.

I.

THE advent of the Christmas season began again to affect the Study with those allegorical influences felt in greater measure or less throughout polite literature at the holiday time. It found itself haunted by a tendency to apologue that became at last irresistible, and it gracefully made a virtue of yielding to inspirations which it could no longer withstand. It drowsed, and almost instantly it perceived with a not wholly unexpected shock of agreeable surprise that its windows were once more looking out on the great public square in the metropolis of the United Sympathies of Altruria. The vast space was thronged with Altrurians of every age and sex, who appeared to be engaged in the celebration of some public rite of unusual solemnity. Not only were the citizens of the metropolis present in festive multitudes, but all the different Sympathies of the republic were represented by deputations of their principal men and women, sent to take part at the capital in a ceremony observed on a varying scale of magnificence throughout the nation. The Study was vaguely aware of the nature and significance of much that was going forward, but it was painfully perplexed as to the exact symbolical value of the whole. From time to time a joyous procession came forward to the centre of the great square through the orderly myriads that gave way on either side without the aid of a policeman's club, and performed what was clearly an Act of Renunciation; when another procession, not apparently so gay or light-hearted, advanced to meet the first, and performed in its turn what was as clearly an Act of Recipience. But what was renounced and what was received, the Study was at a loss to determine, so great was the space traversed by its vision, and so wild and prolonged were the plaudits attending the orations with which the several acts were accomplished. Bursts of minstrelsy, conveniently arranged at different points in the square, drowned the roar of happy human voices, and amidst these floods of harmony the owners of the voices were seen to embrace with tears of rapture. It was a noble and affecting spectacle; it stirred the Study with the profoundest emotion; but in the absence of a precise interpretation, it lacked the final charm of intelligibility.

In an interval of the ceremony the Study cast its windows eagerly out over the multitude in the hope of seeing some disengaged Altrurian to whom it might appeal for information, and it had no difficulty in discovering, almost at its very threshold, The Christmas Boy.

II.

The Christmas Boy was loaded down like a scapegoat with turkeys and toys, champagne and celery, coal and cranberries, and holiday editions of favorite authors, for the poor; but as there were no poor in Altruria, except at those moments when some Altrurian had reduced himself to destitution by giving everything he had to his neighbor, and had not yet been overwhelmed with benefits himself by the witnesses of his good deeds, the Christmas Boy was in the act of laying down his burden and sitting on it, when the Study recognized him. The Study was quite sure of him, but it felt the need of confirmation at the same time, and it called out, a little tremulously, "Our good boy! Is that you?"

"Yes," said the Christmas Boy, "it's me," and the Study rejoiced in his unimpeachable identity.

The Study said, "You must be rather tired," but the Boy answered, "Oh no. This kind of a load never tires a fellow. Besides, I couldn't get really tired, because I'm only a Tradition, anyway."

"That is true," the Study assented. "But we wanted to ask you a few questions about this affair here, and we thought it might be a little more convenient if you came in and rested while we talked."

"Thank you," said the Boy. "I know what you do to Traditions when you get them up there. And I've got to keep a close watch and catch some fellow down here in an instant of destitution, or I can never get rid of this stuff. But go on with your questions, and I'll answer; and the harder they are the better."

"They won't be hard," said the Study, and it began cautiously, "What day is it?"

"What day?" and the Christmas Boy betrayed all the scorn that an Altrurian ever allows himself to feel. "Why, Christmas!"

"Of course! But what year?"

"Why, 2091. It's the bicentennial of the International Copyright."

"Oh, exactly! It's the celebration of that great legislative act of Common Honesty."

"No, *not* exactly. It's Solution day."

"Solution day?" the Study repeated, with the meekness of a competitive examiner. "Solution of what?"

"Of the problem that remained to be solved after Congress had legislated common honesty to foreign authors."

"You mean the uncommon dishonesty of the law distinguishing between literary property and other property?"

"Correct! You see, the thing became more ridiculous, more scandalous, as you may say, after the passage of the International Copyright Law, and people began to realize the enormity of the wrong that they had been guilty of."

"Yes; there is nothing that opens one's eyes to the sinfulness of sin like leaving off sinning," the Study could not help noting. "Well! You were saying?"

III.

"After the passage of the International Copyright Law," said the Christmas Boy, "the sense of wrong began to work of itself in the public conscience. The people, when they had got their eyes open to the injustice they had been doing the foreign authors, could not get them shut again to the injustice they were still doing to the native authors. They lost sleep, and were uncomfortable everyway. The authors themselves did not have to move; they simply had to lie low, and let the public misery work itself out. The Altrurians had always prided themselves on the equality of all classes and conditions of men before the law, and now they had suddenly become aware that the law actually distinguished against the very best class of citizens: the most industrious, refined, and modest."

"The literary class?" asked the Study, feeling a glow of diffidence suffuse its façade. "Well, perhaps."

"No perhaps about it!" retorted the Christmas Boy. "Here was a class, and the noblest and truest class in the whole republic, who had no lasting claim to the property they had created. All other

kinds of property were fully protected and warranted in perpetuity to the owners; crimes against other property were more unerringly punished, and on the whole more severely punished than crimes against life and honor. Any Altrurian who had cheated another in a horse trade, and come into the possession of a valuable animal which he had not fairly paid for, was presumed to be the owner of it, and if you stole it you got six years in State's prison. The Altrurian who lent his brother money at such ruinous usury that he could not pay it might foreclose his mortgage on his brother's farm, or house, or shop, and become its owner at a half or third of its real value; and the law confirmed him in possession with every safeguard, and he might transmit it to his children and his children's children to the remotest generation. Any number of Altrurians who combined to build a railroad, or to wreck one, were secured in its tenure against all the stockholders they had robbed, and protected in their franchises by the most solemn statutory obligations. The idler who inherited his estates could leave them intact to the drones who bore his name; the gambler who won a hundred thousand dollars on the rise or fall of a fictitious value could build himself a castle in which he and his could be as secure forever as the fabled Englishman in his house."

"We suppose that was right," said the Study. "Property is the corner-stone of civilization. The law cannot inquire how a thing became property."

"That was what all the legal talent in Altruria told us, and that was what we all believed. So we carefully defended every imaginable kind of owner in everything that was his by every imaginable legislative and juridical device. The poor man who had bought a little cottage with the painful savings of a lifetime we defended as faithfully in perpetual possession as the plutocrat who had wrung the money to build his town houses and his country houses, his yachts and his private cars, from the sweat of his mill hands or his miners. We said we would make no distinctions; that all the Altrurians should be equal before the law. But after the passage of the International Copyright Law we found there had always been a little oversight."

"Yes?" said the Study, beginning to be greatly interested, and rousing itself from a tacit admiration of the Christmas Boy's eloquence. "What was that?"

"Why, we found that there was one class of proprietors who were not only not equal with the others before the law, but who were actually branded with a stamp of inequality, of inferiority, by the law. That was the class of proprietors who *created* their property. You might beg, borrow or steal a thing, and if you did it under the forms of law it was yours and your heirs' and assigns' for ever. You might sell your soul or your honor for it, and it should be inalienably yours. But if you *made* it; if you actually *created* it, *if you gave material form to something out of the ideal world which would never have been here but for you,* then it was *not* yours forever, but only for a certain term of years; and if any one stole it, in whole or in part, the law did not arrest the thief on your complaint, and punish him upon proof of his guilt, but it allowed you to bring suit for damages in a civil action! That was the position of the author before the law of Altruria at the time the famous International Copyright Act was passed in 1891."

The Christmas Boy paused for breath, and the Study observed, "It *was* rather droll."

IV.

"That act of justice," the Christmas Boy proceeded, after running down a tender hen turkey and restoring her to the group of captives from which she had escaped, "rendered the fact of injustice so conspicuous that it became intolerable. Every conscience in Altruria was aroused, and there was a unanimous appeal to the legislature for relief. The Congress elected on this issue passed a bill declaring property in copyrights perpetual, and protecting it from aggression by fine and imprisonment. The constitutionality of the law was questioned, and the first case under it was carried up to the Supreme Court. There the defence urged that there was an essential difference between the property that a man created, and the property that a man earned, or won, or legally stole; that created property was of such a volatile or elusive nature that it could be secured to its owner for a brief term of years only, and protected by such penalties only as left him liable for costs if he failed in a civil suit for damages. It was contended that he was a public benefactor and must be made to feel it. The court inquired if this contention were not a legal fiction, and upon the admission of the defence that it was a legal fiction, the court ordered the defence to copyright it, like other fictions, under the old law, while it reserved its decision."

"Well, they copyrighted the legal fiction for twenty-eight years, just like a novel, and then they renewed the copyright for another term of fourteen years, after which anybody might appropriate it. But the lawyers who had created this fiction protested against the com-

munization of their property, and the courts were filled with the noise they made about it, and the interests of justice suffered so much that the people began to lose all patience. The agitation involved the whole country, and became a political question again. There was talk of secession and of a dictatorship, but at last the parties came together on a measure proposed by the All-Altruria Committee of Common-Sense, and the measure was made a part of the organic law through the act of Congress and the result of the popular vote on the referendum. The committee discovered, after a good deal of hard thinking and talking, that it was no use to enact perpetual patent or copyright; the people had got used to a limited tenure in this kind of property, and they would never consent to perpetuity. At the same time their sense of right was so outraged by the inferiority of authors to other owners before the law, that something must be done to appease them. The only thing to be done was to make the tenure of created property the norm, and declare every species of property tenable for forty-two years only, whether earned, inherited, begged, borrowed, or (legally) stolen. The notion took immensely. It appealed to the two strongest principles in the nature of the Altrurians: their humor and their piety. It was such a good joke on all the other proprietors that folks could not help laughing. At the same time the churches found authority for it in the Old Testament idea of the year of jubilee, when every Israelite was to start fair with the rest on a new half-century's race of self-interest. So the term of tenure was extended from forty-two to fifty years, in deference to religious sentiment, and the plan worked like a charm.

"Of course there were some disorders the first time. Fellows got up and rode off other fellows' horses before the other fellows were awake, Jubilee morning, and some ladies moved in on their neighbors before their neighbors could get out of their houses. It was pretty curious to have a man ploughing up your lawn for potatoes before you realized that he was the new owner, and there were some hot words when a lively chap stepped into an old banker's parlor and said he would trouble him for the combination of his safe. But they all remembered that this sort of thing was what the authors had always had to stand, and the day passed without bloodshed. The statute of limited property-hold was more popular than ever, because the majority got the most, and the details of administration that had proved vexatious were overhauled and rectified. The celebration of Solution day was established by law, and now it falls, every fiftieth year, on Christmas, when people are feeling good, anyway."

V.

"And does the new order of things work well?" inquired the Study. "Isn't it contrary to human nature?"

"What is human nature?" demanded the Christmas Boy. "Once it was human nature for men to eat men. Once it was human nature for men to enslave men. Once it was human nature for men to work men to death in mines, and mills, and sweaters' dens. Once it was human nature for men to hold large tracts of land idle while other men were starving. Once it was human nature for men to say to one class of men that they should have a right to their own for forty-two years, while every one else was secured in his own forever. But human nature changes, and now it isn't human nature for men to eat men, enslave men, sweat men; and it's been found out in Altruria that if it is right for one class of men to be limited in the tenure of their property it is right for all."

The Christmas Boy became so heated with argument that the Study almost feared to provoke him farther by saying: "Oh yes, it's right, of course. But you can't legislate righteousness, you know."

"Stuff!" roared the Christmas Boy, in a voice so loud that all the male turkeys in his keeping gobbled wildly. "All the righteousness in the world is legislated righteousness, and has been ever since the legislation of the Ten Commandments. Now you think of it."

The Study perceived that the Christmas Boy was an Enemy of Society in disguise. But it preferred not to irritate him until it had got out of him everything it wanted to know. "And do the Altrurians like it, this new arrangement?"

"Well, you watch and see," said the Christmas Boy, and instantly vanished.

There was indeed an extraordinary gladness visible in the myriad faces of the Altrurians as they went and came in rapid processions of renunciation and recipience. It was truly a jubilee. The countenances of those who renounced their property were radiant with the relief from its care; those who assumed it wore a look of solemn responsibility qualified with a benevolence as different as possible from the greed that the Study had always supposed inseparable from the possession of the bounty of providence. In its mystification the Study cast about for some kindly person who would explain the fact, when the Christmas Boy materialized again. He was grinning from ear to ear, and turning hand-springs so that his grin formed a wheel in the air four feet in diameter.

"Where are your turkeys and toys, your champagne and celery, your coal and cranberries, your holiday editions of favorite authors?" demanded the Study, holding its larger curiosity in abeyance for the moment.

"Got them all off on a renouncing millionaire down there before he had time to think. And now he'll have to see that I don't come to want till next Jubilee, and I shall merely have to *work* for my daily bread, not beg for it, bleed for it, lie for it, cheat for it."

"Oh, that's the way, is it?"

"Yes; those that assume the property assume the responsibility, and covenant with the Sympathies to see that those who renounce it share equally with themselves in its enjoyment, if they will work. No man can starve or freeze in Altruria, I tell you."

The Christmas Boy disappeared in a vivid hand-spring; and with a deep sigh the troubled Study awoke, happy to find itself again in the good old familiar world where everybody has a right to his own forever, except the author, who has a right to his own for forty-two years.

---

[1] See pp. 288a–292b for discussion of the "Synthesized Sympathies of Altruria."

January, 1892

Editor's Study.

I.

A LITTLE more, and "The Common Man," which seems to us the best in *An Idyl of the Sun and other Poems,* would have been a very fine poem. As it is, it comes near saying surpassingly well what we all feel to be the truth about the superiority of the general humanity over any other expression of human superiority. There is a strong rise of imagination in it that lifts the thought to the command of those wider prospects where heaven and earth are always seen meeting; and there is here and there some phrasing that gives the pleasure one finds in artistic mastery.

"His strength is as the braces of the sky,"

is a good line, with a biblical largeness of stroke; and the suggestion of repose and the sufficiency of life's simple means to life's simple needs could hardly have been better made than in such terms as these:

"Not from rare moments' tenuous chalices,
Flame-filled and flashing with infinities,
But from a cumbrous cup of common clay,
Drinks he the lasting joys of his long day.

"He has long leisure, yet he wastes no time;
He waxes old, but still enjoys his prime;
And what another in despair has sought,
He finds, at last, without one troublous thought.

"Behold! he daily does the world's wide will,
Makes what is good, and masters what is ill;
And when the race has reached its earthly span,
The common shall appear the perfect man."

It would be hard to say just how this real poem fails of being a really great poem; but somehow it does, while it fails so little that it seems as if the artist might take it again into his mind, and give it back to us wrought to the completeness of form and texture we long to have it wear.

In the same volume "The Laggard," which prolongs and deepens something of the same strain of thought, is lacking in much the same indefinable way; but there is enough promise in it and in most of the pieces in the book to make us wish to hear again from Mr. Orrin Cedesman Stevens when his touch is a little firmer and his patience a little finer.

II.

We might say this, or something like it, of Mr. Meredith Nelson, the author of *Short Flights;* though we are afraid we could give less reason for saying it, unless the fine implications of this poem, the first and best in his book, are enough:

"Seasons that pass me by in varied mood,
As on the impressionable land you leave a trace,
Moulding sometimes a delicate flower's sweet face,
Touching again with green the sombre wood,
Or drawing all beneath a sunny hood,—
Am I not worthy as they to have a place
In your remembrance? Am I made too base
To know what weed and thorn have understood?
Fair vernal time, I need your quickening
Even as the sleeping earth! O Summer heat,
Make flowers and fruit in me that I may bring
Full hands to Autumn when above me beat
The serious winds; and, Winter, make me strong
Like the glad music of your battle song!"

III.

There is a want of carefulness or technique in both these poets, which is rather surprising, in the presence of their excellence in other things. This is true, too, of the verse of Mr. William Wilfred Campbell, who has printed a volume of *Lake Lyrics and other Poems,* and true in about the same degree. But we find in him also traits of imaginative thoughtfulness, and a freshness of fancy which make us indifferent—perhaps too indifferent—to the blemishes we cannot deny in his workmanship. He is at his best, we think, in the poem of "Lazarus," where the old parable is transfigured in the light of modern altruism, and the unity of all humanity, which is intimated in "The Common Man," is affirmed in the conception of a heaven that pities hell, a redemption that is not bliss as long as perdition endures. But the teeth are set on edge by the elision of the indefinite article in passages that stir and kindle the mind and move the heart.

"'O Father Abram, I can never rest,
Here in thy bosom in the whitest heaven,
Where love blooms on through days without
an even,
For up through all the paradises seven
There comes a cry from some fierce anguished
breast.

"'I hear it crying through the heavenly night,

When curvèd, hung in space, the million
  moons
Lean planetward, and infinite space attunes
Itself to silence; as from drear gray dunes
A cry is heard along the shuddering light,

"'Of wild dusk-bird, a sad, heart-curdling cry,
  So comes to me that call from out hell's
    coasts.
  There is no heaven, with all its shining hosts,
  There is no heaven, until that hell doth die.'

"So spoke the soul of Lazarus, and from thence

. . . .

"Hellward he moved, like radiant star shot out
  From heaven's blue with rain of gold at even,
  When Orion's train and that mysterious seven
  Move on in mystic range from heaven to
    heaven.
Hellward he sank, followed by radiant rout.

"'Tis ages now long gone since he went out,
  Christ - urged, love - driven, across the jasper
    walls,
  But hellward still he ever floats and falls,
  And ever nearer come those anguished calls;
And far behind he hears a glorious shout."

IV.

As one writes of these little volumes of verse certain threads of association, too filmily impalpable, perhaps, to be made evident to the reader at second hand, connect them with one another. It is possibly a sense of the modern enlargement of the allegory in the one case and in the other that carries us from Mr. Campbell's "Lazarus" to Mr. Denton J. Snider's "Homer in Chios." In very passable English hexameters, this young poet fancies the "Ionian father of the rest," surrounded in his wise and happy age by pupils from all Greece, and pilgrims from the barbaric world, who study to transmit his art and to carry the Hellenic light to distant times and lands. Into this liberal scheme it is easy for Hesiod, Sappho, and David to fit, and the effect is by no means so grotesque as the bare statement of it would suggest. In fact, one cannot regard such an attempt without respect, which is also a hope for its author's efforts in the future.

V.

The future of Mr. J. P. Irvine's efforts, as we infer from the title, *The Green Leaf and the Gray*, which he has given his book of verse, is less to be taken into the account in making up one's mind about him. There is great inequality in his performance, and some offences which it is not easy to forgive, and yet two or three of the descriptive pieces are as good landscape art in the modern sort as we could well find. The best of these are "Summer Drought," "Indian Summer," and "November;" and here is a poem which seems to us very graphic, and which we take to be autobiographic:

THE HALT.

The day was lost, and we were sent
  In haste to guard the baggage train,

And all the night, through gloom and rain,
Across a land of ruin went.

But halting once, and only then
  We turned aside to let the corps
  Of ambulances pass before,
That hauled a thousand wounded men.

And leaning, drowsy and oppressed,
  Upon my gun, I wondered where
  The comrade was I helped to bear
Slow rearward, wounded in the breast.

When lo! I heard a fainting cry,
  As wheels drew near and stopped aside:
  "The man in here with me has died;
Oh, lift him out, or I shall die!"

"All right," the one-armed driver said;
  "The horse can hardly pull the load.
  We leave them all along the road;
It does no good to haul the dead!"

And so we turned by lantern light,
  And laid him in a gloom of pines,
  When came an order down the lines:
"Push on, and halt no more to-night!"

VI.

All or nearly all of these books bear to the experienced eye the sad evidences of having been published by or for the authors; and the reader must not infer a pecuniary boom in poetry from their appearance. But they are interesting for another reason, and they bear witness to the truth of the Study's theory that in "this fair land," as the politicians call it, there is properly no literary centre. Mr. Irvine's book comes from Kirkwood, Illinois; Mr. Snider's from St. Louis; Mr. Campbell's from New Brunswick; Mr. Nelson's from Indianapolis; Mr. Stevens's from central New York. We have, besides, a volume from Mr. James Whitcomb Riley, of Indianapolis, whom all the world now knows, and another from Mr. Madison Cawein, of Louisville, whose quality we have already tried to acquaint our readers with; and from all these appearances one might argue that the centre of poetry, if we have any, was now, like the centre of population, far beyond the Alleghanies. With this active Western competition, literature, like agriculture, may become an effete industry at the East, and we may yet hear of the abandoned studies of New England, as we now hear of the abandoned farms. The poets of the older sections in another generation may leave their haunts in charge of the State, and we shall perhaps have the commonwealth of Massachusetts advertising them by counties and townships, with full descriptions of each and the price annexed.

It has not quite come to this yet; but the Western pressure is very great, and unless something is done to bring up the worn-out fields of thought at the East by the lavish use of fertilizers, or a new system of cultivation, the future is sure to be anxiously awaited there. Perhaps the application of electricity, or the use of hot-water pipes, as in the new horticulture in France, may be found beneficial. But, after all, the Western product will have its own flavor; and no watering-pot process will give us the color and perfume of Mr. Riley's *Old-fashioned Roses*, grown in the open air, and fanned by the breath of the prairies.

His volume bears a London imprint, and decidedly has not been published by or for the author, whose gentle fame commands a public on both sides of the sea. The sweetness that lies at the heart of these old-fashioned roses, and of all those wilding growths which their author calls his "Hoosier dialect" poems, is a very genuine and tender love of the simplicity and humility of the past. The poet has divined, what Tolstoï has thought strenuously out: that the real happiness, the unmistakable bliss of each man's life is something that lurks far back in the memory of his childish innocence; and it is to the sense of this that he makes his touching appeal. The earlier conditions of our national life, before our craze for wealth began, and the millionaire had not yet become the American ideal, inspire his retrospective longing, and it is the memory of the childhood of a people which he appeals to, as well. Of course man cannot live by remembrance alone; but in waking again and again the note that sounds through all his verse, the poet performs a noble office in a vulgar, noisy, and sordid time; and we cannot hearken ever so little to him without being refreshed and strengthened.

VII.

The direction of Mr. Cawein's poetry is less definite, but its range is wider. Here is the impassioned endeavor of art striving to include and express for beauty's sake; and achieving effects which, if too often only effects, are such successes as are deigned only to the very poet. There are bits of painting, strains of music in *Days and Dreams* that make the heart glow and throb, almost at the same moment that the reason censures the poet for his abandon to the delight of much mere beautiful wording, the ecstasy of a really marvellous decorative feeling. Passages of his new volume exceed any others in lustre and color of phrase, but no single piece that seems to us so good as some in his former books.

"Now Time grants night the more and day the less;
  The gray decides; and brown
  Dim golds and reds in dulling greens express
  Themselves, and broaden as the year goes down.
  Sadder the croft where, thrusting gray and high
  Their balls of seed the hoary onions die,
  Where, Falstaff-like, buff-bellied pumpkins lie;
  Deeper each wilderness;
  Sadder the blue of hills that lounge along

The lonesome west; sadder the song
  Of the wild red-bird in the leafage yellow;
  Deeper and dreamier, aye,
  Than woods or waters leans the languid sky
  Above live orchards where the cider-press
  Drips and the russets mellow."

VIII.

A genuine and delicate gift seems to be that of Miss Gertrude Hall, whose Boston book of *Verses* comes round by way of London, like Mr. Riley's. The touch is light and the sense is fine in the brief fancies, as we suppose all these slight and graceful poetries will be called by folks who pretend to know the difference between the fancy and the imagination. Here is something that is perhaps even imaginative, and is certainly touching and lovely:

IN THE ART MUSEUM.

He stands where the white light showers
  In his wonted, high recess;
The dust has woven a soft veil
  Over his comeliness.

Beneath the massive eyebrows
  And lids that never beat,
The same glance floats forever,
  So sad, and solemn sweet.

The same peace seals forever
  The full lips finely curled.
I'm come to this, his dwelling,
  To bring him news of the world:

"Once more the Spring hath mantled
  With green the lasting hills,—
Hast thou no faint remembrance
  Of daisies and daffodils?

"Their stems will lengthen sunward,
  As when thou wast of us.
My heart swells with its sorrow
  For thee, Antinous."

IX.

The name, and perhaps something in the feeling here, beckons our indolent course to *A Garden of Hellas*, where the immortal flowers of Greek epigram have bloomed anew in English verse, at the breath of an American poet. Those who know Mrs. Lilla Cabot Perry's work in her own volume of poems, *The Heart of the Weed*, will allow that few writers could bring a finer or deeper sense of beauty to her present task than she; for that book, which still awaits its full recognition, had qualities of feeling and thinking as rare in recent verse as its strenuousness of expression. Those who know her version of Tourguénief's *Prose Poems* will have been prepared for the artistic conscience of this group of translations from the Anthology, where she has aimed to give some sense of the qualities of that most wonderful collection of antique literature, and some notion of its range and variety besides. The pieces chosen are ninety in number, and they represent fifty-eight different poets. The modern sentiment of most of these epigrams is best imparted in our familiar rhythms, and the translator has judged wisely in employing English metres rather than adhering to forms that would have been false to the spirit of the original in our tongue. There is, in fact, nothing more striking in the poems of the Anthology than their modernity; so that an epigram from Meleager might well seem a bit of society verse from some poet of our own day, or at the furthest from some airy trifler of the first Charles's time. Dobson might have written this one, or Herrick:

" Tell her this, Dorcas ! Tell her once again ;
 A third time, Dorcas, tell her everything.
 Run, don't delay, fly ! Wait a minute, wait
 A moment longer, Dorcas ! Whither haste
 Before the whole thou knowest ? Add only this
 To what I said before—but trifle not.
 Say, only say—no, Dorcas, tell her all.
 Why should I send you, Dorcas ? for with you
 I go myself ! My message I precede."

Perhaps a good half of the pieces here are more or less love-poems; of the rest, the most have to do with death, which, after love, is the thing that the minor poets like best to talk about. Of many epitaphs, one of the subtlest is this by Paul the Silentiary :

" My name—why tell it ? Country—matters not.
 From famous blood—what if from poor thou
   came ?
 Of honorable life—hadst thou been bad, then
   what ?
 Here I lie now. Who says this, and to whom ?"

Certain of the slighter elegiacs mourn dead partridges, or crickets and locusts; and the seasons duly share the poets' songs with the landscape. But the themes are not many; the same note is struck again and again; it is the divine temperance, the implicit as well as the explicit beauty that pleases. To these characteristics, which we all understand to be most Greek, the sweet, elect English of the translator is as faithful as it is to the universal meaning of the epigrams. They are really imparted to us; they are fairly naturalized in our speech; and it is a garden of Hellas, indeed, but on our own ground. The flowers are Greek, but they blow in English air under an American sky, and many of them we find as familiarly dear in scent and color as Mr. Riley's old-fashioned roses themselves. The world itself is new to every generation; and under the hoary ashes of antiquity the latest of the moderns feels the appeal of a kindred life that once was.

X.

" High noon,
  And from the purple-veiled hills
  To where Rome lies in azure mist,
  Scarce any breath of wind
  Upon this vast and solitary waste,

These leagues of sunscorch'd grass
Where i' the dawn the scrambling goats maintain
A hardy feast,
And where, when the warm yellow moonlight
   floods the flats,
Gaunt laggard sheep browse spectrally for hours,
While not less gaunt and spectral shepherds
   stand
Brooding, or with hollow vacant eyes
Stare down the long perspective of the dusk.
Now not a breath :
No sound ;
No living thing,
Save where the beetle jars his crackling shards,
Or where the hoarse cicala fills
The heavy heated hour with palpitant whirr.
Yet hark !
Comes not a low deep whisper from the ground,
A sigh as though the immemorial past
Breathed here a long, slow breath ?
Lost nations sleep below ; an empire here
Is dust ; and deeper, deeper still,
Dim shadowy peoples are the mould that warms
The roots of every flower that blooms and blows."

These lines, so pure and clear, are from a little volume of English verse printed for Mr. William Sharp at Rome, and called *Sospiri di Roma*. We have had our misgivings of Mr. Sharp before now; but it seems to us that in the thirty three or four bits of musical rhythm, he has gone far to free himself from his past, and to become one of the important poets of the future. The pieces are for the most part landscape work, or studies in color, where the figure is used decoratively; but the observation is close and true, the aspects of earth and air accurately caught, and the prevailing excellence of the performance is so great that we easily forgive the artist some moments of absent-mindedness in which he hands us his palette instead of giving us a picture.

XI.

It would be well, we suppose, if at some such point as this we could put on the prophet, and read the future in the signs of poetical life present in all this verse. But that is a function which we have always rather shrunk from, and we should not be willing even to generalize very boldly now. The reader, however, can do this for himself, and if he has a mind for prophecy, he can expect almost anything he likes from poets who have each given distinct promise. It is always possible that we are on the point of encountering a very great poet like those of the past; but if none such is on the way to us, it is certainly charming and refreshing to meet these young and earnest and conscientious artists, so finely in tune with their time and place. Never before has there been closer affinity between the poets and the universal life; never have its local expressions been more lovingly and faithfully studied. Perhaps in poetry, as in fiction, we are to have a democratic republic of letters, instead of the old oligarchy.

The growth of simplicity, the passion for plainness, the impatience of symbols, and the desire for the very thing, are indications of some such eventuality; and when we have work like that of the Belgian, Maurice Maeterlinck, in the drama, we may almost believe that the hour of a new art has struck. We group him with the poets because it seems to us that the two little plays of his which Mrs. Mary Violé has given us in very unaffected English transcend the form of prose, and ally themselves in effect with the effect of verse. In a kind of elemental directness, they are far beyond Ibsen, while they deal with no social or individual problems, but touch us through our mere humanity, not to say mortality, where we are not citizens, and scarcely men or women, but only Man. One of the pieces is called *The Intruder*, and expresses the advent of death in the circle of a family sitting together after the birth of a child, while the mother lies in the next room. The way in which death is realized as something objectively appreciable to the nerves, is tremendous; but hardly anything less than the quotation of the whole brief drama would give the notion of its finely graduated climax.

The other piece is perhaps even more[1] horrific. A company of blind people have been led from their asylum to a distant wood near the wintry sea, by an old priest, who suddenly dies and sits silent and cold in the midst of their helplessness. At last the priest's dog finds them, and now they think that they are safe, that the dog will lead them back to the asylum. But the dog will not leave the body.

XII.

In Middle Harbor and other Verse, chiefly Australian, is a book whose author has deeply felt the quality of his native landscape and the local life, and has here and there vividly intimated it to the reader. It is a striking effort, and worthy attention; for this poet of far-off scenes is writing from his full sense of them, and not writing merely at a public strange to them. The world appreciably widens in the light his poetry casts; here is something that has a claim upon our knowledge and sympathy which scarcely seemed within our horizons before.

XIII.

Mr. R. W. Gilder's *Two Worlds and other Poems* happens to lie at the bottom of the fortuitous find of fairy-gold which we have been mining. It needs no stamp of the assayer to commend it; the metal and its purity are known. But it is a pleasure to recognize value, if only to show that one knows it, and we wish to praise certain pieces in the volume because, for the moment at least, they have made life richer. One of these is "A Midsummer Meditation"; another, "Non sine Dolore." "The Prisoner's Thought" is a singularly powerful poem, with suggestion in it that will not soon leave the reader, who again could not part if he would with the truth of "Great Nature is an Army Gay." These are all strictly a poet's contribution to the feeling, the unrestful hope, and far-striving thought of our day. Æsthetically the book, we think, reaches its perfectest expression in the peculiarly beautiful poem called "Moonlight," where the sense imparted is of an image plastically shaped of the moonlight itself.

---

[1] Maeterlinck's play outlined by Howells is The Blind, (Les Aveugles).

February, 1892

Editor's Study.

I.

WHEN an author has expressed for the first time a quality of a place or a people, he has added something to literature, and this is what Mr. Thomas A. Janvier has done in his volume, *The Uncle of an Angel, and other Stories*. The distinctive quality of New England has been often in literature; the rank flavors of the Far West are familiar to the critical palate; we know the savor of the South, in Tennessee, Virginia (Mr. Frank Hopkinson Smith's Colonel Carter of Cartersville stands for the simple-hearted, high-minded Virginia gentleman, as Don Quixote stands for Spain), Louisiana, and Carolina; New York has imparted a characteristic taste to many books; but till now Philadelphia had awaited the chymic art that could distil the peculiar gust and aroma of her society life and present it in unmistakable types. It is a great little triumph that Mr. Janvier has achieved, and it takes nothing from the genuineness of the result that it is penetrated and perfumed with a humor that is as finely his as his people and conditions are Philadelphian. It is all the more a triumph because the material which embodies it is slight, and the structure of his stories is sometimes fantastically airy. It is always the work of an artist who feels keenly and clearly the things he renders evident with a touch so gay and bold. *The Uncle of an Angel* is a conception so freshly charming, and a performance so delicately and surprisingly original, in the character of the Angel as well as the Uncle, that we are in little danger of overpraising it, though we praise it a great deal. The wilful young girl who "works" her parents and guardians has probably existed since the world began, but she had wanted her historian till now; and the kind of elderly relative whom she finds an easy victim had never been studied, apparently, till Mr. Janvier came to him. Then he found a master to portray him, and she fell into the hands of an artist with the courage to be true to her at every hazard. Nothing in the whole fine affair is finer than letting the Angel marry the staid old crony of the Uncle, as she would actually have done, instead of *making* her marry the dashing young reprobate swell whom she had simultaneously flirted with. That kind of young girl needs some one whom she can work through life, and the Angel always had her heavenly orbs wide open.

II.

In some studies of East-side German life in New York, Mr. Janvier is very gratifyingly faithful to localities and conditions, but in the stories that he evokes from them he wanders too far for our following in the *selva oscura* of romanticism. We could not ask him to do more than take a lesson from himself as he will find it in *The Uncle of an Angel*: a man is his own best model where he is at his best; and something like this is what we should like to suggest to the author of *Iduna, and other Stories*, whom we find too often lingering on romantic ground. Mr. George A. Hibbard's work must have impressed the magazine reader long before his volume appeared with a certain felicity of execution and a certain ideal of performance which are not common. The wish to deal with poetic material in the region of psychical conjecture is curiously blended with the desire of portraying the life of the society world as one begins to find it in the country colonies where society makes longer or shorter sojourn. We have now a society that "rides to hounds," and though it is still a "far cry" from it to the English original, the American imitation is worth the artist's study. Some notion of what this sort of society is like gets into Mr. Hibbard's brilliant and animated story of *The Dark Horse*, though we fancy the report of it is more or less hampered and hindered by the artist's just reluctance to take snap-shots with the kodak at localities and characters. The result is a picture a little conventionalized, but still valuable as the first of its kind. One aches to have a closer semblance, even while one respects the artist's forbearance; by-and-by it will be possible for him somehow to give us a more perfect sense of society conditions without trenching upon private

conditions. From Mr. Hibbard's cleverness we may hope almost anything, unless he should be content to let it remain
cleverness. His attitude toward life reminds us much of Mr. Henry James's in
his earlier work: there is the same acquaintance with society material, the same
love of the purely ideal, the same feeling
for dramatic effect, the same limitation
of perspective. Mr. Hibbard's *Iduna*,
the girl who never heard of death, is a
poetical motive delicately treated; *The
Woman in the Case* is a deeply tragical
episode approaching the melodramatic;
The Dark Horse is a vivid society piece;
and these things tolerably suggest his
range. But none of them quite indicates his potential scope, which we find
more distinctly given by another art; for
he is, like Mr. Janvier, able to express
himself in two sorts, and is a painter as
well as a poet. It is a picture which
represents this author at his best, and
which those who saw it at an Academy
exhibition of some four or five years
ago cannot have forgotten. Through a
bleak foreground of snowy country road,
overhung by leafless trees, and sparsely
bordered by dead weeds and naked shrubs
thrusting stiffly from the livid drifts, approaches a bob-sled with an elderly man
and woman on the seat in front; his
right hand rests on her hands folded in
her lap; in the wagon body behind stretches a coffin. Another sled follows from
the middle distance, out of a background
of cold sky meeting the level of a frozen
lake. Beside it a farmer-like figure in
high boots drags itself over the snow.
That is all. But the picture's solemn
realism expresses an anguish of pent
pathos that wrings the heart; and it
shows a mastery that we believe Mr.
Hibbard capable of in literature when he
remembers there that humanity is wider
than any world, and that its simplest
facts and nearest are its greatest.

III.

A sense of this is what gives their austere charm to the studies of New England
life which Mrs. Rose Terry Cooke calls
Huckleberries. The name intimates the
whimsical humor which relieves their
sadness and grimness, and imparts its
freakish color to their tragedy. They
are such stories as Miss Wilkins has
made us familiar with of late; but we
ought in justice to remember how long
ago Mrs. Cooke began to write them, and
how true she was in her art, when truth
in art was considered a minor virtue if
not a sordid detail. They are longer and
looser in structure than Miss Wilkins's
tales; they are not so fine as Miss Jewett's; but they are faithful and strong,
and they are as important as any work

of their kind, which, as the reader of the
Study ought to know by this time, we
think a very high and good kind. The
present group does not vary greatly in
kind or quality from that called *Somebody's Neighbors*, and other groups of
Mrs. Cooke's short stories, which are all
to be commended as the work of a poet
and a moralist.

IV.

For some estimate of the kind and
quality, we advise our readers to go to
Mr. W. M. Griswold's excellent *Descriptive Lists of Novels*, which have now included Novels of American Country Life,
Novels of American City Life, International Novels, Romantic Novels, and British Novels. The reader who happens not
to have seen these *Lists* can have little
notion of their interest and value. They
are really very full catalogues of the
different sorts of novels, but they are
critical catalogues, and intended to embrace not everything, but the best of
everything. The title of each book is
given, with the author's and publisher's
names, and the place and date of publication; then follow passages of one or more
reviews from the most respectable authorities, which are chosen not merely
to embody the reviewers' opinion of the
book, but also to show what the book is in
scope and plot. So they form a body of
good criticism as well as offer a prospect
of the whole field of fiction. The careful
and faithful work which their selection
implies, and the vastness of the editor's
reading in contemporary fiction and criticism, are facts which will strike every one;
and we wish every one might gratefully
feel how fresh and important a service
Mr. Griswold has done not only the
reader who is seeking a novel for his
own entertainment, but the librarian, the
teacher, the parent, who is choosing novels for others. Simply, it is incalculable,
and the Study finds it a pleasure as well
as a duty to recognize these agreeable
and valuable lists, which may be had of
the author, at Cambridge, Massachusetts.
In any branch of inquiry concerning fiction, they are indispensable.

V.

The originator of the scheme they so
delightfully realize could not help being
original at several points, and the Study
wishes to express its joy in the reformed
spelling which Mr. Griswold uses, and
has apparently invented. It is not radical, it does not go all lengths, but its
simplifications of our orthography are
many and very great. The surprising
thing is that while they commend themselves to the reason, they do not affront
the eye, accustomed though it is to the

established barbarities. The time must come, of course, when these will no more be suffered than cannibalism, slavery, or polygamy; and Mr. Griswold has gone a long way to meet that time. He has done it quietly and straightforwardly, as if there were no other course for a thoughtful and self-respectful writer to take.

VI.

The Study gathers courage from the spectacle of his boldness to perform one of those acts of contrition and of reparation which it always finds so difficult and distasteful. We accepted the estimate of Mr. Thomas L. Harris given in the *Life of Laurence Oliphant*, without going behind that record and seeking to verify its statements. That is what the whole cry of reviewers did, but we had the less excuse because we felt, as few of them seem to have felt, the grotesqueness of Mrs. Oliphant's suggestion that her brilliant kinsfolk were lured into Mr. Harris's community and kept there by hypnotic influences. Since our criticism appeared we have learned from friends of Mr. Harris, whom it wounded, that the Oliphants' association with him was not only wholly voluntary, but that when they left him, it was to take from the community much more money value than they put into it. We think it right to let these assertions meet the light here, though we have no means of supporting them, and can only testify to our respect for the people who make them. Mr. Harris is a mystic of the most incomprehensible to the world, but these life-long friends and followers of his affirm his generosity of purpose, and his absolute unselfishness of deed. One of them, a member of his community at Fountaingrove, California, writes:

"All his life, Mr. Harris's one aim has been to bring relief to human suffering ....and for this end he has taken to his heart and home, for the last thirty years, all sorts and conditions of men and women....If people have brought money, he has been glad of the help it gave in taking care of those who brought none; but for himself he wants too little to be bothered with any one's possessions. At this place, for instance, he has organized three beautiful and even luxurious homes for his friends, who carry on the business of the estate; but he is rarely here, preferring his simple little mountain hermitage, that all told, to build and furnish, did not cost over a thousand dollars."

Mr. Harris himself makes a passing reference to the accusations of Mrs. Oliphant in a recent pamphlet, *The Brotherhood of the New Life*, saying merely that "the real facts have long been known," and that these have been embodied in a statement to the English public; he declares that he has been "greatly wronged," and has "been in no case the wrong-doer." The whole matter is apparently susceptible of proof, and it is mere justice to make known that there are two sides to the question.

VII.

Mr. Harris apparently does not care a great deal about it. He has for the last three years been trying to solve the far vaster question, namely: "By what process shall the man who, by consequence of inspiration opened into God and the resultant life of service rendered to mankind, has fitted himself mentally and socially for that service, with powers amplified from an hundred to a thousand fold, overcome the universal social tendency to physical deterioration and disease, and renew the outer structures of his person, and lead on a renaissance of the vitalities and vigors of the prime? How, in a word, without passing through physical decease, shall man practically embody and realize the resurrection?" Mr. Harris thinks he has found the answer, and he says that by virtue of it he is "no more an old man of seventy, but" is "now renewed in more than the physical and mental prowess of the early prime."

VIII.

This faith, exultantly proclaimed, can be no less than pathetic to many; to those who are able to make it their own, it must be precious; and we will confess that we have no heart to deride it. At the same time we cannot understand why any one should wish twice to describe the round of human experience. To be again young is to be again old; to be restored is to be doomed to a second decay. The dream would be futile if it were possible.

Yet we must respect the dreamer; it may be, in fact, that we stand at the verge of a great realm, hitherto strange, which our steps are about to penetrate. In his wonderful romance of *Peter Ibbetson*, Mr. Du Maurier has shown how sleep might become a city of refuge from waking, and the soul, even in earthly bonds, find there a contemporaneous life, richer and fuller, than any that mind or body knows in the world of their activities. The plummet of his suggestion plunges into depths not sounded before, and his fancy intimates a consolation and a fruition divinely satisfying. It is a beautiful story, not to be judged by the ordinary canons, but to be valued aright only by the most recondite consciousness of the reader, where he is aware of the encounter and co-operation of reason and passion, elsewhere dissevered by the sordid exigencies of life in a remorseless enmity.

IX.

In the artist, in the poet, the union of principles apparently antagonistic is by no means a rare or strange experience, and the supreme poet has his being in their mystical convergence. This is what makes Dante's dream of Hell and Purgatory and Heaven at once drama and vision, and sublimely real as to all things material and spiritual. It is not inconceivable that the things he had imagined must have remained to him afterwards as vivid as the things he had done, and that his journey through the world of souls should have seemed as veritable as his exile from Florence and his sojourn in Verona and Ravenna. We shall never get any precise answer to such conjectures, however closely we press them; but we must be grateful for any new approach to his presence, any fresh opportunity to interrogate him, as it were, for ourselves. It is some such approach, some such opportunity, that Professor Charles Eliot Norton has offered us in his prose version of the "Divine Comedy." [2]

Translation no longer assumes to content us by telling us what an author is like; it does its best to tell us what an author is; and in this it obeys the universal artistic impulse towards reality. The history of the different versions of Dante would alone form a most interesting prospect of the movement from the time when the translator authoritatively proclaimed that his office was to impart the "spirit" of the original, to the present day, when he faithfully seeks to repeat his very thoughts in the exactest equivalents that can be found for his very words. It is extremely interesting to see a man of Professor Norton's scholarly

and conservative quality practically ranging himself with the boldest of the literary reformers. He has peculiar gifts for metrical translation; doubtless his work in that sort can be equalled, but we doubt whether it has ever been excelled. His knowledge is not only fine and close; it is sensitive and sympathetic; he is a poet without the poet's egoism; his passion for beauty is so impersonal that it does not imply appropriation. He loves a beautiful thing too generously to wish to make it his own; to take it from the hand of its creator, and to offer it unqualified and as little as possible changed, to such as can receive it only at second hand, is his conception of the translator's office, as we find it expressed in his prose rendering of Dante.

Some such version was almost the only word left to say about Dante. Longfellow had followed the Italian step by step; it was with his own gait, to be sure, but it was with a fidelity that must amaze whoever examines and compares the original and the imitation. But Longfellow discarded rhyme, and aimed only to keep the measure of the Italian, for the rhythm was hopeless. Professor Norton goes farther in his endeavor at an exact report of meanings, and frankly trusts himself to the movement and temper of prose. He will not be satisfied with less than the closest analogue. Another word, almost as good, and metrically preferable, he will not use because it is not the utmost truth to Dante. This is his will, and this is his deed, in the latest English for the "Divine Comedy." What that English is in itself, how elect, how clean, how clear, those who know his work know already without our superfluous praises, which could convey no true sense of it to others.

[1] See pp. 337b–339a.

[2] Dante Alighieri, The Divine Comedy of Dante Alighieri, Charles Eliot Norton, trans. (Boston and New York: Houghton, Mifflin and Company, 1891–92).

March, 1892

Editor's Study.

I.

IN one of his suggestive essays on social questions Mr. William Morris points out that in our present conditions there are two epochs or civilizations existing in every household, and that in spite of their frequent contact, these never really mix, and scarcely affect each other. Materially they are united by a common bond, and in a degree their interests are the same, but essentially they are alien and distrustful: the dining-room and drawing-room floors are of one period, and the basement and attic of another; they do not really speak the same language.

It would take us too far if we followed Mr. Morris through his proofs and reasons, which besides are too damaging to the present social fabric to be fully reproduced; and in fact we wished merely to shed the light of his interesting theory in illustration of a diversity doubtless apparent in a certain literary household. In this the differences are between nominal equals, and spring from no injustice of condition. We have often fancied them something like those varying temperaments of the church which express themselves in High and Low and Broad, yet never quite transcend the just authority of the Church, which includes all temperaments, if not all opinions. The Easy Chair or the Study or the Drawer can each consistently think but one thing; the Magazine can consistently tolerate every variety in their thinking. At the end of the ends it is doubtless temperament rather than condition which results in this type or that. In spite of every adversity, the civilized man or woman is often to be rung up from the basement, and in spite of every advantage the savage, male or female, is to be feared in the drawing-room. Mr. Morris is mainly right, perhaps, but the effect of temperament is so prodigious that it must never be left even apparently out of the account. There was nothing but temperament which hindered the Study from emulating the civility of the Chair, when it opened its doors (with something too much of a bang), five or six years ago; for though the civility of the Chair is of so fine and rare a kind, it is most distinctly of the kind that is within the scope of every one. It is shocking, in view of the fact that we might all be gentle and patient and decent, if we would, to reflect how few of us are so, simply because we will not. It is the golden will to be all this which makes the Easy Chair the throne it is, and establishes it above contemporary principalities and powers in its influence and dominion. If the reader will take the pretty book lately made "From the Easy Chair" and look through [1] it, he can hardly fail to be charmed with what is said and how it is said; but if he is the reader we fancy him, we think he will be yet more concerned with the spirit than with the fashion or the matter of the book. Other men (how many other men!) have commented upon manners and morals before; have lightly lashed the follies of "the town"; have satirized "the world"; have rebuked the vices of "the great," and have stood the friends of innocence and virtue in "ages" that seemed as breakneck bent on ruin as our own; but these many long years that Mr. Curtis has occupied the Easy Chair it has been his singular gift never to let the reader fail of something deeply, ultimately serious in his intention, of a concern for what is important and eternal in all these superficial expressions of life. On one side the questions treated of are often slight as questions of decorum; on the other they have the gravity of spiritual things; and it is an art at once gracious and earnest that so sweetly entreats due interest in every aspect of them.

The Easy Chair is probably that part of the Magazine which the greatest number of readers open to first; yet it may be doubted whether those who have so long enjoyed its essays have always consciously recognized their very great excellence. We are sometimes very civil about the regularity and variety of the seasons, but probably we should take more notice of their merit if they happened at odd times, and not with their present periodicity. If something could be done to reobjectivize the phenomenon of their recurrence, we should appreciate it more fully, and this, we trust, will be the effect of the reobjec-tivization of the Easy Chair by the collection of certain of its discourses in the little book lately made from it.

In the perspective which it affords the observer can realize the diversity and the value of the affairs treated from month to month and from year to year with a luminous intelligence which custom has come to accept as insensibly as if it were so much noonday. It is indeed so much noonday; but how shall we persuade a world so long in the usufruct of noonday that noonday is one of the most marvellous and precious possessions of the race? That is the great difficulty, as we have been trying to say, in the estimation of Mr. Curtis's work. If it were a question of form or of matter instead of quality, it would be very simple; one would only have to put one's finger upon this point or that and praise it; but how is one to put one's finger on quality, especially if the quality is almost more a moral than an æsthetic quality? For that is what the transcendent excellence of the Easy Chair essays springs from; so that if we were to hold them up as an example to the Young Writer desirous to Form a Style, we should have to say to him: "Go first of all and be a man, in the widest and deepest sense of that much-abused word; a man so genial that tolerance, which is as modern among the virtues as music among the arts, is a birthright and not an acquisition with him, and whose impulses are all as kind as they are wise; who finds the bewildered spirit of humanity in vulgarity itself; whose smile never wounds, and whose brows are lifted in patient deprecation when other brows would frown; who knows too much ever to despair, yet who is himself trying to learn from every lesson he teaches. Be that kind of man, Young Writer, and all the rest shall be added unto you: beauty of phrase, refinement of manner, subtlety of perception, delicacy of touch, all that you admire and that you have been told can be acquired by the study of good models, you will find in yourself; and they will clothe you like your own flesh and blood, and not like those slop-shop things that you have got ready-made from the Chatham Street pullers-in of the schools." You will say it is extremely difficult to be a man of that kind. Well, we own it is; we perceive the obstacle in your way; and yet it is not impossible. The supreme counsel was a counsel to perfection.

II.

The Study, to be sure, during its five or six years' occupation by the tenant about to quit it, has never apparently profited by its proximity to the Chair.

Very likely, if the neighborhood had lasted a quarter of a century, some effect of its sweetness and light might have been felt by the departing tenant; but that must now remain a question; while there can be no question about his actual condition. With so good a cause as his, the cause of Common Honesty in literature, the Chair would have persuaded every one to think well of it, while as it is, it seems to have rather fewer friends than it had when the tenant of the Study began to belabor its enemies. The spectacle has not been seemly; the passions of the followers of fraud and humbug were aroused; they returned blow for blow, and much mud from afar, so that for months together this haunt of the muses looked rather more like a resort of barn-swallows, in the heart of Donnybrook, at the supreme moment of hostile activities. Not content with the passing result of his monthly ministrations of gall and wormwood, the ill-advised Study-presence thought to bottle a portion of it, and offer it to the public, with the label, "Criticism and Fiction," and a guaranty of its worst effects in any climate, which has been everywhere received with wry faces and retchings, and among the inhabitants of the British Isles has produced truly deplorable consequences. We will not now enter upon any analysis of this drastic potion; partly because we would not fall under the reproach of giving the Study-as-it-has-been a free advertisement; but partly also because we think our time and space may be better employed in recognizing the charm and virtue of that third volume of extracts from these departments. "As we were saying" in the Drawer will soon be "As we are saying" in the Study, with such modifications, doubtless, as will suit the dark associations of the place. At least, this may be the case, we suppose, for a time; but the end may be safely trusted to nature, which gifted Mr. Warner with a gay and sunny wit, whose sparkle will soon irradiate the gloomiest recesses of the Study and make another thing of it. We all know that humor of his, so keen, so quaint, so *sudden*, so apt to take you off your guard, and have its point through you before you are aware. It is at its best in the collection of his essays from the Drawer: little prodigies, every one, of grace and light; with a playful suffusion, so fine, so elusive, that it often seems flatteringly like the gleam of one's own eye on the page.

Many a time has the envious Study looked round its corner (the feat was architecturally difficult, but jealousy accomplished it) at the treasures of the Drawer, and coveted them for its own adornment; and now that the author of those shrewd and brilliant essays is actually coming to make it his home, as the homely phrase is, in the Study, it is hard to realize that it is not wholly for the honor and advantage of the lingering occupant. In a certain sort it is so. The human race, speaking largely, will be the cheerfuler and wiser for the essayist's presence here, and even he who goes out to make room for him will not be denied his share of the common blessing in his evanishment.

III.

It is not given us entirely to rejoice in our successors; it is not, somehow, perfectly pleasing to be inherited; even a voluntary abdication does not necessarily implicate a rapturous welcome of the new prince; the retiring personage probably always carries a critical spirit with him into private life; he wishes the coming ruler well; but he has his little doubts and misgivings, his anxious but-yets and howevers; he cannot help them. The great question is, what changes will the successor make, and will they be all for the public good? It is this question which the paulo-post-future of the Study cannot undertake to answer for its Future: let him have the capital letter; this is not the moment to begrudge such a thing. The paulo-post-future knows a difference of opinions and ideals between himself and the Future, which he will only characterize by saying that it is very much mitigated in practical application; but this difference certainly exists, and we cannot help fancying that it will affect the attitude of the Future towards some cherished objects of the paulo-post-future's veneration. We imagine his looking curiously at the collection of moral bric-à-brac of the latter, and asking himself, "What strange gods are these?" when he comes to the little side altars with the pictures or the busts of canonized realists above them. They strike him as a rabble of unnaturalized foreigners, these literary divinities from France, and Italy, and Norway, and the furthermost parts of Spain, who have long been the cult of the Study, and he sentences the poor gods to exile with his humorous smile, more inexorable than the austerest frown. He has the Christmas Boy remove them, one by one, and takes out a romanticist, and dusts him off, and puts him up in each vacant place, till he comes to that great first of all realists, the supreme artist, the incomparable master of fiction, him with the look of the baffled peasant, the troubled deity, whose plain sad face is perplexed with the vain endeavor to live some Christ-like solution of the riddle of the painful earth. Before this august and pathetic image he pauses a moment, and then not unkindly

but firmly he bids the Christmas Boy, "Take him away; it is the locoed novelist"; and the place that has known Tolstoï knows him no more forever. Up goes the bust of Thackeray on his empty shrine, and all the newspapers think Walter Scott has come to his own again.

It is not harshly done; the paulo-post-future cannot imagine harshness of the Future; but the Future is not so patient with some other objects that he finds in nooks and corners of the Study. He is shocked to find in one of these the blood-stained bludgeon with which the paulo-post-future smote Jack the Giant-killer and Puss-in-Boots, and other romantic forms, and, "Good heavens!" he cries, "here is some of Puss's poor hair adhering to it!" and he hurls the savage weapon out of the window. In another place he stumbles upon something in the obscurity which he has to carry to the light. "Oh, a kodak! Well, I have pronounced against the photographic school; but I have found a kodak convenient, too. Is it the sort that will button under the waistcoat? Put it by, my boy, where I shall not be tempted by it. What is this hanging here? A map of Altruria? It is an outlandish region inhabited by people of heart, a sort of economic Pays du Tendre. It ought not to be tolerated; and yet I traversed parts of it in my *Little Journey in the World*, and the inhabitants, though not much better than early Christian socialists, seemed to mean well. Leave the map for a while!"

So he goes round the whole place, finding much to condemn, to deprecate, but also something, now and then, to tolerate, even to approve. He, too, is of our time, and he has not escaped the influence of the *Zeitgeist*, and if he has sometimes had a question as to whether the *Zeitgeist*, after all, was not the little pocket-goblin of the modern English, instead of that great over-soul, faithful at once and free, which has breathed its life into the literature of all the world outside of the Unhappy Isles, his own work has been of no uncertain response. It is impossible for a humorist to be very romantic, for a humorist is, at the bottom of his heart, always a serious person, and you cannot, at this day, be serious about romanticism: it is too much of a joke. For this reason, if for no other, the paulo-post-future feels that in spite of schools, or rather the names of schools, the true interests of literature will be safe with the Future. He loves them with a devotion which every line of his beautiful work attests, and in his keeping the Study will be the study to serve them, as it has been the study of the paulo-post-future. What matter if the fashion is different? The fashion might very well have been better, though the motive could not, as the paulo-post-future, now on the sidewalk below the Study windows, avers, with some inevitable sorrow at heart. He is gathering up his exiled gods from the kerb-stone where the Christmas Boy has hastily dropped them, and making as portable a bundle of them as he can; not, indeed, with the intention of setting them up in another place, but chiefly to save them from the derision and dishonor of the street. Let us suppose that the Future, now the Present, looks down at the spectacle from the Study windows, and feels its queer pathos with a sympathy that dims the sunny glitter of his *pince-nez*. Let us suppose that he breathes a generous sigh for his predecessor, and that this gentle suspiration, if it could be translated into words, would say: " Well, he may have been an angel unawares. But if he was, he does himself the injustice to look like a professional traveller of uncertain destination and doubtful relations to order and society."

[1] George William Curtis, From the Easy Chair (New York: Harper & Brothers, 1892).

EXPLANATION OF INDEX

Material in parentheses () following the title of a work indicates the author or editor of that work.

An "a" following a page number designates the left-hand column on the page; "b" indicates the right-hand column, and "n" refers to a note on that page.

Material in brackets [] indicates information not found in the text, usually an anonymous author.

Beneath each author entry is an alphabetical listing of his works cited in the text, occasionally including biographical subheadings; each work, in turn, is listed separately in the index.

An italicized page reference indicates a substantial discussion of that entry; numbers not italicized refer to less substantial or incidental references.

The index also serves as a list of names and titles to clarify vague references in the text.

INDEX

Group of Noble Dames (Thomas
Hardy), 334b-335b
"Guinevere, A" (Madison Julius
Cawein), *137b*
Gunnar (Hjalmer Hjorth Boyeson),
206a, 206b, 210n
Guthrie, Thomas Anstey, 65b,
68n
"Guy of the Temple" (John Mil-
ton Hay), 273b

H

Haggard, Rider, *88b-89a*, 278b,
309b;
She, 88b-89a
Hale, Edward Everett, 66b
Haliburton, Thomas Chandler,
11n
Hall, Gertrude, 352b;
"In the Art Museum," *352b*;
Verses, 352b
Halleck, Fitz-Greene, 234a, 235n
"Halt, The" (J. P. Irvine), *351a-b*
Hamerton, Philip Gilbert, 5b,
231a-232a, 234b;
*French and English, 231a-
232a; Paris in Old and Pre-
sent Times,* 5b
Hamet ben Engeli, Cid, 232b
Hamilton, Alexander, 144b
Hamlet (William Shakespeare),
201b
Hammett, Samuel Adams, 11n
Hancock, John, 144b
Hannay, David, 59n;
Admiral Blake, 59n
Happy Boy, The (Björnstjerne
Björnson), 178a
Harding, Chester, *306b-307a;*
Sketch of Chester Harding

Harding, Chester (cont'd)
*Drawn By His Own Hand,
306b-307a*
Hardy, Thomas, 49a-50a, 65b,
75a, 88b, 95b, 194a, 226b,
276b, 334b-335b;
Far From the Madding Crowd,
49b; *Group of Noble Dames,
334b-335b; Mayor of Caster-
bridge, The, 49a-50a; Pair of
Blue Eyes, A,* 50a; *Under the
Greenwood Tree,* 49b; *Wood-
landers,* 88b
Harland, Henry, 29a, 31b-32a,
76b, 195a-b;
*Grandison Mather, 195a-b;
Latin Quater Courtship, A,
195a-b; Mrs. Peixada, 29a*
Harper and Brothers, 5a
Harper's Fifth Reader, 234a-b
Harper's Magazine, 1a, 4b, 62a,
110b, 157b, 161n, 246b,
265a-b, 266a, 328b
Harrigan, Edward, *26a-27a*, 201a-
203b, 244a, 329a;
*Dan's Tribulations, 30b; Leather
Patch, 31a; Waddy Googan,
202a-b*
Harris, Joel Chandler, 67a, 179a,
180n
Harris, Thomas Lake, 337b, *338a-
339a*, 340n, *357a-b;
Brotherhood of the New Life,
The,* 357a
Harris, William Torrey, 25a;
*Life and Genius of Goethe,
25a-26a*
Harrison, Benjamin, 232a, 235n
Harte, Bret, 8b, 66b, 179a, 180n,
332a, 343b
"Has America Produced a Poet?"
(Edmund Gosse), *176a-b*, 179n

.